SECOND EDITION

Beginning Behavioral Research

A CONCEPTUAL PRIMER

Ralph L. Rosnow
Temple University

Robert Rosenthal
Harvard University

PRENTICE HALL
Upper Saddle River, New Jersey 07458

Library of Congress Cataloging-in-Publication Data

Rosnow, Ralph L.
    Beginning behavioral research : a conceptual primer / Ralph L.
Rosnow, Robert Rosenthal. — 2nd ed.
        p.   cm.
    Includes bibliographical references and indexes.
    ISBN 0-13-436916-5
    1. Psychology—Research—Methodology. 2. Social sciences—
Research—Methodology.   I., Rosenthal, Robert,
II. Title.
BF76.5.R64   1996
300'.72—dc20   95-10444
                                                                          CIP

Acquisitions editor: Peter Janzow
Project Manager: Maureen Richardson
Manufacturing buyer: Tricia Kenny
Interior design: Carmela Pereira
Cover design: Carmela Pereira
Illustrations: Hadel Studio

To our students and colleagues
in research methods
past, present, and future

Copyright © 1996 by Prentice-Hall, Inc.
Simon & Schuster Company / A Viacom Company
Upper Saddle River, New Jersey 07458

Printed in the United States of America

10 9 8 7 6 5 4 3

ISBN   0-13-436916-5

Prentice-Hall International (UK) Limited, *London*
Prentice-Hall of Australia Pty. Limited, *Sydney*
Prentice-Hall Canada Inc., *Toronto*
Prentice-Hall Hispanoamericana, S.A., *Mexico*
Prentice-Hall of India Private Limited, *New Delhi*
Prentice-Hall of Japan, Inc., *Tokyo*
Simon & Schuster Asia Pte. Ltd., *Singapore*
Editora Prentice-Hall do Brasil, Ltda., *Rio de Janeiro*

Contents

PART III   *Design and Implementation*

PART IV *Describing and Hypothesis Testing*

Preface

Beginning Behavioral Research is intended for undergraduate students who, as part of a beginning course in research methods, are required to plan an empirical study, to analyze and interpret the data, and to report the findings and conclusions. It is also designed to encourage students to be analytical and critical not only in interpreting research findings in this course but in seeing what is behind the claims and conclusions in news reports of research findings.

ORGANIZATION

Material is presented in a linear sequence corresponding to the steps involved in conducting an empirical research study. The reader is led step by step through the following process:

1. Crafting a testable idea for research:
   Empirical reasoning and the scientific method (Chapter 1); creating, shaping, and polishing a research idea (Chapter 2); weighing and balancing ethical considerations (Chapter 3)
2. Choosing methods of data collection and measurement:
   Using primary and secondary observational methods (Chapter 4); using self-report observations (Chapter 5); assessing reliability and validity (Chapter 6)
3. Designing and implementing the research study:
   Experimenting and controlling for artifacts (Chapter 7); using nonrandomized research designs (Chapter 8); using survey methods in descriptive research (Chapter 9)
4. Analyzing the research data:
   Describing the overall results (Chapter 10); identifying relationships between variables (Chapter 11); significance testing, effect size estimation, and power analysis (Chapter 12)

5. Performing inferential analyses:
Using t to compare two conditions (Chapter 13); computing F in one-way and two-way designs (Chapter 14); analyzing tables of counts by the chi-square (Chapter 15)
6. Reporting the research project (Appendix A)

OUR APPROACH

In our long experience of teaching research methods (over 50 years and several thousand students between the two of us), we have noted the questions and uncertainties of students engaged in empirical research for the first time. The vast majority have not planned to pursue a career in research, but all of them have recognized the vitality and ubiquitousness of research in their daily lives. So we have tried to anticipate and confront questions and uncertainties from their perspective not as potential professional producers of research, but as consumers of scientific results. It is essential for educated consumers to understand the utility and limitations of empirical research as well as the fundamental differences between scientific and pseudoscientific claims of truth. Our aim in chronicling a wide range of older and newer research studies is to show the continuity and stability of science. Once students have mastered this material, they should be able to understand more deeply what scientists mean when they proclaim that they have found something or not found something to be true.

Instructors who know our earlier work will recognize that this book—as well as our advanced text, *Essentials of Behavioral Research: Methods and Data Analysis* (Rosenthal & Rosnow, 1991)—grew from a 117-page paperback book that we wrote many years ago, *Primer of Methods for the Behavioral Sciences* (Rosenthal & Rosnow, 1975a). Over the course of the intervening period, we have had an opportunity to develop and refine that material. Most of our students have been psychology majors required to take a research methods course as part of their concentration, but a substantial proportion have been in fields as diverse as communications, mathematics, accounting, biology, education, sociology, marketing, and even English and physical education. Whether they took this course as part of their major or as an elective, many dreaded the thought of having to wrestle again with statistics. On the assumption that few readers have total recall of statistics or will come away from a statistics course with an intuitive understanding of what was taught, we describe basic aspects of data analysis procedures, purposely avoiding the use of any mathematics beyond the high school level.

Most students with no college training in statistics will find that they can also master basic data-analytic skills by reading the chapters and repeating the exercises in the order in which they are presented. In this age of the computer, the speediest method of doing complex calculations is with the aid of a statistical package. We treat statistics (in Chapters 10–15 and Appendix C) by showing, through intuitive reasoning and simple examples, what the results tell us. We also show how to do basic computations on a pocket calculator. For example, we review how to compute measures of location and spread, effect sizes, measures of simple relationships, and the comparison of means. Instructors who plan to teach students to perform their main calculations on a computer will find that our emphasis on the concrete and arithmetical aspects of data analysis will complement any computer package they may choose. We also describe some useful data-analytic procedures that are not typically found in basic computer packages (e.g., standardizing the margins of chi-square tables, teasing out the residuals to interpret an interaction, and performing a simple meta-analysis).

Instructors familiar with *Essentials of Behavioral Research* will recognize that *Beginning Behavioral Research* can be used for students up to, but just below, the level of *Essentials,* and that the conceptual and philosophical treatment of methods and data analysis is similar in both texts. We again emphasize the utility of the Pearson *r* as an effect size measure that can be conveniently interpreted as an index of practical importance. We also introduce students to statistical power analysis in a way that they should be able to apply in their individual studies. The chapter on ethics is intended to raise questions that project well beyond this book. Students interested in advanced or more detailed analyses of the topics treated here will find such discussions in *Essentials.* In both texts, we have sought to communicate the richness, diversity, and excitement—as well as the basic or advanced technical aspects—of human subjects research that we ourselves find so challenging and stimulating.

SPECIAL FEATURES AND ADDITIONS

In an effort to make this book more useful and more "user-friendly" to students, we have incorporated a number of pedagogical devices. Each chapter begins with a set of *preview questions,* which readers can refer to as they progress. *Boxed discussions* highlight and enliven concepts with practical examples and illustrations. Each chapter concludes with a *summary* of the main ideas, followed by a list of *key terms* pegged to particular pages, and finally a number of *review questions* (with the answers on pp. 320–334) to stimulate thought and discussion. A *glossary* at the end of the book defines key terms and notes the primary chapter(s) or appendix where each term is discussed. Appendix A, on writing the research report, contains an annotated sample manuscript in two alternative formats, with the choice left to the instructor. Appendix C is an optional discussion of meta-analysis, an approach that many students will encounter even in a cursory glance at the journal literature. And finally, the Instructor's Manual accompanying this text contains class-tested exercises, teaching tips, and other ideas that complement each chapter.

We have been gratified by the response to the first edition of this book and wish to thank the many instructors and students who have written to us with comments and suggestions. We asked a number of instructors whether they preferred the sample report in Appendix A to be in the format of a journal submission (i.e., including compositor's notes and so on) or in the more flexible style of a student term paper. The responses were about evenly split, and so we illustrate both formats, one based on the American Psychological Association's (1994) publication manual and the other based on Rosnow and Rosnow's (1995) guide to writing term papers and research reports. Both sample reports follow the APA style in reference citations, nonsexist language, and certain other practical considerations. In the format of the term paper, departures from APA style include, for example, not requiring a "running head" and suggesting that the introduction section start with a center heading (to provide a structure and a constant reminder of the paper's focus). Another departure is the addition of an appendix in which students can report raw data, the statistical calculations performed on the results, and any questionnaires or other relevant material.

Instructors familiar with the previous edition will find that the chapter on the *F* test has been simplified. Chapters 10–15 and Appendix C focus on applications of statistical reasoning in exploring data and testing hypotheses. Throughout the book we have added new examples to expand the range of research areas covered (including human and nonhuman examples). We again invite instructors and students to send us their comments and suggestions for further improvements.

ACKNOWLEDGMENTS

We thank David B. Strohmetz of Shenandoah University for preparing the Instructor's Manual and we thank Margaret Ritchie for her creative, elegant, and helpful copyediting of both editions of this text. We thank Mary Lu Rosenthal for preparing the indexes in this book, and we thank Bruce Rind for again allowing us to include an edited version of his work in Appendix A. We thank Robert E. Lana for permission to borrow a number of ideas and research illustrations from *Introduction to Contemporary Psychology* (Lana & Rosnow, 1972). We thank a long line of teaching assistants and students at Temple University and Harvard University for their valuable comments on and criticisms of the lectures, handouts, and drafts on which the first edition of this book was based. The first edition was published by Macmillan Publishing Company, which has been absorbed by Prentice-Hall, and we thank the following consultants of these publishers for their constructive feedback: Bernard C. Beins, Ithaca College; Patricia R. DeLucia, Texas Tech University; Paul W. Foos, University of North Carolina at Charlotte; Allan J. Kimmel, Fitchburg State College; John W. Webster, Towson State University; Paul J. Wellman, Texas A. & M. University; and Jon L. Williams, Kenyon College. We both thank Mimi Rosnow and Mary Lu Rosenthal for counseling us in ways too numerous to mention.

Certain tables, figures, and passages (specifically acknowledged in the text) have by permission been reproduced in part or in their entirety, for which we thank the following authors, representatives, and publishers: E. Earl Baughman; Leonard Berkowitz; Donald T. Campbell; Jacob Cohen; Mihaly Csikszentmihalyi; J. A. Hagenaars; R. Vance Hall; Howard Kahane; David P. Phillips; Paul Slovic; Alan Sockloff; Laurence Steinberg; Steven Stern; Academic Press; American Association for the Advancement of Science; American Psychological Association; American Sociological Association; American Statistical Association; Biometrika Trustees of the Imperial College of Science, Technology & Medicine; Brooks/Cole Publishing Company; Elsevier Science Publishers; Lawrence Erlbaum Associates, Inc.; HarperCollins Publishers; Helen Dwight Reid Educational Foundation and Heldref Publications; Holt, Rinehart and Winston; Houghton Mifflin Company; Iowa State University Press; *Journal of Applied Behavior Analysis;* McGraw-Hill, Inc.;

W. W. Norton & Company, Inc.; Oxford University Press; The Rand Corporation; Sussex Publishers, Inc. and Psychology Today Magazine; The University of Chicago Press; Wadsworth Publishing Company; and John Wiley & Sons, Inc. We are also grateful to the Longman Group UK Ltd., on behalf of the Literary Executor of the late Sir Ronald Fisher, F.R.S., and Dr. Frank Yates, F.R.S., for permission to reprint Table V from *Statistical Tables for Biological, Agricultural and Medical Research* (6th ed., 1974).

This is our 10th book together in a collaboration that began 30 years ago, and the beat goes on.

Ralph L. Rosnow
Robert Rosenthal

Getting Started

The Scientific Outlook

WHY STUDY RESEARCH METHODS?

Scientists in all fields find research methods intrinsically interesting, but this interest is not shared by everyone. So why study the ways in which science opens the world to scrutiny and investigation if you do not plan to become a scientist? There are at least five good reasons.

One reason is that our modern way of life is largely the creation of science, and we enhance our understanding of our world by improving our understanding of the full range of the influence of science on our lives. By analogy, viewing paintings, drawings, and sculpture in a museum becomes more meaningful when we know something about the techniques involved in producing works of art. Similarly, reading that a public opinion poll predicts that so-and-so will win the election, or that researchers have discovered a new cure for insomnia or have announced a new dietary supplement for increasing longevity, has more meaning when we understand how the conclusions were reached.

Besides providing a richer appreciation of the information that science brings to modern life, a second reason for studying research methods is that *not* having a clear understanding of how scientists cast and address questions can cost us dearly. Physicians, teachers, lawyers, the clergy, politicians, the police—these people also have an influence on our daily lives, and everyone seems to know how men and women in these fields go about their work. But few of us seem to have even a vague idea of how researchers use the scientific method to enlarge our understanding of the world (Medawar, 1969), and we may succumb to misleading allegations based on supposedly scientific research. Becoming familiar with the nature of *empirical reasoning* (i.e., a use of logic that is aided by observation and measurement)—especially by designing and carrying out a research study under the watchful eye of an experienced guide—can teach us the difference between good science and *pseudoscience* (i.e., bogus claims masquerading as scientific fact).

A third reason for studying research methods, particularly in the context of behavioral science, is to acquire information and skills that you can use later. For example, by learning how professional pollsters properly sample opinions, and how they avoid certain pitfalls in asking people what they feel or think, you learn skills that you can apply to real-life questions. The same is true of other information and skills that you will learn, including sharpening your powers of empirical reasoning and improving your data-analytic abilities. For example, not only will you be able to think of probing questions to ask about how sensational claims were reached, but you will often be able to evaluate them independently once you understand certain basic ideas of causal inference, the use of control conditions, and the use of statistics to make numerical conjectures.

A fourth reason for studying and doing research is to learn about the limits of empirical methods and why generalizations, including scientific principles, are said to be based partly on a "leap of faith." In physics, for example, if researchers were to insist that the only acceptable claims are those based on direct scientific observations, they would be unable to accept the venerable laws of mechanics. Newton's first law of motion tells us that a body not acted on by any force will continue in a state of rest or uniform motion in a straight line forever. Of course, no human being has ever seen a "body not acted on by any force" (e.g., friction or gravity), much less observed its "motion in a straight line forever" (M. R. Cohen, 1959). Yet this time-honored law is accepted as one of science's most faithful generalizations. You will see that there are also limits on the empirical methods used in behavioral science, such as those derived from studying human subjects who are aware that they are being observed for scientific purposes (see Box 1.1). We will have more to say about this problem later in the book, where we describe techniques that experimenting psychologists use to address this problem. These techniques are also limited, but despite the intrinsic limits, psychologists and others use the scientific method to formulate powerful and faithful generalizations about how and why people behave as they do.

A final reason for studying and doing research is that some of you will find this enterprise so much fun and so absorbing that you may want to make a career of it!

BOX 1.1   The Hawthorne Effect

The fact that a person is being studied experimentally sometimes affects how the person behaves even more than the experimental manipulation does. This conclusion, traditionally known as the *Hawthorne effect* (French, 1950), grew out of a series of human factors experiments performed in the 1920s and 1930s at the Hawthorne Works of the Western Electric Company in Illinois. The experiments were designed to examine how workers' productivity and job satisfaction might be affected by workplace conditions (lighting, temperature, rest periods, and so on). Although the results, in retrospect, have proved difficult to unravel because of design ambiguities (J. G. Adair, 1984; Gillespie, 1988), they are often cited to support the idea that subjects tend to be overly accommodating in behavioral science experiments. Later in this book, we describe 1960s and 1970s research demonstrating that this idea is sometimes not far off the mark. Therefore, in devising any methodological strategy, it is prudent to take into consideration the subjects' perceptions.

PEIRCE'S METHODS OF "FIXING BELIEF"

Of course, the scientific method is not the only strategy that people use to make sense of things. Philosophers, novelists, theologians, and many others also seek to give us a coherent picture of our world, but they do not use the scientific method to organize their ideas and give us information. What distinguishes the various strategies that people use to formulate a sense of understanding and belief? Charles Sanders Peirce (1839–1914), an American philosopher whose work had a strong influence on William James, the founder of experimental psychology in the United States, suggested an answer to this question. Peirce (pronounced "purse") described four distinct strategies for "the fixation of belief" (i.e., the formulation of a sense of conviction): (1) tenacity, (2) authority, (3) a priori method, and (4) the scientific method (see Box 1.2). Each strategy, although limited in some ways, essentially contains a formula or guiding principle that, once it becomes inculcated as a habit of mind, influences whether we will draw one inference rather than another in a given situation (Peirce, 1966).

Peirce believed the most primitive approach of all to be the *method of tenacity.* In this method, people cling stubbornly (tenaciously) to beliefs or claims just because they seem obvious or make "common sense." The problem is that sometimes holding one's ground is based on an illusion. Like an ostrich that buries its head in the sand, people who cling to false ideas (i.e., dogmatic or closed-minded people) go through life systematically excluding anything that might change their beliefs (see Rokeach, 1960). Sometimes an entire society seems to have fallen victim to false ideas, and it is not easy to shake them loose or to open up dogmatic minds. For example, for centuries people considered it obvious that the earth is

BOX 1.2	The Scientific Method

The term *scientific method* is actually a misnomer because this "method" is not synonymous with any single, fixed procedure; it is instead a philosophical *outlook* as much as an evolving collection of tools and techniques. This outlook is primarily characterized by empirical reasoning, which in turn encompasses experimental and nonexperimental techniques, methods of external observation and self-report, and quantitative as well as qualitative procedures. As one leading psychological researcher put it, the scientific method as used in human behavioral science helps us sort out what we know about human nature from what we only think we know (Milgram, 1977).

fixed and immobile, and that it is at the center of the universe. Elaborate explanations using myths to embellish this belief persisted until they were finally swept away by what has been characterized as the "witness of the naked eye"—that is, by *observational* (i.e., empirical) astronomy (Boorstein, 1985, p. 305).

In our own time, we recognize that the method of tenacity still has a pernicious hold on many people's beliefs. Myth, folklore, superstition, cyclic rumor—all thrive on burying one's head in the sand and keeping out of view all that might change one's beliefs. As a consequence, many people accept weird or astounding allegations as factual, and once accepted, such beliefs feed on people's anxieties and uncertainties (e.g., Kimmel & Keefer, 1991; Rosnow, 1980, 1991; Rosnow & Fine, 1976). For example, Carl Jung (1910, 1959), the eminent Swiss psychiatrist and psychologist, wrote about the old rumor of "flying saucers," unidentified flying objects (UFOs) piloted by extraterrestrials. This weird claim, a recurrent theme for centuries, usually tells either of benevolent superior beings from another planet who have come to save humanity or of menacing creatures who, by threatening all earthlings, unify diverse ideologies against a common foe. When gullible people believe what they want to believe, they become easy victims of hucksters who use fakery and showy methods to prey on human weaknesses. According to Jung, belief in the UFO rumor is a way of expressing fears and uncertainties about the world situation and the universal wish for a redeeming supernatural force.

A second strategy—which Peirce viewed as at least minimally superior to the method of tenacity—is the *method of authority,* in which certain claims (some true and others false) are accepted because someone in a position of authority says they are true. Peirce noted that false accusations of witchcraft resulted in atrocities of the most horrible kind, as people obeyed the word of authority to carry out their cruelties. A somewhat more benign case occurred in the 15th century, when Nicolaus Copernicus was asked by the Pope to help with calendar reform. Copernicus postulated that the sun, not the earth, was the center of all things. However, that idea, being at odds not only with "common sense" but also with the authority of ecclesiastical doctrine, was rejected by the Church. In fact, it was not until the 16th and 17th centuries, and the revolutionary thinking of Galileo and Newton, that there was a successful intellectual uprising against the strictures of ecclesiastical authority.

Again, we do not need to look very far to find examples of the method of authority's benevolent or malevolent influence in our daily lives. On the positive side, civilized society would cease to exist without people's willingness to obey laws and to carry out reasonable orders. Other examples on the benevolent side are the physician who prescribes a drug or regimen to cure an illness, the electrician who advises replacing wiring that is about to blow out, and the mechanic who informs us that the spark plugs in our car are shot and need replacing; we depend on their honesty and the authority of their expertise. On the negative side are unscrupulous people who practice deceit in the name of authority, such as medical quacks, food faddists, cult leaders, and eccentric sexual theorists (M. Gardner, 1957). Let the buyer beware, however, for the authority of these claims is in the eyes of the beholder.

In a third approach, which Peirce called the *a priori method,* we use our individual powers of pure reason and logic to know and explain our world. This method—which Peirce characterized as "far more intellectual and respectable from the point of view of reason" than either of the previous two (Peirce, 1966, p. 106)—has proved itself quite robust in the hands of mathematicians and philosophers. It is sometimes an effective defense against hucksters who depend on gullibility. We can approach their dubious claims with a questioning mind that, as one author put it, resists "being overly impressed" even if the evidence seems to be immediately before us (Gilovich, 1991, p. 187). For example, although the immediate source of a story may be quite credible, we may question the trustworthiness of the person with whom it originated. When we hear things described to us as secondhand, we may question whether they are not thirdhand or even more distant from the original source (Gilovich, 1991).

However, Peirce also recognized that the a priori method is constrained by the limits of pure reason. Suppose you claim that A causes B, and I disagree. Do we just have to let it go at that? What we need, he argued, is a way of drawing on nature to help us resolve matters of disagreement. In other words, we may use the scientific method, which attempts to draw on independent realities to evaluate claims rather than depending on reason alone. Of course, the scientific method is also limited in specific ways (see Box 1.3). How, then, can we distinguish it from Peirce's other strategies for "fixing belief"? The scientific method, more than any other method, is characterized by empirical reasoning.

What Is Empirical Reasoning?

In its dictionary definition, *empirical* refers to the use of experience or observation. In the context of the scientific method, empirical reasoning relies not on armchair theorizing, political persuasiveness, or personal position, but (as noted previously) on observation and measurement. As one author put it, trying to unlock a door with a set of previously untried keys, a person says, "If this key fits the lock, then the lock will spring when I turn the key" (Conant, 1957, p. xii). The same is true in empirical science. The scientist has a choice of "keys," decides on one, and then

BOX 1.3	Limits of Science

One limitation of the scientific method has been imposed by the scientists themselves, that is, what research procedures are morally or ethically permissible. There are also intrinsic limits, however, such as our limited cognitive capacity as human beings to perceive and process all of the rich and disorderly world in which we live. By analogy, we can bend our arms forward at the elbow, but not backward; nature has imposed a limit on how far the human forearm can be bent. The language of science enables researchers in all fields to bend their experiences into prose, but human nature has imposed a limit on our cognitive capacity to evaluate and communicate all of the world's richness of information.

says in essence, "Let's try it." Thus the scientific method calls for a reliance on techniques that are available to *anyone* who is skilled enough to use them to open up the world for scrutiny and investigation. In fact, it is this primary dependence on empirical reasoning that connects scientists working in different fields, even though they may use quite different empirical methods in their research. We will have more to say about the basic kinds of empirical strategies used in behavioral research, but let us pause for a moment to sample how empirical reasoning has been applied to a variety of real-world problems.

A well-known example in physics involved the investigation of the space shuttle *Challenger*'s tragic accident on January 28, 1986 in which seven people lost their lives. A panel of experts and other authorities was convened to look into the disaster and to figure out what had caused it. One member of the panel was Richard P. Feynman, a brilliant physicist, who thought of an innovative way to demonstrate, through empirical reasoning, what had gone wrong in the frigid weather on the day of the launch. The rocket that boosted the shuttle contained two rubber seals in the form of rings, called *O-rings*, that were expected to be resilient but had not actually been tested in freezing temperature. A lack of resilience of the O-rings when it was freezing would explain why the rocket exploded the moment it was ignited. That is, highly flammable fuel leaked out through the seals, then caught fire and exploded.

At the end of an exhausting day of listening to testimony and arguments, Feynman (1988) had a sudden inspiration when he returned to his hotel room:

> I'm feeling lousy and I'm eating dinner; I look at the table, and there's a glass of ice water. I say to myself, "Damn it, *I* can find out about that rubber *without* having NASA [National Aeronautics and Space Administration] send notes back and forth: I just have to *try* it! All I have to do is get a sample of the rubber." (p. 146)

Early the next day, Feynman went to a hardware store, where he bought screwdrivers, pliers, and the smallest C-clamp he could find. He then went to NASA and used the screwdriver to peel away a sample of the rubber used in the O-rings.

When the hearing resumed, he used the pliers to squash the rubber, which he then clamped and placed in a glass of ice water. When he removed the rubber and undid the clamp, the rubber did not spring back. In other words, for more than a few seconds, there was no resilience in the rubber when it was at a temperature of 32°F.

Empirical reasoning entered into behavioral science during the late 19th century when the creative advances inspired by the earlier applications of the scientific method in physics and biology led to the development of psychology as a science. In Leipzig, Wilhelm Wundt (1832–1920), trained in medicine and experimental physiology, developed the first formal experimental laboratory to study psychological behavior. Around the same time, William James (1842–1910), with a background in philosophy and physiology, announced a graduate course at Harvard University in which the students participated in psychological experiments that James arranged. Of course, psychological science is not practiced only in the laboratory. In Britain, another pioneering scientist and writer, Francis Galton (1822–1911), was demonstrating the application of empirical reasoning to behavioral questions that had been thought to lie completely outside its application (Forrest, 1974).

In one of his numerous investigations, Galton decided to see whether there might be empirical grounds for believing that prayers are answered. Of course, the sincerity of all prayers is not equal. However, Galton thought, one way to get at this problem was to look at something prayed for with tremendous frequency. In England, the health and longevity of the royal family is prayed for weekly or even daily nationwide. Galton wondered: Do members of the royal family therefore live longer than individuals of humbler birth? In 1872, he published the results of his inquiry. What he found, after a painstaking gathering and analysis of actuarial data, was that, of 97 members of royal families, the mean age attained by males had been 64.04 years. Compared to 945 members of the clergy who had lived to a mean age of 69.49, 294 lawyers who had lived to 68.14, 244 physicians who had lived to 68.14, and so forth, the members of the royal family had actually fared worse than he expected based on the many prayers on their behalf.

Of course, Galton did not reject the hypothesis that prayer has a powerful effect in other ways, such as by strengthening people's resolution to face hardships or by bringing serenity in distress. Galton's empirical reasoning, as one writer put it, "was thus 'scientific' in the territory in which he exercised it, but also in the territory he disclaimed" (Medawar, 1969, p. 5). Let us look at one more example before moving on, this one involving the *experimental* application of empirical reasoning to a question in forensic (legal) psychology.

Stephen J. Ceci, a developmental psychologist, was interested in the accuracy of children's eyewitness testimony. To study this problem in a real-life setting, he and his coworkers designed a simple demonstration experiment in which a character named "Sam Stone" was described to 3- to 6-year-olds as someone who was very clumsy and broke things (Ceci & Bruck, 1993; Ceci, Leichtman, & White, 1995). Then, a person identified as Sam Stone visited the children's nursery school, where he chatted briefly with them during a storytelling session—but did not behave clumsily or break anything. The next day, the childen were shown a ripped book and a soiled teddy bear and were asked if they knew how the objects had been damaged. Over the course of the next 10 weeks, the children were reinterviewed. Each time, they were asked two leading questions such as "I wonder whether Sam Stone was wearing long pants or short pants when he ripped the book?" or "I wonder if Sam Stone got the teddy bear dirty on purpose or by accident?"

What the researchers observed—and also videotaped so that others could see for themselves—was that the planted stereotype of Sam Stone carried over into the children's eyewitness reports. When asked, 72% of the 3- to 4-year-olds said that Sam Stone had ruined either the book or the teddy bear, and 45% of these children claimed they had actually seen him do it (and then embellished their accounts with other details). A vital ingredient of experimentation is the use of a comparison condition (called a *control group*) against which to evaluate the effect of the experimental manipulation. Ceci's control group received the suggestive interviews but no planted stereotypical information about Sam Stone. As we would predict, they made fewer false claims than the children in whom the stereotype had been planted.

SHARED FEATURES OF THE SCIENTIFIC METHOD

Although the scientific method is uniquely identified by its reliance on observation and measurement, it shares some features with other strategies of explanation. One feature of all methods of explanation is that they are expressed in the accepted *rhetoric* (or language) of the area they represent (Gross, 1990; Pera & Shea, 1991). As in learning a new language, one must be familiar with the linguistic and grammatical mode of a particular field in order to understand what people in that area are talking about. In other words, psychologists talk like psychologists, philosophers like philosophers, lawyers like lawyers, theologians like theologians, physicians like physicians, police like police, and so on. Later on, you will see that the *rhetoric of behavioral science* encompasses the proper use of technical definitions, methods of quantitative analysis, and hypotheses and theories, all of which must satisfy standards that have come to be regarded as "good scientific practice" (see also Box 1.4).

Besides using empirical reasoning and a specialized rhetoric, scientists—indeed, like all of us (Bauer & Johnson-Laird, 1993; Johnson-Laird, 1983; Johnson-Laird & Byrne, 1991)—also use *mental imagery*. In fact, the history of ideas teaches us that good scientific theories, to be influential, must reflect a way of thinking that includes images. We will have more to say about the nature of theories, but it will suffice here to note that theories have to be perceptible in a way that can be seen as "making sense," that is, given accepted truths. In the same way that Michelangelo began with a mental image in creating his *Pietà,* so did Newton in developing his laws of motion, and so do behavioral scientists in constructing their theories (e.g., Nisbet, 1976). Indeed, the annals of science are full of such visualizations (e.g., A. I. Miller, 1986; Randhawa & Coffman, 1978). The reaction to failures in perceptibility is often "I just don't see it!"

A legendary case in modern science occurred when the quantum theorists in physics found it difficult to persuade the physical determinists that it is

Writing Scientific Reports

Robert A. Day (1983), a biologist and the author of an excellent writing manual for research scientists, observed:

> Scientists, starting as graduate students, are measured primarily not by their dexterity in laboratory manipulation, not by their innate knowledge of either broad or narrow scientific subjects, and certainly not by their wit or charm; they are measured, and become known (or remain unknown), by their *publications*. . . . It is not necessary for the plumber to write about pipes, nor is it necessary for the lawyer to write about cases [except for the writing of "briefs"]. . . , but the research scientist, perhaps uniquely among the trades and professions, must provide a written document showing what he or she did, why it was done, how it was done, and what was learned from it. (pp. ix, x)

If you turn to Appendix A (pp. 360–374), you will see what a student's scientific paper might look like if it were written up in the style prescribed by the *Publication Manual of the American Psychological Association* (American Psychological Association, 1994). This particular style has evolved over many years, and it serves several purposes: First, it allows busy readers to read published reports more easily because the reports all conform to similar publishing procedures. Second, it contains notes that are important to compositors and editors, such as telling them where tables and figures belong in the printed article. Third, it provides a basic structure used by researchers to organize their thoughts as they summarize their research project for others.

plausible—given a very great many atoms, all capable of certain definite changes—to tell what proportion of atoms will undergo each change but impossible to tell which particular changes any given atom will undergo. God "does not play dice with the world" is the way Einstein responded.* He could not see that, at the level of simple atomic processes, activity may be ruled by blind chance (see Clark, 1971; Jammer, 1966). Only after mainstream modern physicists were able to accept as "perceptible" the generalizations proposed by the quantum theorists did those principles enter the textbooks as a precise model of knowledge.

Finally, although it would be wrong to claim that art is the same as science, another characteristic of both is the role of *aesthetics* (i.e., having a sense of the beautiful). The chemist Primo Levi (1984) told how, as a young student, he was first struck by the fact that "Mendeleev's Periodic Table. . . was poetry, loftier and more solemn than all the poetry we had swallowed. . . ; and come to think of it, it even rhymed!" (p. 1). Indeed, scientists and philosophers have long been aware

---

*Einstein's exact words, contained in a letter to a colleague, were "Quantum mechanics demands serious attention. But an inner voice tells me that this is not the true Jacob. The theory accomplishes a lot, but it does not bring us closer to the secrets of the Old One. In any case, I am convinced that He does not play dice" (Jammer, 1966, p. 358).

of the basic similarity of the creative act found in the arts and poetry to that found in the sciences (Chandrasekhar, 1987; Garfield, 1989a, 1989b; Nisbet, 1976; Wechler, 1978). "Beauty is truth, truth beauty," the poet Keats wrote in his "Ode on a Grecian Urn," which is as much a visual metaphor of value in science as it is in art and poetry (Gombrich, 1963). Twenty-five hundred years ago, Plato likened the creative work of the astonomer to that of the painter. In your reading, you may find words such as *beauty* and *poetry* used to describe some scientific laws, equations, theories, and so on. Behavioral scientists, like all scientists, love intellectual beauty and strive for it as they attempt to envisage some aspect of the psychological world. There may be no greater praise of a colleague's work than to say of it that the experiment or the set of findings is "just beautiful."

Thus the scientific method is characterized not only by empirical reasoning, but by the accepted terminology in a given area, by perceptible images, and by the aesthetic appeal of those images. But for scientists, the essential criteria are always observation and measurement. In other words, conviction in science rests not just on the rhetorical force of argument, the visual force of imagination, or the aesthetic force of beauty, but also on subjecting ideas to empirical confrontation.

WHAT IS BEHAVIORAL SCIENCE?

The examples that we have mentioned cover a wide range of disciplines, including psychology, physics, and astronomy. However, this book is not just a trip into the realm of science in general; it is a journey into the domain of behavioral science in particular. *Behavior* is what you do and how you act; *behavioral science* is an "umbrella" term that also includes cognitive functioning. The wide range of interests of behavioral scientists covers the study of early primitive humans, humans as political animals, economic animals, social animals, talking animals, and logicians. These aspects of human nature are the concern of psychologists (e.g., clinical, cognitive, developmental, experimental, industrial-organizational, and social), mass communication and educational researchers, sociologists, physical and cultural anthropologists, economists, psycholinguists, behavioral biologists, neuroscientists, and even some statisticians. But no matter what the preferred label, the objective in all fields of behavioral science is the same: to describe and explain how and why people behave as they do, including how and why they feel and think as they do (Kimble, 1989).

For many purposes, it may make little difference whether we can distinguish among those various disciplines; there are differences nonetheless. For instance, the experimental psychologists use laboratory instruments and techniques to study human experiences in controlled settings. The social and industrial-organizational (I-O) psychologists, particularly those trained in a psychology graduate program, also often conduct experiments, but they are apt to be performed in the field as well as in the laboratory. By contrast, the sociologists are more likely to perform survey studies in the field. Nonetheless many behavioral researchers borrow from one another's storehouse of methods. Thus some sociologists conduct experiments and some social psychologists perform survey studies. The point is that, in spite of the fences separating different departments in colleges and universities, the boundary lines in behavioral science are by no means rigid.

You will also see that behavioral scientists study real-life problems not only in naturalistic settings (e.g., Galton's and Ceci's studies) but in the laboratory as well. For example, in the area known as *psychophysics* (i.e., the study of the relationship between physical stimuli and our experience of them), experimental psychologists working in the laboratory discovered many years ago that the amount by which stimulus intensity must be increased to cause a noticeable change in the perception of the stimulus is a constant proportion of the intensity of the original stimulus. Following this line of reasoning, they showed that it is possible to write a mathematical statement of the theoretical relationship between the intensity of a stimulus and the intensity of a sensation, which can then be applied to a range of real-life situations. If, say, your dormitory room is lighted by a 100-watt bulb, and if 15 watts of light must be added before you can detect a difference in the amount of light, then in a room with a 50-watt bulb, 7.5 watts must be added before the difference is detectable.

In many areas of behavioral science, research has evolved since the early 1970s to embrace what is described as a *multiplistic* (or *pluralistic*) *viewpoint,* that is, the use of multiple methods of observation and explanation instead of a single method of observation or a single theoretical perspective (see Houts, Cook, & Shadish, 1986; Jaeger & Rosnow, 1988; Rosnow, 1981). Thus we now see many *interdisciplinary* research projects, as researchers strive to develop a more complete and integrated picture of human nature. Sometimes a whole new field is created when researchers combine the methods and theories of different fields. Examples include behavioral medicine, mathematical psychology, sociobiology, psychobiology, ethnopsychology, psycholinguistics, psychological anthropology, and, perhaps most broadly, neuroscience.

An example is the hybrid discipline of mass media research. Joshua Meyrowitz (1985), a leading theorist in this field, speculated that our home life "is now a less bounded and unique environment because of family members' access and accessibility to other places and other people through radio, television, and telephone" (p. vii). There are more radios than people in the United States, and there are a television and a telephone in nearly every U.S. home. The old notion of disciplining children by sending them to their room takes on a new meaning when the room is equipped with the latest audiovisual hardware. What used to be a restriction becomes a conduit to an uncensored larger world. At the touch of a button or the turn of a dial, the young person can summon a range of experiences that were formerly technologically inaccessible. To examine scientifically the myriad aspects of this situation, social psychologists, communication researchers, developmental psychologists, educational researchers, and many others have joined hands in interdisciplinary research studies.

BROAD RESEARCH APPROACHES

We have touched on a number of research techniques, such as the use of actuarial data to study the efficacy of prayer, the "Sam Stone" manipulation used to study children's eyewitness testimony, and the laboratory investigation of physical stimuli and our perception of them. But even a cursory glance at the many research journals in behavioral science will reveal that there are countless techniques of empirical inquiry. To give an overview, it is convenient to lump together the specific orientations of behavioral research into three broad types: *descriptive, relational,* and *experimental.* Table 1.1 gives illustrations of each type in three general research areas (psycholinguistics, the social psychology of rumor behavior, and methodological research). As you study these illustrations, you will see that descriptive conclusions tell us *how things are,* relational conclusions tell us *how things are in relation to other things,* and experimental conclusions tell us *how things are and how they got to be that way.*

As you become better acquainted with the literature in your area, you will see that the research usually involves more than one approach, although a given study can usually be described as *primarily* descriptive, relational, or experimental. As a program of research progresses, the investigators may need to alternate among these three types, or they may follow a natural progression from descriptive to relational to experimental studies. The hypothetical case presented in the following paragraphs on instructional research in educational psychology will show more clearly what we mean by a "natural progression" in a program of empirical studies (Rosenthal & Rosnow, 1975a).

TABLE 1.1	Descriptive, Relational, and Experimental Conclusions in Three Research Areas

Psycholinguistics
Descriptive: When a 2-year-old child listens to a message spoken by his or her mother and is asked to repeat it, the child typically repeats only part of the message (Brown, 1965).
Relational: On the average, frequently used words tend to be shorter than infrequently used words. This statement is called *Zipf's law* (G. A. Miller & Newman, 1958; Zipf, 1935, 1949).
Experimental: When interfering background noise is present, a speaker tends to use more words and fewer abbreviations than when there is no interfering background noise (Heise & Miller,1951).

Rumor Behavior
Descriptive: Of more than 1,000 rumors collected from all over the United States during World War II, approximately two-thirds were divisive in their intent (Knapp, 1944).
Relational: Rumors that forecast unpleasant consequences for the rumormonger (called *dread rumors*) are passed on to others with greater frequency than rumors that predict pleasant consequences (called *wish rumors*) for the rumormonger (Rosnow, 1991; Rosnow, Esposito, & Gibney, 1987; C. J. Walker & Blaine, 1991).
Experimental: College students who were made to feel anxious required less verbal prodding to repeat a rumor than students who had been told the rumor but were not made to feel anxious (C. J. Walker & Beckerle, 1987).

Methodological Research
Descriptive: College or university students are the most widely used research participants in psychological studies (Rosenthal & Rosnow, 1975b).
Relational: Volunteer subjects tend to be higher in the need for social approval than nonvolunteer subjects (Rosenthal & Rosnow, 1975b; Rosnow, 1993).
Experimental: Subjects made to experience a conflict between "looking good" and cooperating with the experimenter are likely to try to look good, whereas subjects not made to experience such a conflict are likely to help the experimenter (Rosnow, Goodstadt, Suls, & Gitter, 1973; Sigall, Aronson, & Van Hoose, 1970).

DESCRIPTIVE RESEARCH

First, in *descriptive research,* the goal of the investigation tends to be the careful mapping out of a situation or a set of events. The research objective is to describe what is happening behaviorally. Causal explanations are not of direct concern except perhaps speculatively. For example, if we are interested in the study of children's failure in school, we may spend a good deal of time measuring and evaluating the classroom behavior of children who are doing poorly. We would then describe as carefully as possible what we have observed. Our careful observation of failing pupils may lead to some revision of our traditional concepts of classroom failure, to suggestions about factors that may contribute to the development of failure, and perhaps to speculative ideas for the remediation of failure.

This descriptive orientation is usually considered a necessary first step in the development of a program of research because it establishes the cornerstone of any future undertaking. But it is rarely regarded as sufficient, because sooner or later someone will want to know *why* something happens or *how* what happens is related to other events. If our interest is in children's classroom failure, we are not likely to be satisfied for very long with even the most careful description of that failure. We will want to know the antecedents of the failure and the outcomes of various procedures designed to reduce it. Even if we were not motivated directly by the practical implications of knowing the causes and cures of failure, we would believe our understanding to be considerably improved if we knew the conditions that increase and decrease its likelihood. To learn about the increase or decrease of failure, or any other behavior, we must focus on at least two variables at the same time; that is, we must make two sets of observations that can be related to one another.

RELATIONAL RESEARCH

At this point, the second broad type of approach, *relational research,* begins. Research is relational when two or more variables or conditions are measured and related to one another. As we continue with the classroom example, let us suppose we have noted that the teachers of many of the failing students rarely look at or address them and seldom expose them to new academic information. At this stage, we may have only an impression about the relation between learning failure and teaching behavior. Such impressions are a frequent, and often valuable, by-product of descriptive research, but if they are to be taken seriously, they cannot be left at the impressionistic level for very long.

Because we want to find out whether the researcher's impressions are accurate, we now arrange to make a series of "coordinated" observations on a sample of pupils who adequately represent the target population of pupils. We note whether each pupil in the sample is learning anything or to what degree the pupil has been learning; we also note to what degree the teacher has been exposing the pupil to the material to be learned. From these coordinated observations, we should be able to make a quantitative statement concerning the relationship or correlation between the amount of the pupils' exposure to the material to be learned and the amount of this material they have in fact learned. We then indicate not just (1) whether "*X* and *Y* are significantly related" (i.e., whether this nonzero relationship is unlikely to have occurred by chance alone), but also (2) the form or pattern of the relationship (e.g., linear or nonlinear) and (3) the strength of the relationship. (Later in this book, we will illustrate what these statistical terms mean.)

EXPERIMENTAL RESEARCH

To carry the example into the third broad approach, *experimental research,* suppose that the pupils exposed to less information are also those who tend to learn less. The discovery of this relationship may tempt us to conclude that children learn less because they are taught less. Such an *ad hoc hypothesis* (i.e., a conjecture or supposition developed "for this" special result), although plausible, is not warranted by the relationship reported. It may be that teachers teach less to those they know to be less able to learn; that is, differences in teaching behavior may be a result of the pupils' learning as much as a determinant of that learning. To pursue this conjecture, we make further observations that allow us to infer whether differences in the information presented to the pupils, apart from any individual differences among them, have affected the pupils' learning. We can best answer such questions by manipulating the conditions that we believe to be responsible for the effect. That is, we introduce some change into the situation, or we interrupt or terminate the situation in order to identify some causes.

That is what is *generally* meant by experimental research, the focus of which is the identification of causes (i.e., *what* leads to what). Relational research only rarely provides such information, and then only under very special conditions. The difference between the degree of focus on a causal explanation in relational and experimental research can be expressed in the difference between the two statements "*X* is related to *Y*" (relational research) and "*X* is responsible for *Y*" (experimental research). In our example, teaching is *X* and learning is *Y*. Our experiment is designed to reveal the effects of teaching on pupil learning. Let us select a sample of youngsters and, by tossing a coin or some other random method of selection, divide them into two equivalent groups. The teachers will give more information to one of these groups (the experimental group) and will give the other group (the control group) less information. We can then assess whether the experimental group surpasses the control group in learning achievement. If we find this result, we can say that giving the experimental group more information was *responsible* for the outcome.

There might still be a question of what it was about the better procedure that led to the improvement. It is, in fact, characteristic of research that, when a new procedure is shown to be effective, many questions arise about what *specific* aspects of the procedure are producing the benefits. In the case of increased teaching, for example, we may wonder whether the improvement was due to the nature of the additional material; the increased attention from the teacher while presenting the additional material; any accompanying increases in eye contact, smiles, or warmth; or other possible correlates of increased teaching behavior. In fact, these alternative hypotheses have already been investigated. The results indicate that the amount of new material that teachers present to their pupils is sometimes predictable not so much by the children's learning ability as by the teachers' beliefs or expectations about their pupils' learning ability. The teachers' expectations about their pupils' performance may serve as a "self-fulfilling prophecy," in which the expectations become responsible for the outcome in behavior (Babad, 1993; Raudenbush, 1984; Rosenthal, 1966, 1976, 1985, 1991b; Rosenthal & Jacobson, 1968; Rosenthal & Rubin, 1978).

ORIENTING ATTITUDES OF THE SCIENTIST

We have described the scientific method, and we will now concentrate our attention on the appropriate orienting attitudes of individual researchers. The term *attitude* refers to a kind of "posture of the mind," and it is usually assumed that attitudes are the impetus that leads a person to behave one way and not another. In behavioral science, and in science in general, several orienting attitudes of researchers are prescribed or expected in all fields (J. A. Hall, 1984). The technical language of different research fields often makes science seem to be divisive, but at the individual level, there is an attitudinal unity—in our expectations, at least.

1. *Enthusiasm.* A wise researcher, the experimental psychologist Edward C. Tolman (1959), best summed up this aspect of the scientist's orienting attitude: "In the end, the only sure criterion is to have fun" (p. 152). He did not mean that the attitude of the scientist is that research is just fun and games without any ethical or societal implications or consequences; he meant that, for individual scientists, conducting a research study is as absorbing as any game that requires skill and concentration and that fills a person with enthusiasm.

2. *Open-mindedness.* The practice of good research requires an attitude of open-mindedness. That is, good scientific practice requires that the scientist observe with a keen, attentive, inquisitive, and open mind—because many great discoveries are made by accident (called *serendipity* in the next chapter). To practice science, as another writer put it, is to raise incessant questions, both broad and narrow, concerning *all* of our experiences in the world (Koch, 1959, p. 5). An attitude of open-mindedness also allows us to learn from our mistakes and from the advice and criticisms offered by others.

3. *Good sense.* An attitude that values good sense is important in our daily lives and also in scientific practice. For example, one axiom of science is the *principle of the drunkard's search:* A drunkard lost his house key and began searching for it under a street lamp even though he had dropped the key some distance away. Asked why he didn't look where he had dropped it, he replied, "There is more light here." This principle teaches that all the book learning in the world cannot replace good sense in the planning and conduct of research. Much effort is lost when people fail to use good sense and instead look in a convenient place, rather than the most likely place, for the answers to their questions.

4. *Role-taking ability.* Good scientific practice also calls for an ability to take the role of the research consumer. In that role, behavioral scientists ask themselves what the practical implications and moral consequences of their research are. To anticipate criticisms when they submit their work for publication, scientists must be able to take the role of the critic or objective observer. As we saw in Box 1.1, the subjects being studied constitute yet another group inextricably connected with the research, and their unique role is part and parcel of the results of the research. Behavioral scientists must put themselves in their subjects' place so that they can ferret out any unintended cues that the research procedure may offer the subjects about what the research hypothesis is.

5. *Inventiveness.* An orienting attitude that values inventiveness, such as the ability to develop good hypotheses and to recognize the uniformity of nature (Chandrasekhar, 1987), is greatly prized. Inventiveness is also used in finding financial resources, laboratory space, and equipment; recruiting and scheduling research participants; responding to emergencies during the conduct of research; finding new ways to analyze data, if they are called for; and coming up with convincing interpretations of the results.

6. *Confidence in one's own judgment.* Tolman (1959) also said:

> It seems to me that very often major new scientific insights have come when the scientist. . . has been shaken out of his up-until-then approved scientific rules. . . Since all the sciences, and especially psychology, are still immersed in such tremendous realms of the uncertain and the unknown, the best that any individual scientist, especially any psychologist, can do seems to be to follow his own gleam and his own bent, however inadequate they may be. (pp. 93, 152)

In other words, still another prized attitude is confidence in one's own judgment, or as another writer put it:

> You have to believe that by the simple application of your own mind to the facts of experience, you can discover the truth—a little part of it anyway—the truth about nature and how it works. (Regis, 1987, p. 209)

7. *Consistency and care about details.* Taking pride in one's work provides a constructive attitude toward the relentless detail involved in good research. In science there is no substitute for accuracy and for the hours of care needed to keep complete records, organize and analyze data accurately, state facts precisely, and proofread carefully.

8. *Ability to communicate.* Whether or not one subscribes to the notion that writing is an "unnatural act" (as procrastinators joke), an attitude that values the ability to communicate is another essential aspect of good scientific practice. It has been stated:

> The literature of science, a permanent record of the communication between scientists, is also the history of science: a record of truth, of observations and opinions, of hypotheses that have been ignored or have been found wanting or have withstood the test of further observation and experiment. Science is a continuing endeavor in which the end of one investigation may be the starting point for another. *Scientists must write,* therefore, so that their discoveries may be known to others. (Barrass, 1978, p. 25)

9. *Integrity and honest scholarship.* Finally, an orienting attitude that values integrity and honest scholarship, and that abhors dishonesty and sloppiness, is paramount in good scientific practice (see American Association for the Advancement of Science, 1988; Bridgstock, 1982; Koshland, 1988). Social psychologists speak of "primacy" and "recency" effects in attitude formation. That is, statements tend to produce their greatest impact when presented at the very beginning (primacy effect) or the very end (recency effect) of a lengthy discussion (Rosnow, 1966), so we have listed this orienting attitude last in this discussion not because it is less important than the rest, but because it is the *most important* characteristic of good scientific practice. Because it undermines the basic respect for the literature on which the advancement of science depends, dishonesty (e.g., "rigged" experiments or the presentation of faked results) is devastating to science. Safeguarding against dishonesty is the responsibility of each scientist, and it is a duty that must be taken very seriously.

SUMMARY OF IDEAS

1. Five reasons for studying research methods are (a) to provide a richer appreciation of the information that science brings to modern life; (b) to avoid falling prey to hucksters whose claims are based on pseudoscience or bad science; (c) to learn information and skills that are transferable beyond the research setting; (d) to learn that there are limits to science and that generalizations are always based in part on a "leap of faith"; and (e) to consider research as a career.

2. The *Hawthorne effect* refers to one of the potential limits of research on human subjects: Changes in subjects' behavior are sometimes due to being studied rather than to the experimenter's manipulation; therefore it is prudent to consider subjects' perceptions as a part of any methodological strategy.

3. Four alternative strategies for the "fixation of belief" were characterized by Peirce as (a) the method of tenacity; (b) the method of authority; (c) the a priori method; and (d) the scientific method.

4. The *scientific method* is a misnomer, in that it is not any single, fixed procedure but a philosophical outlook as much as an arsenal of research tools.

5. *Empirical reasoning,* using observation and measurement as an aid to reasoning, is a primary characteristic of the scientific method. Examples applied to real-life problems were (a) Feynman's demonstration of the probable cause of the *Challenger* disaster; (b) Galton's actuarial study of prayer; and (c) Ceci's experimental study of children's eyewitness testimony.

6. The scientific method, although uniquely distinguished by its reliance on empirical reasoning, also relies on rhetoric, perceptible images, and aesthetics.

7. The language (or *rhetoric*) of science is limited in some ways and is not always an exact representation of the way in which creative ideas are formulated.

8. Behavioral science comprises different fields that emphasize the use of different methodologies, but all are concerned with how and why people behave as they do, including how and why they feel and think as they do.

9. To develop a more complete or integrated picture of human nature, interdisciplinary fields of behavioral science (e.g., mass media research) have been developed.

10. Descriptive research, which maps out a situation, tells "how things are."
11. Relational research, which describes the relation between two sets of observations, tells "how things are in relation to other things."
12. Experimental research, which aims at the identification of causes, tells "how things are and how they got to be that way."
13. Good scientific practice values (a) enthusiasm, (b) an open mind, (c) good sense, (d) role-taking ability, (e) inventiveness, (f) self-confidence, (g) consistency and carefulness, (h) communication ability, and, most important, (i) integrity and honest scholarship.

KEY TERMS

ad hoc hypothesis   *p. 16*
aesthetics   *p. 11*
a priori method   *p. 7*
behavior   *p. 12*
behavioral science   *p. 12*
control group   *p. 10*
descriptive research   *p. 15*
empirical reasoning   *p. 4*
experimental research   *p. 16*
Hawthorne effect   *p. 5*
interdisciplinary   *p. 13*

mental imagery   *p. 10*
method of authority   *p. 6*
method of tenacity   *p. 5*
multiplistic viewpoint   *p. 13*
principle of the drunkard's search   *p. 17*
psychophysics   *p. 13*
relational research   *p. 15*
rhetoric   *p. 10*
rhetoric of behavioral science   *p. 10*
scientific method   *p. 6*
serendipity   *p. 17*

REVIEW QUESTIONS

1. A Wayne State researcher is interested in the effects of children's viewing TV violence on the children's level of aggression on the playground. The amount and type of viewing will be assessed through a standard procedure: TV diaries sent to parents. Aggression will be rated by two judges. The researcher hypothesizes that children who spend more time watching violent TV at home are more aggressive on the playground than their peers who watch relatively little violent TV at home. Of the three general research types (i.e., descriptive, relational, and experimental), which type is this?

2. A Wichita State researcher plans to assign fifth-grade children to one of two conditions. Half the children (Group A) will be shown a relatively violent movie at 10:30, and half (Group B) will be shown a nonviolent movie at the same time. Each film will be equally engaging. Two observers will code the children's behavior when both groups are brought back together on the playground for their 11:00 recess. This procedure will continue daily for six weeks. The researcher predicts that Group A will be more aggressive than Group B. What type of research is this?

3. A researcher at the University of New Hampshire wants to measure the prevalence of shyness in the undergraduate community. She administers the well-

standardized Shyness Scale to volunteers in a main dining hall, collecting data on a respectable 35% of all undergraduates. What type of research is this?

4. A North Dakota State student wants to study other students' creativity, and he wants to use all three types of research approaches—descriptive, relational, and experimental—in this project. Think of a concrete example of each type that he could use.

5. A student at Foothill College claims that it is not possible to study such nonscientific concepts as prayer because prayer falls in the domain of theology rather than of science. Is the student correct?

Answers to review questions are found on pages 320–334.

CHAPTER 2

Strategies of Discovery

PREVIEW QUESTIONS

➤ Where do good research ideas come from?

➤ How can I use the library to help sharpen my ideas?

➤ How can I run a literature search using a computer?

➤ How should I go about defining concepts?

➤ What is the distinction between regulative principles, hypotheses, models, and theories?

➤ What constitutes an "acceptable" hypothesis?

➤ What is the purpose of a construct?

➤ What is meant by the terms *independent variable* and *dependent variable*?

➤ What is the role of exploration in discovery?

THE STAGES OF DISCOVERY

How do scientists get their ideas? Often they find cues by simply reading the research literature, where they may uncover basic problems that still need probing or questions that have gone unanswered. On the other hand, sometimes ideas seem to be thrust on them by circumstances. For example, Edwin H. Land invented the Polaroid Land Camera after his 3-year-old daughter asked him why a camera could not produce pictures instantly. Thinking about her question while out for a stroll, he suddenly hit on the idea of a camera that would produce developed photographs.

In another case, Ronald Ley, an experimental psychologist, was on a trans-Atlantic flight when an important research question occurred to him. He had just completed several years of exhaustive detective work for a book about the activities of Wolfgang Köhler (the founder of Gestalt psychology) during World War I. Köhler was presumed only to be researching animal behavior on Tenerife, an island off the coast of Africa, but Ley (1990) discovered that Köhler had been a spy for the German military, and that the research station had been a cover for his activities. On his flight back to the United States, Ley was reflecting on his three-year odyssey when his thoughts were interrupted by the passenger sitting next to him, a middle-aged woman who had told him earlier about her anxieties about flying:

> Since anxiety is so commonly associated with flying, I wasn't alarmed by her remarks. But now her chest heaved rapidly as she sat, mouth wide open, gasping for air. In the moment before I turned to offer my help, I wondered if hyperventilation played a part in the initiation and maintenance of anxiety. Could it be that the effects of stress-induced hyperventilation were antecedents of anxiety as well as consequences? I wondered where this question would take me. (p. 255)

It took him, in fact, to the development of a program of empirical research on panic disorder (e.g., Ley, 1993).

In this chapter, we examine what goes on during the initial phase of research, in which the scientist comes up with an idea and crystallizes it into a testable supposition (i.e., a *working hypothesis*). The traditional name for this phase is *discovery* (Reichenbach, 1938), a term reflecting the idea of the scientist as "an adventurer into the domain of what is not yet known or not yet understood" (Medawar, 1969, p. 2). (In later chapters, we discuss what goes on in the second phase of the research process, called *justification*, in which scientists test their working hypotheses and then logically defend their conclusions, usually with the aid of statistics.) It is convenient to divide discovery into three stages: (1) initial thinking, (2) plausibility, and (3) acceptability (Kordig, 1978). We discuss all three stages, beginning with a number of broad scenarios in which research ideas may spring up: (1) the use of an intensive case study; (2) the effort to make sense of a paradoxical incident; (3) the use of metaphors; (4) the attempt to resolve conflicting results; (5) the effort to improve on older ideas; and (6) *serendipity,* or the exploitation of an unexpected observation or experimental result.

Once you have a promising idea, you need to shape and polish it into a working hypothesis. We describe what criteria you need to keep in mind and also how you can use the resources of your college library to get started in your literature search. It is also important to understand the distinction between a number of basic terms, such as *hypotheses, theories,* and *independent* and *dependent variables,* all of which are discussed in this chapter. Finally, we examine the idea of using exploratory observations as a basis of discovery, because no absolute rule says that you *must* follow a traditional path. Such a rule, in fact, would be the antithesis of the advice given to scientists by Edward C. Tolman (in Chapter 1), when he recommended that each researcher "follow his own gleam and his own bent." Nonetheless, it is expected that reports of empirical research in behavioral science will conform to certain conventions (described in Appendix A). One reason for these conventions is to allow busy people to read research reports more easily.

USING AN INTENSIVE CASE STUDY

In the first general scenario, psychologists, sociologists, psychiatrists, and others have used interviewing, testing, and other potentially informative methods to gather information for *intensive case studies*. In this approach, investigators describe or record what happens when people do something, or they describe and analyze why people behave (or say they behave) as they do. Case studies are also used in educational research, policymaking studies, organizational and management studies, city and regional planning, and many other situations that call for descriptive or relational information (Merriam, 1991; Yin, 1989).

For example, going back to the classic work of Sigmund Freud (1856–1939), the intensive case study has been used on an individual basis by psychoanalytically inclined researchers to generate ideas about human motivation and subsequent behavior. Freud developed ideas by using the *free association method* (i.e., the subject tells whatever passes through his or her mind) to tease out the concealed psychological bases of people's neurotic symptoms that apparently had no organic cause. Using information from individual cases, and from fellow psychiatrists, Freud formulated his theory of motivation. Countless examples of intensive case studies of individual patients or clients (as some clinical and counseling psychologists prefer to call them) have helped to enrich our understanding of the etiology (i.e., the causes) of psychological disorders. Some of these ideas have in turn spawned research in such diverse areas of behavioral science as memory, animal behavior, and cognitive development, among others (Kazdin, 1980).

An intensive case study of a quite different kind was done by Perry London, a clinical psychologist. Hannah Arendt's (1963) insightful book on the Adolf Eichmann trial in Jerusalem generated considerable interest in developing an understanding of the character traits and motivations of Christians who saved Jews from the horrors perpetrated by the Nazis during World War II. London and his colleagues carried out intensive case studies of 27 rescuers and 42 rescued people by tape-recording and then analyzing open-ended interviews with each of them. Because the respondents were not a random sample, the researchers could not generalize from this group of rescuers to the majority of those who aided Jews during World War II. At best, then, this study could be used only to generate some tentative hypotheses, or as London (1970) put it, "The lacunae in our data are so great that we cannot even conjecture about the generality of our hypotheses" (p. 249).

A number of interesting leads were developed out of the case studies. One observation was that the behavior of the rescuers could not be boiled down to any simplistic definition. Some of them had been well compensated for their efforts, others had spent fortunes and had been left destitute, and still others had started out with little and had shared their meager resources with the rescued. Motives were even harder to pin down. Some of the rescuers were fanatically religious, and others were atheists; some of the rescuers had deep affiliations with the Jewish community, and others were anti-Semitic. Three promising clues emerged as the basis of a plausible hypothesis to be evaluated more critically at a later time. First, almost all the rescuers interviewed possessed a spirit of adventure. Second, they also had an intense identification with a parental model of moral conduct. Third, they appeared to be socially marginal in terms of German culture. London (1970, p. 249) hypothesized a scenario in which a zest for adventure and chance were important in the initiation of rescue behavior, but what gave the rescuers the impetus and endurance to do what they did was their strong identification with a very moralistic parental model and the experience of social marginality.

A classic example of the case study method in experimental psychology was the work of Hermann Ebbinghaus (1850–1909), another early pioneer in the development of psychology as a science. Using himself as the case studied, Ebbinghaus developed theoretical curves to describe the rates at which information is actually learned and forgotten. To do this, he carefully measured his own ability to learn and relearn thousands of nonsense syllables, each consisting of a random combination of two consonants and a middle vowel, pronounceable as words but uniformly lacking in meaning (e.g., *XOT, BOK, LUM, ZAT*). With himself as the sole subject, he first recorded how long it took him to master a list of nonsense syllables. He waited until he had forgotten the syllables and then relearned the list. He then repeated the procedure again, each time making a careful record of his learning and forgetting.

MAKING SENSE OF A PARADOXICAL INCIDENT

We mentioned earlier that some research questions are thrust on us by circumstances, which is usually the case in the second general scenario: the attempt to make sense of a *paradoxical incident* (i.e., an event that seems contradictory). Social psychologists Bibb Latané and John Darley were puzzled by contradictory aspects of the circumstances surrounding a lurid murder in Queens, New York. A nurse was coming home from work at 3 A.M. when she was attacked by a man who stabbed her repeatedly. When they heard her cries of terror, more than three dozen of her neighbors came to their windows to see what was happening. According to Latané and Darley, not one of them went to her aid, even though it took the stalker over half an hour to murder her. The social psychologists were struck by the paradox that, even though there were so many witnesses, none had bothered to call the police. They wondered whether *so many* people failed to intervene because each believed someone else was likely to. Latané and Darley developed their hypothesis—which they called the "diffusion of responsibility"—predicting that the more witnesses to an emergency, the less likely it is that any one of them will offer help.

The researchers then proceeded to test their diffusion-of-responsiblity hypothesis in a series of experiments (see Latané & Darley, 1970). For example, in a study at Columbia University, they demonstrated that the larger the number of students present, the less likely any of them was to volunteer to help in an emergency (Latané & Darley, 1968). The students in this experiment had agreed to take part in a discussion of problems related to life at an urban university. As the discussion progressed, a stream of smoke began to puff into the room through a wall vent. The researchers found that, if one student was in the room, she or he was about twice as likely to report the emergency than if the student were in the room with as few as three others. Instead of reporting the emergency, students in a group tended to be passive and to dismiss their fears through rationalization. In a similar study with introductory psychology students at New York University, who had also agreed to take part in a discussion group, each was much more likely to report a (simulated) epileptic seizure that he or she happened to hear if alone than if he or she believed that others were also aware of the emergency (Darley & Latané, 1968).

METAPHORS

A third general scenario calls for the use of *metaphorical themes* that allow a particular view of the world. In Chapter 1, we spoke of the mental imagery that is characteristic of scientific (indeed all) beliefs; an example is how metaphors are used. In common parlance, a *metaphor* is a word or phrase applied to something it does not literally denote. "Her life was an uphill climb" and "He is between a rock and a hard place" are metaphors: Each suggests a comparison with another situation. Whether used in everyday speech or in science, such comparisons allow us to see new connections by making us think about one thing in terms of another (Billow, 1977; Gigerenzer, 1991). The history of science, including behavioral science (Leary, 1990; Weiner, 1991), is replete with metaphorical themes that have been used to explain novel and unfamiliar events (see also Box 2.1). A classic example goes back to the 17th and 18th centuries, when scientists and philosophers began to argue that the mechanical systems of Galileo and Newton, which had proved an efficient way of reorganizing the clutter of medieval physics, were metaphors for the mechanical nature of all reality. In the formative years of behavioral science—and carrying over, to an extent, into modern psychology (see Rosnow, 1981)—it was widely believed that human beings might also be understood as a complex piece of machinery.

BOX 2.1   Shock Waves and Ocean Waves

In astronomy recently, the metaphor of ocean waves breaking on a beach has been used to explain shock waves in the atmosphere of a pulsating star (Wallerstein & Elgar, 1992). As the authors of this theoretical idea put it:

> One of the values of recognizing a scientific analogy is the opportunity for scientists investigating one phenomenon to gain insights by studying the analogous phenomenon. In comparing waves on beaches with waves in stellar atmospheres, astronomers may have more to learn from oceanographers than vice versa because the former can only observe the whole star (except for the sun), whereas the latter can place instrument packages at selected points on beaches of various gradients, thereby observing the small-scale structure of the phenomenon. (p. 1535)

In this case, the researchers were using a metaphor as a kind of *simile*—that is, as an explicit comparison—by, in effect, saying, "Shock waves are like ocean waves."

In a more recent example, a metaphor was used as the basis of another theory in the work of a social psychologist, William McGuire (1964). He organized an extensive series of studies based on a biological inoculation model in order to discover techniques for inducing resistance to propaganda messages. He began with the assumption that some beliefs are so widely accepted in American society that they are almost truisms (e.g., "Mental illness is not contagious," "It's a good idea to brush your teeth after every meal," and "Cigarette smoking is bad for your health"). McGuire's impression was that such beliefs can be easily modified by propaganda for two reasons. First, recipients of propaganda, seldom having been called on to defend their beliefs, are unpracticed in mustering a defense. Second, they are not motivated to develop a defense because they probably view such beliefs as established and unattackable.

In other words, McGuire's tentative idea was that cultural truisms exist in a kind of "germ-free" environment. Because they are so seldom attacked, the individual is especially vulnerable to their reversal when faced with massive propaganda. This belief in a truism, McGuire reasoned, can be likened to being unvaccinated for smallpox. The person brought up in a germ-free environment and appearing vigorously healthy may be highly vulnerable to a massive viral attack if he or she has not been vaccinated. On the other hand, a weakened dose of the smallpox virus stimulates the person's defenses so that he or she can later overcome a massive attack. Generalizing from this metaphor, it follows that, to immunize people against massive propaganda, one exposes them to some of the propaganda in advance, so that they can build up their defenses by rehearsing arguments against the propaganda. Exposing them to too much preliminary propaganda may produce the opposite effect, causing them to reverse their attitude. The problem—which McGuire worked out in his empirical research—is to establish the precise amount of "live virus" in an "inoculation" that, without giving the subjects the "disease," will help build a defense against a future massive attack by the same "virus."

RESOLVING CONFLICTING RESULTS

In a fourth possible scenario, the scientist comes up with an insight by trying to *account for conflicting results*. In some cases, it is even possible to argue that both sides are right, which was the strategy used by Marshall B. Jones and Robert S. Fennell (1965). During the 1940s, there was a protracted dispute between Clark L. Hull and Edward C. Tolman concerning the nature of animal learning. Hull, inspired by Pavlov's research on conditioned reflexes, had developed a systematic behavior theory that asserted that the stimulus (S) affects the organism (O), but that the resulting response (R) depends on O as well as on S. According to this so-called S-O-R model, learning is a mechanistic process, in which S-R connections are automatically strengthened only because they occur in association with reinforcement. On the other hand, Tolman's "S-S model" (also called *purposive behaviorism* and *expectancy theory*) stressed the cognitive nature of learning: Behavior is goal-directed and makes use of environmental supports, but this process is a discontinuous one that depends on exploratory behaviors from which the animal learns what leads to what. Docility, Tolman argued, is thus a mark of purpose, because the animal is learning by acquiring expectations and forming "cognitive maps."

Not only were there distinct theoretical and methodological differences between these two camps, but they also used different strains of selectively bred rats. The Tolmanians, centered at the University of California, used a strain of rats that had been selectively bred by others from matings of wild males and laboratory albino females. The Hullians, at Yale under Hull's direction and a second camp at the University of Iowa under Kenneth W. Spence, used another strain of rats that had originally been bred for nonemotionality. It occurred to Jones and Fennell that genetic differences might explain the different results obtained by the Tolmanians and the Hullians, as the two strains of rats had been separated for over 30 years (during which time they had been differently and selectively bred). To test this idea, Jones and Fennell used rats from both strains to replicate the animal learning experiments by the Tolmanians and the Hullians. The Hullian rats, in the words of Jones and Fennell (1965), "popped out of the start box, ambled down the runway, around the turn, and into the goal box," while the Tolman rats "seemed almost oblivious to their environment." Presumably, Hull and Tolman were both correct (see also Box 2.2).

Another example of how scientists sometimes come up with an innovative discovery by trying to account for conflicting results is illustrated by the work of Robert Zajonc (pronounced "zy-ence," rhymes with *science*). He proposed a hypothesis that he termed "social facilitation" (Zajonc, 1965) to account for some conflicting published data: Some reports indicated that performance in humans and animals improved when passive observers were present, whereas other reports

---

BOX 2.2　　　When Dayyans and Scientists Agree

Jones and Fennell's adjudication of the Tolman–Hull conflict is reminiscent of an old Yiddish anecdote and its reincarnation as a maxim of modern science. A dayyan, or rabbinical judge, was asked by a couple to mediate a lingering controversy in which they were embroiled. The woman told her story, and the dayyan commented, "You are right." Then the man told his side, and the dayyan responded, "You are right." A young student, overhearing the conversations, pointed out to the dayyan, "Surely they both can't be a hundred percent right." To which the dayyan replied, "You are right, too."

In modern science, the physicist Neils Bohr stated that "the opposite of a great truth is also true," while the behavioral scientists Donald T. Campbell and Julian C. Stanley (1963) put it this way:

> When one finds, for example, that competent observers advocate strongly divergent points of view, it seems likely on a priori grounds that both have observed something valid about the natural situation, and that both represent a part of the truth. (p. 3)

Of course, even when all agree, this is no certain proof of accuracy. In science, the test for accuracy (as noted in Chapter 1) is empirical confrontation.

showed performance becoming poorer in the presence of others. For instance, in one experiment, subjects were required to learn a list of nonsense syllables, either alone or in the presence of others. The number of trials needed to learn the list was the criterion variable. Those subjects who learned the list alone averaged more than 9 trials, and those who learned the syllables before an audience averaged more than 11 trials (Pessin, 1933). In other experiments, subjects who performed a familiar task in groups did better than when they performed the task alone (Bergum & Lehr, 1963). It seemed that the presence of others enhanced performance on some tasks but not on others.

How could these seemingly inconsistent results be explained? One important finding in experimental psychology is that a high drive level causes people to give the dominant response to a stimulus. When the task is familiar and well learned, the dominant response will probably be correct; when the task is novel and the correct responses are unknown or not well learned, the dominant response will be incorrect. Zajonc started with the idea that the presence of others serves to increase the individual's drive level and that this increase leads to dominant responses. Therefore, Zajonc reasoned, the presence of others must inhibit learning new responses but facilitate the performance of well-learned responses. If this is true, then it follows that students should study alone, preferably in an isolated cubicle, and then (once they have learned the correct responses) take examinations with many other students on a stage before a large audience.

However, Zajonc also intuitively recognized some plausible limitations on his social facilitation hypothesis. For example, when confronted with a highly complex and ambiguous problem to which the answer is not immediately apparent or well learned, we should expect to solve the problem more quickly alone than in a group. On the other hand, if a problem is one whose solution will be easily recognized when suggested by others, groups would probably fare better in solving it than isolated individuals because the correct response is likely to be given by someone in the group. This example not only illustrates the fourth possible scenario but also shows how good intuition and role-taking ability—two of the orienting attitudes listed in Chapter 1—help to move an initial idea forward.

IMPROVING ON OLDER IDEAS

A fifth scenario involves *trying to improve on an influential older idea*. For example, one of many contributions by the noted experimentalist B. F. Skinner was to show that it is possible to look at two sets of older ideas in a new light, those of the Russian physiologist Ivan Pavlov and those of the American psychologist E. L. Thorndike. In the 1930s, Skinner's clear distinction between Pavlov's and Thorndike's ideas of conditioning opened the way to a long series of innovative laboratory studies by Skinner and a great many others (e.g., Ferster & Skinner, 1957; Skinner, 1938).

Pavlov had done pioneering work on classical conditioning. In the experimental procedure that produces this type of conditioning, a neutral stimulus is paired with one that always brings about some desired behavior or response. Suppose we, like Pavlov, wish to condition a hungry dog to salivate at the sound of a bell. After the animal becomes accustomed to the apparatus, we sound the bell to make sure that the dog does not automatically salivate to it. The dog pricks up its ears or barks, but it does not salivate. We now know that the bell will not cause the animal to respond as it does to food. The next step is to ring the bell and present meat to the dog. If we do this a number of times, we find that the dog begins to salivate at the sound of the bell, before we present the meat.

In contrast, E. L. Thorndike, who experimented at about the same time as Pavlov, in the early 1900s, worked with what he called "trial-and-error learning." For example, he studied how cats learned to escape from a puzzle box to gain food. He was convinced that the cats did not reason out a solution. Instead, he thought that their getting out and eating the food he provided somehow strengthened the connection between successful escape movements and the actual escape.

Skinner perceived a clear distinction between Pavlov's and Thorndike's types of conditioning. Skinner pointed out that in Pavlovian conditioning the major factor is the stimulus that precedes the response. The response is elicited reflexively. In Thorndike's trial-and-error conditioning, the major factor is the stimulus consequence (i.e., the reinforcement of escaping the puzzle box), which follows the response. Skinner focused his own work on the latter type of conditioning, called *operant* or *instrumental*. In operant conditioning, first, the organism responds to a stimulus, and then something is done that will either increase or decrease the probability of its making the same response again. Say that we wish to train a dog to sit on command, and we prepare the animal by withholding food for a time. An operant-conditioning procedure requires that we reward the dog with food *after* it sits (or approximates sitting) following the command. The work on operant conditioning, in turn, paved the way for applications in the military, educational institutions, and the treatment of behavior disorders.

Another classic illustration of this fifth possible scenario is Stanley Milgram's series of experiments (1974) on how far people will go in subjecting another person to pain at the order of an authority figure. We will have more to say about this research in the next chapter, but it will suffice here to note that Milgram (1977) came up with the idea for the obedience experiments as a way to make a set of earlier experiments done by Solomon Asch "more humanly significant" (p. 12). Asch's research had been designed to determine under what conditions people will remain independent of their groups and when they will conform. He designed an experiment in which he used confederates to influence an individual subject's expressed judgment concerning which of three lines was closest in length to a standard line.

Milgram (1977) recalled the moment when he suddenly hit on the idea for his obedience experiments:

> I was dissatisfied that the test of conformity was judgments about *lines*. I wondered whether groups could pressure a person into performing an act whose human import was more readily apparent, perhaps behaving aggressively toward another person, say by administering increasingly severe shocks to him. But to study the group effect you would also need an experimental control; you'd have to know how the subject performed without any group pressure. At

that instant, my thought shifted, zeroing in on this experimental control. Just how far *would* a person go under the experimenter's orders? It was an incandescent moment, the fusion of a general idea on obedience with a specific technical procedure. Within a few minutes, dozens of ideas on relevant variables emerged, and the only problem was to get them all down on paper (p. 12).

SERENDIPITY

Serendipity, which is defined in ordinary language as the faculty for making lucky or accidental discoveries, is also a sixth possible scenario (see Box 2.3). For example, without the question asked by Edwin Land's daughter, he might never have

---

BOX 2.3　　Serendipity in the Art World

Serendipity comes from Serendip, once the name for Sri Lanka, because it was claimed that the three princes of Serendip made lucky discoveries. As this etymology suggests, serendipity also plays a role in the discovery process in daily life. One day in May 1984, a young artist named J. S. G. Boggs was sitting in a Chicago diner having a doughnut and coffee and doodling on a napkin. As the waitress kept refilling his cup, the doodle evolved into an abstracted one-dollar bill. Fascinated, the waitress asked if she could buy it, causing Boggs to wonder why anyone would want a greasy napkin covered with coffee stains and perspiration. "Tell you what," he said, "I'll pay you for my doughnut and coffee with this drawing." To his astonishment she took the "dollar" and gave him a dime's change!

Inspired by this lucky incident, Boggs began using colored ink and pencils to launch a career of drawing fairly exact representations of existing denominations of actual currency, and then photocopying them and successfully "spending" them in a kind of artistic performance for goods and services (Weschler, 1988). That is, he always insists on receiving a receipt and change in real money; he then sells the change and receipts to collectors, who in turn track down the people who accepted the art currency. The performance ends when all the elements are encased in a frame on the collector's wall.

The story does not end here, however. Boggs, according to an article in *The New York Times* (December 6, 1992), suddenly found himself under scrutiny of the law in several countries. In 1987, he was tried in England on charges of producing counterfeit British currency. When he was found not guilty, he paid his lawyers in drawings. He was also prosecuted in Australia and, this time, was found not guilty and awarded $20,000 in damages. In the United States, the Secret Service seized some of his work, calling it "counterfeit money." They also searched his office at Carnegie Mellon University and stopped him as he was leaving his apartment one day to attend a ceremony where he planned to announce a new project to print $1-million in his own bills. Boggs was quoted in the *Times:* "They said I was a counterfeiter; they don't understand the difference between art and crime."

invented instant photography. Another illustration of serendipity is a fortuitous event that stimulated one of the authors of this book to begin investigating the psychology of rumor.

In 1969, the Beatles were at the height of their popularity when a rumor concerning them began to circulate (Rosnow & Fine, 1974). According to the rumor, Paul McCartney of the Beatles had been decapitated in an automobile accident and replaced by a double. The basic core of the story, which was a preposterous fiction, swept across American colleges and universities with numerous variants and deviations. What made this rumor theoretically interesting was that it was behaving not at all like the rumors that had been described by experts. The authors of one widely cited book had stated that, because of the porosity of human memory, rumors always become shorter (Allport & Postman, 1947). The McCartney rumor was not shrinking; it was growing by leaps and bounds as each person improvised details.

As a consequence of this serendipitous event, the author's incipient interest in rumor was crystallized. The more he looked into this area, the more it became clear to him that accepted explanations of rumor had been largely speculative and untested. He and his associates began a program of investigation that led to a new hypothesis, which was then tested and, in turn, became the basis of a set of ideas for the control of damaging rumors (e.g., DiFonzo, Bordia, & Rosnow, 1994). According to this hypothesis, the process of rumor generation and transmission is like loading and firing a gun. The gun is the public, and the bullet is the rumor, which is loaded in an atmosphere of anxiety and uncertainty. The trigger is pulled when it is believed that the rumor will hit the mark, much as an involving rumor is likely to be passed on if it is perceived as credible. However, when anxiety is intense, passing a rumor is like a shot in the dark because highly anxious people are unlikely to scrutinize rumors very critically (Rosnow, 1980, 1991).

In experimental psychology, a fascinating case of serendipity involved Joseph V. Brady and his work at Walter Reed Army Hospital (see Sidman, 1960). He was running experiments with monkeys, using long-term conditioning, electric shocks, food reinforcements, and brain stimulation. There was an unusually high mortality rate among the monkeys, which he might have continued to treat simply as an unavoidable problem were it not for a remark made to him. R. W. Porter, a pathologist at Walter Reed, heard about the large number of deaths and asked Brady for permission to do postmortems on the next five monkeys that died. During the next few months, Porter occasionally appeared in Brady's office holding a piece of freshly excised monkey gut. Somewhere in the tissue would be a clear round hole, which (Porter explained to Brady) was a perforated ulcer. One day, Porter remarked that, of several hundred monkeys he had examined before coming to Walter Reed, not one had shown any sign of an ulcer.

Porter's observation changed the course of Brady's research. He asked himself: Could the ulcers have something to do with the role the monkeys had been obliged to play in the stress situation? He then did experiments in which monkeys were subjected to electric-shock-avoidance training and were paired with other monkeys who received the same shocks but without the opportunity to avoid them. When the monkeys were examined, those that had been assigned to make "executive" decisions in the stress situation had stomach ulcers, but the "subordinate" monkeys showed no unusual pathology (Brady, 1958; Brady, Porter, Conrad, & Mason, 1958). Porter's remark had led Brady to begin a program of systematic research to pinpoint the psychological factors causing the ulcers.

Interestingly, when a great deal of research is stimulated in a given area, additional discoveries may even contradict earlier results. Later work in this area demonstrated that rats that lacked control over stressful events suffered weight loss and ulcers from *not* being made the executive (Weiss, 1968).

FOCUSING AND ASSESSING IDEAS

Although innovative ideas typically originate from intuitions and an inquisitive nature, we have also seen how reason and logical thought (i.e., Peirce's a priori method) enter into this initial thinking process. They play an even more deliberate role in what may be thought of as the second phase of discovery: the *plausibility stage*. The scientist asks himself or herself whether the initial idea will measure up in, or is worthy of, actual testing, that is, whether there are plausible reasons to support the feasibility of the idea. To help them in this deliberative effort, scientists customarily turn to the pertinent literature in their area of interest. In your own case, an afternoon perusing the variety of reference materials available in the library (e.g., periodicals, standard texts, and abstracts) should get you started on this path. As you approach this task, you might keep in mind the advice given by the philosopher Francis Bacon more than 350 years ago: "Read not to contradict and confute, not to believe and take for granted . . . but to weigh and consider" (Beveridge, 1957, p. 6, quoting from Bacon's 1620 *Novum Organum*).

Following Bacon's advice, look for the most relevant work related to your research idea, and then make detailed notes and analyses, being careful to document the page numbers of any quotations. A good strategy is to write each useful idea and quote on a separate index card along with an exact citation: author and year, title of publication, source of publication, and pages. Not only will having detailed notes pay off as you start pulling your analyses and quotes together to use as background material for your writing, but it will also help you to avoid committing plagiarism accidentally. *Plagiarism* means taking someone else's words and representing them as one's own, and "accidental" plagiarism occurs when one copies someone else's work but forgets to credit it or to put it in quotes (see also Appendix A). Plagiarism is a serious crime of scholarship, and you can guard against it by making precise notes and citing the sources of your material.

SEARCHING THE LITERATURE

If all you need are a few key studies, the simplest approach is to do a by-hand search of *Psychological Abstracts*. This monthly periodical, available in most college and university libraries, gives brief descriptions (abstracts) of thousands of works in psychology and related disciplines. In Figure 2.1 we see that each abstract begins with a *Psychological Abstracts* code number, so that we can easily find the abstract again by going back to this volume (Volume 77) and issue (Number 2) and looking up this code number. The author's name is then listed; if there are many

3460. **Yakimoff, Naum; Lánský, P. & Radil, T.** (Bulgarian Academy of Sciences, Inst of Physiology, Sofia, Bulgaria) **Systematic error in estimating the orientation of random dot patterns.** 23rd Conference of the Higher Nervous Functions (1987, Mariánské Lázně, Czechoslovakia). *Activitas Nervosa Superior,* 1988(Dec), Vol 30(4), 275–276. —A systematic deviation in 10 Ss' estimations of orientation of dot patterns toward visual meridia provided evidence for at least 2 visual axes, other than horizontal and vertical, that might be accepted as standards for obliqueness.

3815. **Cornell, Carole E.; Rodin, Judith & Weingarten, Harvey.** (U Florida, Gainesville) **Stimulus-induced eating when satiated.** *Physiology & Behavior,* 1989(Apr), Vol 45(4), 695–704. —Two studies investigated factors that promote the desire for food when satiated. In Study 1, 20 Ss (aged 16–33 yrs) tested under conditions of either hunger or satiety, were exposed to 1 of 2 palatable foods (pizza or ice cream) and then given more of that food to eat. Operationally-satiated Ss still ate pizza or ice cream, and the sight of these foods enhanced reported desire for them. The amount of these foods consumed was predicted by the Ss' self-reported desire for the food. In Study 2, 28 males (aged 16–28 yrs) were fed to satiety, then primed with either pizza or ice cream (or not primed at all) and then given both pizza and ice cream to eat. Results suggest that a brief taste of a desirable food enhanced its intake relative to the other, equally-preferred food.

4282. **Taylor, Ronald L.** (U Connecticut, Storrs) **Black youth in crisis.** Special Issue: Black America in the 1980s. *Humboldt Journal of Social Relations,* 1987(Fal–Win–Spr–Sum), Vol 14(1–2), 106–133. —Reviews major social indicators that highlight the negative trends among Black adolescents and young adults during the past 2 decades and underscores the need for corrective action. These negative trends include the growth in single-parent families with children under 18 yrs, the significant differences between Black and White youths in the rate of delayed education and in nonattendance, the dramatic increase in the unemployment of Black youth, the disproportionate representation of Black youth in arrest statistics on crime and delinquency, and the continued rise in out-of-wedlock childbearing among Black teens. Programs and policies designed to reverse these negative developments are discussed.

4451. **Hammer, Torild & Vaglum, Per.** (U Oslo, Norway) **The increase in alcohol consumption among women: A phenomenon related to accessibility or stress? A general population study.** *British Journal of Addiction,* 1989(Jul), Vol 84(7), 767–775. —Explored the relative importance of accessibility and stress variables in explaining the increasing level of women's alcohol consumption. Survey data from 3,997 Norwegian women (aged 16+ yrs) and their husbands indicate that population density and husbands' alcohol consumption had a significant impact on women's consumption. Employment among women was not significantly related to their alchohol use when controlling for the husband's consumption. Stress variables had no significant influence on consumption when controlling for accessibility variables. Accessibility variables with a close relationship to lifestyle had a greater impact on consumption than general accessibility to alcoholic beverages.

6383. **Lynn, Michael.** (U Missouri, Columbia) **Scarcity effects on desirability: Mediated by assumed expensiveness?** *Journal of Economic Psychology,* 1989(Jun), Vol 10(2), 257–274. —Conducted 2 studies to examine whether scarcity effects on desirability are due to a tendency for people to assume that scarce things cost more. Study 1, with 392 undergraduates, found that scarcity increased the desirability of art prints only when Ss had been primed to think about the expensiveness of art prints in general. Findings from Study 2, with 171 undergraduates, further supported the hypothesis by finding that scarcity enhanced the desirability of wine only when Ss did not know how much the wine cost. Economic and marketing implications are discussed.

FIGURE 2.1 *Sample abstracts from* Psychological Abstracts. *(Reproduced from* Psychological Abstracts, *Vol. 77, No. 2; reprinted with permission of the American Psychological Association, publisher of* Psychological Abstracts, *all rights reserved.)*

authors, the first author's name is followed by *et al.* (an abbreviation for *et alia,* "and others"). The first author's institutional affiliation is given next, followed by the work's title and the journal (or other) source where the work appeared. If the work was written in a foreign language, the original title is followed by the translated title. A synopsis (summary or abstract) of the work follows.

You should not stop with the abstract, even if it was written by the original author of the work, but go to the work itself and read it. This advice applies even to a summary of a classic work that you find consistently cited and described by many authors. Mark Twain once defined a classic as "a book which people praise and don't read." Ironically, in the area of eyewitness testimony research, classic demonstration studies of information distortion have been misreported in published works for years (Treadway & McCloskey, 1989). It seems many authors have not bothered to read the original work; instead, they copied one another's erroneous descriptions of it.

If you need more than a few key studies, or if your aim is to compile a comprehensive bibliography, ask if your library has PsycLIT. This is a service purchased by your library from the American Psychological Association (APA); it allows you to do a literature search using a computer. PsycLIT comes in the form of a removable disk that stores information contained in the *Psychological Abstracts;* the disks are updated quarterly by the APA. Using PsycLIT is faster and more fun than doing a by-hand search of the *Psychological Abstracts.* Once you have PsycLIT on your screen, you can press the "F3" key to display a list of topics or the "F1" key to get help with the retrieval software. If the terminal is equipped with a printer, you can press the "F6" key to display a menu that will allow you to make a printed copy of your results. You will find that it becomes easier to do a literature search as your experience grows, although inexperienced users will find PsycLIT friendly and time-saving. Ask in the library if you can borrow PsycLIT's "Quick Reference Guide"; it is a written summary of the commands used by PsycLIT and also shows how to define your search. For additional helpful pointers, see Box 2.4.

You will find many other useful collections of abstracts besides *Psychological Abstracts,* and some of these are also accessible by computer. Examples are the *Sociological Abstracts,* ERIC (Educational Resources Information Center), and the *Social Sciences Index.* Indeed, you can find abstracts and indexes for just about every discipline and area of interest (e.g., *Biological Abstracts, Art Index, Abridged Index Medicus,* and *Humanities Index*). The card file or an information librarian can direct you to the most relevant indexes and abstracts in your field of interest. Even with a computer search of the literature, you will need to weed out irrelevant work manually. As you examine the articles and books that your search turned up, you will find earlier works cited (e.g., classic works), and you can go back to the stacks (the rows of books in the library) to look those up. This is called the *ancestry approach,* because you are looking up the work from which the current work descended. You will find additional hints on using the resources of your college library in various manuals for psychology students (e.g., J. G. Reed & Baxter, 1983; Rosnow & Rosnow, 1995).

BOX 2.4	Using PsycLIT

Steven E. Stern (personal communications, September 9, 1993; February 9, 1994), a social psychologist who has taught research methods at Beaver College and Temple University, offers his students the following practice tips to get them started on PsycLIT:

- Pressing the "F2" key on your keyboard puts the word "Find" on the screen; you now tell the computer what you want it to find. Most researchers simply type in the topic. It is easier, however, to use the following abbreviations in your search: AU = personal author(s); DE = descriptors; JN = journal name; PO = population.
- Suppose you are doing research on prejudice. At the "Find" prompt, type "prejudice in DE" (don't type the quotes). You have told the computer to find citations where prejudice is important enough to be listed as a descriptor of the title or synopsis.
- Suppose you are studying aggression and want to find out what a leading researcher has published. Type "Bandura in AU," which instructs the computer to look for work *by* Bandura but not for work that merely *refers* to Bandura.
- Suppose you want studies on attribution but your library takes only one journal in social psychology, the APA's *Journal of Personality and Social Psychology*. Type "attribution and (journal of personality-and-social-psychology in JN)," which tells the computer to narrow its search; the hyphenated title signifies how the journal field is entered in the data base.
- Suppose you wanted studies using humans. Typing "human in PO" (population) roots out any studies using animals ("animal in PO" does just the opposite).
- Now press the "F5" key, which is the "Index" key. If you type in a term or name, the computer will list all alphabetically close words.
- Pressing the "F9" key brings up the "Thesaurus" prompt, and by entering a term, you elicit synonymous or related terms. For example, type "hallucination" after the "Thesaurus" prompt and see what it turns up.
- Notice that there is something called "ISSN#" that comes with every citation. If you cannot find what you want in your college library, you can report this code number and ask if your library can borrow what you need from another library.

OPERATIONAL AND THEORETICAL DEFINITIONS

As you study the material you have gathered, think carefully about the plausibility of your initial idea in the context of the published work. Does the idea still make sense to you in view of what experts have written about the subject? We return to this question later, when we consider the "payoff potential" of the hypothesis. At this juncture, you will also need to think about naming and defining the things you want to study. There are two general types of definitions for you to consider: *operational* and *theoretical* definitions. If you are at the stage of finding terms for what you are interested in studying, you can start by consulting standard texts and encyclopedic works for leads.

For example, you will find psychological terms and concepts defined in V. S. Ramachandan's *Encyclopedia of Human Behavior* (1994), R. Harré and R. Lamb's *Encyclopedic Dictionary of Psychology* (1983), B. B. Wolman's *International Encyclopedia of Psychiatry, Psychology, Psychoanalysis, and Neurology* (1977), and R. J. Corsini's *Encyclopedia of Psychology* (1984). Other useful encyclopedic works are the *International Encyclopedia of the Social Sciences* (1968, 18 volumes) and *The Encyclopedia of Education* (1971, 10 volumes). If you would like a reference book *about* reference books, look for E. P. Sheehy's *Guide to Reference Books*; it is a comprehensive, annotated listing of reference books. If you want the best unabridged dictionary of the English language, look for the multivolume *Oxford English Dictionary* (called the *OED*); you will find it a fascinating resource if you are interested in the etymology of words.

Operational definitions identify terms on the basis of the empirical conditions or operations used to measure or to manipulate them. For example, an experimental psychologist may define hunger operationally by using laboratory equipment to measure stomach contractions. A social psychologist may define prejudice operationally by a person's score on an attitude questionnaire. A developmental psychologist may define frustration operationally by stopping a child from playing with a set of attractive new toys. In another example, clinical psychologists Phillip C. Kendall, Bonnie L. Howard, and Rebecca C. Hays (1989) had college students and inpatients at a psychiatric institution respond to an inventory of "thoughts" by indicating how frequently, if at all, each thought had occurred to them over the past week. Some thoughts listed were positive ("I feel very happy" and "This is super!"); others were negative ("My life is a mess" and "There must be something wrong with me"). The researchers used simple statistics to compare their results with previous data and thus developed a way of operationalizing clinical depression by using the proportion of people's positive and negative thoughts.

Theoretical definitions assign the meanings of terms more abstractly or generally, as in defining *hunger* by a connection between the feeling of being hungry and the experience of certain internal and external cues. The social psychologist may define *prejudice* theoretically as "a disposition to hasty or premature judgment." The developmental psychologist may define *frustration* theoretically as "the condition that exists when people's goals are blocked by internal or external barriers." In their research, the team of clinical investigators mentioned above (Kendall et al., 1989) defined *depression* theoretically as the preponderance of negative thinking. Their research findings were, in fact, consistent with this definition: People who had been clinically defined as depressed reported a high proportion of negative thoughts and a low proportion of positive thoughts.

DETAILED EXAMPLE: STUDYING INTELLIGENCE

Before we move on, it will be instructive if we illustrate all we have discussed so far (i.e., coming up with an idea, then doing a literature search, and finally defining it operationally and theoretically) with a concrete example. Suppose we are interested in studying a particular aspect of intelligence. We know that people from different countries and cultures have different ideas about intelligence, but the aspect we have in mind, the ability to deal effectively with one's physical and social environment, seems to cross national and cultural boundaries. For example, buying a pig in southern France gives a farmer a chance to display socially valued judgment. A priest on the Greek island of Cephalonia uses his social skills to settle a dispute between two members of his parish by making each believe that he or she has won. His parishioners say he is wise, by which they seem to mean intelligent in interpersonal matters. These examples illustrate in a preliminary fashion the notion of intelligence we have in mind; they also imply that intelligence, as a general concept, embraces a number of different abilities. Given this crude conception, where do we go next?

We do a literature search to find out more about the notion of intelligence as encompassing multiple abilities. This search, let us say, turns up the early work of J. P. Guilford (1967), who envisioned 120 different ways of being intelligent. We have made a promising beginning, but it does not relate specifically to the notion of intelligence we have in mind. It appears that we will have to be more dogged in our literature search. We consult recent texts and encyclopedic works, and we also ask professors who work in developmental, educational, or social psychology for leads. Let us suppose we hit pay dirt by turning up a body of more recent work on multiple intelligence by developmental, educational, and social psychologists (e.g., Cantor & Kihlstrom, 1989; Ceci, 1990; H. Gardner, 1985, 1993; Sternberg, 1985, 1990; Sternberg & Detterman, 1986; Wyer & Srull, 1989).

All of these researchers stress the existence of intellectual capacities beyond mathematical and language skills, but we are interested in one particular set of skills, called *social intelligence* in social psychology (Cantor & Kihlstrom, 1989, 1989; Wyer & Srull, 1989) and *interpersonal intelligence* in developmental psychology (Gardner, 1985). Howard Gardner (1985) described the core capacity of interpersonal intelligence as "the ability to notice and make distinctions among other individuals and, in particular, their moods, temperaments, motivations, and intentions" (p. 239). This is a good theoretical definition, and we also find others that we can quote later; Gardner (1985) wrote that interpersonal intelligence is a system that "turns outward, to other individuals" (p. 239), and another leading researcher wrote that it involves "understanding and acting upon one's understanding of others" (Sternberg, 1990, p. 265). All of these descriptions are quite consistent with our illustrations of the French farmer and the Greek priest.

All we need now is a research idea to test, and we find many interesting ideas throughout this work. But let us suppose the issue that attracts us most is Gardner's proposal (1985) of a developmental trajectory in interpersonal intelligence. In its most elementary form, interpersonal intelligence entails the ability "to discriminate among individuals . . . and to detect their various moods" (Gardner, 1985, p. 239); in its advanced form, it "permits a skilled adult to read the intentions and desires—even when these have been hidden—of many other individuals and, potentially, to act upon their knowledge" (Gardner, 1985, p. 239). Gardner also hypothesized a number of end-state skills that we can borrow (and cite, of course) to help us develop an operational definition. Aided by his conception, we can now think of more accessible situations in which to tap this type of intelligence (e.g., Rosnow, Skleder, Jaeger, & Rind, 1994). For example, the ability of a child to detect the meaning of another's schoolyard behavior would seem to be, according to this conception, an indicator of the child's level of interpersonal intelligence.

REGULATIVE PRINCIPLES, HYPOTHESES, MODELS, AND THEORIES

By reading, thinking, and keeping our eyes and minds open, we find we are able to zero in on ideas and on possible operational and theoretical definitions. We are ready to tackle the final phase of the discovery process (*acceptability*), in which the scientist accepts the plausibility of the idea and molds it into a testable supposition. This testable supposition is generally referred to as the *working hypothesis* or (in experimental research) the *experimental hypothesis*. Before we go on, however, it will be useful to clarify the usual distinction made between hypotheses, theories, and models. Keep in mind, as you read the following cases, that a *hypothesis* is basically a conjectural statement; a *theory* is a larger set of such statements that are connected by logical arguments and certain hidden (or implicit) assumptions; and a *model* is a conceptual representation that is narrower than a theory but broader than a hypothesis.

Let us start with the idea of a model because we have already noted some cases in this chapter. One example is McGuire's idea of biological inoculation as a model for inducing resistance to propaganda. When we spoke of this work, we also used the term *theory* to describe McGuire's work, and in fact there is a thin line between models and theories. Some authors think generally of models as "theorizing that is built on an analogy" (N. Miller & Pollock, 1994, p. 459), although it is quite possible to have a simple model in the form of a *flow diagram* (i.e., a graphic representation of a sequence of events or operations in which one event or operation leads to another). One dictionary definition of a model is that it is an "example for comparison," and this idea seems to capture what scientists also mean by the term *model*, including analogies and flow diagrams. Because models are in part speculative generalizations, it is easy to see why they are said to represent a type of "theorizing." This also reminds us that models and theories, like all generalizations (as discussed in Chapter 1), are based in part on a leap of faith.

Because theories are not as narrow as models, theories also are usually more speculative and contain more hidden assumptions in the form of implicit premises (e.g., assumptions about the nature of reality). In philosophy, these implicit premises (or presuppositions) are also called *regulative principles* (see Apel, 1982; Rosnow, 1983). They are essentially intuitive assumptions that have a strong influence on how people (including scientists) theorize and try to paint a coherent picture of reality. For example, a hallowed assumption in social psychology is the idea that humans are "social animals." This does not mean that humans are necessarily sociable, but it does mean that society is "wired into" human nature—a principle that goes back to Aristotle.

Another favorite assumption of the past in behavioral science was *strict determinism,* the principle that there is a causal law for every behavior or action. This principle was a carryover from Newtonian physics, which stresses that there is a causal law for everything. Newton believed that if we know the present exactly, we can calculate the future precisely. In this century, however, the work of Werner Heisenberg and other quantum physicists has taught us that the changes that atoms undergo from one energy level to another are *not* strictly deterministic. The modern physicist, using the rules of probability, can describe the average behavior of a large number of atoms but cannot predict with *certainty* which of several possible actions will occur within an individual atom. The modern behavioral scientist also assumes that much of human activity is not governed by strict causal laws; therefore we cannot predict with 100% certainty how a person or group will behave at a given moment.

So far, we have given a general flavor of scientific models and theories, and now it is time to take a closer look at some examples. For our first example, we will consider the case of balance theory. Behavioral researchers, including many social psychologists, have for some time been interested in both the internal and the external sources of motivation. One of the first concepts used to explain *why* an animal becomes active when it is deprived of food or water was introduced by the French physiologist Claude Bernard in the 19th century and was developed in its modern form by W. B. Cannon in the 1930s. This concept, called *homeostasis,* assumes that there are various states of balance (equilibrium) in the physiological patterns of an organism and that these states can be identified. In the case of food or water deprivation, the concept assumes that the body has a built-in ability to maintain its cellular ingredients (water, protein, and other constituents) at certain optimal levels. Thus the internal environment of an animal cell tends to return to a constant level by the process of cellular intake from, and discharge into, the fluid surrounding it. The water, salt, sugar, protein, calcium, and fat contents of the blood are all kept constant by the natural physiological processes of the body.

Seizing on the concept of homeostasis as a model for human cognitive processing, Fritz Heider (1946, 1958), a leading psychological theorist, saw people as trying to develop a sense of dynamic equilibrium in the networks of interpersonal emotions. Heider defined this interpersonal homeostasis as a situation in which the relations among the entities fit together harmoniously. There is no stress toward change when this state is reached, he assumed. To explicate this process, he devised a set of conceptual propositions in the form of a more general theory of interpersonal relations. In other words, he took the biological concept as a model on which to build a more general theory containing the hidden assumption that people strive toward a sense of dynamic equilibrium.

Following Heider's theoretical lead, two other social psychologists, Dorwin Cartwright and Frank Harary (1956), restated his conceptual propositions not in the prose form Heider used, but by narrowing them down into the form of a model using linear graphs. Figure 2.2 gives some simple examples. A linear graph, as these diagrams show, is a finite collection of points, together with lines connecting all or some of the points. Let us assume that the points represent people and that the lines indicate whether two persons like one another (a solid line) or dislike one another (a dashed line). We can think of a solid line as being positively signed (+) and a dashed line as being negatively signed (−). The rule for determining whether the graph is balanced is that the product of all the different signs must be positive. If we give the solid lines the value of +1 and the dashed lines the value of −1, we see that the graph on the left is balanced but the graph on the right is not balanced. This idea can also be stated in the form of two hypotheses:

1. In a three-person network, if A and B like each other, and if a third person, C, is introduced, the tendency is to develop mutual liking between A, B, and C.
2. However, if A and B do not like each other, the tendency is for one of them to like and the other to dislike C.

Cartwright and Harary also described more complex situations, but the theoretical basis of the hypotheses in all situations is the same: When imbalance occurs, the resultant tension is presumed to act as a force to effect a state of balance.

Let us look at another example. Another popular concept in the field of social psychology is *attribution,* that is, how people explain the causes of interpersonal events. Heider (1944, 1958) also originally assumed that people have a "commonsense" psychology by which they explain the significance of causal relationships in everyday life. He thought that one goal of this explaining is to assign responsibility for the perceived causal relationships: "Was it my fault or yours?" or "Did he intend to hurt me or not?" Heider reasoned theoretically that people attribute behavior either to internal causes (such as personality traits and moods) or to external causes (such as the weather). Thus there would seem to be two alternatives, Heider theorized: You can attribute an occurrence to an external event (e.g.,

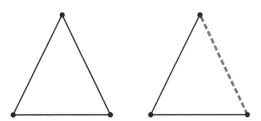

FIGURE 2.2   *Examples of linear graphs. Solid lines denote positively valenced connections between two points, and dashed lines denote negatively valenced connections. The linear graph on the left is balanced, and the linear graph on the right is not balanced.*

you might tell your friend that you are late because you were caught in a traffic jam), or you can attribute it to an internal event (e.g., you might tell your friend that you forgot the time).

Again following Heider's lead, social psychologists who study the cognitive rules of "causal attributions" have derived and tested a number of specific hypotheses. For example, Edward Jones and Richard Nisbett (1972) speculated on how people change their preferences for attributions depending on who is being judged. When we ourselves are "on the spot," we should tend to attribute responsibility for our actions to the situation, especially if we have behaved questionably. When we make attributions to others, however, we should tend to place emphasis on those others (the "actors"). Underlying these two hypotheses is the assumption (i.e., the regulative principle) that we literally do not *see* ourselves as actors when we behave; we see only what is around us. When we watch others, our attention is focused on them and not on their surroundings.

What do these examples teach us about the distinction between regulative principles, hypotheses, models, and theories? First, theories are the most comprehensive and hypotheses the least so. Second, regulative principles are usually untested (like people's prejudices), but hypotheses, models, and theories are presumed to be testable. Third, hypotheses are often derived from models and theories. Fourth, because they are not as comprehensive as theories, hypotheses are more amenable than theories to *focused* (i.e., specific) empirical testing.

We also see that hypotheses, models, and theories are similar in many ways. First, they may range from being precise (e.g., the hypothesis that "Frustration leads to aggression") to quite diffuse (e.g., the hypothesis that "Something will happen if I thwart individuals by interfering with the fulfillment of their expectations"). Second, they fall back on hidden (or implicit) assumptions (i.e., regulative principles). Third, they give direction to researchers' observations, a direction researchers cannot do without. To illustrate, an eminent professor once told his students, "Take pencil and paper; carefully observe, and write down what you have observed." They immediately asked, of course, *what* it was he wanted them to observe, because observation needs a chosen object, a definite task, an interest, a point of view, and a problem (Popper, 1934, 1963). Hypotheses, models, and theories "select" what is to be observed by the researcher.

MOLDING IDEAS INTO ACCEPTABLE HYPOTHESES

We can now ask what constitutes an *acceptable* hypothesis in behavioral science. The answer, as in other scientific areas, is that there are three essential criteria: (1) correspondence with reality; (2) a combination of coherence and parsimony; and (3) falsifiability.

First, *correspondence with reality* refers to the extent to which the hypothesis agrees with accepted truths based on reliable empirical findings. Hypotheses that correspond most closely to such accepted truths are believed to have a higher *payoff potential* when subjected to empirical testing themselves. That is, they are expected to be much more easily corroborated than hypotheses that come out of the blue. There is no way, of course, to be absolutely sure that your working hypothesis will pay off when it is tested, but you can increase the odds in your favor by making sure it agrees with known facts.

Incidentally, many scientists now also use a technique called *meta-analysis* (described in Appendix C) to address the payoff potential question, by grouping the results of previously published studies with the aid of statistical techniques. Using meta-analysis, they ascertain whether they are apt to find small, medium, or large effects, so that they can anticipate how difficult it will be (e.g., how many subjects they will need, discussed in a later chapter) to corroborate their hypothesis if it is correct.

Second, the joint criteria of coherence and parsimony provide another standard by which scientists evaluate the quality of working hypotheses. *Coherence* refers to whether the hypothesis "sticks together," and *parsimony* refers to how "sparing" or "frugal" it is. Scientists believe that, to be acceptable, a hypothesis must be only as complicated or wordy as is absolutely necessary. They "cut away" what is superfluous by means of a ruminative and winnowing process that is known as *Occam's razor,* after William of Occam, a 14th-century Franciscan philosopher who insisted that we cut away what is unwieldy. What can be explained on fewer principles is explained needlessly by more, he stated.

A word of caution: Occam's razor is not a description of nature (because nature is often very complicated); it is instead a prescription for hypotheses. That is, it is important not to cut off too much—"beards" but not "chins." How can you find out whether your hypothesis cuts off too much or does not cut off enough? A straightforward approach is to ask your instructor for critical feedback and suggestions to help you avoid any missteps.

The final criterion is *falsifiability,* which is synonymous with *refutability.* Beginning in the 1930s, the philosopher Karl Popper, recognizing that it is possible for those with a fertile imagination to find support for even the most preposterous propositions, put forth the criterion of falsifiability as the sine qua non of scientific hypotheses. Propositions that cannot, in principle, be shown to be false are not within the realm of science, he argued (Popper, 1934, 1961). As you peruse the journal literature on your research topic, you will find many models of refutable hypotheses and will thus begin to get a sense of the nature of acceptable propositions for testing in behavioral science.

An example of a proposition that is not refutable is, "All behavior is a product of the good and evil lying within us." Superstitions and prejudices are other examples of nonrefutable propositions, because people who believe them *want* to believe and will not open their minds to any evidence to the contrary (see the method of tenacity, as described in Chapter 1). In sum, your working hypothesis has to be stated in a potentially falsifiable way, because a proposition not refutable by any conceivable observation cannot be called scientific.

CONSTRUCTS AND VARIABLES

In Chapter 1, we mentioned that the rhetoric of science involves the use of technical terms. Two terms, which refer to key aspects of scientists' theories and hypotheses, are *constructs* and *variables. Constructs* are   theoretical   concepts formulated (i.e., constructed) to serve as causal or descriptive explanations. We discuss constructs and their validation more fully later in this book, but an example is the "diffusion of responsibility" construct mentioned earlier. Latané and Darley used this construct (or concept) to explain why each bystander in a group feels that he or she is not chiefly responsible for summoning help, and that others should and will help. As described in a later chapter, constructs act as a kind of "theoretical scaffolding" between variables, particularly between what are called *independent* and *dependent variables*.

A *variable* is an event or condition that the researcher observes or measures or plans to investigate and that is liable to variation (or change). The rhetoric of behavioral science recognizes a further distinction between *dependent variables* and *independent variables*. The *dependent variable* (usually symbolized as Y) is the "effect" (or outcome) in which the researcher is interested; the *independent variable* (usually symbolized as X) is the presumed "cause," changes in which lead to changes in the dependent variable. For example, in the statement "Jogging makes you feel better," the independent variable (X) is jogging or not jogging, and the dependent variable (Y) is feeling better or not feeling better. It is important to recognize, however, that *any* event or condition may be an independent *or* a dependent variable. Thus we might also imagine "feeling" affecting "jogging." How a variable should be labeled depends on its context.

EXAMPLES OF INDEPENDENT VARIABLES

You may ask whether there is any agreed-upon way of classifying independent variables in behavioral science, in the way, for instance, that chemists can turn to the periodic table to see how a particular element is classified. The answer is no. There are, in fact, scores of different independent variables in the research literature of behavioral science.

One broad category of independent variables is physiological mechanisms. To illustrate, let us say we are interested in the mechanisms of eating behavior. One example of a physiological mechanism is seen when blood from a well-fed animal, as compared to the blood of a hungry animal, is injected into another animal that is hungry: The hungry animal stops feeding (Davis, Gallagher, & Ladove, 1967). This finding suggests that a physiological stimulus for satiation is somehow carried by the blood: Information about a cell need must be transmitted to a part of the central nervous system that is well supplied with blood and that can control and organize the food-getting activities of the whole animal.

Here is another example in this broad category. Physicians have observed that tumors in the region of the brain near the hypothalamus and the pituitary gland cause the symptoms (described as Fröhlich's syndrome) of tremendous obesity and atrophy of the genital organs. It was unclear, before classic experiments on animals, whether the syndrome was due to damage of the pituitary or to damage of the hypothalamus by the tumor. When the pituitary gland of normal animals was surgically removed, no obesity resulted, but subsequent damage to the hypothalamus was followed by obesity (Bailey & Bremer, 1921). The hypothalamus, not the pituitary gland, was clearly involved in the physiological regulation of food intake.

Another broad class of independent variables is social mechanisms. Feeding by both humans and other species is strongly affected not only by internal factors but also by many external conditions. Having learned to eat at particular times, for example, clearly affects one's experience of hunger (e.g., Schachter, 1968), as anyone who has crossed several time zones during an airplane trip can testify. Taste, appearance, and consistency also strongly influence what foods humans prefer and how much food they will eat.

Physiological and social mechanisms also occur in combinations, or *interactions*. Obese humans, for example, are highly sensitive to the taste of food. If ice cream is adulterated with quinine in increasing quantities, obese people will refuse to eat it before normal-weight people will refuse it. Obese humans will also eat more of an expensive, good-tasting ice cream than will normal-weight people, but they will not work as hard as normal-weight or underweight people to obtain food (Schachter, 1968).

EXAMPLES OF DEPENDENT VARIABLES

It is also true that dependent variables have no single typology in behavioral science. Suppose you wanted to study pain avoidance as a source of drive somewhat different from the appetitive drives of hunger, thirst, and sex. There is no distinct element that is characteristic of pain avoidance and that compares with the drive for food, water, or a mate. What would you choose as the dependent measure? If you imagine yourself quickly withdrawing your hand from a shock-producing stimulus, this thought suggests that measuring the time it takes to withdraw from the stimulus (i.e., the latency of withdrawal) is a good dependent measure. However, suppose you are interested instead in the pain connected with extreme sexual deprivation. This topic seems more complex than food or water deprivation, though similarities certainly exist. If the subjects were hungry, sexually starved male rats, you might record their actions as they were faced with choosing between food and a female rat in heat.

In animal learning and conditioning experiments, four broad categories of dependent variables have frequently served as outcome measures: (1) the *direction* of any observed change in behavior; (2) the *amount* of the change; (3) the *ease* with which this change is effected; and (4) the *persistence* of the changes over time (Rosenthal & Rosnow, 1975a). For example, in a learning experiment that consists of teaching a thirsty rat to run through a complex maze toward a thimbleful of water, the measurements might focus on (1) the direction the rat chooses on each trial (i.e., whether it turns toward or away from the water); (2) the amount of change, as reflected in how long the rat persists in the correct response when the water is no longer available at the end of its run; (3) the ease with which the rat reacquires the correct response when the reward is again made available; and (4) how long the correct response persists after it is reacquired and the reward is permanently removed.

We can easily imagine parallels of these dependent variables in a social psychology experiment. A researcher interested in attitude change, for example, might measure participants' reactions to being exposed to a message treatment or to a no-treatment comparison condition. The independent variable is exposure (experimental group) or nonexposure (control group) to the message. Among the researcher's outcome (dependent) measures would be (1) the direction of each person's attitudinal response (which determines whether the results in the experimental group are different from those in the control condition); (2) the intensity of the new attitude, or how deeply felt it is; (3) the ease with which the subjects are able to express or defend their newly acquired attitude; and (4) how long the new attitude lasts and whether the level of belief diminishes with time.

When you peruse the journal literature in your field, you will see that these examples barely scratch the surface of the many kinds of dependent variables examined by behavioral scientists. As a more exotic example from the field of developmental psychology, infants have always fascinated their parents by balancing precariously on the edge of a chair or table in apparent imitation of a tightrope walker. The fascination is usually liberally mixed with fear for the safety of the infant. Obviously, an infant is not yet a fully competent and accurate judge of size and distance in its exploration of the space around it. The child's ability to perceive depth was a subject of intense interest to psychologists Eleanor J. Gibson and Richard D. Walk (1960). These investigators worked with a "visual cliff," a board laid across a large sheet of glass that was raised a foot or more above the floor. A checkerboard pattern covered half the glass. On the other half, the same checkerboard pattern appeared on the floor directly under the glass. The visual cliff was created by the perceptual experience of the difference between the two sides.

In one study, Gibson and Walk (1960) tested infants ranging in age from 6 to 14 months on the visual cliff. Each child was placed on the central board and was called by its mother from the "cliff" side and the "shallow" side successively. Most of the infants moved off the central board onto the glass, and all of these crawled out to the "shallow" side at least once. Only a few of them, however, moved to the glass suspended above the pattern on the floor. Thus most infants would not cross the apparent chasm to their mothers. The dependent variable in this example was crossing versus not crossing the apparent chasm. As a consequence of having developed this not-so-ordinary variable, Gibson and Walk were able to conclude that most human infants discriminate depth as soon as they are able to crawl.

DISCOVERY AS EXPLORATION

So far, we have characterized discovery as a linear process of inspiration, library research, and critical rumination. But no rule says the scientist cannot explore by simply keeping his or her eyes and ears open and then developing an ad hoc hypothesis as a tentative explanation of an observed phenomenon. For example, William Beveridge (1957, pp. 128–129), a professor of animal pathology at Cambridge University, told of how Louis Pasteur, the 19th-century chemist and bacteriologist, came up with a hypothesis to explain an epidemic. Pasteur found anthrax organisms on the surface of the graves of dead sheep that had been buried as long as 12 years, and he grew curious about how the organisms could resist the deteriorating effects of sunlight. While out for a walk one day, he observed an oddly colored patch of farm soil with a large number of worm casings on the surface. He asked the farmer what was in the soil and was told that sheep that had died of anthrax the previous year were buried there. Pasteur reasoned that the worms had carried anthrax spores with them while traveling up from the depth of the graves to the surface, thus creating epidemic conditions by which anthrax could recur in the same fields at intervals of several years.

As Beveridge (1957) pointed out, "Had Pasteur done his thinking in an armchair it is unlikely that he would have cleared up this interesting bit of epidemiology" (p. 129). Milgram's creative style in rigging up his initial obedience experiments is also a prototypical example of this approach. In his words, "You try to determine whether particular incidents lead up to a definable pattern; you attempt to find an underlying coherence beneath the myriad surface phenomena. . . . You generalize from your own experience and formulate a hypothesis" (Milgram, 1977, p. 2).

In fact, Milgram was a master of exploratory discovery. In an interview with Carol Tavris of *Psychology Today* magazine,* he described how the routine incidents that he encountered while commuting to work in Manhattan by train led him to hit on another ad hoc hypothesis (the "familiar stranger") and to research questions with societal implications:

MILGRAM: I noticed that there were people at my station whom I had seen for many years but never spoken to, people I came to think of as *familiar strangers*. I found a peculiar tension in this situation, when people treat each other as properties of the environment rather than as individuals to deal with. It happens frequently. Yet there remains a poignancy and discomfort, particularly when there are only two of you at the station: you and someone you have seen daily but never met. A barrier has developed that is not readily broken.

TAVRIS: How can you study the phenomenon of the familiar stranger?

MILGRAM: Students in my research seminar took pictures of the waiting passengers at one station. They made duplicates of the photographs, numbered each of the faces, then distributed the group photographs the following week to all the passengers at the station. We asked the commuters to indicate those people whom they knew and spoke to, those whom they did not recognize, and those whom they recognized but had never spoken to. The commuters filled out the questionnaires on the train and turned them in at Grand Central Station.

Well, we found that the commuters knew an average of 4.5 strangers, and the commuters often had many fantasies about these people. Moreover, there are sociometric stars among familiar strangers. Eighty percent of the commuters recognized one person, although very few had ever spoken to her. She was the visual high point of the station crowd, perhaps because she wore a miniskirt constantly, even in the coldest months.

TAVRIS: How do our dealings with familiar strangers differ from those with total strangers?

*Reprinted with permission from Psychology Today Magazine, Copyright © 1974 (Sussex Publishers, Inc.).

MILGRAM: The familiar-stranger phenomenon is not the absence of a relationship but a special kind of frozen relationship. For example, if you wanted to make a trivial request or get the time of day, you are more likely to ask a total stranger, rather than a person you had seen for many years but had never spoken to. Each of you is aware that a history of noncommunication exists between you, and you both have accepted this as the normal state.

But the relationship between familiar strangers has a latent quality to it that becomes overt on specific occasions. I heard of a case in which a woman fainted in front of her apartment building. Her neighbor, who had seen her for 17 years and never spoken to her, immediately went into action. She felt a special responsibility; she called the ambulance, even went to the hospital with her. The likelihood of speaking to a familiar stranger also increases as you are removed from the scene of routine meeting. If I were strolling in Paris and ran into one of my commuter strangers from Riverdale, we would undoubtedly greet each other for the first time.

And the fact that familiar strangers often talk to each other in times of crisis or emergency raises an interesting question: Is there any way to promote solidarity without having to rely on emergencies and crises? (Milgram, 1977, pp. 3–4).

By simply observing people—keeping his eyes and ears open and coming up with a causal explanation to describe the events—Milgram invoked ad hoc hypotheses. Such hypotheses must then stand up to the challenges of empirical testing in order to be absorbed into the scientific literature as valid generalizations.

SUMMARY OF IDEAS

1. A convenient way to organize our thinking about the scientific method is in terms of (a) a *discovery* phase (in which scientific ideas are fashioned) and (b) a *justification* phase (in which the ideas are tested and any conclusions defended). In this chapter, we described three stages in the discovery phase as (a) initial thinking, (b) plausibility, and (c) acceptability.

2. In Stage 1, *initial thinking*, some general scenarios that produce good research ideas include (a) an intensive case study (e.g., Freud's studies of neurotic symptoms, London's study of rescuers, and Ebbinghaus's studies with nonsense syllables); (b) a paradoxical incident (e.g., Latané and Darley's studies of bystander intervention); (c) a metaphor (e.g., mechanistic thinking in physics and psychology, and McGuire's inoculation model); (d) a conflicting result (e.g., Jones and Fennell's adjudication of the Tolman–Hull debate and Zajonc's social facilitation hypothesis); (e) an old idea that needs improving (e.g., Skinner's improvement on traditional learning theories and Milgram's refinement on Asch's classic research); and (f) an unexpected observation (serendipity).

3. Serendipity—in which discovery results from unexpected incidents—can be seen in daily life situations as well as in scientific situations (e.g., Boggs's artistic inspiration, the implications of the Paul McCartney rumor, and Brady's work on "executive" monkeys).

4. In Stage 2 of discovery (*plausibility*), reason and logic, aided by the critical reading of relevant work, are usually used to evaluate initial ideas.

5. To look for relevant published work, we may do a by-hand search using the *Psychological Abstracts* or the ancestry approach, or we may do a computer search using PsycLIT if we want to save time or need to compile a comprehensive bibliography.

6. Operational and theoretical definitions are the two primary kinds of definitions used by scientists.

7. A detailed example of the preliminary stages of discovery was the development of a researchable topic in the area of interpersonal intelligence.

8. Regulative principles are presuppositions that usually go untested; theories are sets of statements connected by a logical argument; models are conceptual representations that are less comprehensive than theories; hypotheses are testable suppositions that may be derived from a theory or a model.

9. Basic criteria to be met by scientific hypotheses in Stage 3 of discovery are (a) that they correspond with reality; (b) that they be coherent and parsimonious; and (c) that they be potentially refutable, or falsifiable.

10. Constructs are explanatory concepts (e.g., "diffusion of responsibility") that provide a kind of "scaffolding" between variables.

11. The independent variable *(X)* refers to the status of the determining event or condition (e.g., physiological and social mechanisms); such events or conditions may also occur in combinations (*interactions*).

12. The dependent variable *(Y)* refers to the status of the effect or consequence (e.g., direction, amount, ease, and persistence of changes in behavior).

13. In exploratory discovery, the idea is to keep one's eyes and ears open and to develop plausible ad hoc hypotheses as the work progresses (e.g., Pasteur in biology and Milgram in social psychology); the hypotheses are then tested in a more controlled fashion later.

KEY TERMS

acceptability stage   *p. 39*
accounting for conflicting results   *p. 27*
ancestry approach   *p. 35*
coherence   *p. 43*
constructs   *p. 43*
correspondence with reality   *p. 42*
dependent variable   *p. 44*
discovery   *p. 23*
experimental hypothesis   *p. 39*
falsifiability (Popper)   *p. 43*
free association method   *p. 24*
hypothesis   *p. 39*
improving on older ideas   *p. 29*

independent variable   *p. 44*
initial thinking stage   *p. 23*
intensive case study   *p. 24*
interactions   *p. 45*
justification   *p. 23*
meta-analysis   *p. 43*
metaphor   *p. 26*
model   *p. 39*
Occam's razor   *p. 43*
operational definitions   *p. 37*
paradoxical incident   *p. 25*
parsimony   *p. 43*
payoff potential   *p. 42*
plagiarism   *p. 33*

REVIEW QUESTIONS

1. A Northern Illinois University student wants to see whether self-esteem affects academic performance. He asks 30 randomly selected students from his dormitory to fill out a self-esteem measure, and he divides them into groups having high and low self-esteem on the basis of their test scores. He then compares the self-reported grade-point average (GPA) of the two groups and concludes that high self-esteem does lead to a higher GPA. How did he operationalize his independent and dependent variables? If he finds these variables to be highly related, how well justified will he be in claiming that self-esteem affects academic performance?

2. A Virginia Tech student is interested in the personality trait of extraversion. Give an example of both an operational and a theoretical definition of this construct that she can use.

3. A friend tells a George Washington University student that astrology is a science and reminds her that no less than a recent president of the United States consulted an astrologer. How should the student respond to her friend? Can you think of a way for her to do an empirical study to test her friend's assertion?

4. A San Diego State student is interested in studying revenge. Can you devise a causal hypothesis for her to test? How can you assess your hypothesis on scientific grounds of acceptability before passing it on to her?

5. A "wolf-boy" was discovered in Alaska and brought to a learned doctor for study. The doctor conducted many exploratory tests to determine the boy's reactions. The doctor slammed the door, and though everyone else flinched, the boy remained calm and unmoving. The doctor called out to his secretary, who was taking notes, "Write: Does not respond to noise." A nurse who was looking after the boy protested, "But, sir, I have seen the boy startle at the sound of a cracking nut in the forest 30 feet away!" The doctor paused and then instructed his secretary, "Write: Does not respond to *significant* noise." How was the doctor's exploratory observation flawed? How would you instead propose to study the wolf-boy?

Answers to review questions are found on pages 320–334.

CHAPTER 3

Ethical Considerations

PREVIEW QUESTIONS

➤ **W**hy are some methodological practices seen as leading to ethical dilemmas?

➤ **I**s the use of deception or the invasion of privacy ever justified in behavioral research?

➤ **W**hat accounts for "unfairness" in human subjects research?

➤ **W**hat is the purpose of a peer review, and how can I prepare for it?

➤ **A**re there ethical guidelines to help me in planning my study?

➤ **W**hat is the purpose of debriefing, and how do I go about it?

➤ **I**n what ways is animal research bound by ethical rules?

What Is an Ethical Dilemma?

In the day-to-day conduct of human subjects research, certain dilemmas may arise from concerns about the problems investigated and the methodological procedures used to study them. As a consequence, ethicists as well as scientists themselves (e.g., Blanck et al., 1992; Kimmel, 1981, 1988, 1991; Rosnow et al., 1993; Schuler, 1982; Sieber, 1982a, 1982b, 1983, 1992) have raised and debated difficult questions such as:

1. Is it right to withhold information from subjects if I think that a full disclosure will bias their responses?

2. Am I justified in misleading subjects by using a deception if it is necessary to study an important societal issue?

3. Is it permissible for me to invade the privacy of subjects if there is no other way to gather essential facts?

Such questions involve *ethical dilemmas* because they imply conflicts in values or moral standards. In each of these cases, the scientist is torn between making the most ethical use of the human subjects available to her or him and also ensuring the integrity of her or his research data (see Box 3.1). These are not easy questions to answer, because deciding not to do a study that the scientist thinks ought to be done is also a moral judgment. What makes these issues even more challenging is that there seems to be a double standard in our society. That is, in some circumstances, people withhold information, use deception, or invade the privacy of others, and few individuals seem to object.

In a recent case, the producers of CBS-TV's news program "60 Minutes" consulted Leonard Saxe (1991), an applied social psychologist, about examining polygraphy. Supposedly representing a photography magazine owned by CBS, the "60 Minutes" people chose four polygraph examiners randomly from the telephone directory and asked each to identify which of the magazine's employees had stolen more than $500 worth of camera equipment. No one had actually stolen anything, but a different person was "fingered" by the "60 Minutes" staff for each polygrapher. These "culprits" were confederates who were paid $50 by the program staff if they could convince the polygrapher of their innocence. The testing situation was filmed without the polygraphers' knowing they were being recorded. The film record showed each polygraph examiner trying to get the "guilty" person to confess. Dramatically, the "60 Minutes" report showed that these polygraphers did not necessarily "read" the psychophysiological information to make their diagnoses of deception (Saxe, 1991, p. 409).

Where was the moral conflict in this study? It was between a duty to scientific truth and a duty to protect human rights to privacy and informed consent (e.g., Kimmel, 1988; Schuler, 1982; Sieber, 1991). As Saxe wrote, "The demonstration was very clever, but dishonest: CBS lied to the polygraphers. The four polygraphers unwittingly starred in a television drama viewed by millions . . . yet it is hard to think of a way to do this study without deception" (p. 409). In other words, informing the polygraphers that they were research subjects for a "60 Minutes" exposé would have made the study—and no doubt the results—quite different. Were the elaborate deceptions used in this study justified? Before you answer, consider the deception that appears in a variety of roles in everyday life. For example, is it all right that lawyers manipulate the truth in court on behalf of their

| BOX 3.1 | Two Basic Moral Obligations |

To make the most ethical use of the human resources available to you, it is important that you understand what behavioral scientists and others perceive as formal and informal moral obligations. In human subjects research, they can be boiled down to the obligation (1) *not to do* physical or psychological harm to research participants and (2) *to do* research in a way that is most likely to produce valid results (so that the participants' time and effort, as well as other valuable resources, will not have been wasted).

clients, or that physicians withhold information from dying patients to delay their fear and anxiety, or that police investigators use entrapment to gain the knowledge they seek (see Bok, 1978, p. xvii)?

In particular, we will have much to say in this chapter about ethical dilemmas arising from the use of deceptive practices because this issue has received so much attention in psychology (e.g., Carlson, 1971; Menges, 1973; Schuler, 1982; Seeman, 1969; Stricker, 1967). Deceptive practices include deliberately misinforming individuals, sometimes called *active deception,* and intentionally withholding information, sometimes called *passive deception.* We will also discuss some other sources of ethical dilemmas in fundamental and applied behavioral research, and we will have something to say about animal experimentation. But the primary purpose of this chapter is to help focus your intuitions about human subjects research. That is, we want to sharpen your critical thinking and reduce the initial tendencies of many students to "play it safe" by eschewing any study that appears to involve deception or an invasion of privacy. You will see that it is important to consider different vantage points, including the societal, the scientific, and your own ethical biases (see also Rosenthal, 1994; Rosnow, 1990; Strohmetz & Skleder, 1992). To get you thinking about these and other issues, we will pose a series of questions for you to reflect on, because in the end it is each person's individual responsibility to decide how to proceed in a given situation.

DECEPTION IN DAILY LIFE

To begin with, what if someone were to say that all deception is wrong because it violates the implicit moral contract we accept as decent human beings? Would you simply agree, or would you instead argue that the consequences of all deceptions are not the same? For example, would you agree that the mugger who conceals his nefarious intent behind an innocent countenance while waiting for the right moment to strike his victim engages in a more dangerous deception than the parent who untruthfully tells a child that the candy is "all gone"? Presumably, the parent's underlying motive is to protect the child from rotting teeth; that is, it is a "little white lie," like the kind people use to avoid hurting one another's feelings. Keeping a secret is also a kind of lying (Bok, 1983); it involves deception by omission rather than commission (see Box 3.2). On the one hand, well-meaning people, such as clergy and doctors, keep secrets. On the other hand, so do unscrupulous people who engage in various scams, from financial confidence (or "con") games to medical quackery.

For example, John Paulos (1990), a mathematician, described a stock market scam based on probability. Suppose that, for six weeks, a "stock-market adviser" sends you a free letter correctly predicting the following week's performance on a certain stock index and then asks you to pay $500 to learn the seventh such prediction. Predicting correctly six weeks in a row that a stock index will go up or down is nothing to sneeze at! A person might think, "If I had had this information before the stock crash of October 19, 1987, I could have saved a bundle and made a fortune." However, as explained by Paulos, the six predictions are nothing but a confidence game, an unscrupulous hoax.

BOX 3.2	Commission and Omission in Deception

Deception by commission (i.e., active deception) includes deliberately misrepresenting the purpose of the research, lying about the identity of the researcher, falsely promising something to the participants, lying about the purpose of the equipment and procedures, using confederates (also called *pseudosubjects*), and (in biomedical or clinical research) secretly using placebos, medications, or other drugs. *Deception by omission* (i.e., passive deception) includes observing people without telling them they are being studied (also called *unobtrusive observation*), secretly recording some negatively evaluated behavior, and using projective tests and other measurement techniques without fully disclosing their purpose to the subjects (Arellano-Galdames, 1972).

The way the con game works is that the would-be adviser buys a mailing list of 32,000 names of potential investors. Then, putting an impressive logo on fancy stationery, he writes to 16,000 of those people predicting that the index will rise and to the other 16,000 predicting that the index will decline. The following week he sends a follow-up letter to 8,000 of the 16,000 who received the correct "prediction" and tells them the index will rise; he sends another letter to the remaining 8,000 who previously received the correct "prediction" and tells them the index will decline. This process is repeated six times until 500 people have received six straight correct "predictions," and they are then told that they must each send a $500 check for the seventh prediction. Deceptions like this succeed all the time, Paulos notes, because "there's always enough random success to justify almost anything to someone who *wants* to believe" (p. 44).

The lesson? Scam artists are not simply using "little white lies" to deceive, as does the parent who tells a child the candy is "all gone." Thus, although we can agree that deception violates the implicit moral contract that decent human beings accept as the basis of all relationships, we can see that the moral obligation to be open and honest is not absolute (Sieber, 1982a, 1983). In other words, most of us are able to draw a sharp distinction between the deception involving the mugger or the one described by Paulos and the benign deceptions that people use in everyday life. In the same way, many researchers find the use of "little white lies" morally defensible in certain instances, even though they all believe it important to be open and honest in their interactions with research participants. As explained by one ethicist:

> The underlying guiding research principle is to proceed both ethically and without threatening the validity of the research endeavor insofar as possible. It thus is essential that investigators continually ask how they can conduct themselves ethically and still make progress through sound and generalizable research. (Kimmel, 1988, p. 9)

We will return to this idea, but deception is sometimes seen as permissible as long as (1) it is necessary to the validity of the research; (2) the research is worth doing; (3) the physical and psychological risks to the participants are minimal; and (4) adequate *debriefing* will be carried out (to be discussed later). Nevertheless, even in cases where all four criteria are met, an ethical dilemma may still arise because of competing values or interests. To illustrate, we return to Stanley Milgram's classic experiments on obedience to authority. In Chapter 2, we alluded to Solomon Asch's use of deception to study the effects of group pressure on conformity (see also Box 3.3). In contrast to Asch's studies (although stimulated in part by them), Milgram's experiments sparked ethical debate both inside and outside behavioral science from the moment they were reported. As you read about this research, think about the first two questions we posed: (1) Is it right to withhold information from subjects if I think that a full disclosure will bias their responses? And (2) Am I justified in misleading subjects by using a deception if it is necessary to study an important societal issue?

THE MILGRAM EXPERIMENTS

Milgram did not make the decision to perform these experiments lightly, as he had an important societal and scientific purpose in mind. The purpose of the Milgram experiments stemmed from his profound dismay about the horrifying effects of blind obedience to Nazi commands in World War II. During that nightmarish period, the unthinkable became a reality when millions of innocent men, women, and children were systematically slaughtered in gas chambers. The purpose of Milgram's experiments was to study the psychological mechanism that links blind obedience to destructive behavior, by determining how far ordinary adults will go in carrying out the orders of a legitimate authority to act against a third person.

BOX 3.3   Asch's Deception Studies

In Solomon Asch's research, a subject arrived at the psychology laboratory along with several others who were confederates of the investigator. Once seated together at the same table, all subjects were told by the experimenter that they would be asked to make judgments about the length of several lines. Each subject was to judge which of three lines was closest in length to a standard line. The confederates (i.e., pseudosubjects) always stated their judgments first, after which the subject gave his or her opinion. The confederates, acting in collusion with the experimenter, sometimes gave obviously incorrect judgments.

The result was that one third of the subjects gave the same opinion as the others in the situation. When interviewed later, these subjects gave three distinct motives for yielding to the pressure exerted by the incorrect majority: (1) unawareness of being incorrect; (2) doubts about their own perceptions and lack of confidence in them; and (3) wanting to appear the same as the majority (Asch, 1952). Most research problems can be pursued in more than one way, but can you imagine how this experiment could have been performed properly without deception?

Briefly, the experimenter tricked volunteer subjects, placed in the role of the "teacher," into believing that they would be giving varying degrees of painful electric shock to a third person (the "learner") each time the learner made a mistake in a certain task. Milgram also varied the distance between the teacher and the learner, to see whether the teacher would be less ruthless in administering the electric shocks as he or she got closer and the learner pressed the teacher to quit. The results were, to Milgram as well to others, almost beyond belief. A great many subjects (the "teachers") unhesitatingly obeyed the experimenter's "Please continue" or "You have no choice, you must go on" and continued to increase the level of the shocks no matter how much the learner pleaded with the "teacher" to stop. What particularly surprised Milgram was that *no one* ever walked out of the laboratory in disgust or protest. This remarkable obedience was seen time and time again in several universities where the experiment was repeated. "It is the extreme willingness of adults to go to almost any lengths on the command of an authority that constitutes the chief finding of the study and the fact most urgently demanding explanation," Milgram later wrote (1974, p. 5).

Although the "learner" in these studies was a pseudosubject (i.e., a confederate of Milgram's) and no actual shocks were transmitted by the "teacher," concerns about ethics and values arose and have dogged these studies ever since they were first reported. One leading critic, Diana Baumrind (1964), a clinical psychologist, pointed to descriptions by Milgram of the reactions of some of his participants, for example:

> I observed a mature and initially poised businessman enter the laboratory smiling and confident. Within 20 minutes he was reduced to a twitching, stuttering wreck, who was rapidly approaching a point of nervous collapse. He constantly pulled on his earlobe, and twisted his hands. At one point he pushed his fist into his forehead and muttered: "Oh God, let's stop it." And yet he continued to respond to every word of the experimenter and obeyed to the end. (Milgram, 1963, p. 377)

Baumrind argued that Milgram, once he had seen how stressful the manipulation was, should have terminated the experiments. She insisted that there was "no rational basis" for even doing this kind of research unless the participants were aware of the psychological dangers to themselves and unless effective steps were taken to ensure the restoration of their well-being afterward.

Milgram responded that the chief horror was not that a stressful deception was carried out, but that the subjects obeyed. The signs of extreme tension that appeared in some subjects were quite unexpected, and his intention had not been simply to create anxiety, he stated. Indeed, before carrying out the research, he had asked professional colleagues about their expectations, and none of the experts had anticipated the blind obedience that resulted. Like those experts, he had thought the subjects would refuse to follow orders, Milgram said. Furthermore, he was skeptical about whether there had been any injurious effects on the subjects, in spite of the dramatic appearance of anxiety in some subjects. To ensure that the subjects would not feel worse after the experiment than before, he had taken elaborate precautions to debrief them. They were given an opportunity for a friendly reconciliation with the "learner" after the experiment and were shown that the "learner" had not received dangerous electric shocks but had only pretended to receive them.

To discover any long-range negative effects, Milgram also sent questionnaires to the subjects to elicit their reactions after they had read a full report of his investigation. Less than 1% of those who received this questionnaire said that they regretted having participated; 15% were neutral or ambivalent, and over 80% responded that they were glad to have participated. Milgram regarded such results as providing a compelling moral justification for his research:

> The central moral justification for allowing my experiment is that it was judged acceptable by those who took part in it. Criticism of the experiment that does not take account of the tolerant reaction of the participants has always seemed to me hollow. This applies particularly to criticism centering on the use of technical illusion (or "deception," as the critics prefer to say) that fails to relate this detail to the central fact that subjects find the device acceptable. The participant, rather than the external critic, must be the ultimate source of judgment in these matters. (Milgram, 1977, p. 93)

Do you agree with Milgram that the research participants, not the experimenter, are the ultimate arbiters of what is morally acceptable in this situation? If you answer yes, how would you implement this idea in this situation so that you could anticipate the subjects' judgments before they participated in the research? Incidentally, it should be noted that *when* Milgram did his work, it was well within the norms of deception then in use. We will have more to say about this research, but it is not just the use of "technical illusion" that is at issue as behavioral researchers wrestle with moral imperatives. Another source of ethical conflict arises from perceptions of *fair-mindedness,* or impartiality. In the 1970s, a famous incident involved a field experiment, referred to as the *Rushton study,* that had been designed to improve the quality of work life in a mining operation in rural Pennsylvania.

ISSUES OF FAIR-MINDEDNESS

The Rushton study, sponsored by the Rushton Mining Company, began innocently enough. Developed from earlier research in the United Kingdom, the study's specific aims were to improve employee skills, safety, and job satisfaction while raising the level of performance and company earnings (Blumberg & Pringle, 1983). After months of careful preparation by the researchers and the managers of the mine, a call was issued for volunteers for a work group that would have direct responsibility for the production in one section of the mine. The experimental induction called for the workers in this group to abandon their traditional roles and to coordinate their own activities after extensive training in safety laws, good mining practices, and job safety analysis. Paid at the top rate—that for the highest-skilled job classification in that section—they became (not surprisingly) enthusiastic proponents of "our way of working."

BOX 3.4   Unfairness in Daily Life

Just as deception as an ethical dilemma is not limited to research situations, neither is unfairness. For example, a drug company recently announced a new medicine that slows the course of multiple sclerosis (Lewin, 1994). The problem is that the company is unable to produce enough of the new medicine to treat everyone who wants it, and the ethical question is how to select people for treatment. The company's answer was to have people register for a lottery and then to draw names at random as the medicine becomes available. Each person in the lottery has the same likelihood of being chosen, in the same way, for example, that a lottery may be used in wartime to select conscripts for the military. Is this a "fair" procedure, because everyone has an *equal chance* of being selected for life or death? Suppose people were selected to receive the new medicine not randomly, but on the grounds of who is most likely to benefit from it. Similarly, suppose that conscripts for the military were selected on the basis of who is the biggest and strongest. Which approach, in your view, is *more fair*—a random lottery or selection on the basis of who is more likely to benefit or survive (see also Broome, 1984)?

Unfortunately, trouble soon reared its head. Workers in the rest of the mine (who were the "control" group) were resentful of and angered by the haughtiness they perceived in the volunteers: "Why should these inexperienced volunteers receive special treatment and higher pay than other miners with many more years on the job?" Rumors circulated through the mine that the volunteers were "riding the gravy train" and being "spoon-fed," and that the project was a "communist plot" because all the volunteers received the same rate and the company was "making out" at their expense. As a consequence, the study had to be terminated prematurely.

In contrast to Milgram's experiments and the "60 Minutes" demonstration study, the Rushton study involved neither deception nor invasion of privacy. Instead the problem was what a sizable number of workers (nonvolunteers, to be sure) viewed as a lack of fair-mindedness, because they had not received the benefits enjoyed by those in the experimental group (see Box 3.4). We see that ethical dilemmas arise not only because of the researcher's actions, but because of people's perceptions of those actions. Can you think of a way to anticipate problems that may arise from people's perceptions or sensitivities? Assuming we can anticipate them, what should we do about them?

THINKING ALOUD

So far, we have described dilemmas arising from differences in moral interests or values. What if someone told you that being open and honest prevents all such dilemmas? Would you agree? Before you answer, imagine an experiment like Milgram's in which the experimenter greeted the subjects by saying something like the following:

Hello. Today we are going to do a study on blind obedience to a malevolent authority, particularly emphasizing the effects of physical distance from the victim on willingness to inflict pain on her or him. You will be in the "close" condition, which means that you are expected to be somewhat less ruthless. In addition, you will be asked to fill out a test of your fascist tendencies because we believe there is a positive relation between scores on our fascism test and blind obedience to an authority who requests that we hurt others. Any questions?

A completely open and honest statement to a research subject of the intention of an experiment might involve a briefing of this kind, but would it result in fewer problems? Clearly, such a briefing would be absurd if we were serious in our efforts to learn about blind obedience to authority. If the subjects had full information about our experimental purpose, plans, procedures, and hypotheses, it seems unlikely they would behave as Milgram's subjects did. They might instead base their behavior on what they *thought* the world was like or what they believed the *experimenter* thought the world was like. If you agree that Milgram's experiments were worth doing, do you also agree that the use of deception was necessary in this case?

In fact, there are very few (if any) behavioral scientists who would advocate the use of deception merely for its own sake. At the same time, there are few researchers who feel that behavioral science can do entirely without deception. For instance, no behavioral scientist would seriously advocate giving up the study of prejudice or discrimination. But if all measures of prejudice and discrimination had to be openly labeled, continuing this research might not be worth the effort. The point is that adopting a rigid moral orientation that decries deception as wrong would mean banishing *all forms* of deception. However, most people—behavioral scientists included—are willing to weigh and measure their "sins" of commission and omission, judging some to be larger than others.

For example, refraining from telling a subject that an "experiment in the learning of verbal materials is designed to show whether earlier, later, or intermediate material is better remembered" is *not* a particularly serious deception. The reason most of us would probably not view this deception with alarm seems, on first glance, that it involves an omission (a passive deception) rather than a commission (an active deception). A truth is left unspoken; a lie is not told. But what if the same experiment were presented as a "study of the effects of the meaningfulness of verbal material on retention or recall"? That is a direct lie, designed to misdirect the subject's attention from a crucial aspect of the experimental treatment to another factor that really does not interest the scientist. Even this change, however, does not seem to make the deception awful, although the "sin" is now one of commission and the scientist has not withheld information from, but actively lied to, the subject.

In other words, it does not seem that the active or passive style of a deception is its measure. Instead, its probable effect on the subject is what is significant. Very few people would care whether subjects focused on a noncrucial aspect of verbal material rather than on a crucial aspect of the experimental treatment, because this deception seems to have no consequence (positive or negative). It is not simply deception so much as it is potentially *harmful* deception that we would like to minimize. But how shall we decide what is potentially harmful? Does it come down to personal opinion, and if so, whose opinions should prevail?

On the one hand, can we agree that most researchers (and the subjects themselves) would concur that it is not very harmful to tell subjects that a test they are taking anonymously as part of a research project is one of "personal reactions" (which it is) rather than a test of their need for social approval, schizophrenic tendencies, or authoritarianism (which it may also be)? On the other hand, can we also agree that most researchers (and the subjects themselves) would concur that it may be harmful to falsely tell college-age students that a test shows them to be "abnormal" even if they are later told that they have been misled? In other words, the investigator, her or his colleagues, and, to some extent, ultimately, the general community might decide whether a particular potentially harmful deception is worth a possible increase in knowledge. In fact, that is exactly how such decisions are made, that is, by using an analysis that weighs costs and benefits.

A COST–BENEFIT ANALYSIS

What we have said so far should be read not as a blanket defense (or a blanket indictment) of deception, but as an illustration of the kind of reasoning that researchers and others undertake in assessing the pros and cons of doing a given study. This reasoning involves estimating the costs and benefits of studies on scales of *perceived* methodological and societal values or interests. With the help of Figure 3.1, we see that such an analysis depends very much on how people choose to define costs and benefits in a given situation (Rosenthal, 1994; Rosenthal & Rosnow, 1984; Rosnow, 1990). For instance, their perception of the "cost of doing" might include possible annoyances or inconveniences to subjects, institutional

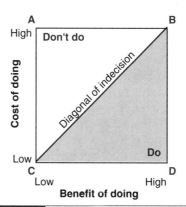

FIGURE 3.1   *A decision-plane model of the costs and benefits of doing research. Studies falling at A are not carried out; studies falling at D are carried out; and studies falling along the B-C diagonal are too hard to decide about. (Rosenthal & Rosnow, 1984.)*

time, expenditures of money and effort, and so on, whereas their perception of the "benefit of doing" might include educational or psychological advantages to the subjects, to other people at other times and places, to the investigator, and so on. Studies that are well thought out and ethically acceptable, and that address important issues, are usually judged to be more beneficial than studies that are not well thought out, that involve physical or psychological risks, or that address trivial issues. Studies falling in the area labeled A *would not* be recommended because the costs are high and the benefits low; studies falling in the area labeled D *would* be recommended because the benefits are high and the costs low. Studies falling along the "diagonal of indecision" (B-C) would have to go back to the drawing board because they are so hard to decide about.

A limitation of this assessment is that it focuses only on the costs and benefits of *doing* research and ignores the costs of *not doing* research. Shouldn't the *failure* to conduct a potentially important study also be subject to evaluation on moral grounds? For example, the biomedical researcher who could conceivably find a cure for acquired immunodeficiency syndrome (AIDS), but who decides not to do the research because it seems risky, is making a decision that must be evaluated on moral grounds as surely as must be the decision to investigate AIDS with a procedure that carries some risk. The behavioral scientist whose study might reduce violence or prejudice (or report on the links of blind obedience to destructive behavior), but who decides not to do the study (or is prevented by a review group from doing the study) because it involves deception, has not solved the moral problem but has only traded one moral problem for another.

REVIEW BOARDS AND PEER REVIEW

Since the 1970s, the U.S. government has mandated as a condition of receiving federal funding that all researchers using human subjects must submit their proposed projects for ethical evaluation by an *institutional review board* (IRB). A central responsibility of IRBs is to ensure that the potential benefits to the individual research participants (and to society) will be greater than any potential risks to the participants in the research (Rosnow et al., 1993). It is likely that your research will also be subject to an ethical evaluation, but the "IRB" is likely to consist of your instructor and your classmates, constituting a *peer review* group. To help prepare you for such a review, Table 3.1 shows the kinds of questions that may be asked of researchers. As your proposal progresses, try answering the particular questions that are relevant to your investigation.

In addition to this information, researchers are often required to prepare a "subject consent form" for the participants to sign. An example of such a form is shown in Figure 3.2. The purpose of this form is *not* to ask subjects to waive, or appear to waive, any of their legal rights or to release the institution from liability for negligence. Its purpose is to make sure that, before agreeing to participate, the subjects have been told (1) the basic nature of the study; (2) the nature of any risk or inconvenience to them; (3) the planned procedure for ensuring the confidentiality of the data; and (4) the voluntary nature of their participation and their freedom to withdraw from the study at any time without prejudice or consequence. As Section

TABLE 3.1	Sample Questions for Ethics Review

Investigator
1. Who is the primary investigator, and who is supervising the study?
2. Will anyone be assisting you in this investigation?
3. Have you or the others whose names are listed above had any experience with this kind of research?

Nature of the Study
4. What is the purpose of this research? That is, what is it about?
5. What will the research participants be asked to do, or what will be done to them?
6. Will deception be used? If the answer is yes, why is it necessary?
7. What is the nature of the deception, and when will the debriefing (dehoaxing) take place?
8. Will the subjects risk any harm—physical, psychological, legal, or social—by participating in this research?
9. If there are any risks, how do you justify them? How will you minimize the risks?

Research Participants
10. How will you recruit the research participants? Will you be offering an incentive?
11. How do you plan to explain the research to your potential subjects and obtain their informed consent? How will you make clear that they can quit the study at any time?
12. What should be the general characteristics of your research participants (e.g., age range, sex, institutional affiliation, and the projected number of subjects)?
13. What, if any, are the special characteristics you need in your research participants (e.g., children, pregnant women, racial or ethnic minorities, mentally retarded, prisoners, or alcoholics)?
14. Are other institutions or individuals cooperating in or cosponsoring the study?
15. Do the subjects have to be in a particular mental or physical state to participate usefully?

Material
16. If electrical or mechanical equipment will be used, how has it been checked for safety?
17. What standardized tests, if any, will be used? What information will be provided to the subjects about their scores on these tests?

Confidentiality
18. What procedure will you use to ensure the confidentiality of the data?

Debriefing
19. How do you plan to debrief the subjects?

B notes, another purpose of this form is to make sure that the subjects have been adequately debriefed after the study is completed.

ETHICAL GUIDELINES

To help review groups—and individual investigators (such as yourself)—decide what aspects of a study may pose an ethical problem, national and international organizations of scientists have published explicit guidelines in the form of codes of ethics (for detailed discussions, see Beecher, 1970; Bok, 1978; Delgado & Leskovac, 1986; Doob, 1987; Holton & Morison, 1978; J. Katz, 1972; Kelman, 1968; Kimmel, 1981, 1988; Schuler, 1982; Sieber, 1982b). In the 1970s, in the wake of

Instructions to participant: Please print and then sign your name in the space provided in Section A before you participate in this study. Once the study is over and you have been debriefed, you will be asked to initial the three statements listed in Section B to indicate your agreement.

Section A

I, _____ , voluntarily give my consent to participate in this project. I have been informed about, and feel that I understand, the basic nature of the project.

I understand that I may leave at any time and that my anonymity will be protected.

_____   _____

Signature of Research Participant   Date

Section B

Please initial each of the following statements once the study has been completed and you have been debriefed:

_____ I have been debriefed.

_____ I was not forced to stay to complete the study.

_____ All my questions have been answered satisfactorily.

FIGURE 3.2   *Example of subject consent form.*

growing concern over what were seen as moral issues, the American Psychological Association (APA) published a code of ethical practices to govern research with human participants. A revision of the *APA ethics code* appeared during the following decade, and another revision is due to appear in this decade. The thrust of the current version is essentially the same as the set of principles paraphrased in Table 3.2, based on the 1982 revision (American Psychological Association, 1982).

Note that Principle 5 does not rule out deception but implies that, if deception is to be used, it must be fully justified on scientific grounds. This principle (and items 7 and 19 in Table 3.1) also mentions *debriefing*. The term was first used during World War II to refer to the process of interrogating pilots who had returned from bombing missions. The purpose of debriefing in behavioral research is to remove any misconceptions and anxieties the participants may have so that their sense of dignity remains intact and they feel that their time has not been wasted (Blanck et al., 1992; Harris, 1988). When deception has been used, debriefing also removes any "detrimental impact on the participant's feeling of trust in interpersonal relationships" (American Psychological Association, 1973, p. 77).

TABLE 3.2	American Psychological Association's Code of Research Ethics (Paraphrased)

1. As early as the planning stage, the researcher is personally responsible for weighing the scientific and human values and interests of the study. If it becomes necessary to compromise or deviate from some ethical value, the researcher must seek ethical advice and make an even stronger effort to protect the rights of the research participants.
2. Of primary concern in weighing human values should be the question of whether any of the participants will be "at risk" either psychologically or physically.
3. The researcher is responsible not only for his or her own ethical behavior, but also for the behavior of collaborators, assistants, students, and employees—all of whom incur ethical responsibilities themselves.
4. All promises and commitments to the participants (e.g., promising them anonymity or promising to keep their individual responses confidential) must be honored. If any aspects of the study might influence whether they will want to participate, these aspects must be fully disclosed before participation is requested (except in the case of children or participants who have impairments that limit their intellectual or communication ability). If there is an essential reason not to make full disclosure before requesting subjects' participation, a further effort must be made to ensure the welfare and dignity of the participants.
5. The use of deception or concealment requires that its use be absolutely necessary, that there be no acceptable alternative procedures, and that the subjects be debriefed as soon as possible.
6. Participants who wish to remove themselves from the study at any time must be allowed to do so, without penalty or coercion.
7. Any physical or mental risks must be outweighed by significant benefits of the research. The participants must be informed of such risks, and the researcher must be available to them after the study, should stress, potential harm, or related concerns arise in the future.
8. After the data have been collected, the participants should be provided further information about the study, including the removal of any misconceptions they may have. If it is necessary to delay informing them or to withhold such information for a time, there must be a sound justification for doing so and a strong belief that such a delay will have no damaging consequences.
9. If participants suffer any undesirable consequences, the researcher is obligated to find out about them and to correct them.
10. Any information about individual participants must be kept confidential unless the participants agree otherwise in advance.

Notice the reference to debriefing again in Principle 8 of the APA ethics code. The researcher is advised to debrief participants with information about the nature of the study as soon as it is over. In the next chapter, we describe the unobtrusive observations of public, anonymous behavior, a method that does not require debriefing. A full debriefing may also be inadvisable if it might produce stress or be ineffective, for example, when the participants are children, are mentally ill, or are retarded (Blanck et al., 1992). In many instances, however, debriefing is seen as ethically essential, particularly if (as stated in Principle 5) any deception was used. Before we present specific guidelines for debriefing in your own research, it will be instructive to return to Milgram's experiments to see the elaborate lengths to which he went to debrief his subjects.

DEBRIEFING PARTICIPANTS

We mentioned previously that Milgram's subjects were given the opportunity to have a friendly reconciliation with the "learner." They were also given an opportunity to engage in an extended discussion with the experimenter about the purpose of the study and why it was necessary to use deception. Subjects who had obeyed the experimenter when he told them to keep administering the electric shocks were assured that their behavior was normal and that the conflict or tension they had experienced had been felt by other participants. All subjects were told that they would receive a comprehensive written report at the conclusion of the research; this report detailed the experimental procedures and findings, treating the subjects' own part in the research with dignity. All subjects also received a questionnaire that asked them once again to express their thoughts and feelings about their behavior. A year later, a psychiatrist intensively interviewed 40 of the experimental subjects, to identify any possible injurious effects resulting from the experiment.

As you can see, Milgram's debriefings were unusually extensive—far more so, in fact, than is characteristic in most experiments, or than what is felt to be necessary in most studies. But as a result of his having duped the participants into believing that they were administering painful electric shocks to another person, Milgram felt it was necessary to go to elaborate lengths in order to remove any possible stresses and anxieties. Most studies do not require debriefing covering so wide an area or so great a span of time as Milgram's, but the debriefing procedure used should be sufficiently focused to satisfy the subjects about having participated in the study (Sieber, 1982a, 1983). The following guidelines (Aronson & Carlsmith, 1968; Sieber, 1982a, 1983) may be incorporated into more typical debriefings.

First, as noted in Principle 5 of the APA ethics code, if your study involved any sort of deception, it is important to give whatever explanation is needed to reveal the truth about the research and your careful consideration of the use of the deception. For example, it may be explained that science is the search for truth and that it is sometimes necessary to resort to deception to uncover truth. Recall, however, that debriefing may not be advisable in all cases of deception, as in the unobtrusive observations of public, anonymous behavior (discussed in the next chapter).

Second, despite your sincere wish to treat your participants responsibly, some subjects may leave the experiment feeling gullible, as if they have been "had" by a fraudulent procedure. Whatever the deception used, you should clearly explain it to your subjects and at the same time assure them that being taken in does not reflect in any way on their intelligence or character but simply shows the scientific *effectiveness* or validity of the study's design. You presumably went to some pains to achieve an effective design in order not to waste the subjects' time and effort in your search for truth.

Third, you should proceed gradually and patiently, with the chief aim of "gently unfolding" the details of any deceptions used. A patient discussion will go far to reduce the subjects' negative feelings. Instead of thinking of themselves as "victims," they may more correctly realize that they are "coinvestigators" in the search for truth. If you ask each person what he or she thought of the research situation, you may also uncover valuable scientific and theoretical information.

Fourth, never use *double deception,* that is, a second deception in what the subject thinks is the official postinvestigation debriefing. Double deception can be terribly damaging: Instead of restoring your subjects to the frame of mind in which they entered the study, you are leaving them with a lie. Also, if any subject wishes to withdraw from the study, you must treat this request with dignity because to do otherwise would be a violation of Principle 6 of the APA ethics code (see again Table 3.2).

THE USE OF ANIMALS IN RESEARCH

Although the focus of this book is on research on human subjects, we did mention in Chapter 2 the Pavlovian conditioning of a dog, Thorndike's studies of cats in puzzle boxes, and the use of rat subjects by the Tolmanians and Hullians. Given the biological continuities between animals and human beings, animals may be used as research subjects in justifiable circumstances. For example, the use of in-bred mice allows researchers to compare different procedures on subjects that are genetically similar. Animals bred for defects have been used by scientists working in immunology research or studying behavioral correlates of genetic disorders. Discoveries have also been made by the use of animal subjects in neuroscience and other areas involving research on the brain. Not only humans benefit from animal research; many of the same methods that have been developed to prevent and treat disorders in humans have also been used to improve the lives of animals (Committee on the Use of Animals in Research, 1991).

Another series of studies illustrative of the use of animals in behavioral science was the work on individual development by Harry Harlow (1959) and his associates, in which it would have been ethically impossible to use human subjects. Harlow was interested in the effects of loving mother–child relationships on the psychological health of the offspring. To use humans to investigate this problem experimentally, we would be required to assign half our sample of young children to loving mothers and half to rejecting mothers and to follow up the development of the children's adult personality. Such an experimental plan is an ethical absurdity, although no special problems of *experimental logic* are involved. Does this mean that we can never do experimental work on important questions of human development and human personality? Harlow's answer was to use primates because they share enough attributes with humans to make them a valuable, even if far from exact or even very accurate, model of human development. Harlow could not, for the sake of furthering our knowledge of personality development, separate a human baby from its mother, but the important lessons we might learn from such a separation seemed to justify separating a nonhuman primate from its mother.

In one phase of the research, infant monkeys were separated from their mothers just a few hours after birth and were raised by bottle with great success. Harlow had been advised by a colleague to have available for his infant monkeys some soft, pliant surfaces, so folded gauze diapers were made available to all the baby monkeys. The babies became so attached to these diapers that removing the diapers for laundering was very difficult. This serendipitous observation led to an experiment designed to show more systematically the shorter- and longer-term effects of access to a soft material. Because his research was also planned to shed light on the relative importance in the development of the infant's attachment to its mother of being fed by her as opposed to being in close and cuddly contact with her, Harlow came up with an innovative manipulation.

Two pseudomothers were built: one a bare, welded-wire cylindrical form with a crude wooden head and face, and the other, a similar apparatus covered with terry cloth. Newborn monkeys were given equal access to the wire and cloth mother figures, but half the monkeys were fed at the breast of the wire mother and half were fed at the breast of the cloth mother. The monkeys fed by the two "mothers" drank about the same amount of milk and gained about the same amount of weight. However, regardless of which mother had fed them, the baby monkeys spent much more time climbing up on the cloth mother and clinging to her than they did on the wire mother. This finding was valuable not only in demonstrating the importance of "contact comfort" (as Harlow called it) but also in showing the oversimplification of an earlier theory that mothers become prized because they are associated with the reduction of hunger and thirst. The results obtained by Harlow and his associates showed quite clearly that being the source of food is not nearly as good a predictor of a baby's subsequent preference as being a soft and cuddly mother. When the monkeys were about 100 days old, they spent an average of about 15 hours a day on the cloth mother but only about 1.5 hours on the wire mother, no matter which mother had fed the baby monkey.

In the period since Harlow's research, specific guidelines have been developed to ensure that the use of experimental animals will conform to a number of ethical requirements. As a consequence, animal research in behavioral science, as in other fields, is subject to a host of federal laws and licensing requirements that spell out the responsibilities of animal facilities to ensure the well-being of experimental animals consistent with the advancements made possible by research. It is beyond the scope of this book to give a detailed account of such policies; it will suffice to say that all research institutions in this country are held accountable by the U.S. government to treat the animals used in research humanely and in full compliance with very stringent regulations. For example, the Animal Welfare Act of 1966 (which has been amended several times) sets specific standards for the use of animals in research—their handling, housing, feeding, use in studying drugs, and so forth. Research institutions are also subject to unannounced inspections by the U.S. Department of Agriculture at any time, and if violations are uncovered, the institution's license to run animal facilities may be revoked.

Beyond these federal regulations, animal researchers are also subject to institutional and professional requirements. Institutions with animal care facilities make a point of informing animal experimenters of their ethical responsibilities, and proposed animal research also routinely undergoes ethical review. In addition, the APA and other professional and scientific organizations around the world have expanded on the ethical obligations of investigators of animal behavior. For example, the APA reminds researchers that they must make every effort to minimize discomfort, illness, and pain in their experimental animals. Any procedure that subjects animals to pain, stress, or privation may be used only when no alternative procedure is available and the goal of the research is justified by its prospective scientific, educational, or applied value. Thus, just as the scientific community recognizes both an ethical and a scientific responsibility for the general welfare of human subjects, it also assumes responsibility for the humane care and treatment of animals used in research.

SUMMARY OF IDEAS

1. Ethical questions arise because of competing values or interests related to perceived moral responsibilities.
2. In general, researchers are obliged *not to do* physical or psychological harm to research participants and *to do* research in a way that is most likely to produce valid results.
3. Active deceptions (deception by commission) and passive deceptions (deception by omission) come in many different forms in science as well as in day-to-day life.
4. Milgram's obedience experiments first aroused the ire of those who criticize the use of deception in psychological experiments, although he went to elaborate lengths to debrief his subjects after the data were collected.
5. Questions about fair-mindedness are a source of ethical conflict in science as well as in everyday life.
6. Being completely open with research participants sometimes produces biased results, as when participants respond with what they believe the experimenter wants to hear.
7. Behavioral scientists (like everyone else) weigh and measure their "sins" of commission and omission, using cost–benefit analyses to judge the seriousness of potential moral conflicts.
8. The true measure of a deception seems to be its potential to harm subjects rather than whether the deception is active or passive.
9. Federal guidelines for protecting the rights and welfare of human subjects mandate that federally supported institutions have IRBs review proposed and ongoing research projects.
10. In the presentation of research for peer review, the questions to be answered concern many aspects of the research, including the way in which the participants will be recruited, the procedures to be used, confidentiality, the risks to the subjects, and so on.
11. The insufficiency of the decision-plane model used to weigh the costs and benefits of doing research is that it ignores the moral costs of not conducting (or of being prevented from conducting) a given study.
12. The APA has developed a code of 10 ethical standards to guide behavioral researchers who study human subjects.
13. Debriefing subjects after the data have been collected is the final step in the data collection process and is considered essential when there has been a deception or when there is any residual anxiety.
14. Just as the scientific community has an ethical and scientific responsibility for the general welfare of human subjects, it also assumes responsibility for the humane care and treatment of animals used in research.

KEY TERMS

active deception   *p. 53*
APA ethics code   *p. 64*
cost–benefit analysis   *p. 60*
debriefing   *p. 64*
deception by commission   *p. 54*
deception by omission   *p. 54*
double deception   *p. 65*
ethical dilemmas   *p. 52*
fair-mindedness   *p. 57*

informed consent   *p. 61*
institutional review board (IRB)   *p. 61*
Milgram experiments   *p. 55*
openness in research   *p. 59*
passive deception   *p. 53*
peer review   *p. 61*
randomness   *p. 58*
Rushton study   *p. 57*

REVIEW QUESTIONS

1. A study proposal is submitted to the Tufts University Human Subjects Committee for review. The researchers plan to administer a two-hour-long questionnaire to people hanging out on the street in Boston's Combat Zone (the red light district). The questionnaire contains questions on these people's lifestyles and attitudes toward criminal behavior. What are some potential costs to subjects for their participation in the study?

2. A University of Richmond student is interested in studying helping behavior. She designs an experiment to take place in a corner drugstore. Enlisting the aid of the owner, the student has confederates, varying in age and manner of dress, commit a robbery at the store. Another confederate, posing as a customer, observes the real customers, noting who helps, what they do, how long it takes, and so on. What are some ethical problems in this research? What costs and benefits would you consider in deciding whether this project should be done?

3. A UCLA student wants to run a study in which he will deceive subjects into believing that they have done poorly on a test of their sensitivity to others. At the end of the experimental session, he plans to pay the subjects, thank them for participating, and tell them they can call him later if they have any questions about the study. How has the student failed in his ethical responsibilities to the subjects? What should he do?

4. A peer review group tells a student at SMU that his proposed study falls on the "diagonal of indecision" in their view. What do they mean, and what are the implications for the student?

5. An Arlington student proposes to replicate Asch's experiment with Texas students. If his IRB requires an informed-consent form, what might it state?

6. A Whittier College student is interested in conducting a study of the effects of various financial incentive programs in a large organization. Because her research involves no deception or invasion of privacy she tells her adviser that no ethical issues are raised by her research. The adviser's reply is "Remember the Rushton study!" What does she mean?

Answers to review questions are found on pages 320–334.

PART 2

Observation and Measurement

CHAPTER 4

Systematic Observational Methods

PREVIEW QUESTIONS

➤ **H**ow does systematic observation in science differ from everyday observation?

➤ **W**hat is the purpose of "triangulation"?

➤ **H**ow do researchers simultaneously participate and observe?

➤ **W**hat is ethnography, and what substantive questions organize it?

➤ **H**ow is content analysis used to impose structure on archival research?

➤ **W**hat is the role of simulation in laboratory experimentation?

➤ **H**ow do behavioral scientists do field experiments?

➤ **W**hat is meant by *unobtrusive observation*, and how do I go about it?

➤ **H**ow are judges chosen to code behavior?

THE RESEARCHER AS OBSERVER

For scientists everywhere, the world is a cornucopia filled with fascinating questions waiting to be addressed by systematic observational methods. The term *systematic observation* simply means that what the scientist observes or records is guided by or influenced by preexisting questions or hypotheses (that is, as contrasted with the more casual and random nature of most of our everyday observations). In Chapter 2, we discussed the art of "discovery" and also mentioned the term *justification,* which in general refers to the confirmation and defense of scientific explanations and interpretations. In this and the following chapter, we will show that the "let's-try-it-and-see" attitude that characterizes successful justification in science calls for resourcefulness and access to multiple research methods (see also Box 4.1).

| BOX 4.1 | Anything Goes? |

Paul Feyerabend (1988), a philosopher, described how success in science often depends on scientists' bending or breaking rules and doing whatever works. As Feyerabend put it, "Not every discovery can be accounted for in the same manner, and procedures that paid off in the past may create havoc when imposed on the future. Successful research . . . relies now on one trick, now on another" (p. 1). Feyerabend's description has been called the *anything-goes view of science.*

The reason for multiple methods is that all are limited in some ways, and therefore the best we can do in a given case is to try to "zero in" (called *triangulation*) on the effect of interest (Campbell & Fiske, 1959). Behavioral scientists do not agonize over whether any particular method puts them in touch with "absolute truth"; instead they view all accepted scientific methods as sufficient tools for opening up the world to empirical scrutiny (Regis, 1987, p. 212). A convergence, or triangulation, of the findings of methodologically varying studies lends credence to the effect. When a finding remains constant though tested under a variety of circumstances, it is said to be *robust.* In this chapter, we will concentrate on two broad categories of systematic observational methods: qualitative and quantitative. *Qualitative* means that the raw data exist in a nonnumerical form (e.g., reports of conversations); *quantitative* means that the raw data exist in a numerical form (e.g., observers' or judges' ratings).

Within each of these two broad categories of observational methods lie many possible strategies and applications. For example, in recent years we have seen a burgeoning literature on qualitative methodology in fields such as organizational management, social psychology, anthropology, social work, aging, and family studies (e.g., H. R. Bernard, 1994; Crabtree & Miller, 1992; Denzin & Lincoln, 1994; Gilgun, Daly, & Handel, 1992; Gubrium & Sankar, 1993; Morse, 1993; Riessman, 1993; D. Silverman, 1993). We will first discuss the use of qualitative methods in participant observer research, ethnographic research, and archival research. Then we will discuss the use of quantitative methods in laboratory and field experimentation. We will point out the advantages and the limitations of each approach and will give a flavor of the procedures used. In many research cases, it is possible—and indeed advisable—to use qualitative *and* quantitative methods to enrich our understanding of the problem studied (see Box 4.2). We will also describe several categories of "unobtrusive observation" and list alternative ways to choose judges to serve as raters or coders.

PARTICIPANT OBSERVATION RESEARCH

The term *participant observation* is somewhat ambiguous in its current usage by behavioral scientists; it is sometimes used interchangeably with *fieldwork, field observation,* and even *ethnography* (Judd, Smith, & Kidder, 1991; Spradley, 1970, 1980). The methodology of participant observation is also nebulous, and in some

---

BOX 4.2   The Look

An analogy by the philosopher Jean-Paul Sartre (1956) illustrates the idea that different perspectives are needed to give us access to the world. When we look at someone who is looking at us, it is hard for us to perceive the watcher behind the look at the same time that we apprehend the precise properties of the organ of vision, the eyes. If we focus on the look, we cease to apprehend the eyes, even though they are still in our field of perception as pure presentations; they are neutralized, put out of play, by a consciousness requiring that they be disconnected. To apprehend the "whole," we shift our concentration back and forth, attending first to one thing and then to another—in the same way that the behavioral scientist uses multiple methods, each of which is limited in some ways, but which together may allow us to catch a glimpse of the whole.

---

cases it is hard to distinguish this method from the reporting methods used by investigative journalists. One basic difference is that the scientist is not under the extreme time pressure of the news reporter. Because there is no instant deadline to meet, the scientist can patiently and methodically plumb aspects of the situation to his or her heart's content. A second difference is that, whereas the investigative reporter's goal is to prove a point or to make a story, the scientist allows nature (i.e., human nature) to tell its own tale.

Participant observer research is one of several examples of watching and recording behavior in its natural state, also called *naturalistic observation*. Other examples of naturalistic methods in human subjects research include ethnography and field experiments, although naturalistic observation is also used by students of animal behavior (e.g., ethologists and comparative psychologists) to make hypothesis-testing observations of animals in the wild. Illustrative of this approach is the work of Ronald Baenninger, a comparative psychologist, who watched and recorded the actions of a troop of baboons when it encountered a cheetah drinking in an East African river (Baenninger, Estes, & Baldwin, 1977). Other researchers had claimed that adult male baboons actively defend their troops against predators, but there were few accepted records of this behavior at the time of the study by Baenninger et al. (cf. DeVore & Washburn, 1963). Field notes made by Baenninger and his colleagues dispelled any doubts about the reality of the baboons' defensive behavior. As the researchers watched, they recorded that two male members of the baboon troop continued to harass the cheetah until they had successfully chased it far away from the main body of the troop.

What factors distinguish participant observation from other naturalistic methods? The basic answer to this question is that other methods of naturalistic observation (e.g., ethnography and field experiments) typically use a more standardized methodology than do participant observers—whose methodology is reminiscent of the "anything-goes" approach described in Box 4.1 (e.g., Judd et al., 1991). For example, in the case of animal research, prescribed naturalistic methods of collecting and handling data have evolved over many years (e.g., Martin & Bateson,

1993). The methodology of participant observation (in particular, the subjective analysis of qualitative results), on the other hand, makes it especially susceptible to criticisms of *interpreter effects* (Rosenthal, 1976); that is, the researcher's interpretation of the observational records may be unwittingly biased or slanted. In a similar vein, sample sizes are reported in a rather casual way in participant observer research, possibly because sampling is often opportunistic and quantitative methods are not used. This vagueness in methodology may be changing, however, as users of participant observation attempt to converge on a set of acceptable practices (e.g., D. Silverman, 1993; Spradley, 1980).

Basically, participant observation describes how people behave by watching and recording what they do and say. What the researcher looks for is material that is sufficiently rich in content to reveal consistent themes. The researcher may use a tape recorder or make field notes largely from memory (Judd et al., 1991, p. 320). As in all methods of systematic observation, the researcher is guided by specific research questions or hypotheses, so that the observation is not random but theoretically selective. However, in contrast to laboratory research, in which the experimenter makes a concerted effort *not* to intercede in the lives of the people he or she studies (except, of course, for the intercessions that define the independent variables), the opposite is frequently true in participant observer research. As the name implies, the participant observer interjects himself or herself into an actual situation in an effort to draw out and document people's reactions.

An interesting example of participant observer research was a study by Louise H. Kidder (1972), who helped focus attention on this method (see Judd et al., 1991). In this study, she investigated the steps that a group of clinical psychologists went through at a three-day hypnosis workshop, during which they gradually learned to become hypnotized. Using a tape recorder and written notes to make a permanent record of her observations, Kidder kept verbatim accounts of the interactions between the experienced hypnotists and the psychologists. What she chose to record was guided by two research questions: (1) How do skeptics become convinced that they have been hypnotized? And (2) does becoming convinced reflect a change in the subject's definition of hypnosis, a change in the subject's definition of his or her own experience, or both? Her interest in these questions was reinforced by the vagueness and ambiguity she perceived in the reactions of most participants coming out of hypnosis for the first time: "How do I know if I was hypnotized?" or "I still don't consider it an experience any different from others" (p. 317).

At one point, for example, Kidder observed and recorded the interaction between a "guest subject" (who had been brought into the workshop to be hypnotized by one of the experts) and several of the other participants, who were given an opportunity to interview the guest subject:

Question: How did it feel?

Answer: Just very good. Very, very relaxed.

Question: Have you felt anything like this before?

Answer: Yeah, well it's sort of like smoking grass. The first few times I used it I just fell asleep.

Question: I want to ask what other experiences it was like.

Answer: It's like being very tired. Or like sitting in an airport and feeling tired and hearing other people around you talking—sort of hazy. (p. 321)

Kidder reported that the experts gave a great deal of feedback to the participants, seemingly manipulating the participants' attitudes, just as they might be shaped in a conditioning study. Her interpretation was that, by the last session, most of the participants had learned how to *behave* like good hypnotic subjects and had come to accept the experts' definitions of hypnosis and new definitions of their own feelings. She inferred that becoming hypnotized is similar to a social interaction and that those persons who are most hypnotizable proceed through the learning cycle more rapidly than others. In effect, Kidder's interpretation was that they learn to notice new sensations and to *feel* that maybe they have been hypnotized, whereas some people never go beyond the "I-don't-think-I-was-hypnotized state" (p. 322). While not a substitute for a more tightly controlled study, Kidder's conversational records flesh out her explanation of how people learn to become hypnotized.

ETHNOGRAPHY

Ethnography can be seen as a more standardized variant of participant observation, in which the objective is to document the customs, habits, and actions of a group of people, usually a culture. Thus it is also another example of naturalistic observation (see Box 4.3), but ethnographers often do interviewing (discussed in the next chapter) as well as make careful records of behavior and conversations. In *ethnomethodological research*, an approach pioneered by Harold Garfinkel in the 1960s, ethnographic methodology is used to explore how people "make sense" of

---

BOX 4.3	Advantages of Naturalistic Observation

Karl E. Weick (1968), an organizational psychologist, cataloged the special advantages of naturalistic observation:

1. It enables us to watch events in their "wholenesss," thereby giving us a sense of the relevant parameters during the preliminary stage of an investigation.
2. It allows us to watch fleeting events that may not be easily or realistically captured or simulated in the experimental laboratory.
3. It permits us to record events *as* they occur, so that we need not rely only on public records of past events made by nonscientists or on people's memories.
4. It allows us to explore the generalizability of laboratory findings in order to see whether changing the context changes the phenomenon.
5. It allows us to observe events that may be too risky or dangerous to create in the laboratory.

things—also called *sensemaking*. Although used primarily by sociologists and social and cultural anthropologists to study culture, ethnography is not limited to cultural studies. For example, one organizational researcher made an ethnographic (and ethnomethodological) study of how people assigned blame in a public inquiry concerning a fatal pipeline accident (Gephart, 1993).

The qualititative data resulting from this approach are often in the form exemplified by Kidder's data (i.e., conversations noted verbatim or notes based on memory), but the conversations may be technically analyzed word by word as well as interpreted in a more gross way. As in Kidder's participant observer research, the ethnographer may also collect and record many pages of detailed observations, constantly adding his or her own interpretation of the meaning of particular passages. Table 4.1 provides examples from the work of John Haviland (1977), an anthropologist, who kept meticulous records while living for 10 years in Zinacantan, a small village in Mexico. The table contains excerpts of conversations he tape-recorded and translated, along with his interpretation of each entire fragment. Haviland was interested in the sociology of gossiping and, on the basis of his wide sampling of conversations, explored the many functions of gossip in this community. He concluded, in general, that gossiping in Zinacantan encouraged spying between households at the same time that it isolated households from one another.

In the early development of ethnography, sociologists and anthropologists had yet to find out how to obtain the most precise and objective results or how to make the most reliable records. But over many years, various techniques have been tested and refined, so that certain procedures are now routinely used in many studies. For example, ethnographers who are interested in describing cultural differences usually work in teams insofar as possible, in order to control for possible idiosyncratic biases in their classifications and evaluations of events. When the language of the target culture is not the native language of the researchers, they also seek out assistance in framing interview questions in the indigenous language of the culture. This approach requires *back-translation;* that is, one bilingual person translates the questions from source to target language, and then another bilingual person translates the questions back into the source language. In this way, the researchers can compare the original with the twice-translated version (i.e., the back-translation) to see if anything important has been lost in the translation. It is also considered essential to identify the language used for each field-note entry, for example, "investigator's native language," "the language of Group X," or "technical language of social science" (Spradley, 1980).

Haviland's field notes were guided or influenced by specific questions that he formulated. The following are a set of *generic* (or general) *questions* formulated by a leading ethnographer (Goodenough, 1980), which might serve as descriptive guideposts in an ethnographic or a participant observation study of the type done by Haviland or Kidder:

1. *What is the purpose of the activity?* That is, what are the goals and their justifications? In his study, Haviland classified several objectives of gossiping, which

TABLE 4.1	Fragments of Zinacanteco Gossip and Their Analysis
Examples	Interpretations
"Didn't I hear that old José was up to some mischief?" "Perhaps, but that never became public knowledge. It was a secret affair." "The magistrate settled the whole business in private." "Yes, when a dispute is settled at the townhall, then a newspaper report goes out to every part of town. . . . Ha ha ha." "Yes, then we all hear about it on the radio. . . . Ha ha ha." "But when the thing is hushed up, then there's nothing on the radio. There are no newspapers. Then we don't hear about it. Ha ha ha."	Shows how some villagers even gossip about gossip.
"Is it true that old Maria divorced Manuel?" "Yes. She complained that she awoke every morning with a wet skirt. Old Manuel used to piss himself every night, just like a child." "When he was drunk, you mean?" "No, even when he was sober. 'How it stinks!' she said." "Ha ha ha. She spoke right out at the townhall."	Shows how some gossip trades on a separation, but also on a connection, between the public and the private domain.
"This is what I told him: All right, I'll see how deeply I must go into debt to take this office. But I don't want you to start complaining about it later. If I hear that you have been ridiculing me, saying things like: 'Boy, he is just pretending to be a man; he is just pretending to have money to do ritual service. He stole my office, he took it from me'. . . . If you say such things, please excuse me, but I'll drag you to jail. I'll come looking for you myself. I don't want you to tell stories about me, because you have freely given me your ritual office. If there is no dispute, then I too will behave the same way. I won't gossip about you. I won't ridicule you. I won't say, for example, 'Hah, I am replacing him; he has no shame, acting like a man, asking for religious office when he has no money.' I won't talk like that. 'He wanted to serve Our Lord, but he ran away. I had to take over for him.' I won't say things like that, if we agree to keep silent about it. . . ."	Shows a common theme in gossip about shady dealings and how the villagers take pains to ensure that the matter is kept quiet.

Source: Reproduced from "Gossip as Competition in Zinacantan" by J.B. Haviland, 1977, *Journal of Communication, 27,* pp. 186–191. Copyright ©1977; *Journal of Communication,* Oxford University Press. Used with permission of the publisher.

led him to conclude that, despite the fences erected between households, the actors were constantly scrutinizing one another's dealings.

2. *What procedures are used?* What are the operations performed, the media or raw materials used, the skills and instruments involved, if any? In Haviland's study, the medium of gossip was word of mouth; he carefully categorized the linguistic and psychological skills required in effective gossipmongering.

3. *What are the time and space requirements?* How much time is needed for each operation, what areas or facilities are required, and are there any obstacles in

the way of the activity? Haviland noted when and where gossiping occurred, as well as what natural obstacles there were to the transmission of information.

4. *What are the personnel requirements?* How many actors participate, and what are their specializations, if any? Haviland classified and evaluated the elaborate conversational devices by which certain people in positions of authority protected themselves against charges of slander.

5. *What is the nature of the social organization?* What are the categories of actors; their rights, duties, privileges, powers; and the types of sanctions used by them? Haviland classified and evaluated the ways in which Zinacanteco gossip was used by the villagers to manage their social faces and at the same time to protect their privacy.

6. *What are the occasions for performance?* When is the activity mandatory, permitted, and prohibited, and what is the relationship of the initiator's role to the roles of others? Haviland noted the occasions that were most and least conducive to gossiping, and he categorized and analyzed the particular role interactions of the gossipmongers within those circumstances.

CONTENT ANALYSIS OF ARCHIVAL MATERIAL

Generally speaking, an *archive* is any relatively permanent depository of data or material (see Box 4.4), such as a library containing books and journals. Other examples of archival material include (1) actuarial records (e.g., the birth, marriage, and death records in town hall ledgers); (2) political and judicial records (e.g., the voting records of legislators and speeches printed in the *Congressional Record*); (3) other governmental records (e.g., weather reports, invention records, and crime reports); (4) information from the mass media (e.g., stories, news reports, advertising, and editorials); (5) sales records (e.g., sales at airport bars, sales of trip-

---

BOX 4.4   Behavioral Science Archives

For students interested in using behavioral science archives, raw data depositories are available at the Human Relations Area Files at Yale University and elsewhere, the University of Chicago's National Opinion Research Center (NORC), and the University of Michigan's Survey Research Center. The Roper Center of the University of Connecticut, for instance, offers survey data collected by the NORC going back to the early 1950s. Data are available from personal interviews of national samples; these NORC interviews used a standardized questionnaire, with the same questions appearing in every survey or according to a rotation pattern. All the data are in the public domain and are readily accessible to researchers for duplication, analysis, and publication without clearance from the NORC. A wide range of variables is tapped, including demographic, sociopsychological, political, and socioeconomic variables. If you are interested in using such data, consult with a librarian about what data are available and what costs there may be.

insurance policies, and decreased sales of airline tickets, all constituting plausible indicators of increased anxiety); (6) industrial and institutional records (sicknesses and absences from the job, complaints and unsolicited commendations from the public, and accident reports); and (7) various other written documents (e.g., diaries and letters of captured soldiers in wartime, letters of protest to large companies, and rumors recorded by rumor control centers).

The use of archival material falls into the category known as *secondary observation,* which means that the observation of the researcher is "twice removed" from the source: The reporter is once removed, and the researcher is removed by another degree. A popular method of decomposing written messages in archives and then evaluating and classifying their content is called *content analysis.* Proposed by a political scientist (Harold Lasswell), and with details worked out by a sociologist (Bernard Berelson), the general procedure consists of burrowing through written records in order to discover their characteristics (see, e.g., Berelson, 1952; Holsti, 1969; Krippendorff, 1980; Rosengren, 1981; Stone, Dunphy, Smith, & Ogilvie, 1966; Weber, 1985). However, content analysis also calls for systematic observation to classify the materials precisely and objectively. We will give an example in a moment, but the basic procedure consists of using judges to count symbols, words, sentences, ideas, or whatever other category of information is of interest.

In a content analysis, three general guidelines should be kept in mind (Berelson, 1954):

1. It is important that the analyses be consistent among the judges; that is, the different coders should produce close to the same results. If each category and unit of analysis are carefully defined, and if the judges are properly trained, the *intercoder reliability* (i.e., the consistency among the judges) should be satisfactorily high. We will have more to say about how to choose judges later in this chapter.

2. It is essential that the specific categories and units be relevant to the questions or hypotheses of the study. In choosing categories, it is a good idea to ask, "What is the communication about?" and "How is it said?" These questions will help to focus the analysis on the substance (the *what*) and the form (the *how*) of the subject matter. It is also a good idea to consider several different units of analysis before settling on any one unit. For example, we might consider coding words and word compounds (or phrases) or perhaps themes (or assertions).

3. And finally, it is important to decide on a good sampling procedure. Because content analysis is so time-consuming, one must be sure that the materials to be analyzed are representative enough to justify the effort. We will have much to say about different sampling plans later in this book, including approaches that call for (a) random samples from listings of all relevant units; (b) stratified samples, which break up units into subgroups and sample from them; and (c) systematic samples, which involve selecting every *n*th unit of a list.

Although this procedure has limitations (cf. Weber, 1985)—as have all methods—content analysis has four distinct advantages when used properly (Woodrum, 1984). First, developing a coding system and then implementing it requires little more than commonsense logic. Second, content analysis is a "shoestring" methodology in that, although labor-intensive, it requires a minimal capital investment. Third, it is a "safe" methodology, because the researcher can add necessary information if it is missed or incorrectly coded (if there are changes in what is being measured over time, it is not usually possible to do this in the typical experimental or survey study). Fourth, it forces researchers to scrutinize the material that they are evaluating and classifying by specifying category criteria and assessing their success in measuring qualitative phenomena.

As an illustration of the use of content analysis, Peter B. Crabb and Dawn Bielawski (1994) used this approach in a study of how influential books written for children portrayed female and male roles. The researchers chose for their study all picture books that had been awarded the Caldecott Medal over a 53-year period, on the assumption that these books have a high profile in libraries and book stores. The books contained 1,613 illustrations, including 416 showing female characters and 1,197 showing male characters. Crabb and Bielawski then drew a proportionate sample of 300 representative illustrations by gender and decade and gave these to two judges to code on a list of criteria.

For example, the coding sheets used by the judges asked them (1) to record the sex of each character shown; (2) to categorize the depiction of any household artifacts, such as those used in food preparation, cleaning, repair, and family care; (3) to categorize the depiction of any nonhousehold artifacts, such as those used in construction, agriculture, and transportation; (4) to list any artifacts not falling into the above two categories; and (5) to code other features of the characters and the situation (e.g., age of character: child, teenager, adult). The ratings by the two judges were in strong agreement with one another (i.e., they had high intercoder reliability). Among the findings were that household artifacts were generally associated with female characters and that nonhousehold artifacts were generally associated with male characters. It was also observed that the proportion of male characters using household artifacts increased over time, but that the proportion of female characters using nonhousehold artifacts did not change very much.

THE LABORATORY EXPERIMENT

In its general scientific usage, the term *experiment* means to test or to try out something in order to identify its causes; in later chapters we will discuss specific categories of experiments and the causal reasoning associated with them. Suppose you wanted to do a laboratory experiment to study why people's ears buzz and tickle as they listen to a hard rock band up close. You could position a loudspeaker next to the subject, present carefully calibrated sounds, and ask the subject to report the sensations he or she feels. If the subject's ears buzz and tickle, the sound pressure may well be above 120 decibels, which can produce feelings of discomfort, prickling, and pain. After each exposure to such sounds, the sensitivity of the ear may be temporarily reduced. (To find out whether people who have a steady diet of hard rock have hearing difficulties, you could study the minimum audible noise detected by subjects who listen to a lot of hard rock or no hard rock. However, such an investigation would not be an experimental study but a relational study.)

The principal advantage of the laboratory experiment is that it allows us to mimic a causal relationhip in a highly controlled setting in which we can actually manipulate the causal condition (i.e., the independent variable). However, using a *simulation* (i.e., a procedure modeled on an actual situation) may sometimes fall short of the real-life situation—even if, for ethical reasons, we are limited to a simulation. For example, an early laboratory experiment was designed to assess the effects of marijuana and alcohol on automobile driving. In the 1960s, when this study was conducted, there were volumes of statistics on the relationship between alcohol use and accident rates, but comparable data for marijuana were unavailable. A laboratory experiment that investigated the effects of drugs on simulated driving performance was ethically acceptable and could also be better controlled. What was lost in the laboratory approach, though, was the actual stress of driving in traffic.

In this experiment (Crancer et al., 1969), the effects of marijuana, alcohol, and no drug at all were compared in simulated driving tests. In Test 1, experienced marijuana smokers were tested 30 minutes after smoking two marijuana cigarettes, and the same subjects were tested when their blood alcohol concentration reached 0.10% (the legally defined intoxication level in 1969), the equivalent of about 6 ounces of 86-proof liquor in a 120-pound subject. In the no-drug control condition, neither marijuana nor alcohol was given. In the driving test, the subject sat in a specially constructed console mock-up of a recent-model car and observed a large screen on which a driver's-eye movie film was projected. Normal and emergency situations on urban and suburban streets appeared on the screen, and the subject was instructed to respond to them by operating the accelerator, brake, turn signals, and steering, and by checking the speedometer. It was possible to make up to 405 errors during the 23-minute film. Test 2 was taken by the subject 2 1/2 hours after taking the first test, and Test 3 was taken 1 1/2 hours after Test 2. All tests were the same.

The results were revealing, but decidedly ambiguous. Under the effects of alcohol, the subjects did worse than in either the marijuana or no-drug condition. In the alcohol condition over all three tests, they made a mean of 97 errors; they made a mean of 85 errors in the marijuana condition and in the control condition. In the marijuana condition, compared to the control condition, the only bad effect was an increase in speedometer errors. Under the effects of alcohol, there was an increase in all types of errors except steering errors. Later in this book we will discuss how to anticipate and control for certain experimental design problems, but how many flaws do you recognize intuitively in this study?

PLAUSIBLE RIVAL HYPOTHESES

One possible flaw is reminiscent of the Hawthorne effect in Chapter 1, in which merely being studied experimentally sometimes affects how a person behaves (see Box 1.1 on p. 5). In this case, the subjects were experienced marijuana users, were probably motivated to do well in the marijuana condition, and may even have been motivated to do poorly in the alcohol condition. A second possible flaw is that the drug doses may not have been comparable. Two marijuana cigarettes may not have made the subjects nearly as "high" as 6 ounces of 86-proof alcohol; if the alcohol and marijuana treatments had made the subjects equally "high," the resulting errors might have been more nearly equal, and both might have been greater than those accumulated in the no-drug condition. In studies such as this, another possible flaw is that the sequence of the treatments may be a source of confounding. To avoid such a problem, the sequences must be "counterbalanced" (discussed in a later chapter).

This critical evaluation is typical of those used routinely on all research studies. It will give you an idea of what your instructor may expect as you begin to put together a background review of the literature on your research topic or to write the discussion section of your final report. That is, the instructor will expect you to think carefully about alternative explanations (also called *plausible rival hypotheses*) for the reported results and about possible ways of improving the studies you review (as well as your own research, as illustrated in the sample report in Appendix A). As a further illustration of this kind of critical thinking, we will turn to another laboratory experiment. This simulation focuses on how human beings select from their perceptual environment those objects and events that are significant to them because of their life experience. Several classic laboratory studies have shown that individuals' personal values affect how they perceive certain aspects of their environment.

In one such study (Postman, Bruner, & McGinnies, 1948), the researchers determined the predominant value attitudes of a group of subjects by having them fill out a questionnaire designed to measure whether their orientation was predominantly aesthetic, theoretical, economic, social, political, or religious. For example, the answers of a person who valued the search for truth above most other things would tend to receive a high "theoretical" score, and a subject whose values were dominated by the usefulness of things received a high "economic" score. The "political" subject was concerned with power, the "social" subject with the needs of others, the "aesthetic" subject with criteria of beauty, and the "religious" subject with the meaning of life as it related to his or her conception of God. The subjects in this study were then presented with a series of words through a tachistoscope projector, a device that briefly presents various stimuli by flashing them on a screen for a fraction of a second. The words reflected the six value orientations of the subjects.

On the whole, the subjects tended to identify the words associated with their own value orientations more rapidly than the words not so associated. This interpretation was later challenged by other researchers (Solomon & Howes, 1951), who argued that persons with a specific value orientation may have been exposed to these words in print more often than other individuals (presumably individuals read more literature relevant to *their* own values). Therefore, a person oriented to "political" words, for example, would recognize them more rapidly than other words because of their familiarity and not because they were visually perceived more quickly. This criticism paved the way for follow-up studies that were designed to reconcile such differences in interpretation. Scientists typically do this kind of critiquing of research studies as they plot their own plans to do research in a given area, so that they will not repeat the mistakes of earlier studies and will instead increase our understanding of the problem of interest. In this way, scientists build on one another's systematic observations, or as Isaac Newton put it more than 300 years ago, "If I have seen further, it is by standing upon the shoulders of giants."

THE FIELD EXPERIMENT

In another variant of naturalistic observation, called *field experimentation*, the researcher evokes behavior by modifying some aspect of the situation or by introducing an experimental variable (i.e., a manipulated independent variable) in a field setting. The advantage of this method is that it may have more mundane and experimental realism than a similar study conducted as a laboratory simulation. *Mundane realism* means that the various dimensions of the experiment are very similar to those in the real world (Aronson & Carlsmith, 1968). The more the manipulation of the independent variable resembles the real-world phenomenon, the greater the mundane realism is. *Experimental realism* refers to the extent to which the subject is drawn into or is affected by the treatment (Aronson & Carlsmith, 1968). The more involving the manipulation of the independent variable, or the greater the degree to which the subject's attention is "turned on" by the treatment, the more experimental realism there is.

Illustrative of this approach is a field experiment in which one of the authors of this book investigated whether teachers' expectations of their students' intellectual performance may come to serve as self-fulfilling prophecies (Rosenthal & Jacobson, 1968). In the spring of 1964, all the children in a public elementary school in South San Francisco were given a standard nonverbal intelligence test. The test was represented to the teachers as a measure of intellectual "blooming," and approximately 20% of the children (the experimental group) were said to be capable of marked intellectual growth. The difference between these supposed potential bloomers and the other students (the control group) existed solely in the minds of their teachers, because the bloomers had been picked entirely at random. The dependent variable in this study was the children's performance on the same intelligence test after one semester, again after a full academic year, and again after two full academic years.

The overall results revealed that, although the greatest differential gain in total intelligence appeared after one school year, the bloomers clearly held an advantage over the other children, the control subjects, even after two years. To account for this finding, the researchers speculated that the teachers may have been more encouraging and friendly to the children in whom they expected greater gains, and that they perhaps unwittingly motivated the children to greater achievement. Similar observations have been made in a wide variety of settings, and we will refer to this general finding again in a later chapter. The implication is that interpersonal expectations may become self-fulfilling prophecies (Merton, 1948); that is, someone who predicts or expects an event may unwittingly behave in ways that are likely to increase the probability that the event will occur. Because it is plausible that an experimenter's expectancies may also serve as self-fulfilling prophecies, the scientist needs to understand this phenomenon and learn how to control for it. (We return to this problem in a later chapter.)

Another example of field experimentation was a classic study by George W. Hartmann (1936), in which he investigated the role of emotional and rational political messages in an actual voting campaign and election. He was struck by the fact that much of the persuasive communication to which we are subjected in daily life is designed to appeal more to our emotions than to our reason. The purpose of such communication seems to be to arouse certain needs and to offer simple solutions that, if we adopt them, will supposedly satisfy those needs. Every day we are bombarded by a host of advertisements on radio, TV, and so forth, each commercial in its own way claiming that it will make us feel better because we will be more sexually appealing or more companionable or more sweet-smelling. Around elec-

---

Leaflet A

You've heard of intelligence tests, haven't you? Well, we have a little examination right here which we are sure you will enjoy taking, even if you didn't care much for school when you were a youngster. The beauty of this test is that you can score it yourself without any teacher to tell you whether you passed or failed.

This is how it works. First read each one of the seven statements printed below. If you *approve* the idea as it stands, *underline* the word AGREE; if you *disapprove* of the idea, underline the word DISAGREE. Simple, isn't it? All right, then. Get your pencil ready. All set? Go!

1. We would have much cheaper electric light and power if this industry were owned and operated by the various governmental units for the benefit of all the people. AGREE—DISAGREE.

2. No gifted boy or girl should be denied the advantages of higher education just because his parents lack the money to send him to college. AGREE—DISAGREE.

3. The Federal Government should provide to all classes of people opportunity for complete insurance at cost against accident, sickness, premature death and old age. AGREE—DISAGREE.

4. All banks and insurance companies should be run on a non-profit basis like the schools. AGREE—DISAGREE.

5. Higher income taxes on persons with incomes of more than $10,000 a year should be levied immediately. AGREE—DISAGREE.

6. The only way most people will ever be able to live in modern sanitary homes is for the government to build them on a non-profit basis. AGREE—DISAGREE.

7. Many more industries and parts of industries should be owned and managed co-operatively by the producers (all the workers) themselves. AGREE—DISAGREE.

Have you answered them all? Fine. Now go back and count the number of sentences with which you AGREED. Then count the number with which you DISAGREED. *If the number of agreements is larger than the number of disagreements, you are at heart a Socialist*—whether you know it or not!

Now that you have tested yourself and found out how much of a Socialist you really are, *why don't you try voting for the things you actually want?* The Republicans and Democrats don't propose to give these things to you, because a mere look at their records will show that they are opposed to them. Do you get the point?

HELP BUILD THE AGE OF PLENTY!

VOTE: SOCIALIST X

FIGURE 4.1   *Rational (A) and emotional (B) leaflets. (G. W. Hartmann, "A Field Experiment on the Comparative Effectiveness of 'Emotional' and 'Rational' Political Leaflets in Determining Election Results,"* Journal of Abnormal and Social Psychology, *1936, 31, p. 101. Reprinted by courtesy of the American Psychological Association. (Continued)*

tion time, political commercials become a complex fusion of excitement, resentment, vague enthusiasms, aroused fears, and hopes. While he was working at Columbia University in the 1930s as a postdoctoral fellow, Hartmann decided to do a field experiment to test whether emotional or rational advertisements are more persuasive in politics.

During the 1935 statewide election campaign in Pennsylvania, Hartmann's name had been placed on the ballot as a Socialist Party candidate in Allentown. To study the role of emotional and rational messages, he created two political leaflets, one designed to appeal to Allentown voters' reason and the other to appeal to their emotions. The leaflets (reproduced in Figure 4.1) were distributed in different

---

Leaflet B

Allentown, Pennsylvania
November 1, 1935

Dear Mother and Father:

We youngsters are not in the habit of giving much thought to serious things. You have often told us so and we admit it.

But while we like to play football and have a good time dancing and cause you a lot of amusement as well as worry with our "puppy loves," we sometimes think long and hard. You ought to know what many of us young folks are quietly saying to ourselves.

Our future as American citizens in 1940 looks dark. We want jobs—and good jobs, too—so that we can help in the useful work of the world. But we know that many of our brightest high-school and college graduates find it absolutely impossible to get any kind of employment. We also know that this condition is not temporary, but that it will last as long as we stick to harmful ways of running business, industry and government.

We want to continue our education, but we haven't the heart to ask you to make that sacrifice. With Dad working only part-time on little pay and Mother trying to make last year's coat and dress look in season, we feel we ought to pitch in and help keep the family's neck above water. But we can't. The world as it is now run has no use for us.

Many of our teachers know what is wrong, although we can see that most of them are afraid to say what they really think. Luckily, the text-books and school magazines keep us in touch with new ideas, and we have learned how to read between the lines of the ordinary newspaper. Please don't be frightened if we tell you what we have decided!

We young people are becoming Socialists. We have to be. We can't be honest with ourselves and be anything else. *The Socialist Party is the only party which is against all wars*—and we have learned from our history courses what awful wars have taken place under both Republicans and Democrats. We refuse to be slaughtered (like Uncles Bob and Charles were in 1918) just to make profits for ammunition manufacturers.

The Socialist Party seeks to create a world in which there will be no poverty. In our science classes we learn how power machinery and other modern inventions make it possible for all of us to have enough of all the goods and services we need. Yet look at our town with its unpainted shacks, suffering parents, half-starved children! We might have everything, but we continue to live on next to nothing.

It is all so unnecessary. You have had to lead a poor workingman's life, because you and most of the workers and farmers of this country have regularly voted for either the Republican or Democratic parties, between which there is no real difference. These old machines are not for us.

The youth of 1935 want to Build a Better America, in which there will be no poverty, no fear of unemployment, no threat of war. We ask you to follow the lead of the Socialist Party this year because that is the most direct way for you to *help hasten the day when Peace and Plenty and lasting Prosperity will be the lot of all men.* Good parents such as you desire these things for us. But we can never have them as long as you are controlled by your old voting habits.

We are profoundly earnest about this. Our generation cannot enjoy the beauty and justice of the *New America* if you block our highest desires. There was a time when you too were young like us. We beg you in the name of those early memories and spring-time hopes to *support the Socialist ticket in the coming elections!*

Your Sons and Daughters

FIGURE 4.1   *Continued*

wards matched on the basis of their size, population density, assessed property valuation, previous voting habits, and socioeconomic status. The main dependent variable in this study was the objective record of the polls. The results of Hartmann's analysis were that the wards that had received the emotional leaflet increased their Socialist votes more than the wards receiving the rational leaflet. In a more in-depth comparison, Hartmann also found that even the "rational" wards showed a greater increase in Socialist votes than a number of control wards that had received neither leaflet.

Unobtrusive Observation

Hartmann's use of voting behavior as his dependent variable is also an illustration of *unobtrusive observation,* so called because those being studied are unaware that they are being observed for the purpose of research. A further distinction is made between *reactive observation* and *nonreactive observation;* the terms are used to differentiate between observations that do (reactive) from those that do not (nonreactive) affect the behavior being systematically observed. The idea of a reactive observation can be viewed as another variation on the Hawthorne effect. For example, in an experiment on therapy for weight control, the initial weigh-in may be a reactive stimulus to weight reduction, even without the therapeutic intervention (Campbell & Stanley, 1963).

Unobtrusive observation, because it involves the use of concealment, is illustrative of nonreactive observation. For example, using hidden recording devices to eavesdrop on conversations exemplifies unobtrusive observation. Another variant involves *partial concealment* (Weick, 1968); the researcher does not conceal the fact that he or she is making observations but does conceal who or what is being observed. For example, in studies of mother–child interaction, the researcher implies that it is the child who is being observed when both the mother *and* the child are being studied (Weick, 1968).

As noted in the previous chapter, these types of studies may cause ethical conflicts, which need to be carefully considered. For example, the threat to privacy is made worse by the lack of permission in this situation and the fact that debriefing is not typically used. The defense of unobtrusive observation usually assumes that the individuals observed are anonymous, so that their privacy is protected. That is, the behavioral scientist's goal (unlike, for example, the investigative reporter's) is not to obtain individually identified information. The American Psychological Association's code of ethics (see Chapter 3) reminds us that individual researchers are responsible for protecting the dignity of those they study. Thus the ethical obligation of researchers who use unobtrusive observations is to ensure that any information to be published will not damage a person by subjecting him or her to ridicule or scorn.

Another example of unobtrusive observation is the "lost-letter" technique, which involves dropping addressed, stamped, but unposted letters in public places. The person who comes across such a letter must decide whether to mail it, disregard it, or destroy it. In the original field experiment that used this technique (Merritt & Fowler, 1948), two kinds of stamped, fully addressed envelopes, one containing a trivial message and the other a lead slug about the size of a half-dollar, were "lost." By recording the return rates, the experimenters attempted unobtrusively to gauge the honesty of various samples of subjects in large cities around the country without the subjects' suspecting that they were participating in an experiment. The result was that significantly fewer letters with slugs than without them were mailed. Variations on the "lost-letter" technique have been used by other researchers to study other kinds of behavior unobtrusively (e.g., Milgram, Mann, & Harter, 1965; Walker & Blaine, 1991).

A major work on unobtrusive observation was written by a team of interdisciplinary authors headed by Eugene J. Webb (Webb, Campbell, Schwartz, & Sechrest, 1966; Webb et al., 1981). It is a fascinating gem of a book that contains hundreds of unobtrusive measures collected by Webb and his group. In general, they classified all their measures into four broad categories: (1) archival records; (2) physical traces; (3) simple observations; and (4) contrived observations. Previously, we discussed archival records, and we will conclude this section by giving examples of the other three classes described by Webb et al.

First, *physical traces* include the kind of material evidence that a detective might use as a clue in solving a crime. For example, in one detective case, a car's radio buttons were clues to the driver's geographic location. By studying the commercial station frequencies to which the buttons were tuned, the detective could identify the general area where the car had been garaged. In one application of this strategy, a car dealer used radio dial settings in an audience measurement study. The dealer had his mechanics record the position of the dial in all the cars brought in for service. He then used this information to choose the radio stations that would carry his advertising to old and potentially new customers.

Other examples of the use of physical traces include measuring the wear and tear (particularly on the corners of pages) of library books as an unobtrusive measure of what books are actually read (not just books checked out and possibly never opened, never read, or never finished). In another case, the relative popularity of children's museum exhibits was measured unobtrusively. The exhibits had glass fronts, and each evening they were dusted for children's noseprints. Those exhibits with more noseprints on the glass were more frequently or more closely observed, the researchers speculated. The distance of the noseprints from the floor even provided a crude index of the ages of the children. Another example in this category is studying language behavior by analyzing the content of messages that people have composed on floor-sample personal computers in department stores.

Second, *simple observation* occurs when one observes events unobtrusively without trying to affect them in any way. For example, Webb's group described a correlation between the methodological and theoretical disposition of psychologists and the length of their hair. The researchers unobtrusively evaluated and classified the hair styles of psychologists at professional meetings and also categorized the meetings by whether they involved "tough-minded" or "tender-minded" areas of research. They reported that the tough-minded psychologists had shorter hair than the tender-minded psychologists.

Third, in *contrived observation,* the observer introduces some variable of interest into a situation and then unobtrusively observes its effect on behavior. It is what Hartmann did in his field experiment, described earlier. For example, you might estimate the degree of fear induced by a ghost story by observing the shrinking diameter of a circle of seated children. Some investigators have "bugged" cocktail parties and recorded the conversations after introducing some variable of interest (e.g., introducing a stranger or an oddly dressed guest). Before the days of audiotapes, Francis Galton, the pioneering English empiricist mentioned in Chapter 1, carried with him paper in the shape of a cross and a small needle for punching holes in the paper. He used this device to count whatever he was observing at the time; a hole at the head of the cross meant "greater," on an arm "equal," and at the foot "less."

USING JUDGES AS OBSERVERS

Except for secondary observations using archival records, we have considered only the researcher himself or herself as the primary observer. Among the other observational "tools" that scientists use in field and laboratory studies are independent *judges* (coders, raters, decoders, etc.) to assist in describing and categorizing ongoing events or existing records of events (film records, narratives, etc.). Judges use *checklists* and *tally sheets* to impose a sense of structure on their observations; as the names imply, these are simply systematic ways of counting (checking off or tallying) the frequency of occurrence of particular acts or events. For example, we mentioned how Crabb and Bielawski used two independent judges to content-analyze a sample of pictures from children's books. In general, researchers choose judges in one of three ways: (1) on the basis of intuition; (2) by consulting the relevant research literature; or (3) by doing pilot testing.

The first approach is to decide intuitively on the type of judges needed (graduate students, community members, college students, clinical psychologists, linguists, mothers, etc.) and then to regard each judge within that sample as equivalent to (or interchangeable with) any other judge within the sample. For example, if you wanted a sample of educated judges, you might be content to select college students. If you wanted judgments of nonverbal expressions of neuroses, you would choose experienced professionals for your judges, such as clinical psychologists, psychiatrists, or psychiatric social workers. If you wanted judgments of nonverbal expressions of discomfort in infants, you might select pediatricians, developmental psychologists, or mothers. If you wanted judgments of nonverbal cues of persuasion, you might invite trial lawyers, fundamentalist ministers, or salespersons. You would also want to make sure that the judges are not relying on stereotypes that may not be accurate (e.g., salespersons recruited to watch people give persuasive messages might rely on their stereotypes to tell you which of the nonverbal cues were most persuasive).

A second approach is to consult the relevant research literature, in which case you might do even better by making a special selection of judges. For example, if you wanted to obtain the highest possible general accuracy in judgments of nonverbal cues, your selection of judges might be based on prior research that had identified the specific characteristics of people who are more sensitive to nonverbal cues. This research (Rosenthal et al., 1979) suggests that to optimize overall sensitivity to nonverbal cues you should probably select judges who are (1) female, (2) college-aged, and (as measured by psychological tests) both (3) cognitively complex and (4) psychiatrically unimpaired.

A third way to select judges is to do a *pilot test* in which you compare all recruits in your pool of potential judges for their accuracy of judgments on some relevant criterion. Suppose you were interested in selecting judges for a study in which they would have to categorize the emotions expressed by participants in encounter groups. You might begin by showing your pool of potential judges pictures of people exhibiting different emotions, such as anger, disgust, fear, happiness, sadness, and surprise. You would ask the subjects to identify the emotion expressed in each picture, score the answers given by the participants, and then use the most accurate judges in your study.

A FINAL NOTE

You have seen examples of how systematic observation provides much of the empirical content of behavioral science. We have noted a range of primary and secondary observational methods (e.g., participant observation, ethnography, laboratory experimentation, and field experimentation), yet our discussion barely scratched the surface of what is possible. In the following chapters we will describe a number of other research methods. We will turn our attention in the next chapter to methods in which the observations are directed "inward" rather than "outward."

SUMMARY OF IDEAS

1. Systematic observation is guided by preexisting questions or hypotheses in descriptive, relational, and experimental research.
2. Because each qualitative and quantitative method is limited in some ways, behavioral scientists use multiple methods to try to fill in the gaps through triangulation.
3. Participant observation, which resembles investigative journalism in some respects, is used to study a group from within by watching and recording how people behave and what they talk about (e.g., Kidder's study of participants in a hypnosis workshop).
4. Students of animal behavior use a variant of naturalistic observation to study animal life in the wild.
5. Ethnography is a more standardized variant of naturalistic observation in which the researcher is guided by questions about (a) the purpose of the activity being observed; (b) the procedures used in the activity; (c) its time and space requirements; (d) its personnel; (e) the nature of its social organization; and (f) the occasions for performance (see e.g., Haviland's study of gossiping in Zinacantan).
6. In ethnomethodological research, ethnography is used to study how people make sense of things (i.e., sensemaking).

7. Content analysis is used in archival research to code and sort secondary observations (e.g., Crabb and Bielawski's study of gender roles in children's picture books).
8. In doing a content analysis, it is important (a) to ensure intercoder reliability; (b) to develop specific, relevant content categories for the judges to code; and (c) to choose a good sampling procedure.
9. Doing a laboratory experiment generally means "testing" or "trying out" something in a tightly controlled artificial setting in order to study causality, and in many cases using a simulation (e.g., the experiment to simulate the effects of marijuana and alcohol use on automobile driving).
10. All research studies, including tightly controlled laboratory experiments, are subject to critical reexamination for plausible rival hypotheses (e.g., the study in Number 9 above and the tachistoscopic study of word recognition).
11. Field experiments are a quantitative variant of naturalistic observational research (e.g., the experimental study of teachers' expectations as unwitting determinants of students' intellectual performance and Hartmann's study of the effects of emotional and rational political leaflets on voting behavior).
12. Unobtrusive observation is nonreactive; examples include (a) archival records, (b) physical traces, (c) simple observations, and (d) contrived observations.
13. When choosing judges to classify events, we can use (a) intuition, (b) previous research results that help us select the most accurate individuals, or (c) pilot testing.

KEY TERMS

archive *p. 80*
back-translation *p. 78*
checklist *p. 90*
content analysis *p. 81*
contrived observation *p. 90*
ethnography *p. 77*
ethnomethodological research
  p. 77
experimental realism *p. 85*
field experimentation *p. 85*
generic questions *p. 78*
intercoder reliability *p. 81*
interpreter effect *p. 76*
judges *p. 90*
justification *p. 73*
mundane realism *p. 85*
naturalistic observation *p. 75*

partial concealment *p. 88*
participant observation *p. 74*
physical traces *p. 89*
pilot test *p. 91*
plausible rival hypotheses *p. 84*
qualitative methods *p. 74*
quantitative methods *p. 74*
reactive observation *p. 88*
robust relationship *p. 74*
secondary observation *p. 81*
sensemaking *p. 78*
simple observation *p. 89*
systematic observation *p. 73*
tally sheet *p. 90*
triangulation *p. 74*
unobtrusive observation *p. 88*

REVIEW QUESTIONS

1. An Iowa student is given the task of describing two possible uses of archival measures not mentioned in this chapter. Can you suggest some possibilities?

2. An Arizona State student wants to test the hypothesis that people's level of aggression predicts their preference of sports; that is, more aggressive people like more aggressive sports. How might the student test this hypothesis using non-reactive measures? Can you think of one strength and one weakness of each of your suggested measures?

3. A Towson State student wants to use content analysis to study the comic pages in the *Baltimore Sun*. Can you think of a particular hypothesis to guide the data collection? What steps would you advise the student to take in carrying out her study?

4. A Fitchburg State College student wants to do a participant observation study of tourists and local residents in Provincetown. What advice would you give him about systematizing his observations?

5. A student at the University of Massachusetts at Boston wants to illustrate the application of triangulation to the question of whether inhaling cigarette smoke is unhealthy. Can you help by giving an example of a descriptive, a relational, and an experimental study, all addressing the same question?

6. An Ohio University student has found that teachers' ratings of their students' intellectual ability are highly correlated with the students' IQ test scores and concludes that this reflects the effects of teachers' expectations on students' intellectual performance. What might be a plausible rival hypothesis to that interpretation?

Answers to review questions are found on pages 320–334.

Self-Report Methods

> ➤ What are the uses and limits of open-ended and closed measures?
> ➤ What is the role of projective tests?
> ➤ What scales are used when people rate themselves?
> ➤ What errors are possible?
> ➤ What is meant by *standardized scale*?
> ➤ When is a questionnaire used?
> ➤ How is a research questionnaire constructed?
> ➤ What are the dynamics of an interview?
> ➤ How is an interview schedule developed?
> ➤ How are telephone interviews conducted?
> ➤ How are "diaries" used in research?

OPEN-ENDED AND CLOSED MEASURES

Behavioral scientists not only watch and record, frequently calling on judges to make systematic observations, but they often ask research participants to look within themselves and describe their impressions. For example, suppose you received the following telephone call:

> Hello, is this _____? My name is _____, and I'm calling from the Survey Institute at Central University. We are conducting a short random survey to determine how people feel about gun control issues so that we can get a true picture of people's attitudes. It will only take about two or three minutes, and we would greatly appreciate your help. May I ask you some questions?

If you answer yes, you will be read a series of questions and asked to report how you personally behave, feel, or think (e.g., Lavrakas, 1987).

This kind of methodological approach is one example of the use of *self-report methods,* which are techniques of data collection in which the research participants describe their own behavior or state of mind. As you will learn in this chapter, some self-report methods (characterized as *open-ended*) offer the research participants an opportunity to express their feelings and impressions quite spontaneously. Other methods (characterized as *closed*) use a more structured approach, providing the research participants with fixed response options such as yes-no or multiple-choice alternatives. We will show how open-ended and closed measures play a role in personality tests, attitude and survey questionnaires, interviews, and self-recorded diaries. The purpose of this chapter is to help you develop an intuitive sense of the uses and limits of self-report methods, as the method chosen should match the dimensions of interest and the kind of information desired. Let us start with the advantages and disadvantages of open-ended and closed measures (Scott, 1968).

An example of an open-ended format would be "How do you feel about the National Rifle Association?" When analyzing the data, the researchers would categorize the responses to this question and then correlate the coded data with the responses to other questions. The advantages of open-ended measures are that (1) they do not lead the research participant by suggesting specific answers; (2) their approach is exploratory, allowing the researcher to find out whether the respondent has anything at all to say; and (3) they invite the research participant to answer in his or her own language, a procedure that sometimes helps to increase rapport. By contrast, the disadvantages of open-ended formats are that (1) they are time-consuming for both the researcher (who must code and analyze the responses) and the research participant; (2) they sometimes invite rambling and off-the-mark responses that may never actually touch on the topic the researcher is interested in; and (3) they may be hard to assess for reliability (which is discussed in the next chapter).

An example of a closed (or structured) format would be "How do you feel about a 10-day waiting period for permission to buy a gun? Would you say that you feel strongly in favor, moderately in favor, moderately against, or strongly against this idea?" A response that would not be read to you is "don't know," but if that is your answer, the interviewer would note it down. The advantages and limitations of closed measures are the reverse of the open-ended format. For most researchers, the major advantage of a structured format is that, when properly used, it forces respondents' replies into the dimensions of interest to the researcher rather than producing large proportions of irrelevant or uncodable answers (Scott, 1968). We begin our discussion of self-report measures by focusing on some of the tools used by researchers, clinical and counseling psychologists, school psychologists, and others to get subjects to reveal aspects of their personality.

PERSONALITY MEASURES

As ideas of personality developed, from the time of Sigmund Freud to the present, methods of assessing various personality characteristics of individuals, particularly as part of the therapeutic process, also developed. Much of the testing of personality characteristics consisted of diagnosing the existing state of the individual by examining that part of the personality relevant to therapy, a process that led to the development of a wide variety of personality measures (see Box 5.1). One of the oldest types of personality measures, still frequently used, is the *projective test,* of which the Rorschach inkblot test is among the best known and most widely used. The *Rorschach test* consists of a set of inkblots on pieces of cardboard; the inkblots are presented to the subject one by one in a standard order, each for as long as the subject likes. The researcher instructs the subject to describe whatever he or she sees in the blot and keeps a verbatim record of everything the subject says, noting any peculiarity of facial expression or bodily movement.

Once the subject has responded to all the cards, the task of scoring begins. Hermann Rorschach, the psychiatrist who developed this instrument, also provided a scoring procedure for the responses, but the scoring method has been modified by several other researchers over the years (Kleinmuntz, 1982). The scoring and analysis procedures call for supervised experience, so that the Rorschach is out of the reach of most undergraduate students. However, because it is used by behavioral scientists around the world and you may find references to it in your literature search, you will find useful an appreciation of its purposes. Illustrative of its use in ethnomethodological research was the work done by George A. De Vos, an anthropologist, and L. Bryce Boyer, a psychiatrist. Using a scoring system they developed for cross-cultural studies, these researchers analyzed the verbal responses of Japanese, Algerian Arabs, and Apache Native Americans in order to identify universal concepts and symbols. Used in this way, the Rorschach revealed various adaptive

---

BOX 5.1   The Big Five

Current thinking in personality assessment generally supports the idea of five broad domains of individual personality, also called the *big-five factors* (Goldberg, 1993). Each factor is presumed to be made up of hundreds, possibly thousands, of specific traits. The factors go by several different names but in general refer to:

1. *Surgency,* or the degree of talkativeness, assertiveness, and activity.
2. *Agreeableness,* or the degree of kindness, trust, and warmth.
3. *Conscientiousness,* or the degree of organization, thoroughness, and reliability.
4. *Emotional stability,* or the degree of nervousness, moodiness, and temperamentality.
5. *Openness to experience,* or the degree of imagination, curiosity, and creativity.

It is presumed, in turn, that each trait will be revealed by a personality measure, which may exist (see, e.g., Box 5.4 on p. 110) or which may need to be developed.

properties of symbolic thinking within and across the cultures studied (De Vos & Boyer, 1989).

Another well-known projective measure is the *Thematic Apperception Test* (TAT), developed by Henry Murray. The TAT is composed of a number of pictures of people in various life contexts. The respondent is asked to make up a story explaining each picture. Because the situations depicted are adaptable to a number of interpretations, a variety of stories are appropriate. The stories the subject tells may reveal one or more themes that disclose certain concerns and personality characteristics. The TAT is a useful tool for studying what the ethnomethodologists term *sensemaking* (discussed in the previous chapter), or how people impose a sense of meaning on an event. For example, it was used recently by a team of personality researchers to probe subjects' implicit motives (i.e., enduring nonconscious needs) when they attribute causes to events (Peterson & Ulrey, 1994).

In a classic example of personality research, David McClelland and his coworkers (McClelland, Atkinson, Clark, & Lowell, 1953) used the TAT to map out the personality features of the need to achieve. The researchers asked college students to construct a story from TAT pictures. As each picture was presented, the student was asked: (1) What is happening? Who are the persons? (2) What has led up to this situation? That is, what has happened in the past? (3) What is being thought? What is wanted? By whom? (4) What will happen? What will be done? Once the students made up their stories about the pictures, they were scored on their need for achievement. The researchers also used other tools of personality measurement to elicit their subjects' high and low need for achievement. As a consequence, they were able both to describe the structure and intensity of the need for achievement in each research participant and to develop a model of the situational factors that increase or decrease a need for achievement.

In contrast to the Rorschach and the TAT, another widely used personality tool, the *Minnesota Multiphasic Personality Inventory* (MMPI), has a structured (closed) rather than an open-ended format. It contains statements such as "I often cross the street to avoid meeting people," "I am afraid of losing my mind," "I believe I am no more nervous than most others," and "I have a great deal of stomach trouble." The hundreds of such statements in the MMPI were selected after studies had determined which items best discriminated normal individuals and various types of psychiatric patients. Items were also selected to reflect general health, sexual attitudes, religious attitudes, emotional states, and so on. From these items, clinical scales were developed, which are related to diagnostic categories such as depression, paranoia, and schizophrenia. Subjects or patients taking the MMPI are usually scored on all scales, and the scores are then compared with those of normal control subjects.

All of the tools described in the remainder of this chapter can be used quite routinely by the general public, but the Rorschach, the TAT, and the MMPI call for supervised experience to prevent unintended negative consequences of their use. Gaining access to these three measures also requires certification to the publisher that the user has had such training in testing. Students interested in the standards to which educational and psychological testers are bound will find a detailed account in the most recent edition of the American Psychological Association's *Standards for Educational and Psychological Testing*. The point of describing these tools is that you may find them referred to in your literature search, and knowing more about them will give you a more intuitive sense of the research in which they have been used.

NUMERICAL SCALES

By far, the most commonly used measurement tools (in both observation and self-report) are *rating scales* of the numerical, forced-choice, and graphic kinds. Whether you are testing subjects and scoring the results yourself or using a computer to administer and score rating scales, you will find that they are easy to use and easy to score and have widespread application. Indeed, a number of standardized tests and measures (as illustrated later) routinely incorporate rating scales.

We begin by describing the *numerical scales,* a class of rating scales distinguished by the fact that the respondents work with a sequence of defined numbers. These numbers may be stated for the subject to see and use, or they may be implicit categories (e.g., 1–0 for "yes–no"). To illustrate, here is a question taken from a 20-item standardized scale that measures attitudes toward mathematics (Aiken, 1963):

My mind goes blank, and I am unable to think clearly when working math.
_____strongly disagree
_____disagree
_____undecided
_____agree
_____strongly agree

In this example, the numbers are implicit rather than explicit. For instance, we might think of "strongly disagree" as −2, "disagree" as −1, "undecided" as 0, "agree" as +1, and "strongly agree" as +2. Alternatively, we might think of "strongly disagree" as 1, "disagree" as 2, "undecided" as 3, "agree" as 4, and "strongly agree" as 5 (see also Box 5.2). Either way, we will get equivalent results when we code and analyze the subjects' responses.

Because there are five response categories in the item above, it is called a *5-point numerical scale*. Researchers also use more or fewer response categories and use different styles. For example, a team of developmental researchers led by Laurence Steinberg used several different forms of numerical scales in a machine-scored questionnaire they gave to 6,400 high school students in Wisconsin and northern California. The purpose of this study was to examine whether student achievement could be best predicted from general parenting practices, parental encouragement of success, or parental involvement in schooling (Steinberg, Lamborn, Dornbusch, & Darling, 1992). Shown in Figure 5.1 is a sequence of items that, in turn, used a 2-point format (Question 24), a 3-point format (25 and 26), a 4-point format (27), and finally a 5-point format (28). The overall finding of this research, incidentally, was that parental involvement was the best predictor and that this rela-

BOX 5.2	Nudging the Undecideds

In the item used to measure attitudes toward mathematics, the subject is given the option to respond "undecided" (i.e., a neutral option). Some researchers prefer pushing the respondents to one or the other side rather than giving them the neutral option. For example, the following item is taken from a 10-item questionnaire that measures attitudes toward vivisection (Lana, 1959):

Animals in pounds would normally be destroyed; therefore, they should be used in animal experiments.

_____I agree strongly
_____I agree moderately
_____I agree slightly
_____I disagree slightly
_____I disagree moderately
_____I disagree strongly

tionship was strengthened or weakened by general parenting practices. In other words, if you have terrific parents, it is better to have them involved in your schooling, but if you have bad parents, then it is better not to have them involved.

We will have more to say about standardized numerical (and other) scales, but there are three minimal considerations in constructing rating scales (Robinson, Shaver, & Wrightsman, 1991). One is that the items must adequately sample the "universe of content" that the scale claims to represent. A way to confirm the adequacy of the sampling is to have experts in the content area examine the instrument for possible omissions. The second consideration is that the items must be easily understood; that is, they must be written in plain language without any double-talk (ambiguities) or out-of-date expressions. A way to evaluate the clarity of the test items is to do *pilot-testing* with a sample of individuals from the target population. The third consideration is whether the subjects are responding to items in the manner intended. Their responses can be checked through some method of *item analysis*. We will have more to say about item analysis when we turn to standardized attitude measures later in this chapter.

FORCED-CHOICE SCALES

A second class of rating scales is called *forced-choice* because these scales "push" responses by presenting equally favorable (or equally unfavorable) alternatives and instructing the respondent to choose among them. Suppose you want subjects to describe themselves in both favorable and unfavorable terms, but you have encountered resistance when you asked them to describe their unfavorable traits. If you ask them, "Which characteristic *best* describes you—honest or intelligent?" you are *forcing* them to choose between two favorable attributes. You may also present two negative choices, of which the subject can reject only one, or three negative choices (or three positive choices), so that the subject must select the most descriptive one and the least descriptive one.

24. In your family, are there any rules about your watching television?

○ Yes   ○ No

25. How much do your parents TRY to know . . .

	Don't try	Try a little	Try a lot
Who your friends are?	○	○	○
Where you go at night?	○	○	○
How you spend your money?	○	○	○
What you do with your free time?	○	○	○
Where you are most afternoons after school?	○	○	○

26. How much do your parents REALLY know . . .

	Don't know	Know a little	Know a lot
Who your friends are?	○	○	○
Where you go at night?	○	○	○
How you spend your money?	○	○	○
What you do with your free time?	○	○	○
Where you are most afternoons after school?	○	○	○

27. Do your parents have the right to tell you:

	They definitely have the right.	They probably have the right.	They probably do not have the right.	They definitely do not have the right.
How to spend time after school?	○	○	○	○
Who your friends can be?	○	○	○	○
How late you can stay out at night?	○	○	○	○
How to handle your school work?	○	○	○	○

28. Answer this question for the parents or guardians you now live with. How much do your mother (stepmother, guardian) and father (stepfather, guardian) agree with each other on:

	They almost always agree.	They usually agree.	They sometimes agree.	They rarely agree.	Doesn't apply (I live with one parent).
How you should behave	○	○	○	○	○
What to do when you do something wrong	○	○	○	○	○
How hard you should work in school	○	○	○	○	○

FIGURE 5.1 *Consecutive items appearing in a questionnaire used by Steinberg, Lamborn, Dornbusch, and Darling (1992) to study the impact of parenting practices on school achievement in adolescents. Reprinted by permission of Laurence Steinberg.*

As you might surmise, this approach is resisted by some subjects, who object to having to make a choice between equally favorable or equally unfavorable alternatives (Cronbach, 1960). Why use such scales at all, then? The forced-choice approach was developed to overcome a response set called the *halo effect,* which is the tendency to surround some persons with a halo when judging them. We will return to the halo effect, but the forced-choice format that seems to arouse the least antagonism (and also to produce the most valid results) presents four favorable options and instructs the respondent to select the two *most descriptive* options in this group (Highland & Berkshire, 1951; cited in Guilford, 1954).

To illustrate, suppose you were interested in testing a new incentive program, which is intended to improve the reward system and morale in a company. To test the effectiveness of the projected program, you plan to expose a sample of workers (i.e., the experimental group) to a one-month treatment condition and to compare their reactions with those of other workers (i.e., the control group) who are not assigned to the condition. The dependent measures will consist of self-ratings, ratings by managers, and nonreactive measures of performance. Among the self-ratings are some forced-choice items, such as:

Circle the *two* characteristics that *best describe* how you feel in your work:
rewarded   relaxed   appreciated   trusting

Your hypothesis is that, if the incentive program has the effect of improving the reward system and morale, the experimental group will be more likely to circle characteristics such as "rewarded" and "appreciated" than will the control group.

GRAPHIC SCALES

Graphic scales are a third basic type of rating scale. Usually, a graphic scale is a straight line resembling a thermometer, presented either horizontally or vertically. It can be used as either an observational or a self-report method. For example, high-school teachers might use the following items to rate each student in a class (i.e., an observational method), or each student might be asked to rate himself or herself (i.e., a self-report method):

Unpopular   ————————————————   Popular
Shy   ————————————————   Outgoing
Solitary   ————————————————   Gregarious

The respondent makes a check mark, and we would then transform that mark into a number by placing a ruler under the line and reading the number from the ruler. Notice that another characteristic of these items is that they are *bipolar;* that is, the ends of the scale are extreme opposites.

It is much easier, however, to divide the line into segments, transforming the thermometer into a numerical rating scale (also called a *segmented graphic scale*), as in the following 6-point example:

Unpopular	____:____:____:____:____:____	Popular
Shy	____:____:____:____:____:____	Outgoing
Solitary	____:____:____:____:____:____	Gregarious

Here, we ask the teacher or student to make only a decision that reflects positively or negatively on the person being rated, because a scale with an even number of segments does not allow for an undecided response (see again Box 5.2). This example also vaguely resembles a forced-choice measure, but without asking the subject to select from equally favorable or equally unfavorable choices.

It is important that the respondent really understand what to do on the scale. Particularly when a response category is not labeled with *cue words* (i.e., guiding labels), it is prudent to give the respondent some guiding examples. For instance, you might precede the actual scales with the following sample case if the subjects are to rate themselves:

If you would like to rate yourself *quite closely* to one or the other end of the scale (but not extremely), you should place your check mark as follows:

Unpopular	____:____:____:____:√__:____	Popular
	or	
Unpopular	____:__√_:____:____:____:____	Popular

We will return to this point in a moment, when we illustrate the use of the semantic differential.

RATING ERRORS AND THEIR CONTROL

The use of numerical, forced-choice, and graphic rating scales assumes that the respondent is capable of an acceptable degree of rating precision and objectivity. However, in constructing such measures it is important to think about how to overcome certain *rating errors*. We mentioned that the forced-choice method was invented to overcome a potential rating error called the *halo effect*. This effect occurs when the observer (i.e., a judge) forms a favorable impression of someone based on one central trait and extends that impression to all of the person's characteristics. For example, a student who is athletic or good-looking may be judged to be more popular than she or he really is.

An old finding in behavioral science (Symonds, 1925) is that the halo effect is most prevalent when the trait or characteristic to be rated (1) is not easily observable; (2) is not clearly defined; (3) involves relations with other people; and (4) is of some moral importance. As noted earlier, the forced-choice rating method was developed to overcome this error. Suppose the respondent is dominated by a desire to make the person being rated "look good" and to avoid making her or him "look bad." A numerical scale would allow the respondent simply to pile up favorable ratings, whereas on a forced-choice scale, the respondent is forced to select among equally favorable or equally unfavorable choices.

A second type of rating error is *leniency bias,* which occurs when respondents rate someone who is very familiar, or someone with whom they are ego-involved, in an unrealistically positive manner. A possible way to overcome this bias is to give only one unfavorable cue word (e.g., *poor*); the rest of the range is then made up of favorable responses in different degrees (e.g., *fairly good, good, very good, excellent*), such as the following extended scale:

Poor	Fairly good	Good	Very good	Excellent

However, we treat or analyze the cue words numerically so that *good* is only a 3 on a 5-point scale.

A third type of error, *central tendency bias,* occurs when the respondent hesitates to give extreme ratings and instead clusters her or his responses around the center choice. This bias can usually be overcome in the same way that the positive range was expanded in the example above. If, for instance, you wanted to have a range of at least 5 points, you might use a 7- or 9-point scale, assuming that some subjects may be reluctant to use the end points in any circumstances (see also Box 5.3).

In a fourth type of response bias, the *logical error in rating,* the respondents give similar ratings for variables or traits that they connect as logically related in their own minds but that may not occur together in the target person. This bias is similar to the halo effect in that both erroneously intercorrelate variables or traits that are being rated. The difference is that, in the halo effect, the respondent extends one favorable trait to the person as a whole, whereas in the logical error, the respondent interrelates certain variables or traits irrespective of individuals. The standard way to overcome a logical error in rating is to construct very precise definitions and to make the instructions as explicit as possible.

BOX 5.3 | Ceiling and Floor Effects

Suppose you are using 5-point rating scales as before-and-after tests in an experiment using a manipulation designed to move the subjects' responses in a given direction. If the subjects make extremely high or extremely low scores on the *pretest* (i.e., the test given before the manipulation), there will be a problem if you then want to produce further change in that direction. That is, you have a *ceiling effect* or a *floor effect,* which limits the amount of change that can be produced. You could try extending the ends of the scale after pilot-testing it, so that a 5-point scale becomes a 9-point or an 11-point scale. But if you find no changes from pretest to posttest, make sure the result is not due to ceiling or floor effects.

In a fifth type of response bias, the *acquiescent response set,* some respondents (called *yea-sayers*) go along with almost any statement. If they are asked whether they agree or disagree with even the most unlikely item, they will almost invariably agree with it. To control for this problem, we would use both anti and pro items. For example, in a vivisection questionnaire, we would use both antivivisection items (e.g., "Many times, the same vivisection experiment is performed again and again without conclusive results.") and provivisection items (such as the one in Box 5.2). Yea-sayers can easily be identified (and eliminated from the sample) from the fact that they agree with both anti and pro items.

These cases give a flavor of rating errors and their control, although there are other possibilities besides these five. Numerical, graphic, and forced-choice rating scales, as noted, are also used in many *standardized measures* of judgment and attitude. *Standardized* means that certain rules (or standards) must be followed in the development, administration, and scoring of these measures. We turn now to three standardized measures that you may encounter if you are doing a literature search in the attitude area: the semantic differential and the Likert and Thurstone scaling methods.

THE SEMANTIC DIFFERENTIAL

The *semantic differential* was developed for the study of the connotative meaning of things in everyday life, as opposed to their denotative meaning. *Denotative* refers to the dictionary or assigned meaning (e.g., *Canis familiaris* is the denotative definition of *dog*), whereas *connotative* refers to the representational meaning, that is, one's own subjective associations (e.g., a warm, furry animal that shows unconditional acceptance of its master). The inventors of this method (Osgood, Suci, & Tannenbaum, 1957) discovered that most things in life (dogs, chairs, continents, ethnic groups, flowers, college majors, and so forth) are perceived in terms of three primary dimensions of subjective meaning, which they named *evaluation, potency,* and *activity,* and which they defined in terms of bipolar cue words. Osgood et al. also showed that it is possible to assess such perceptions by using segmented graphic scales with these bipolar cue words to tap the full dimension of interest to the researcher.

Suppose you were interested in comparing two music groups, Pearl Jam and Arrested Development, in terms of their respective connotative meanings to a sample of high school students. To tap the evaluative dimension, you could choose from among the following bipolar anchors: *bad-good, unpleasant-pleasant, negative-positive, ugly-beautiful, cruel-kind, unfair-fair,* and *worthless-valuable.* To measure the potency dimension, you could choose from among *weak-strong, light-heavy, small-large, soft-hard,* and *thin-heavy.* For the activity dimension, any of the following could be used: *slow-fast, passive-active,* and *dull-sharp.* The scales might look as follows—though you will probably want to use more than just three items—and the instructions to the students would be to rate each group by checking the appropriate space:

Ugly	____:____:____:____:____:____:____	Beautiful
Soft	____:____:____:____:____:____:____	Hard
Dull	____:____:____:____:____:____:____	Sharp

The reason for using more than one scale for each dimension is to increase reliability (discussed in the next chapter). To score the responses, you would assign numbers to the ratings, as follows, and you then might compute a composite index such as a median or mean (defined in Chapter 10):

Ugly ____:____:____:____:____:____:____ Beautiful
$\quad$ -3 $\quad$ -2 $\quad$ -1 $\quad$ 0 $\quad$ $+1$ $\quad$ $+2$ $\quad$ $+3$

Previously, we noted the importance of ensuring that the subjects understand what each response category signifies, particularly when the segments in graphic scales are unlabeled. The numbers above stand for something like "extremely beautiful" (+3), "quite beautiful" (+2), "slightly beautiful" (+1), "neutral" (0), "slightly ugly" (−1), "quite ugly" (−2), and "extremely ugly" (−3). Figure 5.2 shows a typical set of instructions based on those provided by the inventors of the semantic differential (Osgood et al., 1957), which you might use in your comparison of music groups. These instructions incorporate a number of sample items to ensure that the respondents understand the meaning of each alternative. If you were actually doing this study, the instructions would appear on the first page of your semantic differential questionnaire.

THE LIKERT SCALE

Another standardized measure, which produces what is called a *Likert scale,* is based on an item analysis method called the *summated ratings method* by its inventor (Rensis Likert). In appearance this method produces a type of numerical attitude scale. That is, numbers are associated with different responses (e.g., "strongly agree," "agree," "undecided," "disagree," "strongly disagree") to statements that are easily classifiable as favorable or unfavorable. Although most students will not have occasion to develop their own Likert scale, it is useful to understand generally how such scales are constructed in case you decide to borrow one for use in your work (see, e.g., Robinson et al., 1991; Shaw & Wright, 1967).

Briefly, the first step in developing a Likert scale is to gather a large number of statements on the topic of interest. We give these to a sample of subjects from the target population, who indicate their evaluations, usually by means of a 5-point rating scale. We then sort through the data in order to select the best statements for the final scale. This sorting consists of finding out the extent to which all of the responses to individual statements are correlated with the total score (the sum of the scores for all the items). Statements that correlate well with (i.e., show a strong relationship to) the total score are then chosen for the final scale. The rationale is that statements that have low correlations with the total score will not discriminate those respondents with positive attitudes from those with negative attitudes.

The purpose of this questionnaire is to measure the *meanings* of some music groups to various people by having them judge these groups against a set of descriptive scales. We would like you to judge each group on the basis of what the group listed means *to you*. On each page of this booklet, you will find a different group to be judged and beneath it a set of scales. You are to rate the group on each of these scales in order.

If you feel that the group at the top of the page is *very accurately described* by the word at one end of the scale, place your check mark as follows:

Dull   _____:_____:_____:_____:_____:_____:__√__ Sharp

or

Dull   __√__:_____:_____:_____:_____:_____:_____ Sharp

If you feel that the group is *quite* (but not extremely) *accurately described* at one end of the scale, place your check mark as follows:

Dull   _____:_____:_____:_____:__√__:_____ Sharp

or

Dull   _____:__√__:_____:_____:_____:_____ Sharp

If the group seems *only slightly described* by one end as opposed to the other end (but is not really neutral), place your check mark as follows:

Dull   _____:_____:_____:__√__:_____:_____ Sharp

or

Dull   _____:_____:__√__:_____:_____:_____ Sharp

The placement of your check, of course, depends on which of the two ends of the scale seems most descriptive of the music group you are judging. If you see the group as *neutral* on the scale (that is, if both ends of the scale are *equally descriptive* of the group), or if the scale is *completely irrelevant* (that is, unrelated to the group), place your check mark in the middle space:

Dull   _____:_____:__√__:_____:_____:_____ Sharp

FIGURE 5.2   *Semantic differential instructions.*

The result of using this procedure is presented in Figure 5.3, which shows a scale that was pared down to 20 items by the method of summated ratings (Mahler, 1953). Items 2, 4, 6, 9, 10, 11, 14, and 15 (called "pro-socialized-medicine" statements by the author of this scale) are in favor of a compulsory health program and against the system of private practice. Items 1, 3, 5, 7, 8, 12, 13, 16, 17, 18, 19, and 20 (called "anti-socialized-medicine" statements) are against a compulsory health program and in favor of the system of private practice. In using this scale, you might weight the responses to the pro-socialized-medicine statements from 5 ("strongly agree") to 1 ("strongly disagree"). For the anti-socialized-medicine statements, you would simply reverse this scoring procedure. A person's score is the sum of the responses, a high score indicating an

Instructions to Subjects

Please indicate your reaction to the following statements, using these alternatives (circle your choice):

Strongly agree = SA

Agree = A

Undecided = U

Disagree = D

Strongly disagree = SD

1. The quality of medical care under the system of private practice is superior to that under a system of compulsory health insurance.

SA   A   U   D   SD

2. A compulsory health program will produce a healthier and more productive population.

SA   A   U   D   SD

3. Under a compulsory health program there would be less incentive for young men and women to become doctors.

SA   A   U   D   SD

4. A compulsory health program is necessary because it brings the greatest good to the greatest number of people.

SA   A   U   D   SD

5. Treatment under a compulsory health program would be mechanical and superficial.

SA   A   U   D   SD

6. A compulsory health program would be a realization of one of the true aims of a democracy.

SA   A   U   D   SD

7. Compulsory medical care would upset the traditional relationship between the family doctor and the patient.

SA   A   U   D   SD

8. I feel that I would get better care from a doctor whom I am paying than from a doctor who is being paid by the government.

SA   A   U   D   SD

9. Despite many practical objections, I feel that compulsory health insurance is a real need of the American people.

SA   A   U   D   SD

10. A compulsory health program could be administered quite efficiently if the doctors would cooperate.

SA   A   U   D   SD

11. There is no reason why the traditional relationship between doctors and patient cannot be continued under a compulsory health program.

SA   A   U   D   SD

12. If a compulsory health program were enacted, politicians would have control over doctors.

SA   A   U   D   SD

13. The present system of private medical practice is the one best adapted to the liberal philosophy of democracy.

SA   A   U   D   SD

14. There is no reason why doctors should not be able to work just as well under a compulsory health program as they do now.

SA   A   U   D   SD

15. More and better care will be obtained under a compulsory program.

SA   A   U   D   SD

16. The atmosphere of a compulsory health program would destroy the initiative and the ambition of young doctors.

SA   A   U   D   SD

FIGURE 5.3 *The "Socialized Medicine Attitude Scale." Reproduced from "Attitudes toward Socialized Medicine" by I. Mahler, 1953,* Journal of Social Psychology, 38, *pp. 273–282. Used by permission of the Helen Dwight Reid Educational Foundation. Published by Heldref Publications, 1319 Eighteenth St., N.W., Washington, D.C. 20036-1802. Copyright © 1953. (Continued.)*

17. Politicians are trying to force a compulsory health program upon the people without giving them the true facts.

    SA   A   U   D   SD

18. Administrative costs under a compulsory health program would be exorbitant.

    SA   A   U   D   SD

19. Red tape and bureaucratic problems would make a compulsory health program grossly inefficient.

    SA   A   U   D   SD

20. Any system of compulsory insurance would invade the privacy of the individual.

    SA   A   U   D   SD

FIGURE 5.3   *Continued*

accepting attitude toward a compulsory health program and a low score indicating an unaccepting attitude toward a compulsory health program. The highest and lowest possible scores, then, would be 100 (most strongly in favor of a compulsory health program) and 20 (most strongly against a compulsory health program).

THE THURSTONE SCALE

Another widely used method of item analysis, developed by L. L. Thurstone (1929), is called the *method of equal-appearing intervals.* It takes its name from the idea that judges, who are asked to sort statements into different piles, can presumably keep the piles psychologically equidistant. The term *Thurstone scale* is ambiguous in some respects, because Thurstone also pioneered the development of other scaling methods. Fortunately, most behavioral researchers, when they speak of a *Thurstone attitude scale,* actually mean that it has been constructed by the method of equal-appearing intervals. Again, we will describe this method not because you are likely to construct a Thurstone scale for your own research, but because you may find examples of attitude or personality scales constructed in this way that you can use in your research.

Briefly, this method also begins with a large number of statements, each typed on a separate slip of paper or an index card. Judges (not the subjects to be tested later) then sort the statements into 11 piles, numbered from 1 (labeled "most unfavorable statements") to 11 ("most favorable statements"). The judges are allowed to place as many statements as they wish in any pile. A scale value is calculated for each statement, which is the average (usually calculated as the *median,* or midmost value) of the responses of all judges to that particular item. In selecting statements for the final Thurstone scale, the researcher chooses those that are (1) most consistently rated by the judges and (2) spread relatively evenly along the entire attitude range.

Shown in Figure 5.4 is a Thurstone scale developed during World War II by Day and Quackenbush (1942) using the method of equal-appearing intervals. Notice that the subjects are asked to respond to each statement three times, once for each type of war. Shaw and Wright (1967) obtained the following scale values for these statements from a sample of 15 women and 35 men (and the reliability

Instructions to Subjects

This is a study of attitudes toward war. Below you will find a number of statements expressing various degrees of attitudes toward war or tendencies to act in case of war.

In expressing your agreement or disagreement with the statements, please put yourself in three possible situations. First, imagine that the United States had declared a *Defensive War* (war for the purpose of defending the United States in case of an attack). Please indicate in the first set of parentheses, designated by roman numeral I, your agreement, disagreement, or doubt. Put a check mark (✓) if you agree with the statement, put a minus sign (−) if you disagree with the statement, and a question mark (?) if you are in doubt about the statement.

Second, imagine that the United States has declared a *Cooperative War* (war in cooperation with the democratic countries of Europe for the defense of democracy). Go over the statements again and indicate in the second set of parentheses, designated by roman II, your agreement, disagreement, or doubt in a similar way.

Third, imagine that the United States has declared an *Aggressive War* (war for the purpose of gaining more territory). Read the statements again and indicate in the third set of parentheses, designated by roman III, your agreement, disagreement, or doubt by a similar method.

I	II	III	
( )	( )	( )	1. I would support my country even against my convictions.
( )	( )	( )	2. I would immediately attempt to find some technicality on which to evade going to war.
( )	( )	( )	3. I would immediately go to war and would do everything in my power to influence others to do the same.
( )	( )	( )	4. I would rather be called a coward than go to war.
( )	( )	( )	5. I would offer my services in whatever capacity I can.
( )	( )	( )	6. I would not only refuse to participate in any way in war but also attempt to influence public opinion against war.
( )	( )	( )	7. I would take part in war only to avoid social ostracism.
( )	( )	( )	8. I would not go to war unless I were drafted.
( )	( )	( )	9. If possible, I would wait a month or two before I would enlist.
( )	( )	( )	10. I would go to war only if my friends went to war.
( )	( )	( )	11. I would refuse to participate in any way in war.
( )	( )	( )	12. I would disregard any possible exemptions and enlist immediately.
( )	( )	( )	13. I would not enlist but would give whatever financial aid I could.

FIGURE 5.4 *The "Attitudes toward War Scale." Reproduced from "Attitudes toward Defensive, Cooperative, and Aggressive War" by D. D. Day and O. F. Quackenbush, 1942, Journal of Social Psychology, 16, pp. 11–20. Used by permission of the Helen Dwight Reid Educational Foundation, Heldref Publications, 1319 Eighteenth St., N.W., Washington, D.C. 20036-1802. Copyright © 1942.*

of the scale was based on the responses of 326 male students at the University of Mississippi):

Statement	Scale Value		Statement	Scale Value
1	2.5		8	5.9
2	7.5		9	4.6
3	0.8		10	5.1
4	7.9		11	8.2
5	2.5		12	1.4
6	8.4		13	3.5
7	6.3			

We see that the lowest scale value (0.8 for Statement 3) corresponds to the most pro-war statement and that the highest scale value (8.4 for Statement 6) corresponds to the most anti-war statement in this set. If you were to use this scale in your research, the attitude score for each referent (defensive war, cooperative war, and aggressive war) is the median (or midmost value) of the scale values of the statements that the subject endorsed (i.e., checked) for that referent. The higher the median, the more unfavorable the subject's attitude toward that war referent. For example, if the subject checked Statements 2, 4, 6, and 11 under Roman numeral I, it tells us that the subject is very strongly opposed to defensive war (median = 8.05, or midway between the scale values of 7.9 for Statement 4 and 8.2 for Statement 11). (See also Box 5.4.)

PILOT-TESTING YOUR QUESTIONNAIRE

In developing a questionnaire—as much as in developing an interview (discussed next)—*pilot-testing* is absolutely essential. This testing will enable the researcher to determine whether the items are worded properly, for example, whether terms like *approve* and *like* (or *disapprove* and *dislike*) are being used as synonyms or whether there are differences in implication. Suppose you wanted to examine people's perceptions of the quality of a mayor's performance, and you phrased the item as

BOX 5.4	Useful Source Books

If you are looking for a Likert or Thurstone attitude or personality scale to use in your research, you will find many existing scales in the public domain. Two excellent sources of such scales are Marvin E. Shaw and Jack M. Wright's *Scales for the Measurement of Attitudes* (1967) and John P. Robinson, Philip R. Shaver, and Lawrence S. Wrightsman's *Measures of Personality and Social Psychological Attitudes* (1991). Both books reproduce specific instruments and describe their characteristics (e.g., reliability and validity) and scoring. The book edited by Robinson et al. provides background information on groups of alternative scales that can be used to measure aspects of personality, such as subjective well-being, self-esteem, social anxiety and shyness, and depression and loneliness.

follows: "How do you feel about the mayor? _____I like him. _____I dislike him." The item is quite useless because it does not distinguish between liking and approving. It is possible, for example, for people to like someone (or something) without approving of him or her (or it), and vice versa (Bradburn, 1982).

You must also be sure that the way in which the items are worded and present-ed does not lead the respondent into giving an unrealistically narrow answer. A poor question will produce a very narrow range of responses or will be misunder-stood by the respondents. Take the following item: "Do you approve of the way the mayor is handling her duties? _____Yes. _____ No." One might approve of the way a mayor handled the school crisis but not the snow removal crisis or might disapprove of the way a mayor handled the strike threat by sanitation workers but not the threatened tax increase.

Thus a number of different items are needed to cover the various issues on which we want an opinion about a mayor's effectiveness, and the issues must be spelled out if we are to prevent any misunderstanding on the part of the respon-dents. For example, suppose the school crisis and the sanitation workers' threat both involved union confrontations, but the first was resolved without a strike and the second resulted in a protracted strike. We need a separate question, or set of questions, regarding each situation and whether the respondent approved or dis-approved of the handling of it.

The researcher must also avoid a leading question that produces a biased answer: "Do you agree that the mayor has an annoying, confrontational style? _____Yes _____ No." The phrasing of the question *invites* the respondents to be overly negative or critical. How should such a question be phrased? In coming up with an alternative, the researcher will want to be sure that the new question is not worded so as to produce another meaningless answer: "Do you agree with the mayor's philosophy of city government? _____Yes _____ No." What would a yes or no really tell us? We need to do some probing to get meaningful information.

Problems such as these can be identified during the pilot-testing and can usually be resolved with rewording or with a set of probing items instead of a single item. The question of whether to use open-ended or more structured items (or a combi-nation of both) can also be answered in pilot-testing. Like personality measures, the questionnaires used by many survey researchers come in a variety of open and closed styles. For example, structured questions may take the form of multiple-choice, yes-no, either-or, or acceptable-unacceptable items. A fill-in-the-blank form is useful when more specific responses are sought. Of course, these structured forms are effective only if the material to be covered allows this amount of simplification.

In your pilot-testing, think about asking exploratory questions such as "What did the whole item mean to you?" "What was it you had in mind when you said _____?" "Consider the same item this way, and tell what you think of it: _____", "You said _____, but would you feel differently if the question read _____?" (Converse & Presser, 1986, p. 52). It is also impor-tant that the information elicited reflect what the subject *really* feels or believes. As a rule, people have not thought very much about most issues that do not affect them directly; their replies may reflect only a superficial feeling or understanding, or they may try to "put on a good face." Survey researchers often ask the respondent how he or she feels about a topic (e.g., "How deeply do you feel about it?"). In this way, they attempt to determine whether the respondent *truly believes* what he or she has reported (Labaw, 1980). Another useful procedure is to ask subjects to rate their confidence in their answers so that they reveal how much they are guessing.

INTERVIEWS VERSUS QUESTIONNAIRES

We turn next to how to plan a research interview, but it will be instructive if we first note the respective advantages of questionnaires and interviews. In general, questionnaires are convenient to use because (1) they can be administered to large numbers of people (e.g., in mail surveys); (2) they are relatively economical (because a mail survey eliminates travel time and cost); and (3) they provide a type of "anonymity" (in that, instead of meeting the researcher face to face, the respondent sends a mail survey, for example, to an impersonal research center).

However, a *face-to-face interview* has advantages: (1) It provides an opportunity to establish rapport with the subjects and to stimulate the trust and cooperation often needed to probe sensitive areas; (2) it provides an opportunity to help the subjects in their interpretation of the questions; and (3) it allows flexibility in determining the wording and sequence of the questions by giving the researcher greater control over the situation (e.g., by letting the interviewer determine on the spot the amount of probing required).

Just as the researcher who uses a questionnaire needs to do pilot-testing, the researcher who uses an *interview schedule* (i.e., a script containing the questions the interviewer will ask in the face-to-face interview) needs to pilot-test it. This pilot work and the planning that precedes it, which we discuss next, cover four steps: (1) stating the objective; (2) outlining a recruitment strategy; (3) structuring the interview schedule; and (4) testing it and making appropriate revisions.

PILOT-TESTING YOUR INTERVIEW SCHEDULE

First, the *objectives* of the interview need to be spelled out. What are the research hypotheses? What kind of data does the researcher need to test those hypotheses? What kinds of subjects will produce the relevant responses? Suppose a researcher's objective is to interview the "opinion leaders" in a community. During the testing phase (Step 4), she or he will have to locate some of the potential interviewees and try out the questions on them. This step requires patience, because the researcher may need a long series of interviews with many randomly selected individuals to find the appropriate subjects.

Second, the researcher needs to formulate a *recruitment strategy,* that is, a plan for locating the potential interviewees. Part of this plan will include (a) devising relevant questions and specifying how the replies will be analyzed; (b) pretesting the interview schedule; and (c) recruiting and training the interviewers.

Third, the researcher must *structure the interview schedule* by (a) checking each item for relevancy; (b) determining ranges of response for some items; (c) establishing the best sequence of questions; and (d) establishing the best wording of questions:

a. In this third step each question or item should be examined for its relevance to the research hypotheses or exploratory aims of the study. The interview schedule may require the pruning of "Occam's razor" to cut away undesirable or unnecessary items. In addition, the interviews should not be too long; 60–90 minutes seems to be the outermost limit before respondents become bored (cf. Pareek & Rao, 1980).

b. Also, in developing structured items, researchers construct ranges of responses. For example, if you want to know someone's salary, it is better to present ranges of income levels than to ask an exact amount. A potential problem (to which we will return in a moment) is that some questions may make unrealistic demands on the subjects' memory. Even with a range of responses, the subjects may make *false-negative reports* (i.e., they may fail to report information) because of true memory lapses or because of carelessness or an unwillingness to make the effort necessary to give a fuller account of past events (Cannell, Miller, & Oksenberg, 1981).

c. Another consideration in this third stage is the best sequence of items. Broadly speaking, specific questions seem to be less affected by what preceded them than are general questions (Bradburn, 1982). And when sensitive topics are to be discussed, it is usually better to ask these questions at the end of the interview. Some interviewees find questions about their age, education, and income an invasion of privacy and/or a threat to their continued anonymity. When asked at the beginning of an interview, such questions may interfere with the establishment of trust. However, even when they are asked at the end of the interview, it is helpful to preface such questions with a reassuring statement. In one study, the student interviewer stated, "Some of the questions may seem like an invasion of your privacy, so if you'd rather not answer any of the questions, just tell me it's none of my business" (C. Smith, 1980).

d. A final consideration in this third stage is to work out the best wording of the items. It is essential that all the subjects readily understand the wording in equivalent ways. The pilot stage (the next step) should show what jargon and expressions are inhibitors and facilitators of communication in the particular circumstances. Especially important is the phrasing of the opening question, which should show the subject immediately that the interviewer is pursuing the stated purpose. Interestingly, research evidence suggests that disclosing as little as possible about the interview in the introduction has no methodological benefits in terms of refusals, rapport, cooperation, or bias (Sobal, 1982). As noted in Chapter 3, we want to be as open and honest as possible in our communications with our subjects, just as we want them to be forthcoming in their responses.

The fourth and final step before going into the field is to pilot-test the interview schedule and make modifications wherever necessary. At this stage, just as during the actual survey, it is important that the interviewers listen *analytically* to the subjects' responses (Downs, Smeyak, & Martin, 1980). The skilled interviewer does not jump in and interrupt before the subject has developed an idea but is patient, gets the main ideas, hears the facts, makes valid inferences, hears details, and demonstrates other good listening skills (Weaver, 1972).

OPEN AND CLOSED INTERVIEW ITEMS

As in the research questionnaire, a basic consideration in developing an interview schedule is whether to use open-ended or structured questions (see, e.g., Bradburn, 1983; Dohrenwend & Richardson, 1963). Figure 5.5 is an example of a brief interview schedule. This particular schedule was part of an in-depth study of children in the rural South (Baughman & Dahlstrom, 1968). As is typical of most interview schedules, some items are more structured than others. The more structured items are 2, 4, and 9, and the most unstructured one is 3.

Of course, open-ended questions can be asked in other ways. For example, the *critical incident technique,* which has special status in clinical and organizational research (Flanagan, 1954), involves asking the subject to give an open-ended description of an observable action. The purpose of the action must be fairly clear to the observer, and the consequences must be sufficiently definite to leave little doubt about its effects. In a recent study for example, the critical incident technique was used with company managers in the United States and India, who were interviewed as part of an investigation of how managers deal with damaging rumors (DiFonzo et al., 1994). The managers were asked to describe as fully and concretely as possible a real situation that was important to their company, in which they had to confront a harmful or a potentially harmful rumor. The resulting narratives revealed some of the circumstances in which rumor control strategies may or may not succeed.

This method is used in questionnaire as well as interview research (e.g., Fung, Kipnis, & Rosnow, 1987). For example, Edwin P. Hollander and his coworkers used the critical incident technique in their studies of leaders and followers (e.g., Elgie, Hollander, & Rice, 1988; Hollander, 1992; Kelly, Julian, & Hollander, 1992). In one aspect of the research, the investigators presented a sequence of four questions to sketch a profile of bad leadership in organizations (E. P. Hollander, personal communication, May 27, 1992). The first question was "Think of a group or organization to which you belong, or did belong. Please describe a situation or event there that occurred between you and a superior in which you consider that *bad* leadership was displayed. Try to be as clear as possible in describing the conditions and behavior involved." Next, the subject was asked, "Indicate what you found rewarding or not from what that superior did or said as the leader there." Then the subject was asked, "What, if anything, was your response?" And the final question in this set was "What effect did this event have on your relationship with this superior?"

INTERVIEWS BY TELEPHONE

Beginning in the 1960s, various changes in society led many researchers to turn to the *telephone interview* and the mail survey as substitutes for face-to-face interviews. Among the changes contributing to this shift were (1) the increased costs of conducting face-to-face interviews (because interviewing is a labor-intensive activity); (2) the invention of random digit-dialing methods for random sampling of telephone households; and (3) the development of computer-assisted methods of recording responses, in which questions are flashed on a cathode ray screen and the

MOTHER INTERVIEW SCHEDULE

CHILD'S NAME _____ INTERVIEWER _____

DATE _____

We are interested in spending time with your four-year-old child, _____ . We believe there are many things that children can learn when they are young. There are some things you may be able to tell us about _____ that will help us to know him (her) better.

I will be asking you about what _____ is like and some of the things he (she) may or may not like to do.

1. Could you tell me what X is usually like?

   a. Happy _____   d. Silly _____
   b. Serious _____   e. Other _____
   c. Sad _____

2. Would you describe him (her) as:

   a. Shy _____   h. Needs encouragement _____
   b. Active _____   i. Always in a hurry _____
   c. Careful _____   j. Plays well alone _____
   d. Fearful _____   k. Would rather play by himself (herself) _____
   e. Tries things _____   l. Would rather play with others _____
   f. Shows off_____   m. Does he (she) have to do things just right (just so)? _____
   g. Laughs a lot _____   n. Asks a lot of questions _____

3. Do you have any special concerns about X?

   a. _____
   _____
   b. _____
   _____

4. Has X had a chance to spend time doing some of these things?

   _____ a. Marking with crayon _____
   _____ b. Marking with a pencil _____
   _____ c. Cutting with scissors _____
   _____ d. Pasting _____
   _____ e. Collecting things _____
   _____ f. Working puzzles _____
   _____ g. Building with blocks or sticks _____
   _____ h. Looking at magazines or catalogs _____

5. Does anyone read story books to him (her)? _____

   (If yes) Does he (she) seem to listen? _____
   (If no) Does he (she) listen to someone tell stories? _____
   Does he (she) seem to enjoy the stories? _____
   What kind does he (she) seem to like most? _____
   Does he (she) ever tell a story that he (she) has heard? _____
   _____
   Does he (she) ever make up a story to tell? _____
   _____
   Does he (she) ever try to tell a story that he (she) has seen on television? _____

6. Does X get to play with children other than his (her) brothers and sisters? _____
   _____

7. Where does he (she) see other children? _____
   _____

8. Does he (she) get to spend much time with his (her) daddy? _____

9. Does he (she) like to:

   _____ a. Throw a ball   _____ f. Jump
   _____ b. Run   _____ g. Play games
   _____ c. Climb   _____ h. Make believe (play house, play grown-up)
   _____ d. Dance   _____ i. Other things (list) _____
   _____ e. Sing   _____
   _____

10. Does X try to help around the house or farm? _____

FIGURE 5.5 *Example of an interview schedule. Reproduced from E. E. Baughman and W. G. Dahlstrom,* Negro and White Children: A Psychological Study in the Rural South, *Academic Press, 1968. Used by permission of E. E. Baughman and Academic Press.*

interviewer directly keys in the response for computer scoring (Rossi, Wright, & Anderson, 1983).

Telephone interviewing has both advantages and disadvantages (Downs et al., 1980; Lavrakas, 1987; P. V. Miller & Cannell, 1982). Among the advantages are that (1) it allows a quick turnaround (i.e., information can be got more promptly than by face-to-face interview or mail survey) and (2) refusal rates are usually lower in telephone interviewing (because it is not necessary to allow a stranger into one's home). Among the disadvantages are that (1) interviewing is restricted, first, to households that own a telephone and, then, to those that answer the telephone (instead of having an answering machine constantly on duty to screen calls) and (2) fewer questions (and less probing questions) can be asked because it is harder to establish rapport than in a face-to-face interview and people are more impatient to conclude a telephone interview.

Generally speaking, whether telephone or face-to-face interviewing is used, the same procedures are followed in developing an interview schedule and training the interviewers. One difference, however, is that telephone interviewers have less time to establish rapport; the subject can always hang up without listening to the introduction. One strategy used to foster "commitment" on the part of the subject is to point out the important goals of the research and to use "positive feedback" as a means of reinforcing good responding: "Thanks . . . this is the sort of information we're looking for in this research . . . it's important to us to get this information . . . these details are helpful" (P. V. Miller & Cannell, 1982, p. 256).

MEMORY AND THE USE OF SELF-RECORDED DIARIES

Autobiographical questions may yield inaccurate answers when the subjects are asked to rely on memory (e.g., how often they have done something or how much of something they have bought or consumed). Some examples are "For how many weeks have you been looking for work?" and "How much have you paid for car repairs over the previous year?" Problems surface because recall is limited (H. B. Bernard & Killworth, 1970, 1980; S. K. Reed, 1988; Webber, 1970; Zechmeister & Nyberg, 1982).

An innovative tool that overcomes this problem is the *self-recorded diary,* an idea based on the use of field notes in participant observation and ethnographic research (discussed in the previous chapter). The basic procedure is to ask the subjects to keep a diary of events at the time they occur. It is recommended that only a few minutes (e.g., 10 minutes) per day be required to keep the diary (Conrath, 1973). To reduce the time required, the researcher must develop checklists or tally sheets that the subject can use quickly and accurately. The particular times at which the data are to be recorded in the diary should also be precisely specified. Such diaries have been used in a wide variety of situations to supplement the researchers' own records (e.g., Conrath, 1973; Wickesberg, 1968).

For example, this method was used by Mihaly Csikszentmihalyi and Reed Larson (1984), who were interested in studying teenagers' day-to-day lives. The subjects in this study were 75 teenagers, who were given beepers and then signaled at random by the researchers. When the beeper went off, the subject recorded his or her thoughts and feelings at that moment. Figure 5.6 shows a week in the life

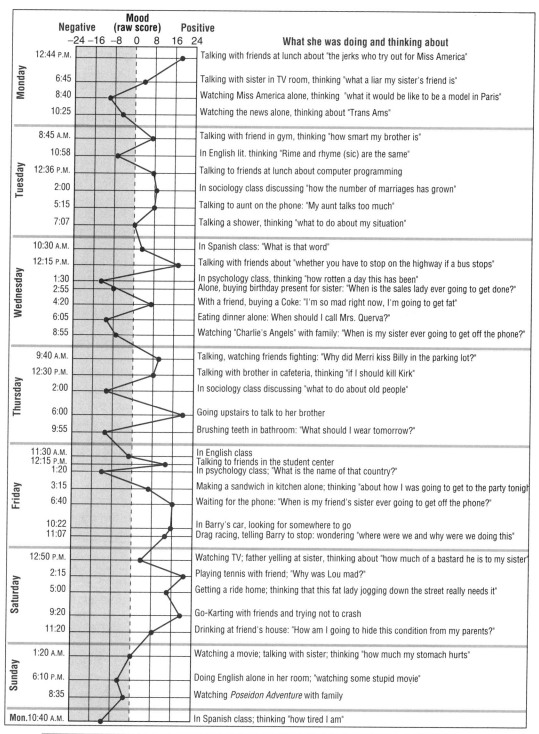

		Mood		
Negative		(raw score)		Positive
−24 −16	−8	0	8	16 24

What she was doing and thinking about

Monday
- 12:44 P.M. — Talking with friends at lunch about "the jerks who try out for Miss America"
- 6:45 — Talking with sister in TV room, thinking "what a liar my sister's friend is"
- 8:40 — Watching Miss America alone, thinking "what it would be like to be a model in Paris"
- 10:25 — Watching the news alone, thinking about "Trans Ams"

Tuesday
- 8:45 A.M. — Talking with friend in gym, thinking "how smart my brother is"
- 10:58 — In English lit. thinking "Rime and rhyme (sic) are the same"
- 12:36 P.M. — Talking to friends at lunch about computer programming
- 2:00 — In sociology class discussing "how the number of marriages has grown"
- 5:15 — Talking to aunt on the phone: "My aunt talks too much"
- 7:07 — Talking a shower, thinking "what to do about my situation"

Wednesday
- 10:30 A.M. — In Spanish class: "What is that word"
- 12:15 P.M. — Talking with friends about "whether you have to stop on the highway if a bus stops"
- 1:30 — In psychology class, thinking "how rotten a day this has been"
- 2:55 — Alone, buying birthday present for sister: "When is the sales lady ever going to get done?"
- 4:20 — With a friend, buying a Coke: "I'm so mad right now, I'm going to get fat"
- 6:05 — Eating dinner alone: When should I call Mrs. Querva?"
- 8:55 — Watching "Charlie's Angels" with family: "When is my sister ever going to get off the phone?"

Thursday
- 9:40 A.M. — Talking, watching friends fighting: "Why did Merri kiss Billy in the parking lot?"
- 12:30 P.M. — Talking with brother in cafeteria, thinking "if I should kill Kirk"
- 2:00 — In sociology class discussing "what to do about old people"
- 6:00 — Going upstairs to talk to her brother
- 9:55 — Brushing teeth in bathroom: "What should I wear tomorrow?"

Friday
- 11:30 A.M. — In English class
- 12:15 P.M. — Talking to friends in the student center
- 1:20 — In psychology class; "What is the name of that country?"
- 3:15 — Making a sandwich in kitchen alone; thinking "about how I was going to get to the party tonigh
- 6:40 — Waiting for the phone: "When is my friend's sister ever going to get off the phone?"
- 10:22 — In Barry's car, looking for somewhere to go
- 11:07 — Drag racing, telling Barry to stop: wondering "where were we and why were we doing this"

Saturday
- 12:50 P.M. — Watching TV; father yelling at sister, thinking about "how much of a bastard he is to my sister"
- 2:15 — Playing tennis with friend; "Why was Lou mad?"
- 5:00 — Getting a ride home; thinking that this fat lady jogging down the street really needs it"
- 9:20 — Go-Karting with friends and trying not to crash
- 11:20 — Drinking at friend's house: "How am I going to hide this condition from my parents?"

Sunday
- 1:20 A.M. — Watching a movie; talking with sister; thinking "how much my stomach hurts"
- 6:10 P.M. — Doing English alone in her room; "watching some stupid movie"
- 8:35 — Watching *Poseidon Adventure* with family

Mon. 10:40 A.M. — In Spanish class; thinking "how tired I am"

FIGURE 5.6 *The self-recorded diary record of a week in the life of one teenage subject. (Figure 8.4 "The week of Lorraine Monawski" from* Being Adolescent: Conflict and Growth in the Teenage Years *by Mihaly Csikszentmihalyi and Reed Larson. Copyright © 1984 by Basic Books, Inc. Reprinted by permission of BasicBooks, a division of HarperCollins Publishers, Inc.)*

of one subject. This person had hoped to spend her first year after high school studying abroad but learned that she would not be allowed to go. The scale at the top shows a continuum from bad to good moods, and the zig-zagged line reveals that this subject's mood fluctuated tremendously as she tried to cope with everyday events. Clearly she was happiest when with friends and unhappiest when alone.

The assumption is that such a diary gives more reliable data than questionnaires or interviews that elicit answers to autobiographical questions. To test this assumption, a team of researchers (Conrath, Higgins, & McClean, 1983) collected data from managers and staff personnel in three diverse organizations (a manufacturer of plastic products, an insurance brokerage company, and a large public utility). Each participant was instructed to keep a diary of 100 consecutive interactions, beginning on a specific date and at a specific time. The instructions were to list the other party to the interaction, the initiator of the activity, the mode of the interaction, the elapsed time, and the process involved. The diary was constructed in such a way that the subject could quickly record all this information with no more than 4 to 8 check marks next to particular items. At a later time, each participant was asked to answer a questionnaire covering the same interactions.

The data from all the self-recorded diaries and questionnaires were compared afterward. If one person reported talking to particular others, the researchers checked the diaries and questionnaires of those others to see whether they had also reported that activity. In this way a separate measure of reliability was obtained for the self-recorded diary and for the questionnaire data (i.e., concerning the reporting of specific events at the time of the events as opposed to a later time). As hypothesized, the results were that the questionnaire data (the recalls from autobiographical memory) were less reliable than the self-recorded diary data.

SUMMARY OF IDEAS

1. Two forms of self-report measures are those that allow the respondents to express their feelings and impressions quite spontaneously (i.e., *open-ended*) and those that use a fixed response format (i.e., *closed*).

2. The general advantages and limitations of open-ended measures are basically the reverse of the advantages and limitations of closed measures.

3. The Rorschach inkblot test and the TAT operate on the principle that, in the spontaneous responses that come to his or her mind, the respondent will project some unconscious aspect of his or her life experience and emotions onto ambiguous stimuli.

4. The "big-five" factors of personality are (a) surgency, (b) agreeableness, (c) conscientiousness, (d) emotional stability, and (e) openness to experience.

5. Three kinds of rating scales are the numerical, the forced-choice, and the graphic scales.

6. In a numerical scale, the numbers may be explicit or implicit, but the statements, if any, must always be unambiguous and easily understood.

7. The forced-choice scale was invented to counteract the halo effect.

8. Graphic scales resemble a thermometer, and they may or may not be segmented.
9. Rating biases include the halo effect, the error of leniency, the error of central tendency, the logical error in rating, and the acquiescent response set; there are specific techniques for dealing with each of these problems as well as with "undecided" responses and the ceiling and floor effects (described in Boxes 5.2 and 5.3).
10. The semantic differential, which is used to measure subjective (connotative) meaning, usually focuses on the evaluative, potency, and activity dimensions by means of 7-point graphic scales with bipolar cue words.
11. Item analysis (which is part of the method of summated ratings) is used to construct a Likert scale (e.g., the "Socialized Medicine Attitude Scale" in Figure 5.3).
12. The purpose of pilot-testing is to enable the researcher to fine-tune the data collection instrument and procedures.
13. The four steps in developing an interview schedule are (a) working out the objective; (b) formulating a general strategy of data collection; (c) writing the questions and establishing the best sequence; and (d) pilot-testing the material.
14. Telephone interviews have both advantages and limitations, but in general, they follow the same procedures used in developing any interview schedule.
15. The major advantage of the self-recorded diary is that events are recorded as they happen, and there is no need to rely on longer-term recall (e.g., Csikszentmihalyi and Larson's study of teenagers' day-to-day lives).

KEY TERMS

acquiescent response set (yea-saying) *p. 104*
big-five factors *p. 96*
bipolar scale *p. 101*
ceiling effect *p. 103*
central tendency bias *p. 103*
closed (structured) items *p. 95*
critical incident technique *p. 114*
cue words *p. 102*
equal-appearing intervals method *p. 108*
evaluation, potency, and activity *p. 104*
face-to-face interview *p. 112*
false-negative report *p. 113*
floor effect *p. 103*
forced-choice scales *p. 99*
graphic scales *p. 101*
halo effect *p. 102*

interview schedule *p. 112*
item analysis *p. 105*
leniency bias *p. 103*
Likert scale *p. 105*
logical error in rating *p. 103*
Minnesota Multiphasic Personality Inventory (MMPI) *p. 97*
numerical scales *p. 98*
open-ended (unstructured) items *p. 95*
pilot-testing *p. 99*
projective test *p. 96*
rating errors *p. 102*
rating scales *p. 98*
recruitment strategy *p. 112*
Rorschach test *p. 96*
segmented graphic scale *p. 102*
self-recorded diary *p. 116*
self-report methods *p. 95*
semantic differential *p. 104*

REVIEW QUESTIONS

1. An Austin Peay State student wants to develop numerical and graphic items to measure attitudes about abortion. What advice would you give him on how to get started?

2. A Central Michigan student is asked by his instructor to tell which rating error each of the following descriptions represents: (a) rating too positively someone you know; (b) tending to respond in an affirmative direction; (c) not using the extremes of a scale; (d) rating a central trait and other traits in the same way. Do you know the answers? Do you also know how to control for each of these errors?

3. A Northwestern student who has a job selling used cars is thinking about developing a questionnaire to discover the motivations of people who buy and don't buy used cars. What methodological pointers would you give him?

4. A Wheaton College student wants to develop a Thurstone scale to measure attitudes about eliminating final exams for graduating seniors. Describe the steps she will need to take in developing this scale.

5. The student in Question 4 has a boyfriend who is a psychology major at Rhode Island College. He tells her that he is planning to develop a Likert scale to measure the same attitudes. Do you know the differences between these two approaches?

6. A student at the City University of New York wants to use the semantic differential to study people's reactions to certain *New York Times* advertisements. If you were this student, how would you design this instrument?

7. A student at Ohio Wesleyan who is running for student body president reads *The Selling of the President,* in which Joe McGinniss wrote about the use of the semantic differential by advertising researchers who worked for Richard M. Nixon when he began assembling a team for his 1968 presidential campaign. The researchers traveled all through the United States asking people to evaluate the presidential candidates (Nixon, Hubert Humphrey, and George Wallace). They then plotted an "ideal presidential curve" (i.e., a line connecting the points that represented what the researchers thought would be the ideal candidate) and compared the candidates' profiles with this ideal. The Ohio Wesleyan student is also running against two rivals and wonders whether it might be possible to do a similar study. What methodological pointers would you give her?

8. A student at the University of South Africa, a correspondence university, works in a company that wants to study the morale of its employees. The student thinks it might be instructive to ask a sample of the employees one or two critical incident questions. How should they be worded?

9. What is the major advantage of the self-recorded diary over a questionnaire?

Answers to review questions are found on pages 320–334.

Reliability and Validity

RANDOM AND SYSTEMATIC ERROR

Whenever we measure something—whether we are using a ruler to measure physical distance, a scale to measure weight, or a psychological test to measure an individual's personality—our measurements are subject to fluctuation (also called *error*). Suppose a grocer weighs the same bunch of grapes a number of times in a row. In an ideal world, the grocer's measurements would give the same result every time he (or someone else) weighed the same bunch of grapes. But no matter how precisely he does it, his measurement will probably come out a bit differently each time it is repeated. Sometimes, the more careful and precise the repeated measurements, the more noticeable are the chance fluctuations.

For example, the National Bureau of Standards in Washington, D.C., is concerned with checking weights and measures, which it does by comparing measuring instruments with certain standards. One such standard is that for 10 grams, a prototype weight that is owned by the bureau. This prototype, acquired around 1940, has been weighed about once a week ever since. At each weighing, an attempt has been made to control all the factors known to affect the results (e.g., air pressure and temperature), but still there have been noticeable fluctuations. For instance, the first five weighings in the series yielded 9.999591 grams, 9.999600 grams, 9.999594 grams, 9.999601 grams, and 9.999598 grams. Although the first four digits are identical, the numbers are nevertheless shaky in the last three digits. As careful and precise as these measurements were, we can clearly see chance fluctuations at work (Freedman, Pisani, Purves, & Adhikari, 1991, pp. 91–94).

Another name for chance fluctuations is *random error,* which can be distinguished from *systematic error* (also called *bias*). The difference is that random error tends to push measurements up and down around an exact value, so that the average of all measurements over many trials is very close to the exact value. Systematic error, on the other hand, tends to push measurements in the same direction and causes the average or mean value to be too big or too small. Another way of saying this is that random errors are likely to cancel out, on the average, over repeated measurements; systematic errors do not cancel out but affect all measurements in roughly the same way. The grocer who always weighs grapes with a thumb on the scale will inflate the price of grapes by tacking extra ounces onto the exact weight (a systematic error).

The purpose of this chapter is to explain the role of measurement fluctuations as they enter into the assessment of reliability and validity. *Reliability,* broadly speaking, refers to consistency or stability, for instance, whether the grocer's measurements can be repeated and confirmed by further competent measurements. *Validity,* broadly speaking, refers to whether the measurements measure what they are supposed (or claim) to measure. In an ideal world, the grocer's measurements would not be contaminated by a thumb on the scale and would consistently give only the true weight of the grapes.

In behavioral research, knowing that a measuring "instrument" (e.g., a personality test, an electroencephalogram for monitoring brain waves, a group of judges, or an attitude questionnaire) is both reliable and valid shortens the time needed to discover the characteristics of what is being measured. If the instrument is not reliable, it is often less likely to be valid, but it can be very reliable without being at all valid. For example, it is possible to imagine that subjects blink their eyes the same number of times a minute under a variety of circumstances (i.e., the measure has high reliability), but under no conditions could one predict the subjects' running speed from their eye-blink rate (i.e., the measure has low validity as a predictor of running speed).

TEST–RETEST RELIABILITY

Suppose you are thinking about using a psychological test or other assessment procedure (see Box 6.1) to make predictions in research. It is important to know the *test-retest reliability* (also called "retest reliability"). The reason is that retest

| BOX 6.1 | Ancient Roots of Behavioral Assessment |

In previous chapters we described the use of various assessment tools, including both observational and self-report methods (e.g., projective tests that measure aspects of an individual's personality or attitude scales that measure an individual's views on controversial issues). The idea of behavioral assessment goes far back into history. For example, the Bible tells us that the Gileadites used a one-item ability test to ferret out the Ephraimites who were hiding in their midst (Wainer, 1990). The test was to pronounce the word *shibboleth;* the Ephraimites could not pronounce *sh* (which came out as *s*), and those who failed this test were put to death. Such a test may have cut down on the number of Ephraimites, but it left no opportunity for anyone to assess the test–retest reliability from one measurement session to another.

reliability gives an estimate of the degree of fluctuation of the instrument, or of the trait it is designed to measure, from one administration to another. To find out the instrument's test–retest reliability, we would administer the test and then readminister the same instrument to the same subjects later. The degree of test–retest reliability can be represented by a *correlation coefficient* between the scores on the test administered at different times. We will have more to say about correlation coefficients in a later chapter, but if you have had a course in statistics, you know that the basic measure of association is the *Pearson r correlation coefficient.*

To jog your memory a little, you will recall that the Pearson r measures the strength of association (i.e., the degree of relatedness) of two variables, such as height and weight. One characteristic of the Pearson r is that it ranges only from -1.0 through 0 to $+1.0$. A value of 0 means that the two variables being correlated have no relation, for example, that taller people are not heavier (or lighter) on average than shorter people. A value of $+1.0$ means that the variables have a perfect positive relation; as scores on one variable increase, there are perfectly predictable increases in the scores on the other variable. A value of -1.0 means the opposite; as the scores on one variable increase, there are perfectly predictable decreases in the scores on the other variable.

Given these characteristics of the Pearson r, what would you want the correlation between the scores at the initial testing and at the retesting to be if you were thinking about using a particular instrument in your research? The answer, of course, is that you would want the Pearson r to be a positive value as high as possible, because the higher the test–retest coefficient, the more "dependable" the test. In other words, the closer the r is to $+1.0$, the more impressive is the measured temporal stability (or dependability) of the instrument.

In actuality, many useful measuring instruments used in behavioral science have reliabilities substantially lower than 1.0. To give us a feeling for what the test–retest r means, Henry Braun and Howard Wainer (1989, p. 181)—researchers at the Educational Testing Service, the organization that revises and administers the SAT (Scholastic Assessment Test)— noted some typical reliabilities. For example, the test–retest *r* for essay scores in the humanities is usually between .3 and .6, and for chemistry problems it is usually between .6 and .8. If we measured the height of a group of boys at ages 6 and 10 and then correlated these values, the reliability coefficient would usually be greater than .8.

INTERNAL-CONSISTENCY RELIABILITY

Test–retest reliability is one of two basic types of reliability employed in test assessment. The other type is *internal-consistency reliability,* which is the degree of relatedness of the individual items. Suppose you want to assess your fellow students' views of the course in which this book is being used, and you have made up a three-item attitude test to do the job. Your instructor suggests that you compute the test's internal-consistency reliability and perhaps, if this value seems too low, think about adding more items. In order to follow the instructor's suggestion, you administer the three-item test to a group of students and then compute the average correlation of each pair of items. That is, you begin by correlating Item 1 with Item 2, Item 1 with Item 3, and Item 2 with Item 3.

Let us say you find $r = .45$ between Items 1 and 2, $r = .50$ between Items 1 and 3, and $r = .55$ between Items 2 and 3. Summing the values gives $.45 + .50 + .55 = 1.50$, and dividing by the number of pairs gives the test's internal-consistency reliability. Your three-item test's internal-consistency reliability could be reported as the average correlation, which is $\bar{r} = .50$ (because $1.50/3 = .50$). (The reason for putting a bar over the *r* is to indicate that it is an *average* correlation.) This average correlation is the reliability of any single item, but it is not the reliability of the test made up of all three items. That reliability can be computed from the *Spearman–Brown formula:*

$$R = \frac{n\bar{r}}{1 + (n - 1)\bar{r}}$$

where R = the new overall internal consistency, n = the total number of items you plan for your test, and $\bar{r}$ = the average intercorrelation. You set n equal to 3 (because you have a three-item test) and $\bar{r}$ equal to .50. Substituting in the formula, you find

$$R = \frac{3(.50)}{1 + (3 - 1).50} = \frac{1.5}{1 + 1.0} = .75$$

If you were to use six items instead of three and the average correlation remained .50, the internal consistency reliability would be

$$R = \frac{6(.50)}{1 + (6 - 1).50} = \frac{3.0}{1 + 2.5} = .86$$

What if you wanted to further increase the length of the test, going to nine items? With $n = 9$, you find

$$R = \frac{9(.50)}{1 + (9 - 1).50} = \frac{4.5}{1 + 4.0} = .90$$

There is not much difference between .90 and .86, but it does seem (as the instructor implied) that you can keep on increasing internal-consistency reliability by steadily adding new, homogeneous items. However, there is a practical limit to how long a test can be. Put yourself in the situation of having to take a test of not 9, but 99, items. It would be hard to concentrate after a point because you would begin to feel bored or fatigued. When this happens, the consistency of accurate responding is frequently reduced as the amount of random error increases.

What you will need to figure out, and to state in your research proposal, is how many items you feel are optimal to achieve the level of reliability you want, without making the scale so cumbersome as to give your respondents a headache. Thus an important question becomes: What is an acceptable range of reliability? Unfortunately, there is no simple answer because the acceptable range depends on the situation in which the instrument is to be used and the purpose or objective of the research. Besides asking your instructor for advice, you can begin to develop a sense of the answer in your particular case by reading test reviews by experts in the *Mental Measurements Yearbook* series published by the Buros Institute of Mental Measurements and also by examining standard texts on psychological testing (e.g., Anastasi, 1988). To get started, let us look at the reliabilities of the standardized tests discussed in the previous chapter.

WHAT IS ACCEPTABLE RELIABILITY?

You will recall that the MMPI (Minnesota Multiphasic Personality Inventory) and the Rorschach inkblot test are both personality tests. As previously noted, the MMPI consists of several hundred statements to which the subject responds by indicating whether or not they apply to him or her; the Rorschach consists of inkblots, and the subject tells what he or she perceives in each blot. A team of psychologists (Parker, Hanson, & Hunsley, 1988) collated information reported in articles between 1970 and 1981 concerning the internal consistency and test–retest correlations of these two instruments—the Rorschach and the MMPI—and similar information about another well-known test, the *Wechsler Adult Intelligence Scale* (WAIS). Developed by David Wechsler (a clinical psychologist who had been connected with New York's Bellevue Hospital for many years), the WAIS is the most widely used individually administered intelligence test. It is divided into verbal and performance subtests, the former depending more on school-related abilities than the latter.

Parker et al. found that the average internal-consistency reliability was .87 for the overall WAIS, .84 for the MMPI, and .86 for the Rorschach. They also found that the average test–retest correlation was .82 for the overall WAIS, .74 for the MMPI, and .85 for the Rorschach. Internal-consistency correlations are expected to be higher than test–retest correlations, unless the test–retest intervals are very short. These results, then, are consistent with that expectation, although in the case of the Rorschach the difference is hardly noticeable.

More is known about the reliability (and validity) of the WAIS, the MMPI, and the Rorschach than about most other psychological tests in current use, including the two attitude tests described in the previous chapter. Let us look first at the test that was built to measure attitudes toward defensive, cooperative, and aggressive war (see Figure 5.4). The authors of this scale (Day & Quackenbush, 1942) reported only its internal-consistency reliability, which was in the .80 to .87 range for all three referents measured. Let us look next at the socialized-medicine attitude test shown in Figure 5.3. Its internal-consistency reliability was reported by its author (Mahler, 1953) to be .96. This test is interesting for another reason having to do with reliability: It actually comprised two comparable 10-item forms.

The advantage in having comparable forms of a test is that we do not have to administer the same items twice. Subjects' familiarity with certain items may artificially inflate test–retest reliability. When comparable forms with different questions are available, it is important to know whether they actually measure the same attribute (called *equivalent-forms reliability*). To find out, we give the forms to the same individuals and then compute the equivalent-forms correlation. That is, we find out how much agreement there is between the two forms by correlating the subjects' scores on one form with their scores on the second form. If there is not much agreement, the equivalent-forms correlation is close to 0. Thus the more that the scores on one form are correlated with those on the other, the better is the equivalent-forms reliability. In this case, the author (Mahler, 1953) reported equivalent-forms reliability in the .81 to .84 range (see also Box 6.2).

BOX 6.2   Cronbach's Alpha and K-R 20

In your reading, you may find references to other measures of reliability, such as Cronbach's alpha and K-R 20. Briefly, *Cronbach's alpha* (invented by Lee J. Cronbach), also called the *alpha coefficient,* is another measure of internal-consistency reliability. If you have had a course in statistics that covered the analysis of variance (reviewed in a later chapter), it may be of interest to you that the alpha coefficient is related to the analysis of variance. You may also recall that another name for the "p value" is alpha; however, that alpha (which refers to the probability of a Type I error) does not mean the same thing as the alpha coefficient (which refers only to internal-consistency reliability). *K-R 20* is also a measure of internal-consistency reliability; it is used when the items of the test are scored dichotomously, that is, scored "1" if marked correctly and "0" if marked otherwise. It is beyond the scope of this text to give detailed examples of Cronbach's alpha and K-R 20, but the same rule applies in both cases: The more highly correlated the scores, and the more items there are, the higher is the reliability.

THE RELIABILITY OF JUDGES

As we first mentioned in Chapter 4, reliability is also a basic consideration in observational studies that use judges or raters. For example, in one popular observational procedure used by developmental psychologists to study attachment behavior in infants and maternal responses, the judges code positive and negative actions in a number of situations. They may do this coding, for example, when the mother and infant are together, when the mother leaves the infant in the presence of a stranger, when the mother returns, when the infant is left by itself, and so forth (Ainsworth, Bell, & Stayton, 1971). Suppose a developmental researcher uses three judges (A, B, and C) to code the maternal behavior of five mothers (a, b, c, d, and e) in one situation on a 7-point scale from "very secure" (1) to "very anxious" (7). The results are shown in Part A of Table 6.1. After calculating the correlations between pairs of judges (A with B, A with C, and B with C), the researcher obtains the mean of these correlations. The results are given in Part B of Table 6.1, in which the mean correlation is shown as .676, calculated as $(.645 + .800 + .582)/3 = .676$. This value does *not* tell the researcher the reliability of *all three* judges (called the *effective reliability* and also called the *aggregate reliability*); instead it estimates the reliability of any *single* judge (also characterized as the *judge-to-judge reliability*).

To assess the effective (or aggregate, which means *overall*) reliability (symbolized as R), the researcher uses the same approach that we used in the previous section to determine how many items to include in the test. Using the Spearman–Brown formula, the researcher calculates the effective reliability as

$$R = \frac{n\bar{r}}{1 + (n-1)\bar{r}}$$

TABLE 6.1	Ratings and Intercorrelations for Three Judges

A. Judges' ratings

	Judges		
Mothers	A	B	C
a	5	6	7
b	3	6	4
c	3	4	6
d	2	2	3
e	1	4	4

B. Judge-to-judge correlations
$r_{AB} = .645$
$r_{AC} = .800$
$r_{BC} = .582$
$\bar{r} = .676$

but where R = the homogeneity of the *total* set of judges (i.e., the effective reliability), n = the number of judges, and $\bar{r}$ = the mean correlation among all the judges (the judge-to-judge reliability). Substituting in the formula gives

$$R = \frac{3(.676)}{1 + (3 - 1).676} = \frac{2.028}{1 + 1.352} = .862$$

The researcher then reports that the effective (or aggregate) reliability of the three judges' ratings is .862, and that the reliability of any single typical judge is .676. The researcher reports both reliabilities and, of course, labels each to avoid reader misunderstandings. The two reliabilities described in Box 6.2 (Cronbach's alpha and K-R 20), incidentally, are both effective (or aggregate) reliabilities.

USING A TABLE OF ESTIMATED VALUES

Table 6.2 is a useful summary table based on this adaptation of the Spearman–Brown formula (Rosenthal & Rosnow, 1991). It gives the effective reliability, R, for values of n ranging from 1 to 20 judges or raters. When $n = 1$, we see that the effective reliability (R) is equivalent to the reliability of a single judge ($\bar{r}$). The table will yield approximate answers to questions such as the following:

1. Given an obtained or estimated mean reliability, $\bar{r}$, and a sample of n judges, what is the approximate effective reliability, R, of the mean of the judges'

TABLE 6.2	Effective Reliability of the Mean of Judges' Ratings

Number of judges (n)	.05	.10	.15	.20	.25	.30	.35	.40	.45	.50	.55	.60	.65	.70	.75	.80	.85	.90	.95
1	05	10	15	20	25	30	35	40	45	50	55	60	65	70	75	80	85	90	95
2	10	18	26	33	40	46	52	57	62	67	71	75	79	82	86	89	92	95	97
3	14	25	35	43	50	56	62	67	71	75	79	82	85	88	90	92	94	96	98
4	17	31	41	50	57	63	68	73	77	80	83	86	88	90	92	94	96	97	*
5	21	36	47	56	62	68	73	77	80	83	86	88	90	92	94	95	97	98	*
6	24	40	51	60	67	72	76	80	83	86	88	90	92	93	95	96	97	98	*
7	27	44	55	64	70	75	79	82	85	88	90	91	93	94	95	97	98	98	*
8	30	47	59	67	73	77	81	84	87	89	91	92	94	95	96	97	98	*	*
9	32	50	61	69	75	79	83	86	88	90	92	93	94	95	96	97	98	*	*
10	34	53	64	71	77	81	84	87	89	91	92	94	95	96	97	98	98	*	*
12	39	57	68	75	80	84	87	89	91	92	94	95	96	97	97	98	*	*	**
14	42	61	71	78	82	86	88	90	92	93	94	95	96	97	98	98	*	*	**
16	46	64	74	80	84	87	90	91	93	94	95	96	97	97	98	98	*	*	**
18	49	67	76	82	86	89	91	92	94	95	96	96	97	98	98	*	*	*	**
20	51	69	78	83	87	90	92	93	94	95	96	97	97	98	98	*	*	*	**

Note: Numbers in body of table should be read as two decimal places (e.g., 05 is read as R = .05). Single asterisk (*) denotes R approximately .99, and double asterisks (**) denote R approximately 1.00.

Source: Reproduced from *Essentials of Behavioral Research: Methods and Data Analysis* (2nd. ed.) by R. Rosenthal and R.L. Rosnow, 1991, McGraw-Hill, p. 53. Used by permission of McGraw-Hill, Inc.

ratings? The value of R is read from the table at the intersection of the appropriate row (n) and column ($\bar{r}$). Suppose an investigator wants to work with a variable believed to show a mean reliability of .50 and can afford only four judges. The investigator believes he should go ahead with his study only if the effective reliability will reach or exceed .75. Shall he go ahead? The answer is yes, because the table shows R to be .80 for an n of 4 and an $\bar{r}$ of .50.

2. Given the value of the obtained or desired effective reliability, R, and the number of judges actually available, n, what will be the approximate value of the required mean reliability, $\bar{r}$? The table is entered in the row corresponding to the n of judges available and is read across until the value of R closest to the one desired is reached; the value of $\bar{r}$ is then read as the corresponding column heading. Suppose an investigator who will settle for an effective reliability no less than .90 has a sample of 20 judges available. In the investigator's selection of variables to be rated by these judges, what should be their minimally acceptable average individual reliability? From this table we see the answer is $\bar{r} = .30$.

3. Given an obtained or estimated mean reliability, $\bar{r}$, and the obtained or desired effective reliability, R, what is the approximate number of judges (n) required? The table is entered in the column corresponding to the mean reliability, $\bar{r}$, and is read down until the value of R closest to the one desired is reached; the value of n is then read as the corresponding row title. For example, we know our choice of variables to have a mean reliability of .40, and we want to achieve an effective reliabiity of .85 or higher. How many judges must we allow for in our preparation of a research budget? The answer is nine judges.

Table 6.2 can be used equally well in estimating the increase in internal-consistency reliability of tests when new, homogeneous items are added. In that case we would relabel the n of judges as the n of items, $\bar{r}$ as the average inter-correlation of items, and R as the estimated internal-consistency reliability with n items. In the previous section we gave the example of a three-item test with an average item-to-item correlation of .50; the researcher wanted to estimate the effect of using three, six, or nine items. The table is entered in the column corresponding to this mean reliability, and we then read down the column until we reach the Spearman–Brown value closest to the one desired. Let us say we want to achieve an internal-consistency reliability of .90 or higher. How many homogeneous items will we need? When we read across the row, the answer is nine.

REPLICATION AND RELIABILITY

In the same way that researchers want to know the dependability of measuring instruments, they are also interested in the dependability of scientific observations. Knowing that a set of observations is dependable means that it is subject to *replication* (i.e., it can be repeated or duplicated by others). Students interested in a detailed discussion of replication may refer to Rosenthal (1990c); here we will give a general sense of what this term implies—and does not imply. Clearly, the *same* set of observations can never be "exactly" repeated by a different worker, because at the very least the subjects would be older. Thus, to avoid the not very helpful conclusion that there can be no exact replication, researchers speak of *relative* replications. This means that in the replication attempt, the research procedure is modeled very closely on that in the original study. For the replication attempt to be successful, the pattern of results must not be markedly different in magnitude.

A convenient way to decide whether the results are comparable is to examine the *effect size,* which is the size of the relation between the independent variable *(X)* and the dependent variable *(Y)*. The effect size can be directly expressed by the correlation between *X* and *Y*. The closer this correlation in the replication study is to that observed in the original study, the more *homogeneity* the set of results is said to have. If the effect sizes are markedly different, the conclusion is that the studies show *heterogeneity.*

For example, suppose you wanted to replicate an experimental finding in which the effect size was originally given as $r = .50$ (i.e., a large effect). In your study, the effect size is calculated as $r = .40$ (i.e., a somewhat smaller effect), but by some easy calculations (given in Appendix C on meta-analysis), you find that .40 and .50 are not significantly different. In other words, the set of studies is not significantly heterogeneous; that is, you have replicated the original relation reasonably well. Correlations that scattered closely around zero would have told you that not much was going on. But both correlations cluster on the same side of zero and fairly far from zero, so you know that something reliable was probably going on. As Appendix C describes, it is also possible to combine these results and to compute other informative statistics.

Just as reliability has different facets, so has *validity.* In general, assessing the validity of a test or questionnaire means finding out the degree to which it measures what it is supposed to measure. This assessment is considered the most important criterion in instrument evaluation and, in test or questionnaire construction, involves accumulating evidence in three categories: (1) content validity; (2) criterion validity; and (3) construct validity.

CONTENT VALIDITY

Content validity means that the test or questionnaire items represent the kinds of material (or content areas) they are supposed to represent, which is usually a basic consideration in the construction phase of any test or questionnaire. Thus a test or questionnaire with good content validity covers all major aspects of the content areas that are relevant. For example, when the development of the MMPI was begun, the researchers tried to select a range of statements that would be endorsed in a certain direction by each of several different clinical groups. In this way they hoped to differentiate among a number of different clinical conditions by including a wide range of items that tapped different content areas. To help them during this initial phase, they called on expert judges to make subjective evaluations of the relevance or appropriateness of each item for assessing different content areas.

Less formal methods are possible in other situations. For instance, a teacher who is making up a final exam and wants it to have content validity may start by asking, "What kinds of material should students be able to master after studying the readings and taking this course?" The teacher would make a list of all the material the exam should sample and then make up questions to represent this material. As students we have all experienced exams with poor content validity. They are the ones about which we say, "The prof never even mentioned this material, and it was a two-line footnote in the appendix!"

CRITERION VALIDITY

Criterion validity (also called *empirical validity*) is the degree to which the test or questionnaire correlates with one or more outcome criteria (a variable with which our instrument should be reasonably correlated). Researchers who were developing a test of college aptitude might use as their criterion the successful completion of the first year of college or maybe the grade-point average (GPA) after each year of college. If they were developing a test to measure anxiety, they might use as their criterion the pooled judgments of a group of highly trained clinicians who rate (e.g., on a numerical scale of anxiety) each person to whom the researchers administered the test. In assessing criterion validity, researchers usually try to select the most sensitive and meaningful criterion in the present (also called *concurrent validity*) or future (also called *predictive validity*) and then correlate performance on the test or questionnaire with that criterion.

For example, clinical diagnostic tests are ordinarily assessed for concurrent validity, because the criterion of the patient's "real" diagnostic status is in the present with respect to the tests being validated. The concurrent validity of shorter forms of longer tests is also often evaluated, the longer test being used as the criterion (see also Box 6.3). The practical advantage to the researcher of using a criterion in the present is that it is less expensive and less time-consuming than using a criterion that is in the future.

Nevertheless, predictive validity also plays an important role in measurement. Tests of college aptitude are normally assessed for predictive validity, inasmuch as the criteria of graduation and GPA are criteria of the future. The aptitude test scores are saved until the future-criterion data become available; the scores are

---

BOX 6.3   Criteria Evaluated against Criteria

Sometimes researchers must consider the validity of the criterion itself. Suppose a personality researcher wants to develop a short test of anxiety that will predict the scores on a longer test of anxiety. The longer test serves as the researcher's criterion, and the new short test may be relatively valid with respect to the longer test. But the longer test may be of dubious validity with respect to some other criterion (e.g., clinicians' judgments). In other words, criteria must sometimes be evaluated with respect to other criteria, but there are no firm rules (beyond the consensus of the researchers in that area) about what constitutes an "ultimate" criterion.

then correlated with them. The resulting correlation coefficient serves as an index of criterion validity. GPA tends to be a fairly reliable criterion, but clinicians' judgments (e.g., about complex behavior) may be a less reliable criterion. Table 6.2 showed how the reliability of pooled judgments can be increased if more judges are added, and researchers can increase the reliability of pooled clinical judgments by adding more clinicians to the group whose pooled judgments will serve as their criterion (Rosenthal, 1973, 1982, 1987).

CONSTRUCT VALIDITY

More sophisticated views of the validation of tests require that researchers be sensitive not only to the correlation between their measures and some appropriate criterion, but also to the correlation between their measures and some "inappropriate" criterion. Suppose a researcher in clinical psychology developed a test of adjustment for a field experiment and found that the test correlated positively and substantially with the pooled judgment of expert clinicians, an attractive outcome of a concurrent validation effort. Imagine, however, that the researcher administered a test of verbal aptitude to all the subjects and found that the correlation between the adjustment scores and verbal aptitude was also positive and substantial. Would the new test be a reasonably valid measure of adjustment, of verbal aptitude, of both, or of neither?

That question is difficult to answer, but the researcher could not claim on the basis of such results to understand the new test very well. It was not intended, after all, to be a measure of verbal aptitude. In short, the new test has good concurrent validity but fails to discriminate: It does not correlate differentially with criteria for different types of observation. This "ability to discriminate" is a characteristic of *construct validity.*

In a seminal paper, Donald T. Campbell and Donald W. Fiske (1959) sought to formalize this process on a statistical basis by proposing two kinds of construct validation evidence: (1) the testing for "convergence" across different measures or manipulations of the same trait or behavior (called *convergent validity*) and (2) the testing for "divergence" between measures or manipulations of related but conceptually distinct behaviors or traits (called *discriminant validity*). To give you a clearer idea of how this is done, we turn next to a classic illustration of construct validation research, performed by personality researchers Douglas Crowne and David Marlowe in the 1950s.

CROWNE AND MARLOWE'S RESEARCH

The original purpose of Crowne and Marlowe's research was to develop a psychological scale that would measure a source of systematic error in personality test taking called *social desirability responding,* in which individuals give answers that make them look good (rather than give the most candid or honest answers). As the research progressed, Crowne and Marlowe realized that the scale they were building might be tapping a more general personality variable, which they termed the *need for social approval* (to reflect the idea that people differ in their need to be thought well of by others). In developing this scale—the *Marlowe-Crowne Social*

Desirability Scale (MCSD)—the researchers wanted to measure the degree to which people vary on the need-for-approval dimension independent of their level of psychopathology, and they were also interested in validating the need-for-approval construct.

Crowne and Marlowe began by considering hundreds of personality test items (including a few from the MMPI) that could be answered true or false. To be included, an item had to be one that would reflect socially approved behavior but that would also almost certainly be untrue (i.e., behavior too good to be true). In addition, answers to the items could not have any implications of psychological abnormality or psychopathology. By having a group of psychology graduate students and faculty judge the social desirability of each item, Crowne and Marlowe developed a set of items that would reflect behavior that was too virtuous to be probable, but that would not be primarily influenced by personal maladjustment. The final form of the MCSD was reduced to 33 items by item analysis and the ratings of experienced judges (Crowne, 1979; Crowne & Marlowe, 1964). In about half the items a "true" answer reflected the socially desirable response (i.e., the higher need for approval), and in the remainder a "false" answer reflected this type of response. An example of the former type of item might be "I have never intensely disliked anyone," whereas the latter type might be "I sometimes feel resentful when I don't get my way."* The MCSD showed a high degree of relationship to those variables with which the scale scores were expected to converge (i.e., convergent validation evidence). It also showed only a low degree of relationship to those variables with which it was expected not to converge but that it was expected to discriminate (i.e., discriminant validation evidence).

For example, although the test did show moderate correlations with measures of psychopathology, there were fewer of these correlations and they were smaller in magnitude than those of an earlier developed scale of social desirability. Also encouraging was an impressive correlation ($r = .88$) between the two testings of a group of subjects who were tested one month apart (i.e., evidence of test–retest reliability). In other words, the test seemed to be measuring what it measured in a stable manner.

These were promising beginnings for the MCSD, but it remained to be shown that the concept of need for social approval (and the scale developed to measure it) was useful beyond predicting responses on other paper-and-pencil measures. As part of their program of further validating their new scale and the construct that was its basis, the researchers undertook an ingenious series of varied replications relating scores on the MCSD to subjects' behavior in a number of non-paper-and-pencil test situations. They reasoned that "dependence on the approval of others should make it difficult to assert one's independence, and so the approval-motivated person should be susceptible to social influence, compliant, and conforming" (Crowne, 1991, p. 10). A series of relational studies produced results that were generally consistent with this hypothesis.

---

*This scale, along with related measures of response bias, is available in Robinson et al. *Measures of Personality and Social Psychological Attitudes* (1991).

In the first of these studies, the subjects began by completing various tests, including the MCSD, and then were asked to get down to the serious business of the experiment. This "serious business" required them to (1) pack a dozen spools of thread into a small box, (2) unpack the box, (3) repack the box, (4) reunpack the box, and so on for 25 minutes while the experimenter appeared to be timing the performances and making notes about them. After these dull 25 minutes had elapsed, subjects were asked to rate how "interesting" the task had been, how "instructive," and how "important to science" and how much the subject wanted to participate in similar experiments in the future. Those subjects who scored above the mean on social desirability said they found the task more interesting, more instructive, and more important to science and were more eager to participate again in similar studies than those subjects who had scored below the mean. In other words, just as we would have predicted, subjects higher in the need for social approval were more compliant and said nicer things to the experimenter about the task that he had set for them.

In still other research, Crowne and Marlowe used a variant of Asch's (1952) conformity procedure (described in Chapter 3). That is, a group of subjects is required to make judgments on specific issues, and all the confederates make the same uniform judgment, one that is quite clearly in error. Conformity is defined as the real subject's "going along with" the majority in his or her own judgment rather than giving the objectively correct response. In one of these experiments, Crowne and Marlowe had the subjects listen to a tape recording of knocks on a table and then report their judgment of the number of knocks. Each subject was led to believe that he or she was the fourth participant. To create this illusion, the experimenter played for the subject the tape-recorded responses of three prior subjects to each series of knocks that were to be judged. The earlier three subjects were the confederates, and they all gave an incorrect response in 12 of 18 trials. It was therefore possible to count the number of times out of 12 that the real subject yielded to the wrong but unanimous majority. The results supported Crowne and Marlowe's hypothesis that the approval-motivated person is conforming: The subjects who had scored higher in the need for social approval went along with the majority judgment more than did the subjects who scored lower in the need for social approval.

Many additional studies were performed by these and other investigators (see, e.g., Allaman, Joyce, & Crandall, 1972; Crowne, 1979; Crowne & Marlowe, 1964; Weinberger, 1990). As in any well-researched area of behavioral science, some of the follow-up studies produced different results, and an exhaustive literature review (using the search methods described in Chapter 2) will turn up these additional studies. However, the point of this example is to illustrate a systematic approach to construct validity.

WHAT IS ACCEPTABLE VALIDITY?

Previously, we asked the question: What is an acceptable level of reliability? We turned to convention for the answer. The same question can be asked about the validity of standardized tests, and we can again turn to texts and annual reviews to help us get a sense of precedents. To get you started in your thinking, we will return to the tests noted in our discussion of reliability. Although not much can be said about the validity of the attitude scales discussed previously (because the published data are limited), much is known about the validity of the WAIS, the MMPI, and the Rorschach.

Like the MCSD, the socialized-medicine attitude scale developed by Mahler (1953) has also been found to discriminate between known groups (e.g., Stanford University students who were identified by interview as having pro- or anti-socialized-medicine attitudes; see Shaw & Wright, 1967, p. 153). However, regarding the scale developed by Day and Quackenbush (1942) to measure attitudes toward defensive, cooperative, and aggressive war, little evidence is available beyond the finding that a nonrandom sample of law students had more favorable attitudes than other students—a finding that might (or might not) have some relevance (Shaw & Wright, 1967, p. 217).

In the review cited earlier (Parker et al., 1988), the convergent validity of the WAIS, the MMPI, and the Rorschach was examined along with their internal-consistency reliability and their stability. The criteria against which the WAIS—the standard of comparison in this examination—was validated were typically other intelligence tests. Generally, those other tests had higher validity and reliability than the measures against which the MMPI and the Rorschach were validated (e.g., clinical diagnoses). As a consequence, we might expect higher validity coefficients for the WAIS than for the MMPI or the Rorschach, and that is what Parker and his group found to be true. For the WAIS, the average validity was .62; for the MMPI it was .46; and for the Rorschach it was .41. Because of such results, these tests are generally considered acceptable for research purposes, as long as researchers know what they are looking for and use the tests appropriately.

INTERNAL, CONSTRUCT, AND EXTERNAL VALIDITY OF EXPERIMENTS

In the next chapter we will discuss the logic of experimental design, which also involves thinking about a number of validity-related criteria. The most often considered criteria are *internal, construct,* and *external validity,* although other types of validity are also of some concern to experimenters (see Box 6.4). In concluding this discussion, we will give a flavor of these three types of validity as a prelude to the following chapter.

First, *internal validity* is concerned with ruling out *plausible rival hypotheses* that jeopardize statements made about whether *X* causes *Y*. Suppose a male student and a female student decide to conduct, as a team, an experiment on verbal learning. Their particular interest is the effect of stress, in the form of loud noise, on the learning of prose material. In order to divide the work fairly, the experimenters flip a coin to determine which of them will run the subjects in the stress condition and which of them will run the subjects in the no-stress condition. They find that better learning occurred in the stress condition. Can we confidently ascribe the effect to the experimental stress? We cannot, because we have a plausible rival hypothesis to the working hypothesis that the result was due to stress. Our plausible rival hypothesis is "The result is due to experimenter differences" (e.g., personality and

BOX 6.4   Ecological, Face, and Statistical-Conclusion Validity

Before ending this discussion of validity, we should note that you may come across other uses of the term *validity* besides those defined here. For example, the term *ecological validity* (like the term *mundane realism,* defined in Chapter 4) is generally used to refer to whether an experimental situation reflects the outside world. An experiment set up in an artificial setting that appears to bear little resemblance to the real-world setting that it is intended to mirror may be criticized as lacking ecological validity. The experimenter may produce a "law" of human nature that is true only for the subjects tucked away in the artificial setting. Another term for validity—*face validity*—is one you may particularly encounter if you are working with, or reading about, tests. It refers to the extent to which the test seems on its surface (or "face") to be measuring what it purports to measure. To be sure, the appearance of a test may not always be a good clue to precisely what it is trying to measure (e.g., the Rorschach and the TAT). A third type of validity is *statistical-conclusion validity,* which refers to the accuracy of drawing statistical conclusions and involves concepts that are discussed in later chapters.

gender differences). This rival hypothesis could have been fairly well ruled out in this experiment if each of the two experimenters had run half the subjects in the stress condition and half the subjects in the no-stress condition. Such a plan would prevent the "confounding" (or intermixing) of the effects of stress and the effects of experimenter differences. Preventing such confounding increases the internal validity of an experiment.

Second, *construct validity* is here concerned with the psychological qualities constituting what has been characterized as the *theoretical scaffolding* between X and Y (Cronbach & Meehl, 1955). As Crowne and Marlowe's research illustrated, one strategy for developing construct validation evidence is to examine a range of situations in which particular results can be hypothesized on the basis of the construct. Another example, discussed in Chapter 2, was Latané and Darley's (1968, 1970) series of experiments in which they used the construct "diffusion of responsibility" as a theoretical scaffolding to explain why the more witnesses to an emergency *(X),* the less likely it is that any one of them will offer help *(Y).* As in any well-researched problem, we will usually find that not all studies support our expectations. Strictly speaking, constructs (like theories) can never actually be "verified" because we can never complete *every* possible test (Cronbach & Quirk, 1971). For this reason, the term *validate* is perhaps too strong, because a construct cannot be proved; it can only be falsified. Nevertheless, repeated failures to falsify a hypothesis provide some support for the hypothesis.

Third, *external validity* refers to the generalizability of a causal relationship to circumstances beyond those experimentally studied or observed by the scientist. We might ask, for example, how robust the causal relation between X and Y is in its generalizability across both persons and settings. For example, Irwin Horowitz

(1969) noticed that some classic studies in social psychology showed that people were more persuaded by scary communications as the messages became more threatening; however, other classic studies showed the opposite relationship. On closer inspection of the procedures used in these studies, Horowitz also noticed that volunteer subjects had participated in the former studies, whereas *captive subjects* (samples consisting of available subjects) had participated in the latter studies. Was it just a coincidence, Horowitz wondered, or did results with volunteer subjects not generalize to the wider population in this research area?

To answer this question, he performed an experiment in which he assigned volunteers and nonvolunteers to two groups. In one of the groups, a high level of fear was aroused, and in the other, a low level of fear was aroused. The high-fear group read pamphlets on the abuse and effects of drugs and watched two films that depicted the hazards of LSD and other hallucinogens and the dangerous effects of amphetamines and barbiturates. The low-fear group did not see the films; instead, they read pamphlets on the hazards of drug abuse that omitted the vivid verbal descriptions of death and disability to which the high-fear group was exposed. Afterward, the subjects filled out a questionnaire of opinion scales corresponding to statements contained in the pamphlets. To assess the subjects' perceptions of the fear manipulation, Horowitz also conducted an *internal manipulation check,* that is, a check on whether the manipulation had actually been perceived correctly by the subjects. Such a check is considered essential by some experimenters and is therefore often part of any research plan. In Horowitz's internal manipulation check, the subjects were given another scale that asked them to tell the extent, if any, to which they had been concerned and upset.

The results of this experiment were quite illuminating in relation to the role of external validity. The manipulation check confirmed that the high-fear treatment had been more distressing than the low-fear treatment. But more important, the volunteer subjects had been more persuaded by the high-fear than by the low-fear message, and the nonvolunteer subjects had been more persuaded by the low-fear than by the high-fear message. Horowitz's initial observation was of more than just a coincidence, as he was able to show by confirming his suspicions empirically. The lesson? When subjects are volunteers, it may be necessary to consider the possible interdependence of their volunteer status and the X variable of interest—that is, if the conclusions are to have external validity. We will return to this idea in the following chapter and again in a later chapter when we discuss procedures for overcoming the problem of volunteer subject bias.

SUMMARY OF IDEAS

1. All measurements are subject to random errors and systematic errors, which may affect reliability and validity.
2. Test–retest reliability (i.e., stability or dependability) and internal-consistency reliability (i.e., the relatedness of the items) are usually denoted by a correlation coefficient, the Pearson *r*.

3. Using the Spearman–Brown formula, we can predict an improvement in internal-consistency reliability as a function of adding items to a test.
4. The degree of reliability and validity of widely used tests (e.g., the MMPI, the Rorschach, and the WAIS) provides standards by which to assess what convention specifies as acceptable reliability and validity.
5. The logic of the Spearman–Brown formula can be applied to estimating the effective (or aggregate) reliability (i.e., as opposed to the judge-to-judge reliability) of a group of raters.
6. We can use the same table of values of R (Table 6.2) to estimate the optimal number of judges or the optimal number of test items.
7. To say that a replication attempt was successful implies that the research procedure was modeled closely on the original study and that the overall pattern of results was similar.
8. The effect size can be denoted by a correlation coefficient (the correlation between the independent variable and the dependent variable).
9. Validity in testing usually means accumulating evidence in three categories: (a) content-related validity; (b) criterion-related validity (e.g., predictive, concurrent); and (c) construct validity.
10. In assessing criterion-related validity, researchers must be attuned to the validity of the criterion as well as to other aspects of the situation.
11. Convergent and discriminant validity are essential in construct validity.
12. Crowne and Marlowe's research had as its purpose the development and validation of the construct of approval need and a test that would measure it.
13. Three kinds of validity-related evidence in experimental research are (a) internal validity; (b) construct validity; and (c) external validity.
14. The volunteer status of the research participants may affect the external validity of the results.

KEY TERMS

aggregate reliability   *p. 127*
alpha coefficient   *p. 126*
bias   *p. 122*
captive subjects   *p. 137*
concurrent validity   *p. 131*
construct validity   *pp. 132, 136*
content validity   *p. 130*
convergent validity   *p. 132*
correlation coefficient   *p. 123*
criterion validity   *p. 131*
Cronbach's alpha   *p. 126*
discriminant validity   *p. 132*
ecological validity   *p. 136*
effective reliability   *p. 127*

effect size   *p. 130*
empirical validity p. 131
equivalent-forms reliability
   p. 126
error   *p. 121*
external validity   *p. 136*
face validity   *p. 136*
heterogeneity   *p. 130*
homogeneity   *p. 130*
internal-consistency reliability
   p. 124
internal manipulation check
   p. 137
internal validity   *p. 135*

REVIEW QUESTIONS

1. An Emory student is trying to make her mark in the field of psychology by developing a new scale measuring fear of public speaking. How might she assess her scale's predictive and construct validity?

2. On a quiz, a University of Lethbridge student is asked how we know that the Marlowe–Crowne scale (MCSD) measures need for social approval. What is the answer?

3. A University of Houston student has piloted his observational study using two judges and has found a moderate interrater reliability ($r = .50$). Because he wants to achieve a higher reliability coefficient, he is distressed by the prospect of having to modify his coding criteria and training procedures. Another student suggests, "Don't bother with all that. Simply add two more judges to improve the reliability." Would you consider the second student's advice sound?

4. A Penn State researcher wants to study the effects of the texture of toys on the frequency with which toddlers touch them. She uses the following toys: a brown teddy bear, a smooth blue plastic ball, a green wooden cube, and an orange corduroy-covered rattle. She finds that male toddlers are more likely to touch the ball and the cube than the teddy bear and the rattle, whereas female toddlers are more likely to touch the teddy bear and the rattle than the other two toys. When she reports the results, a member of the audience raises the possibility that male toddlers must therefore prefer hard, less variegated textures to soft, more variegated textures, whereas female toddlers show the reverse preference. What is one rival hypothesis that would also be consistent with the researcher's results? How might the rival hypothesis be ruled out?

5. A Northeastern University researcher wants to build a 20-item test to measure need for power. She assigns several students to assess the internal consistency of her new test based on data recently collected from a large sample. They tell her that the effective reliability equals .50 and the mean inter-item reliability equals .40. She asks them to check their work. Why?

6. A student at the State University of New York at Binghamton is interested in assessing a new 20-item scale of optimism-pessimism. Describe how he ought to go about assessing the reliability of this scale. The student is also advised by his instructor to measure several different traits using several different methods to demonstrate empirically the convergent and discriminant validity of the new scale. Why did the instructor give this advice?

7. A student at Bridgewater State College weighs an object known to weigh 10 pounds five times. She obtains readings on the scale of 14, 8, 7, 10, and 11 pounds. Describe the systematic error and the random errors characterizing the scale's performance.

Answers to review questions are found on pages 320–334.

PART III

Design
and
Implementation

CHAPTER 7

The Design of Randomized Experiments

PREVIEW QUESTIONS

➤ **W**hat is the purpose of random assignment, and how is it achieved?

➤ **W**hat are basic forms of between-subjects and within-subjects designs?

➤ **W**hat constitutes a causal inference, and what conditions undermine such inferences?

➤ **W**hy are history, maturation, instrumentation, and selection said to constitute threats to internal validity?

➤ **W**hat are the relative strengths and weaknesses of pre-post and posttest-only designs?

➤ **W**hat can the Solomon design teach us about the logic of control conditions?

➤ **W**hat do demand characteristics have to do with the "good subject" effect and quasi-control groups?

➤ **W**hat is an experimenter expectancy effect, and how can it be controlled?

A BASIC FRAMEWORK

Now that you have an understanding of the general methods of data collection in behavioral science, the time is ripe to think about the design of your study. One option (discussed in this chapter) is to design a randomized experiment, if that seems appropriate to your hypothesis or the research question that interests you. It is not your only option, of course, and in the following two chapters we will discuss descriptive and relational research designs. Although you have seen that experiments frequently take different forms in different fields, the general idea (as introduced in previous discussions) is that experimental observations are designed to tell how things are and how they got to be that way. Another way of saying this is that the purpose of scientific experiments is to record empirical results that are causal and that are observed deliberately and carefully (Fisher, 1971).

If you have had a course in chemistry, you know that "doing an experiment" usually means mixing reagents in a test tube in order to *cause* a certain reaction to occur. If you follow the instructions in the lab manual very carefully (e.g., by using clean test tubes and pure reagents, and by measuring, stirring, or heating precisely), you are very likely to produce the predicted reaction. However, we said in Chapter 1 (where we mentioned the Hawthorne effect in Box 1.1), our "test tubes" (i.e., psychology laboratories) are frequently contaminated by the fact that the "reagents" (i.e., the research subjects) know perfectly well that they are research subjects and that they are to play this role in interaction with another human being, the experimenter. Insofar as we can evaluate the bias resulting from uncontrolled aspects of the interaction between the experimenter and the subjects, we should be able to draw more accurate conclusions. We will return to this problem toward the end of this chapter.

However, our primary interest in this chapter is the nature of what are called *true experimental designs.* This class of experiments is characterized by (1) the controlled arrangement or manipulation of certain treatment conditions and (2) *randomization* (also called *random assignment*), which is the unbiased allocation of the elements or experimental units of the design (also called the *sampling units*) to treatment conditions. These sampling units (i.e., the subjects or groups or objects being studied) may be people, schools, countries, agricultural crops, and so forth. The term *true* does not refer to *absolute truth;* it means that the design uses a genuinely unbiased method (i.e., random assignment) to allocate the sampling units to the treatment conditions. Research designs that approximate true experimental designs but do not randomly assign the sampling units to the treatment conditions are generally classified as *quasi-experimental designs* (discussed in the next chapter).

Table 7.1 gives an overview of the four broad classes of research designs that we will discuss in this and the following chapter. The term *between-subjects design* (i.e., designs of the A and C type) means that the sampling units are exposed to one treatment condition each. In drug trials, for example, the subjects in the experimental condition receive the new drug while the subjects in the control condition may be given a *placebo* (i.e., a substance without any pharmacological benefit given as a pseudomedicine to a control group). This class of designs can be contrast-

TABLE 7.1	Four Classes of Research Designs	
	Order of treatments	
Random assignment	Between-subjects	Within-subjects
Yes	Type A	Type B
No	Type C	Type D

ed with another class (i.e., designs of the B and D type), in which the sampling units receive two or more treatments (called *within-subjects designs*). If all the subjects receive the new drug *and* the placebo in a counterbalanced order, and if the subjects are assigned to the various sequences (e.g., treatment then placebo versus placebo then treatment) in a random manner, then the design constitutes a within-subjects *true* experiment. In the next chapter, we will turn our attention to designs of the C and D type, including what are called *single-case experimental designs* as well as various nonexperimental research designs. In this chapter, we will focus on designs of the A and B type.

We will begin with an overview of some basic A and B designs and describe how random assignment may be achieved. We then turn to what the experimenter means by *causation* and the criteria he or she uses to decide whether something causes something else to occur. It is also important to understand the limits (or "uncertainty") of causal inference, and so we give a detailed example. Next, we briefly review the history of the concept of control before turning to examples of specific threats to validity and how they are controlled. To give you a further idea of the logic of experimental design and how the effects of causal factors are teased out, we then concentrate our attention on one illustrative design, the Solomon design. Randomization is not a panacea for all experimental design problems, and we conclude by examining some further implications of doing experiments with human research participants.

RANDOMIZATION IN BETWEEN- AND WITHIN-SUBJECTS DESIGNS

As conceived by the statisticians who invented it, random assignment (randomization) is meant to serve as a safeguard against the experimenters' subconsciously letting their opinions and preferences influence which sampling units will receive any given treatment (Gigerenzer et al., 1989). Randomization does not guarantee equality in the characteristics of the sampling units assigned to the different conditions, but the idea is to give each unit an equal chance of being assigned to any condition. To guard against unsuspected sources of bias that can be effectively controlled in this way, researchers use a randomized procedure to determine how the sampling units will be allocated to the treatment conditions (e.g., Snedecor & Cochran, 1989).

An experimenter may use a variety of procedures to achieve random assignment. For example, if the experimental manipulation is in the form of a booklet or questionnaire, a simple procedure is to sort the booklets so that they represent the particular treatments and then to administer the booklets in this presorted arrangement. For example, if there are two treatments, A and B, the first subject receives Booklet A or B (decided by a flip of a coin), and the second subject receives the other booklet. For the next two subjects this random procedure is repeated, so that we end up with an equal number of subjects in each of the two conditions. Alternatively, we can arrange the booklets so that, of every 4 or 6 or 8 booklets, half will be A's and half will be B's (also determined by coin flips). If the same experiment were being run on a computer, it would be even easier because we could have the machine randomly assign the treatments and tabulate the results.

Suppose that, instead of a booklet or a questionnaire, the subjects in one condition receive a new drug while the subjects in the second condition receive a placebo. An easy way to assign subjects in equal numbers to these two conditions is, first, to write each person's name on a slip of paper and then to "blindly" draw pairs of names. We flip a coin to decide which member of a pair will receive the new drug.

Another standard procedure uses a table of random numbers. Imagine we wanted to assign 120 subjects at random to either an experimental or a control condition based on the following 120 random digits (taken from a longer table on page 194):

10097	32533	76520	13586	34673
37542	04805	64894	74296	24805
08422	68953	19645	09303	23209
99019	02529	09376	70715	38311
12807	99970	80157	36147	

Suppose we decide to read across and down the first five-digit column (10097, 37542, and 08422) and have any odd numbers (1, 3, 5, 7, 9) designate the subjects assigned to the experimental group and any even numbers (0, 2, 4, 6, 8) designate those assigned to the control group. We would assign Subject 1 to the experimental condition (1), Subjects 2 and 3 to the control condition (0, 0), Subjects 4 through 8 to the experimental condition (9, 7, 3, 7, 5), Subjects 9 through 15 to the control condition (4, 2, 0, 8, 4, 2, 2), and so forth.

The technical name for a Type A design consisting of two groups is *simple randomized design;* we will have more to say about this design in a later chapter, where we show how to analyze the results statistically. However, suppose the subjects were to receive both treatments instead of just one treatment. We now have a Type B design, also called a *repeated-measures design* because the subjects are measured successively after each treatment. We will be using the subjects more efficiently because we are making use of the same subjects repeatedly, but a problem is that the order in which the treatments are administered may produce differences between successive measurements. For example, in developmental research, the children may be nervous when first measured, and they may perform poorly; later on, they may be less nervous, and they may perform better. To deal with problems of systematic differences between successive measurements, we use a method called *counterbalancing;* that is, some subjects randomly receive Treatment A before Treatment B, and the others randomly receive B before A (see also Box 7.1).

Another favorite *between-subjects* design is called a *simple factorial design,* because the two or more levels of each independent variable (or "factor") are administered in combination with the two or more levels of every other factor. For example, suppose a clinical researcher designed a study using the 2 × 2 layout in Table 7.2 (also called a *two-by-two factorial design*); it represents a between-subjects design in which a computer-simulated "male" or "female" therapist administers a standard form of psychotherapy to male and female college students (who play the role of patient). An easy way to assign "patients" in equal numbers to the four groups would again be to write each subject's name on a slip of paper

BOX 7.1	Latin Square Designs

One type of repeated-measures design that has counterbalancing built in is called the *Latin square design*. It is characterized by a square array of letters (representing treatment conditions) in which each letter appears once and only once in each row and in each column. For example, shown below is a Latin square representing the case in which the four treatments (A, B, C, and D) will be administered to all the subjects in a counterbalanced pattern:

	Order of administration			
	1	2	3	4
Sequence 1	A	B	C	D
Sequence 2	B	C	D	A
Sequence 3	C	D	A	B
Sequence 4	D	A	B	C

The subjects randomly assigned to Sequence 1 receive the treatments in the sequence A, then B, then C, and finally D. In Sequences 2 through 4, the treatments are administered in different sequences, BCDA, CDAB, and DABC, respectively. You will find discussions of these and other repeated-measures designs in more advanced texts (e.g., Keppel, 1991; Kirk, 1982; Rosenthal & Rosnow, 1991).

and to separate the names by sex. We then randomly draw one woman's name at a time and assign the first female subject to Condition A and the second to Condition B. We do the same for the men in order to assign male subjects at random to Conditions C and D, until we have filled our quota of male and female "patients" in the four cells (see also Box 7.2).

FOUR KINDS OF CAUSATION

Our previous discussions have noted that the purpose of scientific experiments is to show "what causes what," and before going any further in this chapter, it is important that you understand what scientists themselves mean by *causation*. Imagine the flight of a curve ball thrown by a pitcher at a professional baseball game. The batter swings and misses, while you ask yourself, "What caused the ball to break

TABLE 7.2	Two-by-Two Factorial Design	
	"Therapist's" Sex	
"Patient's" sex	Female	Male
Female	A	B
Male	C	D

BOX 7.2   Historical versus Random Controls

Some researchers deliberately avoid using randomization. For example, in bio-medical research it has been pointed out that the majority of published clinical trials have used historical controls rather than random controls (Sacks, Chalmers, & Smith, 1982). The term *historical control* means that subjects in the control condition(s) are recently examined patients with the same disorder as those in the experimental condition. Researchers who use historical controls justify their actions on the basis of ethical and practical considerations, the argument being that they avoid exposing the control subjects to possibly ineffective therapies and uncertainties.

Unfortunately, the use of historical controls may also result in poorly controlled experimental comparisons, because the experimental and historical-control groups may differ in important ways other than whether they have received the treatment or not. This problem was analyzed by a team of bio-medical researchers (Sacks et al., 1982) based on a literature search they conducted in several clinical areas (e.g., coronary artery surgery, the treatment of cirrhosis, the use of anticoagulants in heart attack cases, and the treatment of certain forms of cancer). In each area, Sacks et al. found that whether the controls were historical or randomized, the treated patients responded similarly to the same therapy but that the historical controls generally did worse than the randomized controls. The implication of this finding is that studies using historical rather than random controls yield results exaggerating the benefits of the treatment procedures investigated. The best protection against this problem is to assign the subjects to experimental and control conditions by some random procedure.

---

that way?" This is a question also pondered by Isaac Newton—not about baseballs, but about tennis balls. When you think carefully about questions of causation (such as this one), you begin to see that they have more than a single answer. Indeed, more than 2,300 years ago, Aristotle thought carefully about questions of causation (although it was not baseballs or tennis balls that stimulated his interest) and came to realize that they can be answered in four distinct ways.

One answer concerns what is called the *material cause,* which is the substance or substances necessary for the movement or coming into being of the effect. According to the physics of baseball (R. K. Adair, 1990), the roughness on the surface of the ball and the nature of fluid flow constitute the material cause of its unusual movement—and make it hard to hit. A ball with a smooth surface tends to have a smooth flight to the plate, especially if it passes through the air at a speed less than 50 miles per hour. A ball with rough seams that travels at a speed over 50 miles per hour begins to encounter turbulence, particularly when it is thrown in a special way to take advantage of the nature of airflow.

A second answer concerns the *formal cause,* which is the plan or development that gives meaning to the event. In this instance the idea of throwing a curve ball is formally initiated in the mind of the catcher, who then communicates the plan to the pitcher, who in turn thinks "curve ball" up to the moment the ball is released.

A third answer, termed the *final cause* (also called *teleological*, which means the action is "goal-directed"), refers to the objective or end purpose of the event. In this case it is the objective of having a ball "break" as it nears the plate, so that the batter will not be able to hit the pitch squarely.

And finally, a fourth answer is the *efficient cause,* or the activating force or event that was responsible for the effect. In the baseball example, the efficient cause is the actual throwing of the ball, which causes it to travel at an optimal velocity and causes its trajectory to deviate from the original horizontal direction of motion.

How may we translate these four causes in the case of human behavior? For human development, for instance, we may say that (1) cellular structure is the material cause; (2) DNA or genetics is the formal cause; (3) physiological aging in relation to time is the final cause; and (4) parenting as an environmental variable is the efficient (i.e., activating or instigating) cause. It is this fourth cause that experimenting scientists generally have in mind when they say that something *causes* something else to occur.

THREE CRITERIA OF EFFICIENT CAUSATION

How do scientists actually arrive at the conclusion that one thing activates or instigates something else (e.g., "Smoking causes cancer" or "Frustration causes aggression")? This question has three answers: covariation, temporal precedence, and internal validity.

First, scientists look for evidence that the independent variable *(X)* and the dependent variable *(Y)* are mutually related (or *covary*). That is to say, they ask whether the presence (and absence) of *X* (the cause) is actually correlated with the presence (and absence) of *Y* (the effect). When they find that *X* and *Y* show a satisfactory correlation, they have evidence of *covariation*. What constitutes "satisfactory" correlation? We will save this question for Chapter 12, where we return to the idea of effect size (described in the previous chapter) and also discuss the mechanics of statistical significance testing.

Second, scientists look for evidence that *Y* does not occur until after *X* occurs or is set in motion (called *temporal precedence*). In other words, they ask whether there is clear-cut evidence to support the assumption that the "cause" actually came before the "effect." In relational research it is frequently hard to find incontrovertible evidence of temporal precedence because we are looking at *X* and *Y* in retrospect. We will have more to say about this subject in the next chapter, but it can sometimes be argued on logical grounds, even retrospectively, that *X* must surely have come before *Y*. Suppose we have found satisfactory evidence of covariation between gender and height and want to underscore which is the independent variable and which is the dependent variable. Common sense leads us to conclude that gender is more likely to determine height than that height is to determine gender, because a person's gender is biologically established at conception.

Third, scientists look for logical and evidential ways to rule out competing explanations of the relation between *X* and *Y*. In other words, they try to rule out plausible rival hypotheses that may undermine the causal interpretation (i.e., they look for evidence of *internal validity*). To be sure, human beings are not clairvoyant, and therefore there is a human limit on how successful this effort can be. That is, we cannot realistically expect to anticipate all plausible rival hypotheses because we cannot look into the future. Nevertheless, some methodologists have attempted to compile lists of conditions that may undermine validity; we will have more to say about this approach later.

The bottom line, however, is that working even within the limited framework of these three criteria (covariation, temporal precedence, and internal validity), scientists find they must settle for the most compelling evidence *available* of efficient causality, even if that evidence is inconclusive. In other words, *causal inference* is always subject to some degree of uncertainty.

UNCERTAINTY OF CAUSAL INFERENCE

As an illustration, imagine we discovered an outbreak of strange psychological symptoms and wanted to explain them in causal terms. We might begin by interviewing some or all of those afflicted, with the aim of finding an event they have in common. Our interviews suggest that all of them have been taking a new prescription drug whose side effects have not yet been fully established. We now suspect the drug may be the efficient cause of the strange symptoms in some persons at least. Shall we take a sample of subjects and arrange to give half of them the suspected drug? That procedure would allow us to compare two groups of people to see whether those given the drug are more likely to develop the strange symptoms. But the ethical cost of such experimental research would be too high, because we would *not* be willing to expose people to a drug we had good reason to believe harmful.

As a practical alternative, we could compare persons who have been given the new drug by their physicians with those persons whose physicians have not prescribed the drug. If only those given the drug developed the new symptoms, the drug would be more seriously implicated. But its causal role would still not be fully established, because those patients given the new drug may differ in a number of ways from those not given the drug. Not the new drug, but a correlate of being given the drug may be the causal variable.

However, among those patients given the drug, some will very likely have been given large dosages, whereas others will have been given small dosages. If it turns out that persons on larger dosages suffer more severely from the new symptoms, will this evidence implicate the drug more strongly? We cannot be certain about the causal role of the drug, because those given larger dosages may have been more ill to begin with. In this case, the illness for which the drug was prescribed, rather than the drug itself, may be the "cause" of the symptoms.

How have we done? "Not very well," you might answer. To prove temporal precedence, we need to show that taking the drug preceded the symptoms. Unless our medical records go back far enough, however, we cannot prove that the symptoms did not occur until after the drug had been taken. The covariation proof requires us to show that the drug is related to the symptoms. Even if we can show that taking the drug is correlated with the mysterious symptoms, it might be argued that, in order to be susceptible to the drug, a person already has to be in a given state of distress. According to this argument, it is not the drug, or *not only* the drug, that is related to the symptoms. If the subjects who were in a state of distress are the only ones who have been given the drug, it is possible to explain the observed relationship by arguing that the subjects have been "self-selected" into the treatment groups. Thus the subjects' state of distress has determined the particular group in which they find themselves. What we seem to need is a comparison group of other subjects who were in a similar state of distress but have not been given the drug.

Despite the difficulty of clear inference in this example, we might still be convinced by strong circumstantial, though inconclusive, evidence. Thus, if persons taking the drug are more likely to show the symptoms, if those taking more of the drug show more of the symptoms, and if those taking it over a longer period of time show more of the symptoms, we would be reluctant to say that the drug is *not* the efficient cause of the symptoms. Even if we were unwilling to say that the drug is *surely* at the root of the symptoms, at least on the basis of the type of evidence outlined, it might well be prudent to act "as though" it were.

If there were not a troublesome question of ethics, a simple randomized design—in which the drug is given to subjects randomly assigned to an *experimental group* and is not given to subjects in a *control group*—would allow us a more controlled comparison of the rates at which distress occurs. Such control also embodies certain "logical methods" (or propositions) popularized by the 19th-century English philosopher John Stuart Mill—after whom they came to be known as *Mill's methods*. As we see next, two of those methods—agreement and difference—together provide the logical basis of all simple randomized designs.

MILL'S METHODS AND THE LOGIC OF CONTROL

First, the *method of agreement* states, "If X, then Y," X symbolizing the cause and Y the effect. The statement means that, if we find two or more instances in which Y occurs, and if only X is present on each occasion, it follows that X is a *sufficient condition* of Y. That is, X is "adequate" to bring about the effect, or stated another way, an effect will be present when the cause is present. In baseball, we would say that the cause (X) of getting on base (Y) is a "sufficient condition" because it is brought about by getting a hit $(X1)$, being walked $(X2)$, or being struck by a pitch $(X3)$.

Second, the *method of difference* states, "If not-X, then not-Y." The statement means that if Y does not occur when X is absent, X is a *necessary condition* of Y. That is, X is "absolutely essential" to bring about the effect, or stated another way, the effect will be absent when the cause is absent. To win in baseball (Y), it is "necessary" to score the most runs (X); not scoring any runs (not-X) will therefore result in not winning (not-Y).

To take these ideas one step further, suppose that X represents a new and highly touted tranquilizer, and Y represents a change in measured tension. We give a group of subjects who complain of tension a certain dosage of X, and they show a reduction in measured tension. Can we conclude from this before-and-after observation that the tranquilizer caused the reduction in tension? Not yet, because even if we had repeatedly found that giving X was followed by tension reduction, we would have implied only that X is a sufficient condition of Y. What we seem to require is a control group with which to compare the reaction in the first group. For our control, we use a group of comparable subjects to whom we do not give drug X. If these subjects show no tension reduction, we have implied that X may be a necessary condition of Y.

We can diagram this research design as follows, and we see that it corresponds precisely to Mill's methods:

Experimental group	Control group
If X, then Y	If not-X, then not-Y

Can we now conclude that taking the drug led to tension reduction? Yes—but with the stipulation that "taking the drug" implies something more than getting a chemical into the blood system. "Taking the drug" means among other things (1) having someone give the subject a pill; (2) having someone give the subject the attention that goes with pill giving; (3) having the subject believe that relevant medication has been administered; and (4) having the ingredients of the drug find their way into the blood system of the subject.

Usually, when testing a new drug, the researcher is interested only in the subject's physical reaction to the active ingredients of the medication. The researcher does not care whether the subjects will feel better if they merely *believe* they are being helped, because this fact (i.e., the power of suggestion) has already been established. But if researchers know about the power of suggestion, how are they to separate the effects of the drug's ingredients from the effects of pill giving, of the subjects' expectations of being helped, and of other psychological variables that may also be sufficient conditions of Y? The answer is by the choice of a different (or an additional) control group. So this time, we use not a group given nothing, but a group given something that differs only in the ingredients whose effects we would like to establish. The need for this type of control is so well established in drug research that virtually all trained investigators routinely use a *placebo-control group*. The general finding is that placebos are often effective and are sometimes even as effective as the far more expensive drug for which they serve as the control.

In this research we used a no-pill control group (called a *zero-control group* because it receives nothing, not even a placebo) and a placebo-control group. Assuming there is often a choice of groups, how can we decide what design to use? If there are two groups, the groups should be as similar as possible except for the effect of interest. If the groups to be compared differ in some factor other than that effect, the influence of this factor is said to be *confounded* (i.e., mixed up) with the effect of interest. In choosing a design, the researcher tries to control for potentially confounding effects while isolating the effect of interest. In practice, there are two complementary approaches to this problem, and we will describe each of them.

CAMPBELL'S APPROACH TO RESEARCH DESIGN

One approach is that pioneered by Donald T. Campbell and his associates (e.g., Campbell & Stanley, 1963; Cook & Campbell, 1976, 1979), who developed master lists to help us check for plausible threats to validity. The idea is to look up all the plausible threats we can think of and, accordingly, to choose the most adequate design. Table 7.3 shows a portion of such a master list for finding the plausible threats to internal validity (i.e., the approximate validity by which we can infer that a causal relationship exists). We will give a more detailed description of each design in a moment, but *history,* as the term is used here, refers to an uncontrolled event that occurs between the premeasurement and the postmeasurement and that can bias the postmeasurement. *Maturation* refers to certain intrinsic changes in the research participants, such as their growing older, wiser, stronger, or more experienced between the premeasurement and the postmeasurement. *Instrumentation* refers to intrinsic changes in the measuring instruments, such as deterioration. *Selection* also refers to the subjects, but in this case the threat to internal validity comes from the selection of the subjects or their assignment to particular treatments.

Notice that Designs 1 and 2 are called *preexperimental designs,* by which Campbell et al. meant that these designs lack comparison (or *control*) conditions. Unless an outside standard of comparison is available, neither 1 nor 2 is of much help to us in establishing causality. The symbols are defined as follows: X = the exposure of

TABLE 7.3	Sources of Internal Invalidity for Two Preexperimental Designs and the Solomon Four-Group Experimental Design			
	Sources of invalidity			
	History	Maturation	Instrumentation	Selection
1. Preexperimental: one-shot case study X O	–	–	not relevant	–
2. Preexperimental: one-group pre-post O X O	–	–	–	+
3. True experimental: four-group design I R O X O II R X O III R O O IV R O	+	+	+	+

Note: A minus (–) means the source of invalidity is not controlled, while a plus (+) means the source of invalidity has been controlled.

Source: Experimental and Quasi-Experimental Designs for Research. by D. T. Campbell and J. C. Stanley, 1963, Rand McNally. Copyright © 1966 by Houghton Mifflin Company. Reprinted with permission.

a treatment group to an experimental variable or event; O = an observation or measurement; R = the random assignment of subjects to separate treatment groups; a negative (−) sign indicates a definite weakness in terms of internal validity; and a positive (+) sign denotes that the source of internal invalidity is controlled. We can now flesh out the three designs with some examples.

First, an illustration of Design 1 (called a *one-shot case study* by Campbell) would be the introduction of a new educational treatment designed to improve students' concentration and then the use of an achievement test to measure their performance. Because no allowance is made for a comparison with the reactions of students who have not been subjected to the educational treatment, the design is deficient in almost all categories of internal validity. However, instrumentation is not a factor, because the subjects are measured only once in the study.

Second, Design 2 (labeled a *one-group pre-post study*) is a slight improvement on the first design, in that the students are measured before and after exposure to our educational treatment. Still, no allowance is made for a comparison with the reactions of other students who have not been exposed to that treatment. Before going on, let us examine each of the four threats to internal validity listed in Table 7.3: history, maturation, instrumentation, and selection.

SOME THREATS TO INTERNAL VALIDITY

 First, history is a threat when the inferred causal relationship is confounded by an irrelevant event that occurs between the pretest and the posttest. As noted in Table 7.3, Designs 1 and 2 are especially vulnerable to such confounding because specific contaminating events occurring before the postmeasurement are not controlled for and assessed by either design. Suppose that a sudden snowstorm results in an unexpected cancellation of classes. Neither design allows us to isolate the effects on motivation of a school closing, or to assess that factor apart from the effects of the new educational treatment designed to improve concentration.

 Second, maturation is a threat when it is not the variable of interest, but the inferred causal relationship is nevertheless confounded by the respondents' growing older, wiser, stronger, more experienced, and the like between the pretest and the posttest. Imagine a study in which the posttest is given one year after the pretest. If the students' concentration has improved as a result of their getting older, so that they have become better at the task, we cannot tell whether the gains are due to their maturing or to their being subjected to a particular educational treatment.

 Third, instrumentation is a threat when an effect may be due to unsuspected changes in the measuring instruments between the pretest and the posttest. As noted in this table, this potential source of confounding is relevant to Design 2 but not to Design 1. In the case of our educational treatment, we might ask whether the effect is caused by the instability (i.e., deterioration) of the measuring instrument or to changes in the students that are caused by the treatment. Or suppose the "instruments" are actually judges who are asked to rate the subjects. Over time, judges may become better raters of student concentration, in which case the confounding is due not to "instrument" deterioration but to "instrument" improvement.

Fourth, selection is a threat when there are important, unsuspected differences between the subjects in each condition. (This problem is especially salient in certain quasi-experimental designs, discussed in the next chapter.) In Design 1 there is no way of knowing beforehand anything about the state of the participants, because they are observed or measured only after the treatment has been administered. The addition of an observation before the treatment in Design 2 results in an improvement over Design 1; it enables us to ascertain the prior state of the participants.

The master lists developed by Campbell and his associates describe and catalog other threats to internal validity, as well as specific threats to external validity (discussed later) and construct validity. In the case of construct validity, for example, Campbell et al. advocated the use of many methods, rather than a single method, to assess how results may converge (or zero in) on the particular construct used as a "scaffolding" between the independent and dependent variables. The threats to internal validity in Table 7.3 give us a flavor of how Campbell's suggested approach works, and we turn now to Design 3 as a way of drawing a link between Campbell's and a more traditional approach to choosing experimental and control groups and then teasing out the effects.

This third design in Table 7.3, which is another example of a two-by-two factorial design, is known as the _Solomon design_, after Richard L. Solomon, the experimental psychologist who first proposed it (Solomon, 1949). There are many possible factorial designs, but this one provides an elegant introduction to the logic of a more traditional approach to experimental design. This approach relies on logic to make broad comparisons—sometimes even multiple comparisons (as will be shown in a moment)—instead of relying on a master list to reveal all the plausible threats to validity associated with specific designs. The assumption behind the traditional approach (also a limitation of Campbell's approach) is that, in principle, it is impossible to enumerate and rule out all validity threats. To illustrate how the traditional approach works, we will describe a research problem that was investigated by Solomon and his associate Michael Lessac (Lessac & Solomon, 1969). Afterward, we will return to Campbell's procedure, in order to underscore the complementary nature of the two approaches.

SOLOMON'S APPROACH TO RESEARCH DESIGN

The primary purpose of Lessac and Solomon's study was to discover the effect of isolation on behavioral development in order to confront certain hypotheses proposed as plausible alternatives to the so-called critical-period hypothesis. This hypothesis postulates that there are optimum periods in the life of an infant during which it learns to make adaptive responses to its environment (see, e.g., Columbo, 1982). On the basis of the critical-period hypothesis, it had been predicted that withholding certain stimulation early in an organism's development would impede the learning of sensory and motor associations important in adult behavior. However, Lessac and Solomon took issue with this prediction, because in their view the critical-period hypothesis ignored two alternative explanations of the same effect. First, they reasoned that early deprivation may destroy not the opportunity to learn, but an already-formed perceptual-motor pattern that triggers further development. Second, they reasoned that early deprivation may result in unusual patterns that interfere with already-formed perceptual-motor patterns.

In other words, whereas the assumption of the critical-period hypothesis kept normal perceptual-motor patterns from forming, the two rival hypotheses raised by Lessac and Solomon were that normal perceptual-motor capabilities exist at birth but are destroyed (Rival Hypothesis 1) or are interfered with (Rival Hypothesis 2) by the experience of deprivation. To rule out these two rival hypotheses, Lessac and Solomon realized that they needed to know the organism's capabilities before it underwent the experimental treatment. That is, they needed to know whether the organism had had the perceptual-motor skills before it was subjected to a state of isolation. The design question they faced was how to find out this information without actually contaminating the organism by specifically testing it.

It is actually not a very hard question to answer—and you may already have guessed the answer based on what you know about the purpose of randomization—but the answer does present ethical problems. Simply stated, to uncover such evidence, we would need to test the organisms at birth. The design problem, of course, is that we must also figure out a way to control for this pretesting, because it constitutes extraneous stimulation that may be confounded with the effects of the experimental treatment. However, all we need to do is randomly assign a sample of newborn infants to two groups, one of which is tested on perceptual-motor capabilities at birth and the other of which is placed in isolation. Afterward, we would use the pretest scores from the group tested at birth to estimate how the unpretested group *would have* responded had it also been tested at birth. Randomization is designed to minimize any biased differences between the two groups by giving each infant an equal opportunity of being assigned to either group by chance. The ethical problem, however, is that it would be absurd even to consider working with human subjects. Facing this insurmountable problem, Lessac and Solomon decided on an alternative procedure (although many people may have ethical objections to this procedure as well), which was to work with an animal model (in this case, beagle pups).

Still, the elegance of the Solomon design is illustrated not by the way it allows us to get the pretest scores without actually contaminating the subjects, but instead by the ability of this design to address a more subtle question: Besides wanting to discover the effects of isolation, Lessac and Solomon were also interested in finding the effect of measuring an organism on the effect of isolation. This more subtle effect—which we refer to as the *confounding of pretesting and* X— involves the possibility that the pretest sensitizes the organism to respond differently to the experimental treatment than if the organism had not been pretested (also called *pretest sensitization*). How does this design allow us to tease out this effect? Once you grasp the answer to this question, you will have a better understanding of the logic of experimental design. Before proceeding, however, you need to understand clearly what is going on in each of the four groups.

In Part A of Table 7.4, we see the Solomon design displayed in the form of a two-by-two factorial design. Notice that Group I is pretested, then receives the experimental treatment, and later is retested. Group II is not pretested but does undergo the same experimental treatment as Group I. Group III is pretested and retested but is treated normally instead of being subjected to the experimental treatment. Group IV gets only the posttest. In Lessac and Solomon's (1969) experiment, the subjects were beagle pups that were randomly assigned to one of the four groups shown in Table 7.4. Those pups assigned to Groups III and IV were reared normally, in the same way that they would have been in a kennel, whereas those assigned to Groups I and II were raised in isolation in $18 \times 24 \times 30$-inch aluminum cages through which light entered only by a 2½-inch space between the bottom tray and the door. All the pups were fed and medicated at the same time, and the dependent measures (e.g., how they responded to their physical environment and on various tests of learning) were obtained for all groups after one year had passed.

ANALYZING THE SOLOMON DESIGN

Now that you know what went on in each condition, we return to the logical problem of how to separate the effects.

First, we use Groups I and III (the pretested groups) to estimate the pretreatment performance levels in Groups II and IV (the unpretested groups). In other words, without actually pretesting Groups II and IV, we can make a good guess of

---

TABLE 7.4　The Solomon Four-Group Research Design

A. Displayed as 2 × 2 Table

| | Treatment conditions | |
Pretest procedure	Isolation	Control
Pretested	Group I	Group III
Not pretested	Group II	Group IV

B. Plausible Causal Events

| | Outcome Measures | | | |
Causal Events	$\overline{Y}_I$	$\overline{Y}_{II}$	$\overline{Y}_{III}$	$\overline{Y}_{IV}$
Pretest–posttest effect	*	0	*	0
Experimental treatment effect	*	*	0	0
Pretest and X sensitization	*	0	0	0
Extraneous effects	*	*	*	*

Note: Asterisks (*) refer to the presence—and zeros (0) to the absence—of the causal events shown in the left-hand column.

Source: Reproduced from *Essentials of Behavioral Research: Methods and Data Analysis* (2nd ed., p. 86) by R. Rosenthal and R. L. Rosnow, 1991, McGraw-Hill. Used by permission of McGraw-Hill, Inc.

the pretest scores in both groups. This guess will require a leap of faith because we cannot be *absolutely* sure what the pretest performance in the unpretested groups would have been. Even if the value of the pretest in Group I is identical to that in Group III, we can only *assume* that the values are close to those that would have been obtained by Groups II and IV. Suppose that, in randomly allocating subjects to conditions, the experimenter was very careful with some groups and not as careful with others. If the pretest values in Groups I and III differ greatly (because of bias in the assignment of subjects), there is still a possibility that the unknown pretreatment performance in Groups II and IV would have been similar to the mean of Groups I and III (because of the greater attention paid to the random allocation of subjects to these conditions).

Second, on the basis of our estimate of the pretreatment performance levels in Groups II and IV, we can enrich our comparison of the performance scores in these groups. That is, we can estimate the pre-to-post effects of isolation without having contaminated the experimental and control groups by pretesting. In the study by Lessac and Solomon, such a comparison led to the conclusion that psychomotor development is not merely retarded by isolation but is distorted by it.

Third, this design can tell us whether there was any *confounding of pretesting and* X. To find this out, we can use a subtraction-difference procedure, in which we systematically compare the different cell means. For a demonstration of this comparison, we refer to Part B of Table 7.4, which shows the four plausible causal events affecting the performance outcomes in each treatment group. The symbol $\overline{Y}$ (with a bar) indicates that these are mean values. An asterisk (*) indicates that the event noted (the pretest, the treatment, pretest sensitization, or extraneous events) is considered a plausible causal event; a zero (0) indicates that the event is not considered relevant.

We see that the average outcome in Group I ($\overline{Y}_I$) can be affected by the pretest, the treatment, pretest sensitization, and extraneous events. The average outcome in Group II ($\overline{Y}_{II}$) can be affected only by the treatment and any extraneous events, because there was no pretest to produce a sensitization effect. The performance outcome in Group III ($\overline{Y}_{III}$) can be affected by the pretest and any extraneous events, but by no other conditions because there was no treatment to produce a sensitization effect. The performance outcome in Group IV ($\overline{Y}_{IV}$) can be affected by extraneous events, but by no other conditions. To assess the direction and magnitude of any pretest sensitization, we compare $(\overline{Y}_I - \overline{Y}_{III}) - (\overline{Y}_{II} - \overline{Y}_{IV})$. A positive difference-between-differences tells us that the confounding of pretesting and X enhances the effect of the treatment; a negative score tells us that it has a weakening effect (see also Box 7.3).

CAMPBELL'S PROCEDURE REVISITED

We return now to Campbell's procedure, and Table 7.5 shows several designs recast into the checklist framework, with the additional listing of two threats to *external validity* (i.e., the approximate validity by which we can infer that the causal relationship can be generalized across alternate types of persons, settings,

---

BOX 7.3   Pretest Sensitization

Although the confounding of pretesting and *X* is not always a problem (Lana, 1969), it does seem to surface in certain kinds of studies. For example, Solomon (1949) conducted an experiment in which teachers equated grammar school classes for spelling ability. Solomon pretested different groups of children on a list of words of equal difficulty by having the children spell the words. The children were then given a lesson on the rules of correct spelling and afterward were tested on the same list of words. The results suggested that taking the pretest made the children more resistant to the spelling lesson.

In another study, Doris R. Entwisle (1961) investigated her subjects' ability to learn the state locations of large U.S. cities. The results suggested that pretest sensitization aided recall in high-IQ subjects and was "mildly hindering" in average-IQ subjects. In an experiment involving attitude measurements, Rosnow and Suls (1970) used the Solomon design to study pretest sensitization to a persuasive message. They found that pretest sensitization enhanced receptivity to the message in volunteer subjects and reduced receptivity in nonvolunteer subjects.

---

times, and measures of the cause and effect). The table also shows two experimental designs that were not previously shown in Table 7.3, but that can be carved out of the Solomon design. One threat to external validity is the confounding of pretesting and *X,* that is, the pretest sensitization problem. The second threat to external validity is the *confounding of selection and* X, as illustrated by the study performed by Horowitz (described at the end of the previous chapter). For example, this second threat might be illustrated by the confounding of the subjects' volunteer status with the effects of the experimental treatment (to be discussed in Chapter 9).

Specifically, we see that Design 4 (called here a *pre-post control-group design*) consists of Groups I and III of the Solomon design, and that Design 5 (labeled a *posttest-only control-group design*) consists of Groups II and IV of the Solomon design. Except for the two sources of external invalidity noted, there is no loss in the relative validities of the two-group designs as compared to the Solomon four-group design. Design 4, however, is deficient in its control of the possible confounding of pretest sensitization, which may be a problem in attitude change and learning experiments (as noted in Box 7.3). Design 5 is not flawed in this way because the subjects are measured only after the manipulation of *X*. Design 5, even though unconfounded in this respect, would not have been a good choice in the Lessac and Solomon study because they raised specific questions that could be answered only by estimating the state of the pups' psychomotor skills before the isolation began. Design 5, although perhaps less precise and less powerful than Design 4, would be clearly preferable when the situation does not warrant pretesting.

TABLE 7.5	Some Sources of Internal and External Invalidity for Three Randomized Experimental Designs					
	Sources of Internal Invalidity				Sources of External Invalidity	
	History	Maturation	Instrumentation	Selection	Confounding of Pretesting and X	Confounding of Selection and X
3. Solomon four-group design I R O X O II R X O III R O O IV R O	+	+	+	+	+	?
4. Pre-post control-group design I R O X O III R O O	+	+	+	+	–	?
5. Posttest-only control-group design II R X O IV R O	+	+	+	+	+	?

Note: A minus (–) means the source of invalidity is not controlled; a plus (+) means the source of invalidity has been controlled; a question mark (?) indicates a possible source of concern.

Source: *Experimental and Quasi-Experimental Designs for Research,* by D. T. Campbell and J. C. Stanley, 1963, Rand McNally. Copyright © 1966 by Houghton Mifflin Company. Reprinted with permission.

All three designs are subject to concerns about the possible threat to external validity resulting from the confounding of selection and X. *

Subject and Experimenter Artifacts

In Chapter 4 the terms *reactive* and *nonreactive* were used to distinguish measurements or observations that do (reactive) from those that do not (nonreactive) affect the object being measured or observed. When an engineer carefully takes the dimensions of a large piece of metal, we do not suppose that the act of measurement will have an effect on the metal. Similarly, when a biologist observes the movements of a paramecium, we should not expect that the paramecium will change its behavior when the scientist is looking at it through a microscope. However, one may be less sure of the risks of reactive observation when beagle pups or

*Tables 7.3 and 7.5 are by no means an exhaustive list of the sources of internal and external invalidity. Interested readers will find additional discussions in Cook and Campbell (1976, 1979) and Brinberg and Kidder (1982).

primates are the object of study. Is the pup's or the chimpanzee's behavior apt to be affected by its awareness of having captured the attention of the behavioral scientist? With human subjects, of course, the problem of reactive observation is even more salient.

The term used to refer to this problem is *artifact*, which means a finding that results from conditions other than those intended by the experimenter (see Rosenthal & Rosnow, 1969). However, artifacts are not simply serendipitous findings, but findings resulting from uncontrolled factors that may jeopardize the validity (internal, construct, and external) of the researcher's conclusion about what went on in the study or about the implications of the results. In the remainder of this chapter we will give an overview of the work in this area (called the *social psychology of the experiment*) and note some ways that subject and experimenter artifacts are addressed.

THE GOOD SUBJECT EFFECT

The notion of subject artifacts proceeds from the idea that much of the complexity of human activity described by behavioral scientists lies in the nature of the human organism that serves as the model: the research subject. We know, for example, that no two research subjects behave identically, and therefore the "same" careful experiment conducted in one place at one time may yield results very different from those of an experiment conducted in another place at another time. Although it is generally accepted that much of this complexity is due to the complexities of human nature, it is recognized that most subjects know perfectly well that they are research participants and that they are to play this role in interaction with the experimenter. The role of research subject appears to be well understood by most normal adults who find their way into behavioral scientists' subject pools (J. G. Adair, 1973; Danziger, 1988; Rosenthal & Rosnow, 1969, 1975b; Silverman, 1977; Strohmetz & Rosnow, 1994; Suls & Rosnow, 1988). Therefore, what one researcher interprets as a causal relation between X and Y, another researcher may theorize to be the relation between some role variable and Y (i.e., a plausible rival explanation).

Pioneering work in the *social psychology of the experiment* was done by Martin T. Orne, whose interest in subject artifacts grew out of his research on hypnosis. The results of that research led him to theorize that the trance manifestations that subjects exhibit on entering hypnosis are partly determined by their motivation to "act out" the role of a hypnotized person. Both their preconceptions of how a hypnotized person ought to act and the cues communicated by the hypnotist of how the subjects should behave—called "demand characteristics" by Orne (see also Box 7.4)—were viewed by Orne as plausible determinants of the subjects' expectations concerning how this role was to be enacted (Orne, 1962, 1969, 1970). In particular, Orne postulated that typical volunteers for hypnosis research have a predisposition to act out the role of the *good subject*, which is to say the kind of subject who tries to give experimenters what they ostensibly want to find.

For example, Orne (1959) tested whether subjects in experimental hypnosis would behave in whatever ways the demand characteristics led them to believe

BOX 7.4	Demand Characteristics and the Good Subject

The extent to which some research participants will comply with demand characteristics sometimes surprises even the experimenter. At one point in his hypnosis research, Martin Orne (1962) tried to devise a set of dull, meaningless tasks that nonhypnotized persons either would refuse to do or would try for only a short time. One task was to add thousands of rows of two-digit numbers. Five and a half hours after the subjects began, the experimenter gave up. When the subjects were told to tear each worksheet into a minimum of 32 pieces before going on to the next, they *still* persisted.

Orne suggested that the subjects were so compliant because they gave meaning to a meaningless chore. Perhaps they thought that no matter how trivial and inane the task seemed to them, the experimenter certainly had an important scientific purpose that justified their work. Feeling that they had a stake in the outcome of the study, the students may have rationalized that they were making a useful contribution to science by acquiescing in the experimenter's demands. This motive is not uncommon among many research subjects, Orne contended. The "good subject" tries to comply with what he or she sees as the experimenter's scientific desires.

were characteristic of hypnotized subjects. He first concocted a novel characteristic of hypnosis, "catalepsy of the dominant hand," which he demonstrated to a large college class by using volunteers in a lecture on hypnosis. The volunteers were given the posthypnotic suggestion that on entering a "trance" they would manifest catalepsy (rigidity) of the dominant hand. The class was instructed that catalepsy of the dominant hand was a "classical" reaction of the hypnotized subject, and attention was called to the fact that the right-handed subject exhibited catalepsy of the right hand and the left-handed subject exhibited catalepsy of the left hand. In another lecture section, intended to serve as a control group, the demonstration of hypnosis was also performed, but there were no demand characteristics concerning catalepsy of the dominant hand. A few weeks later, students from both classes were invited to serve as the research subjects in a study of hypnosis. When they arrived at the laboratory and were hypnotized, catalepsy of the dominant hand was found to be present in almost all the subjects who had attended the lecture asserting that the response was characteristic of the hypnotized state. None of the subjects in the control condition exhibited the catalepsy response.

To help researchers eliminate any confounding effects of demand characteristics, Orne has proposed that *quasi-control subjects* be used (Orne, 1962, 1969). These are subjects who step out of their traditional roles and serve as "co-investigators" (that is, rather than as "objects of study" for the experimenter to investigate). Such subjects are usually drawn from the same population as the experimental and control subjects, but the quasi-control subjects are instructed to reflect on the context in which the experiment is being conducted. They then talk about how they think the situation might influence their behavior if they were in the experimental group. For example, the participation of a few subjects in the experimental group may be interrupted at different points during the course of the experiment. They then become quasi-control subjects, who are carefully interviewed about what they perceived to be the demand characteristics of the experiment.

EXPERIMENTER EXPECTANCY AND ITS CONTROL

On the other side of the artifact coin are experimenter artifacts, that is, sources of bias (or systematic error) resulting from uncontrolled intentions or actions of experimenters themselves. There are a number of such sources (see Rosenthal, 1966), but the one we describe here is by far the most intriguing because it occurs when the experimenter's expectations serve as *self-fulfilling prophecies* (an idea raised in Chapter 4). In a self-fulfilling prophecy, someone prophesies an event, and this prophecy or expectation then changes the behavior of the prophet in such a way as to make the predicted event more likely to occur. For example, a teacher who believes that certain pupils are especially bright may act more warmly toward them, teach them more material, and spend more time with them. Over time, this behavior may result in greater gains in achievement for those students than would have occurred in the absence of the teacher's positive expectation (Rosenthal & Jacobson, 1968).

In one early study of *experimenter expectancy*, 12 student experimenters were each given five rats that were to be taught to run a maze with the aid of visual cues (Rosenthal & Fode, 1963). Half the students were told their rats had been specially bred for maze-brightness, and the remaining students were told their rats had been bred for maze-dullness. Actually, there were no differences in the rats. At the end of the experiment the results were clear. Rats run by experimenters expecting brighter behavior showed significantly better learning than rats run by experimenters expecting dull behavior. The study was repeated, this time using a series of learning experiments, each conducted in a Skinner box (Rosenthal & Lawson, 1964). Half the student experimenters were led to believe their rats were "Skinner-box-bright," and half were led to believe their animals were "Skinner-box-dull." Once again, there were not really any differences in the two groups of rats, at least not until the results were analyzed at the end of the study. Then, the allegedly brighter animals really were brighter, and the alleged dullards were really duller. We should emphasize that the experimenters' expectations acted on the actual performance of the animals, not simply on the evaluation of the animals' performance. In addition, neither of these studies showed any evidence that the experimenters were trying to generate false data (i.e., they were not cheating).

One strategy for dealing with this problem calls for the use of *blind experimenters*, that is, experimenters who are unaware of ("blind" to) which subjects have received the experimental treatment and which the control treatment. The assumption is that if experimenters do not know what treatment the subject has received, they are unlikely to communicate expectancies about the efficacy of that treatment. The necessity of keeping the experimenters blind (i.e., unaware) is well recognized in the area of biomedical research. No pharmacological study is taken completely seriously unless it has followed elaborate *double-blind* procedures (i.e., in which neither the subjects nor the experimenters know who is in the experimental and control groups).

This principle of ensuring "blindness" may also be applicable to the role of other participants in the research. For example, cognitive psychologists Kathy Hirsh-Pasek and Roberta Michnick Golinkoff (1993) used a novel method to study language comprehension in infants and toddlers, which the researchers called the "preferential looking paradigm." Suppose we want to study noun comprehension in order to find out how early in their lives infants and toddlers are able to distinguish a shoe from a hat. An infant is seated on a blindfolded parent's lap approximately 2½ feet away from a pair of television monitors. By means of a concealed speaker, the word *shoe* is sounded at the same time that one of the monitors shows a shoe and the other monitor shows a hat. A camera records the child's preferential looking behavior over a series of paired-comparison trials using many different stimuli. Blindfolding eliminates the possibility of the parent's unintentionally signaling the correct response by some reflex or other movement.

Another approach to the experimenter expectancy problem is to use a factorial design that not only assesses whether an expectancy effect is present but also allows a direct comparison of that effect with the phenomenon of theoretical interest (called an *expectancy control design*). To achieve this design, the scientist uses certain conditions of experimenter expectancy as a second independent variable to be varied along with the factor of theoretical interest (Rosenthal, 1966, p. 381).

Table 7.6 sketches a two-by-two expectancy control design. Cell A represents the condition in which the experimental treatment is administered to subjects by a data collector who expects the occurrence of the treatment effect. Cell D represents the condition in which the absence of the experimental treatment is associated with a data collector who expects the nonoccurrence of the treatment effect. But ordinarily the investigator is interested in the treatment effects unconfounded with experimenter expectancy. The addition of the appropriate expectancy control groups will permit the evaluation of the treatment effect separately from the expectancy effect. Subjects in Cell B are those who will receive the experimental treatment but who will be contacted by an experimenter who does not expect a treatment effect. Subjects in Cell C are those who will not receive the experimental treatment but who will be contacted by an experimenter who expects a treatment effect.

Illustrative of the use of this between-subjects design in animal research is a study reported by J. Randolph Burnham (1966), with the results shown in Table 7.7. Each of 23 student experimenters ran one rat in a T-maze discrimination task (i.e., a runway with the starting box at the base and the goal at one end of the

TABLE 7.6	Basic Expectancy Control Design	
	Expectancy	
Actual treatment	Experimental	Control
Experimental	A	B
Control	C	D

TABLE 7.7	Expectancy Control Design Used to Study Discrimination Learning in Rats as a Function of Brain Lesions and Experimenter Expectancy		
	Expectancy		
Brain state	Lesioned	Unlesioned	Totals
Lesioned	46.5	49.0	95.5
Unlesioned	48.2	58.3	106.5
Totals	94.7	107.3	

Source: Burnham (1966), as reanalyzed by Rosenthal (1976).

crossbar). Portions of the brains of approximately half the rats had been surgically removed. The remaining rats had received only sham surgery, which involved a cut through the skull but no damage to brain tissue. The purpose of the study was explained to the student experimenters as an attempt to learn the effects of lesions on discrimination learning. Expectancies were manipulated by labeling each rat as lesioned or unlesioned. Some of the really lesioned rats were labeled accurately as lesioned, but some were falsely labeled as unlesioned. Similarly, some of the really unlesioned rats were labeled accurately as unlesioned, but others were falsely labeled as lesioned.

By comparing the totals in the row and column margins, we get an idea of the relative effectiveness of (1) the manipulation of the brain state of the animals and (2) the manipulation of the students' expectancies concerning the brain state of the animals. The higher the scores, the better were the rats' performances. We see that rats that had been lesioned did not perform as well as those that had not been lesioned. We also see that the rats that were believed to be lesioned did not perform as well as those that were believed to be unlesioned. The logic of this design is that it enables us to compare the magnitude of the effect of experimenter expectancy with the magnitude of the effect of the actual removal of brain tissue. We see that, in this case, the two effects were similar.

SUMMARY OF IDEAS

1. A "true" experimental design calls for randomization, which guards against potential sources of bias.
2. Randomization (i.e., random assignment) procedures include coin flipping and using a table of random digits to allocate the sampling units or treatment condition in an unbiased way.
3. Between-subjects and within-subjects designs—which are distinguished, respectively, by whether each sampling unit is measured on one or more than one occasion—include simple randomized and factorial between-subjects designs and Latin square within-subjects designs.

4. Aristotle described four kinds of causality: material, formal, efficient, and final (or teleological).
5. To help us decide when one thing is the efficient cause of another, we attempt to establish covariation, temporal precedence, and internal validity.
6. In practice, we find that we must frequently settle for the best available evidence even if it is inconclusive.
7. The notion of control embodies Mill's methods of agreement and difference, as basically reflected in simple randomized designs.
8. Campbell's approach to research design uses a checklist of threats to validity, including threats to internal validity such as history, maturation, instrumentation, and selection.
9. Preexperimental designs, such as a one-shot case study or a one-group pre-post study, make no effort to control for threats to internal validity.
10. The Solomon design, a type of factorial design, enables us to isolate the effect of pretest sensitization.
11. The pre-post control-group design and the posttest-only control-group design are components of the Solomon design.
12. The *good subject* (a term coined by Orne) is sensitive and accommodating to demand characteristics.
13. The use of quasi-controls, in addition to regular controls, helps us to ferret out potential demand characteristics.
14. Experimenter expectancy may cause the experimental hypothesis to become a self-fulfilling prophecy.
15. Blind procedures are used to control for expectancy effects; an expectancy control design allows us to isolate and compare the expectancy effect with the effect of the independent variable of theoretical interest (e.g., Burnham's study of discrimination learning in rats).

KEY TERMS

artifact *p. 161*

between-subjects designs *p. 144*

blind experimenters *p. 163*

causal inference *p. 150*

confounding *p. 152*

confounding of pretesting and *X*
    p. 156

confounding of selection and *X*
    p. 159

control conditions *p. 151*

counterbalancing *p. 146*

covariation *p. 149*

demand characteristics *p. 161*

double-blind *p. 163*

expectancy control design *p. 164*

experimenter expectancy *p. 163*

external validity *p. 158*

factorial designs *p. 146*

final cause *p. 149*

formal cause *p. 148*

good subjects *p. 161*

historical controls *p. 148*

history *p. 153*

instrumentation *p. 153*

internal validity *p. 150*

Latin square designs *p. 147*

material cause *p. 148*

maturation *p. 153*

method of agreement *p. 151*

method of difference *p. 151*

REVIEW QUESTIONS

1. A Colby student wants to evaluate the effectiveness of a popular method of boosting self-esteem called *I'm-better-than-OK* therapy. In this therapy, clients read pop psychology books, compliment themselves while looking in a mirror, and have group touch-a-lot sessions. What kind of subjects would you recommend be used in the student's control group(s)?

2. A Villanova student believes that positive reinforcement increases self-esteem. To test this hypothesis, she administers a self-esteem scale to 40 other students and correlates the scores with their grade-point averages. Can you think of any limitations in this research design?

3. An Auburn student tells his subjects that he is interested in identifying the characteristics associated with good leadership skills. He then administers two measures titled Social Intelligence Survey and Interpersonal Problem-Solving Ability. Do you see any potential problem in this method?

4. A student at the University of New Mexico wants to prove that eating chocolate chip cookies will cure depression. What basic requirements of inference would he have to meet, according to J. S. Mill?

5. An American University student wants to use an expectancy control design to assess a program offering individual tutoring to enhance students' performance on achievement tests. How might she set up this design?

6. A well-known manufacturer of pain relievers wants to market what seems to be a revolutionary new product: a near-cure for the common cold. Researchers in the R & D division select 1,000 persons to participate in a test study. Each participant is observed for six months. For the first three months, baseline data are collected. For the last three months, the participants take a weekly dose of the common-cold cure. Sure enough, 15% of the participants contracted a cold during the first three months, whereas only 5% do so in the second three months. The investigators rush their findings to the company president, who must decide whether the data are convincing enough for the company to put

the product on the market. Can you think of any weakness in the research design?

7. On a quiz, University of Arkansas students are asked how the Solomon design allows researchers to rule out the possibility of confounding the pretest and the results of the treatment. What is the answer? The same students are also asked to define the following threats to internal validity: history, maturation, selection, and instrumentation. Do you know the answers?

8. A Howard University medical student designs an experiment to test the effects of a new drug. In consultation with her faculty mentor, she decides to include both a placebo-control group and a zero-control group. Do you know the difference?

Answers to review questions are found on pages 320–334.

CHAPTER 8

Nonrandomized Research Designs

PREVIEW QUESTIONS

➤ **W**hen are between-subjects and within-subjects designs called *quasi-experimental?*

➤ **W**hat circumstances invite the use of nonrandomized research designs?

➤ **H**ow do nonequivalent-groups designs attempt to compensate for possible initial differences?

➤ **H**ow are necessary and sufficient causation inferred from circumstantial evidence?

➤ **H**ow are graphs used to display time-series results?

➤ **H**ow do single-case experimental designs allow us to make a comparison of effects?

➤ **H**ow do cross-lagged panel designs attempt to identify causation?

➤ **H**ow might cohort and cross-sectional designs lead to different conclusions?

USES OF QUASI EXPERIMENTATION

In the previous chapter, you saw how "true" experiments use randomized treatment conditions to make causal inferences. The basic idea is to use an unbiased procedure to allocate sampling units (e.g., research subjects) to treatment conditions so that the groups differ only in respect to the treatment of interest. For either practical or ethical reasons, true experiments are not always possible, however. The term *quasi* means "resembling," and the between-subjects and within-subjects designs we now discuss are called *quasi-experimental* because in some ways they resemble true experiments. That is, quasi experiments also have treatments, outcome measures, and sampling units, but they do not use randomization to allocate sampling units to treatment conditions.

For example, suppose we wanted to study whether cigarette smoking causes heart disease and lung cancer in human beings. To perform a true experiment, we would have to randomly assign some nonsmokers to a treatment condition that requires them to smoke for many years. Because that procedure would be an ethical absurdity, we might instead conduct a relational or a quasi-experimental study in which we observed the association of heart attack and lung cancer to smoking. Association is not the same thing as "causation" because some hidden confounding factor may make people smoke—and also give them heart attacks and lung cancer. However, the best we may be able to do under the circumstances is to try to make sure that the nonsmokers in our study are as similar as possible to the smokers on as many relevant variables as possible (Freedman et al., 1991).

We will describe the causal reasoning in quasi-experimental studies, which may be like that used by an epidemiologist trying to uncover the cause of an outbreak of food poisoning based only on circumstantial evidence (see also Box 8.1). In particular, we will describe three broad categories (and several subtypes) of nonrandomized research designs of either the between-subjects or within-subjects type: (1) nonequivalent-groups designs; (2) time-series designs (e.g., single-case experimental designs); and (3) correlational designs (e.g., cross-lagged designs and longitudinal designs using cohorts).

NONEQUIVALENT-GROUPS DESIGNS

Nonequivalent-groups designs are between-subjects designs in which the subjects are assigned to experimental and control groups by means other than randomization and are measured before and after the treatment. Suppose that a court-ordered treatment program for reducing drinking and driving is to be evaluated by a team of behavioral researchers (Vaught, 1977). Based on joint decisions by the judge, the research institution's administrators, the volunteer program coordinator, and the researchers, the subjects are to be assigned to one of four condi-

BOX 8.1	Causal Reasoning in the Doctor's Office

In one class of quasi experiments discussed later, the reasoning sometimes resembles that used by a doctor working with a single case. For example, suppose your hand has been bitten by a dog. You go to a doctor, who prescribes a tetanus shot and an oral antibiotic. You ask the doctor to give the tetanus shot in your bad arm so that you will have your good arm to use. But the doctor points out that if she did so and you had a reaction to the tetanus, she would not be able to separate it from the possible continued reaction to the dog bite—which could, in the worst-case scenario, also cause the arm, not just the hand, to swell. For this reason, she gives the shot in your good arm, so any swelling due to an allergy to the tetanus will not be confounded with a possible reaction to the dog bite. Her causal reasoning will be based on a comparison of her before and after observations.

tions: (1) use of the drug Antabuse (which causes an unpleasant reaction if alcohol is consumed); (2) group psychotherapy administered by clinical psychologists or psychiatric social workers; (3) a volunteer program along the lines of Alcoholics Anonymous (AA); and (4) a zero control condition (i.e., no treatment of any kind). The construct to be investigated—that is, examined both before and after the intervention or control treatment—is the subject's set of attitudes, as measured by interviews and an attitude questionnaire.

This design would be a true experimental design if subjects were assigned randomly. What makes it into a quasi-experimental design is a number of unanticipated problems. First, the volunteer program (AA) accepts only individuals who attend of their own accord. True experimental designs require that the assignment of the subjects to the treatments be unbiased, but AA insists that subjects choose for themselves whether to enter this treatment condition (i.e., it insists on *self-selection*). Second, the judge feels a moral obligation to assign the worst offenders to the drug or group psychotherapy conditions, and certainly not to the zero control condition. Third, administrators at the institution conducting this research are worried about the legal risks of random assignment. They believe that the institution may be sued by repeat offenders who find themselves assigned to a condition not to their liking, or by future victims of participants assigned to the zero control condition.

Faced with such considerations, a true experiment will be impossible because the researchers cannot assign the subjects to the treatments at random. The compromise design is as follows:

$$
\begin{array}{ccc}
O & X_1 & O \\
\hline
O & X_2 & O \\
\hline
O & X_3 & O \\
\hline
O & & O
\end{array}
$$

where X_1 = the drug Antabuse; X_2 = the group psychotherapy; X_3 = the AA program; and O = the attitudinal measures at the beginning and the end. The absence of R (randomization) signifies that random assignment will not be used.

What are some alternative ways of increasing the likelihood that the groups to be compared will actually be similar to one another? One way to try to overcome objections to random assignment is to propose randomization *after* assignment (Vaught, 1977). After the subjects are assigned to Groups I, II, and III, each group might be randomly divided into experimental and control subgroups; the experimental subgroups will receive the assigned experimental treatment, and the controls will receive nothing. Within the groups, the experimental and control subgroups should be comparable because both are a part of the original assignment group. Of course, the reasons we cannot randomize to begin with (e.g., legal and ethical constraints) may also prevent randomizing after assignment. Nevertheless, this approach works when the treatment programs are oversubscribed and cannot accept all candidates at once in any case. Thus the random allocation of some candidates to a waiting-list control condition is sound both scientifically and ethically.

Another alternative is to try to match the groups as closely as possible on demographic variables, such as age, sex, and socioeconomic status. However, matching implies the biased dropping of subjects if the groups differ on the matching variables, and the judge would no doubt find this alternative unacceptable. One alternative is to include these nonmatching subjects in the treatment programs, but not in the data analysis.

INFERRING CAUSATION FROM CIRCUMSTANTIAL EVIDENCE

We have noted that inferential risk must be considered in *any* investigation, and we will return to this issue in a later chapter when we discuss statistical significance testing. In quasi-experimental research, we see that the primary risk results from the nonrandom assignment of the sampling units to the treatment conditions. In the previous chapter, we alluded to this problem when we talked about "selection" as a threat to internal validity. In quasi-experimental research, investigators often emulate the causal reasoning of the experimental approach in order to reach causal inferences that are as sound as possible (i.e., working within the intrinsic limitations of the research; see Cook & Campbell, 1979). For example, imagine we want an epidemiological question answered, but we have only circumstantial evidence. We may still be able to simulate the "experimental" approach to causal inference by using Mill's methods (see again pages 151–152) to reach highly justified conclusions about the necessary and sufficient conditions of Y.

By analogy, Table 8.1 helps to illustrate this approach (Kahane, 1986). Imagine that we are trying to track down the cause of food poisoning in five people (Mimi, Nancy, Michele, John, and Sheila). Initially, we learn that they all ate at the same fast-food restaurant. We discover that one of them drank a milkshake (which *may*

TABLE 8.1	Illustration of Agreement and Difference Methods			
Persons	Ate burger	Ate fries	Ate salad	Drank shake	Got food poisoning
Mimi	Yes	Yes	No	No	Yes
Connie	No	Yes	No	No	No
Greg	No	No	Yes	Yes	No
Nancy	Yes	Yes	Yes	No	Yes
Jeffrey	No	Yes	No	No	No
Michele	Yes	Yes	Yes	Yes	Yes
John	Yes	Yes	Yes	No	Yes
Sheila	Yes	No	No	No	Yes

Source: Adapted from *Logic and Philosophy: A Modern Introduction* (6th ed.) by H. Kahane, 1989, Wadsworth. Used by permission of Howard Kahane and Wadsworth Publishing Co.

have contained spoiled ingredients that no other milkshakes contained); three of them ate a salad (which *may* have had spoiled dressing that no other salads had); four of them ate particularly greasy french fries; and all five of them ate a particularly greasy hamburger. What should we conclude? If we can safely assume that all the people in Table 8.1 would have been found healthy in a pretest, maybe we have a "kind" of nonequivalent-groups design.

On the surface, the one common factor is the greasy hamburger. However, the owner tells us that the food handler was feeling ill the day these people were served. He worked for a while but then asked to be excused after he complained of feeling dizzy and nauseous. Is it possible the food handler was the culprit? Suppose he touched some but not all of the foods eaten that day; maybe he passed on his germs in this way. His possible handling of Mimi's and Sheila's burger, Nancy's salad dressing, and Michele's and John's fries would be another factor common to all the cases. It is possible, in other words, that these particular foods were *sufficient* to bring about poisoning *(Y)*, but that the food handler's handling of them *(X?)* was the *necessary* condition.

We think we can safely rule out the food handler because he must have touched many more items than those implicated above. If he were the cause *(X)*, then others who ate at the restaurant should have become ill *(Y)*. However, this table shows that Connie, Greg, and Jeffrey did not get food poisoning (not-*Y*) even though they ate some of the same things the others ate *(X?)*—except for the greasy hamburger (the true *X?*). Only the burger was absent in every case in which there was no food poisoning. On the basis of this circumstantial evidence, we now believe that the greasy hamburger was the necessary and sufficient condition *(X)* that brought about food poisoning *(Y)*. This kind of causal reasoning on the basis of circumstantial evidence is typical of that used in certain quasi-experimental studies.

INTERRUPTED TIME-SERIES DESIGNS

A second basic class of quasi-experimental designs is the *interrupted time-series design,* in which the effects of a "treatment" are inferred from a comparison of the outcome measures obtained at different time intervals before and after the treatment is introduced. This data structure is called a *time series* because there is a single data point for each point in time, and it is called an *interrupted time series* because, presumably, there is a clear dividing line at the beginning of the *intervention* (i.e., a line analogous to the beginning of an experimental treatment). The level of statistical sophistication needed to analyze such designs properly is beyond the scope of this text (see, e.g., Cryer, 1986; Judd & Kenny, 1981), but it is nevertheless useful to have a general knowledge of how such designs work.

An early example is the work of social psychologists Leonard Berkowitz and Jacqueline Macaulay (1971), who were interested in whether highly publicized violent crimes are "infectious" (i.e., capable of causing a "contagion of violence" in the population). In the 19th century, a French sociologist (Gabriel de Tarde) argued that a number of violent crimes, having been sensationalized in news reports, had prompted similar crimes. For instance, news of the Jack the Ripper murders in London in 1888 had had this effect, Tarde argued, for within less than a year as many as eight identical crimes had been committed. To test Tarde's idea, Berkowitz and Macaulay decided to do a time-series analysis of FBI monthly counts of specific violent crimes in each of 40 cities for the seven years 1960–1966.

Berkowitz and Macaulay wanted to see whether Tarde's hypothesis held up for two sensational crimes in the United States: the assassination of President John F. Kennedy in Dallas on November 22, 1963, and the murder of eight nurses by Richard Speck in Chicago in July 1966. Two pieces of circumstantial evidence that seemed to support the contagion hypothesis were the murders committed by Charles J. Whitman and Robert Smith in the aftermath of the Speck crime. A month after the Speck murders, Whitman, an engineering student and former marine, killed his wife and mother in their homes and then went on a shooting spree from the top of a tower at the University of Texas, killing 14 and wounding 30 before he was shot to death by a police officer. About three months later, Robert Smith, an 18-year-old high school senior, walked into a Mesa, Arizona, beauty school and killed four women and a child. Afterward, Smith told the police that he had got his idea after reading the news stories of the Speck and Whitman crimes.

In choosing this approach, Berkowitz and Macaulay had to satisfy four basic requirements of any time-series analysis. First, they had to define the period of observation broadly enough to allow the outcome variable to be examined before, during, and following the intervention (i.e., the heavily publicized violent crime). Second, the same units had to be used throughout the analysis in order to ensure that the observations and time points would be equally spaced. Berkowitz and Macaulay could not, for example, use monthly observations for one year and then quarterly observations for another year, because they would not be exactly comparable. Third, the time points had to be sensitive to the particular effects of interest (e.g., increases in aggravated assaults). Fourth, the measurements could not fluctuate very much as a result of "instrumentation" changes (i.e., the obervations had to be reliable). Berkowitz and Macaulay reasoned that (1) the FBI data would provide an adequate number of data points (i.e., 84 months); (2) the same unit could be used throughout (i.e., monthly observations); (3) the crime data would be sensitive to the particular effects that interested them; and (4) the FBI crime data would also satisfy the reliability requirement.

Berkowitz and Macaulay sought to obtain a representative sample of cities by selecting four ranging in size from 260,000 to 1.4 million in each of 10 primary zip-code areas. They then ran various analyses of data from these 40 cities for different categories of crimes (e.g., aggravated assaults, robberies, and homicides). Figure 8.1 shows one of a number of such graphs that were constructed to show any increases or decreases in criminal violence during the observed period in the areas covered by the FBI data. This graph shows a significant increase in aggravated assaults during this 84-month period, with sharp increments after the Dallas assassination in particular and also after the Speck murders.

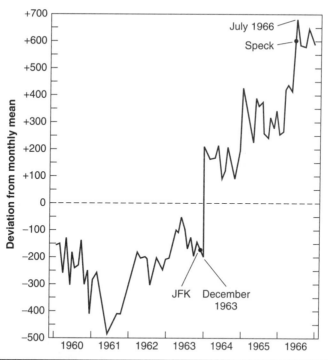

FIGURE 8.1 *Data for aggravated assaults. (Reproduced from L. Berkowitz and J. Macaulay, "The Contagion of Criminal Violence," Sociometry, 1971, 34, p. 251. Used by permission of Leonard Berkowitz and the American Sociological Association.)*

APPRAISING RIVAL AND CONVERGENT PREDICTIONS

A series of follow-up studies by David P. Phillips not only provides a fascinating twist on Berkowitz and Macaulay's work but also illustrates how rival and convergent predictions are tested in quasi-experimental studies. Phillips was interested in using the time-series approach to discover whether highly publicized executions or death sentences might have a deterrent effect on homicides. Earlier investigations of the deterrent effect of capital punishment had failed to find such an effect, but Phillips believed that those failures may have been due to the fact that the studies had examined yearly rather than daily or weekly homicide statistics and had failed to focus on *publicized* executions. Phillips (1980) began his investigation by searching the document sections of major libraries in the United States and England to find a period in which capital punishment had been widely publicized and for which weekly homicide statistics were also available. He noticed that from 1858 to 1921 there had been a number of heavily publicized English executions, and that weekly homicide statistics were also available for this period.

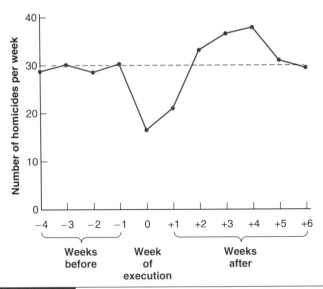

FIGURE 8.2   *The frequency of weekly homicides before, during, and after 22 publicized executions in England from 1858 to 1921. (Reproduced from D. P. Phillips, "The Deterrent Effect of Captial Punishment: New Evidence on an Old Controversy,"* American Journal of Sociology, *1980, vol. 86, pp. 139–148. Used by permission of David P. Phillips and the University of Chicago Press.)*

Figure 8.2 gives a composite picture of the results. It shows the number of homicides per week during each of the four weeks leading up to the week of the execution, as well as the number of homicides during each of the six weeks after the execution. Phillips conceptualized the week of the execution as the intervention period and the two weeks straddling this time as the control period. If there were no deterrent effect, we would expect the number of homicides in the intervention period to be at approximately the same level as in the control periods (i.e., a rival prediction). However, the composite picture tells quite a different story. It shows the number of homicides declining sharply leading into the week of the execution and then increasing sharply over the next few weeks before falling back to "normal." In other words, it seems that heavily publicized executions temporarily deterred some violent crimes, but that afterward there was a kind of "catching-up" period before things returned to normal.

In all research, though especially in quasi-experimental studies, it is important to think of additional predictions to test that should converge on the hypothesized relationship if it is true. In this case, for example, if a publicized execution deters some homicides, we should expect that the more the publicity devoted to the execution, the greater will be the drop in homicides. To test this convergent prediction, Phillips (1986) recorded the number of column inches in *The London Times* of articles devoted to each execution. In this way he was able to correlate the amount of space accorded to the execution and the number of homicides associated with it. Consistent with his additional prediction, he found a significant relationship between the amount of publicity and the drop in homicides in the week of the execution (see also Box 8.2).

SINGLE-CASE EXPERIMENTAL DESIGNS

A subclass of interrupted time-series designs goes by several different names: *single-case experimental designs, small-N experimental designs,* and *N-of-1 experimental designs*. All have the following characteristics: (1) only one unit is studied, or else only a few units are studied; (2) repeated measures are taken of the unit (i.e., a *within-subjects* design, as defined in the previous chapter); and (3) random assignment procedures are rarely used.* Although the unit is frequently a single subject (human or animal), it may also be a group, such as an assembly line, a class of students, or a shift in a plant (see also Box 8.3). In one case, for example, the unit was the offensive backfield on a football team of 9- to 10-year-olds, the purpose of the study being to test a schedule of feedback to improve their execution of plays (Komaki & Barnett, 1977). In another case, the unit was a community, and the objective was to encourage drivers to use child safety seats by rewarding them with coupons they could exchange for a seat and training in its use (Lavelle, Hovell, West, & Wahlgren, 1992).

Single-case experimental designs have also found a niche in educational, clinical, and counseling settings as a tool for evaluating the effects of operant conditioning interventions (Hersen & Barlow, 1976; Kazdin & Tuma, 1982). In operant conditioning (described in Chapter 2), one way to strengthen behavior is to use posi-

---

*It is, of course, impossible to assign a single subject at random to the various treatment procedures. Instead, the occasions (e.g., at intervals of days, weeks, or months) may be assigned at random to the various treatment procedures, and the results are then compared.

| BOX 8.2 | Testing Additional Predictions |

In another study, Phillips and Hensley (1984) tried still another time-series test of their hypothesis. This time, they examined daily homicides in the United States between 1973 and 1979 (comprising more than 140,000 deaths!). Instead of confining their analysis to executions, they examined a range of heavily publicized death sentences, executions, life sentences, acquittals, and even heavyweight championship prize fights. Their idea was that each of these events could be conceptualized as falling along a reward–punishment continuum (with prize fights at the reward end; death sentences, executions, and life sentences at the punishment end; and acquittals somewhere in the middle). When they examined homicide fluctuations from 0 to 4 days after the publicized events, they found that the drop in homicides following the publicized punishments was not canceled out by a subsequent rise in homicides above normal.

BOX 8.3	Superstition in the Pigeon

In a fascinating single-case study by B. F. Skinner (1948), the unit was eight hungry pigeons. The birds were housed in cages in which there was a food hopper (containing grain) that swung into and away from the cage at regular intervals. A timing mechanism automatically moved the hopper into the cage so that all the pigeon had to do was reach into the hopper and eat. But six of the birds developed "superstitious" movements, in that whatever they had been doing in the moment when they were first rewarded with food became imprinted. One pigeon made counterclockwise motions about the cage before taking the grain; another performed a tossing motion of the head; and others persisted in making pendulum-type motions of the head and body or brushing movements toward the floor.

tive reinforcement (i.e., to reward the behavior), and one way to weaken behavior is to use extinction (i.e., no longer reinforcing the response). Such designs use observations of the subject's behavior before the experimental treatment has been applied as a *behavioral baseline,* operationally defined as the continuous, and continuing, performance of the individual (Sidman, 1960, p. 409). When the observations after the treatment are compared with these baseline observations, each subject serves as its own control.

For example, in a seminal study by R. Vance Hall, Diane Lund, and Dolores Jackson (1968), a single-case experimental design was used to track the effects of interventions used in the classroom to modify the behavior of a child named "Robbie." During a class spelling period, the psychologists had observed that Robbie studied only 25% of the time. The rest of the time his behavior was disruptive: He snapped rubber bands, played with toys in his pocket, slowly drank his milk and played with the milk carton, and laughed with those around him. Almost 55% of his teacher's attention was absorbed by this disruptive behavior.

The psychologists believed that the teacher's attention was maintaining Robbie's disruptive behavior. To modify his behavior, they decided to use a twofold intervention: (1) ignoring the nonstudy and disruptive behavior (extinction) and (2) attending to the study behavior (positive reinforcement). Whenever Robbie engaged in 1 minute of continuous study, the observer would quietly signal the teacher and she would come over and compliment him, saying such things as, "Good work, Robbie." The second part of Figure 8.3 shows Robbie's increased study behavior during the nine sessions of this stage. Then, to verify the effect of the teacher's attention, the consequences were reversed. The teacher ignored Robbie, remaining with the group. His study behavior decreased to about 50% over these five sessions. When reinforcement was restored, Robbie's study behavior increased to and leveled off at about 75%. A checkup over the following weeks, when the teacher continued to praise his study behavior, showed that Robbie continued to study. Robbie's academic performance also increased, with a

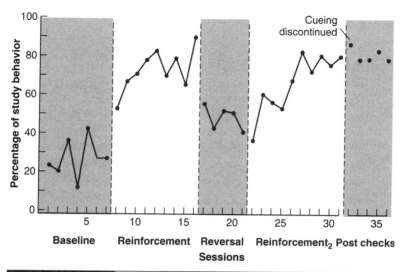

FIGURE 8.3 *Robbie's study behavior record. (Reproduced from R. V. Hall, D. Lund, and D. Jackson, "Effects of Teacher Attention on Study Behavior,"* Journal of Applied Behavior Analysis, *1968, 1, 1–12. Used by courtesy of R. Vance Hall and the* Journal of Applied Behavior Analysis.*)*

jump in spelling accuracy from fewer than 5 words correct out of 10 to 9 correct out of 10.

The design used in this study has a number of variants. Let us start with the basic model, the *A-B-A design*. It evolved out of an even simpler prototype, the *A-B design*, which is the simplest of all single-case designs and is used to study the effects of clinical, counseling, and educational interventions. The so-called A phase is the baseline (or pretreatment) period, and in the B phase, the intervention (i.e., the independent variable) is introduced. In an A-B design the dependent variable is measured repeatedly throughout the baseline and intervention phases of the study. In the A-B-A design the treatment is withdrawn at the end and the behavior is measured; that is, there are repeated measures before the intervention, during the intervention, and then with the intervention withdrawn.

A number of other single-case designs are used in clinical intervention assessment. In the *A-B-BC-B design*, for example, B and C are two therapeutic conditions. The symbol *A* tells us that the individual's behavior is measured or observed (1) before the introduction of either intervention; (2) during Intervention B; (3) during the combination of B and C; and (4) during B alone. The purpose of this design is to evaluate the effect of B both in combination with C and apart from C. Still another basic variant is the *A-B-A-B design*. Here the strategy again ends in a treatment phase of B, but this model provides two occasions (B to A and then A to B) for demonstrating the positive effects of the intervention (Hersen & Barlow, 1976). Although the interpretation of single-case results typically depends on visual inspection, there are also standard statistical techniques for evaluating the effects (see, e.g., Kazdin, 1976; Kratochwill & Levin, 1992).

CROSS-LAGGED PANEL DESIGNS

The largest general class of quasi-experimental designs is called *correlational. Correlation* is actually a catchall term for odds and ends of relational research designs (i.e., designs that allow us to see "how things are in relation to other things"—discussed in Chapter 1). The term *correlational* is not really a helpful description in this case, because correlations are what one looks for in true experiments as well (i.e., evidence that the cause and the effect covary). Nevertheless, we will describe two common examples of designs that are lumped together as correlational: *cross-lagged panel designs* and *longitudinal designs using cohorts*. We will begin with a discussion of the former.

A *cross-lagged panel design* is called *cross-lagged* because, although it is basically another variant of a time-series design, some data points are treated as temporally "lagged" (or delayed) values of the outcome variable. It is called a *panel design* because, in social survey terms, a *panel study* is another name for a *longitudinal study* (i.e., a study that examines the change in a person or a group of people over an extended period of time), and the roots of this design are in longitudinal investigations in sociological survey research. When invented in the 1940s, longitudinal measurements of the same two variables, A and B, were assumed to provide information about any causal relationships between the variables (Lazarsfeld, 1978). In other words, even though nonexperimental, the cross-lagged panel design was originally intended to be a method for choosing among competing causal hypotheses (Campbell & Stanley, 1963; Lazarsfeld, 1978; Pelz & Andrew, 1964; Rozelle & Campbell, 1969).

You will recall that the correlation coefficient is a measure of the mutual relationship between two variables or measurements; we gave as an example the Pearson *r*. It will be recalled that *r*'s can range from −1.0 (a perfect negative relationship) through 0 (no relationship) to +1.0 (a perfect positive relationship). As illustrated in Figure 8.4, A and B represent two variables, each of which has been measured individually at two successive time periods. Three sets of paired correlations are also represented (called *test–retest, synchronous,* and *cross-lagged* correlations).

First, the two *test–retest correlations* (r_{A1A2} and r_{B1B2})—which indicate the reliability of A and B over time—refer to the relationship, respectively, between A1 and A2 and between B1 and B2. Second, the two *synchronous correlations* (r_{A1B1} and r_{A2B2})—which, when compared, indicate the reliability of the association between A and B over time—refer to the relationship, respectively, between A1 and B1 and between A2 and B2. Third, the two *cross-lagged correlations* (r_{A1B2} and r_{B1A2})—which show the relationships between two sets of data points, where one is treated as a lagged value of the outcome variable—in this case refer to the association, respectively, between A1 and B2 and between B1 and A2.

The causal question concerns whether A is a more likely cause of B than B is of A, or whether A causes B to a greater extent than B causes A. The basic logic used

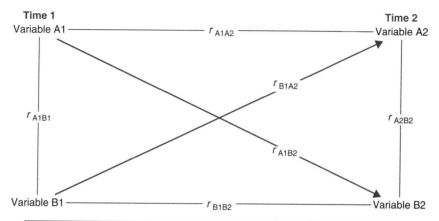

Time 1
Variable A1 ——————— r_{A1A2} ——————— Variable A2 Time 2

r_{B1A2}

r_{A1B1} r_{A2B2}

r_{A1B2}

Variable B1 ——————— r_{B1B2} ——————— Variable B2

FIGURE 8.4 *Design for cross-lagged and other correlations between variables A and B. (Reproduced from R. Rosenthal and R. L. Rosnow,* Essentials of Behavioral Research: Methods and Data Analysis, *2nd ed., McGraw-Hill, 1991, p. 99. Used by permission of McGraw-Hill, Inc.).*

to arrive at the answer is that, given equally reliable test–retest correlations and synchronous correlations equal in magnitude, comparing the cross-lagged correlations should enable us to conclude which is the more likely causal direction, or which variable shows the preponderance of causal influence. Presumably, we would conclude that A is a more important cause of B than B is of A if r_{A1B2} is appreciably higher than r_{B1A2}. On the other hand, we would conclude that B is a more important cause of A than A is of B if r_{B1A2} is appreciably higher than r_{A1B2}. Let us use a real-life example to show how this design is used, and also to reveal the hidden problem of confounded hypotheses (i.e., competing confounded pairs of hypotheses).

Figure 8.5 is taken from a study by Louise H. Kidder, Robert L. Kidder, and Paul Snyderman (1976). These investigators used archival data in the *FBI Uniform Crime Reports* for 1968–1972 to explore the causal relationship between the size of a city's police force and the crime rate. This figure shows correlational analyses for 1968–1969 (as reported in Kenny, 1979, pp. 235–236). The variables noted are the number of police (A) and the number of burglaries (B) in 724 U.S. cities during each year. Looking first at the test–retest correlations (.86 and .89), we see that both the number of police and the number of burglaries were reliable during this two-year period. That is, cities with a lot of police in 1968 had a lot of police in 1969, and also cities with a lot of burglaries in 1968 continued to have a lot of burglaries in 1969. The synchronous correlations of .47 and .39 between the number of police and the number of burglaries for 1968 and 1969, respectively, were substantial in magnitude.

At first glance, our intuition says that burglaries may cause an increase in the number of police. However, there are plausible rival hypotheses. For example, it

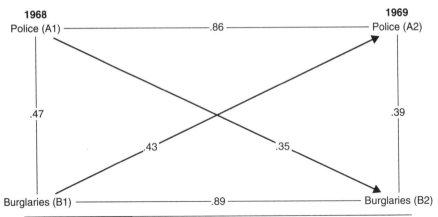

FIGURE 8.5   *Correlation of number of police and number of burglaries per capita measured in 1968 and 1969 in 724 cities. (Adapted from Kidder, Kidder, & Snyderman, 1976, by permission of L. H. Kidder.)*

might just as well be hypothesized that police increase burglaries, because the more police there are available, the more opportunities there are to keep thorough records of all the burglaries reported. That is, when there are not many police, some reported burglaries may go unrecorded. The cross-lagged correlations do not allow us to rule out either hypothesis and, in fact, provide some support for both (.43 and .35). If you think carefully, you are sure to come up with other rival hypotheses. There are statistical ways of trying to rule out rival causal hypotheses in cross-lagged designs, but they are not without problems (cf. Kenny, 1979; Rozelle & Campbell, 1969). As a consequence, such designs—which were used in the past with some frequency—are now treated with "skeptical advocacy" by leading methodologists (see Cook & Campbell, 1979, p. 309).

LONGITUDINAL DESIGNS USING COHORTS

Suppose we wanted to study the life course of some variable of interest. One possibility is to estimate maturational effects by using a cross-sectional design. A *cross-sectional design*, as the term is used in this section, is one that takes a slice of time and examines several age groups during one period. This approach would be a lot easier than, for example, examining people's responses or behavior over an extended period of time (i.e., a *longitudinal design*). An example would be a cross-sectional survey performed in 1994 to study the maturational effects of the variable of interest in cohorts born in 1954, 1964, 1974, and 1984. The purpose of the survey is to develop a growth curve of the effects of interest in people who are 10, 20, 30, and 40 years old.

The problem with this design is that 10-year-olds in 1994 may have had different life experiences from 40-year-olds in 1994, when they were 10 years old. That is, it is likely that children who are born and grow up in one period have quite different life events from children who are born and grow up in another period. Some of these experiences (e.g., schooling and repeated exposure to TV) may, in turn, systematically affect the normal development of the two groups. A *cohort* is a group of individuals who are born and grow up in the same period and thus have generally similar life experiences. The problem in research is that a possible confounding of cohort and maturation would be hidden in a design that failed to look at several cohorts longitudinally. Insofar as such experiences are associated with the variable of interest, we might be led to spurious conclusions about maturational effects if we relied solely on a cross-sectional design to find them (see also Box 8.4).

Table 8.2 illustrates how the relationship between age and another variable may be misinterpreted because of a reliance on the results of cross-sectional studies instead of on the results of longitudinal studies of cohorts. This table shows the results of a sociological study done in the Netherlands by Jacques A. Hagenaars and Niki P. Cobben (1978), in which data were compiled on the percentages of women with no religious affiliation, by age and time period. The results are shown for seven different cohorts (or generations) of women in the Netherlands. The values in the vertical rectangle beneath "Period 4" provide the basic data for a cross-sectional analysis, and the values in the parallelogram for "Cohort 4" provide the

BOX 8.4	Does IQ Bottom Out at 30?

At one time, it was believed that the age curve for intelligence increased to a maximum at age 30 and then declined. This belief was based on the results of cross-sectional studies, in which IQ tests had been given at the same time to younger and older persons (whose scores were then compared as a function of their calendar years). However, a quite different picture has emerged as a result of a longitudinal study of cohorts conducted by K. Warner Schaie (1993, 1994) and his associates. The researchers have gathered information on over 5,000 subjects during six major testing cycles (1956, 1963, 1970, 1977, 1984, and 1991). The participants are repeatedly given a battery of tests, including measures of mental abilities (i.e., spatial orientation, inductive reasoning, word fluency, verbal meaning, and number skill), attitudes, and so forth.

One finding is that there is no uniform pattern of IQ change, although, in general, intellectual abilities that are primarily genetically determined tend to decline before those that are primarily acquired through schooling and experience. Comparing the different cohorts, Schaie has observed that IQ test scores are declining less rapidly now in old age and that younger people are scoring lower now on tests. Other correlational results in this study suggest the possibility that being involved in an intellectually stimulating environment, having a flexible personality style, and having a "high cognitive" spouse slow down intellectual decline.

TABLE 8.2	Percentages of Women in the Netherlands with No Religious Affiliation According to Age and Time Period			
	Period 1 (1909)	Period 2 (1929)	Period 3 (1949)	Period 4 (1969)
Age 20–30	Cohort 4 4.8%	Cohort 5 13.9%	Cohort 6 17.4%	Cohort 7 23.9%
Age 40–50	Cohort 3 3.1%	Cohort 4 11.9%	Cohort 5 17.2%	Cohort 6 22.0%
Age 60–70	Cohort 2 1.9%	Cohort 3 6.7%	Cohort 4 11.9%	Cohort 5 19.4%
Age 80–	Cohort 1 1.2%	Cohort 2 3.8%	Cohort 3 6.6%	Cohort 4 12.2%

Note: An example of a cross-sectional design is shown by the vertical analysis (Period 4), and an example of a longitudinal design is shown by the diagonal analysis (Cohort 4).

Source: Reproduced from "Age, Cohort and Period: A General Model for the Analysis of Social Change" by J. A. Hagenaars and N. P. Cobben, 1978, *Netherlands Journal of Sociology, 14* pp. 58–91. Used by permission of J. A. Hagenaars and Elsevier Science Publishers.

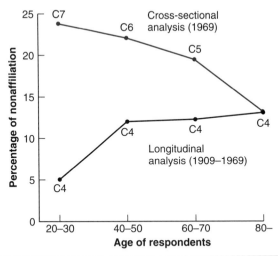

FIGURE 8.6   *Percentages of nonaffiliation with church of women in the Netherlands, as shown by a cross-sectional design in 1969 and a longitudinal design from 1909 to 1969. Cohorts are symbolized as C7 (Cohort 7), C6 (Cohort 6), and so forth. (Reproduced from J. A. Hagenaars and N. P. Cobben, "Age, Cohort and Period: A General Model for the Analysis of Social Change,"* Netherlands Journal of Sociology, *1978, vol. 14, pp. 58–91. Used by permission of J. A. Hagenaars and Elsevier Science.)*

basic data for a longitudinal analysis. Notice that the trends are opposite in these two sets of values and therefore lead to completely opposite conclusions.

A graph showing this difference appears in Figure 8.6; it allows us to compare the cross-sectional data for Period 4 (1969) with the longitudinal data for Cohort 4 in Table 8.2. The cross-sectional curve would mislead us to the conclusion that, with the passing of years and the approach of the end of life, religious observance increased (i.e., the percentage of nonaffiliation decreased) in these women. By contrast, the cohort curve tells us that the opposite was true: Religious observance actually decreased (i.e., the percentage of nonaffiliation increased) in these women as they became older.

Researchers who like to use longitudinal designs—including animal researchers (e.g., Fairbanks, 1993)—also attempt, whenever possible, to examine several cohorts cross-sectionally and longitudinally. In this way they learn about cohort changes as well as age group changes as a function of periods. Other informative uses of longitudinal designs are possible, although each is limited in certain predictable ways (for discussion, see Rosenthal & Rosnow, 1991, pp. 105–109). Thus, as stated earlier, it is a good idea to use several different strategies that allow convergence on the relationship of interest. Each strategy will be limited in some way, but the objective is to use several convergent procedures whose strengths and weaknesses will compensate for one another.

SUMMARY OF IDEAS

1. Three general classes of quasi-experimental designs are (a) nonequivalent-groups designs; (b) interrupted time-series designs; and (c) "correlational" designs.
2. In nonequivalent-groups designs, various strategies are used to try to compensate for nonequivalence, such as matching and randomized subgroups.
3. With quasi-experimental data, we may still be able to identify the necessary and sufficient causes of Y based only on circumstantial evidence.
4. Interrupted time-series designs typically use graphs to compare the effects of an intervention with the situation before and after it occurred (e.g., Berkowitz and Macaulay's study of highly publicized crimes).
5. Especially with quasi-experiments, it is essential to assess rival and convergent predictions (e.g., the series of studies by Phillips of publicized executions).
6. Single-case experimental designs, a subclass of time-series designs, come in many different forms (e.g., A-B-BC-B and A-B-A-B); the unit of study may be one or a few subjects (e.g., Hall et al.'s study of Robbie and Skinner's study of superstition in pigeons).
7. So-called correlational designs are misnamed because correlation (i.e., evidence of covariation) is also what true experiments look for.
8. In the cross-lagged panel approach, some data points are treated as temporally delayed values, and these cross-lagged correlations are analyzed along with test–retest and synchronous correlations for the direction of causation (e.g., Kidder et al.'s study of the number of police and the number of burglaries).

9. In studies in which age is the independent variable, a cross-sectional analysis may lead to spurious conclusions (e.g., the study of women's religiosity in the Netherlands).

10. To achieve optimal understanding, it is best to use multiple methods, each of which has its own but different limitations.

KEY TERMS

A-B design   *p. 179*

A-B-A design   *p. 179*

A-B-A-B design   *p. 179*

A-B-BC-B design   *p. 179*

behavioral baseline   *p. 178*

cohort   *p. 183*

correlational designs   *p. 180*

cross-lagged correlation   *p. 180*

cross-lagged panel design   *p. 180*

cross-sectional designs   *p. 182*

interrupted time-series designs   *p. 173*

longitudinal designs   *p. 182*

N-of 1 experimental designs   *p. 177*

nonequivalent-groups designs   *p. 170*

panel study   *p. 180*

self-selection   *p. 171*

single-case experimental designs   *p. 177*

small-*N* experimental designs   *p. 177*

synchronous correlation   *p. 180*

test–retest correlation   *p. 180*

REVIEW QUESTIONS

1. A University of Toledo student wants to assess the relationship between therapist approval, expressed in tone of voice, and degree of patient progress. Using a sample of 45 therapist–patient dyads, he measures these variables at the beginning and end of treatment. Based on the results shown below, what do you think he will conclude?

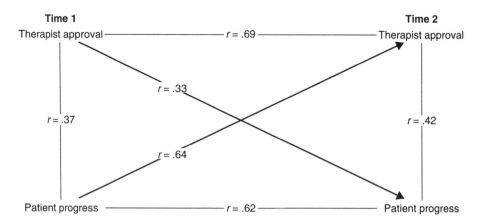

2. Using a cross-sectional design, an Oklahoma University student found a lower degree of androgyny in women aged 40–45 than in women aged 20–25. What confounding variable prevents him from concluding that androgyny decreases with age? Can you think of a better way to do the study?

3. A University of Nevada student wants to evaluate the effects of an educational intervention that is purported to motivate elementary-school children to do their homework. She had hoped to perform an experiment in which she would randomly assign large numbers of children in Reno either to the intervention treatment or to a control group. However, she ran into complications and found that she would not be able to use randomization. Can you think of some other ways that she might evaluate the effects of the intervention without the use of randomization? What are the limitations of each of these ways?

4. A Catholic University student wants to do a time-series analysis of the effects of assassination attempts against U.S. presidents but cannot decide on the dependent variable. What dependent variable would you advise her to track, and how would you suggest she locate the kind of data she needs for such a study?

Answers to review questions are found on pages 320–334.

CHAPTER 9

Survey Designs and Subject Selection

PREVIEW QUESTIONS

➤ What is the purpose of random selection, and how does it differ from random assignment?

➤ What is meant by the avoidance of bias and instability in survey designs?

➤ What is simple random sampling, and how is it done?

➤ What advantages does stratified sampling have over simple random sampling?

➤ What is the role of stratification in area probability sampling?

➤ What is nonresponse bias, and how is it minimized?

➤ How is nonresponse bias related to volunteer bias in experimental research?

➤ How is the direction of volunteer bias estimated, and what recruitment methods minimize this bias?

➤ What is the final step before implementing any study?

SELECTING THE RESEARCH PARTICIPANTS

In the two preceding chapters we examined the logic of some designs used in relational and experimental research, and in this chapter we turn our attention to prototypical designs used in survey research of the descriptive kind. In particular, we will focus on basic designs used to describe "how things are" in a specified larger pool by collecting information on a fraction of that pool. The name for the larger pool is the *population,* and the name for the fraction is the *sample.*

For example, professional pollsters use survey designs to map out people's opinions on a wide variety of issues, such as their fears of crime or their choice of political candidates. Instead of questioning every member of the population (which is usually impossible), the researchers focus on a segment assumed to be typical of the larger pool. Similar methods are used in epidemiological research, forensic research, economic research, and many other areas. For example, when health officials wanted to find out about trends in cases of tuberculosis contracted on the job, they used descriptive surveys of hospitals to make a count of reported employees with TB (Kilborn, 1994). As the federal courts became inundated with mass torts involving asbestos cases (averaging 1,140 per month in 1990, or one third of the federal criminal caseload), one solution was to sample asbestos cases from the total filed within a court's jurisdiction. The assessed damages in randomly sampled cases from each of five disease categories (mesothelioma, lung cancer, other cancer, asbestosis, and pleural disease) were then applied to each larger pool (Saks & Blanck, 1992).

How do researchers know that the segment is *representative* (or typical) of the larger pool? For example, how can they be sure that fears of crime in the sample duplicate percentages in segments of the population as a whole or that reported TB cases in sampled hospitals are representative of trends in all hospitals? To be *absolutely sure*, the researchers would have to know the characteristics of the population in advance. Of course, if they had such information, they would have no need of the sample at all. Instead, they rely on a blueprint for selecting the sample (called the *sampling plan*) that is generally based on *probability sampling*. This means that randomness enters into the selection process (also called *random selection*) at some stage so that the laws of mathematical probability apply (see also Box 9.1). What is the difference between random assignment (discussed in Chapter 7) and random selection? As explained earlier, random assignment refers to the unbiased allocation of sampling units to treatment conditions; it controls the differences in the groups to be compared so that differences will not bias the results of the experiment. As explained in this chapter, random selection increases the sampling units' *representativeness* of the larger pool of units from which they are drawn.

BOX 9.1   What Is Probability?

The term *probability* refers to the mathematical chance of an event's occurring. For example, at a racetrack we see horses that are "20-to-1 shots." This means that in the eyes of the odds setters this particular long shot will win about once in every 21 races, given the conditions under which the horse is currently running. Why should a horse ever beat other horses that are faster? Because of a relative uncertainty in the actions that determine the outcome of a horse race. The lead horse may stumble, the jockey on the second horse may fall off, and so forth. Unlikely? Yes—but that is why the track management is willing to pay 20-to-1 odds. This example gives us two ideas about probability: (1) it expresses uncertainty, and (2) it deals with chance. We will have more to say about this concept in later chapters.

We will begin by describing some basic concepts in survey sampling and will then turn to the logic and implementation of probability sampling plans. We will explain how such plans enable the researcher reasonably to assume—but never with certainty—that the sample is representative of its population. Of course, it is often impossible in experimental research (for practical or ethical reasons) to do probablity sampling. Instead, we may be forced to work with volunteers or some other *opportunity sample* (i.e., a sample made up of the first units that are available). Even in the most carefully conducted survey study, however, not everyone who is invited to participate will accept. We will discuss how survey researchers confront this problem of subject-selection bias (called *nonresponse bias*) and will then examine how experimenters cope with a similar problem called *volunteer bias*. Finally, we will underscore the importance of pilot-testing the research materials before implementing the full-scale study.

BASIC CONCEPTS IN SURVEY SAMPLING

Although survey studies can take many different forms, all are characterized by sampling plans in which every element, or sampling unit, in the population has a known nonzero probability of being selected. Two important statistical requirements of a probability sampling plan are (1) that the sample values be *unbiased* and (2) that there be *stability* in the samples. To be *unbiased*, the values produced by the sample must, on average, coincide with the "true" values of the population—although we can never actually be sure that this requirement has been met in a given study (i.e., unless we know the characteristics of the population). *Stability,* on the other hand, means that there is not much variability (or spread) in the sample values; stability can be directly measured by statistical procedures described in the next chapter.

Figure 9.1 helps us to see more clearly these two technical requirements. In the design, O denotes a particular sampling unit, X represents the true population mean, and the horizontal line indicates the underlying continuum on which the relevant values are determined. Suppose we were trying to estimate the number of widgets that teams of assembly-line workers make in a given period. In the diagram, O = a work team's output, X = the value we are trying to estimate, and the continuum ranges from a low to a high number. The distance between the true population value and the midpoint of the sampling units indicates the amount of *biasedness.* The spread (variability) among the sampling units indicates their degree of instability.

We see that the amount of instability is constant within each row, going from a high amount of instability (or spread) in row 1 to no instability in row 3. The amount of biasedness is constant in each column, going from a high bias in column 1 to zero bias in column 3. Thus, in the three cases in column 3, the sample values are balanced around the population mean, but with much instability in row 1, some in row 2, and none in row 3. In the three cases in row 3 there is no instability, but there is much biasedness in column 1, some in column 2, and none in column 3. The hypothetical case at the intersection of row 3 and column 3 represents the best of all situations, although it is unlikely that we will ever find such complete agreement.

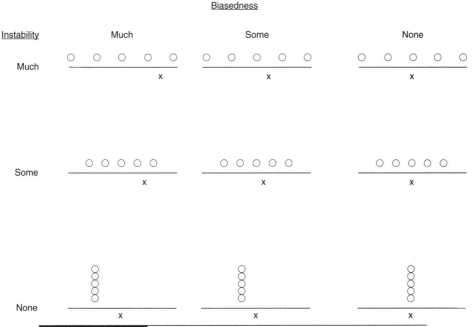

FIGURE 9.1   *Illustrations of biasedness and instability in sampling; the circles represent sampling units located on some dimension, and X represents the population mean.(Reproduced from R. Rosenthal and R. L. Rosnow,* Essentials of Behavioral Research: Methods and Data Analysis, *2nd ed., McGraw-Hill, 1991, p. 208. Used by permission of McGraw-Hill, Inc.)*

Generally speaking, the more homogeneous (alike) the members of the population are, the fewer of them need to be sampled. If all widget makers were exactly alike (i.e., the case in row 3, column 3), *any* sampling unit would provide complete information about the population as a whole. The more heterogeneous (dissimilar) the different teams are, the more sampling units are needed (Kish, 1965).

In connection with our never knowing "for sure" whether there is biasedness in the results, it is sometimes said that election forecasting allows us to know for sure because we can compare the predicted results with the actual results. For example, Gallup Survey records in U.S. presidential elections show discrepancies that are remarkably small (Freedman et al., 1991, p. 314). In the 1988 election, using a sample of 4,089 individuals, the Gallup Survey predicted that George Bush would win by 56.0%, an overestimate of the actual election result by a mere 2.1%: Bush won by 53.9%. In the 1984 election, the Gallup Survey (using 3,456 individual responses) missed by just one-fifth of 1% when it predicted that Ronald Reagan would win by 59.0%. Nevertheless, even in these cases, a true change might have occurred between poll and election, making the poll prediction closer to the election results.

Simple Random Sampling

We said earlier that there is only one *sure way* to find out whether there is biasedness in a survey sample, and that is to examine every member of the population and the sample *at the same time* the sampling is conducted. If the pattern of replies in the sample exactly matches the pattern of replies in the population, we know for certain that there is no biasedness in the survey sample. Such a procedure, of course, makes no sense; we would have no need of a sample if we knew the responses of everyone in the population. Instead, we use a selection process involving probability sampling, of which the basic prototype is called *simple random sampling*.

The *random* tells us that the sample is to be chosen by a process that will give each sampling unit in the population the same chance of being selected (see also Box 9.2). In order for this to occur, the selection of one unit must have no influence on the selection of other units. In the case of simple random sampling, a further requirement is that you have a list of the units in the population. The idea is to draw subjects one at a time until you have as large a sample as you require. The actual method of subject selection might consist of throwing dice, using a table of random digits, or even spinning a roulette wheel or drawing capsules from an urn. In connection with telephone interviewing (discussed in Chapter 5), *random digit dialing* is used to include people with unlisted numbers; the researcher selects the first three digits according to the geographic area of interest and then uses a computer program to select the last digits at random.

Procedures such as drawing capsules from an urn provide the least complex approach, but they are not without potential problems. A famous example of the hazards of "inadequate randomization" occurred in 1970. The previous year, while the war in Vietnam was in progress, the U.S. Congress had passed a bill allowing the use of a random lottery to select conscripts for the armed forces. To give each individual an equal chance of being selected or not selected, the planners decided to pick birthdays out of an urn. The 365 days of the year were written on slips of paper and placed inside tiny cylindrical capsules. Once all the capsules were inside the urn, it was shaken for several hours, and then the capsules were

---

BOX 9.2   Randomness and Aimlessness

Do not confuse randomness with *aimlessness,* or "hit-or-miss" sampling—which, in fact, can seldom be called random. You can prove this to yourself by asking a friend to write down several hundred 1-digit numbers from 0 to 9 in an "aimless" manner. Afterward, tabulate the 0's, 1's, 2's, and so on. If the numbers were truly random, there would be few obvious sequences, and each digit would occur approximately 10% of the time. You will find, however, that the results are inconsistent with the hypothesis of randomness. You will see obvious sequences, and some digits will occur with high frequency, whereas others will appear hardly at all (Wallis & Roberts, 1956).

removed, one by one. However, the results were biased in spite of the precautions taken to ensure a random sample: The birth dates in December tended to be drawn first, those in November next, then those in October, and so on. The reason was that the January capsules were put in the urn first, the February capsules next, and so forth, and layers were formed with the December capsules on top. Even shaking the urn for several hours did not ensure that the capsules would be thoroughly mixed (Broome, 1984; Kolata, 1986).

The use of a table of random digits, such as Table 9.1, helps us to avoid such pitfalls. The 2,250 digits in this list came from a million random digits that were generated by an electronic roulette wheel programmed to produce a random frequency pulse every tiny fraction of a second (Rand Corporation, 1955). As a check on the hypothesis of randomness, the computer also counted the frequency of 0's, 1's, 2's, and so on in the final results. If the probability method were impartial, we would expect an approximately equal number of 0's, 1's, 2's, and so on in the overall table of a million random digits. This equality is exactly what was observed.

In Chapter 7, we showed how to use such a table to allocate subjects to experimental and control conditions (i.e., random assignment). To see how you might use such a table if you were doing a survey (i.e., a random selection), imagine you want to conduct a public opinion poll and decide to interview 10 men and 10 women individually after choosing them at random from a list of 96 men and a list of 99 women. You begin by numbering the population of men consecutively from 01 to 96 and the population of women from 01 to 99. You are now ready to use the 5 × 5 blocks in Table 9.1. To do so, you put your finger blindly on a starting position. You can start anywhere in the table and then move your finger in any direction, as long as you do not pick a set of numbers because they "look right" to you or avoid a set of numbers because they "do not look right" to you. Suppose you put your finger on the first five-digit number in row 5, column 1. Beginning with this number, 12807, you will read across the line two digits at a time, selecting the men numbered 12, 80, 79, 99, and so on, until you have randomly chosen the 10 male subjects. You do the same thing, beginning at another blindly chosen point, to select the 10 female subjects. If you had fewer than 10 persons on each list, you would need to read only one digit at a time; if you had between 100 and 999 persons on your list, you would need to read three digits at a time, and so forth.

Suppose you choose the same two-digit number more than once, or suppose you choose a two-digit number not represented by any name in the population. In either case, you go on to the next two-digit number in the row (that is, unless you are *sampling with replacement;* see Box 9.3). What if your population is so small that you are forced to skip many numbers in the table because they are larger than the largest number of people in your population? For example, what if there are 450 members in the population and you want to select 50 members at random? Because the population is numbered from 001 to 450, you will have to skip approximately one half the three-digit numbers in the section of the table you have chosen. As a simple solution (also acceptable in terms of randomness), you may

BOX 9.3	To Replace or Not to Replace

Two options in simple random sampling are (1) sampling with replacement and (2) sampling without replacement. In *sampling with replacement,* the selected names are placed in the selection pool again and may be reselected on subsequent draws. Thus every element in the population continues to have the same probability of being chosen every time a number is read. In *sampling without replacement,* a previously selected name cannot be reselected and must be disregarded on any later draw. The population shrinks each time you remove a name, but all names remaining still have the same likelihood of being drawn on the next occasion. Either option is technically acceptable, although most survey researchers prefer to do sampling without replacement (because they do not want to use the same sampling units twice).

TABLE 9.1	2,250 Random Digits

	Columns									
Rows	1–5	6–10	11–15	16–20	21–25	26–30	31–35	36–40	41–45	46–50
1	10097	32533	76520	13586	34673	54876	80959	09117	39292	74945
2	37542	04805	64894	74296	24805	24037	20636	10402	00822	91665
3	08422	68953	19645	09303	23209	02560	15953	34764	35080	33605
4	99019	02529	09376	70715	38311	31165	88676	74397	04436	27659
5	12807	99970	80157	36147	64032	36653	98951	16877	12171	76833
6	66065	74717	34072	76850	36697	36170	65813	39885	11199	29170
7	31060	10805	45571	82406	35303	42614	86799	07439	23403	09732
8	85269	77602	02051	65692	68665	74818	73053	85247	18623	88579
9	63573	32135	05325	47048	90553	57548	28468	28709	83491	25624
10	73796	45753	03529	64778	35808	34282	60935	20344	35273	88435
11	98520	17767	14905	68607	22109	40558	60970	93433	50500	73998
12	11805	05431	39808	27732	50725	68248	29405	24201	52775	67851
13	83452	99634	06288	98083	13746	70078	18475	40610	68711	77817
14	88685	40200	86507	58401	36766	67951	90364	76493	29609	11062
15	99594	67348	87517	64969	91826	08928	93785	61368	23478	34113
16	65481	17674	17468	50950	58047	76974	73039	57186	40218	16544
17	80124	35635	17727	08015	45318	22374	21115	78253	14385	53763
18	74350	99817	77402	77214	43236	00210	45521	64237	96286	02655
19	69916	26803	66252	29148	36936	87203	76621	13990	94400	56418
20	09893	20505	14225	68514	46427	56788	96297	78822	54382	14598

Source: Reproduced from *A Million Random Digits with 100,000 Normal Deviates,* 1955, Free Press, by permission of the Rand Corporation.

continued

TABLE 9.1	*(Continued)*								
					Columns				
Rows	1–5	6–10	11–15	16–20	21–25	26–30	31–35	36–40	41–45	46–50
21	91499	14523	68479	27686	46162	83554	94750	89923	37089	20048
22	80336	94598	26940	36858	70297	34135	53140	33340	42050	82341
23	44104	81949	85157	47954	32979	26575	57600	40881	22222	06413
24	12550	73742	11100	02040	12860	74697	96644	89439	28707	25815
25	63606	49329	16505	34484	40219	52563	43651	77082	07207	31790
26	61196	90446	26457	47774	51924	33729	65394	59593	42582	60527
27	15474	45266	95270	79953	59367	83848	82396	10118	33211	59466
28	94557	28573	67897	54387	54622	44431	91190	42592	92927	45973
29	42481	16213	97344	08721	16868	48767	03071	12059	25701	46670
30	23523	78317	73208	89837	68935	91416	26252	29663	05522	82562
31	04493	52494	75246	33824	45862	51025	61962	79335	65337	12472
32	00549	97654	64051	88159	96119	63896	54692	82391	23287	29529
33	35963	15307	26898	09354	33351	35462	77974	50024	90103	39333
34	59808	08391	45427	26842	83609	49700	13021	24892	78565	20106
35	46058	85236	01390	92286	77281	44077	93910	83647	70617	42941
36	32179	00597	87379	25241	05567	07007	86743	17157	85394	11838
37	69234	61406	20117	45204	15956	60000	18743	92423	97118	96338
38	19565	41430	01758	75379	40419	21585	66674	36806	84962	85207
39	45155	14938	19476	07246	43667	94543	59047	90033	20826	69541
40	94864	31994	36168	10851	34888	81553	01540	35456	05014	51176
41	98086	24826	45240	28404	44999	08896	39094	73407	35441	31880
42	33185	16232	41941	50949	89435	48581	88695	41994	37548	73043
43	80951	00406	96382	70774	20151	23387	25016	25298	94624	61171
44	79752	49140	71961	28296	69861	02591	74852	20539	00387	59579
45	18633	32537	98145	06571	31010	24674	05455	61427	77938	91936

mentally subtract 500 from any number in the range from 501 to 999. This additional option will result in fewer unusable selections.

STRATIFICATION IN SAMPLING

Professional polling organizations frequently use another approach to probability sampling: randomly selecting sampling units (e.g., persons or households) from several subpopulations (termed *strata* or *clusters*) into which the population is divided. An application noted previously was the federal court system's sampling of subpopulations of disease categories to deal with asbestos caseloads (Saks & Blanck, 1992). This is a very efficient way of probability sampling, although it requires knowing something about the characteristics of the population. In the example above, the researchers knew exactly how many cases fell into each disease category. The procedure is to divide the population into subclasses and then to sample in such a way as to ensure that each subclass will be proportionally represented.

For example, in *stratified random sampling,* a separate sample is randomly selected from each homogeneous stratum (or "layer") of the population. The stratum means are then statistically weighted to form a combined estimate for the entire population. In a survey of political opinions, it might be useful to stratify the population according to party affiliation, sex, socioeconomic status, and other meaningful categories related to voting behavior. This method ensures that one will have enough men, women, Democrats, Republicans, and so on to draw descriptive or relational inferences about each respective subgroup. We will have more to say about this method of sampling in a moment.

A popular variant of this sampling strategy is called *area probability sampling,* because the population is divided into geographic areas (i.e., population clusters or strata). This method is applicable to any population divisible into geographic areas, such as people living in urban neighborhoods, Inuits in igloos, or nomads in tents. The assumption is that within each of the areas the sampling units will have the same probability of being chosen. The sampling procedure can be more complicated than those described above, but the basic method is very cost-effective because the research design can be used repeatedly with only minor modifications (e.g., Fowler, 1993). Suppose a polling organization needed an area probability sample of 300 out of 6,000 estimated housing units in a city, and a good list of all the dwellings in the entire city does not exist (and would be too costly to prepare). Using a city map, the pollsters can instead obtain a sample of dwellings by selecting small clusters of blocks.

To do this in the simplest case, they divide the entire map of the city into blocks and then select 1 of, say, every 20 blocks for the sample. If they define the sample as the housing units located within the boundaries of the sample blocks, the probability of selection for *any* unit is the selection of its block—which is set at 1/20 to correspond to the desired sampling rate of 300/6,000 (Kish, 1965). In other cases, researchers categorize the blocks by taking into account their size or some other factor of interest and then treat this factor as a stratum to sample in a specific way. Although the procedure gets more complicated as the area gets bigger, the key requirements are to ensure (1) that all areas will have some chance of selection and (2) that units within the areas are chosen impartially (Fowler, 1993). To use the same plan over and over, all that must be altered are the randomly selected units within each area.

Lessons Learned by George Gallup

The late George Gallup, the pioneering survey researcher who founded the Gallup Survey, once noted some of the methodological lessons learned by survey researchers going back to 1936 (Gallup, 1976). That year, Franklin D. Roosevelt (the Democratic presidential candidate) was running against Governor Alfred Landon of Kansas (the Republican candidate). Most people thought Roosevelt would win easily, but a pseudoscientific poll conducted by a current events magazine, the *Literary Digest,* predicted that Landon would win an overwhelming victory. What gave the prediction credence was that the *Digest* had successfully predicted the winner in every presidential election since 1916. Moreover, this time they announced they had based their prediction on a sample of 2.4 million respondents!

They got these 2.4 million by drawing a sample of 10 million people from sources like telephone directories, automobile registration lists, and club membership lists; they then mailed straw vote ballots to each name. The lists had actually been compiled for solicitation purposes, and advertising was included with the straw vote ballot (D. Katz & Cantril, 1937). One problem was that few people in 1936 had a telephone (only one in four households), owned a car, or belonged to a club, so that the final list was biased in favor of wealthy Republican households. Another problem was that there was a large number of nonrespondents, and subsequent analyses suggest that had they responded, the results might have been very different because of the factor of self-selection bias (Squire, 1988); we will return to this problem later.

As it turned out, the election voting was split pretty much along economic lines, the more affluent voting for Landon and the less affluent voting for Roosevelt. The *Digest* predicted that Landon would win by 57% to Roosevelt's 43%, but the election results were Roosevelt 62% and Landon 38% (Freedman et al., 1991). Interestingly, the *Digest* could actually have used the information that its sample was top-heavy in upper-income Republicans to correct its estimate, but it deliberately ignored this information. Instead, the *Digest* proudly proclaimed that the "figures had been neither weighted, adjusted, nor interpreted." After making the largest error ever made by political pollsters in a presidential election, the *Digest* (which had been in financial trouble before the election) declared bankruptcy.

George Gallup was just getting started in those days. Using his own polling method, he was able to predict that Roosevelt would win (although he was off by 6 percentage points)—as well as to predict what the *Literary Digest* results would be! Gallup's method—called *quota sampling*—was an early precursor of current methods; it assigned a quota of people to be questioned and let the questioner build up a sample that was roughly representative of the population. Now, of course, we use random selection procedures instead of leaving the selection of units to the judgment of the questioner. However, the important lesson that Gallup and other pollsters learned from the *Digest*'s debacle was that large numbers do not, in and of themselves, increase the representativeness of a sample.

In the congressional election of 1942, the pollsters encountered a new problem. They had not reckoned with voter turnout, which was at an all-time low because citizens were changing their places of residence to work in war factories or to enter the military. Gallup's polls correctly predicted that the Democrats would retain control of the House of Representatives, but the margin of victory turned out to be much closer than either he or any other pollsters had predicted. The important lesson learned this time was to give far more attention to the factor of voter turnout in making predictions.

In the 1948 presidential election, Harry S Truman, by luring Democratic defectors back into the fold during the last two weeks before Election Day, turned the tide against his Republican opponent, Thomas E. Dewey. However, many public opinion polls predicted that *Dewey* would win. This time, Gallup and other pollsters learned that political polling should be done as close to Election Day as possible.

After 1948, the Gallup Survey (and other political polls) adopted area probability sampling, in which election districts are randomly selected throughout the nation, and then randomly chosen households within these districts are contacted by interviewers. Using this procedure and the lessons learned from the mistakes made in previous polls quickly brought about further improvements. By 1956, the Gallup Survey, based on a little over 8,000 respondents, was able to predict with a margin of error of only 1.7% that Dwight D. Eisenhower would be reelected president. The term *margin of error* means that, based on the laws of mathematical probability, it was predicted that the anticipated percentages would fall within an interval bound by plus and minus 1.7 percentage points. Prudent poll watchers now expect an error of no more than 2 or 3 percentage points in national elections, if the random sampling is properly executed.

POINT AND INTERVAL ESTIMATES

Whatever technique is used, survey researchers are usually interested in making point estimates and interval estimates of the population values in question. *Point estimates* are designed to tell them about some particular characteristic of the population. For example, in a survey of a college population, we might want to make a point estimate of the number of seniors who plan to continue their education after graduating. Other examples noted earlier were the number of widgets made by assembly-line workers and the number of cases of tuberculosis contracted on the job. *Interval estimates* tell survey researchers how much the point estimates are likely to be in error (e.g., because of variability in the composition of the population).

Imagine a simple random survey of 100 college students out of a population of 2,500 graduating seniors at a large state university. Each student is asked, "Do you plan to continue your education after you graduate from college, by going on to graduate school, business school, medical school, dental school, or law school?" In answer to the researchers' question, 25 of them reply yes. In order to make a point estimate, the researchers generalize from this sample value to the population of graduating seniors. They multiply the sample proportion replying yes (.25) by the total number of students in the population (2,500). The result tells them that approximately 625 seniors at this university hope to continue their education.

How "approximate" is this estimate? The interval estimate gives the answer to this question; that is, it tells us the probability that the estimated population value is correct within plus-or-minus some specified interval. Let us say that, using certain statistical procedures, the researchers compute as "95 chances in 100" the probability that an interval of "25% plus-or-minus 9%" contains the true proportion of graduating seniors who plan to continue their education. The point estimate of 625, with its associated interval estimate, enables the researchers to feel fairly confident that the population value falls within the range of 400 to 850 graduating seniors (Cochran, 1963, pp. 57–58).

In this case the researchers randomly selected individual sampling units, using the population of graduating seniors as a single heterogeneous cluster. In most cases of survey research, however, sampling several strata or clusters is more efficient if the population can be conveniently separated into homogeneous strata. The following example illustrates these advantages and shows what is meant by an *unbiased sampling plan* in the case of simple random sampling or stratified random sampling.

BENEFITS OF STRATIFICATION

Suppose we wanted to use a random sampling plan to estimate the mean hourly production of widgets by teams of assembly-line workers. To keep this example simple, we will imagine that the entire population consists of four such teams and that the mean number of widgets produced per hour is

Team A	11.5
Team B	12.5
Team C	13.0
Team D	<u>19.0</u>
	14.0 (true population value)

Adding the means and dividing by four tells us the answer (i.e., true population value = 14.0), but for this example we ask, "How accurate an estimate of the true population value would we obtain by simple random sampling or stratified random sampling?" Finding the answer to this question will reveal what an *unbiased sampling plan* means.

We must initially decide on the size of the sample we wish to use to estimate the population value. To keep it simple, we will define the sample size as any two teams selected at random. For example, were we to randomly select Team A and Team B, we would get a point estimate of 12.0, computed as $(11.5 + 12.5)/2 = 12.0$. How good is this estimate? The answer, called the *error of estimate,* is defined in this case as the closeness of 12.0 to the true population value of 14.0. We figure this answer out by subtracting the population value from the sample mean, or $12.0 - 14.0 = -2.0$. In other words, this particular sample underestimated the true population value by 2.0 (the negative difference means it is an underestimate, whereas a positive difference would indicate an overestimate). Table 9.2 lists all possible combinations of two-member samples, the estimates derived from them, and the error of estimate for each sample. The average of the errors of estimate (when we take account of their signs) gives the *bias* of the general sampling plan. Not surprisingly, we see (at the bottom of column 3) that the general sampling plan produces an unbiased estimate—even though there is error associated with individual sample values.

In stratified random sampling (to which we now turn), we begin by dividing the population into a number of parts. We then randomly sample independently in each part. To get started, notice that column 3 in Table 9.2 shows that every simple random sample containing Team D overestimates the population value, and

TABLE 9.2	Results for All Possible Simple Random Samples of Size Two		
Sample	Sample values	Estimate of population value	Error of estimate
Team A, Team B	11.5, 12.5	12.00	−2.00
Team A, Team C	11.5, 13.0	12.25	−1.75
Team A, Team D	11.5, 19.0	15.25	+1.25
Team B, Team C	12.5, 13.0	12.75	−1.25
Team B, Team D	12.5, 19.0	15.75	+1.75
Team C, Team D	13.0, 19.0	16.00	+2.00
Total		84.00	0.00
Mean		14.00	0.00

that every simple random sample without this team underestimates it. If we had reason to suspect this fact before the sampling, we could make use of such information to form strata so that a heterogeneous population is divided into two parts, each of which is fairly homogeneous (Snedecor & Cochran, 1989). One stratum will consist of Teams A, B, and C, and the second stratum will consist of Team D alone, as Table 9.3 shows. This table helps us to see clearly why this general sampling plan is called *unbiased* and also to see the advantages of stratification in probability sampling.

Starting with the first row, notice under "Weighted sample values" that Team A's score is $11.5 \times 3 = 34.5$, whereas Team D's score is not weighted (19.0). The reason we weight Team A's score by multiplying it by 3 is that it is one of three members of Stratum 1. By the same reasoning, we did not weight Team D's score because it is the sole occupant of Stratum 2. To compute the scores under "Estimate of population value," we add Team A's weighted score to Team D's unweighted score and then divide by the total number of members, or $(34.5 + 19.0)/4 = 13.375$. The "Error of estimate" is obtained by subtracting the true population mean from this result, or $13.375 - 14.0 = -0.625$ (which indicates that the Team A + Team D sample underestimates the true population value by a small amount). This table shows the results of all possible stratified random samples of size two. Again, we find (not unexpectedly) that the general sampling plan is unbiased in that the average of the errors of estimate (bottom of last column) is zero.

TABLE 9.3	Results for All Possible Stratified Random Samples of Size Two			
Sample	Stratum 1	Stratum 2	Weighted sample values	Estimate of population value	Error of estimate
1	Team A	Team D	34.5, 19.0	13.375	−0.625
2	Team B	Team D	37.5, 19.0	14.125	+0.125
3	Team C	Team D	39.0, 19.0	14.500	+0.500
Total				42.000	0.000
Mean				14.000	0.000

By comparing the results in Tables 9.2 and 9.3, you will see in quantitative terms the advantages of separating selections from strata of the population. The most extreme errors in Table 9.2 range from −2.00 to +2.00, a difference of 4.00. By contrast, the most extreme errors in Table 9.3 range from −0.625 to +0.500, a difference of 1.125. Notice that fewer samples are possible of size two in Table 9.3 than in Table 9.2. In summary, not only is the error of an individual sample likely to be greater in simple random sampling than in stratified random sampling—in this case, by a magnitude of $4.00/1.125 = 3.56$, or more than three times the size—but the potential for error is also greater in simple random sampling than in stratified random sampling. Some forethought—and reliable information, of course—is needed about possible mean differences when one is dividing the population into homogeneous strata; these can pay off handsomely in the utility of stratification.

NONRESPONSE BIAS AND ITS CONTROL

A growing problem in the use of polling methods is that, as surveys proliferate, random samples become harder to obtain because more and more people shut the door or hang up the phone on the pollsters. In 1988, an association of survey researchers reported that 38% of consumers had turned down their interviewers. A typical answer by one person who turned down a telephone request to interview her about where she shops was "It was 7 o'clock, I was putting the kids to bed, and it was zoo time around here, which is when these people call" (Rothenberg, 1990, p. A1). As a consequence of many individuals' reluctance to be polled, statisticians and survey researchers have devoted considerable effort to studying the possible effects on accuracy of *nonresponse bias* (i.e., an error due to nonparticipation or nonresponse). The accuracy of estimates of population values may be seriously jeopardized when the researcher fails to collect data from a high percentage of those randomly selected to be in the sample.

Table 9.4 illustrates in quantitative terms the basic idea of nonresponse bias, and it also illustrates one way in which people who conduct large public opinion polls using mailed questionnaires attempt to reduce this bias by sending out questionnaires more than once. The data in this table are based on three waves of questionnaires that were mailed out to peach growers in North Carolina (Finkner, 1950). One variable in this study dealt with the number of peach trees owned, and data were available for the entire population of growers for just this variable. As a consequence, it is possible to quantify the amount of bias due to nonresponse remaining after the first, second, and third waves of questionnaires (Cochran, 1963, 1977). The first three rows provide basic data in the form of (1) the number of respondents to each wave of questionnaires and the number of nonrespondents; (2) the percentage of the total population represented by each wave of respondents and nonrespondents; and (3) the mean number of trees owned by the respondents in each wave. Examination of the third row reveals the nature of the nonresponse bias, which is that the earlier respondents owned more peach trees on the average than did the later respondents.

The remaining five rows of data are based on the cumulative number of respondents available after the first, second, and third waves. For each wave, five items of

TABLE 9.4	Example of Bias Due to Nonresponse in Survey Research				
	Response to Three Mailings				
Basic Data	First Wave	Second Wave	Third Wave	Nonrespondents	Total Population
(1) Number of respondents	300	543	434	1839	3116
(2) Percentage of population	10	17	14	59	100
(3) Mean trees per respondent	456	382	340	290	329
Cumulative Data					
(4) Mean trees per respondent (Y_1)	456	408	385		
(5) Mean trees per nonrespondent (Y_2)	315	300	290		
(6) Difference $(Y_1 - Y_2)$	141	108	95		
(7) Percentage of nonrespondents (P)	90	73	59		
(8) Bias $= (P) \times (Y_1 - Y_2)$	127	79	56		

Source: Reproduced from *The Volunteer Subject* by R. Rosenthal and R. L. Rosnow, 1975, Wiley, p. 4, copyright © by authors. Based on data from Finkner (1950) and Cochran (1963).

information are provided: (4) the mean number of peach trees owned by the respondents up to that point in the survey; (5) the mean number of trees owned by those who had not yet responded up to that point; (6) the difference between these two values; (7) the percentage of the population that had not yet responded; and (8) the magnitude of the bias up to that point in the survey. This last row shows that with each successive wave of respondents there was a decrease in the magnitude of the bias—a fairly typical result in such cases. The implication is that increasing the effort to recruit the nonrespondents should lessen the bias of the point estimates in the sample.

The problem for many survey researchers is not just that nonresponse bias is possible, but that in most circumstances they may not have enough information to estimate its magnitude. That is, they can usually compute the proportion of population participants (P) and the statistic of interest (the point estimate) for these respondents (Y_1), but they may be unable to compute the statistic of interest (the corresponding point estimate) for those who did not respond (Y_2). As a consequence, many survey researchers may be able to suspect bias but may be unable to give an accurate estimate of its magnitude. We will come back to this problem again (in our discussion of volunteer bias), but one obvious way to minimize nonresponse bias is to try to increase the rate of response for telephone and personal surveys.

In the case of mail surveys, the data in this table teach us that drawing nonrespondents into the subject sample may be aided by using one or more follow-ups or reminders. Experts often advise telephoning nonrespondents if the response rate is still not satisfactory. Professional pollsters attempt to increase the initial rate of participation by using various kinds of incentives and attention-getting techniques, such as using special delivery as opposed to ordinary mail, using hand-stamped rather than postage-permit envelopes, and sometimes including a courtesy gift (e.g., a 50-cent piece or a Susan B. Anthony dollar) at the time of the request for participation (Linsky, 1975). In Chapter 5, we discussed the development of questionnaires; to help reduce nonresponse, it is important that the instructions be clear, that the items be easy to read and the layout attractive, and that the task of answering questions not be burdensome (Fowler, 1993).

In the case of telephone surveys, techniques of increasing subject participation were alluded to in Chapter 5. Response rates may be increased by sending an informative advance letter that emphasizes the purpose and importance of the study, by pilot-testing items to ensure that the persons contacted will not feel intimidated by the questions or by the uses to which the data will be put, and by training interviewers and screening out bad ones (Fowler, 1993). Using one or more follow-up telephone calls on evenings and weekends may also improve the response rate.

CHARACTERISTICS OF VOLUNTEER SUBJECTS

So far, we have focused on the prototypical survey study. We turn now to a problem similar to nonresponse bias that occurs in the kinds of studies discussed in the previous two chapters: the *volunteer subject problem*. In experimental fields, for example, most scientists do not concern themselves with the particulars of a probability sampling plan when choosing subjects for research participation. One reason for this lack of concern (noted earlier) is that it is frequently impossible to work within the confines of such a plan (see also Box 9.4). Can you imagine, for example, trying to persuade a randomly selected sample of adults to agree to be assigned to a smoking treatment condition for many years? When scientists recruit volunteers for studies involving risk (e.g., testing the effects of different diets on cholesterol), it is possible that those already at high risk are the most likely to volunteer. The question is how to generalize from the volunteers to the population in general.

In recent years we have come to know a great deal about the personal characteristics of typical volunteers for research participation, and of typical *nonvolunteers*. You may be asking yourself how a researcher can identify the characteristics of someone who refuses to participate in research. One technique used by

BOX 9.4	People Are People?

A more basic reason for most behavioral experimenters' lack of interest in random subject selection, even when it may be perfectly feasible, is that they believe that "people are people" in terms of the psychological mechanisms that regulate behavior. That is, they believe that, as long as subjects are randomly assigned to treatments, it makes little difference whether the subjects in the experimental and control groups are volunteer subjects (i.e., a self-selected sample) or a random sample of the population as a whole. In some cases, as we will show, the use of volunteers may lead to biased conclusions— even when the volunteers are randomly assigned to the experimental and control conditions. Fortunately, we are able to estimate the direction of this bias in many instances, as described in this chapter.

researchers who attempt to compare the characteristics and reactions of volunteers and nonvolunteers is to recruit research participants from a population for which information is already available on all the potential recruits (e.g., biographical data and psychological test results). Requests for research volunteers are then made some time later—sometimes years later—and those who volunteer are compared with those who do not volunteer on all the items of information in which the investigator is interested. For instance, most colleges administer psychological tests and questionnaires to all incoming students during an orientation period. The results, if they are obtainable by researchers, can be used not only to compare those who volunteer with those who do not volunteer for a psychological experiment later that same year, but also to compare the respondents with the nonrespondents to an alumni-organization questionnaire sent out years later.

To explain *volunteer bias* (and to explain how it is controlled), we must first describe these characteristics of typical volunteers and nonvolunteers. Listed below are nine characteristics, ranked in the descending order of their approximate accuracy in describing those who are likely to volunteer (Rosenthal & Rosnow, 1975b). This list was derived from a number of studies, and confidence in the inclusion of a characteristic on the list increased as (1) the inclusion was based on a larger number of studies; (2) a larger percentage of the total number of relevant studies significantly favored its inclusion; and (3) a larger percentage of just those studies showing a significant relationship favored its conclusion:

1. Volunteers tend to be better educated than nonvolunteers, especially in studies in which personal contact between investigator and respondent is not required.

2. Volunteers tend to have higher social-class status than nonvolunteers, especially when social class is defined by the respondents' own status rather than by parental status.

3. Volunteers tend to be more intelligent than nonvolunteers when the volunteering is for somewhat less typical types of research (such as hypnosis, sensory isolation, sex research, and small-group and personality research).

4. Volunteers tend to be higher than nonvolunteers in the need for social approval.

5. Volunteers tend to be more sociable than nonvolunteers.

6. Volunteers tend to be more arousal-seeking than nonvolunteers, especially when the volunteering is for studies of stress, sensory isolation, and hypnosis.

7. Volunteers tend to be more unconventional than nonvolunteers, especially when the volunteering is for studies of sexual behavior.

8. Women are more likely than men to volunteer for research in general, but they are less likely than men to volunteer for physically and emotionally stressful research (e.g., electric shock, high temperature, sensory deprivation, and interviews about sexual behavior).

9. Volunteers tend to be less authoritarian than nonvolunteers.

IMPLICATIONS FOR RESEARCH CONCLUSIONS

Knowing that research volunteers are likely to be brighter (Conclusion 3), higher in approval need (Conclusion 4), less authoritarian (Conclusion 9), and so on than nonvolunteers allows behavioral scientists to predict the direction of volunteer bias. Using the same logic, in some situations you can also predict the likelihood of conclusions that are too liberal or too conservative as a consequence of the employment of volunteer subjects.

To illustrate, imagine that an educational researcher wants to assess experimentally the validity of a new teaching procedure that is purported to make young children less rigid in their thinking. The researcher asks parents and teachers to volunteer their children or pupils as participants in the investigation, because, realistically, it is impossible to draw a random sample for participation. The researcher intuitively expects that the children who are volunteers will—like adults who volunteer themselves—be low in authoritarianism (Characteristic 9). Because people who are low in authoritarianism are also likely to be less rigid thinkers, the researcher suspects that using these volunteered children will lead to a more conservative assessment of the new teaching procedure than if it were possible to use a randomly selected subject sample. The reason is that the experimental group will already be unusually low on the dependent measure (rigidity in thinking). Knowing this, however, the researcher can have greater confidence in the magnitude of the causal relationship to which the visible evidence in this study points, because that magnitude is likely to be even greater in the general population.

We can also imagine the opposite type of inferential error in another situation. Suppose a marketing researcher wants to find out how persuasive an advertisement is before recommending its use in a heavily funded television campaign. The researcher finds it most convenient to pilot-test the advertisement on volunteer subjects, who are assigned at random to an experimental group that sees the advertisement or a control group that sees something else that will fill the same amount of time. The researcher knows that volunteer subjects tend to be relatively high in approval need (Characteristic 4), and also (from working in this area and knowing the background literature) that people who are high in approval need are likely to be more influenced than those who are low in approval need (Buckhout, 1965). Putting this information together, the researcher feels it prudent not to make too strong a claim about the causal relationship evidence in this pilot study. Because the volunteers may have overreacted to the treatment in the experimental condition, the predicted effect of the new advertisement on the general population may be exaggerated.

Knowing that biased conclusions are likely in a given experimental or nonexperimental situation, researchers try to avoid this problem when possible. For example, the use of volunteer subjects may lead to biased conclusions in the standardization of a new intelligence test. As noted in earlier discussions, uniform procedures are established for administering and scoring standardized tests, so that every competent tester is likely to obtain the same "unbiased" results. Many standardized tests are accompanied by *norms,* or tables of values representing the typical performance of a given group. The norms provide a standard of comparison so that we can see how much any person's score deviates from the average of a large group of representative individuals.

For example, if you are planning to apply to law school, you may want to know how much your score on the Law School Admission Test (LSAT) deviates from the scores of other highly qualified college students with similar career plans. A crucial assumption of researchers in developing test norms is that the resulting values are truly representative of the group in question, but suppose that a researcher uses only volunteer subjects to standardize a new intelligence test. Based on Characteristic 3, our hypothesis is that the researcher's estimates of population norms will be artificially inflated, because volunteers can be expected to score higher on such tests than nonvolunteers.

INCREASING PARTICIPATION RATES

Previously, we mentioned some of the techniques used to stimulate participation by typical nonrespondents in survey research. Experimental researchers also use a number of incentives to stimulate participation by typical nonvolunteers (Rosenthal & Rosnow, 1975b), because increasing their participation lessens the likelihood of subject selection bias by drawing a more representative subject sample.

One technique is to inform potential subjects that participation in the research will be interesting. This approach is based on research findings that persons more interested in the topic under investigation are more likely to volunteer. A second technique is to make the appeal as nonthreatening as possible, so that potential subjects will not be put off by unwarranted fears of unfavorable evaluation. The basis of this approach is another set of research findings that persons who expect to be favorably evaluated by the investigator are more apt to volunteer. Other empirically based techniques for stimulating research participation are emphasizing the theoretical and practical importance of the research, offering small courtesy gifts to potential participants simply for considering participation, and avoiding tasks that may be perceived as psychologically or biologically stressful.

A hasty reading of these techniques may give the impression that they are designed only to increase rates of participation. However, there is another, more subtle, benefit. When researchers tell their subjects as much as possible about the significance of the research, avoid doing psychologically or biologically stressful research, and so on, it follows that more care and thought probably went into the planning in order to ensure that the study will stand up to the scrutiny of critical evaluations. In effect, the researchers are treating the participants as if they are another "granting agency"—which in fact they are, granting the researchers time and cooperation. Thus another benefit of these techniques is that they also provide incentives to behavioral scientists to be ethically responsible and humane when they decide what kind of research to do and how to do it (see also Blanck et al., 1992; Rosenthal, 1994).

PILOT-TESTING AS A FINAL STEP

Whatever your research project, whether it involves a survey or an experiment or a quasi-experiment, the final step before implementing the study is to pilot-test the materials. For example, suppose we want to study a sensitive topic and fear that people will be reluctant to tell the truth. We might pilot-test two or three versions of the questionnaire or interview schedule. If we are concerned about nonresponse bias, we might pilot-test different recruitment procedures. Interestingly, even when carrying out the actual survey, researchers sometimes use embedded experiments (e.g., using alternate questionnaires or other variations in procedures on subsets of the sample) in order to test various methodological hypotheses (see Fienberg & Tanur, 1989; Tanur, 1994). As the old saying goes, an ounce of prevention is worth a pound of cure. The purpose of pilot-testing (and embedded experiments in survey studies) is to prevent producing incurably flawed data.

SUMMARY OF IDEAS

1. Probability sampling plans ensure that the selection process will use a random procedure.

2. To be absolutely sure that a sample is representative, we would need to know the characteristics of the population, in which case there would be no reason to study the sample.

3. A *biased* sample overestimates or underestimates the true population value; an *unstable* sample is characterized by sampling units that vary greatly from one another.

4. Inadequate randomization occurs when a probability sampling plan is not implemented properly (e.g., the first draft lottery during the war in Vietnam). One way to avoid this problem is to use a table of random digits to select the sampling units.

5. Two options in simple random sampling are (a) sampling with replacement and (b) sampling without replacement.

6. Area probability sampling is a variant of stratified random sampling in which the strata are geographic clusters.

7. Point estimates are designed to tell us about a particular characteristic of the population, whereas interval estimates describe how much the point estimates are likely to be in error.

8. As the widget example illustrated, both the error of estimate of an individual sample and the likelihood of making that error tend to be greater in simple random samples than in stratified random samples.

9. In survey research that uses a probability sampling plan, bias due to nonresponse is likely to diminish with each successive wave of respondents (e.g., in the survey of peach growers). Other ways to reduce nonresponse bias in survey research include (a) using reminders and follow-up communications; (b) personalizing the contact; and (c) offering an incentive to respond.

10. Political pollsters take their final survey close to election time, and they give attention to the factor of voter turnout.

11. For practical, ethical, and theoretical reasons (e.g., on the premise that "people are people"), behavioral experimenters tend to pay little attention to whether their subjects constitute a random sample.

12. Knowing the relationship between the characteristics of volunteer subjects and the variable of theoretical interest, researchers can sometimes predict the direction of volunteer bias in experimental and nonexperimental studies.

13. Procedures for stimulating subject participation (e.g., telling subjects as much as possible about the significance of the research and avoiding psychologically or biologically stressful manipulations) also provide incentives to researchers to act ethically and humanely.

KEY TERMS

aimlessness *p. 192*
area probability sampling *p. 196*
biasedness *p. 190*
clusters *p. 195*
error of estimate *p. 199*
instability *p. 190*
interval estimates *p. 198*
margin of error *p. 198*
nonresponse bias *p. 201*
norms *p. 205*
opportunity sample *p. 190*
pilot-testing *p. 206*
point estimates *p. 198*
population *p. 188*
probability *p. 189*
probability sampling *p. 189*

quota sampling *p. 197*
random *p. 192*
random digit dialing *p. 192*
random selection *p. 189*
representativeness *p. 189*
sample *p. 188*
sampling plan *p. 189*
sampling without replacement *p. 194*
sampling with replacement *p. 194*
simple random sampling *p. 192*
stability *p. 190*
strata *p. 195*
stratified random sampling *p. 196*
unbiased sampling plan *p. 199*
volunteer bias *p. 204*

REVIEW QUESTIONS

1. Do you know the answer to the following question asked of a University of Vermont student? Given a true population mean of 12 and the following subjects' scores, (a) which group is measured with greatest stability, and (b) which group is the most biased?

Group 1	Group 2	Group 3
10	10	9
11	12	12
12	14	15
13	16	18

2. Fed up with studying for midterms, four Smith College students—Susan, Valerie, Ellen, and Jane—decide to throw darts at Susan's encyclopedia, which contains one volume for each letter of the alphabet. Because the word *midterm* begins with the letter *M,* the *M* volume is chosen as the target. Each person gets three darts. Susan hits the *M* volume every time; Valerie hits the *N* volume every time; Ellen hits the *L* volume, the *M* volume, and the *N* volume once each; and

Jane hits the *M* volume, the *N* volume, and the *O* volume once each. Assuming that each volume of the encyclopedia is the same size, interpret the performance of each person in terms of bias and instability.

3. A Virginia Polytechnic Institute student is interested in the relationship between IQ and sociability. He designs a questionnaire to study this relationship and sends it out to hundreds of people. Twenty percent of the people complete and return the questionnaire. What is a possible source of bias in the results this student will obtain? How would you improve on his design?

4. A University of Kansas student is asked by his instructor to think up experimental cases in which the difference between volunteer subjects and nonvolunteers might lead the researcher (a) to overestimate the effectiveness of the experimental treatment and (b) to underestimate the effectiveness of the experimental treatment. Can you help the student? Can you also think of how these situations might be remedied?

5. A University of Michigan student wants to sample the opinions of all graduating seniors on various issues. However, because the graduating class is so large, she decides it would be best to sample a representative group rather than try to contact every one of the graduating seniors. Describe the steps she should take to develop a representative sampling plan, as well as some further steps she might take to deal with the problem of nonresponse bias.

6. An Eastern College student wants to conduct an interview study using married adults who frequent the King of Prussia shopping mall. Because she is worried about volunteer bias, she would like to make every reasonable effort to obtain as representative a sample as she possibly can. What can she do to induce people to participate in her study?

Answers to review questions are found on pages 320–334.

PART IV

Describing and Hypothesis Testing

CHAPTER 10

Summarizing the Data

PREVIEW QUESTIONS

➤ **H**ow are frequency distributions used to summarize data?

➤ **H**ow do stem-and-leaf plots work?

➤ **W**hen are means, medians, and modes used?

➤ **W**hat are the effects of outliers on measures of location and spread?

➤ **W**hich range should be reported?

➤ **W**hat is the difference between variance and standard deviation?

➤ **W**hat are descriptive and inferential measures?

➤ **W**hat is the role of the standard normal distribution?

➤ **W**hat are Z scores, and how are they used?

STATISTICAL PROCEDURES

In Chapter 1 we noted that the scientific method, like all methods of explanation, is characterized by a distinctive language particular to the area it represents. So far, we have discussed a number of aspects of this rhetoric (e.g., the use of technical definitions and the nature of hypotheses and theories), and we turn now to statistical procedures that also are a part of many research reports. The purpose of the remaining chapters is to help you develop an intuitive understanding of the proper use (and limitations) of these procedures. Some will be particularly useful as you analyze your own results and prepare to write a final report (see also Appendix A), but you will find these procedures instructive even beyond your research. For example, once you understand the logic of using graphs, descriptive and inferential measures, probabilities, correlations, and so on, you will be in a better position to evaluate claims made on the basis of such procedures.

If you are learning to use a computer with a statistics package to analyze data, you will find that the quantitative procedures to be described are among the most common statistical tools. When you understand the logic of these procedures, you will have a better intuitive sense of what your computer churns out. However, these procedures are simple enough so that all you need is a pocket calculator that can compute the standard deviation and variance of a sample (S, S^2) and a population (σ, σ^2). If your budget permits, you will find calculators that compute correlations and t tests quite directly; some give precise p values (so you won't have to root around for a table of values) and can be programmed with your favorite formulas (e.g., for computing effect sizes, as described in later chapters).

In this chapter we review some older and newer procedures to help us visualize and summarize tendencies of the data. We will begin by showing some ways of graphing data to reveal underlying patterns. We then review basic summary statistics that are used to indicate the central or typical value (e.g., mean, median, or mode) and the spread of scores around that value (e.g., range, average deviation, standard deviation, or variance). A valuable piece of information is that population data often take the form of a symmetrical, bell-shaped curve, a fact that will often come in handy, for example, if you want to transform scores to a common metric (by Z-scoring them). In the following chapters we will show how these concepts provide the basic ingredients of more advanced data-analytic procedures.

VISUALIZING DATA

It is often said that a good picture is worth a thousand words, which may be particularly true in reporting research data. If we want to emphasize the overall pattern of the data, we may find it useful to create a *frequency distribution*. Such a "picture" shows the number of times each score or other unit of observation occurs in a set of scores. A frequency distribution can take the form of a figure (e.g., a histogram or a frequency polygon) or a table, such as Table 10.1.

TABLE 10.1	Palatability Evaluation of Two Food Products	
Score	Control product	New product
+3	1	7
+2	5	13
+1	15	16
0	17	11
−1	8	2
−2	3	1
−3	1	0

Source: "Preliminary Evaluation of a New Food Product" by E. Street and M. B. Carroll, 1989, in J. M. Tanur et al. (Eds.), *Statistics: A Guide to the Unknown* (3rd ed.), Wadsworth & Brooks/Cole, p. 166. Used by permission of Brooks/Cole Publishing Company.

This table shows part of the results of an evaluation of a new food product by Elisabeth Street and Mavis B. Carroll (1989). This aspect involved a palatability evaluation, in which Street and Carroll had 50 people taste and evaluate a new food product and a competitive food product (i.e., a control) already on the market. Instead of using a scale with words such as *excellent, very good, good, average, poor, very poor,* and *terrible,* the subjects were given a variation of the pictorial scale in Figure 10.1. In the scoring of the results, each of the pictures was assigned a number (or score) in the sequence +3, +2, +1, 0, −1, −2, −3, with +3 being most acceptable. In Table 10.1, we see, for example, that only one person rated the control product +3, whereas seven people gave the new product this "excellent" rating (see also Box 10.1).

Figure 10.2 recasts the results as two *histograms* (i.e., bar charts) showing the number of times each rating was made. Notice that the score values appear on the horizontal axis (also called the *X axis*) and the number of scores appears on the vertical axis (also called the *Y axis*). Another name for the horizontal, or *X* axis, is the *abscissa;* another name for the vertical, or *Y* axis, is the *ordinate.* (To keep these names straight, remember that the "abscissa sits," or rests on the bottom.) Com-

---

BOX 10.1 | **Tallying Items**

When you are working with batches of numbers and want to count the frequencies, the fastest method involves one pencil (or pen) stroke per unit. For example, if you were counting seven units, the conventional technique is:

I	II	III	IIII	ʼNɄ	ʼNɄ I	ʼNɄ II
1	2	3	4	5	6	7

John W. Tukey (1977), a leading statistician, invented an alternative technique using dots and lines. To use this method, we use first dots, then box lines, then crossed lines to make a final character for 10. For example,

4   is   ∷

8   is   □

10   is   ⊠

The order in which you place the dots around the square, fill in the square, or cross the two diagonals is unimportant. If you use a rolling ball pen, you will find that it gives a more distinct impression than a pencil and is more easily read afterward. Tukey found that his technique results in fewer recording errors than the old method. Here is a list of examples to get you started:

Tally	Count	Tally	Count
.	1		7
. .	2	□	8
.·.	3	◨	9
∷	4	⊠	10
⊡	5	⊠ ⊠	27
⊐	6	⊠ ⊠ ⊠ ⊠ ..	42

PLEASE CHECK THE BOX UNDER THE PICTURE WHICH EXPRESSES HOW YOU
FEEL TOWARD THE PRODUCT YOU HAVE JUST TASTED.

FIGURE 10.1 *Pictorial taste-test scale (the scores +3 to −3 were assigned the figures from left to right) used in a palatability evaluation study. (Based on E. Street and M. B. Carroll, "Preliminary Evaluation of a New Food Product" (1989), in J. M. Tanur et al. (Eds.),* Statistics: A Guide to the Unknown *(3rd ed.), Wadsworth & Brooks/Cole, p. 166. Used by permission of Brooks/Cole Publishing Company.)*

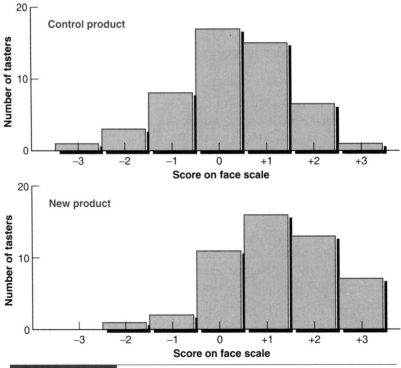

FIGURE 10.2 *A pair of histograms that display the results in Table 10.1.*

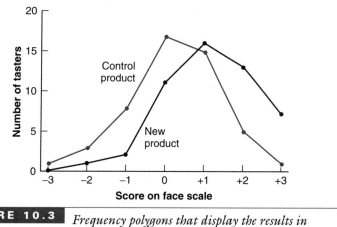

FIGURE 10.3 *Frequency polygons that display the results in Table 10.1*

paring the two histograms allows us to see that the new food product was rated as more acceptable than the control product.

Another conventional way of graphing the frequency of scores is called a *frequency polygon,* as shown in Figure 10.3 (often referred to simply as a *frequency distribution*). You may recall seeing other examples of frequency polygons in Chapter 8, such as Figure 8.1 (page 175) and Figure 8.2 (page 176).

STEM-AND-LEAF DISPLAYS

No hard-and-fast rule insists that graphs always resemble these figures. For example, there is an even more informative display called a *stem-and-leaf display* (Tukey, 1977). The beauty of the stem-and-leaf display is that it preserves the original numbers yet manages to give an economical visual summary of them.

Suppose we ask 15 students to rate a rap group, famous for its social statements and wry political observations, on a scale from 0 ("the most shallow") to 100 ("the most profound"), and we get the following results: 66, 87, 47, 74, 56, 51, 37, 70, 82, 66, 41, 52, 62, 79, 69. Figure 10.4 shows a stem-and-leaf plot of these ratings.

Stems	Leaves
8	2 7
7	0 4 9
6	2 6 6 9
5	1 2 6
4	1 7
3	7

FIGURE 10.4 *A stem-and-leaf display of students' ratings of a rap group.*

BOX 10.2   A Back-To-Back Tally

The figure below shows how we might use Tukey's method of tallying scores (Box 10.1) to summarize the taste-test results in Table 10.1:

Control product	Score	New product
.	+3	
˙˙ —	+2	⊠ .˙
˙˙ ⊠	+1	⊠ ˙⌉
⊠	0	⊠ .
☐	−1	. .
˙˙	−2	.
.	−3	

Notice that the bulk of the tallies shifts further upward (i.e., to higher positive scores) for the new food product than for the control. Not surprisingly, this type of comparison is called a *back-to-back tally*.

Each row label is called a *stem*. Because we are working with two-digit numbers, we save space by listing the leading digits (the "stem ends") only once and recording for each of the stem ends the second digits (the "leaves") attached to them (see also Box 10.2).

Histograms, frequency polygons, and stem-and-leaf displays are a small sample of the kinds of graphics used to display data. If you are interested in learning more about this subject, see Edward R. Tufte's *Visual Display of Quantitative Information* (1983) and *Envisioning Information* (1990), both published by Graphics Press. An article containing tips on what *not to do* is one by Howard Wainer, "How to Display Data Badly" (1984).

PERCENTILES AND THE MEDIAN

The graphics we have looked at were used to summarize *all* the data, but researchers also find it useful to summarize part of the data. For example, there is often a practical value in knowing the point in the distribution below and above which a certain percentage of sampling units fall, called the *percentile*: 25% of the sampling units fall below the 25th percentile, 75% of the sampling units fall below the 75th percentile, and so on. Quantitative summaries of data displayed in stem-and-leaf plots often include a listing of the scores falling at the 25th, 50th, and 75th percentiles (see, for example, Box 10.3).

In most cases, it is highly useful to know the location of the typical score and the spread of scores around that location. We will return to measures of spread in a moment, but one common measure of typical location is the 50th percentile, also called the *median*. It is one of several useful measures of *central tendency*, which

BOX 10.3	Adjusting for No-Shows

In the previous chapter we referred to research on volunteer characteristics (Rosenthal & Rosnow, 1975b). As part of that research a number of investigators were interested in what kind of volunteers become *no-shows* (i.e., volunteers who fail to show up for their scheduled appointments). Suppose we wanted to know how many volunteer subjects we need to ensure that at least 40 will show up. A review of this literature turned up 20 studies that reported the proportion of no-shows. Those proportions are listed in the stem-and-leaf display shown below. In other words, the proportion of no-shows was .40 in one study, .41 in another study, .42 in another study, and so forth.

Stems	Leaves									
.4	0	1	2							
.3	0	0	1	2	6	6	7	7	7	8
.2	4									
.1	0	2	4	6	9					
.0	3									

To summarize this stem-and-leaf display in certain key values of the distribution, the researchers also reported:

Maximum value	.42
75th percentile	.37
Median (50th percentile)	.32 (.315 rounded to nearest even digit)
25th percentile	.17
Minimum value	.03

From the fact that 50% of the studies that were midmost (25% to 75%) had values between .17 and .37 (with a a median no-show rate of .32), a practical recommendation emerges: If we are counting on 40 volunteer participants to show up for our research, we should probably schedule about 60 (i.e., 1/3 of 60 = 20, and 60 − 20 = 40), or one-half more subjects than we absolutely need.

means that such measures tell us the location of central or typical values. In the case of the median, the typical score is defined as the midmost score (i.e., the score below which 50 percent of all the scores fall).

For example, when the number of scores (often designated as N) is an odd number, the median is simply the midmost score. Thus, in the series 2, 3, 3, 4, 4, 5, 6, 7, 7, 8, 8, the median value is 5 because it is midmost, leaving five numbers below it (2, 3, 3, 4, 4) and five numbers above it (6, 7, 7, 8, 8). When the number of scores is an even number (so that there are two midmost scores), the median is computed as half the distance between the two midmost numbers. In the series 2, 3, 3, 4, 4, 7, the median value is 3.5, halfway between the 3 and the 4 at the center of the set of scores.

Ties create a small problem when one is computing medians. The series 3, 4, 4, 4, 5, 6, 7 has one score below 4 and three above. What shall we regard as the median? A useful procedure is to imagine such a series as perfectly ranked, so that a series 1, 2, 3, 3, 3 is seen as being made up of a 1, a 2, a "small" 3, a "larger" 3, and a "still larger" 3. The assumption here is that more precise measurement procedures would have allowed us to break the ties. In the series 1, 2, 3, 3, 3, we regard the "small 3" as the median, because there are two scores below this particular 3 and two above it. In reporting this result, however, the researcher would state "median = 3."

An easy way to locate the median (the 50th percentile) is to multiply $N + 1$ (where N is the number of scores in the set) by .50. In the stem-and-leaf in Box 10.3, the sequence of the reported values (from lowest to highest) is:

(1)	.03	(6)	.19	(11)	.32	(16)	.37
(2)	.10	(7)	.24	(12)	.36	(17)	.38
(3)	.12	(8)	.30	(13)	.36	(18)	.40
(4)	.14	(9)	.30	(14)	.37	(19)	.41
(5)	.16	(10)	.31	(15)	.37	(20)	.42

and the median is .50(20 + 1) = 10.5. In other words, the median is halfway between the 10th score (.31) and the 11th score (.32), which is .315 (rounded to .32, the nearest even value).

We can also use this procedure to locate other percentiles. The 25th percentile score is $.25(N + 1)$, and therefore .25(21) = 5.25th score (i.e., 25% of the distance between the 5th and 6th scores), which gives us .17. The 75th percentile is $.75(N + 1)$, which we calculate as .75(21) = 15.75th score, 75% of the distance between the 15th and 16th scores. In this case the 15th and 16th scores are both .37, so 75% of the distance between them is zero. Therefore, the 15.75th score is still .37.

THE MODE AND THE MEAN

A second measure of central tendency is the *mode*. It is the score, or category of scores, that occurs with the greatest frequency. In the series 3, 4, 4, 4, 5, 5, 6, 6, 7, the modal score is 4. The series 3, 4, 4, 4, 5, 5, 6, 7, 7, 7 has two modes (at values 4 and 7) and is thus described as *bimodal*. For the stem-and-leaf display in Box 10.3, the modal *category* is ".30's" (stem of .3 and leaves of 0, 0, 1, 2, 6, 6, 7, 7, 7, and 8).

A third measure of central location is the ordinary mean or *arithmetic mean*, called the *mean* for short, and symbolized as $\overline{X}$ or M. It is the arithmetical average of the scores. That is, it is the sum of the scores divided by the number (N) of the scores. The formula for the mean is

$$\overline{X} = \frac{\Sigma X}{N}$$

where Σ (the uppercase Greek letter sigma) tells us to "sum" the X scores. In the series 1, 2, 3, 3, 3, the sum of the scores is 12, the number of scores is 5, and therefore $\overline{X} = 12/5 = 2.4$. For the stem-and-leaf values in Box 10.3, the mean is calculated as the sum of the reported proportions (5.65) divided by 20, which gives .2825 (rounded to .28) as the mean proportion of no-shows.

In Table 10.1, how would you calculate the mean of the scores for each of the two food products? You could add up the 50 scores (i.e., +3 to −3 ratings) in each group and divide by 50, which gives .22 for the control product and 1.18 for the new product. An easier way to average these scores is to multiply each score by its frequency, sum the results, and divide by 50.

DEALING WITH OUTLIERS

Distributions of scores may also be described as *symmetrical* or *asymmetrical,* which means that there is *(symmetrical)* or is not *(asymmetrical)* correspondence in arrangement on the opposite sides of the middle plane (see Figure 10.5). What if we have a few scores that lie far outside the normal range (called *outliers*)? When a distribution of scores is strongly asymmetrical because of outliers, researchers frequently prefer a *trimmed mean* to an ordinary mean. The reason for using trimmed means is that ordinary means are the most sensitive to extreme values. Trimming implies giving the series a "light haircut" by cutting off not just the one or more outliers from one side, but the same percentage of the scores from *both* ends of the series.

Consider this strongly asymmetrical series: −20, 2, 3, 6, 7, 9, 9, 10, 10, 10. The −20 is an outlier that clearly disrupts the homogeneity of the series. To expunge outliers fairly, we trim an equal number of scores from each end. In this case, trimming one score from each end leaves 2, 3, 6, 7, 9, 9, 10, 10. What if we had *not* given the series a haircut? Would leaving the outlier in have distorted the average by very much? It depends on how the average is defined in a given situation. The trimmed mean = 7.0 and the untrimmed mean = 4.6, so the answer is yes in the case of the ordinary mean. The median is unaffected by trimming, so the median of these scores is 8 with or without trimming. The mode, which may be affected by trimming, is 10 before trimming but is bimodal at 9 and 10 after trimming (see also Box 10.4).

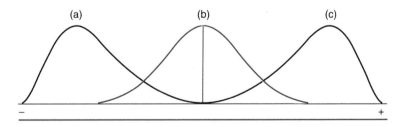

FIGURE 10.5 *Illustrations of symmetry and asymmetry. Only distribution (b) is symmetrical, in that both sides of the middle line are identical. When the pointed end is toward the right (or positive direction) as represented by (a), the distribution is said to be positively skewed. When the pointed end is toward the left (or negative direction) as illustrated by (c), the distribution is said to be negatively skewed.*

| BOX 10.4 | Protecting Against Misleading Interpretations |

Medians and trimmed means protect us in certain cases from possibly mislead-ing interpretations based on very unusual scores. For example, if we listed the family income for 10 families and found 9 of them with 0 income and 1 with a $10 million income, the mean income of $1 million would be highly unrep-resentative compared to the trimmed mean, the median, or (in this case) even the mode. Medians and trimmed means also protect us somewhat against the intrusion of "wild" scores. Imagine the series 4, 5, 5, 6, 6, 6, 7, 7, 8, of which the mean, median, mode, and trimmed mean are all 6. However, suppose we erred and entered the data as 4, 5, 5, 6, 6, 6, 7, 7, 80. Our new (erroneous) mean would now be 14, but our median or trimmed mean would remain unaffected.

THE CRUDE AND EXTENDED RANGE

Besides knowing the central tendency (or *typical value*) of a set of scores, researchers also usually want to know how "spread out" the scores are. That is, they want to know how far the scores deviate from the value of the central tenden-cy measure. Just as there are different measures of central tendency, there are also different measures of *spread, dispersion,* or *variability.* The most widely cited mea-sures are the range (crude or extended), the average deviation, the variance, and the standard deviation.

The ordinary *range* (or *crude range*) is simply the difference between the highest and lowest scores. If you are administering a standardized scale in your research, you will want to know the crude range of both the potential scores and the observed scores. If the crude range of the potential scores is very narrow, it may be impossible to observe appreciable differences among the subjects; that is, there is a flaw in the design. On the other hand, it does not follow that simply having a very wide poten-tial range will automatically result in a substantial observed range. The range must be interpreted within the context of the study's purpose or objective and the nature of the instruments used.

A further distinction is made between the crude range and the *extended range* (also called the *corrected range*). In the series 2, 3, 4, 4, 6, 7, 9, the *crude range* is the highest score minus the lowest score, or $9 - 2 = 7$. The extended range is a refinement that recognizes that, in more precise measurement, a score of 9 may fall somewhere between 8.5 and 9.5 and that a score of 2 may fall somewhere between 1.5 and 2.5. To adjust for this possibility, we view the extended range as running from a high of 9.5 to a low of 1.5. The extended range (or corrected range) is then $9.5 - 1.5 = 8$. The extended range thus adds a half unit at the top of the distribu-tion and a half unit at the bottom of the distribution, or a total of one full unit. Symbolizing the highest score as H and the lowest score as L, we see that crude range $(CR) = H - L$ and that the extended range $(ER) = (H - L) + 1$.

Which range should you report? For most practical purposes, you can use either the crude or the extended range. However, when measurement is not very precise and when the crude range is small, you will obtain a more accurate picture of the actual range when you calculate the extended range. Suppose you use a 3-point rating scale in your research and all the judges' ratings are at the midpoint value (i.e., 2 on your scale of 1 to 3). The crude range would be $2 - 2 = 0$, and the extended range would be $(2 - 2) + 1 = 1$ (because some of your judges might theoretically have rated nearly as high as 2.5 and some nearly as low as 1.5 had those ratings been possible). A simple rule of thumb can help you decide when to report the crude range rather than the extended range. It involves dividing the crude range by the extended range. This *CR/ER* index yields zero in the extreme example just given and .90 if the crude range is 9 and the extended range is 10. With *CR/ER* as high as .90, it seems reasonable to report either of the ranges, but with *CR/ER* much lower, it may be more informative to report only the extended range.

THE AVERAGE DEVIATION AND THE INTERQUARTILE RANGE

Two measures of spread that you may see in a few reports are the *average deviation* and the *interquartile range*. The *average deviation* $(\overline{D})$ tells us the "average absolute distance" of all the scores in a series from the mean of the series. It indicates that the researcher has subtracted the mean $(\overline{X})$ from each score (X); has added these differences (D), disregarding signs; and has divided by the number of scores (N) in the series, or

$$\overline{D} = \frac{\Sigma|X - \overline{X}|}{N} = \frac{\Sigma|D|}{N}$$

For example, given the series of scores 4, 5, 5, 6, 10, we find the mean to be $30/5 = 6$. When we substract the mean from each score, the signed (or *algebraic*) deviations are $-2, -1, -1, 0$, and $+4$, respectively. The sum of the algebraic deviations about the mean is always zero, but the sum of the unsigned (or *absolute*) deviations is not often zero. In this example the sum of the absolute deviations is $2 + 1 + 1 + 0 + 4 = 8$, which, when divided by $N = 5$, gives $\overline{D} = 8/5 = 1.6$. Notice that this measure of spread uses more of the information in a series of scores than does the range, which uses only the largest and smallest scores.

Another measure of spread that you may see mentioned is the *interquartile range*, which is defined as the difference between the 75th percentile and the 25th percentile. For the stem-and-leaf display in Box 10.3, the interquartile range is $.37 - .17 = .20$. The interquartile range is typically reported when the reported measure of location is the median. Two additional measures of spread—the variance and the standard deviation—are the most popular measures; they also play a central role in statistical significance testing (discussed in Chapter 12). As you will see next, the variance and the standard deviation are also very directly related to one another.

The Variance and the Standard Deviation

The *variance* of a set of scores tells us the deviation from the mean of the scores, but instead of using deviation values directly, it squares the deviations and then averages them. In other words, it is the mean of the squared deviations of the scores *(X)* from their mean *(X̄)*. It also is referred to as the *mean square* (i.e., the mean of the squared deviations); you will see this term used again in our discussion of the *F* test, which is employed in the statistical procedure known as *analysis of variance*. The symbol used to denote the variance of a population is σ^2 (read as "sigma-squared"), and the formula used to calculate this value is

$$\sigma^2 = \frac{\Sigma (X - \overline{X})^2}{N}$$

The *standard deviation* is simply the square root of this value, or $\sqrt{\sigma^2}$. Another name for the standard deviation is the *root mean square*, which is shorthand for the square root of the mean of the squared deviations. This measure is by far the most widely used and reported of all measures of spread around the average.

If you do not have a calculator that allows you to compute the standard deviation and the variance directly from "raw" (i.e., obtained) scores, it is still easy to compute these values with the calculator you use to balance your checkbook. Table 10.2 shows the basic arithmetic required. The first column lists six raw scores, which (as ΣX denotes) sum to 30. It also shows the mean *(X̄)* as $30/6 = 5$. The second column lists the algebraic deviations of the individual raw scores from the mean, and the third column lists the squared deviations. Substituting in the

TABLE 10.2	Summary Data for Computing the Variance and the Standard Deviation	
Raw Scores	$X - \overline{X}$	$(X - \overline{X})^2$
2	−3	9
4	−1	1
4	−1	1
5	0	0
7	2	4
8	3	9
$\Sigma X = 30$	$\Sigma (X - \overline{X}) = 0$	$\Sigma (X - \overline{X})^2 = 24$
$\overline{X} = 5$		

$$\sigma^2 = \frac{\Sigma(X - \overline{X})^2}{N} = \frac{24}{6} = 4$$

$$\sigma = \sqrt{\frac{\Sigma(X - \overline{X})^2}{N}} = \sqrt{\frac{24}{6}} = \sqrt{4} = 2$$

variance formula, we find $\sigma^2 = 4$. The standard deviation is the square root of 4 or, in other words,

$$\sigma = \sqrt{\sigma^2} = \sqrt{4} = 2$$

Incidentally, summing the $X - \overline{X}$ differences (column 2) will always give zero if you have done your calculations correctly. The reason, of course, is that when you subtract all the scores in a closed set from the average of the set, the positive differences will cancel out the negative differences. So if you get a number other than zero when you add up your $X - \overline{X}$ differences, you have made a calculation or recording error. As a check on your understanding, you might try computing the standard deviation and the variance of the stem-and-leaf values in Box 10.3. (We will tell you the answer later.)

DESCRIPTIVE AND INFERENTIAL FORMULAS

Another distinction is that made between *descriptive and inferential formulas.* Suppose we are interested in the variability of the batting averages of a favorite baseball team. We collect the scores of all the players and then compute the standard deviation using the formula described above. In this case, the formula for measuring variability is characterized as a *descriptive* one, because it describes a finite population of events—with Greek letters used to symbolize the particular measure (e.g., σ or σ^2).

Researchers are also interested in generalizing from a sample of known events to a population of unknown events that may be either finite or infinite. Suppose, based on samples of sand that have been randomly collected, we want to make a generalization about the variability of all the sand at Atlantic City. Here, we are attempting to make an inference from a finite sample to a population of unknown "events" that is regarded as infinite (because of ecological changes and so on). By contrast, suppose we are interested in estimating the variability of all major-league baseball players' batting averages based on a sample of scores. We are again dealing with a finite sample of known events, but this time the population of unknown events is also a finite set. In either case, the formula that we use to measure variability will be characterized as an *inferential* one—with roman letters used to symbolize the particular measure (e.g., S or S^2).

Except for the denominator and the symbol (Greek or roman), descriptive and inferential formulas for computing variances (and therefore standard deviations) are identical. In the descriptive formulas for variances and standard deviations, the numerator is divided by N (as previously shown). In the inferential formulas, the numerator is instead divided by $N - 1$ (because it can be shown statistically that, with repeated sampling, this procedure gives the most accurate inferences). Thus, if our aim is to estimate the σ^2 of a population, we employ the statistic S^2 (referred to as the *unbiased estimator of the population value of* σ^2), using the following formula:

$$S^2 = \frac{\Sigma\ (X - \overline{X})^2}{N - 1}$$

The inferential formula for the standard deviation thus becomes

$$S = \sqrt{S^2} = \sqrt{\frac{\Sigma (X - \bar{X})^2}{N - 1}}$$

For example, if you wanted to generalize from the raw scores in Table 10.2 to the target population from which the scores were obtained, you would compute

$$S^2 = \frac{(2 - 5)^2 + (4 - 5)^2 + (4 - 5)^2 + (5 - 5)^2 + (7 - 5)^2 + (8 - 5)^2}{6 - 1}$$

$$= \frac{24}{5} = 4.8$$

and

$$S = \sqrt{S^2} = \sqrt{4.8} = 2.19$$

Did you try computing the standard deviation and the variance on the stem-and-leaf values in Box 10.3? The answers are $\sigma = .115$ and $\sigma^2 = .013$. If you use the inferential formulas above, you will find that $S = .118$ and $S^2 = .014$.

THE NORMAL DISTRIBUTION

When scores on a variety of types of sampling units (e.g., intelligence test scores, running speeds of rats, or scores on an attitude scale) are collected by means of a representative sampling procedure, the distribution of these scores often forms a curve that has a distinct bell-like shape (as shown in Figure 10.6). This curve is called a *normal distribution* because of the large number of different kinds of measurements that are assumed to be ordinarily ("normally") distributed in this manner.

The normal distribution is useful because it can be completely described from our knowledge of just the mean and the standard deviation. For example, we can

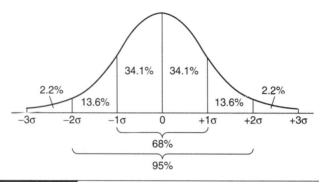

FIGURE 10.6   *The normal distribution divided up into standard deviation units.*

say that roughly two thirds of the area of the normal distribution is within one standard deviation of the average, or we can say that roughly 95% of the area is within two standard deviations of the average, and so on. In other words, the normal distribution is useful because researchers can specify what proportion of normally distributed scores can be found in any region of the curve.

More specifically (as represented in Figure 10.6), 68.3% of normally distributed scores will fall between -1σ and $+1\sigma$, 95.4% will fall between -2σ and $+2\sigma$, and 99.7% will fall between -3σ and $+3\sigma$. Even though over 99% of the scores fall between -3σ and $+3\sigma$, notice that the tails of the normal curve never do touch down on the abscissa (instead, they stretch into infinity).

Because so many measurements are distributed normally, the statistics derived from this bell-shaped curve are very important in the testing of hypotheses. We will return to this topic in Chapter 12, but we must mention here one useful statistical measure, the *standard score* (or *Z* score).

STANDARD SCORES

A normal curve with a mean set equal to 0 and a standard deviation set equal to 1 is referred to technically as a *standard normal curve*. Any score can be *transformed* (i.e., statistically translated or modified) into a *standard score* (or *Z* score) corresponding to a location on the abscissa of a standard normal curve. We make such a transformation by subtracting the mean of all the scores from the particular obtained score and then dividing this difference by the standard deviation of all the obtained scores.

For example, imagine a mean $(\overline{X})$ of 500 and a standard deviation (σ) of 100 for the Scholastic Assessment Test (a standard assumption). It follows that an SAT score of 625 would be equivalent to a standard score of 1.25. That is,

$$Z \text{ score} = \frac{X - \overline{X}}{\sigma} = \frac{625 - 500}{100} = 1.25$$

Turning to Table B.1 in Appendix B (see page 382), we find a listing of standard normal deviates (i.e., *Z* scores). The *Z* column (with rows ranging from .0 to 4.0) lists such scores to a single decimal place. The remaining columns (.00 to .09) carry *Z* to two decimal places. The body of the table shows the proportion of the area of the normal distribution that includes and is to the right of (i.e., above) the value of any particular *Z* on the abscissa.

For example, given $Z = 1.25$, we locate the intersection that corresponds to 1.2 (row 13) and .05 (column 6). That value is .1056, which tells us the proportion of SAT scores including and higher than an obtained score of 625 in the population of students taking the SAT. Multiplying .1056 by 100 transforms the proportion into a percentage, which informs us that 10.56% of those tested scored as high as 625 or higher. Subtracting this percentage from 100 reveals how many scored lower than 625 (i.e., 100 - 10.56 = 89.44% scored lower). It is not necessary for scores to be normally distributed for us to transform them into *Z* scores. However, only if they are distributed approximately normally can we tell from a Z score how many scored above or below a given Z score. We can do so for the SAT scores because they are approximately normally distributed.

Note that the title of Table B.1 refers to "one-tailed" p values. We will have more to say about *one-tailed* (or *one-sided*) significance levels in other chapters, but basically the term means that we are concentrating on one part of the normal distribution. In the case of a positive Z score, we are focusing on the part from the midpoint (0) to the end of the right tail. If the Z were a negative score, we would be concentrating on the part from the midpoint to the end of the left tail.

In summary, a positive Z score is above the mean, a negative Z score is below the mean, and a zero Z score is at the mean. Knowing this, we can use Z scores to compare (and average) raw scores from distributions of widely differing means and standard deviations. For example, by calculating Z scores for height and weight, we can tell whether a person is taller than he or she is heavy, relative to others in the distribution of height and weight.

As an illustration of the utility of Z scores, imagine that an instructor has two measures of course grades on five male (M) and five female (F) students, as shown in Table 10.3. One set of scores is based on an essay exam of 50 points with $\overline{X} = 21.2$ and $\sigma = 11.69$, and another is based on a multiple-choice exam of 100 points with $\overline{X} = 68.8$ and $\sigma = 17.47$. The instructor transforms the raw scores into Z scores, with the results shown in this table. For example, the first student received a score of 42 on Exam 1, which the instructor converts to a Z score by computing $(42 - 21.2)/11.69 = +1.78$. This student's score on Exam 1 is almost two standard deviations above the mean, but the second student's score on the same exam is approximately one standard deviation *below* the mean.

TABLE 10.3	Raw and Standard Scores on Two Exams				
	Exam 1		Exam 2		Average of
Student	Raw score	Z score	Raw score	Z score	Z scores
1 (M)	42	+1.78	90	+1.21	+1.50
2 (M)	9	−1.04	40	−1.65	−1.34
3 (F)	28	+ .58	92	+1.33	+ .96
4 (M)	11	− .87	50	−1.08	− .98
5 (M)	8	−1.13	49	−1.13	−1.13
6 (F)	15	− .53	63	−.33	− .43
7 (M)	14	− .62	68	−.05	− .34
8 (F)	25	+ .33	75	+.35	+ .34
9 (F)	40	+1.61	89	+1.16	+1.38
10 (F)	20	− .10	72	+ .18	+ .04
Σ	212	0	688	0	0
$\overline{X}$	21.2	0	68.8	0	0
σ	11.69	1.0	17.47	1.0	0.98[a]

[a]Note that the averages of two or more Z scores are not themselves distributed as Z scores with $\sigma = 1.00$. If we want the averages of Z scores to be distributed as Z, we must first Z-score these averages.

The *Z* scores take this information into account, allowing the instructor to make easy comparisons within and across students. Here, the instructor counted the two exams equally to get the average score (in the last column), but it is easy enough to weight them. Suppose she had wanted to count the second exam twice as much as the first exam; she would double the Exam 2 *Z* score before averaging the two exams and divide by 3 instead of 2.

SUMMARY OF IDEAS

1. In a frequency distribution, a set of scores is arranged according to incidence of occurrence either in a table or in a figure such as a histogram or a frequency polygon.
2. In a stem-and-leaf display, the original data are preserved with any desired precision.
3. A stem-and-leaf display used to analyze reported proportions of no-shows revealed that it is a good idea to schedule one-half more subjects than are needed.
4. A percentile locates a score in a distribution by defining the point below which a given percentage of the cases fall.
5. The median (or 50th percentile) is the midmost score of a distribution.
6. The mode is the score occurring with greatest frequency.
7. The mean is the arithmetic average of a set of scores.
8. Trimmed means are useful when distributions are strongly asymmetrical.
9. Medians and trimmed means protect us somewhat against the intrusion of wild scores.
10. The range is the distance between the highest and lowest scores, sometimes corrected (extended) to increase precision.
11. The average deviation is the average absolute distance from the mean of all the scores.
12. The variance is the average *squared* distance from the mean of all the scores; the standard deviation is the square root of the variance.
13. Descriptive statistics describe known events, whereas inferential statistics enable us to make better estimates about unknown events based on a sample of values taken from a target population.
14. The normal distribution is a bell-shaped curve that is completely described by the mean and the standard deviation.
15. We calculate *Z* scores by transforming raw scores to standard deviation units. Such units permit the comparison (and averaging) of scores from distributions of widely differing means and standard deviations.

KEY TERMS

abscissa   *p. 215*

absolute deviation   *p. 223*

algebraic deviation   *p. 223*

asymmetrical   *p. 221*

average deviation ($\overline{D}$)   *p. 223*

central tendency   *p. 218*

REVIEW QUESTIONS

1. A University of Oregon student conducted a study on anxiety in 11 business executives. Their scores on a standardized test of anxiety were 32, 16, 29, 41, 33, 37, 27, 30, 22, 38, and 33. Can you reconstruct the student's stem-and-leaf plot for these scores? What is the median of these scores, and what are the extended range and the interquartile range?

2. A Fordham student is interested in studying ways of cutting down noise pollution in Manhattan. Her first step is to buy a machine that will measure the loudness of various sounds. In order to decide which machine to buy, she tests four brands against a standard tone of 85 decibels for five trials each, with the results shown below. Assuming that all the machines have the same price, which should be her first choice?

	Machine A	*Machine B*	*Machine C*	*Machine D*
	76	84	83	85
	82	87	89	81
	78	83	91	93
	84	85	77	89
	80	86	105	77
Mean	80	85	89	85
S	3.16	1.58	10.49	6.32

Oops. . . the manufacturer has run out of her first-choice brand. Which machine would you recommend as her second choice, and why?

3. A Haverford student recorded the following scores: 22, 14, 16, 24, 13, 26, 17, 98, 11, 9, and 21. What measure of central tendency would you advise him to calculate? Why?

4. A Florida State student was looking at her grades for the midterm and the final exam. On the midterm she got a score of 58, and the class mean was 52 with a standard deviation of 12. On the final she got a score of 110; the class mean was 100 with a standard deviation of 30. On which test did she do better?

5. A Brandeis student calls home to tell his family that he just received a score of 2 on a new IQ test. As they wonder why they are spending so much money on his tuition, he reassures them that 2 is his Z score. What percentage of the population did he score above?

6. A University of Missouri professor has three sections with three graduate assistants—Tom, Dick, and Harry—each of whom has six students. The time has come to grade papers. In order to ensure uniform grading standards across the sections, the professor instructs the assistants to give an average score of 8.0 (equivalent to B−) on a scale of 1 to 12 (where 1 represents a grade of F, and 12 represents a grade of A). The assistants submit the following sets of grades:

Tom	Dick	Harry
12	8	7
6	8	7
5	10	8
5	7	5
8	8	6
12	7	9

The professor calls in Harry and says, "You have not followed my instructions. Your scores are biased toward having your section do better than it was supposed to." Calculate the means of each section, and then argue the truth or falsity of the professor's accusation. The professor next calls in Tom and Dick and says, "Although both of your sections have a mean grade of 8.0, Tom's scores look more spread out." Calculate, and then compare, the variance of the scores in the sections to decide whether the professor is right. Which is a better grade (relative to one's own section), a 5 in Tom's section or a 7 in Dick's section?

Answers to review questions are found on pages 320-334

Establishing Relationships

THE CORRELATION COEFFICIENT

We have seen that researchers view variables not in isolation, but as being systematically and meaningfully associated with or related to other variables. In this chapter we examine how correlational procedures are used to measure the strength of association between two variables (referred to as X and Y). In particular, we describe correlation coefficients that reflect the degree to which mutual relations between X and Y resemble a straight line (also called *linearity*). The Pearson r (see Box 11.1) is the correlation coefficient of choice in such situations, with values of 1.0 (positive *or* negative) indicating a perfect linear relation. A positive r means that an increase in X is associated with an increase in Y, whereas a negative r means that an increase in X is associated with a *decrease* in Y.

Causation implies correlation (or covariation), but finding that X and Y are correlated does not necessarily imply causation. In Chapter 7 we noted that, although covariation is essential evidence for making causal inferences, other requirements

BOX 11.1   Karl Pearson (1857-1936)

In an earlier chapter we mentioned Francis Galton's work, and one of his many research projects concerned the relationship between traits of fathers and their adult sons. Galton, who was very intuitive about both research and statistics, invented a way of measuring the strength of association between the two variables. Inspired by his mentor's statistical thinking, Karl Pearson perfected Galton's idea into the more general method of correlation that has come to be known as the *Pearson r* (Stigler, 1986).

of evidence include temporal precedence and internal validity. Another important consideration is whether another variable that is correlated with both X and Y could be the cause of both—called the *third-variable problem*. To illustrate, John Paulos (the mathematician mentioned earlier in this book) gives his students data demonstrating conclusively a high positive relation between the size of children's feet and their spelling ability. "Should we therefore use foot stretchers to increase spelling scores?" he then asks the class (Paulos, 1991, p. A25). The answer, of course, is no. The more likely reason for the high correlation is that children with bigger feet are usually older, and older children spell better. In other words, a third variable (age) could account for the correlation between X and Y (see also Box 11.2).

We will begin by examining what different values of r look like. Then we proceed through the steps in computing the correlation coefficient when the data have different characteristics (previewed in Table 11.1), such as when the values of X and Y are continuous or dichotomous. For example, imagine that a psychophysicist who studies the discrimination of pitch (i.e., the highness or lowness of a tone) wants to correlate changes in the frequency of sound waves with the differing abil-

BOX 11.2   The Third Variable Problem

In his book *Innumeracy: Mathematical Illiteracy and Its Consequences,* John Paulos (1990) mentioned the moderate positive correlation between milk consumption and the incidence of cancer in various societies: "The correlation is probably explained by the relative wealth of these societies, bringing about both increased milk consumption and more cancer due to greater longevity. In fact, any health practice, such as milk drinking, which correlates positively with longevity will probably do the same with cancer incidence" (p. 159). Another example is the small negative correlation between death rates and divorce rates (i.e., more divorce, less death) in various regions of the country. The third variable proposed by Paulos is the age distribution of the various regions: "Older married couples are less likely to divorce and more likely to die than younger married couples. In fact, because divorce is such a wrenching, stressful experience, it probably raises one's risk of death, and thus the reality is quite contrary to the above misleading correlation" (p. 159).

TABLE 11.1	Basic Forms of Product–Moment Correlations
Common name	Characteristics of the data
Pearson *r*	Two continuous variables, such as correlating scores on the Scholastic Assessment Test (SAT) with grade-point average (GPA) after four years of college
Spearman rho	Two ranked variables, such as correlating the ranking of the top 25 college basketball teams by sports writers (Associated Press ranking) with the ranking of the same teams by college coaches (*USA Today* ranking)
Point biserial	One continuous and one dichotomous variable, such as correlating subjects' gender with their performance on the SAT-Verbal
Phi	Two dichotomous variables, such as correlating subjects' gender with their yes-or-no responses to a specific question

ity of subjects to discriminate the changes. The values of both variables are *continuous,* in that we can always imagine another number falling between any two adjacent scores (e.g., 1.5 between 1 and 2, or 1.55 between 1.5 and 1.6). Alternatively, suppose that the psychophysicist wants to correlate the variable of the subjects' gender with their abilities to discriminate pitch. Pitch discrimination is a *continuous variable,* but gender is a *dichotomous variable* (i.e., divided into two parts). Gender is naturally dichotomous (male and female), but we can also sometimes create dichotomies by splitting variables at the median point (the split is called a *median split*; we will return to this idea when we discuss the binomial effect-size display in the next chapter).

VISUALIZING THE CORRELATION COEFFICIENT

In addition to the graphics described in the preceding chapter, another informative visual display is called a *scatter plot* (or *scatter diagram*). It takes its name from the fact that it looks like a cloud of scattered dots. Each dot represents the intersection

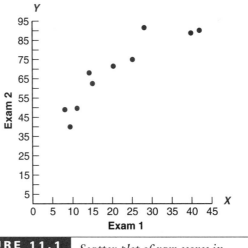

FIGURE 11.1   *Scatter plot of raw scores in Table 11.2.*

of a line extended from a point on the X axis and a line extended from a point on the Y axis. To illustrate, Table 11.2 repeats the data we used in the previous chapter to explain Z scores, and we will continue to discuss these data in this chapter. For now, we will concentrate on the raw scores of these 10 students on the two exams. Figure 11.1 displays these scores in the form of a scatter plot.

By way of comparison, Figure 11.2 shows additional scatter plots (each containing 50 dots) that represent different values of the correlation coefficient, including zero and near-perfect r's. However, remember that even a perfect r is not necessarily indicative of a cause-and-effect relation, because there might be a third variable (i.e., the true cause) that correlates perfectly with both X and Y. Notice that the higher the correlation coefficient is, the more tightly clustered along a straight line are the dots. Observe also that the cloud of dots slopes up for positive correlations and slopes down for negative correlations, whereas the linearity becomes clearer as the correlation becomes higher (see also Box 11.3). From these diagrams, what would you guess is the size of the Pearson r represented by the data in Figure 11.1?

CALCULATING THE PEARSON r

There are many useful formulas for computing Karl Pearson's correlation coefficient, but the following formula (which defines the Pearson r conceptually) can be used quite generally:

$$r_{xy} = \frac{\Sigma Z_x Z_y}{N}$$

It signifies that the correlation between X and Y is equal to the sum of the products of the Z scores of X and Y divided by the number (N) of pairs of X and Y

TABLE 11.2	Raw and Standardized Data for Correlation Coefficients				
	Exam 1		Exam 2		Product of
Student	Raw Score	Z Score	Raw Score	Z Score	Z Scores
1 (M)	42	+1.78	90	+1.21	+2.15
2 (M)	9	−1.04	40	−1.65	+1.72
3 (F)	28	+ .58	92	+1.33	+ .77
4 (M)	11	− .87	50	−1.08	+ .94
5 (M)	8	−1.13	49	−1.13	+1.28
6 (F)	15	− .53	63	− .33	+ .17
7 (M)	14	− .62	68	− .05	+ .03
8 (F)	25	+ .33	75	+ .35	+ .12
9 (F)	40	+1.61	89	+1.16	+1.87
10 (F)	20	− .10	72	+ .18	− .02
Σ	212	0	688	0	+9.03
$\overline{X}$	21.2	0	68.8	0	+ .90
σ	11.69	1.0	17.47	1.0	

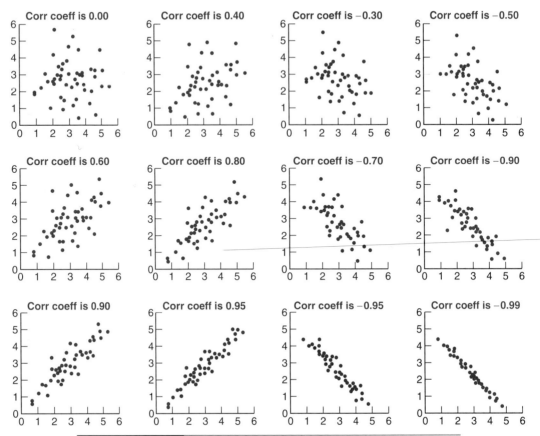

FIGURE 11.2   *Scatter plots representing different values of the correlation coefficient. (D. Freedman, R. Pisani, R. Purves, and A. Adhikari, Statistics (2nd ed.), W. W. Norton, New York. Reproduced from pp. 119, 121 by permission of the first author and the publisher.)*

scores. The Pearson r is also called the *product–moment correlation* because the Z's are distances from the mean (also called *moments*) that are multiplied by each other to form *products*. To use this formula for calculation, you would begin by transforming the X and Y scores (i.e., the raw scores) to Z scores following the procedure described in the previous chapter. That is, you would calculate the mean and the standard deviation of each column of raw scores and then substitute in the $(X - \overline{X})/\sigma$ formula.

In Table 11.2 we see such Z scores corresponding to the students' individual raw scores on Exam 1 and Exam 2. Notice that, for Student 5, the Z score for Exam 1 is identical to the Z score for Exam 2, even though the raw scores are very different. The reason, of course, is that the Z scores for Exam 1 were computed by

| **BOX 11.3** | Linearity and Nonlinearity |

Linearity means that the mutual relation between two variables resembles a straight line. For example, temperature in centigrade can be converted to fahrenheit (and vice versa) by means of a straight line connecting the two scales:

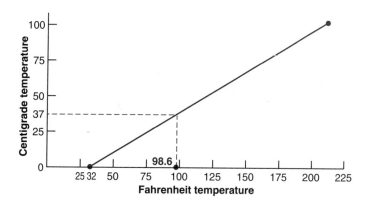

If we computed a correlation coefficient for these data, we would find that r was equal to +1.0, reflecting a perfect positive linear relation.

Nonlinearity, on the other hand, can take many different forms, for example, U-shaped, J-shaped, and wave-shaped curves. Suppose we were studying the relation between age and the latency of some response, and we found that latency decreased up to a certain age and then gradually increased. The curve showing this nonlinear relation would resemble a *U*, with age plotted on the abscissa (*X* axis) and latency of response (from low to high) on the ordinate (*Y* axis). Other examples of nonlinear relations include curves for learning, extinction, dark adaptation, response rate as a function of the amount of reinforcement, and so on (e.g., Grant, 1956; Malmo, 1959).

the use of the mean and standard deviation of Exam 1 (21.2 and 11.69, respectively), whereas the Z scores for Exam 2 were computed by the use of the mean and standard deviation of that exam (68.8 and 17.47, respectively). Instead of averaging the Z scores (as we did in the previous chapter for a very different purpose), the last column gives the *products* of the Z scores and their mean, showing that $r = .90$.

This formula, although clear enough conceptually, requires tedious calculations to arrive at r. If you are working with a statistics program and a computer, this is not a problem. It is also not a problem if you have a pocket calculator that computes r's directly. But there is also an easier way of computing this r if all you have handy is a calculator that cumulates scores and squares of scores. You could use the following formula, which is based on the raw scores alone:

$$r_{xy} = \frac{N\Sigma XY - (\Sigma X)(\Sigma Y)}{\sqrt{[N\Sigma X^2 - (\Sigma X)^2][N\Sigma Y^2 - (\Sigma Y)^2]}}$$

where N is the number of X and Y pairs of scores, and Σ directs us to sum a set of values. This formula may look difficult, but it is not hard to use. All we need are the sums of the scores and of the squared scores.

To illustrate, Table 11.3 shows the basic data required to compute r from the raw scores in Table 11.2. Substituting these numbers into the formula above gives

$$r_{xy} = \frac{10(16,430) - (212)(688)}{\sqrt{[10(5,860) - (212)^2][10(50,388) - (688)^2]}}$$

$$= \frac{164,300 - 145,856}{\sqrt{(58,600 - 44,944)(503,880 - 473,344)}} = \frac{18,444}{\sqrt{(13,656)(30,536)}}$$

$$= \frac{18,444}{\sqrt{416,999,616}} = \frac{18,444}{20,420.57} = .90$$

When using the formula above, don't forget to take the square root of the denominator!

SPEARMAN RANK CORRELATION

Imagine a set of data in which the units are ranks rather than scores on a rating scale. When the data are in this form, the correlation coefficient is called the *Spearman rho* (ρ), but this—as you will see—is nothing more than the product–moment

| TABLE 11.3 | Basic Data for Computing r from Scratch |

	Exam 1		Exam 2		
Student	X	X²	Y	Y²	XY
1	42	1,764	90	8,100	3,780
2	9	81	40	1,600	360
3	28	784	92	8,464	2,576
4	11	121	50	2,500	550
5	8	64	49	2,401	392
6	15	225	63	3,969	945
7	14	196	68	4,624	952
8	25	625	75	5,625	1,875
9	40	1,600	89	7,921	3,560
10	20	400	72	5,184	1,440
Σ	212	5,860	688	50,388	16,430

r calculated on numbers that happen to be ranks. Because ranked numbers are more predictable (in the sense that knowing only the number of pairs of scores tells us both the mean and the standard deviation of the scores that have been ranked), you can work with the formula below for scores that have been ranked:

$$r_{rho} = \rho = 1 - \frac{6\Sigma D^2}{N^3 - N}$$

where 6 is a constant value, and *N* is the number of pairs of scores or ranks. The only new element is *D,* the difference between the ranks assigned to the two members of each pair of sampling units.

To illustrate the use of this formula, we turn to Table 11.4, which shows a portion of the data collected by Paul Slovic (1987) in his investigation of the perception of risk. He was interested in comparing the judgments people make when they are asked to characterize and evaluate hazardous activities and technologies. This table shows the overall rankings made by 15 national experts on risk assessment and 40 members of the League of Women Voters (LWV). We see, for example, that the experts ranked motor vehicles as most hazardous (Rank 1) and skiing as least hazardous (Rank 30), whereas the LWV members ranked nuclear power as most hazardous (Rank 1) and vaccinations as least hazardous (Rank 30). Notice that the sums of the ranks are equal for the two variables (465). The column headed *D* lists the differences between the ranks. For example, the difference in ranking of nuclear power is computed as $D = 1 - 20 = -19$. The sum of the *D* scores is always 0. The column headed D^2 shows such differences squared, so that $(-19)^2 = 361$. The sum of the squared differences—indicated as 1,828 at the bottom of the column headed D^2—is now substituted in the Spearman rho formula:

$$r_{rho} = \rho = 1 - \frac{6(1,828)}{(30)^3 - 30} = .59$$

In interpreting rank correlations, we may use the *D* scores and the ranks to identify similarities and differences in the results. A positive difference tells us that the LWV members perceived the activity or technology as less risky than did the experts, whereas a negative difference indicates the opposite conclusion. For example, we see that these two groups of raters disagreed little about the high risks associated with motor vehicles, handguns, and smoking (*D*'s of +1 or −1). There was little disagreement about the much lower risk associated with power mowers ($D = -1$), but there was strong disagreement about nuclear power ($D = -19$), X-rays ($D = 15$), and mountain climbing ($D = -14$).

To show why we characterized the Spearman rho as a Pearson *r* calculated on numbers that happen to be ranks, we turn next to Table 11.5. The columns containing *Z* scores show the standard scores of the ranks. For example, to find the *Z* score corresponding to the LWV's ranking of nuclear power, we computed

$$Z = \frac{X - \overline{X}}{\sigma} = \frac{1 - 15.50}{8.655} = -1.68$$

TABLE 11.4	Ordering of Perceived Risk for 30 Activities and Technologies			
Activity or Technology	League of Women Voters	Experts	D	D²
Nuclear power	1	20	−19	361
Motor vehicles	2	1	1	1
Handguns	3	4	−1	1
Smoking	4	2	2	4
Motorcycles	5	6	−1	1
Alcoholic beverages	6	3	3	9
General (private) aviation	7	12	−5	25
Police work	8	17	−9	81
Pesticides	9	8	1	1
Surgery	10	5	5	25
Fire fighting	11	18	−7	49
Large construction	12	13	−1	1
Hunting	13	23	−10	100
Spray cans	14	26	−12	144
Mountain climbing	15	29	−14	196
Bicycles	16	15	1	1
Commercial aviation	17	16	1	1
Electric power (nonnuclear)	18	9	9	81
Swimming	19	10	9	81
Contraceptives	20	11	9	81
Skiing	21	30	−9	81
X-rays	22	7	15	225
High school and college football	23	27	−4	16
Railroads	24	19	5	25
Food preservatives	25	14	11	121
Food coloring	26	21	5	25
Power mowers	27	28	−1	1
Prescription antibiotics	28	24	4	16
Home appliances	29	22	7	49
Vaccinations	30	25	5	25
Σ	465	465	0	1828

Source: Reproduced from "Perception of Risk" by P. Slovic, 1987, *Science, 236*, p. 281. Used by permission of Paul Slovic and the American Association for the Advancement of Science.

The last column shows the products of the *Z*-scored ranks, with the sum and mean indicated at the bottom. Recalling that the mean of the products is the Pearson *r*, we see that it is identical to the value we obtained using the Spearman rho formula; that is,

$$r_{rho} = \frac{\Sigma Z_x Z_y}{N} = \frac{17.82}{30} = .59$$

Suppose we were working with raw scores that were continuous but we wanted to recast them as ranks and then use the Spearman rho formula (see also Box

TABLE 11.5	Ranked and Standardized Data for Spearman rho				
Activity or Technology	League of Women Voters		Experts		Product of Z Scores
	Rank	Z Score	Rank	Z Score	
Nuclear power	1	−1.68	20	+ .52	− .87
Motor vehicles	2	−1.56	1	−1.68	+2.62
Handguns	3	−1.44	4	−1.33	+1.92
Smoking	4	−1.33	2	−1.56	+2.07
Motorcycles	5	−1.21	6	−1.10	+1.33
Alcoholic beverages	6	−1.10	3	−1.44	+1.58
General aviation	7	− .98	12	− .40	+ .39
Police work	8	− .87	17	+ .17	− .15
Pesticides	9	− .75	8	− .87	+ .65
Surgery	10	− .64	5	−1.21	+ .77
Fire fighting	11	− .52	18	+ .29	− .15
Large construction	12	− .40	13	− .29	+ .12
Hunting	13	− .29	23	+ .87	− .25
Spray cans	14	− .17	26	+1.21	− .21
Mountain climbing	15	− .06	29	+1.56	− .09
Bicycles	16	+ .06	15	− .06	.00
Commercial aviation	17	+ .17	16	+ .06	+ .01
Electric power	18	+ .29	9	− .75	− .22
Swimming	19	+ .40	10	− .64	− .26
Contraceptives	20	+ .52	11	− .52	− .27
Skiing	21	+ .64	30	+1.68	+1.08
X-rays	22	+ .75	7	− .98	− .74
High school and college football	23	+ .87	27	+1.33	+1.16
Railroads	24	+ .98	19	+ .40	+ .39
Food preservatives	25	+1.10	14	− .17	− .19
Food coloring	26	+1.21	21	+ .64	+ .77
Power mowers	27	+1.33	28	+1.44	+1.92
Prescription antibiotics	28	+1.44	24	+ .98	+1.41
Home appliances	29	+1.56	22	+ .75	+1.17
Vaccinations	30	+1.68	25	+1.10	+1.85
Σ	465	0	465	0	17.82
$\overline{X}$	15.50	0	15.50	0	.59
σ	8.655	1.00	8.655	1.00	—

11.4). Table 11.6 shows how this is done with the data from our continuing example. The students are ranked from 1 (highest raw score) to 10 (lowest raw score), and again the D score is the difference between these rankings. The sum of the squared differences—indicated as 10 at the bottom of the column headed D^2—is substituted in the Spearman rho formula:

$$\rho = 1 - \frac{6(10)}{(10)^3 - 10} = .94$$

BOX 11.4   The Utility of Ranking

Why use rankings when continuous data are available? Suppose you wanted a quick estimate of the correlation between the six pairs of scores shown below:

	Raw score for X	Raw score for Y	Rank of X	Rank of Y
Pair 1	73.8	801.76	2	1
Pair 2	186.2	732.90	1	2
Pair 3	44.4	539.47	3	3
Pair 4	38.6	206.11	4	5
Pair 5	37.5	210.56	5	4
Pair 6	21.8	159.33	6	6

Clearly it would be tedious to calculate r by hand from the raw scores in the first two columns. Transforming the scores into ranks and then calculating rho on the basis of the values in the last two columns is much easier. Another reason for preferring ranks to raw scores in some situations is that raw scores may include extreme outliers that may lead to misleading correlations; ranked scores never have extreme outliers.

POINT-BISERIAL CORRELATION

Another special case of the product–moment r is the *point-biserial correlation,* or r_{pb}. In this case one variable is continuous and the other variable is dichotomous with arbitrarily applied values such as 0 and 1 or −1 and +1. The quantification of the two levels of a dichotomous variable is called *dummy coding* when 0 and 1 are used. Dummy coding is a tremendously useful procedure, for it allows us to quantify certain qualitative variables. For example, suppose the qualitative variable is the treatment condition to which the subjects have been assigned in a study consisting of an experimental and a control group. To dummy-code this variable, we simply record 1 for experimental and 0 for control. Other examples of qualitative variables that can be easily recast into 0's and 1's are gender (female vs. male), survival rate (live vs. die), and success rate (succeed vs. fail).

Going back to our continuing example in Table 11.2, suppose we want to compare males (M) with females (F) on Exam 1. The scores for males and females on the first exam are as follows:

Males	*Females*
42	28
9	15
11	25
8	40
14	20

TABLE 11.6	Raw Data from Table 11.2 Ranked for Spearman Rho					

	Exam 1		Exam 2			
Student	Raw Score	Rank	Raw Score	Rank	D	D^2
1	42	1	90	2	−1	1
2	9	9	40	10	−1	1
3	28	3	92	1	2	4
4	11	8	50	8	0	0
5	8	10	49	9	1	1
6	15	6	63	7	−1	1
7	14	7	68	6	1	1
8	25	4	75	4	0	0
9	40	2	89	3	−1	1
10	20	5	72	5	0	0
Σ	212	55[a]	688	55[a]	0[b]	10

[a]Note that the sum of the ranks is equal for the two variables.
[b]Note that the sum of D is always 0.

Although we have two groups of scores, the arrangement does not look like the typical one for a correlation coefficient—where we would expect to see *pairs* of scores (i.e., X and Y) for each subject, not just one score as above. The data arrangement rewritten into a form that "looks more correlational" is shown in Table 11.7.

Under Variable X we see the raw and standard scores for each student on Exam 1, and under Variable Y we see the dummy-coded raw scores and standard scores for gender (with male students coded 0 and female students coded 1). All the Z scores are calculated in the usual way. For example, to find the Z score for Student 1's gender, you would compute

$$Z = \frac{X - \overline{X}}{\sigma} = \frac{0 - 0.5}{0.5} = -1$$

Notice that, as always, the Z scores sum to zero; another sum would signal a computational or recording mistake. Observe also that the standard deviation scores are $Z = -1$ for a dummy code of 0 and $Z = +1$ for a dummy code of 1, a situation always found when the number of 0 scores equals the number of 1 scores. And finally, the sum of the products of the Z scores corresponding to the X and Y variables is shown as 3.77. When we divide this result by the number of subjects ($N = 10$), we find that

$$r_{pb} = \frac{\Sigma Z_x Z_y}{N} = \frac{3.77}{10} = .38$$

	Variable X		Variable Y		Product of
Student	Exam 1	Z Score	Gender	Z Score	Z Scores
1 (M)	42	+1.78	0	−1	−1.78
2 (M)	9	−1.04	0	−1	+1.04
3 (F)	28	+ .58	1	+1	+ .58
4 (M)	11	− .87	0	−1	+ .87
5 (M)	8	−1.13	0	−1	+1.13
6 (F)	15	− .53	1	+1	− .53
7 (M)	14	− .62	0	−1	+ .62
8 (F)	25	+ .33	1	+1	+ .33
9 (F)	40	+1.61	1	+1	+1.61
10 (F)	20	− .10	1	+1	− .10
Σ	212	0	5	0	+3.77
$\overline{X}$	21.2	0	0.5	0	+ .38
σ	11.69	1.0	0.5	1.0	

TABLE 11.7 Raw, Dummy-Coded, and Standardized Data for Point-Biserial r

which tells us that this sample of students showed a moderate relation between gender and scores on Exam 1.

PHI COEFFICIENT

Not infrequently, both of the variables to be correlated are dichotomous. In Chapter 8, for example, we noted a hypothetical case in which people who ate a greasy hamburger became sick. Going back to Table 8.1 (page 172), suppose we are interested in quantifying the relation between these two variables. In such a situation we have another special case of the product–moment r called the *phi coefficient* (symbolized as either ϕ or r_{phi}). In this instance, both variables are dichotomous (with arbitrarily applied numerical values such as 0 and 1 or −1 and +1). This dichotomy is illustrated below, where we compare five people who ate the burger with three people who did not eat it:

Ate	Outcome	
burger	Sick	Well
No	0	3
Yes	5	0

This 2×2 table of frequencies (or *counts*)—also called a *contingency table*—shows that all five people who ate the burger became sick and that the three people who did not eat it remained well.

However, this configuration does not seem to resemble the more standard situation for a correlation coefficient, where we would expect to find pairs of scores (i.e., X and Y) for each subject. Nevertheless, if you use the dummy coding of the dichotomous variable in the previous example, you know exactly how to convert the data into Z scores and then calculate the Pearson r. Rewriting the data yields the arrangement shown in Table 11.8.

To obtain the value of phi, you need only substitute the sum of the products in the definitional formula for the Pearson r:

$$r_{\text{phi}} = \phi = \frac{\Sigma Z_x Z_y}{N} = \frac{8.0}{8} = 1.0$$

We have treated phi no differently from any product–moment r calculated on the basis of Z scores. There is an alternative formula that takes advantage of the fact that the data come to us in a 2×2 contingency table. In Table 11.9 we return to the previous display, but with parts of the table now labeled as A, B, C, and D. Using that code, you would calculate

$$r_{\text{phi}} = \phi = \frac{BC - AD}{\sqrt{(A + B)(C + D)(A + C)(B + D)}}$$

$$= \frac{(3)(5) - (0)(0)}{\sqrt{(3)\,(5)\,(5)\,(3)}} = 1.0$$

and (not unexpectedly) obtain the same result as with the definitional formula for the Pearson r.

TABLE 11.8 Dummy-Coded and Standardized Data for Phi Coefficient					
	Ate hamburger	Outcome	Standard scores for variables X and Y		
Name	(yes = 1; no = 0)	(sick = 1; well = 0)	Z_x	Z_y	$Z_x Z_y$
Mimi	1	1	.775	.775	.601
Connie	0	0	−1.291	−1.291	1.667
Greg	0	0	−1.291	−1.291	1.667
Nancy	1	1	.775	.775	.601
Jeffrey	0	0	−1.291	−1.291	1.667
Michele	1	1	.775	.775	.601
John	1	1	.775	.775	.601
Sheila	1	1	.775	.775	.601
Σ	5	5	.002	.002	8.006
$\overline{X}$	.625	.625	.000	.000	1.001
σ	.484	.484	1.000	1.000	.516

TABLE 11.9 | 2 × 2 Contingency Table Coded for Computation of Phi

	Sick	Well	
Didn't eat burger	A 0	B 3	(A + B) = 3
Did eat burger	5 C	0 D	(C + D) = 5
	(A + C) = 5	(B + D) = 3	

A FINAL NOTE

We will have more to say about the Pearson r in the following chapters, in which we return to the idea that the correlation coefficient can be a very valuable index of effect size. It is becoming increasingly important in empirical research that scientists routinely report the effect size, and (as we show in the following chapters) the Pearson r is easily computed and interpreted as a measure of the "practical importance" of the size of the effect.

SUMMARY OF IDEAS

1. The Pearson r is a standard index of linear relationship, with values from -1.0 to $+1.0$.
2. The third-variable problem is that another variable that is correlated with both X and Y may be the cause of both.
3. The Spearman rho is the Pearson r calculated on scores that happen to be in ranked form.
4. Calculating r on the unranked scores typically results in a different value for the correlation than calculating r, or rho, on the ranks, and therefore the correlation must be interpreted in the context of the data.
5. The point-biserial correlation is the Pearson r where one of the variables is continuous and the other is dichotomous.
6. Dummy-coding the dichotomous variable allows us to calculate the point-biserial correlation by the Pearson r formula.

7. In dummy-coded data, 0 converts to $Z = -1$, and 1 converts to $Z = +1$ when the number of 0s equals the number of 1's; in general, the 0 converts to a negative Z, whereas 1 converts to a positive Z.
8. The phi coefficient is the Pearson r where both variables are dichotomous.
9. To calculate the correlation between two dichotomous variables, we can (a) dummy-code both variables and then use the corresponding Z scores to compute the Pearson r or (b) compute phi directly from the 2×2 contingency table.

KEY TERMS

contingency table *p. 244*
continuous variable *p. 234*
dichotomous variable *p. 234*
dummy coding *p. 242*
linearity *p. 237*
median split *p. 234*
Pearson r *p. 233*

phi coefficient *p. 244*
point-biserial correlation *p. 242*
product–moment correlation *p. 236*
scatter plot *p. 234*
Spearman rank (rho) correlation *p. 238*
third-variable problem *p. 233*

REVIEW QUESTIONS

1. A St. Bonaventure researcher administers tests of IQ and reading ability to four high school students. In addition, their grade-point average (GPA) is obtained from school records, with the following results:

	IQ	Reading	GPA
Student 1	105	13	2.6
Student 2	113	17	3.4
Student 3	87	10	2.0
Student 4	125	19	3.8

The correlation between IQ and reading ability is $r = .98$. Without doing any direct calculation, the researcher says he knows the correlation between reading and GPA. Do you also know this correlation? What about the correlation between IQ and GPA—without any direct calculation?

2. Twenty subjects take part in a University of Minnesota study on the relationship between socioeconomic status (SES: coded as rich = 1, poor = 0) and shyness (coded as shy = 1, not shy = 0). Given the results shown below, what is the correlation between these two variables? What specific type of Pearson correlation is this?

	SES	Shyness		SES	Shyness
Subject 1	0	1	Subject 11	0	0
Subject 2	0	1	Subject 12	1	1
Subject 3	0	0	Subject 13	0	0
Subject 4	0	1	Subject 14	1	0
Subject 5	1	1	Subject 15	0	1
Subject 6	0	0	Subject 16	1	0
Subject 7	1	1	Subject 17	1	0
Subject 8	1	0	Subject 18	1	1
Subject 9	0	1	Subject 19	0	1
Subject 10	1	0	Subject 20	1	0

3. A student at the University of Waterloo had two judges rate infants' fussiness, with the following results:

	Rater 1	Rater 2
Infant 1	60	30
Infant 2	40	50
Infant 3	30	60
Infant 4	50	40

The interjudge agreement, in terms of r, was not what the student had hoped for: $r = -1.0$. So he got himself two more raters, whose ratings were as follows:

	Rater 3	Rater 4
Infant 1	60	130
Infant 2	40	150
Infant 3	30	160
Infant 4	50	140

What is the agreement, in terms of r, between Raters 3 and 4?

4. A Georgia State student has a job managing a 200-seat summer-stock theater that is filled to capacity on Saturday nights. To study the effect of staff courtesy on audience enjoyment, she asks the ticket taker to smile at 100 randomly selected patrons and to frown at 100 randomly selected patrons. After the show, each member of the audience rates his or her enjoyment of the performance on a 7-point scale. Can you identify the independent and dependent variables and then figure out a way to calculate the correlation between them?

5. A student at California State University at Chico administered two tests to five subjects with the following results:

	Test A	Test B
Subject 1	1	4
Subject 2	2	3
Subject 3	3	2
Subject 4	4	1
Subject 5	5	100

Show a scatter plot of the relationship between the scores on Test A and Test B. Is there anything troubling about this plot? Can you adjust this problem by employing a different version of a Pearson r? Show a scatter plot of the revised or transformed scores on Tests A and B. What is the correlation between the tests if you use (a) the original scores and (b) the revised or transformed scores?

6.   Two students from Foothill College compared their obtained scatter plots. Which plot is associated with the higher correlation? How can you tell just from inspecting the scatter plots? What are the actual r's associated with each plot?

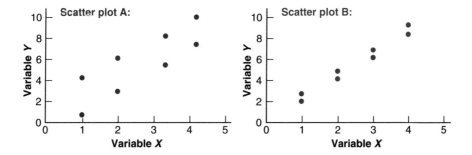

Answers to review questions are found on pages 320–334.

CHAPTER 12

Statistical Significance and Practical Importance

PREVIEW QUESTIONS

➤ **W**hat is the purpose of the null hypothesis in significance testing?

➤ **W**hat is the difference between Type I and Type II errors?

➤ **W**hat does the *p* value tell us?

➤ **W**hy is it also important to know the effect size?

➤ **W**hat is the power of a test, and how is it related to the number of subjects?

USE OF STATISTICS AND PROBABILITIES

Besides describing data (Chapter 10) and looking for mutual relations between variables (Chapter 11), scientists frequently make comparisons among research groups. For example, in Chapter 10 we described a study in which the participants rated the palatability of a new food product and a comparison food product already on the market. The new food product was rated more favorably on the average than was the comparison product. Because the researchers wanted to know whether the difference between these two means might be due to chance, they performed a simple test of significance. Finding the probability associated with the observed difference to be quite small, they concluded that the difference was real and not a result of chance (Street & Carroll, 1989).

In this chapter we explain the logic behind such tests of significance, and in the following chapters we concentrate on the computation and interpretation of the three most popular significance tests: the *t* test, the *F* test, and the chi-square. In describing this logic, we outline a two- or three-step process in which the general aim of the scientist is to gain some degree of information about the research results (Nelson, Rosenthal, & Rosnow, 1986). We review the reasoning and mechanics involved in each step in this process, but let us begin with an overall picture.

Briefly, in one of these steps some degree of information is gleaned when the *null hypothesis* (i.e., a supposition implying no difference between means or a correlation of zero between variables) can be rejected. Particular attention is paid to a level of probability that serves as the basis of this rejection (also called the *significance level*, or the *p value*). In another step, which may precede or follow the step already described, the scientist gains further information from the magnitude of the effect (or the *effect size*), which, interpreted in the context of the study's measurements, implies the "practical importance" of the observed result. In a third step—taken if the null hypothesis has not been rejected, but the effect size is promising—the scientist examines the "power" of the statistical test to see whether there was a realistic chance of rejecting the null hypothesis. However, it is prudent to consider the power of the statistical test even before implementing the study, because power improves with increases in the number of sampling units.

THE NULL HYPOTHESIS IN SIGNIFICANCE TESTING

In discussing these steps, we begin with an analogy based on an idea by Howard Wainer (1972). Imagine you are walking along the Atlantic City boardwalk or the Las Vegas strip when a shady character approaches and whispers he has a quarter that he is willing to sell you for *only* five dollars. What makes the coin worth so much more than its face value? The answer, he tells you, is that this is a quarter with extraordinary properties. When properly used, this quarter can win you fame and fortune because it does not always come up heads and tails with equal regularity. Instead, one outcome is more likely than the other. A smart person can, when flipping the coin, bet on the outcome and win a fortune, he says. "It might sound like a cock-and-bull story," he says, "but flip the coin and see for yourself."

If the coin is not what the street entrepreneur says it is, this means that getting a head or a tail is the result purely of chance. Thinking experimentally, you decide to test whether the probability of heads does or does not equal the probability of tails. You flip the coin once and heads appears. You flip the coin again, and again it comes up heads. Suppose you flip the coin nine times and each time it comes up heads. Would you believe him at this point? If your answer is yes, then would you believe him if, in nine tosses, the coin came up heads eight times and tails once? This is the essential problem in significance testing. You can be as stringent as you like in setting a rejection criterion, but you *may* eventually pay for this decision by rejecting what you perhaps should not.

The classical ideas involved in this process evolved out of the arguments of different statisticians. Let us state these ideas more precisely. When you decide to test whether the probability of heads "does or does not" equal the probability of tails, two hypotheses are implied. One is that the quarter is unbiased (i.e., the probability of heads *does* equal the probability of tails), and the second is that the coin is biased (i.e., the probability of heads *does not* equal the probability of tails). Think of the "experiment" of tossing a coin as a way of trying to determine which of these two hypotheses you cannot logically reject. In statistical terms we call the former the *null hypothesis* (symbolized as H_0) and the latter the *alternate hypothesis* (symbolized as H_1). That is,

> H_0 *(null hypothesis)*: The probability of heads equals the probability of tails in the long run (i.e., the coin is not biased).

> H_1 *(alternate hypothesis)*: The probability of heads is not equal to the probability of tails in the long run (i.e., the coin is biased).

Notice that these two hypotheses are *mutually exclusive,* which means that when one is true the other must be false. Experimenters who do significance testing are usually interested in testing the specific H_0 (i.e., no difference) against a general H_1 (i.e., some difference). Given the typical experimental design, the null hypothesis would imply no difference in performance between the experimental and the control groups. Experimenters try to reject H_0 and yet be reasonably sure that they will not be wrong in doing so. We will return to the coin example in a moment, but first you need to understand what *probability* means and the difference between Type I and Type II errors.

THE NOTION OF PROBABILITY

If we were to ask someone what *probability* means, the reply might be something like "It means things that sometimes happen and sometimes do not." This is not a bad description, because the probability that one particular event will occur is the proportion of times that the event would occur if all the possible events were repeated indefinitely (see Box 12.1). When you throw a die, for example, there are six possibilities, and (unless a die is loaded) the probability of any particular outcome is therefore 1/6, or .167. Thus you can recognize an important characteristic of probabilities. If all the outcomes are *independent* (i.e., one outcome is not influenced by any other), the sum of all the probabilities associated with a particular event is equal to 1. This characteristic means that one of the six sides *must* appear on any one roll of the die.

Instead of throwing a die, suppose we had two fair coins and flipped them simultaneously. There are four possible combinations of heads (H) and tails (T): HH,

---

BOX 12.1   Will It Rain Tomorrow?

We frequently hear weather reports that include a statement like "There is a 70% probability of rain tomorrow." Does this mean that it is going to rain for 70% of the day? No, it means that, when examined over the long run, 70% of all the days that follow weather characteristics like today's have been rainy. In other words, probabilities are long-term measures that deal with uncertain events. As noted, the probability that one particular event, out of many possible events, will occur is the proportion of times out of all outcomes that the event would occur.

HT, TH, TT. In determining probabilities, the general rule is to count the total number of possible outcomes and then to count the number of outcomes that yield the event you are interested in. The probability of that event is the ratio of the number you are looking for (the favorable event) to the total number of outcomes. For example, the probability of two heads (out of the four possible events) can occur in only one way (HH) and is therefore 1/4, or .25. The probability of one head (out of these four possible events) can occur in two ways (HT or TH) and is therefore 2/4, or .5

TYPE I AND TYPE II ERRORS

To see what all this has to do with Type I and II errors, imagine a law-school admissions officer whose job it is to decide between two alternatives. One alternative is that the prospective student will be able to do the work required in the school and will succeed if admitted, and the other alternative is that the student will not be able to do the required work and will flunk out. For the sake of this illustration, think of the first alternative as the "null hypothesis" (i.e., the candidate will succeed because she is no less qualified than the accepted students) and the second alternative as the alternate hypothesis (i.e., the candidate will not succeed because she is less qualified than the accepted students). The dilemma the officer faces is that a risk of error is associated with either alternative. If the officer rejects a student and the student could have done well, the officer commits what would be classified as a *Type I error;* that is, the null hypothesis is true. If, on the other hand, the officer accepts a student and the student flunks out, the officer has committed a *Type II error;* that is, the null hypothesis is false.

In other words, a *Type I error* means that one has mistakenly rejected the null hypothesis when it is, in fact, true and should not have been rejected. A *Type II error* means that one has mistakenly failed to reject the null hypothesis when it is, in fact, false and should have been rejected. The risk (or probability) of making a Type I error is called by three different names: *alpha, significance level,* and *p value.* The risk (or probability) of making a Type II error is known by one name: *beta.* To make the most informed decision, we would, of course, like to know what each risk is in a given case, so that we can balance those risks in some way.

However, we are jumping ahead. Let us return with this newfound knowledge to the analogy of the street entrepreneur with the coin for sale. Suppose you decide that you do not want to be wrong more than 1 time out of 20—called the *5% significance level* (see Box 12.2). You flip the coin 9 times and get 8 heads and 1 tail. To make an informed decision, you need to know about the chances of obtaining this result or a result even more extreme. That is, you need to know the probability of obtaining this result (or a more extreme result) if the null hypothesis (H_0) is true, and so you think, "If this probability is less than 1/20 (i.e., $p < .05$), I will reject the null hypothesis and buy the coin; if not (i.e., $p > .05$), I will not buy the coin." Because it can be shown that the probability of 8 or 9 heads in 9 tosses is less than 1 out of 20 (p approximately .020), you decide to reject the null hypothesis and buy the coin.

In other words, assuming you have no pangs of conscience about accepting a

BOX 12.2	The 5% Solution

The ultimate day-to-day decision about what is a reasonable risk is a personal one. However, as you do your literature search, you will notice that many behavioral scientists use the .05 level of probability as a kind of "critical demarcation point" for deciding whether or not to reject the null hypothesis. The conventional wisdom behind this procedure goes something like this: The logic begins, more or less, with the proposition that one does not want to accept an alternate hypothesis that stands a fairly good chance of being false (i.e., one ought to avoid Type I errors). The logic goes on to state that one either accepts an alternate hypothesis as probably true (not false) or rejects it, concluding that the null is too likely for one to regard *it* as rejectable. The .05 alpha is seen by many behavioral scientists as a good "fail-safe" standard because it is both convenient (most statistical tables show 5% values) and stringent enough to safeguard against accepting an "insignificant" result (i.e., the null hypothesis is true) as significant (Rosnow & Rosenthal, 1989b).

crooked coin, you are doing so for two reasons: (1) because the resultant probability leads you to reject the null hypothesis of a fair coin, with 50% heads, at your chosen significance level of 5% and (2) because you think that the alternate hypothesis (i.e., the coin is biased) is tenable and that the data (i.e., 8 heads and 1 tail, or 89% heads instead of 50%) support this alternative.

GULLIBILITY AND BLINDNESS

This analogy is a simplified one, not an exact representation of what goes on in significance testing. One reason the coin example falls short is that it is not a relational event; that is, there was only one variable: the result of the coin toss. The behavioral scientist, however, usually wants to estimate the probability of claiming that two variables are related when in fact they are unrelated. The Type I error can thus be seen as claiming a relation that truly does not exist; it is the likelihood of this particular risk that initially most interests the scientist. In other words, a question to be answered is "What is the probability of a Type I error?"

Although the scientist is not indifferent to the probability of making a Type II error (i.e., failing to claim a relation that truly does exist), science has traditionally attached greater psychological importance to the risk of making a Type I error than to the risk of making a Type II error (see Box 12.3). The reason the scientist attaches greater weight to alpha (the risk of making a Type I error) than to beta (the risk of making a Type II error) is explained in Table 12.1. The risk of making a Type I error is synonymous with an inferential mistake involving *gullibility,* whereas the risk of making a Type II error is synonymous with an inferential mistake involving *blindness to a relationship.* Traditionally, scientists have been taught to believe that it is worse to risk being gullible than it is to be blind to a relationship, and some philosophers have characterized this choice as the "healthy skepticism" of the scientific outlook (see Axinn, 1966; Kaplan, 1964).

BOX 12.3	Innocent or Guilty?

Imagine that a man is being tried for a brutal murder. If he is convicted, hanging is the likely penalty. As a member of the jury, you have to vote on whether he is innocent or guilty of the charges against him. If you vote "guilty" and in fact he is not guilty, you are sending an innocent man to the gallows. If you vote "innocent" and in fact he is not innocent, you could be turning a murderer loose in the community. In the United States, it is generally accepted that convicting an innocent person is a more serious risk than finding a guilty person innocent. The lesson? Just as most scientists do not weight Type I and Type II errors equally, in everyday life we also give greater weight to some decision risks than to others.

In Table 12.2, we see these ideas translated into the tactical language of significance testing. For researchers, the null hypothesis is the assumption that no relation between two variables is present in the population from which a sample was drawn, or that there is no difference in the responses to the treatments. The researcher considers the possibility of making a Type I error whenever a true null hypothesis is tested. As this table shows, Type I errors occur when the researcher mistakenly rejects the null hypothesis by claiming a relationship that does not exist. Type II errors occur when the researcher mistakenly accepts the null hypothesis by failing to claim a relationship that does exist.

FINDING THE SIGNIFICANCE OF *r*

Especially when a *p* value is low enough to justify rejecting the null hypothesis, the scientist's information about the results is increased by the effect size and its practical implications. The effect size can be measured by the Pearson *r*, and we will return to this idea in a moment. However, you first need to understand how to read *p* values from a table if you are going to compute a test of significance in your own research. Table 12.3, which contains a portion of a longer table in Appendix

TABLE 12.1	Illustration of Definitions of Type I and Type II Errors

	True State	
Your Decision	The Coin is Unbiased	The Coin is Biased
The coin is biased (i.e., it will not come up heads and tails equally)	Type I error (gullibility risk)	No error
The coin is unbiased (i.e., it is an ordinary coin)	No error	Type II error (blindness risk)

TABLE 12.2	Implications of the Decision to Reject or Not to Reject the Null Hypothesis (H_0)

Scientist's Decision	True State	
	H_0 is True	H_0 is False
To reject H_0	Type I error	No error
Not to reject H_0	No error	Type II error

B (see Table B.5 on p. 390), shows *p* levels associated with different values of *r*. In the following chapters we will examine similar tables for *t*, *F*, and chi-square, all three of which are statistics used to test significance. The first column in this table shows $N - 2$ (where *N* is the total number of sampling units), while the other columns indicate *p* levels (i.e., Type I error risks).

Notice that both one-tailed and two-tailed *p* levels are given and that the two-tailed *p*'s are exactly twice the size of the one-tailed. The term *two-tailed* means that the alternate hypothesis (H_1) did *not* specifically predict in which side (or tail) of the probability distribution the significance would be detected. One-tailed *p* values (obtained by halving the two-tailed value) imply that the alternate hypothesis requires the significance to be in one tail rather than in the other tail.

TABLE 12.3	Significance Levels of *r*			

	Probability Level (*p*)				
	.05	.025	.01	.005	one-tail
$N - 2$	.10	.05	.02	.01	two-tail
1	.988	.997	.9995	.9999	
2	.900	.950	.980	.990	
3	.805	.878	.934	.959	
4	.729	.811	.882	.917	
5	.669	.754	.833	.874	
10	.497	.576	.658	.708	
20	.360	.423	.492	.537	
30	.296	.349	.409	.449	
40	.257	.304	.358	.393	
50	.231	.273	.322	.354	
100	.164	.195	.230	.254	
200	.116	.138	.164	.181	
300	.095	.113	.134	.148	
500	.074	.088	.104	.115	
1000	.052	.062	.073	.081	

Note: For a more complete table see Appendix B.5.

As an illustration of how to use Table 12.3 (and Table B.5), suppose you conduct a questionnaire study to test whether people's level of self-esteem (as measured by a standardized personality inventory) is significantly correlated with the extent to which they engage in gossiping (measured by peer ratings). However, you are unsure of the direction this relation will take because (based on your literature review) you feel that a positive *or* a negative correlation is possible (e.g., Jaeger, Skleder, Rind, & Rosnow, 1994). That is, some writers have portrayed the typical gossip as a social isolate, the least popular member of a group, characterized by feelings of little self-worth, social anxiety, and a need for esteem from others, who gossips in order to become the center of attention and to obtain status or esteem from others. By contrast, other writers have characterized the typical gossip as sensitive, curious, social, and involved, a person who gossips out of a need to control or manipulate those he or she perceives to be subordinates. Because you are unable to predict whether the correlation will be positive or negative, you will do a two-tailed (rather than a one-tailed) test of significance.

Continuing with this example, suppose that in a total N of 52 subjects you find that the correlation between self-esteem and the tendency to gossip is $r = .33$. The positive r is consistent with the notion that high gossipers are higher in self-esteem, but you also want to test the .33 for significance to see whether it may have occurred by chance. For your alpha, let us say you pick the conventional 5% significance level as a helpful (but not critical) demarcation point. Looking at the intersection of $N - 2 = 50$ and the column labeled .05 two-tail in Table 12.3, you can see that r needs to be at least .273 to be beyond the level of risk you have picked in order to reject the null hypothesis. As this table shows, the obtained p is somewhere between .02 and .01 two-tailed. That is, $r = .33$ is larger than the listed value for $p = .02$ two-tailed ($r = .322$) and smaller than the listed value for $p = .01$ two-tailed ($r = .354$).

In reporting your results, you have several options. One alternative—which is typically used—is to state only that "$p < .05$ two-tail" (that is, the two-tailed probability of mistakenly rejecting the null hypothesis is less than 1/20). A second alternative—if you want to use this table more precisely—is to state ".01 < two-tailed $p < .02$" (that is, the two-tailed probability of mistakenly rejecting the null hypothesis is more than 1/100 but less than 1/50). A third alternative—recommended by many statisticians—is to state the exact p value. We also prefer this third alternative, but we recognize that it is not always practicable because it requires access to a computer or an expensive statistics calculator. Alternative 1 or 2 will suffice in almost all cases of student research reports.

BINOMIAL EFFECT-SIZE DISPLAY (BESD)

We mentioned that the *practical importance* of the observed result is indicated by the *effect size,* and we now see how the product–moment r gives us this information quite directly. In the following chapters we will present formulas for obtaining the correlation coefficient by means of different significance tests. For now, we will focus on how the BESD—short for *binomial effect-size display*—transforms the product–moment r into a convenient display of practical importance (Rosenthal &

Rubin, 1982a). The BESD is called a *display* because it converts the success rates in the experimental and control conditions into a tabular graphic, and it is called *binomial* (which means "two terms") because the independent and dependent variables are presented as dichotomous.

To illustrate, several years ago a major biomedical experiment found that heart attack risk is cut by aspirin (Steering Committee of the Physicians' Health Study Research Group, 1988). Presumably, aspirin works to reduce mortality from heart attack, or myocardial infarction (MI), by promoting circulation even when fatty deposits have collected along the walls of the coronary arteries. That is, aspirin does not reduce the chances of clotting, but it makes the transport of blood easier as the arteries get narrower. The conclusion that heart attack risk is actually cut by aspirin was based on the results of a five-year study of a sample of 22,071 male physicians, approximately half of whom (11,037) were given an ordinary aspirin tablet (325 mg) every other day, while the remainder (11,034) were given a placebo. Part of the results are shown in Table 12.4.

The top part of this table shows the number of participants in each condition who did or did not have a heart attack. We see that 1.3% suffered an attack, and that this event occurred more frequently in the placebo condition (1.7%) than in the aspirin condition (0.9%). Tests of the statistical significance of these results—using a procedure described in a later chapter—yielded a p value that was considerably smaller than the conventional .05 significance level. It was "p approximately .0000006," which tells us conclusively that the result of *significance testing* was

---

TABLE 12.4 Aspirin's Effect on Heart Attack

A. Myocardial Infarctions (MI) in Aspirin and Placebo Conditions

Condition	No Heart Attack	Heart Attack	Total
Aspirin	10,933	104	11,037
Placebo	10,845	189	11,034
Total	21,778	293	22,071

B. Binomial Effect-Size Display of $r = .034$

Condition	MI Absent	MI Present	Total
Aspirin	51.7[a]	48.3[b]	100
Placebo	48.3[b]	51.7[a]	100
Total	100	100	200

[a]Computed from $100(.500 + r/2)$
[b]Computed from $100(.500 - r/2)$

Source: Based on result reported in "Preliminary Report: Findings from the Aspirin Component of the Ongoing Physicians' Health Study" by Steering Committee of the Physicians' Health Study Research Group, 1988, *New England Journal of Medicine, 318,* pp. 262–264.

very unlikely to be a fluke or a lucky coincidence. However, when we calculate the effect size as a standard phi coefficient—using the procedure described in the previous chapter—the result is only $r = .034$. We say "only" because effect size r's of .1 or less are typically considered small in behavioral science. However, before dismissing this "small" effect as inconsequential, let us see what it means in terms of practical importance.

We see the importance more clearly when we recast this magnitude of effect in the tabular form of a BESD. As has already been noted, in such a display the correlation coefficient is translated into dichotomous outcomes, such as success and failure, improved and not improved, or, in this case, the presence and absence of myocardial infarction. Part B of Table 12.4 provides us with a BESD that corresponds to the $r = .034$ effect size calculated from the results in Part A. We see that the BESD resembles a 2×2 contingency table of the kind from which we calculated the phi coefficient in Chapter 11. However, whereas the rows and columns of ordinary contingency tables may sum to any number, each row and column of the BESD adds up to 100. The purpose of "standardizing" (or equalizing) the row and column totals or margins is to make the numbers in the A, B, C, and D cells easier to interpret and compare as proportions or percentages. This BESD tells us that approximately 3.4% of persons who would probably have experienced a myocardial infarction (i.e., given the particular conditions of this experiment) did not experience one if they followed the regimen as prescribed in the aspirin treatment condition.

One great convenience of the BESD is how easily we can go from the 2×2 display to an r (simply by taking the difference between the outcome rates of the experimental group and the control group) and how easily we can go from an effect-size r to the display (by calculating the experimental success rate as .50 plus one half of r and the control success rate as .50 minus one half of r). In this case, where $r = .034$, the experimental success rate is $.50 + .017 = .517$, multiplied by 100 to change .517 to 51.7%. In the placebo group we calculate $.50 - .017 = .483$ and then multiply by 100 to change the proportion to 48.3%.

Let us give one more example to show how the BESD is used to reveal the practical importance of an effect size whether the dependent measure is dichotomous or continuous. We will stay in the biomedical research area, with an effect that was more than six times larger than aspirin's effect on heart attack. Table 12.5 shows, in the form of a BESD, the results of a study (Barnes, 1986) of the effects of the drug AZT (azidothymidine) on the survival of 282 patients suffering from AIDS (acquired immunodeficiency syndrome) or AIDs-related complex (ARC). The correlation between survival and receiving AZT was $r = .23$, or what might be characterized as a small to medium effect by the conventional standard. The BESD clearly shows, however, that an effect equivalent to reducing the death rate from 61.5% to 38.5% is a dramatic finding (see also Box 12.4).

DON'T SQUARE THE EFFECT SIZE!

In your literature search you may have noticed that some authors, when analyzing the effect size, talk about squaring r. This value (r^2) is also called the *coefficient of determination*, or the *proportion of variability explained*. However, the terms

TABLE 12.5	BESD Showing Effect of AZT in Treatment of AIDS and ARC ($r = .23$)

Condition	Death	Survival	Total
AZT	38.5	61.5	100.0
Placebo	61.5	38.5	100.0
Total	100.0	100.0	200.0

Source: Based on results reported in "Promising Results Halt Trial of Anti-AIDS Drug" by D. M. Barnes, 1986, *Science, 234,* pp. 15–16.

determination and *explained* are used in a technical sense and, despite the names, do not mean that r^2 explains the causal relation between X and *Y*. They mean only that r^2 signifies the fraction or proportion of the variability shared by *X* and *Y*. For example, a positive or negative Pearson *r* of 1.0—in which case r^2 also equals 1.0—implies that the variation in the *Y* scores is perfectly associated with the variation in the *X* scores (and vice versa). The coefficient of determination has its uses in a number of situations, but it is a poor indicator of the effect size because in

---

BOX 12.4   What Is a Breakthrough Effect?

In a small informal poll, some physicians spending the year at a California think tank were asked to tell of some medical "breakthrough" that was of very great practical importance (Rosenthal, 1990b). Their consensus was that the breakthrough was the development of the drug cyclosporine, which is used to suppress the body's rejection of organ transplants. A multicenter randomized experiment was published in 1983 (Canadian Multicentre Transplant Study Group, 1983), which showed that the effect size of cyclosporine was $r = .19$ for the dependent variable of organ rejection and $r = .15$ for the dependent variable of patient survival.

Appendix C of this book describes a classic meta-analysis done by Mary Lee Smith and Gene V Glass (1977) of psychotherapy outcome studies. These authors found the average effect of psychotherapy on patient improvement to be $r = .32$. Critics of psychotherapy who were unaware of the implications of this statistical finding viewed it as indicating not a breakthrough, but a "modest" effect that sounded the "death knell" of psychotherapy. However, an effect size of $r = .32$ is equivalent to increasing the success rate from 34% to 66%, an effect that becomes even more dramatic when we compare it with "breakthrough" effects in other areas. Using the BESD allows us to see how researchers are doing, if we routinely translate the typical answers to research questions into effect sizes such as *r* and compare them with other well-established findings, such as those shown in Tables 12.4 and 12.5.

almost all cases it underestimates the practical importance of the observed outcome. That is, except when $r = 0$ or 1 (in which case r^2 and r will be identical), the use of r squared as a measure of effect size will mislead you into believing that the practical importance of the effect is less than it really is.

For instance, in the AZT study (Table 12.5), squaring $r = .23$ gives $r^2 = .05$. In the aspirin study (Table 12.4), squaring $r = .034$ gives $r^2 = .00$, which tells us there was *no* effect! However, when you think of an r of .034 as reflecting a 3.4% decrease in heart attacks (which was the interpretation given r in Table 12.4), the r does not appear to be quite so small—especially if you can count yourself or a loved one among that percentage (Rosenthal, 1990a, 1990b).

Table 12.6 shows the underestimation of the effect size by the coefficient of determination with different outcome rates. Column 1 shows the result of squaring the r's in column 2 (e.g., $.10 \times .10 = .01$), and columns 3 and 4 show the percentage increases in success rates as they would be revealed by a BESD corresponding to the values in column 2. The final column shows the difference between the values in columns 3 and 4. Multiplying these percentages by .01 changes them back into proportions and gives the values in column 2. In other words, the difference in success rates (e.g., survival rate, cure rate, improvement rate, or selection rate) is *exactly equal* to r. Thus r is a way of quantifying the practical importance of a given experimental outcome, although we must also consider the nature of the variables and the dependent measures to decide how to frame the implications of the results.

TABLE 12.6	Increases in Success Rates Corresponding to Values of r^2 and r			
Coefficient of determination r^2	Effect size r	Success rate increased:		Difference in success rates
		From	To	
.01	.10	45%	55%	10%
.04	.20	40%	60%	20%
.09	.30	35%	65%	30%
.16	.40	30%	70%	40%
.25	.50	25%	75%	50%
.36	.60	20%	80%	60%
.49	.70	15%	85%	70%
.64	.80	10%	90%	80%
.81	.90	5%	95%	90%
1.00	1.00	0%	100%	100%

Source: Based on "A Simple, General Purpose Display of Magnitude of Experimental Effect" by R. Rosenthal and D. B. Rubin, 1982, *Journal of Educational Psychology, 74,* pp. 166–169.

STATISTICAL POWER ANALYSIS

If the null hypothesis has not been rejected in a given study, the scientist analyzes the *power* of the statistical test used in the significance testing procedure. The reason is that the *power of a test* has to do with the sensitivity of the significance test in providing an adequate opportunity to reject the null hypothesis if it warrants rejection (e.g., Cohen, 1988; Keppel, 1991). Thus the purpose of the power analysis is to learn whether there was a reasonable chance of rejecting the null hypothesis and whether the power of the test should be increased in any future study to increase the sensitivity of the significance test.

To illustrate, suppose that young researcher Smith conducts an experiment (with $N = 80$) on productivity and finds that Managerial Style A is better than B (the old standard), with p less than .05 and $r = .22$. That is, Smith's results are statistically significant at the conventional 5% alpha, and the effect size is only slightly smaller than the dramatic effects of AZT (Table 12.5). Old researcher Jones, the creator of Style B, is skeptical and asks his graduate students to try to replicate Smith's results (with $N = 20$). The graduate students, to Jones's perverse delight, report a failure to replicate Smith's results. Their obtained two-tailed p value, they gleefully tell Jones, is *greater* than .30. However, before savoring his victory, Jones tells his graduate students to calculate the effect size of their result (Step 2). They return with glum faces to report that their effect size is *identical* ($r = .22$) to Smith's.

In other words, Jones's students have found exactly what Smith found, even though the p values of the two studies are not very close. The problem, as we will now show, is that the students were working with a level of statistical power that was too low to obtain the p value reported by Smith. Because of the smaller sample size of 20, it turns out that their power to reject the null hypothesis at .05 two-tailed is about .15, whereas Smith's power of about .50 (using an N of 80) is more than three times as great.

You will recall that beta is the probability of a Type II error (i.e., the probability of failing to claim a relationship that does exist). *Power* is simply 1 minus beta, or the probability of not making a Type II error. In the language of statistics, *power* refers to the probability of rejecting the null hypothesis when it is false and needs rejecting. For any given statistical test of a null hypothesis (e.g., t, F, or chi-square), the power of the statistical test is determined by three factors: (1) the level of the risk of drawing a spuriously positive conclusion (i.e., the p level); (2) the size of the study (i.e., the sample size); and (3) the effect size. These three factors are so related that when any two of them are known, the third can be determined. Thus, if you know the values for Factors 1 and 3, you should be able to figure out how big a sample you will need to achieve your desired level of significance.

Table 12.7 provides a compact way of figuring out the total number of subjects needed to detect various effects at the .05 (two-tailed) significance level. Suppose you decide to work with power = .8 or better, because this happens to be a recommended level (see J. Cohen, 1965). Let us also say you anticipate finding a small effect (e.g., $r = .10$), based on your review of the research literature. Given an effect size $r = .10$ and .8 power, you will need a total of approximately 800 subjects

TABLE 12.7	Rounded Sample Sizes (Total *N*) Required to Detect Various Effects *(r)* at .05 Two-Tailed

			Effect Sizes *(r)*				
Power	.10	.20	.30	.40	.50	.60	.70
.15	85	25	10	10	10	10	10
.20	125	35	15	10	10	10	10
.30	200	55	25	15	10	10	10
.40	300	75	35	20	15	10	10
.50	400	100	40	25	15	10	10
.60	500	125	55	30	20	15	10
.70	600	155	65	40	25	15	10
.80	800	195	85	45	30	20	15
.90	1000	260	115	60	40	25	15

Source: Reproduced from *Statistical Power Analysis for the Behavioral Sciences* (2nd ed., pp. 92–93), by J. Cohen, 1988, Lawrence Erlbaum Associates, Inc. Used by permission of Jacob Cohen and Lawrence Erlbaum Associates, Inc.

to reject the null hypothesis at .05 two-tailed. This is a lot of subjects! Had you chosen to work in an area with typically larger effects, your recruitment of subjects would have been made much easier. With an effect size $r = .30$ and power $= .8$, you would need a total *N* of approximately 85 sampling units. With $r = .50$, you would need a total *N* of only 30 sampling units.

You will be happy to know that most reported experimental effects in behavioral science are quite a bit larger than $r = .10$. Besides increasing the total *N*, there are other techniques you may use to increase power, and in the next chapter you will find more information to help you conduct your research with greater statistical power.

SUMMARY OF IDEAS

1. Three procedures in the use of statistics and probabilities are (a) significance testing; (b) effect size estimation; and (c) power analysis.
2. The probability of a particular outcome is the number of favorable events divided by the total number of possible events.
3. In significance testing, we try to see whether we can reject the null hypothesis and yet be reasonably sure that we will not be wrong in doing so.
4. The null hypothesis (H_0) and alternate hypothesis (H_1) are mutually exclusive, which means that when one is true the other must be false.
5. A Type I error is a mistake in rejecting H_0 when it is true, whereas a Type II error is a mistake in failing to reject H_0 when it is false.
6. The probability of a Type I error is called *alpha*, the *significance level*, and the *p value;* the probability of a Type II error is called *beta*.

7. The .05 significance level is commonly used by behavioral researchers as a basis for deciding whether or not to reject the null hypothesis.

8. Traditionally, scientists have believed that it is worse to make a Type I error than to make a Type II error.

9. The binomial effect-size display (BESD) shows the difference in success rates between the experimental and the control conditions based on the effect size, r, itself.

10. Using r^2 (the coefficient of determination) as an effect-size index is misleading under almost all circumstances, because it underestimates the practical importance of the effect when r is not 0 or 1.

11. Power, defined as 1 − beta, refers to the probability of not making a Type II error.

12. Given a particular effect size, r, we can determine how big a sample we need to achieve any desired level of significance, with a known probability of success (i.e., power).

KEY TERMS

alpha *p. 253*
alternate hypothesis *p. 252*
beta *p. 253*
binomial effect-size display (BESD)
  p. 257
blindness *p. 254*
coefficient of determination *p. 259*
effect size *p. 257*
gullibility *p. 254*
mutually exclusive *p. 252*
null hypothesis *p. 251*

power of a test *p. 262*
probability *p. 252*
proportion of variability explained *p. 259*
p value *p. 253*
r *p. 257*
r^2 *p. 259*
significance level *p. 253*
significance testing *p. 255*
Type I error *p. 253*
Type II error *p. 253*

REVIEW QUESTIONS

1. A Notre Dame student manipulated the presence or absence of a confederate in a wheelchair on subjects' willingness to sign a petition urging more handicapped parking spaces for public and private buildings. The effect size of the result was $r = .40$. Can you create and interpret a BESD for this effect size?

2. A Gallaudet student was asked by her teacher to define the Type II error in the context of the aspirin study (Table 12.4) and to tell how it is related to the power of a test. Do you know the answer? Do you know what factors determine the power of a test of significance?

3. A panicking friend asks a University of Texas student for help with a project she is doing at Southern Methodist University on sex differences in scores on a new test of assertiveness. Her study will involve a randomly sampled group of males and a randomly sampled group of females. She tells the Texas student that effect sizes in this area of research have tended to be approximately $r = .20$. She wants

to present her findings at the Southeastern Psychological Association meeting in New Orleans but worries that the study will not be accepted for presentation unless the group difference reaches a significance level (alpha) of $p = .05$ two-tailed. She also tells her Texas friend that the power level she is seeking for her study is .7. Given all this information, how many subjects should the friend advise her to run in each condition?

4. A St. Lawrence student does a study and gets $p = .05$. Exactly what does this p value tell him? What doesn't it tell him that is also important to know?

5. The first three students to complete their course research projects at Minot State College displayed their BESDs to the other students, to inspire them. All three students had developed new methods of teaching vocabulary. What were the r's associated with each of the following BESDs?

Student A:

Method	Above Average	Below Average
New	75	25
Old	25	75

Student B:

Method	Above Average	Below Average
New	55	45
Old	45	55

Student C:

Method	Above Average	Below Average
New	35	65
Old	65	35

Answers to review questions are found on pages 320–334.

PART 5

Statistical Decision Making

CHAPTER 13

The t Test

➤ **H**ow does the *t* test work?

➤ **H**ow is it computed for a comparison of independent groups?

➤ **W**hat do degrees of freedom have to do with *p* values?

➤ **H**ow is the effect size of *t* computed?

➤ **W**hat can be done to maximize *t*?

➤ **H**ow is a matched *t* computed on nonindependent groups?

SIGNAL-TO-NOISE RATIOS

We have examined the logic of using statistics and probabilities to test hypotheses, and with this chapter we begin our discussion of the implementation of the *significance test*. The choice of a significance test (e.g., *t*, *F*, or chi-square) depends on the research question and the design of the study. If we are interested in comparing the means of two groups (e.g., experimental and control subjects), we will find the *t test* (also called *Student's t*) a convenient method (see Box 13.1). It allows us to test the likelihood that the population means represented by the two groups are equal (i.e., the null hypothesis), by setting up a *signal-to-noise ratio*. In this ratio, the *signal* is represented by the difference between the two means and the *noise* is represented by the variability of the scores within the samples. The larger the signal is relative to the noise, the more likely the null hypothesis is to be rejected.

BOX 13.1	Student's *t*

The *t* test is called *Student's t* in honor of William Sealy Gosset, its inventor. Gosset worked for Guinness, the famous Irish brewery, which for security reasons prohibited publication of research done by its staff. Gosset was able to persuade the company to relax this rule for the statistical methods he had developed, but it agreed only on condition that he use a pen name. The one he chose was "Student."

As an illustration, suppose a researcher is conducting an experiment on the effect of vitamins on the academic performance of children from families below the poverty level. In Chapter 7 we described the statistical plan as a *simple randomized design;* that is, the treatments are randomly assigned to the sampling units. The researcher has randomly assigned the children to an experimental group (which has received vitamins at regular intervals) or to a control group (which has received a placebo). The alternate hypothesis (H_1), stated in terms of the experimenter's working hypothesis, is that vitamins will have a positive effect on the children's academic performance. The null hypothesis (H_0) is that vitamins will have no effect on the children's academic performance. Table 13.1 and Figure 13.1 show two alternative outcomes of this experiment and help to illustrate the signal-to-noise idea.

We see that the means of the vitamin groups are identical $(\overline{X} = 15)$, as are the means of the control groups $(\overline{X} = 10)$. The only difference between Results A and B is that one set of results (B) is more variable. That is, the scores of B are less tightly bunched than the scores of A. When we compare the mean differences *between* the groups (15 minus 10), it seems that we should also take into consideration the amount of variability *within* the groups. That is, the 5 points of difference between the groups look larger to us when seen against the backdrop of the small within-group variation of A than when seen against the backdrop of the larger within-group variation of B.

This is the way the *t* test works. It is a test of statistical significance that examines the difference between two means (the "signal") against the background of the within-group variability (the "noise"). The larger the difference between the

TABLE 13.1	Simple Randomized Design with Alternative Results A and B

	Results A		Results B	
	Vitamins	Control	Vitamins	Control
	13	8	9	4
	15	10	15	10
	17	12	21	16
$\overline{X}$	15	10	15	10

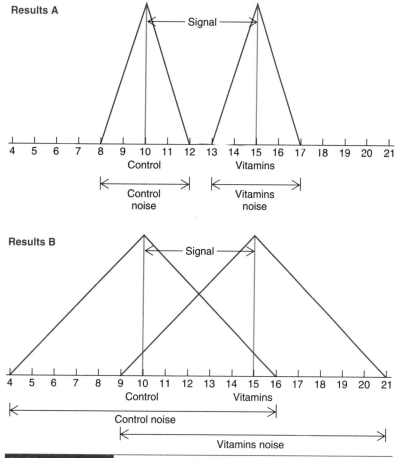

FIGURE 13.1   *Graphical display of the data in Table 13.1. Note that Results A have no overlapping data but that Results B overlap from the scores of 9 to 16.*

means, or the smaller the within-group variability for any given size of study, the greater will be the magnitude of *t*. Because larger *t*'s are associated with differences between means that are more statistically significant, researchers generally prefer larger *t*'s. That is, larger *t*'s have a lower level of probability (*p* value, or alpha), which in turn allows researchers to reject the null hypothesis that there is no difference between the means.

COMPARING INDEPENDENT SAMPLES

In the example we have been considering, the two groups are presumed to be *independent* of one another, which means that the results in one group are not influenced by the results in the other group. Had this been a repeated-measures design, the two scores on each sampling unit would not be independent. We examine this second situation in a moment, but several formulas can be used to calculate t when we want to compare independent samples. A general-purpose one is

$$t = \frac{\overline{X}_1 - \overline{X}_2}{\sqrt{\left(\dfrac{1}{n_1} + \dfrac{1}{n_2}\right) S^2}}$$

in which $\overline{X}_1$ and $\overline{X}_2$ are the means of the two groups; n_1 and n_2 are the number of sampling units in each of the two groups; and S^2 is the pooled estimate of the population variance (i.e., a single estimate of the variance associated with both populations from which the two groups were drawn) computed as

$$S^2 = \frac{\Sigma(X_1 - \overline{X}_1)^2 + \Sigma(X_2 - \overline{X}_2)^2}{n_1 + n_2 - 2}$$

Table 13.2 provides the basic data needed to compute t for the two sets of results in Table 13.1. For each group we compute the sum of the squares of the deviations of the scores from their mean, and we then enter this information in the formula for S^2. With Results A we find

$$S^2 = \frac{8.0 + 8.0}{3 + 3 - 2} = 4.0$$

TABLE 13.2   Basic Data for Calculating t for Results A and B in Table 13.1

Results A

	Vitamin Group			Control Group		
	X_1	$X_1 - \overline{X}_1$	$(X_1 - \overline{X}_1)^2$	X_2	$X_2 - \overline{X}_2$	$(X_2 - \overline{X}_2)^2$
	13	−2.0	4.0	8	−2.0	4.0
	15	0.0	0.0	10	0.0	0.0
	17	+2.0	4.0	12	+2.0	4.0
Σ	45	0	8.0	30	0	8.0
$\overline{X}$	15	—	—	10	—	—

Results B

	Vitamin Group			Control Group		
	X_1	$X_1 - \overline{X}_1$	$(X_1 - \overline{X}_1)^2$	X_2	$X_2 - \overline{X}_2$	$(X_2 - \overline{X}_2)^2$
	9	−6.0	36.0	4	−6.0	36.0
	15	0.0	0.0	10	0.0	0.0
	21	+6.0	36.0	16	+6.0	36.0
Σ	45	0	72.0	30	0	72.0
$\overline{X}$	15	—	—	10	—	—

so

$$t = \frac{15 - 10}{\sqrt{\left(\frac{1}{3} + \frac{1}{3}\right)4.0}} = \frac{5}{1.63} = 3.06$$

Performing the same calculations on Results B gives

$$S^2 = \frac{72.0 + 72.0}{3 + 3 - 2} = \frac{144.0}{4} = 36.0$$

and

$$t = \frac{15 - 10}{\sqrt{\left(\frac{1}{3} + \frac{1}{3}\right)36.0}} = \frac{5}{4.90} = 1.02$$

Not surprisingly, t is larger for Results A than for Results B. We expected this effect because of the difference in variability between A and B. Ordinarily, we would now look up the p values in a suitable table. Because larger t's are rarer events, we expect to find a smaller p associated with Results A than with Results B. Before we move on to this step, some background information will be useful.

USING THE *t* TABLE TO FIND *p*

Although it is convenient to think of t as a single test of statistical significance, it might also be thought of as a family of curves. The reason is that there is a different curve (each resembling the standard normal distribution) for every possible value of what are called the *degrees of freedom (df)* of the t test. In the case we have been considering, the degrees of freedom are defined as $n_1 + n_2 - 2$ (see Box 13.2). One of the great contributions by the inventor of the t test (see again Box 13.1) was to figure out the curve for each number of degrees of freedom. However, instead of having to make our way through scores of different curves, we can use a table that summarizes the most pertinent information from these curves for selected p values. Such information is contained in Table 13.3, which gives the areas found in one or both tails of selected t curves. That is, for one-tailed p values, this table gives the areas found in the right-hand tail, whereas for two-tailed p's, it gives the areas found in both tails.

Studying Table 13.3 teaches us that for any level of p, the t value required to reach that level is smaller and smaller as the *df* increase. In addition, for any *df*, a higher t value is required to reach more extreme (smaller) p levels. One way to think about t is that if the null hypothesis were true (i.e., if the means in the population did not differ), the most likely value of t would be zero. However, even if the population mean difference were truly zero, we would often find nonzero t values by sheer chance alone. For example, suppose the direction of the effect is pre-

---

BOX 13.2	Degrees of Freedom

The origin of "degrees of freedom" *(df)* has to do in a way with the standard deviation, which in turn depends on the deviations from the mean (i.e., the $X - \overline{X}$ values). Suppose we have five raw *(X)* scores: 1, 3, 5, 7, and 9, with sum = 25 and mean = 5. The sum of the deviations has to be 0, because $(1 - 5) + (3 - 5) + (5 - 5) + (7 - 5) + (9 - 5)$ equals zero. Knowing this, if we were given all but one value, we could easily find the missing value. In other words, one deviation in the group is not free to vary, so 1 *df* is eliminated. Thus, with a group of five scores, we have 4 *df* remaining. In the case of the *t* test on independent samples, we have two groups and therefore eliminate 2 *df*, and this is why $df = n_1 + n_2 - 2$.

---

dicted, in which case we may use the one-tailed *p* values. With $df = 8$ we would obtain a *t* value of 1.40 or greater (favoring the predicted outcome) about 10% of the time (i.e., one-tailed $p = .10$ in Table 13.3), or of 1.86 or greater about 5% of the time (one-tailed $p = .05$), or of 3.36 or greater about 0.5% of the time (one-tailed $p = .005$).

TABLE 13.3	*t* Values Required for Significance at Various *p* Levels

	Probability Level *(p)*				
	.10	.05	.025	.005	one-tail
df	.20	.10	.05	.01	two-tail
1	3.08	6.31	12.71	63.66	
2	1.89	2.92	4.30	9.92	
3	1.64	2.35	3.18	5.84	
4	1.53	2.13	2.78	4.60	
5	1.48	2.02	2.57	4.03	
6	1.44	1.94	2.45	3.71	
8	1.40	1.86	2.31	3.36	
10	1.37	1.81	2.23	3.17	
15	1.34	1.75	2.13	2.95	
20	1.32	1.72	2.09	2.84	
25	1.32	1.71	2.06	2.79	
30	1.31	1.70	2.04	2.75	
40	1.30	1.68	2.02	2.70	
60	1.30	1.67	2.00	2.66	
80	1.29	1.66	1.99	2.64	
100	1.29	1.66	1.98	2.63	
1000	1.28	1.65	1.96	2.58	
∞	1.28	1.64	1.96	2.58	

Note: For a more complete table see Appendix B.2.

Notice also that the values of *t* in each column become more stable as the degrees of freedom increase. The reason is that the *t* distribution gradually approximates the standard normal distribution as the size of the samples is increased. At 30 *df,* the *t* distribution is fairly close to that of the standard normal distribution, and with *df* = infinity, the *t* distribution gives values identical to those for the standard normal distribution. This information may come in handy when you read Appendix C on meta-analysis, because the implication is that you may look up the *p* values of *Z*'s in the *df* = ∞ row of a *t* table (such as Table B.2).

We are now ready to look up our two *t*'s, and we will assume that the direction of the effect was predicted. For this step we will use the more comprehensive listing found in Table B.2 (see pp. 383–384). The rows show the degrees of freedom (*df*), which will be 4 for both sets of results because we eliminate 1 *df* in each group (i.e., *df* = 3 + 3 − 2 = 4). We put a finger on the row labeled 4 *df* and read across the columns until we find a value that is the same as or larger than the obtained value of *t*. We see that our *t* of 3.06 is larger than the value listed for *p* = .025 one-tail (2.776) but smaller than the value listed for *p* = .01 one-tail (3.747). Thus the one-tailed *p* of *t* = 3.06 is less than .025 (i.e., *p* < .025 one-tail) but greater than .01 (i.e., *p* > .01 one-tail). We next see that our *t* of 1.02 is larger than the value listed for *p* = .25 one-tail (.741) but smaller than the value listed for *p* = .10 one-tail (1.533). In other words, the one-tailed *p* for *t* = 1.02 is < .25 but > .10.

We must decide for ourselves whether we will regard any given *t* as an event rare enough to make us doubt that the null hypothesis is true. Of course, we cannot simply decide, for example, that "*p* < .20 is a reasonable risk" and then expect that instructors, reviewers, or editors will necessarily accept that decision. If we decide to follow convention—which dictates that the .05 significance level be used as a critical demarcation point—we will conclude that Results A are "statistically significant" and that Results B are "not statistically significant at the 5% level" (see also Box 13.3).

MEASURING THE EFFECT SIZE

In the previous chapter we developed the argument that, in defining the results of research, the significance level alone fails to tell the whole story. We also want to know the effect size so that we can get an idea of the practical importance of the results (using the binomial effect-size display, or BESD) and make plans to do a follow-up study with increased power if necessary. You will recall that the power of a statistical test is determined by (1) the level of the risk of drawing a spuriously favorable conclusion (i.e., the *p* level); (2) the size of the study (i.e., the sample size); and (3) the effect size. Thus, if we know the *p* value we are trying to "reach" and the effect size likely to be found in nature, we can easily figure out how big a sample we need to achieve any desired level of statistical power (see again Table 12.7, p. 263).

We also showed that the effect size tells us something very different from the *p* value. A result that is statistically significant is not necessarily practically important as judged by the magnitude of the effect. Consequently, highly significant *p* values

---

BOX 13.3   How Many Decimal Places for *p*?

As noted in the previous chapter, many statisticians prefer to report the actual descriptive level of significance because it carries more information than the phrases "significant difference" or "no significant difference at the 5% level" (e.g., Mosteller, Fienberg, & Rourke, 1983; Snedecor & Cochran, 1989). There is something absurd, they would argue, in regarding as a "real" effect one that is supported by $p = .05$ and as a "zero" effect one that is supported by $p = .06$. Some pocket calculators automatically give us exact probabilities if we simply punch in the value of the statistical test and its degrees of freedom. With the use of such a calculator, tables such as those in Appendix B become superfluous because the calculator replaces the statistical tables. When *p* values are to be reported accurately, the convention is to report two digits after the initial 0s (e.g., .064, .0071, .00011, .000092), though for many purposes a single such digit will suffice.

---

should not bc interpreted as automatically reflecting large effects. A case in point is that much research on medications results in very small effects, even though many such medications are often advertised as providing relief in a "significant" percentage of cases (Paulos, 1990). On the other hand, if we do not have enough power, small effects of some practical importance may be ignored because of failure to reach statistical significance (i.e., a Type II error). If the effect size is theoretically interesting, the researcher should continue the investigation with a larger sample before deciding that nothing happened (i.e., that the null hypothesis is true).

The procedure for computing the effect size, *r*, from a *t* test is simple enough to be performed on any pocket calculator. As you take notes for your literature review, you can also use this procedure to compute the effect sizes of reported *t*'s as a prelude to synthesizing them (see Appendix C on meta-analysis). To reiterate, we will be emphasizing the product–moment *r* as an index of the effect size, because it can be interpreted by the BESD procedure described in the previous chapter. You may find other indices of effect size in published reports, and if you are interested in converting them to *r*'s, you will find formulas for doing so elsewhere (e.g., Rosenthal & Rosnow, 1991).

When the significance test is a *t* test, the corresponding effect size, *r*, can be calculated as

$$r = \sqrt{\frac{t^2}{t^2 + df}}$$

In the case of Results A in Table 13.2, with $t = 3.06$ and $df = n_1 + n_2 - 2 = 4$, we find

$$r = \sqrt{\frac{(3.06)^2}{(3.06)^2 + 4}} = .84$$

which indicates a "jumbo-sized" effect. In the case of Results B, with $t = 1.02$ and the same *df*, we find

$$r = \sqrt{\frac{(1.02)^2}{(1.02)^2 + 4}} = .45$$

which indicates a substantial effect in spite of the failure of the *t* test to achieve significance at the conventional 5% level.

MAXIMIZING *t*

The *t* test, like any significance test, can be shown mathematically to consist of two components, one having to do with the effect size and the other with the *size of the study* (i.e, the number of sampling units). The way these two components come together can be expressed by the following equation:

Magnitude of significance test = size of effect × size of study

which tells us that the larger the effect or the more subjects used, the greater will be the magnitude of *t*. It also allows us to envision specific ways of maximizing (or strengthening) the *t* test in a given situation (i.e., ways of optimizing the power of the test).

For example, here is another formula in which *t* is mathematically broken down into these two components:

Significance test = Effect size × Size of study

$$t = \frac{\overline{X}_1 - \overline{X}_2}{S} \times \sqrt{\frac{n_1 n_2}{n_1 + n_2}}$$

In this equation the effect size is described differently from the way it was just stated. This different way—called *Hedges's g*—defines the effect size not as a Pearson *r*, but in *Z*-score-like terms. However, the reason for noting this equation is that it suggests we can maximize *t* in three ways: (1) by driving the means further apart; (2) by decreasing the variability within groups; and (3) by increasing the effective size of the study.

First, we might try to strengthen *t* by using a strong treatment that drives the means of the experimental and control groups further apart. For example, if our hypothesis is that longer treatment sessions are more beneficial than shorter treatment sessions, we are more apt to find a significant difference if we compare the control group with an experimental group that has been treated for 45 minutes than if we compare it with a group treated for just 15 minutes. This tactic should increase the numerator of the effect-size component.

Second, by decreasing the variability of response within groups, we decrease the denominator of the effect-size component and thereby strengthen *t*. This is what happened in Results A, in which the variability of response within groups was substantially less than that in Results B. Two ways of decreasing the variability of response are (1) standardizing the research procedures in order to make them more uniform and (2) recruiting subject samples that are fairly homogeneous in those characteristics that are substantially correlated with the dependent variable.

Third, as implied in the previous chapter, we also strengthen t by increasing the size-of-study component. That is, we simply increase the number of subjects. Another way to increase this component is to make the sample size as nearly equal as possible in the two groups. The reason is that t tests thrive more when sample sizes are not very different for any given total N (Rosenthal & Rosnow, 1991, pp. 304–305).

COMPARING NONINDEPENDENT SAMPLES

So far, we have used t to compare the means of two *independent* groups. That is, we regarded the scores in one group as having no inherent relationship to the scores in the other group. However, suppose we measure the *same* subjects more than once (e.g., before and after they are exposed to a learning experience) and want to compare the means of these two measures. Now the two groups of scores are no longer independent because of the *repeated-measures design,* or *within subjects design.* Another example of nonindependence would occur if the two groups consisted of children who were related by birth, and one member of the family were assigned to Group 1 and the other member were assigned to Group 2. The common family membership has again introduced a degree of relatedness between the scores in Group 1 and Group 2.

When nonindependent samples are compared by the ordinary t test, the resulting value is *usually* too small (although it is also sometimes too large). To avoid this problem, we instead use a *matched-t* formula (also called a *correlated t*) for nonindependent groups. To illustrate this approach, we refer to the basic data in Table 13.4, which shows a hypothetical study in which girls were predicted to be more sociable than boys. The scores are ratings by a judge on a 9-point scale of sociability. What makes this study appropriate for a matched t is that these were six

TABLE 13.4	Basic Data for Matched t					
	Group 1	Group 2				
Family	X_1(girls)	X_2(boys)	Mean	D	$(D-\overline{D})$	$(D-\overline{D})^2$
Smith	4	3	3.5	1	−1	1
Ross	6	4	5.0	2	0	0
Kern	8	5	6.5	3	1	1
Jones	4	3	3.5	1	−1	1
Hill	6	4	5.0	2	0	0
Brown	8	5	6.5	3	1	1
Sum	36	24	30.0	12	0	4
Mean	6	4	5.0	2.0		

pairs of girls and boys, each pair from a different family. When we examine the judge's ratings over these pairs, we find that a child's sociability score is to some degree predictable from family membership. For instance, the third column in this table shows that the Smith and Jones children were judged (on the average) to be less sociable than the Kern and Brown children.

In *t* tests for matched (or correlated) data, we perform our calculations on the difference score *(D)* for each pair of lined-up scores. We use the following formula:

$$t = \frac{\overline{D}}{\sqrt{\left(\frac{1}{n}\right)S^2_D}}$$

in which $\overline{D}$ is the mean of the $D = X_1 - X_2$ scores; n is the number of D scores (i.e., the number of lined-up pairs); and S^2_D is the unbiased estimate of the population value of σ^2_D, with S^2_D defined by

$$S^2_D = \frac{\Sigma (D - \overline{D})^2}{n - 1}$$

with *df* now defined as $n - 1$.

Substituting the data in Table 13.4, we find

$$S^2_D = \frac{4}{5} = .80$$

and

$$t = \frac{2.0}{\sqrt{\left(\frac{1}{6}\right).80}} = \frac{2.0}{.365} = 5.48$$

We now look up p as a one-tailed value (because we predicted that girls would score higher than boys) and also compute the effect size. For the p value we turn to Table B.2 (p. 383), but we now read across the row labeled 5 *df* (because the *df* for a single sample are $n - 1$, or $6 - 1 = 5$). Our t of 5.48 is larger than 4.773 but smaller than 5.893, so one-tailed $p < .0025$ but $> .001$. When we calculate the effect size, we find

$$r = \sqrt{\frac{t^2}{t^2 + df}} = \sqrt{\frac{(5.48)^2}{(5.48)^2 + 5}} = .926$$

which leads us to conclude that we have another "jumbo-sized" effect in addition to a statistically significant one.

TABLE 13.5	Binomial Effect-Size Display of Results in Table 13.4

Gender	Sociability		Total
	More Sociable	Less Sociable	
Girls	96.3	3.7	100
Boys	3.7	96.3	100
Total	100	100	200

BOX 13.4   BESD and Phi

In Chapter 11 we described how the phi coefficient can be computed on data in a 2 × 2 contingency table. If we did so for the BESD in Table 13.5, what would you guess the phi coefficient to be?

Recall that we can compute phi from

$$r_{phi} = \phi = \frac{BC - AD}{\sqrt{(A + B)(C + D)(A + C)(B + D)}}$$

where the letters correspond to each of the four cells:

A	B	(A + B)
C	D	(C + D)
(A + C)	(B + D)	

Substituting in this formula gives

$$\phi = \frac{13.7 - 9273.7}{\sqrt{(100)(100)(100)(100)}} = \frac{-9,260}{\sqrt{100,000,000}} = .926$$

which, not surprisingly, is the same value as our effect size, r, computed directly from t. Note that because the denominator has both a positive and a negative square root, the sign of the correlation coefficient has no fixed meaning. In this example if we had coded girls as 1 and boys as 0, and if we had coded more sociable as 1 and less sociable as 0, then being more sociable is positively related to being a girl, so $r = +.926$, or negatively related to being a boy, so $r = -.926$.

Table 13.5 shows what this imaginary effect will look like as a BESD with equal totals in the row and column margins (see also Box 13.4). The cell values should not be mistaken for the actual frequencies that would be obtained in a random sample; instead, they should be seen as standardized values because of the uniform totals that we imposed on the margins for ease of interpretation.

SUMMARY OF IDEAS

1. The *t* test operates like a signal-to-noise ratio used to compare two means relative to the variability of scores within each group.
2. Like any significance test, *t* is made up of two components: the size of the effect and the size of the study.
3. We maximize the *t* test by (a) drawing means further apart; (b) decreasing the variability within groups; and (c) increasing the effective size of the study.
4. Because the *df* (degrees of freedom) for a single sample are $n - 1$, the *df* for an independent *t* are $n_1 + n_2 - 2$ and for a matched *t* are $n - 1$.
5. We look up the *p* value in a table of one-tailed or two-tailed probabilities, depending on whether we predicted (one-tailed) or did not predict (two-tailed) in which side of the *t* distribution the *p* value would be situated.
6. The effect size of *t* can be computed as

$$r = \sqrt{\frac{t^2}{t^2 + df}}$$

and the result is then interpreted by use of the BESD (described in the previous chapter).

KEY TERMS

correlated *t*   *p. 278*
degrees of freedom   *p. 274*
df   *p. 274*
Hedges's *g*   *p. 277*
independent samples   *p. 271*
matched *t*   *p. 278*
noise   *p. 269*

repeated-measures design   *p. 278*
signal   *p. 269*
signal-to-noise ratio   *p. 269*
simple randomized design   *p. 270*
Student's *t*   *p. 270*
t test   *p. 270*
within subjects design   *p. 278*

REVIEW QUESTIONS

1. A Kent State researcher hypothesizes that marijuana use decreases short-term memory. He brings five subjects to his laboratory. Each subject is given a test of short-term memory. Each subject is then given marijuana and administered another test of short-term memory. The results are given on the next page (high scores indicate good memory):

	Test 1	Test 2
Subject 1	5	2
Subject 2	7	5
Subject 3	4	5
Subject 4	8	3
Subject 5	8	4

Can you set up the formula and insert the numbers that would be used to test the hypothesis that the scores on Test 2 are significantly lower than the scores on Test 1? What would be the degrees of freedom? If you found a significant difference and a large effect size, should you conclude that marijuana causes a decrease in short-term memory? Why or why not?

2. A Loyola student conducted a study comparing the creativity scores of four biology and four history majors. The results were

Biology	History
4	7
6	3
3	5
3	6

Can you set up the formula that would be used to compute a t test? What would be the degrees of freedom? How would you compute and interpret the effect size?

3. An experimenter at the University of California at San Diego studied sex differences in nonverbal sensitivity. Her results showed that women were significantly better at decoding nonverbal cues than were men, with $t = 2.34$, $df = 62$, $p < .05$, and $r = .28$. Pretend that the experimenter added an additional 60 subjects, randomly selected from the same population as the original sample. When the analysis is recalculated with the extra subjects added, should the new t be larger, smaller, or about the same size? Should the p value be larger, smaller, or about the same size? Should the r be larger, smaller, or about the same size?

4. A Santa Fe College student has developed a brief training program that increases sensitivity to nonverbal cues. He plans to compare it to a brief training program that increases sensitivity to other people in general. He plans on randomly assigning 10 subjects to each treatment, the subjects having been found through newspaper ads. He describes his plans to his professor, who suggests he think hard about trying to obtain a larger t than he is likely to get in the planned study. What might the student do to get a larger t?

Answers to review questions are found on pages 320–334.

The F *Test*

F AND *t*

The *t* test is useful whenever there are two groups to be compared, but some randomized designs contain more than two groups. A general test of significance for such designs is the *F* test, a statistic based on the *analysis of variance* (ANOVA). The *F* test may also be used whenever a *t* test is useful, so that *F* is an "all-purpose" significance test for comparing two or more groups. In this chapter we illustrate the use of ANOVA in one-way and two-way designs. In a *one-way design,* two or more groups make up a single dimension (e.g., a medication group, a placebo group, and a zero control group). In a *two-way design* (also called a *two-way factorial* in Chapter 7), each entry in the table is associated with a row variable and a column variable (see, for example, Table 7.2, p. 147).

In fact, the *F* and *t* tests are related statistically; $F = t^2$ when there are only two groups to be compared. Because the effect size of *t* is computed as

$$r = \sqrt{\frac{t^2}{t^2 + df}}$$

it follows that whenever there are only two groups to be compared, the effect size of F can be computed as

$$r = \sqrt{\frac{F}{F + df}}$$

where df refers to the degrees of freedom "within conditions," obtained by determining the df within each group (or condition) and then adding. If there are more than two groups, we do not compute the effect size for that dimension because the result will be uninterpretable. One possibility, discussed here, is to compute t tests on paired comparisons and then to compute and interpret the effect sizes of the t's as we did in Chapter 13.

That F is based on the analysis of variance implies that we are analyzing variances (also called *mean squares* in Chapter 10) instead of analyzing means. For example, in two-way designs in which the sampling units are exposed to one treatment condition each, the analysis of variance allows us to apportion the variability of the rows, columns, and so forth, and to test (using F) how large each variance is relative to the variance within conditions (also called the *mean square for error*). We begin by describing the basic ideas involved in computing and interpreting one-way ANOVAs and then discuss factorial designs in which there are two levels of each of two independent variables operating simultaneously. In the course of your literature search you may find designs with additional sources of variation (e.g., three-way or four-way designs). The logic is basically the same as that for the two-way design, but we do not go further than the two-way ANOVA in illustrating calculations. We conclude with an example of an ANOVA table for a repeated-measures design in the context of a two-way layout.

THE LOGIC OF ANOVA

In the previous chapter we began with a hypothetical case to illustrate the signal-to-noise idea; if we look at another example, we will see that the logic is essentially the same for analysis of variance. In this illustration we will imagine that an experimenter interested in the effects of nutrition on the academic performance of children decides to use a four-group instead of a two-group randomized design. One group of randomly assigned children gets a hot lunch daily, another group gets free milk, a third group gets a vitamin supplement, and the fourth group gets nothing extra. Once again, imagine two different sets of results of this experiment, as represented by A and B in Table 14.1.

In examining these results, what conclusions would we be willing to draw on the basis of A compared to B? We note that the outcome in the group receiving no special nutritional bonus (Group 1) has an average of 10 units of academic performance, whereas the average performance of the group receiving milk is 12 (Group 2), of that receiving vitamins (Group 3) is 15, and of that receiving hot lunches (Group 4) is 19. By applying the logic about within-group variance

TABLE 14.1	Fully Randomized Design with Alternative Results A and B

Results A:

	Group 1 Zero	Group 2 Milk	Group 3 Vitamins	Group 4 Hot Lunch
	8	10	13	17
	10	12	15	19
	12	14	17	21
$\overline{X}$	10	12	15	19

Results B:

	Group 1 Zero	Group 2 Milk	Group 3 Vitamins	Group 4 Hot Lunch
	4	6	9	13
	10	12	15	19
	16	18	21	25
$\overline{X}$	10	12	15	19

described in the previous chapter, we find ourselves feeling more impressed by Results A than by Results B. In Results A the subjects have never varied in their performance by more than 2 points from the average score of their group. The few points of difference between the mean scores of the four groups look larger when seen against the backdrop of the small within-group variation of Results A, whereas they look smaller when examined against the backdrop of the large within-group variation of Results B.

The analysis of variance provides researchers with a more formal comparison of the variation between the average results per condition and the average variation within the different conditions. In this kind of analysis, as we see next, a ratio (the *F ratio*, or *F test*) is formed. You will recall that the *t* has a value of 0 when the null hypothesis is true. The *F* ratio has a value close to 1.0 when the variation between conditions is not different from the variation within conditions (i.e., when the null hypothesis is true); we will explain why this is so later. The larger the *F* ratio becomes, the greater is the dispersion of group means relative to the dispersion of scores within groups. In other words, as with the *t*, researchers generally prefer larger *F*'s because they are associated with smaller *p*'s (see also Box 14.1).

DIVIDING UP THE VARIANCE

The calculation of *F* tests is only one purpose of the analysis of variance. A more general purpose is to divide up the variance of all the observations into a number of separate sources of estimation and significance testing. In this illustration of

---

BOX 14.1   Fisher's Idea of Significance and Nonsignificance

The *F* test is named after its inventor, Ronald A. Fisher (1890–1962), who also invented the null hypothesis. Another essential idea of Fisher's was that there is no sharp dividing line between a "significant" and a "nonsignificant" difference, but that the strength of evidence for or against the null hypothesis may be viewed as a fairly continuous function of the magnitude of *p*. In his seminal text, *The Design of Experiments* (1960), Fisher stated that

> convenient as it is to note that a hypothesis is contradicted at some familiar level of significance such as 5% or 2% or 1% we do not...ever need to lose sight of the exact strength which the evidence has in fact reached, or to ignore the fact that with further trial it might come to be stronger or weaker. (p. 25)

Fisher did not specifically advise us how to appraise "the exact strength" of the evidence, but the use of statistical power analysis (Chapter 12), effect-size estimation procedures (Chapters 13–15), and meta-analytic procedures (Appendix C) enables us to do this with relative ease.

---

comparing the means of four groups, the total variation among the 12 scores is broken into two sources: (1) systematic variation between groups or conditions (i.e., the "signal") and (2) error variation within groups or conditions (i.e., the "noise").

It will be useful here to look again at the basic idea of variance:

$$S^2 = \frac{\Sigma(X - \overline{X})^2}{N - 1}$$

where S^2 is the unbiased estimate of the population value of σ^2, and σ^2 differs from S^2 only in that the denominator $N - 1$ is replaced by N. As noted in Chapter 10, the quantity S^2 is also called a *mean square* (abbreviated as *MS*) because when the sum of the squares [i.e., the $\Sigma(X - \overline{X})^2$] is divided by $N - 1$ (or *df*), the result is the squared deviation per *df*—a kind of average.

In the analysis of variance, we are especially interested in the numerators of our various S^2 values (e.g., for between conditions and for within conditions). This interest has to do with the additive property of the numerators, or the *sum of squares* (abbreviated as *SS*) of deviations about the mean. These *SS* values add up to the total sum of squares in the following way:

Total *SS* = between-conditions *SS* + within-conditions *SS*

In one-way designs, the analysis of variance requires the calculation of the between-conditions *SS* and the within-conditions *SS*. If you are doing these calculations using a pocket calculator, compute the total *SS* as a check on your arithmetic. If you are using a computer, running the program on the data in this chapter will allow you to see what the results in your printout actually tell you. Before we start crunching numbers, let us pause for a moment and look at the formulas for each of these three sums of squares.

First, the total *SS* is defined as the sum of squares of deviations of all the measurements from the grand mean. What goes into the total *SS* is given by the following formula:

$$\text{Total } SS = \Sigma\,(X - \overline{X}_G)^2$$

where X is each observation and $\overline{X}_G$ is the grand mean (i.e., the mean of the condition means).

Second, the between-conditions *SS* is defined as the sum of squares of deviations of the condition means from the grand mean. This between-conditions value is computed by the following formula:

$$\text{Between-conditions } SS = \Sigma[\,n_k(\overline{X}_k - \overline{X}_G)^2\,]$$

where n_k is the number of observations in the kth condition, $\overline{X}_k$ is the mean of the kth condition, and $\overline{X}_G$ is again the grand mean.

And finally, the within-conditions *SS* is defined as the sum of squares of deviations of the measurements from their condition means, as given by the following formula:

$$\text{Within-conditions } SS = \Sigma(X - \overline{X}_k)^2$$

where X is each observation and $\overline{X}_k$ is again the mean of the condition to which X belongs.

COMPUTING THE ONE-WAY ANOVA

We will now use these formulas to analyze the scores of Results A in Table 14.1. Table 14.2 provides the basic data for this analysis, with the addition of two new symbols: $\overline{X}_k$ for the group or condition mean and $\overline{X}_G$ for the grand mean.

First, we compute the total *SS*. The formula instructs us to subtract the grand mean from each individual score and then add up the squared deviations:

$$
\begin{aligned}
\text{Total } SS ={}& (8 - 14)^2 + (10 - 14)^2 + (12 - 14)^2 \\
&+ (10 - 14)^2 + (12 - 14)^2 + (14 - 14)^2 \\
&+ (13 - 14)^2 + (15 - 14)^2 + (17 - 14)^2 \\
&+ (17 - 14)^2 + (19 - 14)^2 + (21 - 14)^2 \\
={}& 170
\end{aligned}
$$

TABLE 14.2	Data for ANOVA Based on Results A in Table 14.1		
Group 1 Zero	Group 2 Milk	Group 3 Vitamins	Group 4 Hot Lunch
8	10	13	17
10	12	15	19
12	14	17	21
$\overline{X}_k$ 10	12	15	19

$$\overline{X}_G = (10 + 12 + 15 + 19)/4 = 14$$

Next, we compute the between-conditions *SS*. The formula instructs us to subtract the grand mean from each condition mean and then add up the weighted squared deviations:

$$\text{Between } SS = 3(10 - 14)^2$$
$$+ 3(12 - 14)^2$$
$$+ 3(15 - 14)^2$$
$$+ 3(19 - 14)^2$$
$$= 138$$

And finally, we compute the within-conditions *SS*. The formula instructs us to subtract the appropriate condition mean from each individual score and then add up the squared deviations:

$$\text{Within } SS = (8 - 10)^2 + (10 - 10)^2 + (12 - 10)^2$$
$$+ (10 - 12)^2 + (12 - 12)^2 + (14 - 12)^2$$
$$+ (13 - 15)^2 + (15 - 15)^2 + (17 - 15)^2$$
$$+ (17 - 19)^2 + (19 - 19)^2 + (21 - 19)^2$$
$$= 32$$

As a check on our arithmetic we add the sum of squares between conditions to the sum of squares within conditions to make sure their total equals the total sum of squares:

$$\text{Total } SS = \text{between } SS + \text{within } SS$$
$$170 = 138 + 32$$

THE **ANOVA** SUMMARY TABLE

The results of one-way ANOVAs may be displayed in the form shown in Table 14.3. The rows label the source of variation, in this case the variation between and within conditions. Listed in the *SS* column are sum-of-squares values for each source of variation; the degrees of freedom (*df*) are listed in the next column. Because there were four conditions (symbolized as $k = 4$), three of those means were free to vary once the mean of the means $(\overline{X}_G)$ was determined. We define the degrees of freedom between conditions as

$$df\,\text{between} = k - 1$$

which gives us $4 - 1 = 3\ df$ between.

We obtain the degrees of freedom within conditions by determining the *df* within each condition (defined as $n - 1$) and then adding. The reason we have $n - 1$ degrees of freedom within each condition is that all but one score is free to vary within each condition, and so we eliminate 1 *df* within each condition. Thus the *df* within conditions are found by

$$df\,\text{within} = N - k$$

where *N* is the total number of measurements or sampling units and *k* is the number of conditions, giving us $12 - 4 = 8\ df$ within.

The total *df* (not shown in Table 14.3) are defined as the total number of measurements minus 1, or

$$df\,\text{total} = N - 1$$

which gives us $12 - 1 = 11\ df$ total. After we have computed the *df* for between and within conditions, we can check our calculations by adding these *df* to see whether they agree with the *df* total. In the present case we have

$$df\,\text{total} = df\,\text{between} + df\,\text{within}$$

$$11 = 3 + 8$$

TABLE 14.3	Summary ANOVA Table				
Source	*SS*	*df*	*MS*	*F*	*p*
Between conditions	138	3	46	11.50	.003
Within conditions	32	8	4	—	—

Note: The effect size, *r*, is not reported here because it is uninterpretable when the numerator $df > 1$. That is, we compute the effect size of *F* only when it is based on a single *df* (e.g., the situation we find when two means are being compared).

The *MS* column shows the mean squares, which we obtained by dividing the sums of squares by the corresponding *df*. We divide 138 by 3 to get 46, and we divide 32 by 8 to get 4. Thus the *MS* values can be seen as the amounts of the total variation (measured in *SS*) attributable to each *df*. The larger the *MS* for the between-condition source of variance (the signal) relative to the within-condition source of variance (the noise), the less likely becomes the null hypothesis of no difference between the condition means. If the null hypothesis were true, the variation per *df* should be roughly the same for the *df* between groups and the *df* within groups. The *F* in the next column provides this information. We compute it by dividing the mean square between conditions by the mean square within conditions; the result is a signal-to-noise ratio of $F = 46/4 = 11.50$ (see also Box 14.2).

The final value in this table is the probability that an *F* of this size or larger, with this number of degrees of freedom, might occur if the null hypothesis of no difference among the means were true. In the previous chapter we noted that there is a different distribution of *t* values for every possible value of the degrees of freedom. The situation for *F* is similar but more complicated, because for every *F* ratio there are *two* relevant *df* values to take into account: the *df* between conditions and the *df* within conditions. For every combination of *df* between and *df* within, there is a different curve. As is the case for *t*, small values of *F* are likely when the null hypothesis of no difference between conditions is true, but large values are unlikely and are used as evidence to suggest that the null hypothesis is probably false.

Another important difference between *t* and *F* curves was alluded to earlier, when we said that the expected value of *t* is zero when the null hypothesis is true but that the expected value of *F* is approximately 1 when the null is true. The symmetrical bell shape of *t* curves means that they are centered at 0, with negative values running to negative infinity and positive values running to positive infinity. However, *F* curves are positively skewed, with values beginning at zero and ranging upward to positive infinity. In other words, *F* is intrinsically a one-tailed test of significance. When the null hypothesis is true, the expected value of *F* is $df/(df-2)$, where these *df* are for within conditions. For most values of *df*, then, the

---

BOX 14.2   *F* Ratios and Effect Sizes

To review, *F* is called the *F ratio* to reflect the fact that it is a ratio of two mean squares. The denominator mean square (i.e., the *mean square for error*) serves as a kind of base rate for noise level, or typical variation. The numerator (i.e., the signal) is a reflection of both the size of the effect and the size of the study. That is, a numerator *MS* may be large relative to a denominator *MS* because (1) the effect size is large; (2) the *n* per condition is large; or (3) both are large. As a consequence, large *F*'s should not be automatically interpreted as reflecting large effects. In the case of *F* with numerator $df > 1$, the idea of interpreting the effect size is academic, because we report the effect size only for *F*'s with numerator $df = 1$.

expected value of *F* when the null hypothesis is true is a little more than 1.0, as noted in Table 14.4

Table 14.4 enables us to locate the *p* value of a given *F;* a more comprehensive table can be found in Appendix B (see pp. 385–388). In Table 14.4 notice that the critical values of *F* required to reach the .05 and .01 levels decrease as the *df* within increase for any given *df* between. Similarly, the critical values of *F* decrease as the *df* between increase for any given *df* within—except for the special cases of *df* within = 1 or 2. For *df* within = 1, there is a substantial increase in the *F*'s required to reach the .05 and .01 levels as the *df* between increase from 1 to infinity. For *df* within = 2, only a very small increase in the *F*'s is required to reach the .05 and .01 levels as the *df* between increase from 1 to infinity. In practice, however, there are very few studies with large *df* between and only 1 or 2 *df* within.

To look up our *F* of 11.50 in Table 14.4, we put a finger on the intersection of 3 *df* between conditions and 8 *df* within conditions. The two values listed are 4.07 (the *F* value required for significance at *p* = .05) and 7.59 (the *F* value required for significance at *p* = .01). Because our obtained *F* is larger than 7.59, we know that the corresponding *p* must be less than .01. As implied by the extended table on pages 385–388, the actual *p* is approximately .003. Performing the same calculations on Results B in Table 14.1, we find *F* to be 1.28 (again with 3 and 8 degrees of freedom). Looking up this value in Table B.3, we find it to be too small to be significant at even the .20 level: The actual *p* is approximately .35.

What do the more precise *p* values tell us? The *p* value of .003 for Results A indicates that we would obtain an *F* of 11.50 or larger (for numerator *df* = 3 and denominator *df* = 8) only 3 in 1,000 times if we repeatedly conducted this study under the same conditions and if there really were no differences between the four means (i.e., if the null hypothesis were true). The *p* value of .35 for Results B informs us that we would obtain an *F* of 1.28 with 3 and 8 *df* 1 in every 3 times if we conducted the study under *these* conditions over and over, and if the null hypothesis were true. In reporting the *p* level, there is no need to state that it is one-tailed, because this fact is implicit in *F* (see also Box 14.3).

BOX 14.3	Using *t* to Boost Power

Taking the square root of *F* with numerator *df* = 1 gives us *t*, and we then interpret the effect size, *r*, in the usual way. An interesting characteristic of *F* distributions is that the *p* values, although naturally one-tailed, translate into two-tailed *p* values in *t* curves. Suppose we had computed *F* with numerator *df* = 1 and found *p* = .06 in the predicted direction. If we report *t* instead of *F*, we have the option of reporting "*p* = .03 one-tailed" (because we predicted the direction) or "*p* = .06 two-tailed" (if we choose a more conservative *p*), but we do not have this option with *F*. There is, of course, not much difference between *p* = .06 and *p* = .03, except that they fall on either side of the conventional level of *p* = .05. But the essential point is that there is a potential boost in statistical power if *t* rather than *F* is used when appropriate.

TABLE 14.4	*F* Values Required for Significance at the .05 (Upper Entry) and .01 Levels

Degrees of Freedom within conditions (denominator)	Degrees of Freedom Between Conditions (numerator)						Expected Value of *F* when H_0 True
	1	2	3	4	6	∞	
1	161 4052	200 4999	216 5403	225 5625	234 5859	254 6366	—
2	18.5 98.5	19.0 99.0	19.2 99.2	19.3 99.3	19.3 99.3	19.5 99.5	—
3	10.1 34.1	9.55 30.8	9.28 29.5	9.12 28.7	8.94 27.9	8.53 26.1	3.00
4	7.71 21.2	6.94 18.0	6.59 16.7	6.39 16.0	6.16 15.2	5.63 13.5	2.00
5	6.61 16.3	5.79 13.3	5.41 12.1	5.19 11.4	4.95 10.7	4.36 9.02	1.67
6	5.99 13.7	5.14 10.9	4.76 9.78	4.53 9.15	4.28 8.47	3.67 6.88	1.50
8	5.32 11.3	4.46 8.65	4.07 7.59	3.84 7.01	3.58 6.37	2.93 4.86	1.33
10	4.96 10.0	4.10 7.56	3.71 6.55	3.48 5.99	3.22 5.39	2.54 3.91	1.25
15	4.54 8.68	3.68 6.36	3.29 5.42	3.06 4.89	2.79 4.32	2.07 2.87	1.15
20	4.35 8.10	3.49 5.85	3.10 4.94	2.87 4.43	2.60 3.87	1.84 2.42	1.11
25	4.24 7.77	3.38 5.57	2.99 4.68	2.76 4.18	2.49 3.63	1.71 2.17	1.09
30	4.17 7.56	3.32 5.39	2.92 4.51	2.69 4.02	2.42 3.47	1.62 2.01	1.07
40	4.08 7.31	3.23 5.18	2.84 4.31	2.61 3.83	2.34 3.29	1.51 1.80	1.05
∞	3.84 6.64	2.99 4.60	2.60 3.78	2.37 3.32	2.09 2.80	1.00 1.00	1.00

Note: For a more complete table see Appendix B.3.

AFTER THE *F*: *t* REVISITED

Now we know that for the data in Table 14.2 the group means are not likely to be this far apart if the null hypothesis were true. But knowing that the four groups of our study differ does not tell us whether milk helps in and of itself and whether vitamins help in and of themselves. To address these questions, we need to compare (1) the results in Group 2 with the results in Group 1 (the zero control) and (2) the results in Group 3 with the zero control. These comparisons are called *tests of simple effects*, and an easy way to do them is by *t* tests. Using the formula for comparing independent means given in the previous chapter, we now define S^2 as the pooled value we just calculated for the denominator of our *F* ratio.

To illustrate the test of simple effects using the results in Table 14.2, we substitute the values of Groups 1 and 3 in our general formula:

$$t = \frac{\overline{X}_3 - \overline{X}_1}{\sqrt{\left(\dfrac{1}{n_3} + \dfrac{1}{n_1}\right)S^2}} = \frac{15 - 10}{\sqrt{\left(\dfrac{1}{3} + \dfrac{1}{3}\right)4}} = \frac{5}{\sqrt{2.67}} = 3.06$$

where $\overline{X}_3$ is the mean of Group 3; $\overline{X}_1$ is the mean of Group 1; n_3 and n_1 are the sample sizes of these groups; and S^2 is the value of the within-conditions *MS* shown in Table 14.3. When we test this *t* for significance, we base our *df* not on $n_3 - n_1 - 2$ (as we did previously), but on *df* equal to the within-conditions *SS* (i.e., 8 *df*) because we are using a pooled estimate of S^2. Referring to Table B.2 (see pp. 383–384), we find the significance of $t = 3.06$ to be less than $p = .01$ but more than $p = .005$ one-tailed. The actual one-tailed p is approximately .008 (and the two-tailed $p = .016$, or $.008 \times 2$). If we have planned from the beginning to compute a particular *t* test, we can do so whether our overall *F* is significant or not. However, if we are going to be looking for large differences that we had not specifically predicted, our *t* test results are going to be much more interpretable if our overall *F* is significant.

The next step is to calculate the effect size of our *t* as

$$r = \sqrt{\frac{t^2}{t^2 + df}} = \sqrt{\frac{(3.06)^2}{(3.06)^2 + 4}} = \sqrt{\frac{9.36}{13.36}} = .84$$

indicating another jumbo-sized effect. However, there is something tricky here. When we compute *t* tests after an ANOVA, we use the *df* from the *MS* of the ANOVA (8 in this case) to find the significance level. When we compute the effect size, we use only the *df* from the groups being compared (4 in this case). In terms of the binomial effect-size display (BESD), this *r* of .84 amounts to a difference in success rates of 8% to 92% between nonusers and users of vitamins, respectively (i.e., if half the population used vitamins and also half the population showed improved performance).

TWO-WAY DESIGNS

R. A. Fisher, the British statistician who invented the *F* test, noticed that it is sometimes possible to rearrange a one-way design to form a two-way design of much greater power to reject the null hypothesis. We turn now to an analysis of the simplest two-way design, one in which there are two levels of each factor (i.e., a 2 × 2 factorial). An example is essential, and we study again the hypothetical effects of nutrition on academic performance. However, we slightly change the question we asked earlier about the differences among our four nutritional conditions. Instead we will ask several questions simultaneously:

1. What is the effect on academic performance of daily milk?
2. What is the effect on academic performance of daily vitamins?
3. What is the effect on academic performance of both milk and vitamins? (The hot lunch includes both milk and vitamins.)
4. Is the effect of vitamins different when milk is also given from when milk is not given?
5. Is the effect of milk different when vitamins are also given from when vitamins are not given?

We can answer all these questions by using a two-way design of the kind illustrated in Table 14.5.

Note that the scores in Table 14.5 are the same as those in Table 14.2, while Table 14.6 shows the group means of the sets of individual scores. Table 14.6 also illustrates how factorial designs allow us to answer more questions than one-way designs. In this case, for example, we can learn whether the effect of one of our factors is much the same for each of the two or more conditions of the other factor. As noted earlier, another name for the difference between group means is *simple effects*. Here, a comparison of the differences between the simple effects tells us that there is a two-unit effect (12 − 10 = 2) of milk when no vitamins are given, and that there is a four-unit effect (19 − 15 = 4) of milk when vitamins are given. Similarly, there is a five-unit effect (15 − 10 = 5) of vitamins when no milk is given and a seven-unit effect (19 − 12 = 7) of vitamins when milk is given.

Not only do factorial designs allow us to answer more questions than one-way

TABLE 14.5	Raw Scores of Two-Way Design		
	Milk Treatment		Row
Vitamin Treatment	Present	Absent	Means
Present	17, 19, 21	13, 15, 17	17
Absent	10, 12, 14	8, 10, 12	11
Column means	15.5	12.5	

Note: The milk-present, vitamin-present condition is the hot lunch condition of Table 14.2, as that condition included both milk and vitamins.

TABLE 14.6	Means and Effects			
	Milk Treatment		Row	Row
Vitamin Treatment	Present	Absent	Means	Effects
Present	19	15	17	+3.0
Absent	12	10	11	−3.0
Column means	15.5	12.5	14 (grand mean)	
Column effects	+1.5	−1.5		

designs, but having subjects serve double duty increases the power to reject null hypotheses regarding overall effects if the null hypotheses are false. That is, more of the subjects available for the study are able to contribute to the major comparisons (milk versus no milk; vitamins versus no vitamins). In this case, half of all the subjects of the experiment are in the milk conditions instead of the quarter of all subjects that would be in the milk condition in a one-way design. Thus half of the subjects can be compared to the remaining half of the subjects who received no milk, so that all the subjects of the experiment shed light on the question of the effect of milk. The overall effect (also called a *main effect*) of milk is assessed by a comparison of the milk and no-milk column means (15.5 and 12.5, respectively). At the same time that all subjects are providing information on the milk comparison, they are also contributing information on the effect of vitamins. The main effect of vitamins is assessed by a comparison of the vitamin and no-vitamin row means (17 and 11, respectively).

As described next, another advantage of factorial designs is that they allow us to examine *interaction effects*, or "leftover effects" (also called *residuals*), representing the combinations of independent variables. Thus the interaction here is designated as "rows × columns" (stated as "rows by columns") or "vitamins × milk" (stated as "vitamins by milk") to imply this combination.

EFFECTS AND THE FACTORIAL ANOVA

Previously, we noted that a general purpose of the analysis of variance is to divide up the variance of all the observations into a number of separate sources of estimation and significance testing. To understand how a two-way ANOVA does its job, we think of the group means (as well as each individual score) as comprising a number of separate elements. In a 2 × 2 design, the group means (and measurements) can be broken into (1) the grand mean; (2) the row effects; (3) the column effects; (4) the interaction effects; and (5) error. We will begin by describing how the first four elements (grand mean, row effect, column effect, and interaction effect) are conceptualized in terms of an *additive model* (i.e., a model in which the components sum to the group means).

As noted previously, the *grand mean* $(\overline{X}_G)$ is the mean of all group means, or $(19 + 15 + 12 + 10)/4 = 14$. As shown in Table 14.6, the *row effect* for each row is the mean of that row $(\overline{X}_r)$ minus the grand mean. Thus the row effects are computed as $17 - 14 = +3.0$ for vitamins-present and $11 - 14 = -3.0$ for vitamins-absent. The *column effect* of each column is the mean of that column $(\overline{X}_c)$ minus the grand mean, which gives us $15.5 - 14 = +1.5$ for milk-present and $12.5 - 14 = -1.5$ for milk-absent. Each set of effects sums to zero when totaled over all conditions, which is a result characteristic of all row, column, and interaction effects.

Not visible in Table 14.6 are the *interaction effects* (i.e., the residuals, or leftover effects). These effects are what remain after the grand mean, the row effect, and the column effect are subtracted from the group mean (see, e.g., Rosnow & Rosenthal, 1989a, 1995). In other words,

Interaction effect = group mean − grand mean − row effect − column effect

so for these data, the interaction effects for the vitamins-plus-milk group (VM), the vitamins-only group (V), the milk-only group (M), and zero control (O) are computed as follows:

	Group Mean		Grand Mean		Row Effect		Column Effect		Interaction Effect
VM	19	−	14	−	3.0	−	1.5	=	0.5
V	15	−	14	−	3.0	−	(−1.5)	=	(−0.5)
M	12	−	14	−	(−3.0)	−	1.5	=	(−0.5)
O	10	−	14	−	(−3.0)	−	(−1.5)	=	0.5
Sum	56	−	56	−	0.0	−	0.0	=	0.0

What can we learn about the results of our experiment by studying the above table of effects (see also Box 14.4)? The grand mean tells us the general "level" of our measurements and is usually not of great intrinsic interest. The row effect

---

BOX 14.4   The Additive Model

We said that the idea of ANOVA is based on an *additive model;* that is, the components sum to the group means. We see this clearly when we total all four conditions of our two-way table:

	Group Mean		Grand Mean		Row Effect		Column Effect		Interaction Effect
VM	19	=	14	+	3.0	+	1.5	+	0.5
V	15	=	14	+	3.0	+	(−1.5)	+	(−0.5)
M	12	=	14	+	(−3.0)	+	1.5	+	(−0.5)
O	10	=	14	+	(−3.0)	+	(−1.5)	+	0.5
Sum	56	=	56	+	0.0	+	0.0	+	0.0

The advantages of the additive structure are that it offers a baseline that allows us to compare row, column, and interaction effects with one another, and it makes *F* tests possible.

shows us that the groups receiving vitamins (VM and V) did better than those not receiving vitamins (M and O). The column effect shows us that the groups receiving milk (VM and M) did better than those not receiving milk (V and O). The interaction effect shows us that the group receiving *both* vitamins and milk (VM) and the group receiving *neither* vitamins nor milk (O) both benefited more than did the groups receiving *either* vitamins (V) or milk (M). But although it is slightly better from the viewpoint of the *interaction effect alone* to receive neither treatment, this statistical advantage in the interaction effect (i.e., 0.5) is more than offset by the statistical disadvantage in the row effect (i.e., −3.0) and the column effect (i.e., −1.5) to be receiving neither treatment.

That the mean of each group in a two-way design can be broken into the grand mean, the row effect, the column effect, and the interaction effect does not quite tell the whole story—because *error* is omitted. That is, it is not taken into account that the various scores found in each condition may be rewritten as a deviation from the mean of that condition. The term *error* takes its name from the idea that the magnitude of these deviations reflects how poorly we have done in predicting individual scores from a knowledge of condition or group membership. A particular score shows a large error if it falls far from the mean of its condition but only a small error if it falls close to the mean of its condition.

We can now write error as

$$\text{Error} = \text{score} - \text{group mean}$$

so that

$$\text{Score} = \text{group mean} + \text{error}$$

but

$$\text{Group mean} = \text{grand mean} + \text{row effect} + \text{column effect} + \text{interaction effect}$$

so

$$\text{Score} = \text{grand mean} + \text{row effect} + \text{column effect} + \text{interaction effect} + \text{error}$$

COMPUTING THE TWO-WAY ANOVA

Earlier, when we analyzed the results of the present study as a one-way analysis, we computed the total sum of squares as

$$\text{Total } SS = \Sigma(X - \overline{X}_G)^2 = 170$$

where X is each observation or measurement and $\overline{X}_G$ is the mean of all the condition means. We computed the within-conditions sum of squares as

$$\text{Within-conditions } SS = \Sigma(X - \overline{X}_k)^2$$

where $\overline{X}_k$ is the mean of the group or condition to which each observation or measurement *(X)* belongs. For our two-way ANOVA, we may use the same (above) formulas, but we also need to compute the sums of the squares of the rows, the columns, and the interaction.

The sum of squares of the rows is defined as

$$\text{Row } SS = \Sigma[nc(\overline{X}_r - \overline{X}_G)^2]$$

where n is the number of observations in each condition; c is the number of columns contributing to the computation of $\overline{X}_r$ (the mean of the rth row); and $\overline{X}_G$ is again the grand mean. The sum of squares of the columns is defined as

$$\text{Column } SS = \Sigma[nr(\overline{X}_c - \overline{X}_G)^2]$$

where n is the number of observations in each condition; r is the number of rows contributing to the computation of $\overline{X}_c$ (the mean of the cth column); and $\overline{X}_G$ is the grand mean. And finally, the interaction sum of squares is defined as

$$\text{Interaction } SS = \text{total } SS - (\text{row } SS + \text{column } SS + \text{within } SS)$$

With our newfound knowledge about the effects, at the same time that we compute the formulas above we can take apart the individual scores to help us understand better the various terms of the analysis of variance. The ANOVA summary is presented in Table 14.7, and Table 14.8 reminds us where the *SS* values came from. The only new values in Table 14.8 are those for error, which for each subject is computed as the individual's raw score minus the group mean. Thus, for the VM subject in Table 14.5 who scored 17, we subtract 19 (the mean of this group) to get the error score of −2 in Table 14.8. Beneath each column in Table 14.8 are shown the sums of the listed values (ΣX) and the sums of squares of the listed values (ΣX^2).

In the formula above, the total SS is defined as the sum of the squared deviations between every single score and the grand mean, that is, $(17 - 14)^2 + (19 - 14)^2 + \ldots + (12 - 14)^2 = 170$. Alternatively, we see in Table 14.8 that subtracting the sum of the squared grand means (shown as 2,352) from the sum of the squared scores (shown as 2,522) gives us the same value (i.e., total $SS = 2,522 - 2,352 = 170$). Looking again at Table 14.3, we are reminded that in the one-way analysis of variance this total *SS* is allocated to two sources of variance: a between-

TABLE 14.7	Summary Table for Two-Way ANOVA					
Source	SS	df	MS	F	p	r
Vitamins (rows)	108	1	108	27.0	.0008	.88
Milk (columns)	27	1	27	6.75	.03	.68
Interaction	3	1	3	0.75	.41	.29
Within error	32	8	4	—	—	—
Total	170	11	---	---	---	---

Note: Although the listing of effect sizes for *F*'s with numerator *df* = 1 is not yet standard, it is a practice we strongly recommend.

			Grand		Row		Column		Interaction		
Group	Score	=	Mean	+	Effect	+	Effect	+	Effect	+	Error

TABLE 14.8 Table of Effects for Computing ANOVA

Group	Score	=	Mean	+	Effect	+	Effect	+	Effect	+	Error
VM	17	=	14	+	3.0	+	1.5	+	0.5	+	(−2)
VM	19	=	14	+	3.0	+	1.5	+	0.5	+	0
VM	21	=	14	+	3.0	+	1.5	+	0.5	+	2
V	13	=	14	+	3.0	+	(−1.5)	+	(−0.5)	+	(−2)
V	15	=	14	+	3.0	+	(−1.5)	+	(−0.5)	+	0
V	17	–	14	+	3.0	+	(−1.5)	+	(−0.5)	+	2
M	10	=	14	+	(−3.0)	+	1.5	+	(−0.5)	+	(−2)
M	12	=	14	+	(−3.0)	+	1.5	+	(−0.5)	+	0
M	14	=	14	+	(−3.0)	+	1.5	+	(−0.5)	+	2
O	8	=	14	+	(−3.0)	+	(−1.5)	+	0.5	+	(−2)
O	10	=	14	+	(−3.0)	+	(−1.5)	+	0.5	+	0
O	12	=	14	+	(−3.0)	+	(−1.5)	+	0.5	+	2
ΣX	168	=	168	+	0	+	0	+	0	+	0
ΣX^2	2522	=	2352	+	108	+	27	+	3	+	32

conditions and a within-conditions source. In moving from a one-way to a two-way ANOVA, the within-conditions source of variance (i.e., the source attributable to error) remains unchanged (i.e., "Within error" or "Within conditions" $SS = 32$ in Tables 14.3, 14.7, and 14.8). The between-conditions source of variance in the one-way ANOVA (shown in Table 14.3 as 138) is broken down into three components in our two-way ANOVA: a row effect SS, a column effect SS, and an interaction effect SS.

Table 14.8 shows the origin of these values in the individual measurements, and let us also compute them using our formulas. First, we obtain the row effect sum of squares from

$$\text{Row } SS = \Sigma[nc(\overline{X}_r - \overline{X}_G)^2]$$
$$= [(3)(2)(17 - 14)^2] + [(3)(2)(11 - 14)^2]$$
$$= 108$$

giving us the value shown in the bottom row of Table 14.8.

Next, we obtain the column effect sum of squares from

$$\text{Column } SS = \Sigma[nr(\overline{X}_c - \overline{X}_G)^2]$$
$$= [(3)(2)(15.5 - 14)^2] + [(3)(2)(12.5 - 14)^2]$$
$$= 27$$

again giving the value in Table 14.8.

Finally, we obtain the sum of squares of the interaction from

$$\text{Interaction } SS = \text{total } SS - (\text{row } SS + \text{column } SS + \text{within } SS)$$

which gives us

$$\text{Interaction } SS = 170 - (108 + 27 + 32) = 3$$

and, as anticipated, it is the value shown in Table 14.8.

The logic of computing the degrees of freedom of the two-way ANOVA is the same as that in the one-way analysis, but we must apportion the between-conditions df to the row main effect, the column main effect, and the interaction. The degrees of freedom for rows in Table 14.7 are

$$df \text{ rows } = r - 1$$

where r is the number of rows (i.e., $2 - 1 = 1$ df). The degrees of freedom for columns are

$$df \text{ columns } = c - 1$$

where c is the number of columns (i.e., $2 - 1 = 1$ df). The degrees of freedom for the interaction are

$$df \text{ interaction } = (r - 1)(c - 1)$$

which gives us $(2 - 1)(2 - 1) = 1$ df.

The degrees of freedom for the "Within error" are the same as those in Table 14.3, defined as

$$df \text{ within } = N - k$$

where N is the total number of observations or measurements and k is the number of groups or conditions (i.e., $12 - 4 = 8$). In other words, this is the number of subjects in each group or condition minus 1 totaled over all groups, or $(3 - 1) + (3 - 1) + (3 - 1) + (3 - 1) = 8$ df within conditions. As a check on the degrees of freedom, we compute the df of the total SS as $N - 1$ (i.e., $12 - 1 = 11$) and find this result to be identical to the sum of the df in Table 14.7 (i.e., $1 + 1 + 1 + 8 = 11$).

As before, the mean square *(MS)* values in Table 14.7 are obtained by dividing the sums of squares by the corresponding df. For example, we divide 108 by 1 to get 108, and we divide 32 by 8 to get 4 (i.e., the amounts of the total variation, measured in SS, attributable to each df). The F ratios are computed by dividing the mean squares for rows, columns, and interaction (the signals) by the mean square within conditions (the noise). Thus we divide 108 by 4 to get 27.0, and we divide 27 by 4 to get 6.75, and we divide 3 by 4 to get 0.75. Because the effect sizes of F ratios with 1 df in the numerator are readily interpretable, we calculate the effect size of each of these F values by

$$r = \sqrt{\frac{F}{F + df \text{ within}}}$$

We interpret the results as we would any Pearson r, including using the BESD described in Chapter 11.

Table 14.7 also shows precise values of *p*. The *F* of 6.75 for the effect of milk could have occurred by chance approximately 3 times in 100, and the *F* of 27.0 for the effect of vitamins could have occurred by chance far less often, if the null hypothesis were true. The *F* for interaction, however, is so small that it could easily have arisen by chance. If it were significant and of interest, we would analyze it as before (i.e., as a comparison between the residuals of the diagonal cells). What we learn from the effect sizes is that both milk and vitamins have a beneficial effect, and that more of the effect is attributable to vitamins than to milk. We can also compute tests of simple effects by using the *t* procedure described previously.

REPEATED-MEASURES ANOVA DESIGNS

In earlier discussions we referred to *repeated-measures designs,* so called because the sampling units are measured on the dependent variable more than once. Table 14.9 illustrates such a design, in which one factor is the repeated-measures factor of treatments, and the second factor is subjects. Because there is only a single score for each subject entered for each condition, there can be no estimate of within-cell variability. Previously, each subject was observed only once, but here we see that each subject was observed once a month for a total of four times. The analysis of variance computed on these scores is summarized at the bottom of Table 14.9. The *F* test was computed as a ratio of the mean square for treatments (46) divided by the mean square for treatments × subjects (4), with degrees of freedom defined as 3 and 6.

The statistical analysis of repeated-measures designs involves some intricacies that go beyond the scope of this text, but you will find detailed discussions and illustrations in advanced texts (e.g., Keppel, 1991; Rosenthal & Rosnow, 1991). In analyzing designs of the repeated-measures kind (including mixed designs, in which some variables involve repeated measures), we must be especially sensitive to the error terms to be inserted in the denominators of *F* ratios. The same caution applies to the specification of the appropriate degrees of freedom. However, the

TABLE 14.9	Repeated-Measures Design and ANOVA			
	January Condition 1 (Zero)	February Condition 2 (Milk)	March Condition 3 (Vitamins)	April Condition 4 (Hot Lunch)
Subject 1	8	12	15	21
Subject 2	10	14	17	19
Subject 3	12	10	13	17

Source	*SS*	*df*	*MS*	*F*	*p*
Treatments	138	3	46	11.50	.007
Subjects	8	2	4	—	—
Treatments × subjects	24	6	4	—	—

interpretation of such designs uses a logic similar to that used to interpret all factorial ANOVAs.

SUMMARY OF IDEAS

1. The limitation of the two-sample t is that it can be used only when there are two means to be compared; the advantage of F is that it can be used for any number of groups (i.e., two or more groups).
2. For the special case of the comparison of two groups, $F = t^2$, and in that particular case, we can calculate the effect size for F as $r = \sqrt{F/(F + df\text{ within})}$.
3. In one-way ANOVAs, we compute the between-conditions MS and the within-conditions MS to serve as a kind of signal-to-noise ratio.
4. In factorial designs, two or more levels of each factor (independent variable) are administered in combination with two or more levels of every other factor.
5. Such designs use sampling units more efficiently and address more questions than do ordinary one-way ANOVAs.
6. In the two-way ANOVA, the group means and the individual measurements are broken into additive elements representing the grand mean, the row effects, the column effects, the interaction effects, and error.
7. The error of individual scores (i.e., the deviation of each score from the mean of the group) tells us the extent to which the score can be predicted from a knowledge of group membership.
8. The summary table for the factorial ANOVA differs from the summary table for the one-way ANOVA in reflecting the subdivision of the between-conditions SS.
9. Interaction effects are effects left over (residuals) after the grand mean and the row and column effects are removed from the group (condition) means.
10. In repeated-measures designs, the observations or measurements are repeated on the same sampling units.

KEY TERMS

additive model *p. 296*

analysis of variance (ANOVA)

   p. 283

column effect *p. 296*

degrees of freedom *p. 289*

df *p. 289*

error *p. 297*

factorial designs *p. 283*

F ratio *p. 285*

grand mean *p. 295*

interaction effects *p. 296*

main effect *p. 295*

mean square *(MS)* *p. 286*

mean square for error *p. 284*

one-way designs *p. 283*

repeated-measures designs *p. 301*

residuals *p. 295*

row effect *p. 295*

simple effects *p. 293*

summary ANOVA table *p. 289*

sum of squares *(SS)* *p. 286*

two-way designs *p. 283*

REVIEW QUESTIONS

1. From a population of 50 male professional runners, an Ohio State researcher randomly assigns 10 to each of five groups. Each group receives a different brand of running shoe. The brands are coded A, B, C, D, and E. Each member of a group receives a new pair of the top-of-the-line shoe made by the shoe company and then rates the shoe for comfort. Below are the mean comfort ratings (on a scale from 1 to 20) given to the different brands:

Brand	Rating
A	19
B	13
C	17
D	9
E	10

   Suppose the researcher performs an analysis of variance, and the within-shoe-brands mean square is 94, whereas the mean square for between-shoe-brands is 188. What is the value of the *F* testing the significance of the difference among the shoe brands? What are the associated degrees of freedom?

2. A University of Pittsburgh researcher has the following two sets of data, each of which contains three independent groups. The 12 subjects in each set were randomly assigned to the groups; 4 subjects were assigned to each group. The numbers are scores on some dependent measure.

Set A		Group 1	Group 2	Group 3
		2	5	11
		3	5	10
		2	4	9
		1	6	10
	Mean	2	5	10

Set B		Group 1	Group 2	Group 3
		9	11	23
		−6	−10	10
		4	0	−2
		1	19	9
	Mean	2	5	10

   Which set of data is likely to yield a larger *F* ratio in an analysis of variance? How can you be sure?

3. A University of Colorado student obtains the following set of means in a study that measures the benefits of vacations in rural versus urban areas for subjects who live in rural or urban areas. Higher numbers indicate greater benefits. Figure out the row effects, the column effects, and the interaction residuals, and then decide how they should be interpreted.

	Urban Subjects	Rural Subjects
Urban vacations	5	3
Rural vacations	11	1

4. A University of Maine student obtains the data shown in Table 14.2 and computes the ANOVA shown in Table 14.3. His primary interest, however, is in whether the hot lunch group performed significantly better than did the average of the remaining three groups. How would you advise him to address his question?

Answers to review questions are found on pages 320–334.

Chi-Square

THE UTILITY OF CHI-SQUARE

To review, in our discussion of the correlation coefficient (Chapter 11) we said that it could be viewed quite directly as a measure of the degree of relation between two variables. As noted in Chapter 12, when the number of pairs of scores on which r is computed is small, a very large r may not differ significantly from chance. In that case, although there is a strong relation between the two variables, relations that strong occur quite often by chance even if the true correlation is zero. For that reason we would like to know for any r not only its size but also the probability of its having occurred by chance.

Whereas r tells us immediately how "big" a relation there is between variables, but not how unlikely it is to have occurred by chance, t and F tell us immediately (with the help of a table) how unlikely it is that a given relation has occurred by chance, but not how "big" the relation is. However, by taking a simple additional step, described in Chapters 13 and 14, we can compute the size of a relation that a large t or F (based on two conditions) has convinced us is unlikely to have occurred by chance. Thus r gives us the size of the relation and permits us a further assessment of statistical significance, whereas t and F give us statistical significance and permit us a further assessment of the size of the relation.

The statistic we discuss in this final chapter is the *chi-square*, symbolized as χ^2 (pronounced "ki-square"). Invented in 1900 by Karl Pearson (who also invented the product–moment r), it is a statistic that, like t and F, tells us how unlikely it is that the relation investigated has occurred by chance, and like t and F, it does not tell us immediately about the strength of the relation between the variables. Just as in the case of t and F, any given value of χ^2 is associated with a stronger degree of relation when it is based on a smaller number of sampling units. In other words, a relation must be quite strong to result in a large χ^2 (or t, or F) with only a small number of subjects.

Another name for frequencies is *counts,* and chi-square can be thought of as a comparison of counts. That is, it does its job of testing the relation between two variables by assessing the discrepancy between a theoretically *expected frequency* and an obtained or *observed frequency* (see also Box 15.1). In other words, it differs from the other significance tests we have examined in that it can be used for dependent variables that are not scored or scaled. In all the earlier examples of t and F, subjects' responses were recorded as scores in such a way that some could be regarded as so many units greater or less than other scores. Because chi-square is a comparison of counts, it allows us to deal with categories of response that are not so easily ordered, scaled, or scored.

COMPUTING 2 × 2 CHI-SQUARES

Imagine that we want to study the food preferences of members of two campus organizations, which call themselves the Junk Food Junkies (JFJ) and the Green Earthies (GE). We give each subject a choice of one of two foods, a juicy grilled

---

BOX 15.1   Fisher As Detective

In the 19th century, Gregor Mendel, the legendary Austrian botanist, performed experiments that became the basis of the modern science of genetics. Working with garden peas, he showed how their characteristics could be predicted from the characteristics of their "parents." In a famous piece of scientific detective work, Ronald A. Fisher (the inventor of the F test and the null hypothesis) later used the chi-square to ask whether Mendel's data may have been manipulated so that they would seem to be more in line with his theory. Fisher used the chi-square as a "goodness-of-fit" test of Mendel's reported findings compared with statistically expected values, and he found Mendel's "findings" *too perfect* to be plausible Fisher concluded that Mendel had been deceived by a research assistant, who knew what Mendel wanted to find and who manipulated the data *too* well.

TABLE 15.1	Basic Data for 2 × 2 Chi Square		

A. Observed *(O)* Frequencies

Food Choice	JFJ	GE	Row Sums
Big Jack	24	13	37
Soyburger	12	30	42
Column sums	36	43	79

B. Expected *(E)* Frequencies

Food Choice	JFJ	GE	Row Sums
Big Jack	16.861	20.139	37.000
Soyburger	19.139	22.861	42.000
Column sums	36.000	43.000	79

C. *(O − E)²/E* Values

Food Choice	JFJ	GE	Row Sums
Big Jack	3.023	2.531	5.554
Soyburger	2.663	2.229	4.892
Column sums	5.686	4.760	10.446

hamburger with onions, pickles, relish, and barbecue sauce on a sesame seed bun (called a Big Jack) or a grilled soyburger with lettuce and tomato on whole wheat bread. Table 15.1 provides the basic data for computing a simple chi-square, a 2 × 2 table. Membership in the organizations is thought of as the independent variable, and the preference for a Big Jack or a soyburger is the dependent variable; each member of the two samples of subjects falls into one and only one of the four possible cells. In Section A, the "Observed frequencies" are the number of people in that column (organization) who chose the alternative listed in that row. Of the members of the Junk Food Junkies, 24 chose a Big Jack, and 12 chose the soyburger, and of the members of the Green Earthies, 13 chose a Big Jack, and 30 chose the soyburger.

The following general formula summarizes the steps we will take in analyzing those observed frequencies:

$$\chi^2 = \sum \frac{(O - E)^2}{E}$$

where O is the observed frequency in each cell, and E is the expected frequency in that cell. This formula instructs us to sum the squared differences between the observed frequencies (O) and the expected frequencies (E) after first dividing each squared difference by the expected frequency. If the null hypothesis of no relation between the rows and columns were true, we would expect the O's and E's to be similar in magnitude. In other words, observed frequencies that are substantially larger and smaller than the expected frequencies are needed to throw doubt on the null hypothesis, because the value of chi-square will be small when the difference $O - E$ is small.

To use this formula we must first determine for each of our observed frequencies the number of "expected" entries, that is, the number expected if the null hypothesis of no relation between the independent and dependent variable were true. To compute this expected frequency (E) for each cell, we multiply the column total by the row total where that row and that column intersect in that cell. We then divide this quantity by the grand total of entries. That is,

$$E = \frac{\text{Column total} \times \text{Row total}}{\text{Grand total}}$$

For example, the upper-left cell in Section A of Table 15.1 is at the intersection of the JFJ column and the Big Jack row. The appropiate totals multiplied together and divided by the grand total are $(36 \times 37)/79 = 16.861$. Section B gives all the expected frequencies computed in this way. These values, row by row, are

$$(36 \times 37)/79 = 16.861$$

$$(43 \times 37)/79 = 20.139$$

$$(36 \times 42)/79 = 19.139$$

$$(43 \times 42)/79 = 22.861$$

As a check on our arithmetic, notice that the row totals, the column totals, and the grand total of all the values in Section B are equal to the corresponding totals of the values in Section A. Substituting in the formula for chi-square, we now add up the $(O - E)^2/E$ values (i.e., for each cell, the square of the difference between the observed and expected frequency divided by the expected frequency), which gives us

$$\chi^2 = \sum \frac{(O - E)^2}{E}$$

$$= \frac{(24 - 16.861)^2}{16.861} + \frac{(13 - 20.139)^2}{20.139} + \frac{(12 - 19.139)^2}{19.139} + \frac{(30 - 22.861)^2}{22.861}$$

$$= 10.446$$

These $(O - E)^2/E$ values for each cell also appear in Section C of Table 15.1, which underscores the idea that the total of all these values is the chi-square.

TABLE 15.2	Chi-Square Values for Significance at .10, .05, and .01		
df	*p* = .10	*p* = .05	*p* = .01
1	2.71	3.84	6.64
2	4.60	5.99	9.21
3	6.25	7.82	11.34
4	7.78	9.49	13.28
5	9.24	11.07	15.09

FINDING THE *P* VALUE AND EFFECT SIZE

As is true of *t* and *F*, there is a different chi-square curve for every value of the degrees of freedom. The degrees of freedom *(df)* of chi-square are defined as

$$df = (r - 1)(c - 1)$$

or the number of rows *(r)* minus 1 multiplied by the number of columns *(c)* minus 1. The larger the χ^2, the less likely are the observed frequencies to differ from the expected frequencies only by chance. Table 15.2 gives a sample listing of χ^2 values with *df* 1–5 for *p* = .10, .05, and .01. A more comprehensive listing can be found in Table B.4 (see page 389). Notice that a chi-square must be larger than the degrees of freedom to throw doubt on the null hypothesis (see also Box 15.2).

In this example, the 1 *df* chi-square of 10.446 is larger than the largest value shown for *df* = 1 (6.64 for *p* = .01); the actual *p* is approximately .001. Thus a chi-square value this large or larger would occur 1 time in 1,000 repeated samplings if the null hypothesis were true. That is, there is about 1 chance in 1,000 that a chi-square this large would occur if there really were no relation between organizational membership and food preference.

We now compute the effect size, and it should be obvious that we will do so by

---

BOX 15.2   Chi-Square and the Null Hypothesis

Reminiscent of *F*, all chi-square curves begin at zero and range upward to infinity. You will recall that the expected value of *t* is zero when the null hypothesis is true, and the expected value of *F* is $df/(df - 2)$ where *df* are for the denominator mean square. For chi-square distributions, the expected value (when the null hypothesis of no relation is true) is equal to the *df* defining that chi-square distribution. Thus, for chi-squares based on 1, 2, and 3 *df*, the average value of the χ^2 obtained if the null hypothesis were true would be 1, 2, and 3, respectively.

using the *phi coefficient*. In computing phi in Chapter 11, we used the following general formula:

$$\phi = \frac{BC - AD}{\sqrt{(A + B)(C + D)(A + C)(B + D)}}$$

with the letters defined as follows:

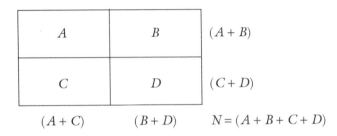

A	B	(A + B)
C	D	(C + D)
(A + C)	(B + D)	N = (A + B + C + D)

Substituting the data in Section A ("Observed frequencies") of Table 15.1, we find

$$\phi = \frac{(13 \times 12) - (24 \times 30)}{\sqrt{(37)(42)(36)(43)}} = \frac{-564}{1551} = .36$$

which indicates a substantial effect. Although we see that the numerator of this phi is negative because of the particular arrangement of the cell counts, we also see that Junk Food Junkiness (scored 1 or 0) is positively correlated with Big Jackness (scored 1 or 0). We can now translate this effect into a binomial effect-size display (BESD) with uniform ("standardized") row and column totals (see also Box 15.3).

PHI AND CHI-SQUARE

Before we leave the phi coefficient, note that a special formula for computing chi-square directly from the observed frequencies in a 2 × 2 table is

$$\chi^2 = \frac{N(BC - AD)^2}{(A + B)(C + D)(A + C)(B + D)}$$

which for the data in Table 15.1 yields

$$\chi^2 = \frac{79[(13 \times 12) - (24 \times 30)]^2}{(37)(42)(36)(43)} = \frac{79(318,096)}{2,405,592} = 10.446$$

If the sample size *(N)* is not too small (e.g., *N* > 20), and if the smallest expected frequency is not too small (e.g., less than 3 or so), we can test the significance of phi coefficients by chi-square tests, because

$$\chi^2 = \phi^2 \times N$$

BOX 15.3	The Aspirin Study Revisited

In Chapter 12 we described a major biomedical experiment that found that heart attack risk was cut by aspirin (Steering Committee of the Physicians' Health Study Research Group, 1988). The raw frequencies are repeated in the table below, which shows the number of participants in each condition who did or did not have a heart attack:

Condition	No Heart Attack	Heart Attack	Total
Aspirin	10,933	104	11,037
Placebo	10,845	189	11,034
Total	21,778	293	22,071

It is sometimes possible to reconstruct a table such as the one above from the information in newspaper articles, but we can always go to the original published study in the library and construct such a table. Once we have this basic information, we can easily find out the magnitude of the effect. As a check on your understanding, first compute the chi-square test on these results, and then the effect size based on your chi-square and *N*, and finally, recast the effect size in the form of a BESD. You will find the answers in Table 12.4 (page 258) and its accompanying discussion in Chapter 12.

Having satisfied these assumptions, we substitute in this equation and find

$$\chi^2 = (.3636)^2 \times 79 = 10.444$$

which, not surprisingly, is the same value of chi-square we obtained before (within rounding error).

Note also that the formula above serves as another example of the conceptual relation between tests of significance and measures of effect size and size of study:

Magnitude of significance test = size of effect × size of study.

In other words, just as in the case of *t* and *F*, a relation must be quite strong (i.e., the effect must be large) to result in a large chi-square with only a small number of subjects (see also Box 15.4).

More often, we will compute the chi-square test first and then calculate the effect size, *r*. To obtain phi from any 1-*df* chi-square value, we substitute in the following equation:

$$\phi = \sqrt{\frac{\chi^2}{N}}$$

BOX 15.4   *Z* and Phi

Related to the chi-square approach for testing the significance of a phi coefficient is an approach using the *standard normal deviate (Z)*, which is equal to $\sqrt{\chi^2}$ with $df = 1$. In this case the relation between the test of significance and (1) the size of the effect and (2) the size of the study is given by

$$\sqrt{\chi^2(1)} = Z = \phi \times \sqrt{N}$$

For the example that we have been discussing, with phi = .36 and $N = 79$, we find

$$Z = .36 \times \sqrt{79} = 3.20$$

which is significant at the .0007 level (one-tailed) from the table of *p* values associated with standard normal deviates in Appendix B (see page 382).

With this procedure and knowledge, you can calculate someone else's phi from their reported *p* value, because

$$\phi = \frac{Z}{\sqrt{N}}$$

For example, suppose a research report states $p = .005$ for a 2×2 chi-square but neglects to report any effect size estimate. If you can find *N* (the total size of the study) in the published report, it is a simple matter to estimate phi. Using Table B.1 (p. 382), you find the *Z* associated with $p = .005$ (one-tailed) to be 2.58. If the *N* reported is 36, then

$$\phi = \frac{2.58}{\sqrt{36}} = .43$$

and this value serves as our effect size index (*r*) of any 1-*df* chi-square and can be interpreted by means of the BESD. In our continuing example, substituting in the above formula gives us

$$\phi = \sqrt{\frac{10.446}{79}} = .36$$

LARGER TABLES OF COUNTS

When there are many cells in a chi-square table (i.e., a *table of counts,* or frequencies), a statistically significant chi-square may be more difficult to interpret than in a 2×2 table. Table 15.3 illustrates this situation in a 2×4 table, constructed by the addition of two new groups to Table 15.1. One new group (designated PC) consists of 35 members of the Psychology Club, and the other new group consists of 11 members of the Mathematics Club (MC). The working hypothesis is that psychology and mathematics students are more like Junk Food Junkies than Green Earthies in choosing grilled beef over grilled soy.

| TABLE 15.3 | Obtained Frequencies for 2 × 4 Chi-Square |

Food Choice	PC	MC	JFJ	GE	Row Sums
Big Jack	21	8	24	13	66
Soyburger	14	3	12	30	59
Column sums	35	11	36	43	125

Table 15.4 shows in Section A the expected frequencies computed from the obtained counts in Table 15.3. For example, in Table 15.3 we see that 21 of the 35 members of the Psychology Club chose grilled beef. To obtain the expected frequency shown as 18.480 in Table 15.4, we multiply the appropriate row total (shown as 66 in Table 15.3) by the appropriate column total (35), and then divide the product by the total number of observations (125); the result is $(66 \times 35)/125 = 18.480$. Notice that the row and column sums in Section A of Table 15.4 are identical to the corresponding values in Table 15.3.

The calculation of the 3-*df* chi-square is accomplished by the general procedure and formula given earlier:

$$\chi^2 = \sum \frac{(O - E)^2}{E}$$

and the entries in Section B of Table 15.4 show the $(O - E)^2/E$ results used in this procedure. The value of this chi-square, then, is the grand total of these cell data, or 14.046. The *p* value of this chi-square (with 3 *df*) is approximately .003.

The larger the value of chi-square, the less likely are the observed frequencies to

| TABLE 15.4 | Expected Frequencies and $(O - E)^2/E$ Values for Table 15.3 |

A. Expected Frequencies

Food Choice	PC	MC	JFJ	GE	Row Sums
Big Jack	18.480	5.808	19.008	22.704	66
Soyburger	16.520	5.192	16.992	20.296	59
Column sums	35	11	36	43	125

B. $(O - E)^2/E$ values

Food Choice	PC	MC	JFJ	GE	Row Sums
Big Jack	0.344	0.827	1.311	4.148	6.630
Soyburger	0.384	0.925	1.467	4.640	7.416
Column sums	0.728	1.752	2.778	8.788	14.046

differ only by chance from the expected frequencies, and this chi-square is interestingly large. However, all it tells us is that *somewhere* in the data the observed frequencies depart noticeably from the expected values. In a way, it reminds us of the case of analysis of variance with $df > 1$ in the numerator of F; a significant F tells us that there is some difference but not where that difference may be found. To help us interpret chi-square tables with $df > 1$, let us review some of the options available.

INTERPRETING LARGE TABLES

One procedure when chi-square $df > 1$ is to examine closely the table of $(O - E)^2/E$ results, because the entries in such a table show which of the cells contributed most to the overall large chi-square. A large cell entry in such a table indicates that the cell in question is "surprising" to us given the magnitude of the row and column totals that are affected by that cell. That is, the cell is surprising (or "unexpected") in terms of chance or likelihood—not necessarily in terms of our research hypothesis, however. In Table 15.4 the largest values in Section B suggest that Green Earthies reacted in a less likely way than would be expected by chance on the basis of the choices of the other three groups.

A second option for dealing with larger tables of counts is to subdivide them into smaller (e.g., 2×2) tables. In this procedure—called *partitioning of tables*—we compute some additional chi-squares based on portions of the overall table. Either a prior theory or hypothesis or the nature of the obtained results can guide our judgment about which additional chi-squares to compute. The number and size of the subtables are guided by certain statistical rules, and the calculations also call for certain statistical adjustments. Readers who would like to know more about partitioning chi-square tables will find a detailed discussion in our advanced textbook (Rosenthal & Rosnow, 1991).

For a third option, all that is required is a pocket calculator and a little patience. This option is called *standardizing the margins* (Mosteller, 1968), and it enables us to take the size of the row and column totals (or "margins") into account by setting all the row totals equal to each other and all the column totals equal to each other. We illustrate this method with our continuing example.

TAKING THE MARGINS INTO ACCOUNT

One of the special problems of trying to understand the data in large tables of counts is that our eye is likely to be fooled by the absolute magnitude of the frequencies displayed. Suppose we were to ask of the data in Table 15.3 which group of subjects is most overrepresented in the Big Jack category. Our eye notes that Psychology Club members (PC) and Junk Food Junkies (JFJ) have the greatest frequency of occurrence in that category, and we might erroneously conclude that one of these groups is most overrepresented in the Big Jack category. Our conclusion would be in error because we looked only into the table and not, at the same time, at the sums in the row and column margins.

A look at these margins suggests that the PC and JFJ groups *should* have larger frequencies in the Big Jack category than the Mathematics Club members (MC)

TABLE 15.5	Steps in Standardizing the Margins

A. Results "Corrected" for Unequal Column Margins in Table 15.3

Food Choice	PC	MC	JFJ	GE	Row Sums
Big Jack	.600	.727	.667	.302	2.296
Soyburger	.400	.273	.333	.698	1.704
Column sums	1.000	1.000	1.000	1.000	4.000

B. Results "Corrected" for Unequal Row Margins in A (above)

Food Choice	PC	MC	JFJ	GE	Row Sums
Big Jack	.261	.317	.291	.132	1.001
Soyburger	.235	.160	.195	.410	1.000
Column sums	.496	.477	.486	.542	2.001

C. Final "Corrected" Results

Food Choice	PC	MC	JFJ	GE	Row Sums
Big Jack	.517	.657	.589	.238	2.001
Soyburger	.483	.343	.411	.762	1.999
Column sums	1.000	1.000	1.000	1.000	4.000

D. Results in C (above) Shown as Deviations from an Expected Value of .500

Food Choice	PC	MC	JFJ	GE	Row Sums
Big Jack	+.017	+.157	+.089	−.262	+.001
Soyburger	−.017	−.157	−.089	+.262	−.001
Column sums	.000	.000	.000	.000	.000

because the PC and JFJ groups have more members than the MC group. In addition, there are slightly more subjects in general in the Big Jack category than in the soyburger category. Taking all these margins into account simultaneously would show us that it is actually the MC subjects who are most overrepresented in the Big Jack category.

In large tables, however, "taking the margins into account" becomes a very difficult matter without the use of systematic aids to eye and mind. Standardizing the margins allows us to "correct" for the unequal column and row margins and thus provides us with a systematic procedure for taking the unequal margins into account. Table 15.5 illustrates the steps taken to correct for the unequal column and row margins in Table 15.3.

The results in Section A illustrate the first step, which is to divide each obtained frequency (in Table 15.3) by its column sum. For example, to obtain the "corrected" values for 21 and 14 in Table 15.3, we divide each by 35; to find the "corrected" values for 8 and 3 in Table 15.3, we divide each by 11; and so on. These calculations yield the results in Section A of Table 15.5, in which we see that the column margins have been equalized but that the row margins remain very unequal. To "correct" for the latter, we now divide each of the new values in Section A by its row margin. To obtain the "corrected" values for .600, .727, .667, and .302, we divide each by 2.296. To obtain the "corrected" values for .400, .273, .333, and .698, we divide each by 1.704. The results appear in Section B of Table 15.5.

Section B has equalized the row margins, at least within rounding error, but now the column margins are no longer equal. By now we know what to do about that: Simply divide each entry of Section B by its new column margin. That process will equalize the column margins but *may* make our new row margins unequal. We repeat this procedure until further repetitions no longer affect the margins. For our present data, the final results obtained by this procedure are shown in Section C of Table 15.5. It shows margins equalized within rounding error, and it allows us to interpret the table entries without worrying about the confusing effects of variations in margins. It shows that in the Big Jack category the Mathematics Club (MC) is overrepresented most, and that in the soyburger category the Green Earthies (GE) are overrepresented most.

There is one final step we can take to throw the results into still bolder relief: We can show the cell entries as deviations from the values we would expect if there were no differences whatever among the groups in their representation in the Big Jack and soyburger categories. If there were no such differences, and given the margins of Section C, all the values in the table would be .500. In forming our final table, we subtract this expected value of .500 from each entry in Section C; the results are shown in Section D.

The interpretation of this final table is fairly direct. Besides the big difference between the Green Earthies, who are overrepresented very heavily in the soyburger category, and all the other groups, which are more modestly overrepresented in the Big Jack category, there are other differences that help us to interpret our earlier results. For example, even though some of the sample sizes are too small to be very stable, we can also raise some tentative questions about differences among the three groups overrepresented in the Big Jack category. The Mathematics Club is substantially more overrepresented in the Big Jack category than is the Psychology Club, which is virtually not overrepresented at all. The Junk Food Junkies fall almost exactly midway between the PC and MC groups in their degree of overrepresentation in the Big Jack category.

Because of the small sample sizes of this study, the differences among these three groups (PC, MC, JFJ) are not significant statistically, but with larger sample sizes they might be. In any case, the purpose of the procedure of standardizing the margins is to highlight the differences among groups, whether these achieve statistical significance or not.

A JOURNEY BEGUN

The *beginning* in the title of this book is intended to have a double meaning, as it not only describes the level of the text but also conveys the idea of a journey. For some students the journey embarked on at the start of this course is now complete, whereas for others it is still just beginning. In either case, it should be recognized that, particularly in some of their statistical aspects, the design of experiments and the comparison of research groups constitute a very specialized and highly developed field. The purpose of these last six chapters was to further your understanding of the logic and meaning of the statistical procedures and concepts associated with the application of the scientific method, an understanding that may have been initiated in a basic statistics course. A thorough knowledge of the characteristics of both the data obtained and the statistics used is assumed by professional researchers in all fields to be an essential aspect of good scientific practice. Whether the conclusion of this chapter represents the start or the end of your journey in behavioral research, you should now have a deeper understanding of the applicability and limitations of the scientific method in many fields.

SUMMARY OF IDEAS

1. Chi-square is used to test the degree of agreement between the data actually obtained (or "observed") and the data expected under a particular hypothesis (e.g., the null hypothesis).
2. The expected value of chi-square when the null hypothesis is true is equal to the degrees of freedom defining the particular chi-square distribution.
3. If the sample size is not too small, and if the variables are split not more than 3 to 1, we can test the significance of phi by chi-square.
4. As in the case of t and F, a relationship must be quite strong to result in a large chi-square with only a small number of sampling units.
5. The value of the square root of chi-square with 1 df is identical to that of the standard normal deviate (Z).
6. Knowing the p value and the size of the study, we can estimate phi as an effect size index.
7. We compute the effect size, r, on 2×2 chi-squares by

$$\phi = \sqrt{\frac{\chi^2}{N}}$$

8. One option in interpreting larger tables of counts is to study the table of $(O - E)^2/E$ results, because the entries in such a table show which of the cells contribute most to the overall large chi-square.
9. A second option is to partition the larger table of counts into smaller, 2×2 chi-square tables.
10. A third option is to standardize the margins (totals) by making all row margins equal and by, at the same time, making all column margins equal.

KEY TERMS

chi-square   *p. 306*   phi coefficient   *p. 310*
expected frequency   *p. 306*   standardizing the margins   *p. 314*
observed frequency   *p. 306*   standard normal deviate *(Z)*   *p. 312*
partitioning of tables   *p. 314*   table of counts   *p. 312*

REVIEW QUESTIONS

1. A clinical psychologist at the University of Alabama examines the relation of three types of psychopathology to socioeconomic status (SES) in 100 subjects. Her table of counts is:

SES	Schizophrenic	Neurotic	Depressed
High	5	5	20
Medium	5	15	20
Low	10	10	10

How should she test the hypothesis that this table of counts is significantly different from what would be expected by chance if there were no relation between these variables? How many degrees of freedom will her statistic have?

2. A Brigham Young student obtained the following data, where the numbers are frequencies (counts). How should he plan to standardize the margins?

Annual Carrot Consumption	Visual Acuity		
	High	Average	Low
11–20 lb.	9	3	1
1–10 lb.	5	8	2
0 lb.	1	8	7

3. A researcher at Rochester Institute of Technology asks 10 engineering students from the freshman, sophomore, junior, and senior classes whether they plan to attend graduate school. The results are

	Frosh	Sophs	Juniors	Seniors
Want advanced degree	7	6	3	1
Want out of school	3	4	7	9

How many degrees of freedom would the chi-square for this table have? How should the researcher calculate the expected frequencies? What is the nature of the relation between year in college and wanting an advanced degree?

4. Three students at Trenton State each conduct the same study with the following results:

	Chi-square (1 *df*)	N	*p*
Student 1	2.00	20	.16
Student 2	3.00	30	.08
Student 3	4.00	40	.05

Student 3 claims a significant relationship between the two levels of her independent variable (0, 1) and the two levels of her dependent variable (0, 1). Students 1 and 2 chide her, saying that they have not found a significant effect and that her results are, therefore undependable and unreplicable. How should Student 3 reply?

Answers to review questions are found on pages 320–334.

Answers to Review Questions

CHAPTER 1

1. This is relational research because the relation of two sets of observations (TV diary entries and playground aggression) is examined. It is not experimental because neither of the variables is manipulated by the investigator.
2. This is experimental research because the investigator has manipulated the type of movie shown.
3. This is descriptive research because the data are collected on student shyness, but these scores are not examined for their relation to any other variable.
4. For his descriptive research he might collect data on the creativity scores of other students. For his relational research he might examine the relationship between creativity scores and SAT scores. For experimental research he might experimentally manipulate the type of music being played in the background while the students' creativity is being measured to see whether Mozart makes students more creative than does hard rock.
5. No, it certainly *is* possible to study the concept of prayer, and Galton conducted a relational study of prayer and longevity. An experimental study might employ prayer for a randomly chosen half of 20 people who are ill and no prayer for the remaining people to see whether prayer causes faster recovery.

CHAPTER 2

1. His independent variable was operationalized by scores on the self-esteem scale; his dependent variable was operationalized by self-reported grade-point average. Because this is a relational study rather than an experimental study, he would not be justified in drawing the causal inference that either variable led to or affected the other.
2. An operational definition might be "score earned on Hans Eysenck's test." A theoretical definition might be "the degree of social ease and smoothness shown in a group setting."
3. Science is defined by its procedures rather than by the status of a person who labels a particular belief system a "science." One study of the accuracy of astrological forecasts might ask a panel of "expert" astrologers to prepare a brief description of the personality of persons born under each of the 12 signs of the

zodiac. A large number of students are then asked to rate each of these 12 descriptions on the extent to which each of the descriptions applies to them. As long as the students know nothing about astrology, evidence for the accuracy of astrology would be obtained if the students rated the personality descriptions of their sign as more characteristic of them than the average of the other 11 descriptions. These students' roommates or friends could also rate the students, assuming the roommates or friends also knew nothing about astrology.

4. A causal hypothesis might be that revenge is more likely to occur when people feel they have been harmed intentionally by another. To evaluate the acceptability of this hypothesis we would examine the correspondence with reality of this hypothesis, its coherence and parsimony, and its falsifiability. On these grounds it seems we are ready to proceed to the stage of operationalizing our independent and dependent variables.

5. The doctor did not take the boy's cultural background or context into account. We might study the boy by administering standard medical, neurological, and psychological evaluations; by giving him a wide choice of cultural artifacts (toys, tools, foods, pictures, videos, etc.) to observe, use, and explore; and by accompanying him to settings (e.g., parks, lakes, and forests) more like those in which he had grown up in order to observe his behavior in a habitat more natural to him.

CHAPTER 3

1. Some possible costs include time, energy, income lost by spending time on the questionnaire items, possible embarrassment at "being studied" in an unsavory location or occupation, and the danger of discovery of subjects' criminal behavior because someone in law enforcement obtains the questionnaire and can link it to the respondents, to name a few.

2. Observing the thefts might be quite upsetting to the real customers, who may be put at risk of, say, anxiety reactions or heart attacks. The confederate "robbers" may also be put at risk of being attacked by a customer trying to foil the robbery. We need to ask whether what we might be able to learn from this research is really worth the risk to the real customers and the confederate "robbers."

3. The student has failed to debrief the subjects, so that they may leave feeling that they were really insensitive to others. He should, of course, debrief them.

4. They mean that the costs and utilities are in such balance that it is very difficult to reach a decision on whether to go ahead with the research. For removal of the study from the diagonal of indecision, the costs of the study should be decreased, the benefits should be increased, or both.

5. That the student understands what the research will require from her or him, that the student may leave at any time, and that he or she will remain anonymous.

6. The Rushton study also raised no questions of deception or invasion of privacy. However, the issue of fair-mindedness *was* raised. Were some of the organization's workers going to be "treated specially," or would they get to ride "the gravy train" in the eyes of other workers?

CHAPTER 4

1. To learn the "effects" of legislation on some outcome behavior (e.g., drunk driving) by comparing the change in behavior in states (or counties) changing their laws with the change in behavior in states not changing their laws. To predict legislators' votes from an analysis of their past votes or the style of communication revealed in their earlier speeches. To predict future intelligence, personality, and psychopathology from archived early childhood drawings.

2. The student could correlate the frequency of reported fights, stampedes, and riots with the aggressiveness of various sports as defined by the average number of injuries per player sustained in each sport. This study offers the advantage of unobtrusiveness of measures but does not ensure that the aggressiveness of fans will be a trait of the fans or will be brought about by the aggressiveness of the sport they have decided to watch.

3. To examine the hypothesis that comic strips featuring children are designed for a younger readership, the mean word length in comic strips featuring children is compared to the mean word length in comic strips not featuring children. The student should check the reliability of two judges' (a) classifying the strips as featuring or not featuring children and (b) counting the word lengths and computing their average. We may also want to sample the comic strips over a period of several weeks or months.

4. The most important advice is that he should be clear about what he wants to learn from this research. Beyond that, he should consider the guideposts suggested by Goodenough and described on pages 78–80.

5. A descriptive study may reveal a high rate of wheezing, coughing, illness, and death among those exposed to cigarette smoke. A relational study may show that those who are exposed to greater amounts of cigarette smoke suffer from higher rates of illness and death. An experimental study may show that animals experimentally exposed to higher dosages of cigarette smoke have higher rates of illness and death than do animals exposed to lower dosages.

6. That the teachers' ratings of their students' intellectual ability were nothing more than the teachers' accuracy of diagnosing IQ. It would take an experimental manipulation of one of these variables to demonstrate that it played a causal role.

CHAPTER 5

1. Define the aspects of attitudes about abortions you want to have covered by your measure; be sure the items are easily understood, and check the items by means of item analysis. Decide how many response categories you want to use in your numerical and segmented graphic scales.

2. Leniency bias, acquiescent response set, central tendency bias, and halo effect, respectively. The section on *rating errors and their leniency* gives suggestions on how to control for each of these rating errors.

3. Most of the chapter contributes to an answer to this question, but you might begin with the answer to Review Question 1 above.

4. Have a large number of judges sort a large number of items into 11 piles numbered 1 to 11 in order of item favorableness. The median rating of favorableness of each item is computed, and items are selected for the final scale on the basis of (a) the judges' agreement on each item's degree of favorableness and (b) the items' being spread fairly evenly throughout the range of attitudes from 1 to 11.

5. The major difference is that the Likert 5-point (or 7-point or 9-point) rating scale is used only if it correlates highly enough with the total score.

6. Select a sample of bipolar cue words that represent the evaluative, potency, and activity dimensions of the so-called semantic space created by these three dimensions.

7. Instead of supposing what the ideal candidate might be like, it may be better to ask respondents about characteristics of candidates that would elicit the respondents' votes.

8. One wording might be: Describe in detail a situation in which you felt pleased and proud to be an employee of the company. What led up to the situation, and what was its outcome? The same question might well be asked again, this time with "unhappy and ashamed" substituted for "pleased and proud."

9. It has been shown to lead to more accurate data.

CHAPTER 6

1. By showing that her scale correlates substantially with future symptoms of fear when subjects are asked to speak in public (convergent validity). In addition, the new scale should not correlate substantially with such less relevant variables as height, spatial relations abilities, and political party preference.

2. Because it correlates highly with behaviors defined as reflecting high need for social approval but not as highly with behaviors not reflecting high need for approval.

3. Yes, because a total of four judges will yield an aggregate reliability of .80 when the typical judge-to-judge reliability is .50 (see Table 6.2).

4. Perhaps female toddlers prefer more complex shapes than do male toddlers. A new study might add four new stimuli: a smooth, hard teddy bear and rattle, and a soft, fuzzy ball and cube. If the plausible rival hypothesis were correct, female toddlers would prefer the new smooth, hard teddy bear and rattle to the new fuzzy ball and cube. Considering all eight stimuli, then, female toddlers would prefer the four complexly shaped stimuli compared to male toddlers, who would prefer the four simply shaped stimuli if the rival hypothesis were accurate.

5. Because Table 6.2 shows that, for 20 items, a mean inter-item reliability of .40 is associated with an effective reliability of .93, not .50.

6. The test–retest reliability can be computed by administering the test twice to the same subjects (for example, four weeks apart) and computing the correlation between the two administrations. The internal-consistency reliability can be computed by correlating all the items with each other and then applying the Spearman–Brown formula to the mean inter-item correlation (or using Table 6.2) to get the effective or aggregate reliability. The reason for administering

the several different measures was that the student could show convergent validity with the measures with which his new scale should correlate substantially and discriminant validity with the measures with which his new scale should not correlate substantially.

7. There is no systematic error because the average reading is accurate (10 pounds). The random errors are + 4, –2, –3, 0, and +1 on the five readings, or errors of +40%, –20%, –30%, 0%, and +10%, respectively, a not very precise performance.

CHAPTER 7

1. A placebo-control group might be used to which clients would be randomly assigned. This placebo-control group would receive a pseudo method of boosting self-esteem, for example, reading material believed to be irrelevant to self-esteem, watching irrelevant movies, and the like. The clients assigned to this placebo-control group should believe that their "treatment" will have beneficial effects to the same degree as do the clients assigned to the "real" treatment.

2. Because the positive reinforcement (grades) was not experimentally manipulated, there is no basis for our concluding that it "caused" the self-esteem scores even if there is a positive correlation between self-esteem and GPA. Self-esteem may as well "cause" grades, or some other variable may "cause" both grades and self-esteem.

3. Telling subjects the hypothesis and the names of the measuring instruments is likely to result in strong demand characteristics.

4. The student should use the methods of agreement and of difference. In that way, he can learn the degree to which eating chocolate chip cookies is followed by reduction in depression (method of agreement) to a greater extent than not eating chocolate chip cookies is followed by reduction in depression (method of difference).

5. The basic plan could be implemented by using the following four conditions:

Actual Treatment	Expectancy	
	Experimental	Control
Tutoring	A	B
Control	C	D

The four conditions shown are analogous to those in Tables 7.5 and 7.6.

6. As in all one-group pre-post studies, history, maturation, and instrumentation all threaten the internal validity of the research.

7. By comparing the difference between the experimental and control groups obtained when pretests were and were not used. The four threats to internal validity were described as part of Campbell's approach to research design.

8. A placebo-control group offers a treatment-like condition that serves to control for subjects' beliefs or expectations about the efficacy of any treatments that might be administered. A zero-control group is characterized by the absence of any intervention, "real" or "pseudo" (placebo).

CHAPTER 8

1. Since (a) the test–retest correlations are similar to each other, (b) the synchronous correlations are similar to each other, and (c) the cross-lagged correlations differ appreciably from each other (.64 versus .33), it might be reasonable for him to conclude a preponderance of causal influence of the patient progress variable over the therapist approval variable.

2. The cohort of the women is confounded with their age, so we cannot tell whether age or cohort differences or both are reflected in the obtained differences. For example, it may be that the women aged 40–45 have been showing an *increasing* degree of autonomy as they developed from age 20–25 to age 40–45. A longitudinal design of the type shown in Table 8.2 would be a better way to do this study.

3. She might try to match the children finding their way into each of the two conditions on as many relevant variables as possible and then perform her data analysis only on the subset of children for whom there are very close matches. Because of the large proportion of children for whom there may be no good matches, and who would therefore be omitted from the design, the generalizability of the study could be decreased substantially. In addition, the lack of randomization could seriously limit the internal validity of the study. If we could randomize after assignment, we would have a true experiment, but with generalizability only to the type of children who found their way into the treatment condition. Data of this type can also be analyzed by means of a variety of "multiple-regression" procedures, but these are beyond the scope of this book. Though these procedures are flexible and useful, they still have associated shortcomings.

4. Some dependent variables that may reflect presidential assassination attempts are stock market figures, mental-health-facility-usage data, gun-control legislative activity, the number of people announcing for elective positions, views of the United States reflected in the foreign press, and changes in party affiliation. Reference librarians can help her find the government and other documents that would carry the needed information. These documents would also be a rich source of ideas for other dependent variables for which data would be available.

CHAPTER 9

1. Group 1 is measured with the greatest stability; its subjects' scores range only from 10 to 13, while Groups 2 and 3 range from 10 to 16 and from 9 to 18, respectively. The means of Groups 1, 2, and 3 are 11.5, 13.0, and 13.5, respectively; therefore, the mean of Group 3 is the most biased.

2. Susan showed no bias with respect to the target volume (her average volume hit was M, the target volume) and no instability (she hit the same volume each time). Valerie showed a one-volume-away bias, hitting volume N on average, instead of volume M; she showed no instability, hitting the same volume each time. Ellen showed no bias (her average volume hit was M, the target volume, but she showed a three-volume instability, hitting three adjacent volumes). Jane

showed a one-volume-away bias, hitting volume *N* on average instead of volume *M;* she showed a three-volume instability, hitting three adjacent volumes. We can summarize the results as follows:

	Bias	No bias
Some instability	Jane	Ellen
No instability	Valerie	Susan

3. Since volunteers or respondents tend to be more intelligent and more sociable than the general population, the correlation between IQ and sociability found in this self-selected sample may be quite different from the correlation we would find in the general population. One way to improve on the design might be to use follow-up questionnaires to increase the representativeness of our sample. Another way to improve on the design might be to try to locate data archives that include data for almost all of a given target population, for example, a college sample all of whom were tested at the time of admission or orientation.

4. In a study of the effects of a placebo on self-reported happiness, volunteers might show a larger placebo effect (i.e., the difference between the placebo and no-treatment condition) than nonvolunteers because volunteers are more likely to want to please the experimenter. In a study of the effects of a treatment designed to increase sociability, volunteers might show a smaller treatment effect than nonvolunteers because volunteers might already score so much higher on sociability that it might be hard to show further changes. Any procedures reducing volunteer bias would help reduce these potential problems.

5. She might draw a random sample of graduating seniors and contact them several times to reduce nonresponse bias. If she knew what characteristics were likely to be highly correlated with questionnaire responses, she might do her random selection within the various strata formed by her subdividing the sample into relatively more homogeneous subgroups.

6. She can try to make her appeal for volunteers as interesting, nonthreatening, and rewarding as possible.

CHAPTER 10

1. The stem-and-leaf plot is

Stem	Leaf
4	1
3	0 2 3 3 7 8
2	2 7 9
1	6

The median score can be found from $.5(N + 1) = .5(12) = 6$; because the 6th score is 32, that is our median. The extended range is the crude range $(41 - 16)$

plus 1, or $25 + 1 = 26$. The interquartile range is from the $.25(N+1)$th to the $.75(N+1)$th score, or from 27 to 37.

2. Her first choice is Machine B because it shows no bias and the least instability or variability. Her second choice might be Machine D because it shows no bias or Machine A because, although it shows a 5-decibel bias, it measures volume more consistently. As long as she remembers to correct for the 5-decibel bias, she might be well advised to get Machine A.

3. Because of the outlier score of 98, he should prefer the median or a trimmed mean to the ordinary mean. In this example, the mean of the 11 untrimmed scores is 24.6, whereas the median is only 17 and the trimmed mean (trimming by 1 on each end) is 18.2.

4. She did better on the midterm $[Z = (58 - 52)/12 = .50]$ than on the final $[Z = (110 - 100)/30 = .33)$.

5. He scored above 97.7% of the population.

6. The professor is correct in thinking Harry's grading to be biased. However, the professor is wrong about the direction of the bias. Harry's average grade is a C+ (7) instead of a B– (8). The professor *is* correct in thinking Tom's grades to be more spread out than Dick's grades. The three standard deviations are 3.00, 1.00, and 1.29 for Tom, Dick, and Harry, respectively. Students earning 5's in Tom's section performed the same as those earning 7's in Dick's section; in both cases, $Z = -1.00$.

CHAPTER 11

1. The correlation between reading ability and GPA is 1.00 because the Z scores for reading and for GPA are identical. Careful inspection of the original reading and GPA scores shows that the GPA scores are always one-fifth the size of the reading scores. If a variable (X) is multiplied by any constant (c), it yields a new variable (cX) that is correlated 1.00 with the original variable (X). The reason is that the old scores are multiplied by c, the old mean is multiplied by c, and the old σ is multiplied by c. Thus

$$Z\text{old} = \frac{X - \overline{X}}{\sigma}$$

$$Z\text{new} = \frac{cX - c\overline{X}}{c\sigma} = \frac{X - \overline{X}}{\sigma}$$

so Znew = Zold, and any variables with identical Z scores are perfectly correlated.

Since reading ability and GPA have the same Z scores, GPA Z scores can be substituted for reading Z scores, and GPA will be correlated .98 with IQ just as reading is correlated .98 with IQ. You can check this out by computing Z scores for all three variables of IQ, reading, and GPA and computing the correlations among these three variables.

2. The correlation is –.20, computed by r_{phi} (ϕ), the two-dichotomous-variables version of the Pearson *r*. It can be computed by the *Z*-score method or by the 2×2 contingency table method; that is,

    $$r_{phi} = \phi = \frac{\Sigma Z_x Z_y}{N}$$

    or

    $$r_{phi} = \phi = \frac{BC - AD}{\sqrt{(A + B)(C + D)(A + C)(B + D)}}$$

3. The correlation between Raters 3 and 4 is also –1.00. We can compute that directly, or we could notice that Rater 3 rates identically to Rater 1 and that Rater 4 rates identically to Rater 2, except for adding a constant of 100 points to each of Rater 2's ratings. Adding a constant *(c)* to each score also adds the constant to the mean, so adding a constant to the raw scores does not change the *Z* scores because

    $$Z \, old = \frac{X - \overline{X}}{\sigma}$$

    $$Z \, new = \frac{(X + c) - (\overline{X} + c)}{\sigma} = \frac{X - \overline{X}}{\sigma}$$

4. The independent variable is smiling (scored 1) or frowning (scored 0). The dependent variable is the rating of enjoyment. For the 200 patrons we correlate the scores on the treatment variable (1 or 0) with the scores on the 7-point enjoyment scale.

5.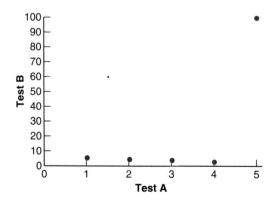

The score of 100 on Test B appears to be an outlier. We can solve the outlier problem by employing rank instead of scores as shown below:

Test A		Test B	
Score	Rank	Score	Rank
1	5	4	2
2	4	3	3
3	3	2	4
4	2	1	5
5	1	100	1

Our scatter plot based on ranks is

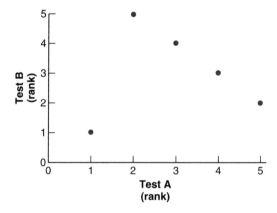

The correlation between Test A and Test B is .69 if we employ the original scores; it is .00 if we employ the ranks. A discrepancy that large is unusual and needs to be evaluated further before we can confidently say we "know" the correlation between Test A and Test B.

6. Scatter plot B is associated with the higher correlation because its points are more tightly clustered around the straight-line relationship between variables X and Y. The correlation between variables X and Y is .83 for scatter plot A and .98 for scatter plot B.

CHAPTER 12

1. The BESD would be

Condition	Signing Petition	Not Signing Petition	Total
Wheelchair present	70	30	100
Wheelchair absent	30	70	100
Total	100	100	200

2. A Type II error would have occurred if it had been concluded that there was a correlation of zero between taking aspirin and having a heart attack when that correlation was not really zero. The power of a test is the probability that results will be found significant at a given p value; power is defined as $1 - $ beta, where beta is the probability of making a Type II error. The power of a test of significance depends on the alpha we set, the actual size of the effect being investigated, and the size of the sample.

3. In Table 12.7, the intersection of the column headed .20 and the row labeled .70 shows the required total N to be 155. Therefore, she should run about half that number in each condition.

4. It tells him that only 5% of the time would he obtain a result that significant, or more significant, if the null hypothesis were really true. It does not tell him about the size of the effect being studied.

5. Since r is simply the difference between the proportions successful in the treatment and the control conditions, the three r's are (A) .75 − .25 = .50; (B) .55 − .45 = .10; and (C) .35 − .65 = −.30. Notice that Result C reflects a negative r; the new method is *worse* than the old.

CHAPTER 13

1. The difference or change scores (D) for the five subjects are −3, −2, +1, −5, and −4. The matched or correlated t can be computed from

$$t = \frac{\overline{D}}{\sqrt{\left(\frac{1}{n}\right) S^2{}_D}} = \frac{[(-3) + (-2) + (+1) + (-5) + (-4)]/5}{\sqrt{\left(\frac{1}{5}\right) 5.30}} = \frac{-2.6}{1.03} = 2.53$$

giving $S^2{}_D$ from

$$S^2{}_D = \frac{\Sigma(D - \overline{D})^2}{n - 1} =$$

$$\frac{[(-3) - (-2.6)]^2 + [(-2) - (-2.6)]^2 + [(+1) - (-2.6)]^2 + [(-5) - (-2.6)]^2 + [(-4) - (-2.6)]^2}{5 - 1}$$

$$= \frac{21.20}{4} = 5.30$$

The *df* are $n - 1 = 5 - 1 = 4$. Had we found a significant and large change in memory test scores, we would not be able to conclude that the change was due to marijuana use. There was no control group to rule out plausible rival hypotheses. Had we been asked to compute the significance level and effect size, we would have used Table B.2 and found our t with 4 *df* to be significant at $p < .05$ one-tailed (but not quite significant at $p = .025$ one-tailed). The effect size r would have been computed from

$$r = \sqrt{\frac{t^2}{t^2 + df}} = \sqrt{\frac{(2.53)^2}{(2.53)^2 + 4}} = .78$$

2. We would compute t from

$$t = \frac{\overline{X}_1 - \overline{X}_2}{\sqrt{\left(\dfrac{1}{n_1} + \dfrac{1}{n_2}\right)S^2}} = \frac{4.00 - 5.25}{\sqrt{\left(\dfrac{1}{4} + \dfrac{1}{4}\right)2.46}} = 1.13$$

The df would be $n_1 + n_2 - 2 = 6$, and the effect size, r, could be computed from

$$r = \sqrt{\frac{t^2}{t^2 + df}} = \sqrt{\frac{(1.13)^2}{(1.13)^2 + 6}} = .42$$

a very substantial r though t is not significant ($p = .30$, two-tailed).

3. From the prose equation:

$$\text{Significance test } = \text{ size of effect} \times \text{size of study}$$

we can see that increasing the size of the study would increase the magnitude of the significance test, and the result would be a smaller (more significant) p value. However, the effect size would not be systematically affected by adding more subjects of the same type. To illustrate, we assume the following original ingredients of t:

$$t = \frac{2.585 - 2.000}{\sqrt{\left(\dfrac{1}{32} + \dfrac{1}{32}\right)1.00}} = 2.34, p = .023, r = .28$$

We then add 60 subjects (30 to each group), yielding

$$t = \frac{2.585 - 2.000}{\sqrt{\left(\dfrac{1}{62} + \dfrac{1}{62}\right)1.00}} = 3.26, p = .0014, r = .28$$

Therefore, with nothing changing but n_1 and n_2, we see that t increases, p decreases, and r remains unchanged.

4. The student might try three approaches. First, he might try to drive the means further apart by using a control group that is not as similar to the treatment group. Second, he might use subjects who are more homogeneous than the subjects who answer newspaper ads. Third, he might use larger sample sizes for each condition.

CHAPTER 14

1. An appropriate table of variance for this study follows:

Source	SS	df	MS	F	p	r
Between brands	752	4	188	2.00	.11	—
Within brands	4230	45	94	—	—	

We find F from MS-between/MS-within, and we find df from $k - 1$ for numerator df and $N - k$ for denominator df. We do not report r because this is an "omnibus" F test (i.e., one with $df > 1$ in the numerator).

2. Set A would yield a larger F because its within-condition variability is much smaller than that of Set B. Since the means of Sets A and B are equal, the MS-between for Sets A and B are equal; therefore, the results with the smaller MS-within will yield the larger F.

3. The following table shows the means, row effects, and column effects (as in Table 14.6):

Type of Vacation	Type of Subjects		Row Means	Row Effects
	Urban (US)	Rural (RS)		
Urban (UV)	5	3	4	−1
Rural (RV)	11	1	6	+1
Column means	8	2	5(grand mean)	
Column effects	+3	−3		

The interaction effects for each of the four conditions are computed from:

	Interaction Effect	=	Group Mean	−	Grand Mean	−	Row Effect	−	Column Effect
UV, US	−2	=	5	−	5	−	(−1)	−	3
UV, RS	+2	=	3	−	5	−	(−1)	−	(−3)
RV, US	+2	=	11	−	5	−	1	−	3
RV, RS	−2	=	1	−	5	−	1	−	(−3)

If we disregard matters of statistical significance, these results show that the type of subjects made the largest difference, the type of vacation made the smallest difference, and the interaction made an intermediate amount of difference. The urban subjects benefited more than the rural subjects, the rural vacations were associated with greater benefits than were the urban vacations, and the interaction showed greater benefits for those vacationing in the setting in which they did *not* live.

4. A t test following the F would address the question appropriately. The two means to be compared would be the hot lunch mean and the mean of the means of the remaining three groups, that is, $(10 + 12 + 15)/3 = 12.33$. The two required sample sizes, n_1 and n_2, would be the n for the hot lunch group (i.e., 3) and the n for the children in the remaining three groups (i.e., $3 + 3 + 3 = 9$).

As in the case of most t tests computed after an ANOVA, the S^2 used in computing t is the S^2 obtained from the ANOVA, the MS-within. Thus

$$t(8df) = \frac{19 - 12.33}{\sqrt{\left(\frac{1}{3} + \frac{1}{9}\right)4}} = \frac{6.67}{1.33} = 5.00, p = .0005$$

Whenever we compute t or F with 1 df in the numerator, we want to know the effect size. So we compute r from

$$r = \sqrt{\frac{t^2}{t^2 + df}} = .87$$

which is a very large effect size.

CHAPTER 15

1. She would compute a χ^2 for which the df would be $(r - 1)(c - 1) = (3 - 1)(3 - 1) = 4$.
2. Following the procedures of Table 15.5, we arrive at the approximate solution:

Annual Carrot Consumption	Visual Acuity			
	High	Average	Low	Σ
11–20 lb.	.64	.20	.14	.98
1–10 lb.	.31	.45	.23	.99
0 lb.	.05	.34	.62	1.01
Σ	1.00	.99	.99	2.98

We can display these results as deviations from an expected value of .33 (i.e., the total of 3.00 divided by 9 cells = 3/9 = .33), yielding the following:

	High	Average	Low	Σ
11–20 lb.	.31	−.13	−.19	−.01
1–10 lb.	−.02	.12	−.10	.00
0 lb.	−.28	.01	.29	.02
Σ	+.01	.00	.00	.01

These results show very clearly that high-visual-acuity subjects are relatively overrepresented among high carrot consumers, whereas low-visual-acuity subjects are relatively overrepresented among low carrot consumers. As a corollary, we find high-visual-acuity subjects underrepresented among low carrot consumers, whereas low-visual-acuity subjects are relatively underrepresented among high carrot consumers. Unless this was a randomized experiment, we should be cautious about inferring causality. While it is possible that eating more carrots leads to better visual acuity, it may also be that better visual acuity leads to finding more carrots in the darker regions of the refrigerator.

3. The *df* for this χ^2 are obtained from $(c - 1)(r - 1) = (4 - 1)(2 - 1) = 3$. The expected frequencies are obtained from

$$E = \frac{\text{Column total} \times \text{Row total}}{\text{Grand total}}$$

which, for these data, results in

	Frosh	Sophs	Juniors	Seniors
Want degree	4.25	4.25	4.25	4.25
Want out	5.75	5.75	5.75	5.75

With each advancing year, a greater proportion of students want out, a result shown clearly in the final results, in deviation form, of standardizing the margins:

	Frosh	Sophs	Juniors	Seniors	Σ
Want degree	.26	.20	−.10	−.36	.00
Want out	−.26	−.20	.10	.36	.00
	.00	.00	.00	.00	.00

Once again, we must be careful in our interpretation of the results. Because this is a cross-sectional study, we cannot distinguish differences in year at college from cohort differences.

4. Student 3 should ask that all three students compute the effect size, *r*, that is associated with their results, using the following equation:

$$r = \phi = \sqrt{\frac{\chi^2(1)}{N}}$$

When the three students compute their *r*'s, they all find exactly the same effect size ($r = .316$). Student 3 shows thereby that the three studies agree with one another remarkably well.

Writing Up the Research

THE RESEARCH REPORT

For scientists in all fields, the research process is not complete until the results have been reported in a written document. Indeed, it is often said that scientists are measured by the quality of their publications (e.g., R. A. Day, 1983). The purpose of reporting the what, why, and how of the study is to enable others to replicate the investigation or to assess for themselves what the researchers believed they have learned. Instructors of research methods courses do not expect that many of their undergraduate students will actually submit their research findings for publication, as the rejection rate of our top journals in psychology is around 80%–90%. But instructors do measure the achievement of their students in part by the logic, clarity, and precision of their written reports. Some instructors prefer that their students go through the exercise of writing up their research findings in the style of a journal article.

In this appendix we describe the basic steps in writing up your research results. If you carefully follow the steps described here, you will find that the reporting process will help you to clarify your thoughts as it leads you to find good reasons for what you want to say. Your instructor will tell you whether your submitted paper should adhere to the term paper format represented in Exhibit A.2 (pp. 342-359) or to the journal submission format represented in Exhibit A.3 (pp. 360-374). Exhibit A.2 is based on Rosnow and Rosnow's (1995, 3rd ed.) simplified guide to writing term papers and undergraduate research reports, and we offer pointers borrowed from that book. Exhibit A.3 is based on the *Publication Manual of the American Psychological Association* (APA, 1994, 4th ed.), which was designed primarily as a guide for journal submissions and not for scientific writing at an undergraduate level. If, in fact, you are writing for possible publication, you will find Robert J. Sternberg's *Psychologist's Companion* (1993) another invaluable guide. For tips on writing style, we recommend that you consult Strunk and White's *Elements of Style* (1979).

Getting Organized

We begin by offering some pointers to help you organize your tasks and to ensure that all assignments will be completed on time. The success of your final report will depend on your ability to meet the expectations of your instructor as much as on your own creativity and writing ability. Thus, before you do anything else, make sure you know what is expected. You can talk with other students to get their impressions, but it is a good idea to check with the instructor or grader to make sure that you are on the right track.

Besides knowing the form of the final report, here are some questions to keep in mind:

- When is the final report due?
- How will it be graded?
- Will there be an opportunity to obtain feedback as the project progresses?
- Is there a specified length for the final report?
- Are intermediate drafts or outlines required, and when are they due?
- Are other sample reports available to provide a further idea of what is expected?

Questions about due dates are very important because missing deadlines—just like unexcused absences on a job—is a sure way to elicit disapproval. If you are someone who has a hard time meeting deadlines, remember that instructors have heard all the excuses. Try keeping a pocket calendar and checking it every morning and evening to see what your responsibilities are for the next several days. If that approach fails, try posting scheduled dates and appointments over your mirror or desk—anywhere you routinely look.

To help you keep on schedule, jot down both self-imposed and assigned dates, such as:

- Completion of proposal for research
- Completion of data collection
- Completion of data analysis
- Completion of first draft of research report
- Completion of revised draft(s) of research report
- Completion of final draft of research report
- Due date for submission of final report

Writing a Research Proposal

Many instructors require one or more preliminary research proposals, in which you sketch your ideas and give a justification of what you propose. You may be asked to tell how you arrived at your ideas and why you believe the topic is interesting and important. The purpose of these questions is (1) to help you crystallize your ideas; (2) to encourage you to focus on a topic you find intrinsically interesting; and (3) to make sure that these are *your* ideas. We will have more to say about the last point, but it is essential that the work be your own even when it builds on previous research by others. A series of preliminary papers will allow the instructor to monitor how your project is developing and how you respond to suggestions and constructive criticisms.

What should a research proposal look like? Instructors may differ in terms of what they require, but Exhibit A.1 proceeds on the assumption that the student has been asked (1) to state the objective of the research; (2) to provide a justification for the hypothesis or research question; (3) to sketch the method and instruments proposed; (4) to state in general terms how the data will be analyzed; and (5) to defend the ethicalness of the research. The proposal in this exhibit shows a set of specific ideas that include a tentative plan for proceeding (although your instructor may ask for additional details). Having put his or her ideas down on paper, the student now awaits feedback concerning modifications and improvements and also the instructor's final approval to proceed with the research.

Research Proposal   **1**

Research Proposal for (Course No.)

Submitted by Bruce Rind

(Date Submitted)

Objective

The purpose of this study will be to examine whether

harsher bail judgments are likely to result when judges

are told that the defendant tested positive for drug usage

than when no testing information is made available. My

hypothesis, based on a preliminary examination of the

relevant literature in forensic psychology and attribution

research, is that such an effect will emerge.

Method

I propose to use a simple randomized design in which

the research participants will be assigned to one of two

EXHIBIT A.1   *Sample Research Proposal*

conditions. The subject sample will consist of approximately 30 students in an undergraduate class. I have been given permission by the instructor to ask these students to participate. I have developed a "crime scenario" that the subjects will read; it describes a man seen running from a burglarized house.

In the experimental condition the scenario will state that the suspect tested positive for drugs while in custody:

> A man was arrested as a suspected burglar.
> He fit the description of a man seen running
> from the burglarized house. While in custody
> the man submitted to a blood test, and it was
> determined that he had very recently used
> drugs.

In the control condition, neutral information (i.e., the suspect ate and phoned someone) will be presented in lieu of the information about having tested positive for drugs:

> A man was arrested as a suspected burglar.
> He fit the description of a man seen running
> from the burglarized house. The man spent
> enough time in custody so that he received
> two meals and made three phone calls.

EXHIBIT A.1 *Continued*

Research Proposal   **3**

The dependent measure will be the subjects' responses to the following question:

> If you were the bail judge, what would you set
> the bail to be? Choose a dollar amount from
> $0 to $50,000.

I am specifying a range in order to give the subjects a common metric, and I chose this range because it seemed realistic and sufficiently wide to allow differences to result between the experimental and control groups. At the beginning of the questionnaire, I will also ask for some general demographic data (e.g., age, sex, year in college, GPA) but will not ask for the respondent's name.

Data Analysis

I anticipate analyzing the results using an independent t and also interpreting the effect size (r).

Ethical Considerations

Although I have the instructor's permission to run my study in this class, I will emphasize at the outset that any student who does not wish to participate may decline to respond. The responses will be anonymous to reduce the likelihood of social desirability bias. The study does not involve deception. At the end of the study, I will debrief the students and answer any questions.

EXHIBIT A.1   *Continued*

Avoiding Plagiarism

Before we go any further, let us return to the point about your work's being original. The cornerstone of science is that it progresses by building on previous work, and it is important that you try to do the same in your research. In Chapter 2 we described how to do a literature search in order to construct a logical foundation for your hypothesis. We also emphasized the importance of taking accurate notes in order to avoid committing plagiarism accidentally. The term *plagiarism* comes from a Latin word meaning "kidnapper," and to plagiarize means to kidnap another person's idea or work and then to pass it off as one's own.

Suppose a student turned in a proposal or research report that, without a citation, contained the following conceptual definition of cognitive dissonance:

> Dissonance—that is, the existence of nonfitting relations among cognitions—is a motivating factor in its own right. By *cognition* is generally meant any knowledge, opinion, or belief about the environment, about oneself, or about one's behavior. Cognitive dissonance can be seen as an antecedent condition that leads to activity oriented toward dissonance reduction, just as hunger leads to activity oriented toward hunger reduction.

Unfortunately, the student has committed plagiarism and will pay the consequences. The reason is that, except for a changed word here and there, the student has lifted this passage directly from Festinger's *Theory of Cognitive Dissonance* (1962). On page 5, Festinger wrote:

> In short, I am proposing that dissonance, that is, the existence of nonfitting relations among cognitions, is a motivating factor in its own right. By the term *cognition,* here and in the remainder of the book, I mean any knowledge, opinion, or belief about the environment, about oneself, or about one's behavior. Cognitive dissonance can be seen as an antecedent condition which leads to activity oriented toward dissonance reduction just as hunger leads to activity oriented toward hunger reduction.

This does not mean that you cannot use others' ideas, but you must clearly indicate what is yours and what is theirs. For example, this student could have written:

> In his book *A Theory of Cognitive Dissonance* (1962), Festinger described cognition as "any knowledge, opinion, or belief about the environment, about oneself, or about one's behavior" and defined cognitive dissonance as "the existence of nonfitting relations among cognitions" (p. 5). He added, "Cognitive dissonance can be seen as an antecedent condition which leads to activity oriented toward dissonance reduction just as hunger leads to activity oriented toward hunger reduction" (p. 5).

Without accurate notes, it is easy to stumble into *accidental plagiarism*. Figure A.1 shows how to take notes on index cards. You can use any system of note taking you like; the essential point is to be thorough and consistent. Notice in Figure A.1 that the student recorded the full reference for the material, as well as the page number, so she would not accidentally mistake the quote for her own words.

Cooke, Gerald (1980). An introduction to basic issues and concepts in forensic psychology. In Gerald Cooke (Ed.), The Role of the Forensic Psychologist (pp. 5–15). Springfield, Illinois: Charles C. Thomas Publisher.

This book defines forensic psychology as a content area in the interface of law and psychology. Cooke writes: "The law is a reflection of societal standards. As these standards change, so does the law. Similarly, the concepts having to do with the relationship between an individual's mental condition and his status under the law are fluid and everchanging ones. For example, the degree to which mental status mitigates responsibility and the specific manner in which the law treats those who are deemed to have diminished responsibility has changed frequently and is related to changing attitudes over the relative weight to be given to the rights of the individual and the rights of society at large." (page 5)

FIGURE A.1   *An example of how to take library notes.*

TITLE PAGE

We turn now to the structure and form of your final report, beginning with the title page. If you have been instructed to use the simplified format of an undergraduate research paper, as represented in Exhibit A.2, notice that the title page contains the student's name, the course number, and the date when the report was submitted. If you have been instructed to use the technical format of a journal submission, illustrated in Exhibit A.3, observe that the page number is preceded by a two- or three-word "header"; its purpose is to allow the editor or printer to pull together pages that may become accidentally separated during the production process. Notice also that this page starts out with a "running head" (typed flush left below the page number and in all uppercase letters). Running heads are abbreviated titles (limited to 50 characters, including punctuation and spaces between words) that appear at the top of the pages of printed articles. Below the running head (separated by four lines) is the full title of the paper (centered and typed in uppercase and lowercase letters), and below this is the place for the author's name and institutional affiliation. However, your instructor may simply tell you to put the number or name of your research course in the institutional affiliation space.

We mentioned Strunk and White's *Elements of Style;* one of Professor Strunk's famous dictums is "Omit needless words. Omit needless words. Omit needless words." If you were writing for publication, this rule would apply to all aspects of your paper; journal space is limited, and editors often insist that authors pare their manuscripts to the essentials. In your case, where space is not at a premium, your instructor will presumably be more lenient as he or she does *not* want you to leave out any relevant details. Thus Bruce's title (although the subtitle is too wordy to include in a journal article) adequately summarizes the main idea of his research. Incidentally, if you started with a working title, do not hesitate to change or polish the final full title if it no longer aptly describes the project.

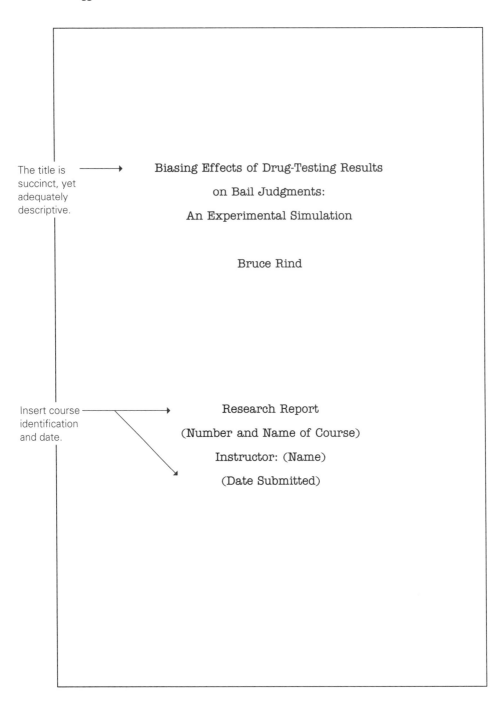

The title is →
succinct, yet
adequately
descriptive.

Biasing Effects of Drug-Testing Results

on Bail Judgments:

An Experimental Simulation

Bruce Rind

Insert course
identification
and date.

Research Report

(Number and Name of Course)

Instructor: (Name)

(Date Submitted)

EXHIBIT A.2 *Format of an Undergraduate Research Report Submitted as a Term Paper (Based on Rosnow & Rosnow, 1995).*

Abstract

This experimental simulation was addressed to a recent legal debate concerning the institution of mandatory drug testing of all suspects upon arrest. The crime control side has held that this testing will have no biasing effects in legal proceedings, whereas the due process side has argued that drug information will have prejudicial effects. Drawing on correspondent inference theory (Jones & Davis, 1965) and the general function of inferring traits (Baron & Byrne, 1987), it was hypothesized that harsher bail judgments are likely to result when judges are informed that the defendant has tested positive for drug usage than when no testing information is made available. The results were in the hypothesized direction but were not statistically significant after an adjustment for heterogeneity of variance was made. The wider implications of this field of research are discussed.

Why was the research important and worth doing?

Pages are numbered consecutively, beginning with the Abstract on page 2.

What was the purpose or objective of the study?

What were the results?

What else appears in the discussion?

EXHIBIT A.2 *Continued*

The title of this section ("Introduction") is a reminder of its purpose.

Abbreviations are first spelled out. The opening paragraph sets the stage in an inviting way.

3

The introduction begins on a new page.

Introduction

In the summer of 1988, the ABC television program "Nightline" featured a debate between a representative from the American Civil Liberties Union (ACLU) and a spokesperson for a national group of prosecutors. The focus of the debate was on whether mandatory drug testing should be performed on all persons arrested. The prosecutors' representative proposed that the institution of mandatory drug testing would be one more weapon for law enforcement officials in fighting the drug war by identifying drug offenders who would otherwise escape detection. The ACLU representative argued that the institution of this program would result in serious threats to individual rights regarding the bail issue. He contended that positive results would unfairly bias the bail judge's decision on how much bail to impose. Drug-positive suspects, the ACLU representative contended, would tend to receive higher bail judgments, which would be a violation of the rights of suspects when there is no necessary connection between drug usage and the particular crime that was committed. The prosecutor responded that the drug information would have no effect on a bail judge's decision.

Forensic psychology (i.e., the application of psychological principles and methods to the legal

Although the left margin is even, the right margin is left ragged.

EXHIBIT A.2   *Continued*

4

Citations buttress the introduction.

process) has been successful in providing insight into a number of legal issues. For example, Loftus, Miller, and Burns (1978) demonstrated the distorting effects of misleading questions on the memories of eyewitnesses. Subjects were shown a sequence of 30 slides depicting successive stages of an automobile-pedestrian accident. In one of the slides half the subjects saw a stop sign while the other half saw a yield sign. Subjects were later asked a question that made reference to the sign they had actually seen or to a sign they had not seen. When they were subsequently asked what sign they had seen, subjects exposed to the misleading question tended to misremember the sign.

The introduction gives a concise history and background of your topic.

How does the study build on, or derive from, previous work?

Summaries are succinct, but precise.

In fact, many studies have demonstrated that eyewitness testimony is often inaccurate. For example, Buckhout (1974) staged an "assault" on a professor which was witnessed by 141 students. When these students were asked seven weeks later to identify the assailant from a group of six photographs, 60% chose an innocent person. Wells, Lindsay, and Ferguson (1979) staged hundreds of eyewitnessed thefts and found that not only did the eyewitnesses have difficulty in correctly identifying the culprits, but other subjects who judged the accuracy of these eyewitnesses were incapable of distinguishing between accurate and inaccurate accounts.

Citations in the text are by authors' surnames and dates.

EXHIBIT A.2   *Continued*

5

E.g. is from
exempli gratia
("for
example").

Aside from the forensic aspects of eyewitness
testimony, other facets of the legal process have also
been investigated, such as defendant attractiveness (e.g.,
Efran, 1974), the judge's instructions to the jury (e.g.,
Sue, Smith, & Caldwell, 1973), juror characteristics
(e.g., Saks & Hastie, 1978), and group decision making
among the jurors (e.g., Kalven & Zeisel, 1966). These
investigations, among others, have demonstrated the
utility of applying psychological principles and methods
to legal situations in order to understand them better. In
the light of this background, the present investigation
addressed the issue raised in the "Nightline" debate
between the ACLU representative and the prosecutors'
spokesperson. That is, will drug information tend to
prejudice a bail judge's decision regarding the amount of
bail to set?

The main task of the bail judge is to set bail at a
certain level so as to make it likely that the defendant
will appear for trial. In making this decision, the bail
judge is perhaps apt to consider factors suggestive of the
defendant's traits (i.e., lasting characteristics) so as to
predict the likelihood that the defendant will skip bail or
show up for the trial. Attribution theory is the area of
psychology concerned with factors such as inferring the
traits of others (e.g., Jones & Davis, 1965; Kelley,

Abbreviation
was defined
previously.

Ampersand
(&) is used
instead of
and for
citations in
parentheses.

EXHIBIT A.2 *Continued*

6

1972) and using this trait information to make decisions
or judgments regarding these other individuals (Baron &
Byrne, 1987).

Jones and Davis (1965) proposed a framework
describing how individuals (i.e., observers) go about
inferring the traits of others (i.e., actors). According to
the theory of correspondent inferences, observers focus
mainly on certain types of observed behavior to infer
traits because they believe that only certain behaviors
are indicative of traits. The primary questions observers
will ask themselves, according to Jones and Davis, are:
(1) Was the behavior freely chosen? (2) Did the
behavior produce uncommon effects? And (3) was the
behavior low in social desirability? The third question is
particularly relevant to the topic of this research report.
Because drug usage is held by our society to be low in
social desirability, it follows from correspondent
inference theory that observers will be likely to focus on
this socially undesirable behavior in judging the actor's
traits. Once observers have inferred traits, they tend to
use this information to predict the actor's future
behavior and to assess and to guide their own actions,
decisions, and judgments regarding the actor (Baron &
Byrne, 1987). Thus I hypothesized that positive results
from a drug test will result in harsher bail judgments

I.e. is from *id est* ("that is").

The introduction leads into the hypotheses, or the questions that guided the research.

What was the researcher's hypothesis?

Connecting points are numbered for clarity.

EXHIBIT A.2   *Continued*

than when no such information is made available.

Method

The method section continues on the same page.

Research Participants

Temple University undergraduate students in an introductory statistics class served as subjects in this study. This sample of 31 subjects consisted of both men and women, and the materials were administered during the class meeting with the permission of the instructor and the consent of the students.

What was the subject pool?

Subheadings are placed at the left margin and underlined.

Materials

Two forms of a crime scenario were developed. Both forms stated that a man was arrested as a suspected burglar because he fit the description of a man seen running from a burglarized house. In the experimental condition (Form A, see Appendix) the scenario stated that the suspect tested positive for drugs while in custody. In the control condition (Form B) the scenario continued with neutral information (i.e., the suspect received two meals and made three phone calls while in custody). Following both versions of the crime scenario was the dependent measure, requesting the subjects to play the role of the bail judge and to set a bail amount between $0 and $50,000.

EXHIBIT A.2   *Continued*

8

Subgroups are denoted by lower-case *n*.

Procedure

Subjects were randomly assigned to the control (n = 16) or experimental (n = 15) condition. The experimental and control handout sheets were mixed together and thus passed out at the same time. Subjects were told to fill out certain preliminary information on their sheets and then to read the scenario and make their judgment. When the subjects were finished, they were completely debriefed.

Center head indicates a major section.

The results section continues on the same page.

Results

The overall findings are given in Table 1 which shows that the mean judgment of the subjects exposed to the drug information was higher than the mean judgment of the subjects exposed to the neutral information. Computing a t test on these data yielded a significant result (t = 2.08, df = 29, p = .023 one-tailed). However, the results in Table 1 also raise the possibility that the variabilities were significantly different in the two conditions. That possibility was tested by dividing the larger of the two variances (277,058,355.31) by the smaller of the two variances (30,798,060.16) and referring the quotient to an F table. The result was highly significant, F(14,15) = 9.0, p < .001, which indicated that the homogeneity of variance required by

Reader is referred to accompanying table.

The *p* value is reported as one-tailed.

Statistical test, degrees of freedom, and significance are reported.

EXHIBIT A.2   *Continued*

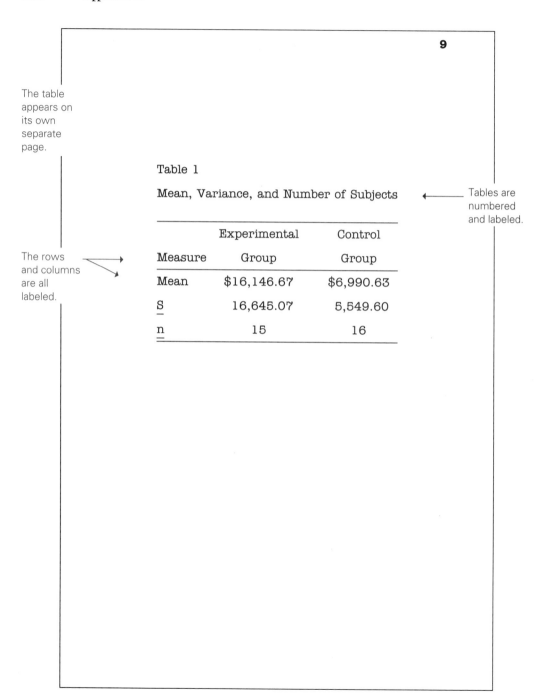

The table appears on its own separate page.

9

Table 1

Mean, Variance, and Number of Subjects

Tables are numbered and labeled.

The rows and columns are all labeled.

Measure	Experimental Group	Control Group
Mean	$16,146.67	$6,990.63
S	16,645.07	5,549.60
n	15	16

EXHIBIT A.2   *Continued*

10

the t test had been violated (Rosenthal & Rosnow, 1991).

In an alternative analysis, the raw scores were transformed by means of a log transformation. Computing a t test on these values yielded a nonsignificant result ($t = 1.09$, $r = .20$). Other methods of analysis were still possible, although a more prudent alternative would be to view the effect size as theoretically interesting but in need of replication with a larger sample. If the results are replicated in follow-up studies, it will also then be possible to employ a meta-analysis in order to increase statistical power and obtain a more reliable estimate of the effect size.

The effect size is reported.

Discussion

This research was an attempt to apply the principles and methods of forensic psychology to clarify certain aspects of the legal system. Specifically, this study addressed the contention of the representative from the ACLU that even drug information unrelated to the crime under consideration will tend to bias bail judgments. One fundamental purpose of our criminal justice system is, of course, to be just and unbiased in all of its aspects. The results, although in the hypothesized direction, were not statistically significant after the appropriate adjustment

The discussion continues on the same page.

The opening discussion reminds the reader of the study's purpose.

EXHIBIT A.2 *Continued*

11

was made for heterogeneity of variance. Nevertheless, the effect size was theoretically interesting and suggested that follow-up studies are warranted.

The discussion should pull together the various parts of th e paper.

If future studies provide stronger support for the ACLU representative's contention, it may be possible to argue on empirical grounds that the goal of being just and unbiased would be jeopardized with the institution of mandatory drug testing upon arrest. It would then follow that this biasing effect could be circumvented if the bail judge were not given access to the results of the drug testing. Such a follow-up finding would, in turn, fit in with correspondent inference theory (Jones & Davis, 1965), because knowledge about socially undesirable behavior (i.e., having taken drugs recently) could be said to lead subjects to infer certain traits of the suspect. This chain of logic is interesting to contemplate, but it is premature at this stage in the research.

The limitations and wider significance of the study are noted.

I believe the criminal justice system can benefit from forensic research such as that performed in this study. At the moment, however, its procedures are mostly based on tradition and precedent, and the courts do not take into strong consideration the results of scientific investigations. For example, jurors who are willing to follow the law that the death penalty should sometimes be imposed are referred to as <u>death qualified jurors</u>.

Any special terms are defined.

EXHIBIT A.2   *Continued*

12

Psychological research has demonstrated that death-qualified jurors are more likely to convict (Ellsworth, 1985). However, in a split decision in 1986, the U.S. Supreme Court overturned a lower court ruling that such jurors are indeed a biased sample. Another example concerns the research finding that the confidence of eyewitnesses is unrelated to their accuracy unless witnessing conditions are very favorable (Wells & Murray, 1984). However, the U.S. Supreme Court declared in 1972 that among the factors that jurors can use in determining the accuracy of eyewitnesses is the level of certainty demonstrated by the witnesses. The results of scientific investigations of the various aspects of the legal system point to the need for the courts to acknowledge and incorporate these and future results so as to build a justice system that is truly just.

Using a sample of college students, the present investigation studied the biasing effect of drug results. Even if these results were statistically significant, they still might not be generalizable to actual bail judges. Therefore, future research should address this potential problem of external validity. Future research should also directly assess subjects' inferences of corresponding traits from socially undesirable behavior. In this study these inferences were hypothesized to occur based on the

The importance of the research is underscored.

Future research is suggested.

EXHIBIT A.2   *Continued*

13

subjects' bail judgments. It is interesting to note that, while the subjects seemingly judged the suspect more harshly based on the drug information in the burglary scenario, there is no necessary connection between drug usage and burglary. However, the subjects may have been drawing on a stereotype to assume that the association was likely because the media often report property crimes that are motivated by the need to get money to purchase drugs. Thus it would be valuable to use other crime scenarios that are not so stereotypically associated with drugs to determine whether the biasing effect is more general.

EXHIBIT A.2   *Continued*

14

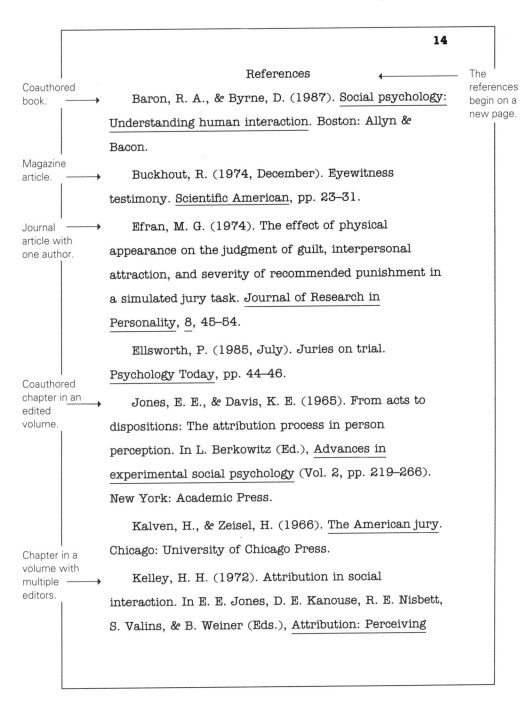

Coauthored book.

Magazine article.

Journal article with one author.

Coauthored chapter in an edited volume.

Chapter in a volume with multiple editors.

References

Baron, R. A., & Byrne, D. (1987). Social psychology: Understanding human interaction. Boston: Allyn & Bacon.

Buckhout, R. (1974, December). Eyewitness testimony. Scientific American, pp. 23–31.

Efran, M. G. (1974). The effect of physical appearance on the judgment of guilt, interpersonal attraction, and severity of recommended punishment in a simulated jury task. Journal of Research in Personality, 8, 45–54.

Ellsworth, P. (1985, July). Juries on trial. Psychology Today, pp. 44–46.

Jones, E. E., & Davis, K. E. (1965). From acts to dispositions: The attribution process in person perception. In L. Berkowitz (Ed.), Advances in experimental social psychology (Vol. 2, pp. 219–266). New York: Academic Press.

Kalven, H., & Zeisel, H. (1966). The American jury. Chicago: University of Chicago Press.

Kelley, H. H. (1972). Attribution in social interaction. In E. E. Jones, D. E. Kanouse, R. E. Nisbett, S. Valins, & B. Weiner (Eds.), Attribution: Perceiving

The references begin on a new page.

EXHIBIT A.2   *Continued*

15

the causes of behavior (pp. 1–26). Morristown, NJ: General Learning Press.

Journal article with multiple authors. → Loftus, E. F., Miller, D. G., & Burns, H. J. (1978). Semantic integration of verbal information into a visual memory. Journal of Experimental Psychology: Human Learning and Memory, 4, 19–31.

Book in second edition. → Rosenthal, R., & Rosnow, R. L. (1991). Essentials of behavioral research: Methods and data analysis (2nd ed.). New York: McGraw-Hill.

Saks, M. J., & Hastie, R. (1978). Social psychology in the court. New York: Van Nostrand Reinhold. ← *Book title is underlined and begins with a capital letter.*

Sue, S., Smith, R. E., & Caldwell, C. (1973). Effects of inadmissible evidence on the decisions of simulated jurors: A moral dilemma. Journal of Applied Social Psychology, 3, 345–353. ← *Journal title is underlined.*

Wells, G. L., Lindsay, R. C. L., & Ferguson, T. (1979). Accuracy, confidence, and juror perceptions in eyewitness identification. Journal of Applied Psychology, 64, 440–448. ← *Volume number of journal is underlined.*

Coauthored chapter in an edited volume. → Wells, G. L., & Murray, D. M. (1984). Eyewitness confidence. In G. L. Wells & E. F. Loftus (Eds.), Eyewitness testimony: Psychological perspectives (pp. 155–170). New York: Cambridge University Press.

EXHIBIT A.2   *Continued*

16

The appendix begins on a new page.

Appendix A: Research Materials

The experimental group's questionnaire (Form A) was as follows:

Please answer the following questions in the spaces provided below:

Questionnaires or tests that you constructed for this project appear in the appendix.

_____ age

_____ sex

_____ year in college

_____ grade-point average (GPA)

_____ major

Now please read the following paragraph carefully, and then answer the question that follows it:

A man was arrested as a suspected burglar. He fit the description of a man seen running from the burglarized house. While in custody the man submitted to a blood test, and it was determined that he had very recently used drugs.

If you were the bail judge, what bail would you set? Choose a dollar amount from $0 to $50,000:

amount of bail _____

EXHIBIT A.2 *Continued*

17

The control group's questionnaire (Form B) was as follows:

___

Please answer the following questions in the spaces provided below:

_____ age

_____ sex

_____ year in college

_____ grade-point average (GPA)

_____ major

Now please read the following paragraph carefully, and then answer the question that follows it:

A man was arrested as a suspected burglar. He fit the description of a man seen running from the burglarized house. The man spent enough time in custody so that he received two meals and made three phone calls.

If you were the bail judge, what bail would you set? Choose a dollar amount from $0 to $50,000:

amount of bail _____

EXHIBIT A.2   *Continued*

18

A second Appendix begins on a new page and is labeled. →

Appendix B: Statistical Calculations

This Appendix displays the raw data and computations of the study.

These data do not have to be typed.

Drug Test		Neutral information	
Raw scores	Log data	Raw scores	Log data
10,000	4.00	10,000	4.00
12,500	4.10	4,000	3.60
2,000	3.30	5,000	3.70
50,000	4.70	350	2.54
20,000	4.30	5,000	3.70
200	2.30	15,000	4.18
500	2.70	500	2.70
30,000	4.48	5,000	3.70
2,000	3.30	· 500	2.70
10,000	4.00	1,500	3.18
5,000	3.70	10,000	4.00
10,000	4.00	10,000	4.00
50,000	4.70	20,000	4.30
30,000	4.48	5,000	3.70
10,000	4.00	10,000	4.00
		10,000	4.00

$$\bar{X} = 16,146.67 \qquad 3.871 \qquad 6,990.63 \qquad 3.625$$

$$S = 16,645.07 \qquad 0.7041 \qquad 5,549.60 \qquad 0.5524$$

$$t_{raw\ scores} = \frac{16,146.67 - 6,990.63}{\sqrt{\frac{3.9 \times 10^9 + 4.6 \times 10^8}{15 + 16 - 2} \left(\frac{1}{15} + \frac{1}{16}\right)}} \qquad t_{log\ data} = \frac{3.871 - 3.625}{\sqrt{\frac{6.941 + 4.577}{15 + 16 - 2} \left(\frac{1}{15} + \frac{1}{16}\right)}}$$

$$t_{29} = 2.08 \qquad r = \sqrt{\frac{2.08^2}{29 + 2.08^2}} = .36 \qquad t_{29} = 1.09 \qquad r = \sqrt{\frac{1.09^2}{29 + 1.09^2}} = .20$$

EXHIBIT A.2   *Continued*

The Running head is flush left and typed in uppercase letters.

Pages are numbered consecutively, beginning with the title page, and contain a short heading.

Biasing Effects   **1**

Running Head: BIASING EFFECTS IN BAIL JUDGMENTS

Biasing Effects of Drug-Testing Results

on Bail Judgments:

An Experimental Simulation

Bruce Rind

(Institutional Affiliation)

The title of the paper is succinct, yet adequately descriptive.

Print the report on 8½ × 11-inch white bond paper.

EXHIBIT A.3 *Format of a Research Report Based on the* APA Publication Manual *(1994).*

Short title
appears on
each page.

Biasing Effects   **2** ← The abstract
begins on a
new page.

Abstract

Abstract is → This experimental simulation was addressed to a recent
not indented.
legal debate concerning the institution of mandatory
Tell why the
research was
drug testing of all suspects upon arrest. The crime
important →
control side has held that this testing will have no
and worth
doing.
biasing effects in legal proceedings, whereas the due

process side has argued that drug information will have

prejudicial effects. It was hypothesized that harsher bail ← What was
hypothesized?
judgments are likely to result when judges are informed

that the defendant has tested positive for drug usage

than when no testing information is made available. The
What were
the results?
results were in the hypothesized direction but were not
Report, but
save
significant at .05 alpha after an adjustment was made
evaluation for
the body of
for heterogeneity of variance. The wider implications of
the paper. →
this field of research are discussed.

EXHIBIT A.3   *Continued*

The text begins on page 3, starting with the full title repeated. →

Abbreviations are first spelled out.

Double-space between all lines of text.

Biasing Effects of Drug-Testing Results

on Bail Judgments:

An Experimental Simulation

In the summer of 1988, the ABC television program "Nightline" featured a debate between a representative from the American Civil Liberties Union (ACLU) and a spokesperson for a national group of prosecutors. The focus of the debate was on whether mandatory drug testing should be performed on all persons arrested. The prosecutors' representative proposed that the institution of mandatory drug testing would be one more weapon for law enforcement officials in fighting the drug war by identifying drug offenders who would otherwise escape detection. The ACLU representative argued that the institution of this program would result in serious threats to individual rights regarding the bail issue. He contended that positive results would unfairly bias the bail judge's decision on how much bail to impose. Drug-positive suspects, the ACLU representative contended, would tend to receive higher bail judgments, which would be a violation of the rights of suspects when there is no necessary connection between drug usage and the particular crime that was committed. The prosecutor responded that the drug information would have no effect on a bail judge's decision.

The opening paragraph sets the stage in an inviting way.

Although left margins are even, right margins are left ragged.

EXHIBIT A.3   *Continued*

Biasing Effects   **4**

Start each →
paragraph
with a five-
space indent.
APA style
uses author-
date method
of citation.

Forensic psychology (i.e., the application of psychological principles and methods to the legal process) has been successful in providing insight into a number of legal issues. For example, Loftus, Miller, and Burns (1978) demonstrated the distorting effects of misleading questions on the memories of eyewitnesses. Subjects were shown a sequence of 30 slides depicting successive stages of an automobile-pedestrian accident. In one of the slides half the subjects saw a stop sign while the other half saw a yield sign. Subjects were later asked a question that made reference to the sign they had actually seen or to a sign they had not seen. When they were subsequently asked what sign they had seen, subjects exposed to the misleading question tended to misremember the sign.

Citations
buttress the
introduction.

Summaries
are succinct,
but precise.

In fact, many studies have demonstrated that eyewitness testimony is often inaccurate. For example, Buckhout (1974) staged an "assault" on a professor which was witnessed by 141 students. When these students were asked seven weeks later to identify the assailant from a group of six photographs, 60% chose an innocent person. Wells, Lindsay, and Ferguson (1979) staged hundreds of eyewitnessed thefts and found that not only did the eyewitnesses have difficulty in correctly identifying the culprits, but other subjects who judged

EXHIBIT A.3   *Continued*

Biasing Effects   **5**

the accuracy of these eyewitnesses were incapable of distinguishing between accurate and inaccurate accounts.

Aside from the forensic aspects of eyewitness testimony, other facets of the legal process have also been investigated, such as defendant attractiveness (e.g., Efran, 1974), the judge's instructions to the jury (e.g., Sue, Smith, & Caldwell, 1973), juror characteristics (e.g., Saks & Hastie, 1978), and group decision making among the jurors (e.g., Kalven & Zeisel, 1966). These investigations, among others, have demonstrated the utility of applying psychological principles and methods to legal situations in order to understand them better. In the light of this background, the present investigation addressed the issue raised in the "Nightline" debate between the ACLU representative and the prosecutors' spokesperson. That is, will drug information tend to prejudice a bail judge's decision regarding the amount of bail to set?

The main task of the bail judge is to set bail at a certain level so as to make it likely that the defendant will appear for trial. In making this decision, the bail judge is perhaps apt to consider factors suggestive of the defendant's traits (i.e., lasting characteristics) so as to predict the likelihood that the defendant will skip bail or show up for the trial. Attribution theory is the area of

E.g. is from *exempli gratia* ("for example").

E.g. is not underlined, because it will not be set in italics.

Ampersand (&) is used instead of "and" for citations in parentheses.

Abbreviation was defined previously.

EXHIBIT A.3   *Continued*

Works by
different
authors are
listed in
alphabetical
order by first
author's
surname.

psychology concerned with factors such as inferring the traits of others (e.g., Jones & Davis, 1965; Kelley, 1972) and using this trait information to make decisions or judgments regarding these other individuals (Baron & Byrne, 1987).

I.e. is from *id
est* ("that
is").

Jones and Davis (1965) proposed a framework describing how individuals (i.e., observers) go about inferring the traits of others (i.e., actors). According to the theory of correspondent inferences, observers focus mainly on certain types of observed behavior to infer traits because they believe that only certain behaviors are indicative of traits. The primary questions observers will ask themselves, according to Jones and Davis, are:

Connecting
points are
lettered for
clarity.

(a) Was the behavior freely chosen? (b) Did the behavior produce uncommon effects? And (c) was the behavior low in social desirability? The third question is particularly relevant to the topic of this research report. Because drug usage is held by our society to be low in social desirability, it follows from correspondent inference theory that observers will be likely to focus on this socially undesirable behavior in judging the actor's traits. Once observers have inferred traits, they tend to use this information to predict the actor's future behavior and to assess and to guide their own actions, decisions, and judgments regarding the actor (Baron &

Biasing Effects   **6**

EXHIBIT A.3   *Continued*

What was the hypothesis?

First-level headings are centered.

Second-level headings are flush left and underlined.

Byrne, 1987). Thus I hypothesized that positive results from a drug test will result in harsher bail judgments than when no such information is made available.

Method

The major sections of the text follow each other without a break.

Research Participants

Temple University undergraduate students in an introductory statistics class served as subjects in this study. This sample of 31 subjects consisted of both men and women, and the materials were administered during the class meeting with the permission of the instructor and the consent of the students.

Materials

Two forms of a crime scenario were developed. Both forms stated that a man was arrested as a suspected burglar because he fit the description of a man seen running from a burglarized house. In the experimental condition the scenario stated that the suspect tested positive for drugs while in custody. In the control condition the scenario continued with neutral information (i.e., the suspect received two meals and made three phone calls while in custody). Following both versions of the crime scenario was the dependent measure, requesting the subjects to play the role of the

EXHIBIT A.3   *Continued*

Biasing Effects   **8**

bail judge and to set a bail amount between $0 and
$50,000.

Subgroups are denoted by lowercase *n*.

Procedure

Subjects were randomly assigned to the control (n =
16) or experimental (n = 15) condition. The
experimental and control handout sheets were mixed
together and thus passed out at the same time. Subjects
were told to fill out certain preliminary information on
their sheets and then to read the scenario and make
their judgment. When the subjects were finished, they
were completely debriefed.

Results

The overall findings are given in Table 1, which
shows that the mean judgment of the subjects exposed to
the drug information was higher than the mean
judgment of the subjects exposed to the neutral
information. Computing a t test on these data yielded a

A one-tailed test is reported here.

significant result (t = 2.08, df = 29, p = .023 one-tailed).

Statistical test, degrees of freedom, and significance.

However, Table 1 also raises the possibility that the
variabilities were different in the two conditions. That
possibility was tested by dividing the larger of the two
variances (277,058,355.31) by the smaller of the two
variances (30,798,060.16) and referring the quotient to

EXHIBIT A.3   *Continued*

Biasing Effects   **9**

an F̲ table. The result was highly significant—$F(14,15)$ = 9.0, p̲ < .001—which indicated that the homogeneity of variance required by the t̲ test had been violated (Rosenthal & Rosnow, 1991). In an alternative analysis, the raw scores were transformed by means of a log transformation. Computing a t̲ test on these values yielded a nonsignificant result (t̲ = 1.09, r̲ = .20). Other methods of analysis were still possible, although a more prudent alternative would be to view the effect size as theoretically interesting but in need of replication with a larger sample. If the results are replicated in follow-up studies, it will also then be possible to employ a meta-analysis in order to increase statistical power and obtain a more reliable estimate of the effect size.

The effect size is reported to two decimal places.

Discussion

This research was an attempt to apply the principles and methods of forensic psychology to clarify certain aspects of the legal system. Specifically, this study addressed the contention of the representative from the ACLU that even drug information unrelated to the crime under consideration will tend to bias bail judgments. One fundamental purpose of our criminal justice system is, of course, to be just and unbiased in all of its aspects. The results, although in the hypothesized direction, were not

The discussion continues without a break in the text, except for the heading.

EXHIBIT A.3   *Continued*

Biasing Effects **10**

statistically significant after the appropriate adjustment
was made for heterogeneity of variance. Nevertheless,
the effect size was theoretically interesting and
suggested that follow-up studies are warranted.

Future
implications
are
projected.

→   If future studies provide stronger support for the
ACLU representative's contention, it may be possible to
argue on empirical grounds that the goal of being just
and unbiased would be jeopardized with the institution of
mandatory drug testing upon arrest. It would then follow
that this biasing effect could be circumvented if the bail
judge were not given access to the results of the drug
testing. Such a follow-up finding would, in turn, fit in
with correspondent inference theory (Jones & Davis,
1965), because knowledge about socially undesirable
behavior (i.e., having taken drugs recently) could be said
to lead subjects to infer certain traits of the suspect. This
chain of logic is interesting to contemplate, but it is
premature at this stage in the research.

Remind the
reader of the
importance
of the
research.

I believe the criminal justice system can benefit from
forensic research such as that performed in this study.
→   At the moment, however, its procedures are mostly
based on tradition and precedent, and the courts do not
take into strong consideration the results of scientific
investigations. For example, jurors who are willing to
follow the law that the death penalty should sometimes

EXHIBIT A.3   *Continued*

Any special → be imposed are referred to as death-qualified jurors.
terms are
defined.   Psychological research has demonstrated that death-

qualified jurors are more likely to convict (Ellsworth,

1985). However, in a split decision in 1986, the U.S.

Supreme Court overturned a lower court ruling that such

jurors are indeed a biased sample. Another example

concerns the research finding that the confidence of

eyewitnesses is unrelated to their accuracy unless

witnessing conditions are very favorable (Wells &

Murray, 1984). However, the U.S. Supreme Court

declared in 1972 that among the factors that jurors can

use in determining the accuracy of eyewitnesses is the

level of certainty demonstrated by the witnesses. The

results of scientific investigations of the various aspects

of the legal system point to the need for the courts to

acknowledge and incorporate these and future results so

as to build a justice system that is truly just.

Using a sample of college students, the present

investigation studied the biasing effect of drug results.

Even if these results were statistically significant, they

still might not be generalizable to actual bail judges.

Future → Therefore future research should address this potential
research is
suggested.   problem of external validity. Future research should also

directly assess subjects' inferences of corresponding

traits from socially undesirable behavior. In this study

EXHIBIT A.3   *Continued*

Biasing Effects **12**

these inferences were hypothesized to occur based on the subjects' bail judgments. It is interesting to note that, while the subjects seemingly judged the suspect more harshly based on the drug information in the burglary scenario, there is no necessary connection between drug usage and burglary. However, the subjects may have been drawing on a stereotype to assume that the association was likely because the media often report property crimes that are motivated by the need to get money to purchase drugs. Thus it would be valuable to use other crime scenarios that are not so stereotypically associated with drugs to determine whether the biasing effect is more general.

EXHIBIT A.3 *Continued*

Biasing Effects   **13**

The first line of each reference is indented.

Coauthored book.

Magazine article.

Journal article with one author.

Coauthored chapter in an edited volume.

Chapter in a volume with multiple authors.

The references begin on a new page.

References are arranged in alphabetical order by the surname of the first author.

Major cities are listed without a state abbreviation.

Smaller cities are listed with a state abbreviation.

References

Baron, R. A., & Byrne, D. (1987). Social psychology: Understanding human interaction. Boston: Allyn & Bacon.

Buckhout, R. (1974, December). Eyewitness testimony. Scientific American, pp. 23–31.

Efran, M. G. (1974). The effect of physical appearance on the judgment of guilt, interpersonal attraction, and severity of recommended punishment in a simulated jury task. Journal of Research in Personality, 8, 45–54.

Ellsworth, P. (1985, July). Juries on trial. Psychology Today, pp. 44–46.

Jones, E. E., & Davis, K. E. (1965). From acts to dispositions: The attribution process in person perception. In L. Berkowitz (Ed.), Advances in experimental social psychology (Vol. 2, pp. 219–266). New York: Academic Press.

Kalven, H., & Zeisel, H. (1966). The American jury. Chicago: University of Chicago Press.

Kelley, H. H. (1972). Attribution in social interaction. In E. E. Jones, D. E. Kanouse, R. E. Nisbett, S. Valins, & B. Weiner (Eds.), Attribution: Perceiving the causes of behavior (pp. 1–26). Morristown, NJ: General Learning Press.

EXHIBIT A.3 *Continued*

Biasing Effects   **14**

Journal article with multiple authors. →
Loftus, E. F., Miller, D. G., & Burns, H. J. (1978). Semantic integration of verbal information into a visual memory. Journal of Experimental Psychology: Human Learning and Memory, 4, 19–31.

Book in second edition. →
Rosenthal, R., & Rosnow, R. L. (1991). Essentials of behavioral research: Methods and data analysis (2nd ed.). New York: McGraw-Hill.

Saks, M. J., & Hastie, R. (1978). Social psychology in the court. New York: Van Nostrand Reinhold.   ← Book title is underlined

Sue, S., Smith, R. E., & Caldwell, C. (1973). Effects of inadmissible evidence on the decisions of simulated jurors: A moral dilemma. Journal of Applied Social   ← Journal name and volume number are underlined.
Psychology, 3, 345–353.   ←

Wells, G. L., Lindsay, R. C. L., & Ferguson, T. (1979). Accuracy, confidence, and juror perceptions in eyewitness identification. Journal of Applied Psychology, 64, 440–448.

Coauthored chapter in a coedited volume. →
Wells, G. L., & Murray, D. M. (1984). Eyewitness confidence. In G. L. Wells & E. F. Loftus (Eds.), Eyewitness testimony: Psychological perspectives (pp. 155–170). New York: Cambridge University Press.

EXHIBIT A.3   *Continued*

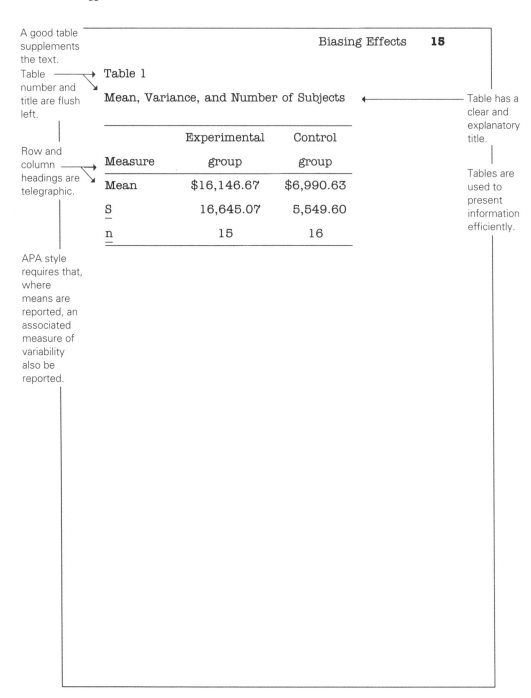

A good table supplements the text.

Table number and title are flush left.

Row and column headings are telegraphic.

APA style requires that, where means are reported, an associated measure of variability also be reported.

Biasing Effects   **15**

Table 1

Mean, Variance, and Number of Subjects

Table has a clear and explanatory title.

Tables are used to present information efficiently.

Measure	Experimental group	Control group
Mean	$16,146.67	$6,990.63
S	16,645.07	5,549.60
n	15	16

EXHIBIT A.3 *Continued*

ABSTRACT

Although the abstract (or summary) is page 2 of your report, it is actually written after you have completed the rest of your paper. The reason is that it is a distillation of the important points covered in the body of your report. It tells the reader what your research is about in one succinct paragraph. In the sample report, Bruce gives a synopsis of the background of his research, his hypothesis, the way he tested it, and the results. The abstract in Exhibit A.3 is slightly shorter than that in Exhibit A.2, reflecting the APA rule that abstracts of reports of research submitted for publication are limited to 960 characters and spaces, or approximately 120 words.

Here are some further questions to guide you as you prepare your abstract:

- What was the problem under investigation or objective of the study?
- What was the principal method used (a laboratory experiment, a survey questionnaire, judges as raters, etc.)?
- Who were the research participants (i.e., their pertinent characteristics)?
- What were the major results?
- What are the primary conclusions and implications that appear in the discussion section?

INTRODUCTION

The introduction should emphasize linking ideas to past research and should lead into your hypotheses. Basically, it describes the point of the research and also provides a framework for your later description of the method used. The idea of writing a strong introduction is to get the reader to think, "Yes, of course, that's what the student *had* to do to test this hypothesis." Bruce begins by describing a debate he saw on television, enabling the reader to view the research in a practical light that is both compelling and significant. He also defines the area of his project—forensic psychology—and develops his hypothesis in such a way that the method section (which follows) will seem a natural consequence of the introduction.

Here are some questions to help you plan the introduction:

- What got me thinking about this study?
- How did I come up with my working hypothesis, and what did I expect to find?
- What terms do I need to define for the reader who may be unfamiliar with this area?
- Do I need to define any terms for special reasons, because they are used differently in different contexts or because I use them in a new way?
- How does the study build on, or derive from, other studies?
- Is each of my hypotheses clearly explained and justified in terms of its logical basis?

If you did not outline your introduction before you drafted it, a useful trick is to outline the introduction *after* it is written. Outlining it at the end will expose any lapses in logic that need to be corrected. You can practice by outlining Bruce's introduction and asking yourself how it might be improved. If you compare

Exhibits A.2 and A.3, you will notice that the APA format (Exhibit A.3) leaves out the word *Introduction* and instead repeats the title of the manuscript. The APA style assumes that it is implicit that the opening section is the introduction, whereas the term paper (Exhibit A.2) uses the word *introduction* as a reminder to the student of what this section should contain.

METHOD

In the method section, you will describe the procedures used and give a detailed account of the pertinent characteristics of the subject sample. Bruce describes where his subjects came from ("an introductory statistics class"), the number that participated in the experimental and control conditions, and the fact that men and women participated who were not volunteers but part of an intact class. Some authors report more detailed demographic data, and you can ask your instructor for further guidance if you are unsure what to report. For example, in your method section you may tell the subjects' ages (average and range), their racial and gender designations, and so on, insofar as any of these characteristics are essential to the generality of the results.

Included in this section is a brief description of the tests and measurements you used. In his materials section, Bruce describes the two forms of his questionnaire. Finally, the procedure for administering the treatments or questionnaires is described. Bruce's procedure is one paragraph long, but other projects may call for more detailed presentations. He describes how the two forms of his questionnaire were distributed so that both he and the subjects were blind to which treatment any individual had received. Bruce ends by noting that he debriefed the subjects.

RESULTS

Beginning with the main results, you will describe your data in this section. Try to strike a balance between being discursive and being overly precise. You might, as Bruce does, present the results in a table (or a figure, e.g., a stem-and-leaf; see Chapter 10). It is important to label your table or figure, both with a caption ("Mean, Variance, and Number of Subjects") and with row headings ("Mean," "$\bar{S}$," "$\bar{n}$") and column headings ("Experimental group," "Control group"). Except for single-case designs (see Chapter 8), you are not expected to list individual scores in this section.

Bruce's results section gets right down to business, as he tells us how he analyzed the results in order to test his hypothesis. He reports the significance test ("$t = 2.08$, $\underline{df} = 29$, $\underline{p} = .023$ one-tailed") and then shows that he consulted an advanced textbook to do a more sophisticated analysis. When he recomputed his results after adjusting for heterogeneity, they were no longer statistically significant. He reports the effect size in anticipation of his discussion section. He does not go into the implications of his data, which go in the discussion section.

A trick to help you pull the results together before you start writing is to set down a list of your statistical findings. Divide the list into coherent sets of results, and then decide the sequence in which you will discuss the sets according to their order of importance or relevance to your study's objective. Experienced authors try to anticipate questions the reader may have, such as questions about ambiguous results that call for clarification or further analysis.

Here are some questions to help you structure this section:

- What were the different results, and what is their order of importance or relevance?
- How can I describe what I found in a careful, detailed way that will make complete sense to someone who is not informed on this topic?
- Have I omitted any necessary details or included superfluous information?
- In reporting my statistical results, am I being precise without being misleadingly or needlessly so?

DISCUSSION

In the discussion section, you will synthesize and interpret the various parts of your report to form a cohesive unit from the facts that you have gathered. Without being overly redundant, Bruce begins by reminding us of the background that he developed in the introduction. That is, he recapitulates his original hypothesis, thereby underscoring the logical continuity of his presentation. Had he found any unexpected results, this would be the place to note how serendipity (see Chapter 2) entered into his investigation.

Bruce also writes "defensively" in that he plays his own devil's advocate. He reminds the reader that "The results, although in the hypothesized direction, were not statistically significant after the appropriate adjustment was made for heterogeneity of variance." In the APA version (Exhibit A.3), he also notes the alpha level used in this decision (as the APA manual asks for this information). However, he does not dwell on the significance level alone but notes that the effect size ($r = .20$) was "theoretically interesting and suggested that follow-up studies are warranted." Incidentally, the APA manual (1994, p. 18) does not recommend r as an effect size index but lists r^2 (i.e., the coefficient of determination) and various other measures. As squaring r can seriously underestimate the practical importance of an effect, we suggest that you not take the APA manual's advice and instead simply report and interpret r (using the BESD, as discussed in Chapter 12). Bruce also points out potential implications and future directions of his research, thus communicating that he has thought deeply about this area.

Questions to consider as you begin to structure this section include:

- What was the major purpose of this study, and were there any secondary objectives?
- How do my results relate to that purpose and those objectives?
- Were there any unexpected findings of interest, and how can I describe them to show their relevance to this project and to possible follow-up research?
- How valid and generalizable are my findings, and what are their limitations?
- What can I say about the wider implications of the results?

REFERENCES

The title page and abstract are on separate pages, but the other sections follow one another without any page breaks (introduction, method, results, discussion). The reference section also begins on a separate page, and you can now see why it was important to make complete and accurate notes. This section is an alphabetized listing of all the sources of information on which you drew, and the index cards you made will now provide a running list of those sources.

List only those references that you have actually discussed or cited. This is not a bibliography (i.e., a comprehensive listing of everything on the subject), but a compilation of the material that you used and discussed. Both versions of Bruce's paper (Exhibits A.2 and A.3) give us examples of the style recommended by the American Psychological Association (1994) in referencing books, journal reports, magazine articles, and chapters in edited volumes. If you run into a problem—and if the instructor is a stickler for having you use the APA style—consult the fourth edition of the *Publication Manual of the American Psychological Association*. Otherwise, just use common sense and Bruce's reference section as a general model.

APPENDIX

The term paper version of Bruce's paper in Exhibit A.2 has an appendix as the final section. However, your instructor may require that you incorporate an appendix into your paper and also use the APA style, in which case you can use the sample appendix in Exhibit A.2 as a model. The purpose of the appendix is to display the raw material and calculations of your study. Here is also where you will display any questionnaires or tests that you constructed but did not fully present in the main body of your report.

Observe in Exhibit A.2 that Bruce's report contains an "Appendix A" (displaying the questionnaires he developed) and an "Appendix B" (showing his raw data and the *t* test and effect size, *r*, he computed). If the student has made a mistake in the data analysis, the grader can easily examine his or her results to trace how far back the error occurred. As a result, the grader will not penalize the student for making what might seem a mistake in interpretation or understanding when it is a less serious typographical error or a recording mistake.

WRITING AND REVISING

Now that you know what is expected, it is time to begin writing a first draft. A good place to start is to compose a "self-motivator" statement that you can refer back to as a way of focusing your thoughts. Such a statement can be posted over your word processor or typewriter to serve as a guidepost to keep you from wandering off on a tangent. Bruce's self-motivator might be "My report will focus on what I know about whether disclosing the results of drug tests influences bail judgments in criminal proceedings."

If you are someone who has trouble getting started, one trick is to begin not at the beginning but with the section you feel will be easiest to write. Once the ideas begin to flow, you can tackle the introductory section. This approach will also bolster flagging spirits, because you can reread the sections you have already written when you begin to feel a loss of energy or determination. Try not to fall into the trap of escaping by napping or watching television. If you recognize these counterproductive moves for what they are, you should be able to avoid them.

Here are some helpful hints to make the writing go more smoothly:

- Find a quiet, well-lighted place in which to write, and do your writing in two-hour stretches.
- Double-space your first draft so you can get an idea of how long the final (double-spaced) paper will be.
- Double spacing will also give you room for legible revisions.
- Number the pages even if you are writing on a note pad.
- Pace your work so that you can complete the first draft and let it rest for at least 24 hours.

LAYOUT AND TYPING

After you have revised your paper and are satisfied with the final version, it is time to "package" it for the instructor. The final report must not contain any typographical errors or spelling mistakes. To help you catch misspellings, use a spell-check if you are processing the paper on a computer. But do not stop here, because there may be technical words that the spell-check missed. Put the final report aside for a day or two and then look at it again with a fresh eye. This is called *proofreading* or *proofing,* and it is the final step before you submit the paper.

It is a good idea to proof the paper more than once, because you will be surprised how elusive some mistakes can be. Ask yourself:

- Are there omissions?
- Are there misspellings?
- Are the numbers correct?
- Are the hyphenations correct?
- Are all the references cited in the body of the paper listed in the reference section, and vice versa?

Make sure the print is dark enough to be easily read, as you do not want to frustrate the grader (frustration can lead to aggression!) by submitting a paper with typescript so light or blurry that it taxes the eyes. Use $8\frac{1}{2} \times 11$-inch white paper, preferably bond (never use onionskin, because it tears easily and does not take corrections well). The APA manual also requires that there be at least 1-inch margins on all four sides of the page, that no typed line exceed $6\frac{1}{2}$ inches, and that there be no more than 27 lines of text on the page. Double-space the printout or typing, and print or type on one side of the paper only, numbering the pages consecutively as illustrated in the appropriate exhibit. Also, words or symbols to be italicized are underlined; do not use the italic typeface on the word processor to create italics.

If you are using a word processor, back up your work routinely. You never know when somebody may playfully touch a couple of keys and erase all your hard work. It also is a good idea to print a hard copy of each day's labors, so you have a double guarantee that you will not lose your work. When the clean, corrected final draft is completed, make an extra copy—just in case. The original is for the instructor, and the duplicate copy ensures that a spare copy will be available if a problem arises.

If you are using a word processor and do not have access to a letter-quality printer (laserjet, inkjet, or daisy wheel), use the strikeover mode rather than the first-draft mode to print your final copy. Notice that both versions of Bruce's paper leave the right margin "ragged" (i.e., uneven), which is also a requirement of the APA manual. In fact, most people seem to find a page with a ragged right margin more readable in typed papers (but not in books or journal articles) than one with a "justified" (i.e., even) right margin.

Give your report a final look, checking to see that all the pages are there and in order, and then turn it in on schedule. Having adhered to these guidelines, you should feel the satisfaction of a job well done.

Statistical Tables

TABLE B.1			Z Values Needed for Significance at One-Tailed p Levels						

Second digit of Z

Z	.00	.01	.02	.03	.04	.05	.06	.07	.08	.09
.0	.5000	.4960	.4920	.4880	.4840	.4801	.4761	.4721	.4681	.4641
.1	.4602	.4562	.4522	.4483	.4443	.4404	.4364	.4325	.4286	.4247
.2	.4207	.4168	.4129	.4090	.4052	.4013	.3974	.3936	.3897	.3859
.3	.3821	.3783	.3745	.3707	.3669	.3632	.3594	.3557	.3520	.3483
.4	.3446	.3409	.3372	.3336	.3300	.3264	.3228	.3192	.3156	.3121
.5	.3085	.3050	.3015	.2981	.2946	.2912	.2877	.2843	.2810	.2776
.6	.2743	.2709	.2676	.2643	.2611	.2578	.2546	.2514	.2483	.2451
.7	.2420	.2389	.2358	.2327	.2296	.2266	.2236	.2206	.2177	.2148
.8	.2119	.2090	.2061	.2033	.2005	.1977	.1949	.1922	.1894	.1867
.9	.1841	.1814	.1788	.1762	.1736	.1711	.1685	.1660	.1635	.1611
1.0	.1587	.1562	.1539	.1515	.1492	.1469	.1446	.1423	.1401	.1379
1.1	.1357	.1335	.1314	.1292	.1271	.1251	.1230	.1210	.1190	.1170
1.2	.1151	.1131	.1112	.1093	.1075	.1056	.1038	.1020	.1003	.0985
1.3	.0968	.0951	.0934	.0918	.0901	.0885	.0869	.0853	.0838	.0823
1.4	.0808	.0793	.0778	.0764	.0749	.0735	.0721	.0708	.0694	.0681
1.5	.0668	.0655	.0643	.0630	.0618	.0606	.0594	.0582	.0571	.0559
1.6	.0548	.0537	.0526	.0516	.0505	.0495	.0485	.0475	.0465	.0455
1.7	.0446	.0436	.0427	.0418	.0409	.0401	.0392	.0384	.0375	.0367
1.8	.0359	.0351	.0344	.0336	.0329	.0322	.0314	.0307	.0301	.0294
1.9	.0287	.0281	.0274	.0268	.0262	.0256	.0250	.0244	.0239	.0233
2.0	.0228	.0222	.0217	.0212	.0207	.0202	.0197	.0192	.0188	.0183
2.1	.0179	.0174	.0170	.0166	.0162	.0158	.0154	.0150	.0146	.0143
2.2	.0139	.0136	.0132	.0129	.0125	.0122	.0119	.0116	.0113	.0110
2.3	.0107	.0104	.0102	.0099	.0096	.0094	.0091	.0089	.0087	.0084
2.4	.0082	.0080	.0078	.0075	.0073	.0071	.0069	.0068	.0066	.0064
2.5	.0062	.0060	.0059	.0057	.0055	.0054	.0052	.0051	.0049	.0048
2.6	.0047	.0045	.0044	.0043	.0041	.0040	.0039	.0038	.0037	.0036
2.7	.0035	.0034	.0033	.0032	.0031	.0030	.0029	.0028	.0027	.0026
2.8	.0026	.0025	.0024	.0023	.0023	.0022	.0021	.0021	.0020	.0019
2.9	.0019	.0018	.0018	.0017	.0016	.0016	.0015	.0015	.0014	.0014
3.0	.0013	.0013	.0013	.0012	.0012	.0011	.0011	.0011	.0010	.0010
3.1	.0010	.0009	.0009	.0009	.0008	.0008	.0008	.0008	.0007	.0007
3.2	.0007									
3.3	.0005									
3.4	.0003									
3.5	.00023									
3.6	.00016									
3.7	.00011									
3.8	.00007									
3.9	.00005									
4.0	.00003									

Source: Reproduced from *Nonparametric Statistics* by S. Siegel, 1956, New York: McGraw-Hill, p. 247. Used by permission of McGraw-Hill, Inc.

TABLE B.2			*t* Values Needed for Significance at One-Tailed and Two-Tailed *p* Levels						
p	.50	.20	.10	.05	.02	.01	.005	.002	two-tail
df	.25	.10	.05	.025	.01	.005	.0025	.001	one-tail
1	1.000	3.078	6.314	12.706	31.821	63.657	127.321	318.309	
2	.816	1.886	2.920	4.303	6.965	9.925	14.089	22.327	
3	.765	1.638	2.353	3.182	4.541	5.841	7.453	10.214	
4	.741	1.533	2.132	2.776	3.747	4.604	5.598	7.173	
5	.727	1.476	2.015	2.571	3.365	4.032	4.773	5.893	
6	.718	1.440	1.943	2.447	3.143	3.707	4.317	5.208	
7	.711	1.415	1.895	2.365	2.998	3.499	4.029	4.785	
8	.706	1.397	1.860	2.306	2.896	3.355	3.833	4.501	
9	.703	1.383	1.833	2.262	2.821	3.250	3.690	4.297	
10	.700	1.372	1.812	2.228	2.764	3.169	3.581	4.144	
11	.697	1.363	1.796	2.201	2.718	3.106	3.497	4.025	
12	.695	1.356	1.782	2.179	2.681	3.055	3.428	3.930	
13	.694	1.350	1.771	2.160	2.650	3.012	3.372	3.852	
14	.692	1.345	1.761	2.145	2.624	2.977	3.326	3.787	
15	.691	1.341	1.753	2.131	2.602	2.947	3.286	3.733	
16	.690	1.337	1.746	2.120	2.583	2.921	3.252	3.686	
17	.689	1.333	1.740	2.110	2.567	2.898	3.223	3.646	
18	.688	1.330	1.734	2.101	2.552	2.878	3.197	3.610	
19	.688	1.328	1.729	2.093	2.539	2.861	3.174	3.579	
20	.687	1.325	1.725	2.086	2.528	2.845	3.153	3.552	
21	.686	1.323	1.721	2.080	2.518	2.831	3.135	3.527	
22	.686	1.321	1.717	2.074	2.508	2.819	3.119	3.505	
23	.685	1.319	1.714	2.069	2.500	2.807	3.104	3.485	
24	.685	1.318	1.711	2.064	2.492	2.797	3.090	3.467	
25	.684	1.316	1.708	2.060	2.485	2.787	3.078	3.450	
26	.684	1.315	1.706	2.056	2.479	2.779	3.067	3.435	
27	.684	1.314	1.703	2.052	2.473	2.771	3.057	3.421	
28	.683	1.313	1.701	2.048	2.467	2.763	3.047	3.408	
29	.683	1.311	1.699	2.045	2.462	2.756	3.038	3.396	
30	.683	1.310	1.697	2.042	2.457	2.750	3.030	3.385	
35	.682	1.306	1.690	2.030	2.438	2.724	2.996	3.340	
40	.681	1.303	1.684	2.021	2.423	2.704	2.971	3.307	
45	.680	1.301	1.679	2.014	2.412	2.690	2.952	3.281	
50	.679	1.299	1.676	2.009	2.403	2.678	2.937	3.261	
55	.679	1.297	1.673	2.004	2.396	2.668	2.925	3.245	
60	.679	1.296	1.671	2.000	2.390	2.660	2.915	3.232	
70	.678	1.294	1.667	1.994	2.381	2.648	2.899	3.211	
80	.678	1.292	1.664	1.990	2.374	2.639	2.887	3.195	
90	.677	1.291	1.662	1.987	2.368	2.632	2.878	3.183	
100	.677	1.290	1.660	1.984	2.364	2.626	2.871	3.174	
200	.676	1.286	1.652	1.972	2.345	2.601	2.838	3.131	
500	.675	1.283	1.648	1.965	2.334	2.586	2.820	3.107	
1,000	.675	1.282	1.646	1.962	2.330	2.581	2.813	3.098	
2,000	.675	1.282	1.645	1.961	2.328	2.578	2.810	3.094	
10,000	.675	1.282	1.645	1.960	2.327	2.576	2.808	3.091	
∞	674	1.282	1.645	1.960	2.326	2.576	2.807	3.090	

TABLE B.2	(Continued)					
p	.001	.0005	.0002	.0001	.00005	.00002	two-tail
df	.0005	.00025	.0001	.00005	.000025	.00001	one-tail
1	636.619	1,273.239	3,183.099	6,366.198	12,732.395	31,830.989	
2	31.598	44.705	70.700	99.992	141.416	223.603	
3	12.924	16.326	22.204	28.000	35.298	47.928	
4	8.610	10.306	13.034	15.544	18.522	23.332	
5	6.869	7.976	9.678	11.178	12.893	15.547	
6	5.959	6.788	8.025	9.082	10.261	12.032	
7	5.408	6.082	7.063	7.885	8.782	10.103	
8	5.041	5.618	6.442	7.120	7.851	8.907	
9	4.781	5.291	6.010	6.594	7.215	8.102	
10	4.587	5.049	5.694	6.211	6.757	7.527	
11	4.437	4.863	5.453	5.921	6.412	7.098	
12	4.318	4.716	5.263	5.694	6.143	6.756	
13	4.221	4.597	5.111	5.513	5.928	6.501	
14	4.140	4.499	4.985	5.363	5.753	6.287	
15	4.073	4.417	4.880	5.239	5.607	6.109	
16	4.015	4.346	4.791	5.134	5.484	5.960	
17	3.965	4.286	4.714	5.044	5.379	5.832	
18	3.922	4.233	4.648	4.966	5.288	5.722	
19	3.883	4.187	4.590	4.897	5.209	5.627	
20	3.850	4.146	4.539	4.837	5.139	5.543	
21	3.819	4.110	4.493	4.784	5.077	5.469	
22	3.792	4.077	4.452	4.736	5.022	5.402	
23	3.768	4.048	4.415	4.693	4.972	5.343	
24	3.745	4.021	4.382	4.654	4.927	5.290	
25	3.725	3.997	4.352	4.619	4.887	5.241	
26	3.707	3.974	4.324	4.587	4.850	5.197	
27	3.690	3.954	4.299	4.558	4.816	5.157	
28	3.674	3.935	4.275	4.530	4.784	5.120	
29	3.659	3.918	4.254	4.506	4.756	5.086	
30	3.646	3.902	4.234	4.482	4.729	5.054	
35	3.591	3.836	4.153	4.389	4.622	4.927	
40	3.551	3.788	4.094	4.321	4.544	4.835	
45	3.520	3.752	4.049	4.269	4.485	4.766	
50	3.496	3.723	4.014	4.228	4.438	4.711	
55	3.476	3.700	3.986	4.196	4.401	4.667	
60	3.460	3.681	3.926	4.169	4.370	4.631	
70	3.435	3.651	3.962	4.127	4.323	4.576	
80	3.416	3.629	3.899	4.096	4.288	4.535	
90	3.402	3.612	3.878	4.072	4.261	4.503	
100	3.390	3.598	3.862	4.053	4.240	4.478	
200	3.340	3.539	3.789	3.970	4.146	4.369	
500	3.310	3.504	3.747	3.922	4.091	4.306	
1,000	3.300	3.492	3.733	3.906	4.073	4.285	
2,000	3.295	3.486	3.726	3.898	4.064	4.275	
10,000	3.292	3.482	3.720	3.892	4.058	4.267	
∞	3.291	3.481	3.719	3.891	4.056	4.265	

Source: Reproduced from "Extended Tables of the Percentage Points of Student's *t*-Distribution" by E. T. Federighi, 1959, *Journal of the American Statistical Association, 54,* pp. 683–688, by permission of the American Statistical Association.

df_2	p \ df_1	1	2	3	4	5	6	8	12	24	∞
1	.001	405284	500000	540379	562500	576405	585937	598144	610667	623497	636619
	.005	16211	20000	21615	22500	23056	23437	23925	24426	24940	25465
	.01	4052	4999	5403	5625	5764	5859	5981	6106	6234	6366
	.025	647.79	799.50	864.16	899.58	921.85	937.11	956.66	976.71	997.25	1018.30
	.05	161.45	199.50	215.71	224.58	230.16	233.99	238.88	243.91	249.05	254.32
	.10	39.86	49.50	53.59	55.83	57.24	58.20	59.44	60.70	62.00	63.33
	.20	9.47	12.00	13.06	13.73	14.01	14.26	14.59	14.90	15.24	15.58
2	.001	998.5	999.0	999.2	999.2	999.3	999.3	999.4	999.4	999.5	999.5
	.005	198.50	199.00	199.17	199.25	199.30	199.33	199.37	199.42	199.46	199.51
	.01	98.49	99.00	99.17	99.25	99.30	99.33	99.36	99.42	99.46	99.50
	.025	38.51	39.00	39.17	39.25	39.30	39.33	39.37	39.42	39.46	39.50
	.05	18.51	19.00	19.16	19.25	19.30	19.33	19.37	19.41	19.45	19.50
	.10	8.53	9.00	9.16	9.24	9.29	9.33	9.37	9.41	9.45	9.49
	.20	3.56	4.00	4.16	4.24	4.28	4.32	4.36	4.40	4.44	4.48
3	.001	167.5	148.5	141.1	137.1	134.6	132.8	130.6	128.3	125.9	123.5
	.005	55.55	49.80	47.47	46.20	45.39	44.84	44.13	43.39	42.62	41.83
	.01	34.12	30.81	29.46	28.71	28.24	27.91	27.49	27.05	26.60	26.12
	.025	17.44	16.04	15.44	15.10	14.89	14.74	14.54	14.34	14.12	13.90
	.05	10.13	9.55	9.28	9.12	9.01	8.94	8.84	8.74	8.64	8.53
	.10	5.54	5.46	5.39	5.34	5.31	5.28	5.25	5.22	5.18	5.13
	.20	2.68	2.89	2.94	2.96	2.97	2.97	2.98	2.98	2.98	2.98
4	.001	74.14	61.25	56.18	53.44	51.71	50.53	49.00	47.41	45.77	44.05
	.005	31.33	26.28	24.26	23.16	22.46	21.98	21.35	20.71	20.03	19.33
	.01	21.20	18.00	16.69	15.98	15.52	15.21	14.80	14.37	13.93	13.46
	.025	12.22	10.65	9.98	9.60	9.36	9.20	8.98	8.75	8.51	8.26
	.05	7.71	6.94	6.59	6.39	6.26	6.16	6.04	5.91	5.77	5.63
	.10	4.54	4.32	4.19	4.11	4.05	4.01	3.95	3.90	3.83	3.76
	.20	2.35	2.47	2.48	2.48	2.48	2.47	2.47	2.46	2.44	2.43
5	.001	47.04	36.61	33.20	31.09	29.75	28.84	27.64	26.42	25.14	23.78
	.005	22.79	18.31	16.53	15.56	14.94	14.51	13.96	13.38	12.78	12.14
	.01	16.26	13.27	12.06	11.39	10.97	10.67	10.29	9.89	9.47	9.02
	.025	10.01	8.43	7.76	7.39	7.15	6.98	6.76	6.52	6.28	6.02
	.05	6.61	5.79	5.41	5.19	5.05	4.95	4.82	4.68	4.53	4.36
	.10	4.06	3.78	3.62	3.52	3.45	3.40	3.34	3.27	3.19	3.10
	.20	2.18	2.26	2.25	2.24	2.23	2.22	2.20	2.18	2.16	2.13
6	.001	35.51	27.00	23.70	21.90	20.81	20.03	19.03	17.99	16.89	15.75
	.005	18.64	14.54	12.92	12.03	11.46	11.07	10.57	10.03	9.47	8.88
	.01	13.74	10.92	9.78	9.15	8.75	8.47	8.10	7.72	7.31	6.88
	.025	8.81	7.26	6.60	6.23	5.99	5.82	5.60	5.37	5.12	4.85
	.05	5.99	5.14	4.76	4.53	4.39	4.28	4.15	4.00	3.84	3.67
	.10	3.78	3.46	3.29	3.18	3.11	3.05	2.98	2.90	2.82	2.72
	.20	2.07	2.13	2.11	2.09	2.08	2.06	2.04	2.02	1.99	1.95
7	.001	29.22	21.69	18.77	17.19	16.21	15.52	14.63	13.71	12.73	11.69
	.005	16.24	12.40	10.88	10.05	9.52	9.16	8.68	8.18	7.65	7.08
	.01	12.25	9.55	8.45	7.85	7.46	7.19	6.84	6.47	6.07	5.65
	.025	8.07	6.54	5.89	5.52	5.29	5.12	4.90	4.67	4.42	4.14
	.05	5.59	4.74	4.35	4.12	3.97	3.87	3.73	3.57	3.41	3.23
	.10	3.59	3.26	3.07	2.96	2.88	2.83	2.75	2.67	2.58	2.47
	.20	2.00	2.04	2.02	1.99	1.97	1.96	1.93	1.91	1.87	1.83
8	.001	25.42	18.49	15.83	14.39	13.49	12.86	12.04	11.19	10.30	9.34
	.005	14.69	11.04	9.60	8.81	8.30	7.95	7.50	7.01	6.50	5.95
	.01	11.26	8.65	7.59	7.01	6.63	6.37	6.03	5.67	5.28	4.86
	.025	7.57	6.06	5.42	5.05	4.82	4.65	4.43	4.20	3.95	3.67
	.05	5.32	4.46	4.07	3.84	3.69	3.58	3.44	3.28	3.12	2.93
	.10	3.46	3.11	2.92	2.81	2.73	2.67	2.59	2.50	2.40	2.29
	.20	1.95	1.98	1.95	1.92	1.90	1.88	1.86	1.83	1.79	1.74
9	.001	22.86	16.39	13.90	12.56	11.71	11.13	10.37	9.57	8.72	7.81
	.005	13.61	10.11	8.72	7.96	7.47	7.13	6.69	6.23	5.73	5.19
	.01	10.56	8.02	6.99	6.42	6.06	5.80	5.47	5.11	4.73	4.31
	.025	7.21	5.71	5.08	4.72	4.48	4.32	4.10	3.87	3.61	3.33
	.05	5.12	4.26	3.86	3.63	3.48	3.37	3.23	3.07	2.90	2.71
	.10	3.36	3.01	2.81	2.69	2.61	2.55	2.47	2.38	2.28	2.16
	.20	1.91	1.94	1.90	1.87	1.85	1.83	1.80	1.76	1.73	1.67

df_1 p df_2	1	2	3	4	5	6	8	12	24	∞
10	.001	21.04	14.91	12.55	11.28	10.48	9.92	9.20	8.45	7.64	6.76
	.005	12.83	9.43	8.08	7.34	6.87	6.54	6.12	5.66	5.17	4.64
	.01	10.04	7.56	6.55	5.99	5.64	5.39	5.06	4.71	4.33	3.91
	.025	6.94	5.46	4.83	4.47	4.24	4.07	3.85	3.62	3.37	3.08
	.05	4.96	4.10	3.71	3.48	3.33	3.22	3.07	2.91	2.74	2.54
	.10	3.28	2.92	2.73	2.61	2.52	2.46	2.38	2.28	2.18	2.06
	.20	1.88	1.90	1.86	1.83	1.80	1.78	1.75	1.72	1.67	1.62
11	.001	19.69	13.81	11.56	10.35	9.58	9.05	8.35	7.63	6.85	6.00
	.005	12.23	8.91	7.60	6.88	6.42	6.10	5.68	5.24	4.76	4.23
	.01	9.65	7.20	6.22	5.67	5.32	5.07	4.74	4.40	4.02	3.60
	.025	6.72	5.26	4.63	4.28	4.04	3.88	3.66	3.43	3.17	2.88
	.05	4.84	3.98	3.59	3.36	3.20	3.09	2.95	2.79	2.61	2.40
	.10	3.23	2.86	2.66	2.54	2.45	2.39	2.30	2.21	2.10	1.97
	.20	1.86	1.87	1.83	1.80	1.77	1.75	1.72	1.68	1.63	1.57
12	.001	18.64	12.97	10.80	9.63	8.89	8.38	7.71	7.00	6.25	5.42
	.005	11.75	8.51	7.23	6.52	6.07	5.76	5.35	4.91	4.43	3.90
	.01	9.33	6.93	5.95	5.41	5.06	4.82	4.50	4.16	3.78	3.36
	.025	6.55	5.10	4.47	4.12	3.89	3.73	3.51	3.28	3.02	2.72
	.05	4.75	3.88	3.49	3.26	3.11	3.00	2.85	2.69	2.50	2.30
	.10	3.18	2.81	2.61	2.48	2.39	2.33	2.24	2.15	2.04	1.90
	.20	1.84	1.85	1.80	1.77	1.74	1.72	1.69	1.65	1.60	1.54
13	.001	17.81	12.31	10.21	9.07	8.35	7.86	7.21	6.52	5.78	4.97
	.005	11.37	8.19	6.93	6.23	5.79	5.48	5.08	4.64	4.17	3.65
	.01	9.07	6.70	5.74	5.20	4.86	4.62	4.30	3.96	3.59	3.16
	.025	6.41	4.97	4.35	4.00	3.77	3.60	3.39	3.15	2.89	2.60
	.05	4.67	3.80	3.41	3.18	3.02	2.92	2.77	2.60	2.42	2.21
	.10	3.14	2.76	2.56	2.43	2.35	2.28	2.20	2.10	1.98	1.85
	.20	1.82	1.83	1.78	1.75	1.72	1.69	1.66	1.62	1.57	1.51
14	.001	17.14	11.78	9.73	8.62	7.92	7.43	6.80	6.13	5.41	4.60
	.005	11.06	7.92	6.68	6.00	5.56	5.26	4.86	4.43	3.96	3.44
	.01	8.86	6.51	5.56	5.03	4.69	4.46	4.14	3.80	3.43	3.00
	.025	6.30	4.86	4.24	3.89	3.66	3.50	3.29	3.05	2.79	2.49
	.05	4.60	3.74	3.34	3.11	2.96	2.85	2.70	2.53	2.35	2.13
	.10	3.10	2.73	2.52	2.39	2.31	2.24	2.15	2.05	1.94	1.80
	.20	1.81	1.81	1.76	1.73	1.70	1.67	1.64	1.60	1.55	1.48
15	.001	16.59	11.34	9.34	8.25	7.57	7.09	6.47	5.81	5.10	4.31
	.005	10.80	7.70	6.48	5.80	5.37	5.07	4.67	4.25	3.79	3.26
	.01	8.68	6.36	5.42	4.89	4.56	4.32	4.00	3.67	3.29	2.87
	.025	6.20	4.77	4.15	3.80	3.58	3.41	3.20	2.96	2.70	2.40
	.05	4.54	3.68	3.29	3.06	2.90	2.79	2.64	2.48	2.29	2.07
	.10	3.07	2.70	2.49	2.36	2.27	2.21	2.12	2.02	1.90	1.76
	.20	1.80	1.79	1.75	1.71	1.68	1.66	1.62	1.58	1.53	1.46
16	.001	16.12	10.97	9.00	7.94	7.27	6.81	6.19	5.55	4.85	4.06
	.005	10.58	7.51	6.30	5.64	5.21	4.91	4.52	4.10	3.64	3.11
	.01	8.53	6.23	5.29	4.77	4.44	4.20	3.89	3.55	3.18	2.75
	.025	6.12	4.69	4.08	3.73	3.50	3.34	3.12	2.89	2.63	2.32
	.05	4.49	3.63	3.24	3.01	2.85	2.74	2.59	2.42	2.24	2.01
	.10	3.05	2.67	2.46	2.33	2.24	2.18	2.09	1.99	1.87	1.72
	.20	1.79	1.78	1.74	1.70	1.67	1.64	1.61	1.56	1.51	1.43
17	.001	15.72	10.66	8.73	7.68	7.02	6.56	5.96	5.32	4.63	3.85
	.005	10.38	7.35	6.16	5.50	5.07	4.78	4.39	3.97	3.51	2.98
	.01	8.40	6.11	5.18	4.67	4.34	4.10	3.79	3.45	3.08	2.65
	.025	6.04	4.62	4.01	3.66	3.44	3.28	3.06	2.82	2.56	2.25
	.05	4.45	3.59	3.20	2.96	2.81	2.70	2.55	2.38	2.19	1.96
	.10	3.03	2.64	2.44	2.31	2.22	2.15	2.06	1.96	1.84	1.69
	.20	1.78	1.77	1.72	1.68	1.65	1.63	1.59	1.55	1.49	1.42
18	.001	15.38	10.39	8.49	7.46	6.81	6.35	5.76	5.13	4.45	3.67
	.005	10.22	7.21	6.03	5.37	4.96	4.66	4.28	3.86	3.40	2.87
	.01	8.28	6.01	5.09	4.58	4.25	4.01	3.71	3.37	3.00	2.57
	.025	5.98	4.56	3.95	3.61	3.38	3.22	3.01	2.77	2.50	2.19
	.05	4.41	3.55	3.16	2.93	2.77	2.66	2.51	2.34	2.15	1.92
	.10	3.01	2.62	2.42	2.29	2.20	2.13	2.04	1.93	1.81	1.66
	.20	1.77	1.76	1.71	1.67	1.64	1.62	1.58	1.53	1.48	1.40

df_2	p	1	2	3	4	5	6	8	12	24	∞
19	.001	15.08	10.16	8.28	7.26	6.61	6.18	5.59	4.97	4.29	3.52
	.005	10.07	7.09	5.92	5.27	4.85	4.56	4.18	3.76	3.31	2.78
	.01	8.18	5.93	5.01	4.50	4.17	3.94	3.63	3.30	2.92	2.49
	.025	5.92	4.51	3.90	3.56	3.33	3.17	2.96	2.72	2.45	2.13
	.05	4.38	3.52	3.13	2.90	2.74	2.63	2.48	2.31	2.11	1.88
	.10	2.99	2.61	2.40	2.27	2.18	2.11	2.02	1.91	1.79	1.63
	.20	1.76	1.75	1.70	1.66	1.63	1.61	1.57	1.52	1.46	1.39
20	.001	14.82	9.95	8.10	7.10	6.46	6.02	5.44	4.82	4.15	3.38
	.005	9.94	6.99	5.82	5.17	4.76	4.47	4.09	3.68	3.22	2.69
	.01	8.10	5.85	4.94	4.43	4.10	3.87	3.56	3.23	2.86	2.42
	.025	5.87	4.46	3.86	3.51	3.29	3.13	2.91	2.68	2.41	2.09
	.05	4.35	3.49	3.10	2.87	2.71	2.60	2.45	2.28	2.08	1.84
	.10	2.97	2.59	2.38	2.25	2.16	2.09	2.00	1.89	1.77	1.61
	.20	1.76	1.75	1.70	1.65	1.62	1.60	1.56	1.51	1.45	1.37
21	.001	14.59	9.77	7.94	6.95	6.32	5.88	5.31	4.70	4.03	3.26
	.005	9.83	6.89	5.73	5.09	4.68	4.39	4.01	3.60	3.15	2.61
	.01	8.02	5.78	4.87	4.37	4.04	3.81	3.51	3.17	2.80	2.36
	.025	5.83	4.42	3.82	3.48	3.25	3.09	2.87	2.64	2.37	2.04
	.05	4.32	3.47	3.07	2.84	2.68	2.57	2.42	2.25	2.05	1.81
	.10	2.96	2.57	2.36	2.23	2.14	2.08	1.98	1.88	1.75	1.59
	.20	1.75	1.74	1.69	1.65	1.61	1.59	1.55	1.50	1.44	1.36
22	.001	14.38	9.61	7.80	6.81	6.19	5.76	5.19	4.58	3.92	3.15
	.005	9.73	6.81	5.65	5.02	4.61	4.32	3.94	3.54	3.08	2.55
	.01	7.94	5.72	4.82	4.31	3.99	3.76	3.45	3.12	2.75	2.31
	.025	5.79	4.38	3.78	3.44	3.22	3.05	2.84	2.60	2.33	2.00
	.05	4.30	3.44	3.05	2.82	2.66	2.55	2.40	2.23	2.03	1.78
	.10	2.95	2.56	2.35	2.22	2.13	2.06	1.97	1.86	1.73	1.57
	.20	1.75	1.73	1.68	1.64	1.61	1.58	1.54	1.49	1.43	1.35
23	.001	14.19	9.47	7.67	6.69	6.08	5.65	5.09	4.48	3.82	3.05
	.005	9.63	6.73	5.58	4.95	4.54	4.26	3.88	3.47	3.02	2.48
	.01	7.88	5.66	4.76	4.26	3.94	3.71	3.41	3.07	2.70	2.26
	.025	5.75	4.35	3.75	3.41	3.18	3.02	2.81	2.57	2.30	1.97
	.05	4.28	3.42	3.03	2.80	2.64	2.53	2.38	2.20	2.00	1.76
	.10	2.94	2.55	2.34	2.21	2.11	2.05	1.95	1.84	1.72	1.55
	.20	1.74	1.73	1.68	1.63	1.60	1.57	1.53	1.49	1.42	1.34
24	.001	14.03	9.34	7.55	6.59	5.98	5.55	4.99	4.39	3.74	2.97
	.005	9.55	6.66	5.52	4.89	4.49	4.20	3.83	3.42	2.97	2.43
	.01	7.82	5.61	4.72	4.22	3.90	3.67	3.36	3.03	2.66	2.21
	.025	5.72	4.32	3.72	3.38	3.15	2.99	2.78	2.54	2.27	1.94
	.05	4.26	3.40	3.01	2.78	2.62	2.51	2.36	2.18	1.98	1.73
	.10	2.93	2.54	2.33	2.19	2.10	2.04	1.94	1.83	1.70	1.53
	.20	1.74	1.72	1.67	1.63	1.59	1.57	1.53	1.48	1.42	1.33
25	.001	13.88	9.22	7.45	6.49	5.88	5.46	4.91	4.31	3.66	2.89
	.005	9.48	6.60	5.46	4.84	4.43	4.15	3.78	3.37	2.92	2.38
	.01	7.77	5.57	4.68	4.18	3.86	3.63	3.32	2.99	2.62	2.17
	.025	5.69	4.29	3.69	3.35	3.13	2.97	2.75	2.51	2.24	1.91
	.05	4.24	3.38	2.99	2.76	2.60	2.49	2.34	2.16	1.96	1.71
	.10	2.92	2.53	2.32	2.18	2.09	2.02	1.93	1.82	1.69	1.52
	.20	1.73	1.72	1.66	1.62	1.59	1.56	1.52	1.47	1.41	1.32
26	.001	13.74	9.12	7.36	6.41	5.80	5.38	4.83	4.24	3.59	2.82
	.005	9.41	6.54	5.41	4.79	4.38	4.10	3.73	3.33	2.87	2.33
	.01	7.72	5.53	4.64	4.14	3.82	3.59	3.29	2.96	2.58	2.13
	.025	5.66	4.27	3.67	3.33	3.10	2.94	2.73	2.49	2.22	1.88
	.05	4.22	3.37	2.98	2.74	2.59	2.47	2.32	2.15	1.95	1.69
	.10	2.91	2.52	2.31	2.17	2.08	2.01	1.92	1.81	1.68	1.50
	.20	1.73	1.71	1.66	1.62	1.58	1.56	1.52	1.47	1.40	1.31
27	.001	13.61	9.02	7.27	6.33	5.73	5.31	4.76	4.17	3.52	2.75
	.005	9.34	6.49	5.36	4.74	4.34	4.06	3.69	3.28	2.83	2.29
	.01	7.68	5.49	4.60	4.11	3.78	3.56	3.26	2.93	2.55	2.10
	.025	5.63	4.24	3.65	3.31	3.08	2.92	2.71	2.47	2.19	1.85
	.05	4.21	3.35	2.96	2.73	2.57	2.46	2.30	2.13	1.93	1.67
	.10	2.90	2.51	2.30	2.17	2.07	2.00	1.91	1.80	1.67	1.49
	.20	1.73	1.71	1.66	1.61	1.58	1.55	1.51	1.46	1.40	1.30

TABLE B.3   *(Continued)*

df₂	p	1	2	3	4	5	6	8	12	24	∞
28	.001	13.50	8.93	7.19	6.25	5.66	5.24	4.69	4.11	3.46	2.70
	.005	9.28	6.44	5.32	4.70	4.30	4.02	3.65	3.25	2.79	2.25
	.01	7.64	5.45	4.57	4.07	3.75	3.53	3.23	2.90	2.52	2.06
	.025	5.61	4.22	3.63	3.29	3.06	2.90	2.69	2.45	2.17	1.83
	.05	4.20	3.34	2.95	2.71	2.56	2.44	2.29	2.12	1.91	1.65
	.10	2.89	2.50	2.29	2.16	2.06	2.00	1.90	1.79	1.66	1.48
	.20	1.72	1.71	1.65	1.61	1.57	1.55	1.51	1.46	1.39	1.30
29	.001	13.39	8.85	7.12	6.19	5.59	5.18	4.64	4.05	3.41	2.64
	.005	9.23	6.40	5.28	4.66	4.26	3.98	3.61	3.21	2.76	2.21
	.01	7.60	5.42	4.54	4.04	3.73	3.50	3.20	2.87	2.49	2.03
	.025	5.59	4.20	3.61	3.27	3.04	2.88	2.67	2.43	2.15	1.81
	.05	4.18	3.33	2.93	2.70	2.54	2.43	2.28	2.10	1.90	1.64
	.10	2.89	2.50	2.28	2.15	2.06	1.99	1.89	1.78	1.65	1.47
	.20	1.72	1.70	1.65	1.60	1.57	1.54	1.50	1.45	1.39	1.29
30	.001	13.29	8.77	7.05	6.12	5.53	5.12	4.58	4.00	3.36	2.59
	.005	9.18	6.35	5.24	4.62	4.23	3.95	3.58	3.18	2.73	2.18
	.01	7.56	5.39	4.51	4.02	3.70	3.47	3.17	2.84	2.47	2.01
	.025	5.57	4.18	3.59	3.25	3.03	2.87	2.65	2.41	2.14	1.79
	.05	4.17	3.32	2.92	2.69	2.53	2.42	2.27	2.09	1.89	1.62
	.10	2.88	2.49	2.28	2.14	2.05	1.98	1.88	1.77	1.64	1.46
	.20	1.72	1.70	1.64	1.60	1.57	1.54	1.50	1.45	1.38	1.28
40	.001	12.61	8.25	6.60	5.70	5.13	4.73	4.21	3.64	3.01	2.23
	.005	8.83	6.07	4.98	4.37	3.99	3.71	3.35	2.95	2.50	1.93
	.01	7.31	5.18	4.31	3.83	3.51	3.29	2.99	2.66	2.29	1.80
	.025	5.42	4.05	3.46	3.13	2.90	2.74	2.53	2.29	2.01	1.64
	.05	4.08	3.23	2.84	2.61	2.45	2.34	2.18	2.00	1.79	1.51
	.10	2.84	2.44	2.23	2.09	2.00	1.93	1.83	1.71	1.57	1.38
	.20	1.70	1.68	1.62	1.57	1.54	1.51	1.47	1.41	1.34	1.24
60	.001	11.97	7.76	6.17	5.31	4.76	4.37	3.87	3.31	2.69	1.90
	.005	8.49	5.80	4.73	4.14	3.76	3.49	3.13	2.74	2.29	1.69
	.01	7.08	4.98	4.13	3.65	3.34	3.12	2.82	2.50	2.12	1.60
	.025	5.29	3.93	3.34	3.01	2.79	2.63	2.41	2.17	1.88	1.48
	.05	4.00	3.15	2.76	2.52	2.37	2.25	2.10	1.92	1.70	1.39
	.10	2.79	2.39	2.18	2.04	1.95	1.87	1.77	1.66	1.51	1.29
	.20	1.68	1.65	1.59	1.55	1.51	1.48	1.44	1.38	1.31	1.18
120	.001	11.38	7.31	5.79	4.95	4.42	4.04	3.55	3.02	2.40	1.56
	.005	8.18	5.54	4.50	3.92	3.55	3.28	2.93	2.54	2.09	1.43
	.01	6.85	4.79	3.95	3.48	3.17	2.96	2.66	2.34	1.95	1.38
	.025	5.15	3.80	3.23	2.89	2.67	2.52	2.30	2.05	1.76	1.31
	.05	3.92	3.07	2.68	2.45	2.29	2.17	2.02	1.83	1.61	1.25
	.10	2.75	2.35	2.13	1.99	1.90	1.82	1.72	1.60	1.45	1.19
	.20	1.66	1.63	1.57	1.52	1.48	1.45	1.41	1.35	1.27	1.12
∞	.001	10.83	6.91	5.42	4.62	4.10	3.74	3.27	2.74	2.13	1.00
	.005	7.88	5.30	4.28	3.72	3.35	3.09	2.74	2.36	1.90	1.00
	.01	6.64	4.60	3.78	3.32	3.02	2.80	2.51	2.18	1.79	1.00
	.025	5.02	3.69	3.12	2.79	2.57	2.41	2.19	1.94	1.64	1.00
	.05	3.84	2.99	2.60	2.37	2.21	2.09	1.94	1.75	1.52	1.00
	.10	2.71	2.30	2.08	1.94	1.85	1.77	1.67	1.55	1.38	1.00
	.20	1.64	1.61	1.55	1.50	1.46	1.43	1.38	1.32	1.23	1.00

Source: Reproduced from Table V of R. A. Fisher and F. Yates, *Statistical Tables for Biological, Agricultural and Medical Research* (6th ed.), 1974, published by Longman Group UK Ltd., London (previously published by Oliver and Boyd Ltd., Edinburgh) and by permission of the authors and publishers. The 0.5% and 2.5% points are reproduced from "Tables of Percentage Points of the Inverted Beta (*F*) Distribution," *Biometrika*, vol. 33 (April 1943), pp. 73–88, by permission of the Biometrika Trustees, Imperial College of Science, Technology, and Medicine, London, England.

TABLE B.4 χ² Values Needed for Significance at Various *p* Levels

df	Probability													
	.99	.98	.95	.90	.80	.70	.50	.30	.20	.10	.05	.02	.01	.001
1	.0³157	.0³628	.00393	.0158	.0642	.148	.455	1.074	1.642	2.706	3.841	5.412	6.635	10.827
2	.0201	.0404	.103	.211	.446	.713	1.386	2.408	3.219	4.605	5.991	7.824	9.210	13.815
3	.115	.185	.352	.584	1.005	1.424	2.366	3.665	4.642	6.251	7.815	9.837	11.345	16.268
4	.297	.429	.711	1.064	1.649	2.195	3.357	4.878	5.989	7.779	9.488	11.668	13.277	18.465
5	.554	.752	1.145	1.610	2.343	3.000	4.351	6.064	7.289	9.236	11.070	13.388	15.086	20.517
6	.872	1.134	1.635	2.204	3.070	3.828	5.348	7.231	8.558	10.645	12.592	15.033	16.812	22.457
7	1.239	1.564	2.167	2.833	3.822	4.671	6.346	8.383	9.803	12.017	14.067	16.622	18.475	24.322
8	1.646	2.032	2.733	3.490	4.594	5.527	7.344	9.524	11.030	13.362	15.507	18.168	20.090	26.125
9	2.088	2.532	3.325	4.168	5.380	6.393	8.343	10.656	12.242	14.684	16.919	19.679	21.666	27.877
10	2.558	3.059	3.940	4.865	6.179	7.267	9.342	11.781	13.442	15.987	18.307	21.161	23.209	29.588
11	3.053	3.609	4.575	5.578	6.989	8.148	10.341	12.899	14.631	17.275	19.675	22.618	24.725	31.264
12	3.571	4.178	5.226	6.304	7.807	9.034	11.340	14.011	15.812	18.549	21.026	24.054	26.217	32.909
13	4.107	4.765	5.892	7.042	8.634	9.926	12.340	15.119	16.985	19.812	22.362	25.472	27.688	34.528
14	4.660	5.368	6.571	7.790	9.467	10.821	13.339	16.222	18.151	21.064	23.685	26.873	29.141	36.123
15	5.229	5.985	7.261	8.547	10.307	11.721	14.339	17.322	19.311	22.307	24.996	28.259	30.578	37.697
16	5.812	6.614	7.962	9.312	11.152	12.624	15.338	18.418	20.465	23.542	26.296	29.633	32.000	39.252
17	6.408	7.255	8.672	10.085	12.002	13.531	16.338	19.511	21.615	24.769	27.587	30.995	33.409	40.790
18	7.015	7.906	9.390	10.865	12.857	14.440	17.338	20.601	22.760	25.989	28.869	32.346	34.805	42.312
19	7.633	8.567	10.117	11.651	13.716	15.352	18.338	21.689	23.900	27.204	30.144	33.687	36.191	43.820
20	8.260	9.237	10.851	12.443	14.578	16.266	19.337	22.775	25.038	28.412	31.410	35.020	37.566	45.315
21	8.897	9.915	11.591	13.240	15.445	17.182	20.337	23.858	26.171	29.615	32.671	36.343	38.932	46.797
22	9.542	10.600	12.338	14.041	16.314	18.101	21.337	24.939	27.301	30.813	33.924	37.659	40.289	48.268
23	10.196	11.293	13.091	14.848	17.187	19.021	22.337	26.018	28.429	32.007	35.172	38.968	41.638	49.728
24	10.856	11.992	13.848	15.659	18.062	19.943	23.337	27.096	29.553	33.196	36.415	40.270	42.980	51.179
25	11.524	12.697	14.611	16.473	18.940	20.867	24.337	28.172	30.675	34.382	37.652	41.566	44.314	52.620
26	12.198	13.409	15.379	17.292	19.820	21.792	25.336	29.246	31.795	35.563	38.885	42.856	45.642	54.052
27	12.879	14.125	16.151	18.114	20.703	22.719	26.336	30.319	32.912	36.741	40.113	44.140	46.963	55.476
28	13.565	14.847	16.928	18.939	21.588	23.647	27.336	31.391	34.027	37.916	41.337	45.419	48.278	56.893
29	14.256	15.574	17.708	19.768	22.475	24.577	28.336	32.461	35.139	39.087	42.557	46.693	49.588	58.302
30	14.953	16.306	18.493	20.599	23.364	25.508	29.336	33.530	36.250	40.256	43.773	47.962	50.892	59.703

Source: Reproduced from Table III of R. A. Fisher, *Statistical Methods for Research Workers*, copyright by Oxford University Press, England. Used by permission of Oxford University Press (originally published by Oliver and Boyd, Ltd.).

TABLE B.5	*r* Values Needed for Significance at Various *p* Levels

	Probability level				
(N–2)	.10	.05	.02	.01	.001
1	.988	.997	.9995	.9999	1.000
2	.900	.950	.980	.990	.999
3	.805	.878	.934	.959	.991
4	.729	.811	.882	.917	.974
5	.669	.754	.833	.874	.951
6	.622	.707	.789	.834	.925
7	.582	.666	.750	.798	.898
8	.549	.632	.716	.765	.872
9	.522	.602	.685	.735	.847
10	.497	.576	.658	.708	.823
11	.476	.553	.634	.684	.801
12	.458	.532	.612	.661	.780
13	.441	.514	.592	.641	.760
14	.426	.497	.574	.623	.742
15	.412	.482	.558	.606	.725
16	.400	.468	.542	.590	.708
17	.389	.456	.528	.575	.693
18	.378	.444	.516	.561	.679
19	.369	.433	.503	.549	.665
20	.360	.423	.492	.537	.652
22	.344	.404	.472	.515	.629
24	.330	.388	.453	.496	.607
25	.323	.381	.445	.487	.597
30	.296	.349	.409	.449	.554
35	.275	.325	.381	.418	.519
40	.257	.304	.358	.393	.490
45	.243	.288	.338	.372	.465
50	.231	.273	.322	.354	.443
55	.220	.261	.307	.338	.424
60	.211	.250	.295	.325	.408
65	.203	.240	.284	.312	.393
70	.195	.232	.274	.302	.380
75	.189	.224	.264	.292	.368
80	.183	.217	.256	.283	.357
85	.178	.211	.249	.275	.347
90	.173	.205	.242	.267	.338
95	.168	.200	.236	.260	.329
100	.164	.195	.230	.254	.321
125	.147	.174	.206	.228	.288
150	.134	.159	.189	.208	.264
175	.124	.148	.174	.194	.248
200	.116	.138	.164	.181	.235
300	.095	.113	.134	.148	.188
500	.074	.088	.104	.115	.148
1000	.052	.062	.073	.081	.104
2000	.037	.044	.052	.058	.074

Note: All *p* values are two-tailed in this table.

Source: Reproduced from *Some Extensions of Student's* t *and Pearson's* r *Central Distributions* by A. L. Sockloff and J. N. Edney, May 1972, Temple University Technical Report 72–5, Measurement and Research Center, with the permission of Alan Sockloff.

Introduction to Meta-Analysis

UTILITY OF META-ANALYSIS

Meta-analysis, a term coined by Gene V Glass (1976), is the use of statistical techniques to sum up a body of similar studies. Meta-analytic techniques have begun to be used widely in behavioral science, medical research, physics, and other fields. Thus students in almost all fields of science are likely to come across meta-analytic reviews of research results even in a casual perusal of the journal literature.

For example, in a classic meta-analysis, psychologists Mary Lee Smith and Gene Glass (1977) synthesized the results of nearly 400 controlled evaluations of psychotherapy and counseling. They coded and systematically analyzed each study for the kind of experimental and control treatments used and the results obtained. They were able to show that, on the average, the typical psychotherapy client was better off than 75% of the untreated "control" individuals.

A more recent example is a two-volume, multiauthored meta-analysis based on a review of randomized controlled clinical trials in perinatal medicine (see report by Mann, 1990). As a consequence of meta-analyzing more than 3,000 studies, the authors were able to document the practical benefits of certain clinical procedures (e.g., vacuum extraction rather than forceps) and the practical costs of others (e.g., repeating caesarean sections routinely).

Although meta-analysts use a number of more advanced techniques, we will concentrate on some basic techniques that incorporate the fundamental tools discussed earlier in this book. We begin by describing the rationale for comparing effect sizes within the context of all scientists' awareness of the importance of replication (see Chapter 6). Students interested in a more detailed discussion of meta-analysis will find a comprehensive overview in Cooper and Hedges's *Handbook of Research Synthesis* (1994) and specialized accounts in a number of basic and advanced texts (e.g., Cooper, 1989; Glass, McGaw, & Smith, 1981; Hedges &

Olkin, 1985; Hunter & Schmidt, 1990; Light & Pillemer, 1984; Mullen & Rosenthal, 1985; Rosenthal, 1991a; Rosenthal & Rosnow, 1991).

REPLICATION AND META-ANALYSIS

Smith and Glass (1977) reported their meta-analytic observations in terms of the "average" effect sizes (but not the simple arithmetic average, as we will show in a moment). The reason why scientists who do this kind of synthesizing work are usually more interested in effect sizes than in p values is illustrated in Table C.1 (Rosenthal, 1990c). Set A shows two results, with the p values both rejecting the null (i.e., both p's = .05) and with a difference in effect sizes of .30 in units of r (i.e., .50 − .20 = .30). The fact that both studies were able to reject the null and at exactly the same p level is a function of sample size, whereas the difference in effect sizes implies the degree of failure to replicate. Set B shows two studies with different p values, one significant at $p < .05$ and the other not significant; the two effect sizes, on the other hand, are in excellent agreement.

The meta-analyst would say, accordingly, that Set B shows more successful replication than does Set A. Set C shows two studies differing markedly in both level of significance and magnitude (and direction) of effect size. Observe that one of the effects is reported as a "negative" r, which in the language of meta-analysis tells us that this result was not in the same direction as the other result. Set C, then, is a not very subtle example of a clear failure to replicate. That the combined probabilities of all three sets are identical to one another (combined $p = .0028$) tells us that the pooled significance level is uninformative in differentiating successful from unsuccessful sets of replication studies.

Another way of looking at the effect size results is illustrated in Figure C.1, which shows the "replication plane" generated by crossing the effect size r of the first study with the results of the second study. All perfect replications (i.e., those

TABLE C.1	Comparison of Three Sets of Replications					
	Set A		Set B		Set C	
	Study 1	Study 2	Study 1	Study 2	Study 1	Study 2
N	96	15	98	27	12	32
p level (two-tailed)	.05	.05	.01	.18	.000001	.33
r (effect size index)	.20	.50	.26	.26	.72	−.18
Combined p (one-tailed)	.0028		.0028		.0028	

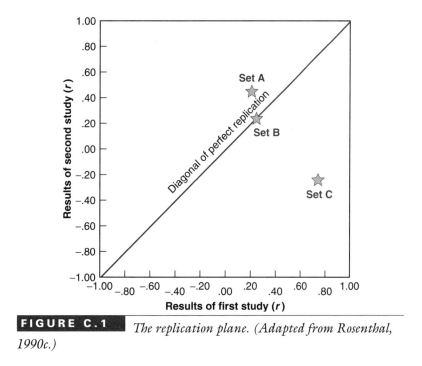

FIGURE C.1 *The replication plane. (Adapted from Rosenthal, 1990c.)*

in which the effect sizes in the two studies are identical) fall on a diagonal rising from the lower left corner $(-1.0, -1.0)$ to the upper right corner $(+1.0, +1.0)$. The results of the studies in Set B from Table C.1 are shown to fall exactly on the diagonal of perfect replication $(+.26, +.26)$. The results of Set A are shown to fall somewhat above the line representing perfect replication.

This diagram shows that, although Set B reflects more successful replication than Set A, Set A is also located fairly close to the line and is therefore a "fairly successful" replication set as well. The results of Set C, however, are shown to fall rather far from the diagonal of perfect replication.

COMPARING TWO EFFECT SIZES

So far, we have examined the results of separate but similar studies, and we now describe how the meta-analyst might use statistical techniques in this process. Before synthesizing the effect sizes of separate studies, the meta-analyst usually finds it instructive to compare the results to learn the degree of their actual similarity. One approach is to define effect size r's as dissimilar *(heterogeneous)* if they are significantly different from one another, and to define them as similar *(homogeneous)* if they are not significantly different from one another.

In statistical terms, such significance testing involves (1) giving the r's the same sign if both studies show effects in the same direction, but different signs if the results are in the opposite direction; (2) finding for each r the associated "Fisher z"

z	.00	.01	.02	.03	.04	.05	.06	.07	.08	.09
TABLE C.2	Fisher z Transformations of r									
.0	.000	.010	.020	.030	.040	.050	.060	.070	.080	.090
.1	.100	.110	.119	.129	.139	.149	.159	.168	.178	.187
.2	.197	.207	.216	.226	.236	.245	.254	.264	.273	.282
.3	.291	.300	.310	.319	.327	.336	.345	.354	.363	.371
.4	.380	.389	.397	.405	.414	.422	.430	.438	.446	.454
.5	.462	.470	.478	.485	.493	.500	.508	.515	.523	.530
.6	.537	.544	.551	.558	.565	.572	.578	.585	.592	.598
.7	.604	.611	.617	.623	.629	.635	.641	.647	.653	.658
.8	.664	.670	.675	.680	.686	.691	.696	.701	.706	.711
.9	.716	.721	.726	.731	.735	.740	.744	.749	.753	.757
1.0	.762	.766	.770	.774	.778	.782	.786	.790	.793	.797
1.1	.800	.804	.808	.811	.814	.818	.821	.824	.828	.831
1.2	.834	.837	.840	.843	.846	.848	.851	.854	.856	.859
1.3	.862	.864	.867	.869	.872	.874	.876	.879	.881	.883
1.4	.885	.888	.890	.892	.894	.896	.898	.900	.902	.903
1.5	.905	.907	.909	.910	.912	.914	.915	.917	.919	.920
1.6	.922	.923	.925	.926	.928	.929	.930	.932	.933	.934
1.7	.935	.937	.938	.939	.940	.941	.942	.944	.945	.946
1.8	.947	.948	.949	.950	.951	.952	.953	.954	.954	.955
1.9	.956	.957	.958	.959	.960	.960	.961	.962	.963	.963
2.0	.964	.965	.965	.966	.967	.967	.968	.969	.969	.970
2.1	.970	.971	.972	.972	.973	.973	.974	.974	.975	.975
2.2	.976	.976	.977	.977	.978	.978	.978	.979	.979	.980
2.3	.980	.980	.981	.981	.982	.982	.982	.983	.983	.983
2.4	.984	.984	.984	.985	.985	.985	.986	.986	.986	.986
2.5	.987	.987	.987	.987	.988	.988	.988	.988	.989	.989
2.6	.989	.989	.989	.990	.990	.990	.990	.990	.991	.991
2.7	.991	.991	.991	.992	.992	.992	.992	.992	.992	.992
2.8	.993	.993	.993	.993	.993	.993	.993	.994	.994	.994
2.9	.994	.994	.994	.994	.994	.995	.995	.995	.995	.995

Source: Reproduced from *Statistical Methods* (8th ed.) by G.W. Snedecor and W.G. Cochran, 1989, Iowa State University Press. Used by permission of Iowa State University Press.

value; and (3) substituting in the following formula to find the standard normal deviate:

$$Z = \frac{z_1 - z_2}{\sqrt{\dfrac{1}{N_1 - 3} + \dfrac{1}{N_2 - 3}}}$$

where Fisher z (i.e., lowercase z to differentiate this statistic from the uppercase Z denoting the standard normal deviate, described in Chapter 10) refers to a set of log transformations of r as shown in Tables C.2 and C.3. The quantity $N - 3$ corresponds to the degrees of freedom for each z. The final step (4) is to look up the result in a table of standard normal deviates (Z's) such as Table B.1 in Appendix B. Let us try some examples.

TABLE C.3		Transformations of *r* to Fisher *z*							
				Second Digit of *r*					
r	.00	.01	.02	.03	.04	.05	.06	.07	.08	.09
.0	.000	.010	.020	.030	.040	.050	.060	.070	.080	.090
.1	.100	.110	.121	.131	.141	.151	.161	.172	.182	.192
.2	.203	.213	.224	.234	.245	.255	.266	.277	.288	.299
.3	.310	.321	.332	.343	.354	.365	.377	.388	.400	.412
.4	.424	.436	.448	.460	.472	.485	.497	.510	.523	.536
.5	.549	.563	.576	.590	.604	.618	.633	.648	.662	.678
.6	.693	.709	.725	.741	.758	.775	.793	.811	.829	.848
.7	.867	.887	.908	.929	.950	.973	.996	1.020	1.045	1.071
.8	1.099	1.127	1.157	1.188	1.221	1.256	1.293	1.333	1.376	1.422

				Third Digit of *r*					
r	.000	.001	.002	.003	.004	.005	.006	.007	.008	.009
.90	1.472	1.478	1.483	1.488	1.494	1.499	1.505	1.510	1.516	1.522
.91	1.528	1.533	1.539	1.545	1.551	1.557	1.564	1.570	1.576	1.583
.92	1.589	1.596	1.602	1.609	1.616	1.623	1.630	1.637	1.644	1.651
.93	1.658	1.666	1.673	1.681	1.689	1.697	1.705	1.713	1.721	1.730
.94	1.738	1.747	1.756	1.764	1.774	1.783	1.792	1.802	1.812	1.822
.95	1.832	1.842	1.853	1.863	1.874	1.886	1.897	1.909	1.921	1.933
.96	1.946	1.959	1.972	1.986	2.000	2.014	2.029	2.044	2.060	2.076
.97	2.092	2.109	2.127	2.146	2.165	2.185	2.205	2.227	2.249	2.273
.98	2.298	2.323	2.351	2.380	2.410	2.443	2.477	2.515	2.555	2.599
.99	2.646	2.700	2.759	2.826	2.903	2.994	3.106	3.250	3.453	3.800

Source: Reproduced from *Statistical Methods* (8th ed.) by G.W. Snedecor and W.G. Cochran, 1989, Iowa State University Press. Used by permission of Iowa State University Press.

Example 1. Suppose you have used 100 subjects to try to replicate an experiment that reported a large effect ($r = .50$) based on only 10 subjects. You find a smaller sized effect ($r = .31$), but it is in the opposite direction of the one previously reported. You code your effect as negative to reflect the fact that it is in the opposite direction, and then consult Table C.3 to find the Fisher *z* corresponding to each *r*. For $r = .50$, you find $z = .549$ at the intersection of the row labeled ".5" and the column labeled ".00." For $r = -.31$, the Fisher *z* is found at the intersection of the row labeled ".3" and the column labeled ".01" (where the value of *z* is shown as .321), which you note as $-.321$ because your result is in the "wrong" direction.

Next, from the previous equation you compute

$$Z = \frac{z_1 - z_2}{\sqrt{\dfrac{1}{N_1 - 3} + \dfrac{1}{N_2 - 3}}} = \frac{(.549) - (-.321)}{\sqrt{\dfrac{1}{7} + \dfrac{1}{97}}} = \frac{.870}{.391} = 2.22$$

as the *Z* of the difference between the two effect sizes. Finally, looking up the *p* value associated with a *Z* of 2.22 in Table B.1 (page 382), you find $p = .0132$ one-tailed, which you can round to .01 one-tailed or .03 two-tailed (i.e., .0132 × 2 = .03 rounded). The *p* value is small enough to convince you that your result differs from the original one significantly and therefore should not be combined with it without careful thought and comment. For example, in describing the results of both studies considered together, we should report the differences between them and try to think of an explanation for their differences.

Example 2. Alternatively, suppose your result is in the same direction as the original one and of a similar magnitude, and you have used the same number of subjects. This time, imagine that the original effect size was $r = .45$ ($N = 120$) and your effect size is $r = .40$ ($N = 120$). Following the same procedure as in Example 1, you find in Table C.3 the Fisher *z*'s corresponding to these *r*'s to be .485 and .424, respectively.

From the preceding equation you compute

$$Z = \frac{z_1 - z_2}{\sqrt{\dfrac{1}{N_1 - 3} + \dfrac{1}{N_2 - 3}}} = \frac{.485 - .424}{\sqrt{\dfrac{1}{117} + \dfrac{1}{117}}} = \frac{.061}{.131} = .47$$

as your obtained *Z* of the difference. In Table B.1 you find the *p* associated with $Z = .47$ to be .3192 one-tailed. Here, then, is an example of two studies that do not disagree significantly in their estimates of the size of the relation between variables *X* and *Y*. They can now be routinely combined by means of a simple meta-analytic technique, as shown next.

COMBINING TWO EFFECT SIZES

Given two effect size *r*'s that are combinable on statistical and/or logical grounds, the formula to be used again employs the Fisher *z* transformation:

$$\bar{z} = \frac{z_1 + z_2}{2}$$

in which the denominator is the number of *z* scores in the numerator; the resulting value is an average (or $\bar{z}$). Example 3 shows how this number crunching proceeds.

Example 3. In Example 2, one $r = .45$ and the other $r = .40$ (both coded as "positive" to show that both results were in the predicted direction). You found the Fisher *z*'s corresponding to these *r*'s to be .485 and .424, respectively. From the equation above you compute

$$\bar{z} = \frac{z_1 + z_2}{2} = \frac{.485 + .424}{2} = .45$$

as the mean Fisher *z*. Looking in Table C.2, you find that a Fisher *z* of .45 is associated with an *r* of .422, which is the effect size estimate of the two studies combined.

COMPARING TWO SIGNIFICANCE LEVELS

Meta-analysts are usually more interested in effect sizes than in p values, but they sometimes evaluate the overall level of significance as a way of increasing power. It is again instructive to find out whether the individual values are homogeneous and therefore combinable without special thought and comment. To make such a comparison, the meta-analyst first obtains an accurate p level—accurate, say, to two digits (not counting zeros before the first nonzero value), such as $p = .43$ or $.024$ or $.0012$. That is, if t with 30 $df = 3.03$, we give p as $.0025$, not as "$p < .05$." Extended tables of the t distribution, such as the one in Appendix B (see Table B.2), are helpful here, but it is even more helpful to have a calculator that spits out accurate p's at the touch of a couple of buttons.

For each p the meta-analyst then finds Z (i.e., not the Fisher z, but the standard normal deviate Z). The table of Z's (Table B.1) will be useful if the meta-analyst does not have a calculator that gives accurate values of p. Both p's should also be one-tailed, and we give the corresponding Z's the same sign if both studies showed effects in the same direction, but different signs if the results are in the opposite direction. The difference between the two Z's when divided by $\sqrt{2}$ yields a new Z. This new Z corresponds to the p value of the difference between the Z's if the null hypothesis were true (i.e., if the two Z's did not really differ).

Recapping,

$$Z = \frac{Z_1 - Z_2}{\sqrt{2}}$$

is distributed as Z, so we can enter this newly calculated Z in a table of standard normal deviates to find the p value associated with a Z of the size obtained or larger.

Example 4. Suppose that studies A and B yield results in opposite directions, and neither is "significant." One p is $.075$ one-tailed, and the other p is $.109$ one-tailed but in the opposite tail. The Z's corresponding to these p's are found in Table B.1 to be $+1.44$ and -1.23 (note the opposite signs which indicate results in opposite directions). Then, from our equation we have

$$Z = \frac{Z_1 - Z_2}{\sqrt{2}} = \frac{(1.44) - (-1.23)}{\sqrt{2}} = \frac{2.67}{1.41} = 1.89$$

as the Z of the difference between the two p values or their corresponding Z's. The p value associated with a Z of 1.89 is $.0294$ one-tailed (rounded to $.03$). The two p values may thus be seen to differ significantly (or nearly so, if we used the two-tailed p of $.0294 \times 2 = .0588$), suggesting that the results in terms of the p values of the two studies are heterogeneous even when we allow for normal sampling fluctuations. Thus the p levels should not be combined without special thought and comment.

Example 5.   Alternatively, suppose that Studies A and B yield results in the same direction. However, although the p levels appear to be very similar, one result is called "significant" by the author of A because $p = .05$, and the other is called "not significant" by the author of B because $p = .07$. The Z's corresponding to these p's are 1.64 and 1.47. From our equation we have

$$Z = \frac{Z_1 - Z_2}{\sqrt{2}} = \frac{1.64 - 1.47}{\sqrt{2}} = \frac{.17}{1.41} = .12$$

as our obtained Z of the difference between a p value of .05 and one of .07. The p value associated with $Z = .12$ is .4522 one-tailed, and thus shows clearly (as noted in Chapter 10) just how trivial the conventional line of demarcation between "significant" and "nonsignificant" results sometimes is.

COMBINING TWO SIGNIFICANCE LEVELS

After we compare the results of two separate studies, it is an easy matter to combine the p levels. In this way, we get an overall estimate of the probability that the two p levels might have been obtained if the null hypothesis of no relation between X and Y were true. To perform these calculations, we modify the numerator of the formula for comparing p values that we just described. We obtain accurate p levels for each of our two studies and then find the Z corresponding to each of these p levels. Also as before, both p's must be given in one-tailed form, and the corresponding Z's will have the same sign if both studies show effects in the same direction and will have different signs if the results are in the opposite direction.

The only change in the previous equation is to add the Z values instead of subtracting them:

$$Z = \frac{Z_1 + Z_2}{\sqrt{2}}$$

That is, the sum of the two Z's when divided by $\sqrt{2}$ yields a new Z. This new Z corresponds to the p value of the two studies combined if the null hypothesis of no relation between X and Y were true.

Example 6.   As an illustration, suppose studies A and B yield homogeneous results in the same direction but neither is significant. One p is .121, and the other is .084; their associated Z's are 1.17 and 1.38, respectively. From the preceding equation we have

$$Z = \frac{Z_1 + Z_2}{\sqrt{2}} = \frac{1.17 + 1.38}{\sqrt{2}} = \frac{2.55}{1.41} = 1.81$$

as our combined Z. The p associated with this Z is .035 one-tailed (or .07 two-tailed).

COMPARING AND COMBINING MORE THAN TWO EFFECT SIZES AND SIGNIFICANCE LEVELS

As might be expected, we will often want to compare or to combine more than two effect sizes or significance levels. The procedures required are quite similar in spirit to the procedures described in this appendix (see, e.g., Rosenthal, 1991a; Rosenthal & Rosnow, 1991).

THE FILE DRAWER PROBLEM

Because many journal editors are reluctant to accept "nonsignificant" results, researchers' file drawers may contain unpublished studies that failed to yield significant results. If there were a substantial number of such studies in the file drawers, the meta-analyst's evaluation of the overall significance level may be unduly optimistic (see, e.g., Bakan, 1967; McNemar, 1960; Sterling, 1959). One solution to this problem is to calculate the number of studies averaging null results that would be required to push the significance level for all studies, retrieved and unretrieved combined, to the "wrong" side of $p = .05$ (Rosenthal, 1979, 1983, 1991a). If the

TABLE C.4	Tolerances for Future Null Results as a Function of the Original Average Level of Significance per Study and the Number of Studies Summarized		

Number of Studies Summarized	Original Average Significance Level		
	.05	.01	.001
1	1	2	4
2	4	8	15
3	9	18	32
4	16	32	57
5	25	50	89
6	36	72	128
7	49	98	173
8	64	128	226
9	81	162	286
10	100	200	353
15	225	450	795
20	400	800	1412
25	625	1250	2206
30	900	1800	3177
40	1600	3200	5648
50	2500	5000	8824

Note: Entries in this table are the total number of old and new studies required to bring an original average p of .05, .01, or .001 down to $p > .05$ (i.e., just barely to "nonsignificance").

overall significance computed on the basis of the retrieved studies can be brought down to the wrong side of p (i.e., $p > .05$) by the addition of just a few more null results, then the original estimate of p is clearly *not robust* (i.e., not resistant to the file drawer threat).

Table C.4 illustrates such a calculation. It shows a table of "tolerance" values in which the rows represent the number of retrieved studies and the columns represent three different levels of the average statistical significance of the retrieved studies. The intersection of any row and column shows the sum of old and new studies required to bring the combined p value for all studies, retrieved and unretrieved combined, down to the level of being just barely "nonsignificant" at $p > .05$. Suppose we meta-analyzed 8 studies and found the average p value to be .05. The 64 that is shown tells us that it will take an additional 56 unretrieved studies averaging null results to bring the original average $p = .05$ based on 8 studies (i.e., $64 - 8 = 56$) down to $p > .05$.

As a general rule of thumb, it has been suggested that we regard as robust any combined results for which the tolerance level reaches $5k + 10$, where k is the number of studies retrieved (Rosenthal, 1991a). In our example of 8 studies retrieved, this means that we will be satisfied that the original estimate of $p = .05$ is robust if we feel that there are fewer than an additional $5(8) + 10 = 50$ studies with null results squirreled away in file drawers. Because Table C.4 shows a tolerance for an additional 56 studies, it appears to us that the original estimate is indeed robust.

Glossary

Note: Indicated in parentheses is the primary chapter(s) or appendix where each term is discussed.

A-B design Simplest $N = 1$ design, in which the dependent variable is measured throughout the pretreatment or baseline period (the A phase) and the treatment period (the B phase). (8)

A-B-A design $N = 1$ design in which there are repeated measures before the treatment (the A phase), during the treatment (the B phase), and then with the treatment withdrawn (the final A phase). (8)

A-B-A-B design $N = 1$ design in which there are two types of occasions (B to A and A to B) for demonstrating the effects of the treatment variable. (8)

A-B-BC-B design $N = 1$ design in which there are repeated measurements before the introduction of the treatments (the A phase), then during Treatment B, during the combination of Treatments B and C, and finally during Treatment B alone; the purpose of the design is to tease out the effect of B both in combination with C and apart from C. (8)

Abscissa The horizontal axis of a distribution. (10)

Absolute deviation An unsigned deviation from the mean. (10)

Acceptability Stage 3 of discovery, in which a working hypothesis is fashioned according to the criteria of correspondence with reality, a combination of coherence and parsimony, and falsifiability. (2)

Accidental plagiarism Unwittingly falling into plagiarism. (Appendix A).

Accounting for conflicting results One of several possible scenarios for coming up with an innovative idea. (2)

Acquiescent response set The tendency of individuals to go along with any request or attitudinal statement. (5)

Active deception See *Deception research.*

Additive model The components sum to the group means in ANOVA. (14)

Ad hoc hypothesis A conjecture or speculation developed on the spot to explain a result. (1)

Aesthetics The idea that intellectual beauty is one criterion of accepted truths. (1)

After-only designs A class of research designs in which subjects' reactions are measured after the treatment or control procedure. (7)

Aggregate reliability See *Effective reliability.*

Algebraic deviation A signed deviation from the mean. (10)

Alpha (α) Probability of a Type I error; synonyms include *significance level* and *p value.* (12)

Alpha coefficient See *Cronbach's alpha.*

Alternate hypothesis The experimental hypothesis, symbolized as H_1. (12)

Analysis of variance *(ANOVA)* Subdivision of the total variance of a set of scores into its components. (14)

Ancestry approach Looking up the work from which the current work descended. (2)

ANOVA See *Analysis of variance.*

APA ethics code A set of principles, developed by the American Psychological Association, to help researchers and review boards decide what aspects of a study might pose an ethical problem. (3)

a priori method The use of individual powers of pure reason and logic to explain why events occur the way they do (Charles Peirce). (1)

Archive A relatively permanent repository of data or material. (4)

Area probability sampling A type of survey sampling in which the subclasses are geographic areas. (9)

Arithmetic mean Arithmetic average. (10)

Artifacts Specific threats to validity, or confounded aspects of the scientist's observations. (7)

Average deviation An index of the average distance of all the scores in a series from the mean of the series. (10)

Back translation Method used in cross-cultural research in which the researcher has one bilingual person translate the questionnaire items from the source to the target language and then has another bi-

lingual person independently translate the items back into the source language. The researcher then compares the original with the twice-translated version to see whether anything important was lost in the translation. (4)

Baseline See *Behavioral baseline.*

Before-after designs A class of research designs in which subjects' reactions are measured both before and after they have undergone the experimental manipulation or a control procedure. (7)

Behavior What someone does or how someone acts. (1)

Behavioral baseline A comparison base, operationally defined as the continuous, and continuing, performance of a single individual in small-N research. (8)

Behavioral science An umbrella term that encompasses scientific disciplines in which empirical inquiry is used to study motivation, cognition, and behavior. (1)

BESD See *Binomial effect-size display.*

Beta (β) Probability of a Type II error. (12)

Between-subjects designs Statistical designs in which the sampling units (e.g., the research participants) are exposed to one treatment each. (7)

Between variability The variability between scores in two or more samples. (14)

Bias Net systematic error; see also *Nonresponse bias* and *Volunteer bias.* (6)

Bias due to nonresponse See *Nonresponse bias.*

Biasedness The extent to which sample values deviate from the true population value. (9)

Big-five factors A collective name for five broad domains of individual personality (surgency, ageeableness, conscientiousness, emotional stability, and openness to experience). (5)

Bimodal A distribution showing two modes. (10)

Binomial effect-size display (BESD) Procedure for the display of the practical importance of an effect size correlation *(r)* of any particular magnitude. (12, 13)

Bipolar scale Rating scale in which the ends of the scale are extreme opposites. (5)

Blind experimenters Experimenters who are unaware of which subjects receive the experimental and control treatments. (7)

Blindness to a relationship A way of characterizing the result of making a Type II error. (12)

Captive subjects A sample consisting of available (as opposed to volunteer) research participants. (6)

Causal inference The act or process of inferring that *X* causes *Y*. (7, 8)

Ceiling effect Situation in which the amount of change that can be produced is limited by the upper boundary of the measure. (5)

Central tendency Location of the bulk of a distribution; measured by means, medians, modes, and trimmed means. (10)

Central tendency bias A type of response set in which the respondent is reluctant to give extreme ratings and instead tends to rate in the direction of the mean of the total group. (5)

Chance errors See *Random errors.*

Checklist Method of counting the frequency of occurrence. (4)

Chi-square (χ^2) A statistic used to test the degree of agreement between the data actually obtained and those expected under a particular hypothesis (e.g., the null hypothesis). (15)

Closed items See *Structured items.*

Clusters Subpopulations in survey sampling. (9)

Coefficient of determination (r^2) Proportion of variance shared by two variables. (12)

Coherence of theories The extent to which the components of a theory "stick together" logically. (2)

Cohort A collection of individuals who were born in the same general period. (8)

Column effect Column mean minus grand mean. (14)

Concurrent validity The extent to which test results are correlated with some criterion in the present. (6)

Confounding The mixing up of the effect of one variable with the effect of another variable. (7)

Confounding of pretesting and *X* The mixing up of the effect of taking a pretest with the effect of the experimental treatment. (7)

Confounding of selection and *X* The mixing up of the volunteer status of the subjects or some other subject variable with the effect of the experimental treatment. (7)

Construct Abstract variable, formulated from ideas or images, that serves as an explanatory concept. (2, 6)

Construct validation The procedure by which a means is devised to measure a construct and is then related to the subjects' performance in a variety of other aspects as the construct implies. (6)

Construct validity A type of test or research validity that addresses the psychological qualities contributing to the relation between *X* and *Y*. (6)

Content analysis A method of categorizing communication content based on frequency of occurrence. (4)

Content validity A type of test validity that addresses whether the test adequately samples the relevant material. (6)

Contingency table A table of frequencies (counts) coded by row and column variables. (11, 15)

Continuous variable A variable for which we can imagine another value falling between any two adjacent scores. (11)

Contrived observation Unobtrusive observation of the effects of some variable that was introduced into a situation. (4)

Control group A condition with which the effects of the experimental or test conditions are compared. (1, 7, 8)

Convergent validity Validity supported by a substantial correlation of conceptually similar measures. (6)

Corrected range See *Extended range.*

Correlated *t* See *Matched t.*

Correlation Degree of relation between variables. (11)

Correlational designs A class of quasi-experimental designs. (8)

Correlation coefficient An index of the degree of association between two variables, typically Pearson *r* or related product–moment correlation. (6, 11)

Correspondence with reality The extent to which a hypothesis agrees with accepted truths based on reliable empirical findings. (2)

Cost–benefit analysis An evaluation of the ethical and/or methodological pros and cons of studies. (3)

Counterbalancing A procedure in which some subjects receive Treatment A before Treatment B, and the others receive B before A. (7)

Counts Frequencies. (11, 15)

Covariation rule The principle that, in order to demonstrate causality, what is labeled as the *cause* should be shown to be positively correlated with what is labeled as the *effect.* (7)

Covary To have variations (in one variable) that are correlated with variations in another variable. (7)

Criterion validity The extent to which a measure correlates with one or more criterion variables. (6)

Critical incident technique Open-ended method that instructs the respondent to describe an observable action the purpose of which is fairly clear to the respondent and the consequences of which are sufficiently definite to leave little doubt about its effects. (5)

Cronbach's alpha A measure of internal-consistency reliability; also called the *alpha coefficient.* (6)

Cross-lagged correlations Correlations of the degree of association between two sets of variables, of which one is treated as a lagged value of the outcome variable. (8)

Cross-lagged panel design A relational research design using cross-lagged correlations, cross-sectional correlations repeated over time, and test–retest correlations. (8)

Cross-sectional design Research that takes a slice of time and compares subjects on one or more variables simultaneously. (8)

Crude range Highest score minus lowest score. (10)

Cue words Guiding labels that define particular points or categories of response. (5)

D The difference between scores or ranks. (13)

$\overline{D}$ The mean of a set of *D*'s. (13)

Debriefing Disclosing to subjects the nature of the research in which they have participated. (3)

Deception by commission Another name for active deception. (3)

Deception by omission Another name for passive deception. (3)

Deception research Any method of research in which the subjects are misled *(active deception)* or not informed *(passive deception)* about the nature of the investigation. (3)

Degrees of freedom The number of observations minus the number of restrictions limiting the observations' freedom to vary. (13, 14, 15)

Demand characteristics The mixture of various hints and cues that govern the subject's perception of his or her role and of the experimenter's hypothesis. (7)

Dependent variable A variable the changes in which are viewed as dependent on changes in one or more other (independent) variables. (2)

Descriptive and inferential formulas See *Descriptive statistical analysis* and *Inferential statistical analysis.*

Descriptive research Research in which the objective is to map out a situation or set of events. (1)

Descriptive statistical analysis Statistical techniques used to compute population values. (10)

Determinism See *Strict determinism.*

df Degrees of freedom. (13, 14, 15)

df **between conditions** Degrees of freedom for the means of conditions. (14)

df **error** Degrees of freedom for the denominator of the *F* ratio. (14)

df **within conditions** Degrees of freedom for observations within conditions. (14)

Diary See *Self-recorded diary.*

Dichotomous variable A variable that is divided into two classes. (11)

Discovery A term in the philosophy of science referring to the origin, creation, or invention of ideas for scientific justification. (2)

Discriminant validity Validity supported by a lack of correlation between conceptually unrelated measures. (6)

Dispersion Spread or variability. (10)

Distribution A visual display of relative frequencies over varying values of the independent variable. (10)

Double-blind Describing a condition in which neither experimenters nor subjects know who is in the experimental and control groups. (7)

Double deception A deception embedded in what the subject thinks is the official debriefing. (3)

Drunkard's search See *Principle of the drunkard's search.*

Dummy coding Giving arbitrary numerical values (often 0 and 1) to the two levels of a dichotomous variable. (11)

Ecological validity The extent to which an experimental situation reflects the outside world it is intended to represent. (6)

Effective reliability The composite (or aggregate) reliability of two or more judges' ratings. (6)

Effects See *Column effect, Residuals, Row effect.*

Effect size The magnitude of an experimental effect (i.e., the size of the relation between X and Y). (6, 12)

Efficient cause The propelling or instigating condition (i.e., the X that sets in motion or alters Y). (7)

Empirical inquiry Any procedure of controlled experience, observation, or experiment used to explain how or why events happen as they do. (1)

Empirical reasoning Reasoning that is aided by observation and measurement. (1)

Empirical validity. Another name for *Criterion validity.* (6)

Equal-appearing intervals method An attitude-scaling technique in which values are obtained for items on the assumption that the underlying intervals are equidistant; also called a *Thurstone scale.* (5)

Equivalent-forms reliability The extent to which different forms of a test are intercorrelated. (6)

Error Fluctuation in measurements; also, deviation of a score from the mean of the group or condition. (6, 9, 14)

Error of estimate Closeness of estimate to actual value. (9)

Error term The denominator of an *F* ratio in the analysis of variance. (14)

Ethical dilemma A conflict in values or moral standards. (3)

Ethics The system of moral values by which behavior is judged. (3)

Ethnography Field observation that documents the customs, habits, and actions of a group of people, usually a culture. (4)

Ethnomethodological research An ethnographic approach pioneered by Harold Garfinkel. (4)

Evaluation, potency, and activity The primary dimensions of subjective meaning that are usually measured by the semantic differential. (5)

E **values** See *Expected frequencies.*

Expectancy control design An experimental design in which the expectancy variable operates separately from the independent variable of interest. (7)

Expected frequencies Counts expected under specified row and column conditions if certain hypotheses (e.g., the null hypothesis) are true. (15)

Experimental group A group or condition in which the subjects undergo a manipulation or an intervention. (7)

Experimental hypothesis See *Working hypothesis.*

Experimental realism The extent to which the subject is drawn into or is affected by the treatment. (4)

Experimental research Research in which sampling units are assigned to conditions at random (also called *true experiments*); the term has also been applied to certain non-randomized designs described as *single-case experimental designs.* (1, 7, 8)

Experimenter-expectancy effect Experimenter artifact that results when the hypothesis held by the experimenter leads unintentionally to behavior toward the subjects that, in turn, increases the likelihood that the hypothesis will be confirmed (also called a *self-fulfilling prophecy*). (7)

Extended range Crude range plus one unit; also called the *corrected range.* (10)

External validity The degree of generalizability. (6, 7)

Face-to-face interview An interview in which the interviewer and the respondent directly interact with one another face to face. (5)

Face validity The extent to which a test seems on its surface to be measuring what it purports to measure. (6)

Factor A dimension. (7)

Factorial designs Statistical designs in which the effects of two or more variables can be evaluated simultaneously. (7, 14)

False-negative reports Failing to report information. (5)

Falsifiability The principle (advanced by Karl Popper) that a theoretical assertion is scientific only if it is stated in such a way that it can, if incorrect, be refuted by empirical tests. (2)

F **distributions** Family of distributions (curves) centered at $(df)/(df - 2)$ (where degrees of freedom are for the denominator of the F ratio) and ranging from zero to positive infinity. (14)

Field experimentation Experimental or quasi-experimental research that is done in a naturalistic setting. (4)

Field notes Observations recorded in a naturalistic setting. (4)

Final cause The end goal toward which a person or thing tends naturally to strive; also called *teleological cause* (Aristotle). (7)

Fisher's *z* transformation Transformation for Pearson r's, making equal differences equally detectable. (Appendix C)

Floor effect Situation in which the amount of change that can be produced is limited by the lower boundary of the measure. (5)

Flow diagram A graphic representation of a sequence of events or operations showing that one event or operation leads to another. (2)

Forced-choice Describing an item format that requires the respondent to select a single item (or a specified number of items) from a presented set of choices, even when the respondent finds none (or more than one) of the choices acceptable. (5)

Formal cause The implicit form or meaning of something (Aristotle). (7)

***F* ratios** Ratios of mean squares that are distributed as *F* when the null hypothesis is true. (14)

Free association method The subject tells whatever passes through his or her mind. (2)

Frequency Incidence of occurrence. (10)

Frequency polygon A set of data scores arranged according to incidence of occurrence. (10)

***F* test** A test of significance used to judge the tenability of the null hypothesis of no relation between two or more variables (or of no difference between two variabilities). (14)

Generic Meaning *general,* as in the generic questions used in ethnographic studies. (4)

Good subjects Research participants who seek to provide responses that will validate the experimenter's hypothesis. (7)

Grand mean The mean of means, or the mean of all observations. (14)

Graphic scales Rating scales in the form of a straight line with cue words attached. (5)

Halo effect A response set in which the bias results from the judge's overextending a favorable impression of someone, based on some central trait, to the person's other characteristics. (5)

Hawthorne effect The effect on research participants' behavior of merely being studied. (1)

Hedges's *g* An index of effect size in *Z*-score-like terms. (13)

Heterogeneity Dissimilarity among the elements of a set. (6)

Histogram A bar chart. (10)

Historical controls Comparison groups in which the subjects are recently examined patients with the same disorder as those subjects in the experimental group. (7)

History A plausible threat to internal validity when an event or incident that takes place between the premeasurement and the postmeasurement contaminates the results of research not employing randomization. (7)

Homogeneity Similarity among the elements of a set. (6)

Hypothesis A research idea that serves as a premise or supposition that organizes facts and guides observations. (2)

Improving on older ideas One of several possible scenarios for coming up with an innovative discovery. (2)

Independent samples The results in one group are not influenced by the results in another group. (13)

Independent variable A variable on which the dependent variable depends; in experiments, a variable that the experimenter manipulates to determine whether there are effects on another variable, the dependent variable. (2)

Inferential statistical analysis Statistical techniques used to estimate population values based on known sample values. (10)

Initial thinking The first stage in the development of a scientific hypothesis; this stage usually involves introspection and intuition. (2)

Institutional review board (IRB) A group set up to make *cost–benefit analyses* of proposed studies. (3)

Instrumentation A plausible threat to internal validity that occurs when changes in the measuring instrument (e.g., deterioration of the instrument) bias the results of research not using randomization. (7, 8)

Intensive case study The description or recording of what happens when people do something or behave (or say they behave) in a particular way. (2)

Interaction effects In factorial designs, condition means minus grand mean, row effects, and column effects. (14)

Intercoder reliability The extent to which raters or judges are in agreement. (4)

Interdisciplinary Combining methods and theories from different fields (disciplines) in order to develop a more complete and integrated picture. (1)

Internal-consistency reliability See *Reliability of components.*

Internal manipulation check See *Manipulation checks.*

Internal validity The degree of validity of statements made about whether X causes Y. (6, 7)

Internal validity rule The principle that, in demonstrations of causality, plausible rival explanations of the relation between X and Y can be ruled out. (6, 7)

Interpreter effect The effect that occurs when the researcher's interpretation of the observational record is unwittingly biased or slanted. (4)

Interquartile range The difference between the 75th percentile and the 25th percentile. (10)

Interrupted time-series designs Research in which the effects of a treatment are inferred from a comparison of the outcome measures obtained at different time intervals before and after the treatment is introduced. (8)

Interval estimates The extent to which *point estimates* are likely to be in error. (9)

Intervention An experimental treatment. (8)

Interview schedule A script that contains the questions the interviewer will ask. (5)

Item analysis A procedure used for selecting items (e.g., for a Likert attitude scale). (5)

Judges Coders, raters, decoders, or others who assist in describing and categorizing ongoing events or existing records of events. (4)

Judge-to-judge reliability The estimated reliability of the typical single judge or rater. (6)

Justification A term in the philosophy of science referring to the defense or confirmation of hypotheses. (2, 4)

k The number of conditions. (14)

K-R 20 A measure of internal-consistency reliability. (6)

Laboratory experiment The use of an experimental induction in a tightly controlled artificial (as opposed to a naturalistic) setting. (4)

Latin square design A repeated-measures design with built-in counterbalancing. (7)

Leniency bias A type of rating error in which the ratings are consistently more positive than they should be. (5)

Likert scale See *Summated ratings method.*

Linearity The mutual relation between two variables that resembles a straight line. (11)

Location measures Measures of central tendency. (10)

Logical error in rating A type of response set in which the judge gives similar ratings for variables or traits that are only intuitively related. (5)

Longitudinal designs Research in which the same subjects are studied over a period of time. (8)

Main effect The effect of an independent variable apart from its interaction with other independent variables. (14)

Manipulation checks Measures of the effectiveness of experimental treatments, which may involve questioning a new group of subjects (external manipulation check) or questioning the research participants themselves (internal manipulation check). (6)

Margin of error Interval within which an anticipated value is expected to occur. (9)

Marlowe–Crowne scale A standardized test that measures social desirability responding and need for social approval. (6)

Matched *t* The *t* test computed on nonindependent samples. (13)

Material cause The substance out of which something is made (Aristotle). (7)

Maturation A plausible threat to internal validity that occurs when the results of research not using randomization are contaminated by the participants' having, for instance, grown older, wiser, stronger, or more experienced between the pretest and the posttest. (7)

MCSD See *Marlowe–Crowne scale*.

Mean The arithmetical average of a set of scores. (10)

Mean square See *Variance*.

Mean square for error See *MS error*.

Median The midmost score of a distribution. (10)

Median split The splitting of a variable or series of scores at the midmost point. (11)

Mental imagery Thinking in which images have a hand, which is an aspect of theoretical reasoning. (1)

Meta-analysis. The use of statistical techniques to sum up a body of similar studies. (Appendix C)

Metaphor A word or phrase applied to a concept or phenomenon it does not literally denote. (2)

Metaphorical theme The use of metaphorical reasoning to come up with an innovative discovery. (2)

Method of agreement If *X*, then *Y*—which implies that *X* is a sufficient condition of *Y* (John Stuart Mill). (7)

Method of authority The acceptance of an idea as valid because it is stated by someone in a position of power or authority (Charles Peirce). (1)

Method of difference If not-*X*, then not-*Y*—which implies that *X* is a necessary condition of *Y* (John Stuart Mill). (7)

Method of equal-appearing intervals See *Equal-appearing intervals method*.

Method of tenacity Clinging stubbornly to an idea because it seems obvious or is "common sense" (Charles Peirce). (1)

Mill's methods See *Method of agreement* and *Method of difference*.

Minnesota Multiphasic Personality Inventory A structured personality test containing hundreds of statements that reflect general health, sexual attitudes, religious attitudes, emotional state, and so on. (5, 6)

MMPI See *Minnesota Multiphasic Personality Inventory*.

Mode The score occurring with the greatest frequency. (10)

Model A conceptual representation narrower than a theory but broader than a hypothesis. (2)

MS Mean square; see also *Variance*. (10, 14)

MS between Mean square between conditions. (14)

MS error Mean square used as the denominator of *F* ratios. (14)

MS within Mean square within conditions. (14)

Multiplistic viewpoint An emphasis on the use of multiple methods of observation and explanation; also called *pluralistic viewpoint*. (1)

Mundane realism A condition in which the various dimensions of the experiment are very similar to those in the real world. (4)

Mutually exclusive Describing the condition: If A is true, then not-A is false. (12)

n The number of scores in one condition or subgroup of a study. (10)

N The number of scores in a study. (10)

Naturalistic observation Research that looks at behavior in its usual natural environment. (4)

Necessary condition A requisite or essential condition. (7, 8)

Need for social approval See *Social-desirability responding.*

Negatively skewed Describing an asymmetrical distribution in which the pointed end is toward the left. (10)

N-of-1 experimental designs See *Single-case experimental designs.*

Nonequivalent-groups design Nonrandomized research in which the responses of a treatment group and a control group are compared on measures collected at the beginning and the end of the research. (8)

Nonreactive observation Any observation that does not affect what is being observed. (4, 7)

Nonresponse bias Error that is due to nonresponse or nonparticipation. (9)

Normal distribution Bell-shaped curve that is completely described by its mean and standard deviation. (10)

Norms Tables of values representing the typical performance of a given group. (9)

No-shows Subjects who fail to show up for their scheduled appointments. (10)

Null hypothesis The hypothesis that there is no relation between two or more variables, symbolized as H_0. (12)

Numerical scales Rating scales in which the respondent works with a sequence of defined numbers. (5)

Observed frequencies Counts obtained in specific rows and columns. (15)

Occam's razor The principle that explanations should be as parsimonious as possible (William of Occam). (2)

One-dimensional design A research design in which two or more groups are compared on the dependent variable. (7)

One-group pre-post design A preexperimental design in which the reactions of only one group of subjects are measured before and after exposure to the treatment. (7)

One-shot case study A preexperimental design in which the reactions of only one group of subjects are measured after the event or treatment has occurred. (7)

One-sided See *One-tailed tests.*

One-tailed tests Tests of significance in which the null hypothesis is rejected only if the results are significant in one of the two possible directions. (10, 12)

One-way design A statistical design in which two or more groups comprise a single dimension. (14)

Open-ended items See *Unstructured items.*

Operational definition The meaning of a variable in terms of the operations necessary to measure it or the experimental methods involved in its determination. (2)

Opportunity sample A sample using the first units that are available. (9)

Ordinate The vertical axis of a distribution. (10)

Outliers Scores lying far outside the normal range. (10)

O values See *Observed frequencies.*

Panel study Another name for a longitudinal study. (10)

Paradoxical incident An occurrence characterized by seemingly self-contradictory aspects. (2)

Parsimony of theories The degree to which the propositions of a theory are "sparing" or "frugal"; see also *Occam's razor.* (2)

Partial concealment Observation in which the researcher conceals only who or what is being observed. (4)

Participant observation A method of observation in which a group or a community is studied from within by a researcher who records behavior as it occurs. (4)

Partitioning of tables Subdividing larger chi-square tables into smaller tables (e.g., into 2×2 tables). (15)

Passive deception See *Deception research.*

Passive participation Noninvolvement of the scientific observer in the events studied during participant observation. (4)

Payoff potential Subjective estimate of the likelihood that the research idea will be corroborated. (2)

Pearson *r* Standard index of linear relationship. (11)

Peer review Ethical review by classmates of a student's proposed research; see also *Cost–benefit analysis.* (3)

Percentile Location of a score in a distribution defining the point below which a given percentage of the cases falls (e.g., a score at the 90th percentile falls at a point where 90% of the scores fall at or below that score). (10)

Perceptibility The idea that scientific explanations, to be influential, should make sense in a visual or other perceptual way. (1)

Phi coefficient (ϕ) Pearson *r* where both variables are dichotomous. (12, 15)

Physical trace Material evidence of behavior. (4)

Pilot test The evaluation of some aspect of the research before the study is implemented. (4, 5, 9)

Placebo A substance without any pharmacological benefit given as a pseudomedicine to a control group. (7)

Placebo-control group A control group that receives a placebo. (7)

Plagiarism Representing someone else's work as one's own. (2, Appendix A)

Plausibility stage That phase in the development of a research hypothesis in which the scientist evaluates the plausibility of an initial lead or idea. (2)

Plausible rival hypotheses Propositions, or sets of propositions, that provide a reasonable alternative to the working hypothesis. (4, 6, 7)

Pluralistic viewpoint. See *Multiplistic viewpoint.*

Point-biserial correlation (r_{pb}) Pearson *r* for which one of the variables is continuous and the other is dichotomous. (11)

Point estimates Estimates of particular characteristics of the population (e.g., the number of times an event occurs). (9)

Population The universe of elements from which sample elements are drawn, or the universe of elements to which we want to generalize. (9)

Positively skewed Describing an asymmetrical distribution in which the pointed end is toward the right. (10)

Posttest-only control-group design An after-only experimental design containing an experimental and a control group. (7)

Power of a test In significance testing, the probability of not making a Type II error, or $1 - \beta$. (12)

Predictive validity The extent to which a test can predict future outcomes. (6)

Preexperimental designs Research designs in which there is such a total absence of control that they are of minimal value in establishing causality. (7)

Pre-post control-group design Before-after experimental design. (7)

Pretest The test given, or the measurement made, before an experimental manipulation or intervention. (5)

Pretest sensitization The confounding of pretesting and *X*, the independent variable of interest. (7)

Principle of the drunkard's search The gathering of data in a convenient place but not a relevant one. (1)

Probability The mathematical chance of an event's occurring. (9, 12)

Probability sampling In survey sampling, a selection procedure in which every unit in the population has a known nonzero probability of being chosen. (9)

Product–moment correlation Standard index of linear relationship, or Pearson *r*. (11)

Projective test A psychological measure that operates on the principle that the subject will project some unconscious aspect of his or her life experience and emotions onto ambiguous stimuli in the spontaneous responses that come to mind (e.g,. the *Rorschach test* and the *Thematic Appercep-tion Test*). (5)

Proportion of variability explained The amount of variation shared by two vari-ables, as indexed by r^2 (the coefficient of determination). (12)

Pseudoscience Bogus claims masquerad-ing as scientific. (1)

Pseudosubjects Confederates of the exper-imenter who pose as research participants. (3)

Psychophysics The study of the relation-ship between physical stimuli and our expe-rience of them. (1)

p **value** Probability value or level obtained in a test of significance; also called *alpha* and *significance level*. (12)

Qualitative method An observational method in which the raw data exist in a nonnumerical form (e.g., reports of con-versations). (4)

Quantitative method An observational method in which the raw data exist in a numerical form (e.g., observers' or judges' ratings). (4)

Quasi-control subjects Participants who reflect on the context in which an experi-ment is conducted and speculate on ways in which the context may influence their own and research subjects' behavior. (7)

Quasi experiments Research that resem-bles an experimental design (in that there are treatments, outcome measures, and experimental units) but in which there is no

random assignment to create the compar-isons from which treatment-caused changes can be inferred. (8)

Quota sampling A procedure that assigns a quota of people to be interviewed and lets the questioner build up a sample that is roughly representative of the population. (9)

r Pearson's product–moment correlation. (11)

$\bar{r}$ The mean correlation in a set of *r*'s. (6)

R Effective or aggregate reliability. (6)

r^2 Pearson's correlation squared; also called *proportion of variability explained* or *coefficient of determination*. (12)

r_{pb} See *Point-biserial correlation.*

Random assignment Random allocation of sampling units to treatment conditions. (7)

Random digit dialing The researcher selects the first three digits of telephone numbers according to the geographic area of interest and then uses a computer pro-gram to select the last digits at random. (9)

Random errors The effects of uncon-trolled variables that cannot be specifically identified; such effects are, theoretically speaking, self-canceling in that the average of the errors will probably equal zero. (6)

Randomization See *Random assignment.*

Random sampling See *Random selection.*

Random selection A sample chosen by chance procedures and with known proba-bilities of selection. (9)

Range Distance between the highest and lowest score. (10)

Rank correlation See *Spearman rank cor-relation.*

Rating errors Biases in responses on rat-ing scales. (5)

Rating scales The common name for a variety of measuring instruments on which the observer or judge gives a numerical val-ue (either explicitly or implicitly) to certain judgments or assessments. (5)

Reactive observation An observation that affects what is being observed or measured. (4, 7)

Recruitment strategy The plan for locating potential respondents to participate in interview research. (5)

Regulative principles A philosophical term for hidden assumptions that come to serve as presuppositions. (2)

Relational research Research in which the investigatory focus is on the relations among variables. (1)

Reliability The extent to which observations or measures are consistent or stable. (6)

Reliability coefficient A generic name for indices of reliability. (6)

Reliability of components Reliability based on the intercorrelations among components of a test, such as subtests or all the individual test items; also called *internal-consistency reliability*. (6)

Repeated measurements Measurements made on the same sampling units. (8, 13, 14)

Repeated-measures design See *Within-subjects design*.

Replicability The ability to repeat or duplicate a scientific observation, usually an experimental result. (6, Appendix C)

Residuals Effects left over when appropriate components are subtracted from scores or means. (14)

Retest reliability See *Test-retest reliability*.

Rhetoric of science The language of a given field, which encompasses the proper use of technical definitions, hypotheses and theories, and so forth. (1)

Rho (ρ) See *Spearman rank correlation*. (11)

Robust relationship An effect that remains constant under a variety of circumstances. (4)

Root mean square See *Standard deviation*.

Rorschach test A projective test that consists of a set of inkblots on pieces of cardboard. (5, 6)

Row effect Row mean minus grand mean. (14)

S Square root of the unbiased estimator of the population value of σ^2. (10)

S^2 Unbiased estimator of the population value of σ^2. (10)

S^2 pooled Variance collected from two or more samples. (13)

Sample A subset of the population. (9)

Sample selection bias Systematic error resulting from the nature of the sampling units. (9)

Sampling plan A design, scheme of action, or procedure that specifies how the participants are to be selected in a survey study. (9)

Sampling stability The extent to which all samples produced by the same sampling plan yield essentially the same result. (9)

Sampling units The elements that make up the sample (e.g., people, schools, or cities). (7)

Sampling with replacement A type of random sampling in which the selected names are placed in the selection pool again and may be reselected in subsequent draws; this procedure is contrasted with *sampling without replacement,* in which a previously selected name cannot be chosen again and must be disregarded in any later draw. (9)

Scatter diagram See *Scatter plot*.

Scatter plot A visual display of the correlation between two variables that looks like a cloud of scattered dots; also called a *scatter diagram*. (11)

Scientific method An outlook (rather than a single method) that focuses on empirical inquiry, uses the particular rhetoric (or language) of the field it represents, incorporates certain regulative principles, and so on. (1)

Secondary observation Observation that is twice removed from the source. (4)

Segmented graphic scale A rating scale in the form of a line that is broken into segments. (5)

Selection A plausible threat to the internal validity of research not using randomization when the kinds of research subjects selected for one treatment group are different from those selected for another group. (7)

Self-fulfilling prophecy The prediction of an event that leads individuals to behave in a way that increases the likelihood that the event will occur as prophesied. (7)

Self-recorded diary Data collection method in which the research participant keeps a record of events at the time they occur. (5)

Self-report methods Techniques of data collection in which the research participants describe their own behavior or state of mind (e.g., interviews, questionnaires, and self-recorded diaries). (5)

Self-selection The subject chooses for himself or herself whether to enter a treatment condition. (8, 9)

Semantic differential A type of rating method in which connotative (or subjective) meaning is judged in terms of several dimensions, traditionally evaluation, potency, and activity. (5)

Sensemaking The use of ethnographic methodology to explore how people "make sense" of things. (4)

Serendipity A lucky or accidental discovery. (1, 2)

Σ Instruction telling us to sum (or add) a set of scores. (10)

σ The standard deviation of a set of scores. (10)

σ² The variance of a set of scores. (10)

Signal-to-noise A ratio of information to lack of information, for example, the ratio of the variability between samples (the signal) to the variability within the samples (the noise). (13)

Significance level The level of *alpha;* also called *p value.* (12)

Significance test Statistical test giving information on the tenability of the null hypothesis of no relation between two or more variables. (12, 13, 14, 15)

Significance testing The use of statistics and probabilities to evaluate the null hypothesis. (12)

Simple effects Differences between group or condition means. (14)

Simple observation Unobtrusive observation of events without trying to affect them. (4)

Simple randomized design A statistical design in which the sampling units are randomly assigned to two conditions. (7, 13)

Simple random selection A sampling plan in which the participants are selected individually on the basis of a randomized procedure (e.g., a table of random digits). (9)

Simulation A procedure modeled on an actual situation. (4)

Single-case experimental designs Repeated-measures designs in which $N = 1$; also called *N-of-1 experimental designs.* (8)

Size of study The number of sampling units. (13, 15)

Skew See *Negatively skewed* and *Positively skewed.*

Small-N designs Repeated-measures designs in which the treatment effect is evaluated within the same subject or a small number of subjects. (8)

Social-desirability responding The tendency of individuals to respond in ways that elicit a favorable evaluation. (6)

Social psychology of the experiment The study of the ways in which subject and experimenter artifacts operate. (7)

Solomon design A four-group experimental design developed by Richard L. Solomon as a means of assessing pretest sensitization effects without contamination by pretesting. (7)

Spearman–Brown formula A traditional equation that measures the overall internal-consistency reliability of a test from a knowledge of the reliability of its components. (6)

Spearman rank correlation Pearson *r* computed on scores in ranked form; also called *rho*. (11)

Spread Dispersion or variability. (10)

SS See *sum of squares*. (14)

SS **between** Sum of squares between conditions. (14)

SS **total** Total sum of squares. (14)

SS **within** Sum of squares within conditions. (14)

Stability The extent to which a set of measurements does not vary. (9)

Standard deviation An index of the variability of a set of data around the mean value in a distribution; also called the *root mean square*. (10)

Standardized measures Measures of judgment and attitude that require that certain rules be followed in the development, administration, and scoring of the measuring instrument. (5)

Standardizing the margins Setting all row totals equal to each other and all column totals equal to each other. (15)

Standard normal curve Normal curve with mean = 0 and $\sigma = 1$. (10)

Standard normal deviate *Z*-score location on a standard normal curve. (10, 15)

Standard score Score converted to a standard deviation unit. (10)

Statistical conclusion validity The relative accuracy of drawing statistical conclusions. (6)

Statistical power See *Power of a test*.

Statistical significance testing See *Significance testing*.

Stem-and-leaf plot The plot of a distribution in which the original data are preserved with any desired precision. (10)

Strata Subpopulations (or layers) in survey sampling. (9)

Stratified random sampling Probability sampling plan in which a separate sample is randomly selected within each homogeneous stratum (or layer) of the population. (9)

Strict determinism The idea that there is a causal law for everything. (2)

Structured items Questions with clear-cut response options; also called *closed items*. (5)

Student's *t* The pen name used by the inventor of the *t* test, William Sealy Gosset, was "Student." (13)

Sufficient condition A condition that is adequate to bring about some effect or result. (7, 8)

Summary ANOVA table A table that shows the results of an analysis of variance. (14)

Summated ratings method A method of attitude scaling (developed by Rensis Likert) that uses *item analysis* to select the best items. (5)

Sum of squares *(SS)* The sum of the squared deviations from the mean in a set of scores. (14)

Symmetrical Characterizing distributions in which the portions to the right and left of the mean are mirror images of each other. (10)

Synchronous correlations Correlations that indicate the degree of relationship of variables at a moment in time. (8)

Systematic error The effect of uncontrolled variables that often can be specifically identified; such effects are, theoretically speaking, not self-canceling (in contrast to the self-canceling nature of *random errors*). (6)

Systematic observation Observation that is guided or influenced by preexisting questions or hypotheses. (4)

Table of counts A table of independent frequencies; also called a *contingency table* or *chi-square table*. (15)

Tally sheet   Method of counting frequency of occurrence. (4)

TAT   See *Thematic Apperception Test.*

t **distributions**   Family of symmetrical distributions, centered at zero and ranging from negative to positive infinity. (13)

Teleological cause   See *Final cause.*

Telephone interview   An interview that is conducted by phone rather than face to face. (5)

Temporal precedence   The principle that what is labeled as the "cause" must be shown to have occurred before the "effect." (7)

Test–retest correlations   Correlations that indicate reliability over time. (8)

Test–retest method   A means of evaluating reliability (stability) in test construction, in which the correlation coefficient is computed on data from the same test but from results obtained at different times. (6)

Test–retest reliability   The degree of consistency of a test or measurement, or the characteristic it is designed to measure, from one administration to another; also called *retest reliability.* (6)

Tests of significance   Statistical tests giving information on the tenability of the null hypothesis of no relation between two or more variables. (13, 14, 15)

Thematic Apperception Test   A projective test that consists of a set of pictures, usually of people in various life contexts. (5, 6)

Theoretical definition   The meaning of a variable in abstract or conceptual terms; also called the *conceptual definition.* (2)

Theory   A set of proposed explanatory statements connected by logical arguments and certain implicit assumptions. (2)

Third-variable problem   A condition in which a variable correlated with X and Y is the cause of both. (11)

Thurstone attitude scale   See *Equal-appearing intervals method.*

Time-series designs   See *Interrupted time-series designs.*

Triangulation   The process of using multiple methods to zero in on the effect of interest. (4)

Trimmed mean   The mean of a distribution from which a specified highest and lowest percentage of scores has been dropped. (10)

Trimmed range   Range of a distribution remaining after a specified highest and lowest percentage of scores has been dropped. (10)

True experimental designs   Research designs characterized by the random assignment of treatment conditions to sampling units. (7)

t **test**   A test of significance used to judge the tenability of the null hypothesis of no relation between two variables. (13, 14)

Two-sided   See *Two-tailed tests.*

Two-tailed tests   Tests of significance in which the null hypothesis is rejected if the results are significant in either of the two possible directions. (12)

Two-way design   A statistical design in which each entry in the table is associated with a row variable and a column variable; also called a *two-way factorial.* (14)

Type I error   The error of rejecting the null hypothesis when it is true. (12)

Type II error   The error of failing to reject the null hypothesis when it is false. (12)

Typology   A classification scheme. (2)

Unbiased   Describing a case in which the values produced by the sample coincide with the "true" values of the population. (9)

Unbiased estimator of the population value of σ^2 Usually written as S^2. (10)

Unobtrusive observation   Measurements or observations used to study behavior when the subjects are unaware of being measured or observed. (4)

Unstructured items   Questions that offer the respondent an opportunity to express feelings, motives, or behavior spontaneously; also called *open-ended items*. (5)

Validity The degree to which what was observed or measured is the same as what was purported to be observed or measured. (6)

Variables Attributes of sampling units that can take on two or more values. (2)

Variance The mean of the squared deviations of scores from their means; also called the *mean square*. (10)

Volunteer bias Systematic error resulting when participants who volunteer respond differently from how individuals in the general population would respond. (9)

WAIS See *Wechsler Adult Intelligence Scale*.

Wechsler Adult Intelligence Scale The most widely used of the individual intelligence tests; divided into verbal and performance subtests. (6)

Wild scores Extreme scores that result from computational or recording mistakes. (10)

Within-subjects design Statistical design in which the sampling units (e.g., the research participants) generate two or more measurements. (8, 13)

Working hypothesis A testable supposition; also called an *experimental hypothesis* in experimental research. (2)

X Any score. (10)

$\overline{X}$ The mean of a set of scores. (10)

$\overline{X}_G$ The grand mean, or mean of the means. (14)

X **axis** The horizontal axis of a distribution; also called the *abscissa*. (10)

Y **axis** The vertical axis of a distribution; also called the *ordinate*. (10)

Yea-saying A type of response set in which the person answers consistently in the affirmative. (5)

Z Standard normal deviate. (10, 15)

Zero control A group that receives no treatment of any kind. (8)

Z **score** Score converted to the standard deviation unit. (10)

References

Adair, J. G. (1973). *The human subject: The social psychology of the psychological experiment.* Boston: Little, Brown.

Adair, J. G. (1984). The Hawthorne effect: A reconsideration of the methodological artifact. *Journal of Applied Psychology, 69,* 334–345.

Adair, R. K. (1990). *The physics of baseball.* New York: Harper & Row.

Aiken, L. R., Jr. (1963). Personality correlates of attitude toward mathematics. *Journal of Educational Research, 56,* 576–580.

Ainsworth, M. D. S., Bell, S. M., & Stayton, D. J. (1971). Individual differences in strange situation behavior of one-year-olds. In H. R. Schaffer (Ed.), *The origins of human social relations.* London: Academic Press.

Allaman, J. D., Joyce, C. S., & Crandall, V. C. (1972). The antecedents of social desirability response tendencies of children and young adults. *Child Development, 43,* 1135-1160.

Allport, G. W., & Postman, L. (1947). *The psychology of rumor.* New York: Holt, Rinehart & Winston.

American Association for the Advancement of Science. (1988). *Project on scientific fraud and misconduct.* Washington, DC: Author.

American Psychological Association. (1973). *Ethical principles in the conduct of research with human participants.* Washington, DC: Author.

American Psychological Association. (1982). *Ethical principles in the conduct of research with human participants.* Washington, DC: Author.

American Psychological Association. (1994). *Publication manual of the American Psychological Association* (4th ed.). Washington, DC: Author.

Anastasi, A. (1988). *Psychological testing* (6th ed.). New York: Macmillan.

Apel, K. (1982). C. S. Peirce and the post-Tarskian problem of an adequate explication of the meaning of truth: Towards a transcendental-pragmatic theory of truth, Part 2. *Transactions of the Charles S. Peirce Society, 18,* 3–17.

Arellano-Galdames, F. J. (1972). *Some ethical problems in research on human subjects.*

Unpublished doctoral dissertation, University of New Mexico, Albuquerque.

Arendt, H. (1963). *Eichmann in Jerusalem: A report on the banality of evil.* New York: Viking Press.

Aronson, E., & Carlsmith, J. M. (1968). Experimentation in social psychology. In G. Lindzey & E. Aronson (Eds.), *The handbook of social psychology* (2nd ed., Vol. 2, pp. 1–79). Reading, MA: Addison-Wesley.

Asch, S. E. (1952). Effects of group pressure upon the modification and distortion of judgments. In G. E. Swanson, T. M. Newcomb, & E. L. Hartley (Eds.), *Readings in social psychology* (rev. ed., pp. 393–401). New York: Holt, Rinehart & Winston.

Axinn, S. (1966). Fallacy of the single risk. *Philosophy of Science, 33,* 154–162.

Babad, E. (1993). Pygmalion—25 years after interpersonal expectations in the classroom. In P. D. Blanck (Ed.), *Interpersonal expectations: Theory, research, and applications* (pp. 125–153). New York: Cambridge University Press.

Baenninger, R., Estes, R. D., & Baldwin, S. (1977). Anti-predator behavior of baboons and impalas toward a cheetah. *Journal of East African Wildlife, 15,* 327–329.

Bailey, P., & Bremer, F. (1921). Experimental diabetes insipidus. *Archives of Internal Medicine, 28,* 773–803.

Bakan, D. (1967). *On method: Toward a reconstruction of psychological investigation.* San Francisco: Jossey-Bass.

Barnes, D. M. (1986). Promising results halt trial of anti-AIDS drug. *Science, 234,* 15–16.

Barrass, R. (1978). *Scientists must write.* London: Chapman & Hall.

Bauer, M. I., & Johnson-Laird, P. N. (1993). How diagrams can improve reasoning. *Psychological Science, 4,* 372–378.

Baughman, E. E., & Dahlstrom, W. G. (1968). *Negro and white children: A psychological study in the rural South.* New York: Academic Press.

Baumrind, D. (1964). Some thoughts on ethics of research: After reading Milgram's "Behavioral Study of Obedience." *American Psychologist, 19,* 421–423.

Beecher, H. K. (1970). *Research and the individual.* Boston: Little, Brown.

Berelson, B. (1952). *Content analysis in communication research.* Glencoe, IL: Free Press.

Berelson, B. (1954). Content analysis. In G. Lindzey (Ed.), *Handbook of social psychology* (Vol. 1, pp. 488–522). Reading, MA: Addison-Wesley.

Bergum, B. O., & Lehr, D. J. (1963). Effects of authoritarianism on vigilance performance. *Journal of Applied Psychology, 47,* 75–77.

Berkowitz, L., & Macaulay, J. (1971). The contagion of criminal violence. *Sociometry, 34,* 238–260.

Bernard, H. B., & Killworth, P. D. (1970). Informant accuracy in social network data, Part 2. *Human Communication Research, 4,* 3–18.

Bernard, H. B., & Killworth, P. D. (1980). Informant accuracy in social network data: 4. A comparison of clique-level structure in behavioral and cognitive network data. *Social Networks, 2,* 191–218.

Bernard, H. R. (1994). *Research methods in anthropology: Qualitative and quantitative approaches.* Thousands Oaks, CA: Sage.

Beveridge, W. I. B. (1957). *The art of scientific investigation.* New York: Vintage Books.

Billow, R. M. (1977). Metaphor: A review of the psychological literature. *Psychological Bulletin, 84,* 81–92.

Blanck, P. D. (Ed.). (1993). *Interpersonal expectations: Theory, research, and applications*. New York: Cambridge University Press.

Blanck, P. D., Bellack, A. S., Rosnow, R. L., Rotheram-Borus, M. J., & Schooler, N. R. (1992). Scientific rewards and conflicts of ethical choices in human subjects research. *American Psychologist, 47,* 959–965.

Blumberg, M., & Pringle, C. D. (1983). How control groups can cause loss of control in action research: The case of Rushton coal mine. *Journal of Applied Behavioral Science, 19,* 409–425.

Bok, S. (1978). *Lying: Moral choice in public and private life*. New York: Pantheon.

Bok, S. (1983). *Secrets: On the ethics of concealment and revelation*. New York: Vintage Books.

Boorstein, D. J. (1985). *The discoverers*. New York: Vintage.

Bradburn, N. M. (1982). Question-wording effects in surveys. In R. Hogarth (Ed.), *New directions for methodology of social and behavioral science: Question framing and response consistency* (No. 11, pp. 65–76). San Francisco: Jossey-Bass.

Bradburn, N. M. (1983). Response effects. In P. H. Rossi, J. D. Wright, & A. B. Anderson (Eds.), *Handbook of survey research* (pp. 289–328). New York: Academic Press.

Brady, J. V. (1958). Ulcers in "executive" monkeys. *Scientific American, 199,* 95–100.

Brady, J. V., Porter, R. W., Conrad, D. G., & Mason, J. W. (1958). Avoidance behavior and the development of gastroduodenal ulcers. *Journal for the Experimental Analysis of Behavior, 1,* 69–72.

Braun, H. I., & Wainer, H. (1989). Making essay test scores fairer with statistics. In J. M Tanur, F. Mosteller, W. H. Kruskal, E. L. Lehman, R. F. Link, R. S. Pieters, & G. S. Rising (Eds.), *Statistics: A guide to the unknown* (3rd ed., pp. 178–187). Pacific Grove, CA: Wadsworth & Brooks/Cole.

Bridgstock, M. (1982). A sociological approach to fraud in science. *Australian and New Zealand Journal of Sociology, 18,* 364–383.

Brinberg, D., & Kidder, L. H. (Eds.). (1982). *Forms of validity in research*. San Francisco: Jossey-Bass.

Broome, J. (1984). Selecting people randomly. *Ethics, 95,* 38-55.

Brown, R. (1965). *Social psychology*. New York: Free Press.

Buckhout, R. (1965). Need for approval and attitude change. *Journal of Psychology, 60,* 123-128.

Burnham, J. R. (1966). *Experimenter bias and lesion labeling*. Unpublished manuscript, Purdue University, West Lafayette, IN.

Campbell, D. T. (1950). The indirect assessment of attitudes. *Psychological Bulletin, 47,* 15–38.

Campbell, D. T., & Fiske, D. W. (1959). Convergent and discriminant validation by the multitrait-multimethod matrix. *Psychological Bulletin, 56,* 81–105.

Campbell, D. T., & Stanley, J. C. (1963). *Experimental and quasi-experimental designs for research*. Chicago: Rand McNally.

Canadian Multicentre Transplant Study Group. (1983). A randomized clinical trial of cyclosporine in cadaveric renal transplantation. *New England Journal of Medicine, 309,* 809–815.

Cannell, C. F., Miller, P. V., & Oksenberg, L. (1981). Research on interviewing technique. In S. Leinhardt (Ed.), *Sociological methodology*. San Francisco: Jossey-Bass.

Cantor, N., & Kihlstrom, J. F. (1989). *Personality and social intelligence*. Englewood Cliffs, NJ: Prentice-Hall.

Carlson, R. (1971). Where is the person in personality research? *Psychological Bulletin, 75*, 203–219.

Cartwright, D., & Harary, F. (1956). Structural balance: A generalization of Heider's theory. *Psychological Review, 63*, 277–293.

Ceci, S. J. (1990). *On intelligence . . . more or less: A bio-ecological treatise on intellectual development*. Englewood Cliffs, NJ: Prentice-Hall.

Ceci, S. J., & Bruck, M. (1993). Suggestibility of the child witness: A historical review and synthesis. *Psychological Bulletin, 113*, 403–439.

Ceci, S. J., Leichtman, M., & White, T. (1995). Interviewing preschoolers: Remembrance of things planted. In D. P. Peters (Ed.), *The child witness: Cognitive, social, and legal issues*. Netherlands: Kluwer.

Ceci, S. J., Peters, D., & Plotkin, J. (1985). Human subjects review, personal values, and the regulation of social science research. *American Psychologist, 40*, 994–1002.

Chandrasekhar, S. (1987). *Truth and beauty: Aesthetics and motivations in science*. Chicago: University of Chicago Press.

Clark, R. W. (1971). *Einstein: The life and times*. New York: World.

Cochran, W. G. (1963). *Sampling techniques* (2nd ed.). New York: Wiley.

Cochran, W. G. (1977). *Sampling techniques* (3rd ed.). New York: Wiley.

Cohen, J. (1965). Some statistical issues in psychological research. In B. B. Wolman (Ed.), *Handbook of clinical psychology* (pp. 95–121). New York: McGraw-Hill.

Cohen, J. (1988). *Statistical power analysis for the behavioral sciences* (2nd ed.). Hillsdale, NJ: Erlbaum.

Cohen, M. R. (1959). *Reason and nature: An essay on the meaning of scientific method*. New York: Dover. (Original work published 1931)

Columbo, J. (1982). The critical period concept: Research, methodology, and theoretical issues. *Psychological Bulletin, 91*, 260–275.

Committee on the Use of Animals in Research. (1991). *Science, medicine, and animals*. Washington, DC: National Academy Press.

Conant, J. B. (1957). Introduction. In J. B. Conant and L. K. Nash (Eds.), *Harvard case studies in experimental science* (Vol. 1, pp. vii–xvi). Cambridge: Harvard University Press.

Conrath, D. W. (1973). Communications environment and its relationship to organizational structure. *Management Science, 20*, 586–603.

Conrath, D. W., Higgins, C. A., & McClean, R. J. (1983). A comparison of the reliability of questionnaire versus diary data. *Social Networks, 5*, 315–322.

Converse, J. M., & Presser, S. (1986). *Survey questions: Handcrafting the standardized questionnaire*. Beverly Hills, CA: Sage.

Cook, T. D., & Campbell, D. T. (1976). The design and conduct of quasi-experiments and true experiments in field settings. In M. D. Dunnette (Ed.), *Handbook of industrial and organizational psychology* (pp. 223–326). Chicago: Rand McNally.

Cook, T. D., & Campbell, D. T. (1979). *Quasi-experimentation: Design and analysis issues for field settings*. Chicago: Rand McNally.

Cooper, H. M. (1989). *Integrating research: A guide for literature reviews.* Newbury Park, CA: Russell Sage.

Cooper, H. M., & Hedges, L. V. (Eds.). (1994). *The handbook of research synthesis.* New York: Russell Sage.

Corsini, R. J. (Ed.) (1984). *Encyclopedia of psychology* (Vols. 1–4). New York: Wiley.

Crabb, P. B., & Bielawski, D. (1994). The social representation of maternal culture and gender in children's books. *Sex Roles, 30,* 69–79.

Crabtree, B. F., & Miller, W. L. (Eds.). (1992). *Doing qualitative research: Multiple strategies.* Thousand Oaks, CA: Sage.

Crancer, J., Dille, J., Delay, J., Wallace, J., & Haybin, M. (1969). Comparison of the effects of marijuana and alcohol on simulated driving performance. *Science, 164,* 851–854.

Cronbach, L. J. (1960). *Essentials of psychological testing* (2nd ed.). New York: Harper.

Cronbach, L. J., & Meehl, P. E. (1955). Construct validity in psychological tests. *Psychological Bulletin, 52,* 281–302.

Cronbach, L. J., & Quirk, T. J. (1971). Test validity. In L. C. Deighton (Ed.), *Encyclopedia of education* (Vol. 9, pp. 165–175). New York: Macmillan and Free Press.

Crowne, D. P. (1979). *The experimental study of personality.* Hillsdale, NJ: Erlbaum.

Crowne, D. P. (1991). From response style to motive. *Current Contents: Social and Behavioral Sciences, 23*(30), 10.

Crowne, D. P., & Marlowe, D. (1964). *The approval motive: Studies in evaluative dependence.* New York: Wiley.

Cryer, J. D. (1986). *Time series analysis.* Boston: PWS-Kent.

Csikszentmihalyi, M., & Larson, R. (1984). *Being adolescent: Conflict and growth in the teenage years.* New York: Basic Books.

Danziger, K. (1988). A question of identity: Who participated in psychological experiments? In J. Morawski (Ed.), *The rise of experimentation in American psychology* (pp. 35–52). New York: Oxford University Press.

Darley, J. M., & Latané, B. (1968). Bystander intervention in emergencies. *Journal of Personality and Social Psychology, 8,* 377–383.

Davis, J. D., Gallagher, R. L., & Ladove, R. (1967). Food intake controlled by blood factors. *Science, 156,* 1247–1248.

Day, D. D., & Quackenbush, O. F. (1942). Attitudes toward defensive, cooperative, and aggressive wars. *Journal of Social Psychology, 16,* 11–20.

Day, R. A. (1983). *How to write and publish a scientific paper* (2nd ed.). Philadelphia: ISI Press.

Delgado, R., & Leskovac, H. (1986). Informed consent in human experimentation: Bridging the gap between ethical thought and current practice. *UCLA Law Review, 34,* 67–130.

Denzin, N. K., & Lincoln, Y. S. (Eds.). (1994). *Handbook of quantitative research.* Thousand Oaks, CA: Sage.

DeVore, I., & Washburn, S. L. (1963). Baboon ecology and human evolution. In F. C. Howell & F. Bourliere (Eds.), *African ecology and human evolution* (pp. 335–367). New York: Viking Fund.

De Vos, G. A., & Boyer, L. B. (1989). *Symbolic analysis cross-culturally: The Rorschach test.* Berkeley: University of California Press.

DiFonzo, N., Bordia, P., & Rosnow, R. L. (1994). Reining in rumors. *Organizational Dynamics, 23,* 47–62.

Dohrenwend, B. S., & Richardson, S. A. (1963). Directiveness and nondirectiveness in research interviewing: A reformulation of the problem. *Psychological Bulletin, 60,* 475–485.

Doob, L. W. (1987). *Slightly beyond skepticism: Social science and the search for morality.* New Haven, CT: Yale University Press.

Downs, C. W., Smeyak, G. P., & Martin, E. (1980). *Professional interviewing.* New York: Harper & Row.

Ebbinghaus, H. (1885). *Über das Gedächtnis: Untersuchungen zur experimentellen Psychologie.* Leipzig, Germany: Duncker & Humblot.

Elgie, D. M., Hollander, E. P., & Rice, R. W. (1988). Appointed and elected leader responses to favorableness of feedback and level of task activity from followers. *Journal of Applied Social Psychology, 18,* 1361–1370.

Entwisle, D. R. (1961). Interactive effects of pretesting. *Educational and Psychological Measurement, 21,* 607–620.

Fairbanks, L. A. (1993). What is a good mother? Adaptive variation in maternal behavior of primates. *Current Directions in Psychological Science, 2,* 179–183.

Federighi, E. T. (1959). Extended tables of the percentage points of student's *t*-distribution. *Journal of the American Statistical Association, 54,* 683–688.

Ferster, C. B., & Skinner, B. F. (1957). *Schedules of reinforcement.* New York: Appleton-Century-Crofts.

Festinger, L. (1962). *A theory of cognitive dissonance.* Stanford, CA: Stanford University Press.

Feyerabend, P. (1988). *Against method* (rev. ed.). London, England: Verso.

Feynman, R. P. (1988). *"What do I care what other people think?": Further adventures of a curious character.* New York: Bantam Books.

Fienberg, S. E., & Tanur, J. M. (1989). Combining cognitive and statistical approaches to survey design. *Science, 243,* 1017–1022.

Finkner, A. L. (1950). Methods of sampling for estimating commercial peach production in North Carolina. *North Carolina Agricultural Experiment Station Technical Bulletin, 91* (whole).

Fisher, R. A. (1960). *The design of experiments* (7th ed.). Edinburgh, Scotland: Oliver & Boyd.

Fisher, R. A. (1971). *The design of experiments* (8th ed.). New York: Hafner.

Fisher, R. A., & Yates, F. (1974). *Statistical tables for biological, agricultural and medical research* (6th ed.). London, England: Longman.

Flanagan, J. C. (1954). The critical incident technique. *Psychological Bulletin, 51,* 327-358.

Forrest, D. W. (1974). *Francis Galton: The life and work of a Victorian genius.* New York: Taplinger.

Fowler, F. J., Jr. (1993). *Survey research methods* (2nd ed.). Newbury Park, CA: Sage.

Freedman, D., Pisani, R., Purves, R., & Adhikari, A. (1991). *Statistics* (2nd ed.). New York: Norton.

French, J. R. P. (1950). Field experiments: Changing group productivity. In J. G. Miller (Ed.), *Experiments in social process: A symposium on social psychology* (pp. 79–96). New York: McGraw-Hill.

Fung, S. K., Kipnis, D., & Rosnow, R. L. (1987). Synthetic benevolence and malevolence as strategies of relational compliance-gaining. *Journal of Social and Personal Relationships, 4,* 129–141.

Gallup, G. (1976, May 21). *Lessons learned in 40 years of polling.* Paper presented before National Council on Public Polls.

Gardner, H. (1985). *Frames of mind: The theory of multiple intelligences.* New York: Basic Books.

Gardner, H. (1986). *The mind's new science: A history of the cognitive revolution.* New York: Basic Books.

Gardner, H. (Ed.). (1993). *Multiple intelligences: The theory in practice.* New York: Basic Books.

Gardner, M. (1957). *Fads and fallacies in the name of science.* New York: Dover.

Garfield, E. (1989a). Art and science: 1. The art-science connection. *Current Contents, 21*(8), 3–10.

Garfield, E. (1989b). Art and science: 2. Science for art's sake. *Current Contents, 21*(9), 3–8.

Gephart, R. P., Jr. (1993). The textual approach: Risk and blame in disaster sensemaking. *Academy of Management Journal, 36,* 1465–1514.

Gibson, E. J., & Walk, R. D. (1960, April). The visual cliff. *Scientific American, 202*(4), 64–71.

Gigerenzer, G. (1991). From tools to theories: A heuristic of discovery in cognitive psychology. *Psychological Review, 98,* 254–267.

Gigerenzer, G., Swijtink, Z., Porter, T., Daston, L., Beatty, J., & Krüger, L. (1989). *The empire of chance: How probability changed science and everyday life.* Cambridge: Cambridge University Press.

Gilgun, J. F., Daly, K., & Handel, G. (Eds.). (1992). *Qualitative methods in family research.* Thousand Oaks, CA: Sage.

Gillespie, R. (1988). The Hawthorne experiments and the politics of experimentation.

In J. Morawski (Ed.), *The rise of experimentation in American psychology* (pp. 114–137). New York: Oxford University Press.

Gilovich, T. (1991). *How we know what isn't so: The fallibility of human reason in everyday life.* New York: Free Press.

Glass, G. V (1976). Primary, secondary, and meta-analysis of research. *Educational Researcher, 5,* 3–8.

Glass, G. V, McGaw, B., & Smith, M. L. (1981). *Meta-analysis in social research.* Beverly Hills, CA: Sage.

Goldberg, L. R. (1993). The structure of phenotypic personality traits. *American Psychologist, 48,* 26–34.

Gombrich, E. H. (1963). *Meditations on a hobby horse.* London, England: Phaidon.

Goodenough, W. H. (1980). Ethnographic field techniques. In H. C. Triandis & J. W. Berry (Eds.), *Handbook of cross-cultural psychology: Methodology* (Vol. 2, pp. 29–55). Boston: Allyn & Bacon.

Grant, D. A. (1956). Analysis-of-variance curves in the analysis and comparison of curves. *Psychological Bulletin, 53,* 141–154.

Gross, A. G. (1990). *The rhetoric of science.* Cambridge, MA: Harvard University Press.

Gubrium, J. F., & Sankar, A. (Eds.) (1993). *Qualitative methods in aging research.* Thousand Oaks, CA: Sage.

Guilford, J. P. (1954). *Psychometric methods* (2d ed.). New York: McGraw-Hill.

Guilford, J. P. (1967). *The nature of intelligence.* New York: McGraw-Hill.

Hagenaars, J. A., & Cobben, N. P. (1978). Age, cohort and period: A general model for the analysis of social change. *Netherlands Journal of Sociology, 14,* 58–91.

Hall, J. A. (1984). *Instructor's manual to accompany Rosenthal/Rosnow: Essentials of behavioral research*. New York: McGraw-Hill.

Hall, R. V., Lund, D., & Jackson, D. (1968). Effects of teacher attention on study behavior. *Journal of Applied Behavior Analysis, 1,* 1–12.

Hamsher, J. H., & Reznikoff, M. (1967). Ethical standards in psychological research and graduate training: A study of attitudes within the profession. *Proceedings, 75th Annual Convention, American Psychological Association, 2,* 203–204.

Harlow, H. F. (1959). Love in infant monkeys. In S. Coopersmith (Ed.), *Frontiers of psychological research* (pp. 92–98). San Francisco: W. H. Freeman.

Harré, R., & Lamb, R. (Eds.). (1983). *Encyclopedic dictionary of psychology.* Cambridge: MIT Press.

Harris, B. (1988). Key words: A history of debriefing in social psychology. In J. Morawski (Ed.), *The rise of experimentation in American psychology* (pp. 188–212). New Haven, CT: Yale University Press.

Hartmann, G. W. (1936). A field experiment on the comparative effectiveness of "emotional" and "rational" political leaflets in determining election results. *Journal of Abnormal and Social Psychology, 31,* 99–114.

Haviland, J. B. (1977). Gossip as competition in Zinacantan. *Journal of Communication, 27,* 186–191.

Hedges, L. V., & Olkin, I. (1985). *Statistical methods for meta-analysis.* New York: Academic Press.

Heider, F. (1944). Social perception and phenomenal causality. *Psychological Review, 51,* 358–374.

Heider, F. (1946). Attitudes and cognitive organization. *Journal of Psychology, 21,* 107–112.

Heider, F. (1958). *The psychology of interpersonal relations.* New York: Wiley.

Heise, G. A., & Miller, G. A. (1951). Problem solving by small groups using various communication nets. *Journal of Abnormal and Social Psychology, 46,* 327–331.

Hersen, M., & Barlow, D. H. (1976). *Single-case experimental designs: Strategies for studying behavior change.* Oxford, England: Pergamon Press.

Highland, R. W., & Berkshire, J. A. (1951). *A methodological study of forced-choice performance rating* (Research Rep. No. 51–9). San Antonio, TX: Human Resources Research Center.

Hirsh-Pasek, K., & Golinkoff, R. M. (1993). Skeletal supports for grammatical learning: What infants bring to the language learning task. In C. Rovee-Collier & L. P. Lipsitt (Eds.), *Advances in infancy research* (Vol. 8, pp. 299–315). Norwood, NJ: Ablex.

Hollander, E. P. (1992). The essential independence of leadership and followership. *Current Directions in Psychological Science, 1,* 71–74.

Holsti, O. R. (1969). *Content analysis for the social sciences and humanities.* Reading, MA: Addison-Wesley.

Holton, G. (1973). *Thematic origins of scientific thought: Kepler to Einstein.* Cambridge: Harvard University Press.

Holton, G., & Morison, R. S. (1978). *Limits of scientific inquiry.* New York: Norton.

Horowitz, I. A. (1969). Effects of volunteering, fear arousal, and number of communications on attitude change. *Journal of Personality and Social Psychology, 11,* 34–37.

Houts, A. C., Cook, T. D., & Shadish, W., Jr. (1986). The person-situation debate: A critical multiplist perspective. *Journal of Personality, 54,* 52–105.

Hunter, J. E., & Schmidt, F. L. (1990). *Methods of meta-analysis: Correcting error and bias in research findings.* Newbury Park, CA: Sage.

Jaeger, M. E., & Rosnow, R. L. (1988). Contextualism and its implications for psychological inquiry. *British Journal of Psychology, 79,* 63–75.

Jaeger, M. E., Skleder, A. A., Rind, B., & Rosnow, R. L. (1994). Gossip, gossipers, gossipees. In R. F. Goodman & A. Ben-Ze'ev (Eds.), *Good gossip* (pp. 154–168). Lawrence, KS: University Press of Kansas.

Jammer, M. (1966). *The conceptual development of quantum mechanics.* New York: McGraw-Hill.

Johnson-Laird, P. N. (1983). *Mental models: Towards a cognitive science of language, inference, and consciousness.* Cambridge: Harvard University Press.

Johnson-Laird, P. N., & Byrne, R. M. J. (1991). *Deduction.* Hillsdale, NJ: Erlbaum.

Jones, E. E., & Nisbett, R. E. (1972). The actor and the observer: Divergent perceptions of the causes of behavior. In E. E. Jones, D. E. Kanouse, H. H. Kelley, R. E. Nisbett, S. Valins, & B. Weiner (Eds.), *Attribution: Perceiving the causes of behavior.* Morristown, NJ: General Learning Press.

Jones, M. B., & Fennell, R. S., III. (1965). Runway performance in two strains of rats. *Quarterly Journal of the Florida Academy of Sciences, 28,* 289–296.

Judd, C. M., & Kenny, D. A. (1981). *Estimating the effects of social interventions.* Cambridge, England: Cambridge University Press.

Judd, C. M., Smith, E. R., & Kidder, L. H. (1991). *Research methods in social relations* (6th ed.). New York: Holt, Rinehart & Winston.

Jung, C. G. (1910). Ein Beitrag zur Psychologie des Gerüchtes. *Zentralblatt für Psychoanalyse, 1,* 81–90.

Jung, C. G. (1959). A visionary rumor. *Journal of Analytical Psychology, 4,* 5–19.

Kahane, H. (1986). *Logic and philosophy: A modern introduction* (5th ed.). Belmont, CA: Wadsworth.

Kahane, H. (1989). *Logic and philosophy: A modern introduction* (6th ed.). Belmont, CA: Wadsworth.

Kallgren, C. A., & Kenrick, D. T. (1990, March). *Ethical judgments and nonhuman research subjects: The effects of phylogenetic closeness and affective valence.* Paper presented at the Eastern Psychological Association meeting, Philadelphia.

Kaplan, A. (1964). *The conduct of inquiry: Methodology for behavioral science.* Scranton, PA: Chandler.

Katz, D., & Cantril, H. (1937). Public opinion polls. *Sociometry, 1,* 155–179.

Katz, J. (1972). *Experimentation with human beings.* New York: Sage.

Kazdin, A. E. (1976). Statistical techniques for single-case experimental designs. In M. Hersen & D. H. Barlow (Eds.), *Single case experimental designs: Strategies for studying behavior change* (pp. 265–316). Oxford, England: Pergamon Press.

Kazdin, A. E. (1980). *Research design in clinical psychology.* New York: Harper & Row.

Kazdin, A. E., & Tuma, A. H. (Eds.). (1982). *Single-case research designs.* San Francisco: Jossey-Bass.

Kelly, D., Julian, T., & Hollander, E. P. (1992, April 4). *Further effects of good and bad leadership as revealed by critical incidents and rating scales.* Paper presented at Eastern Psychological Association meeting, Boston.

Kelman, H. C. (1968). *A time to speak: On human values and social research.* San Francisco: Jossey-Bass.

Kendall, P. C., Howard, B. C., & Hays, R. C. (1989). Self-referent speech and psychopathology: The balance of positive and negative thinking. *Cognitive Therapy and Research, 13,* 583–598.

Kenny, D. A. (1979). *Correlation and causality.* New York: Wiley.

Keppel, G. (1991). *Design and analysis: A researcher's handbook* (3rd ed.). Englewood Cliffs, NJ: Prentice-Hall.

Kidder, L. H. (1972). On becoming hypnotized: How skeptics become convinced: A case of attitude change? *Journal of Abnormal Psychology, 80,* 317–322.

Kidder, L. H., Kidder, R. L., & Snyderman, P. (1976). *A cross-lagged correlational analysis of the causal relationship between police employment and crime rates.* Paper presented at the meeting of the American Psychological Association, Washington.

Kilborn, P. T. (1994, January 23). Alarming trend among workers: Surveys find clusters of TB cases. *The New York Times,* pp. A1, A16.

Kimble, G. A. (1989). Psychology from the standpoint of a generalist. *American Psychologist, 44,* 491–499.

Kimmel, A. J. (Ed.). (1981). *Ethics of human subject research.* San Francisco: Jossey-Bass.

Kimmel, A. J. (1988). *Ethics and values in applied social research.* Beverly Hills, CA: Sage.

Kimmel, A. J. (1991). Predictable biases in the ethical decision making of American psychologists. *American Psychologist, 46,* 786–788.

Kimmel, A. J., & Keefer, R. (1991). Psychological correlates of the acceptance and transmission of rumors about AIDS. *Journal of Applied Social Psychology, 21,* 1608–1628.

Kirk, R. E. (1982). *Experimental design: Procedures for the behavioral sciences* (2nd ed.). Belmont, CA: Wadsworth.

Kish, L. (1965). *Survey sampling.* New York: Wiley.

Kleinmuntz, B. (1982). *Personality and psychological assessment.* New York: St. Martin's.

Knapp, R. H. (1944). A psychology of rumor. *Public Opinion Quarterly, 8,* 22–37.

Koch, S. (1959). General introduction to the series. In S. Koch (Ed.), *Psychology: A study of a science* (Vol. 1, pp. 1–18). New York: McGraw-Hill.

Kolata, G. B. (1986). What does it mean to be random? *Science, 231,* 1068–1070.

Komaki, J., & Barnett, F. T. (1977). A behavioral approach to coaching football: Improving the play execution of the offensive backfield on a youth football team. *Journal of Applied Behavior Analysis, 10,* 657–664.

Kordig, C. R. (1978). Discovery and justification. *Philosophy of Science, 45,* 110–117.

Koshland, D. E., Jr. (1988). Science, journalism, and whistle-blowing. *Science, 240,* 585.

Kratochwill, T. R., & Levin, J. R. (Eds.). (1992). *Single-case research design and analysis: New directions for psychology and education.* Hillsdale, NJ: Erlbaum.

Krippendorff, K. (1980). *Content analysis: An introduction to its methodology.* Beverly Hills, CA: Sage.

Labaw, P. (1980). *Advanced questionnaire design.* Cambridge, MA: Abt Books.

Lana, R. E. (1959). Pretest-treatment interaction effects in attitudinal studies. *Psychological Bulletin, 56,* 293–300.

Lana, R. E. (1969). Pretest sensitization. In R. Rosenthal & R. L. Rosnow (Eds.), *Artifact in behavioral research* (pp. 119–141). New York: Academic Press.

Lana, R. E., & Rosnow, R. L. (1972). *Introduction to contemporary psychology*. New York: Holt, Rinehart & Winston.

Lasswell, H. D. (1927). *Propaganda technique in the World War*. New York: Knopf.

Latané, B., & Darley, J. M. (1968). Group inhibition of bystander intervention in emergencies. *Journal of Personality and Social Psychology, 10*, 215–221.

Latané, B., & Darley, J. M. (1970). *The unresponsive bystander: Why doesn't he help?* New York: Appleton-Century-Crofts.

Lavelle, J. M., Hovell, M. F., West, M. P., & Wahlgren, D. R. (1992). Promoting law enforcement for child protection: A community analysis. *Journal of Applied Behavior Analysis, 25*, 885–892.

Lavrakas, P. J. (1987). *Telephone survey methods: Sampling, selection, and supervision*. Beverly Hills, CA: Sage.

Lazarsfeld, P. F. (1978). Some episodes in the history of panel analysis. In D. B. Kandel (Ed.), *Longitudinal research for drug abuse* (pp. 249-265). New York: Hemisphere Press.

Leary, D. E. (Ed.). (1990). *Metaphors in the history of psychology*. Cambridge, England: Cambridge University Press.

Lessac, M. S., & Solomon, R. L. (1969). Effects of early isolation on the later adaptive behavior of beagles. *Developmental Psychology, 1*, 14–25.

Levi, P. (1984). *The periodic table*. New York: Schocken Books.

Lewin, T. (1994, January 7). Prize in an unusual lottery: A scarce experimental drug. *The New York Times*, pp. A1, A17.

Ley, R. (1990). *A whisper of espionage*. Garden City, NJ: Avery.

Ley, R. (1993). Breathing retraining in the treatment of hyperventilation complaints and panic disorder: A reply to Garssen, De Ruiter, and Van Dyck. *Clinical Psychology Review, 13*, 393–408.

Light, R. J., & Pillemer, D. B. (1984). *Summing up: The science of reviewing research*. Cambridge: Harvard University Press.

Likert, R. A. (1932). A technique for the measurement of attitudes. *Archives of Psychology, 140*, 1–55.

Lindquist, E. F. (1953). *Design and analysis of experiments in psychology and education*. Boston, MA: Houghton Mifflin.

Linsky, A. S. (1975). Stimulating responses to mailed questionnaires: A review. *Public Opinion Quarterly, 39*, 83–101.

London, P. (1970). The rescuers: Motivational hypotheses about Christians who saved Jews from the Nazis. In J. Macaulay & L. Berkowitz (Eds.), *Altruism and helping behavior* (pp. 241–250). New York: Academic Press.

Mahler, I. (1953). Attitudes toward socialized medicine. *Journal of Social Psychology, 38*, 273–282.

Malmo, R. B. (1959). Activation: A neuropsychological dimension. *Psychological Review, 66*, 367–386.

Mann, C. (1990). Meta-analysis in the breech. *Science, 249*, 476–480.

Martin, P., & Bateson, P. (1993). *Measuring behaviour: An introductory guide* (2nd ed.). Cambridge, England: Cambridge University Press.

McClelland, D. C., Atkinson, J. W., Clark, R. A., & Lowell, E. L. (1953). *The achievement motive*. New York: Appleton-Century-Crofts.

McCormick, T. (1982). Content analysis: The social history of a method. *Studies in Communication, 2,* 143–178.

McGuire, W. J. (1964). Inducing resistance to persuasion: Some contemporary approaches. In L. Berkowitz (Ed.), *Advances in experimental social psychology* (Vol. 1, pp. 191–229). New York: Academic Press.

McGuire, W. J. (1973). The yin and yang of progress in social psychology: Seven koan. *Journal of Personality and Social Psychology, 26,* 446–456.

McNemar, Q. (1960). At random: Sense and nonsense. *American Psychologist, 15,* 295–300.

Medawar, P. B. (1969). *Induction and intuition in scientific thought* (Jayne Lectures for 1968). Philadelphia: American Philosophical Society.

Menges, R. J. (1973). Openness and honesty versus coercion and deception in psychological research. *American Psychologist, 28,* 1030–1034.

Merriam, S. B. (1991). *Case study research in education.* San Francisco: Jossey-Bass.

Merritt, C. B., & Fowler, R. G. (1948). The pecuniary honesty of the public at large. *Journal of Abnormal and Social Psychology, 43,* 90–93.

Merton, R. K. (1948). The self-fulfilling prophecy. *Antioch Review, 8,* 193–210.

Meyrowitz, J. (1985). *No sense of place: The impact of electronic media on social behavior.* New York: Oxford University Press.

Milgram, S. (1963). Behavioral study of obedience. *Journal of Abnormal and Social Psychology, 67,* 371–378.

Milgram, S. (1974). *Obedience to authority: An experimental view.* New York: Harper & Row.

Milgram, S. (1977). *The individual in a social world: Essays and experiments.* Reading, MA: Addison-Wesley.

Milgram, S., Mann, L., & Harter, S. (1965). The lost-letter technique: A tool of social research. *Public Opinion Quarterly, 29,* 437–438.

Miller, A. I. (1986). *Imagery in scientific thought: Creating 20th century physics.* Cambridge: MIT Press.

Miller, G. A., & Newman, E. B. (1958). Tests of a statistical explanation of the rank-frequency relation for words in written English. *American Journal of Psychology, 71,* 209–258.

Miller, N., & Pollock, V. E. (1994). Meta-analytic synthesis for theory development. In H. Cooper & L. V. Hedges (Eds.), *The handbook of research synthesis* (pp. 457–483). New York: Sage.

Miller, P. V., & Cannell, C. F. (1982). A study of experimental techniques for telephone interviewing. *Public Opinion Quarterly, 46,* 250–269.

Morse, J. M. (Ed.) (1993). *Critical issues in qualitative research methods.* Thousand Oaks, CA: Sage.

Mosteller, F. (1968). Association and estimation in contingency tables. *Journal of the American Statistical Association, 63,* 1–28.

Mosteller, F., Fienberg, S. E., & Rourke, R. E. K. (1983). *Beginning statistics with data analysis.* Reading, MA: Addison-Wesley.

Mullen, B., & Rosenthal, R. (1985). *BASIC meta-analysis: Procedures and programs.* Hillsdale, NJ: Erlbaum.

Nelson, N., Rosenthal, R., & Rosnow, R. L. (1986). Interpretation of significance levels and effect sizes by psychological researchers. *American Psychologist, 41,* 1299–1301.

Nisbet, R. (1976). *Sociology as an art form.* London, England: Oxford University Press.

Orne, M. T. (1959). The nature of hypnosis: Artifact and essence. *Journal of Abnormal and Social Psychology, 58,* 277–299.

Orne, M. T. (1962). On the social psychology of the psychological experiment: With particular reference to demand characteristics and their implications. *American Psychologist, 17,* 776–783.

Orne, M. T. (1969). Demand characteristics and the concept of quasi-controls. In R. Rosenthal & R. L. Rosnow (Eds.), *Artifact in behavioral research* (pp. 143–179). New York: Academic Press.

Orne, M. T. (1970). Hypnosis, motivation, and the ecological validity of the psychological experiment. In W. J. Arnold & M. M. Page (Eds.), *Nebraska Symposium on Motivation* (pp. 187–265). Lincoln: University of Nebraska Press.

Osgood, C. E., Suci, G. J., & Tannenbaum, P. H. (1957). *The measurement of meaning.* Urbana: University of Illinois Press.

Pareek, U., & Rao, T. V. (1980). Cross-cultural surveys and interviewing. In H. C. Triandis & J. W. Berry (Eds.), *Handbook of cross-cultural psychology: Methodology* (Vol. 2, pp. 127–179). Boston: Allyn & Bacon.

Parker, K. C. H., Hanson, R. K., & Hunsley, J. (1988). MMPI, Rorschach, and WAIS: A meta-analytic comparison of reliability, stability, and validity. *Psychological Bulletin, 103,* 367–373.

Paulos, J. A. (1990). *Innumeracy: Mathematical illiteracy and its consequences.* New York: Vintage Books.

Paulos, J. A. (1991, April 24). Math moron myths. *The New York Times OP-ED,* p. 25.

Peirce, S. C. (1966). *Charles S. Peirce: Selected writings (Values in a universe of chance).* (P. P. Weiner, Ed.). New York: Dover.

Pelz, D. C., & Andrew, F. M. (1964). Detecting causal priorities in panel study data. *American Sociological Review, 29,* 836–848.

Pera, M., & Shea, W. R. (Eds.). (1991). *Persuading science: The art of scientific rhetoric.* Canton, MA: Science History Publications.

Pessin, J. (1933). The comparative effects of social and mechanical stimulation on memorizing. *American Journal of Psychology, 45,* 263–270.

Peterson, C., & Ulrey, L. M. (1994). Can explanatory style be scored from TAT protocols? *Personality and Social Psychology Bulletin, 20,* 102–106.

Phillips, D. P. (1980). The deterrent effect of capital punishment: New evidence on an old controversy. *American Journal of Sociology, 86,* 139–148.

Phillips, D. P. (1986). Natural experiments on the effects of mass media violence on fatal aggression: Strengths and weaknesses of a new approach. In L. Berkowitz (Ed.), *Advances in experimental social psychology* (Vol. 19, pp. 207–250). New York: Academic Press.

Phillips, D. P., & Hensley, J. (1984). When violence is rewarded or punished: The impact of mass media stories on homicide. *Journal of Communication, 34,* 101–116.

Popper, K. R. (1934). *Logik der Forschung.* Vienna, Austria: Springer-Verlag.

Popper, K. R. (1961). *The logic of scientific inquiry.* New York: Basic Books.

Popper, K. R. (1963). *Conjectures and refutations.* London, England: Routledge.

Postman, L., Bruner, J. S., & McGinnies, E. (1948). Personal values as selective factors in perception. *Journal of Abnormal and Social Psychology, 43,* 142–154.

Ramachandran, V. S. (Ed.). (1994). *Encyclopedia of human behavior* (Vols. 1–4). Orlando, FL: Academic Press.

Rand Corporation. (1955). *A million random digits with 100,000 normal deviates.* New York: Free Press.

Randhawa, B. S., & Coffman, W. E. (Eds.). (1978). *Visual learning, thinking, and communication.* New York: Academic Press.

Raudenbush, S. W. (1984). Magnitude of teacher expectancy effects on pupil IQ as a function of the credibility of expectancy induction: A synthesis of findings from 18 experiments. *Journal of Educational Psychology, 76,* 85–97.

Reed, J. G., & Baxter, P. M. (1983). *Library use: A handbook for psychology.* Washington, DC: American Psychological Association.

Reed, S. K. (1988). *Cognition: Theory and applications* (2nd ed.). Pacific Grove, CA: Brooks/Cole.

Regis, E. (1987). *Who got Einstein's office? Eccentricities and genius at the Institute for Advanced Study.* Reading, MA: Addison-Wesley.

Reichenbach, H. (1938). *Experience and prediction.* Chicago: University of Illinois Press.

Riessman, C. K. (Ed.) (1993). *Qualitative studies in social work research.* Thousand Oaks, CA: Sage.

Robinson, J. P., Shaver, P. R., & Wrightsman, L. S. (Eds.) (1991). *Measures of personality and social psychological attitudes.* San Diego, CA: Academic Press.

Rokeach, M. (1960). *The open and closed mind.* New York: Basic Books.

Rosengren, K. E. (Ed.) (1981). *Advances in content analysis.* Beverly Hills, CA: Sage.

Rosenthal, R. (1966). *Experimenter effects in behavioral research.* New York: Appleton-Century-Crofts.

Rosenthal, R. (1973). Estimating effective reliability in studies that employ judges' ratings. *Journal of Clinical Psychology, 29,* 342–345.

Rosenthal, R. (1976). *Experimenter effects in behavioral research* (enlarged ed.). New York: Irvington Press.

Rosenthal, R. (1979). The "file drawer problem" and tolerance for null results. *Psychological Bulletin, 86,* 638–641.

Rosenthal, R. (1982). Conducting judgment studies. In K. R. Scherer & P. Ekman (Eds.), *Handbook of methods in nonverbal behavior research* (pp. 287–361). New York: Cambridge University Press.

Rosenthal, R. (1983). Meta-analysis: Toward a more cumulative social science. In L. Bickman (Ed.), *Applied social psychology annual* (Vol. 4, pp. 65–93). Beverly Hills, CA: Sage.

Rosenthal, R. (1985). From unconscious experimenter bias to teacher expectancy effects. In J. B. Dusek (Ed.), *Teacher expectancies* (pp. 37–65). Hillsdale, NJ: Erlbaum.

Rosenthal, R. (1987). *Judgment studies: Design, analysis and meta-analysis.* Cambridge, England: Cambridge University Press.

Rosenthal, R. (1990a). Evaluation of procedures and results. In K. W. Wachter & M. L. Straf (Eds.), *The future of meta-analysis* (pp. 123–133). New York: Russell Sage.

Rosenthal, R. (1990b). How are we doing in soft psychology? *American Psychologist, 45,* 775–777.

Rosenthal, R. (1990c). Replication in behavioral research. *Journal of Social Behavior and Personality, 5,* 1–30.

Rosenthal, R. (1991a). *Meta-analytic procedures for social research* (rev. ed.). Newbury Park, CA: Sage.

Rosenthal, R. (1991b). Teacher expectancy effects: A brief update 25 years after the Pygmalion experiment. *Journal of Research in Education, 1,* 3–12.

Rosenthal, R. (1994). Science and ethics in conducting, analyzing, and reporting psychological research. *Psychological Science, 5,* 127–134.

Rosenthal, R., & Fode, K. L. (1963). The effect of experimenter bias on the performance of the albino rat. *Behavioral Science, 8,* 183–189.

Rosenthal, R., Hall, J. A., DiMatteo, M. R., Rogers, P. L., & Archer, D. (1979). *Sensitivity to nonverbal communication: The PONS test.* Baltimore: Johns Hopkins University Press.

Rosenthal, R., & Jacobson, L. (1968). *Pygmalion in the classroom: Teacher expectation and pupils' intellectual development.* New York: Holt, Rinehart & Winston.

Rosenthal, R., & Lawson, R. (1964). A longitudinal study of the effects of experimenter bias on the operant learning of laboratory rats. *Journal of Psychiatric Research, 2,* 61–72.

Rosenthal, R., & Rosnow, R. L. (Eds.) (1969). *Artifact in behavioral research.* New York: Academic Press.

Rosenthal, R., & Rosnow, R. L. (1975a). *Primer of methods for the behavioral sciences.* New York: Wiley.

Rosenthal, R., & Rosnow, R. L. (1975b). *The volunteer subject.* New York: Wiley.

Rosenthal, R., & Rosnow, R. L. (1984). Applying Hamlet's question to the ethical conduct of research: A conceptual addendum. *American Psychologist, 39,* 561–563.

Rosenthal, R., & Rosnow, R. L. (1991). *Essentials of behavioral research: Methods and data analysis* (2d ed.). New York: McGraw-Hill.

Rosenthal, R., & Rubin, D. B. (1978). Interpersonal expectancy effects: The first 345 studies. *Behavioral and Brain Sciences, 3,* 377–386.

Rosenthal, R., & Rubin, D. B. (1979a). Comparing significance levels of independent studies. *Psychological Bulletin, 86,* 1165–1168.

Rosenthal, R., & Rubin, D. B. (1979b). A note on percent variance explained as a measure of the importance of effects. *Journal of Applied Social Psychology, 9,* 395–396.

Rosenthal, R., & Rubin, D. B. (1982a). A simple general purpose display of magnitude of experimental effect. *Journal of Educational Psychology, 74,* 166–169.

Rosenthal, R., & Rubin, D. B. (1982b). Comparing effect sizes of independent studies. *Psychological Bulletin, 92,* 500–504.

Rosnow, R. L. (1966). Whatever happened to the "law of primacy"? *Journal of Communication, 16,* 10–31.

Rosnow, R. L. (1980). Psychology of rumor. *Psychological Bulletin, 87,* 578–591.

Rosnow, R. L. (1981). *Paradigms in transition: The methodology of social inquiry.* New York: Oxford University Press.

Rosnow, R. L. (1983). Von Osten's horse, Hamlet's question, and the mechanistic view of causality: Implications for a post-crisis social psychology. *Journal of Mind and Behavior, 4,* 319–338.

Rosnow, R. L. (1990). Teaching research ethics through role-play and discussion. *Teaching of Psychology, 17,* 179–181.

Rosnow, R. L. (1991). Inside rumor: A personal journey. *American Psychologist, 46,* 484–496.

Rosnow, R. L. (1993). The volunteer problem revisited. In P. D. Blanck (Ed.), *Inter-*

personal expectations: Theory, research, applications (pp. 418–436). New York: Cambridge University Press.

Rosnow, R. L., Esposito, J. L., & Gibney, L. (1987). Factors influencing rumor spreading: Replication and extension. *Language and Communication, 7,* 1–14.

Rosnow, R. L., & Fine, G. A. (1974, August). Inside rumors. *Human Behavior,* pp. 64–68.

Rosnow, R. L., & Fine, G. A. (1976). *Rumor and gossip: The social psychology of hearsay.* New York: Elsevier.

Rosnow, R. L., Goodstadt, B. E., Suls, J. M., & Gitter, A. G. (1973). More on the social psychology of the experiment: When compliance turns to self-defense. *Journal of Personality and Social Psychology, 27,* 337–343.

Rosnow, R. L., & Rosenthal, R. (1970). Volunteer effects in behavioral research. In K. H. Craik, B. Kleinmuntz, R. L. Rosnow, R. Rosenthal, J. A. Cheyne, & R. H. Walters, *New directions in psychology* (No. 4, pp. 211–277). New York: Holt, Rinehart & Winston.

Rosnow, R. L., & Rosenthal, R. (1976). The volunteer subject revisited. *Australian Journal of Psychology, 28,* 97–108.

Rosnow, R. L., & Rosenthal, R. (1988). Focused tests of significance and effect size estimation in counseling psychology. *Journal of Counseling Psychology, 35,* 203–208.

Rosnow, R. L., & Rosenthal, R. (1989a). Definition and interpretation of interaction effects. *Psychological Bulletin, 105,* 143–146.

Rosnow, R. L., & Rosenthal, R. (1989b). Statistical procedures and the justification of knowledge in psychological science. *American Psychologist, 44,* 1276–1284.

Rosnow, R. L., & Rosenthal, R. (1991). If you're looking at the cell means, you're not looking at *only* the interaction (unless all main effects are zero). *Psychological Bulletin, 110,* 574–576.

Rosnow, R. L., & Rosenthal, R. (1995). "Some things you learn aren't so": Cohen's paradox, Asch's paradigm, and the interpretation of interaction. *Psychological Science, 6,* 3-9.

Rosnow, R. L., & Rosnow, M. (1995). *Writing papers in psychology: A student guide* (3rd ed.). Pacific Grove, CA: Brooks/Cole.

Rosnow, R. L., Rotheram-Borus, M. J., Ceci, S. J., Blanck, P. D., & Koocher, G. P. (1993). The institutional review board as a mirror of scientific and ethical standards. *American Psychologist, 48,* 821–826.

Rosnow, R. L., Skleder, A. A., Jaeger, M. E., & Rind, B. (1994), Intelligence and the epistemics of interpersonal acumen: Testing some implications of Gardner's theory. *Intelligence, 19,* 93–116.

Rosnow, R. L., & Suls, J. M. (1970). Reactive effects of pretesting in attitude research. *Journal of Personality and Social Psychology, 15,* 338–343.

Rossi, P. H., Wright, J. D., & Anderson, A. B. (1983). Sample surveys: History, current practice, and future prospects. In P. H. Rossi, J. D. Wright, & A. B. Anderson (Eds.), *Handbook of survey research* (pp. 1–20). New York: Academic Press.

Rothenberg, R. (1990, October 5). Surveys proliferate, but answers dwindle. *The New York Times,* pp. A1, D4.

Rozelle, R. M., & Campbell, D. T. (1969). More plausible rival hypotheses in the cross-lagged panel correlation technique. *Psychological Bulletin, 71,* 74–80.

Sacks, H., Chalmers, T. C., & Smith, H., Jr. (1982). Randomized versus historical controls for clinical trials. *American Journal of Medicine, 72,* 233–240.

Saks, M. J., & Blanck, P. D. (1992). Justice improved: The unrecognized benefits of aggregation and sampling in the trial of mass torts. *Stanford Law Review, 44,* 815–851.

Sartre, J-P. (1956). *Being and nothingness.* New York: Washington Square Press.

Saxe, L. (1991). Lying: Thoughts of an applied social psychologist. *American Psychologist, 46,* 409–415.

Schachter, S. (1968). Obesity and eating. *Science, 161,* 751–756.

Schaie, K. (1993). The Seattle longitudinal studies of adult intelligence. *Current Directions in Psychological Science, 2,* 171–175.

Schaie, K. (1994). The course of adult intellectual development. *American Psychologist, 49,* 304–313.

Schuler, H. (1982). *Ethical problems in psychological research.* New York: Academic Press.

Scott, W. A. (1968). Attitude measurement. In G. Lindzey & E. Aronson (Eds.), *The handbook of social psychology* (2d ed., Vol. 2, pp. 204–273). Reading, MA: Addison-Wesley.

Seeman, J. (1969). Deception in psychological research. *American Psychologist, 24,* 1025–1028.

Shaw, M. E., & Wright, J. M. (1967). *Scales for the measurement of attitudes.* New York: McGraw-Hill.

Sidman, M. (1960). *Tactics of scientific research: Evaluating experimental data in psychology.* New York: Basic Books.

Sieber, J. E. (1982a). Deception in social research: 1. Kinds of deception and the wrongs they may involve. *IRB: A Review of Human Subjects Research, 3,* 1–2, 12.

Sieber, J. E. (Ed.) (1982b). *The ethics of social research* (Vols. 1–2). New York: Springer-Verlag.

Sieber, J. E. (1983). Deception in social research: 2. Factors influencing the magnitude of potential for harm or wrong. *IRB: A Review of Human Subjects Research, 4,* 1–3, 12.

Sieber, J. E. (1991). Scientists' responses to ethical issues in science. In W. Shadish (Ed.), *Contributions to social psychology of science.* New York: Guilford Press.

Sieber, J. E. (1992). *Planning ethically responsible research.* Newbury Park, CA: Sage.

Siegel, S. (1956). *Nonparametric statistics.* New York: McGraw-Hill.

Sigall, H., Aronson, E., & Van Hoose, T. (1970). The cooperative subject: Myth or reality? *Journal of Experimental Social Psychology, 6,* 1–10.

Silverman, D. (1993). *Interpreting qualitative data: Methods for analyzing talk, text, and interaction.* Thousand Oaks, CA: Sage.

Silverman, I. (1977). *The human subject in the psychological experiment.* New York: Pergamon Press.

Skinner, B. F. (1938). *The behavior of organisms: An experimental analysis.* New York: Appleton-Century-Crofts.

Skinner, B. F. (1948). Superstition in the pigeon. *Journal of Experimental Psychology, 38,* 168–172.

Skinner, B. F. (1980). *Notebooks.* (R. Epstein, Ed.). Englewood Cliffs, NJ: Prentice-Hall.

Skinner, B. F. (1987). Whatever happened to psychology as a science of behavior? *American Psychologist, 42,* 780–786.

Slovic, P. (1987). Perception of risk. *Science, 236,* 280–285.

Smith, C. (1980). *Selecting a source of local television news in the Salt Lake City SMSA: A multivariate analysis of cognitive and affective factors for 384 randomly-selected news viewers.* Unpublished doctoral dissertation, Temple University School of Communication, Philadelphia.

Smith, M. L., & Glass, G. V (1977). Meta-analysis of psychotherapy outcome studies. *American Psychologist, 32,* 752–760.

Smith, R. A. (1992). Formatting APA pages in WordPerfect 5.1. *Teaching of Psychology, 19,* 190–192.

Snedecor, G. W., & Cochran, W. G. (1989). *Statistical methods* (8th ed.). Ames: Iowa State University Press.

Sobal, J. (1982). Disclosing information in interview introductions: Methodological consequences of informed consent. *Sociology and Social Research, 66,* 348–361.

Sockloff, A. L., & Edney, J. N. (1972, May). *Some extensions of Student's* t *and Pearson's* r *central distributions.* Technical Report 72–5. Temple University Measurement and Research Center, Philadelphia

Solomon, R. L. (1949). An extension of control group design. *Psychological Bulletin, 46,* 137–150.

Solomon, R. L., & Howes, D. (1951). Word frequency, personal values, and visual duration thresholds. *Psychological Review, 58,* 256–270.

Sperling, G., & Melchner, M. J. (1976). Estimating item and order information. *Journal of Mathematical Psychology, 13,* 192–213.

Spradley, J. P. (1970). *You owe yourself a drunk: An ethnography of urban nomads.* Boston: Little, Brown.

Spradley, J. P. (1980). *Participant observation.* New York: Holt, Rinehart & Winston.

Squire, P. (1988). Why the 1936 *Literary Digest* poll failed. *Public Opinion Quarterly, 52,* 125–133.

Steering Committee of the Physicians' Health Study Research Group. (1988). Preliminary report: Findings from the aspirin component of the ongoing physicians' health study. *New England Journal of Medicine, 318,* 262–264.

Steinberg, L., Lamborn, S. D., Dornbusch, S. M., & Darling, N. (1992). Impact of parenting practices on adolescent achievement: Authoritative parenting, school involvement, and encouragement to succeed. *Child Development, 63,* 1266–1281.

Sterling, T. D. (1959). Publication decisions and their possible effects on inferences drawn from tests of significance—or vice versa. *Journal of the American Statistical Association, 54,* 30–34.

Sternberg, R. J. (1985). *Beyond IQ: A triarchic theory of human intelligence.* Cambridge, England: Cambridge University Press.

Sternberg, R. J. (1990). *Metaphors of mind: Conceptions of the nature of intelligence.* Cambridge, England: Cambridge University Press.

Sternberg, R. J. (1993). *The psychologist's companion: A guide to scientific writing for students and researchers* (3rd ed.). Cambridge, England: Cambridge University Press.

Sternberg, R. J., & Detterman, D. K. (Eds.). (1986). *What is intelligence? Contemporary viewpoints on its nature and definition.* Norwood, NJ: Ablex.

Stigler, S. M. (1986). *The history of statistics: The measurement of uncertainty before 1900.* Cambridge: Belknap/Harvard.

Stone, P., Dunphy, D., Smith, M., & Ogilvie, D. (1966). *The General Inquirer: A complete approach to content analysis.* Cambridge: MIT Press.

Street, E., & Carroll, M. B. (1989). Preliminary evaluation of a new food product. In J. M. Tanur, F. M. Mosteller, W. H. Kruskal, E. L. Lehmann, R. F. Link, R. S. Pieters, & G. R. Rising (Eds.), *Statistics: A guide to the unknown* (3rd ed., pp. 161–169). Pacific Grove, CA: Wadsworth & Brooks/Cole.

Stricker, L. J. (1967). The true deceiver. *Psychological Bulletin, 68,* 13–20.

Strohmetz, D. B., & Rosnow, R. L. (1994). A mediational model of artifacts. In J. Brzeziński (Ed.), *Probability in theory-building: Experimental and non-experimental approaches to scientific research in psychology* (pp. 177–196). Netherlands: Rudopi.

Strohmetz, D. B., & Skleder, A. A. (1992). The use of role-play in teaching research ethics: A validation study. *Teaching of Psychology, 19,* 106–108.

Strunk, W., Jr., & White, E. B. (1979). *The elements of style* (3rd ed.). New York: Macmillan.

Suls, J. M., & Rosnow, R. L. (1988). Concerns about artifacts in psychological experiments. In J. Morawski (Ed.), *The rise of experimentation in American psychology* (pp. 163–187). New York: Oxford University Press.

Symonds, P. M. (1925). Notes on rating. *Journal of Applied Psychology, 9,* 188–195.

Tanur, J. M. (Ed.) (1994). *Questions about questions: Inquiries into the cognitive bases of surveys.* New York: Russell Sage.

Thurstone, L. L. (1929). Theory of attitude measurement. *Psychological Bulletin, 36,* 222–241.

Thurstone, L. L. (1929–1934). *The measurement of social attitudes.* Chicago: University of Chicago Press.

Timmons, B., & Ley, R. (Eds.). (1995). *Behavioral and psychological approaches to breathing disorders.* New York: Plenum Press.

Tolman, E. C. (1959). Principles of purposive behavior. In S. Koch (Ed.), *Psychology: A study of a science* (Vol. 2, pp. 92–157). New York: McGraw-Hill.

Treadway, M., & McCloskey, M. (1989). Effects of racial stereotypes on eyewitness performance: Implications of the real and rumored Allport and Postman studies. *Applied Cognitive Psychology, 3,* 53–63.

Tufte, E. R. (1983). *The visual display of quantitative information.* Cheshire, CT: Graphics Press.

Tufte, E. R. (1990). *Envisioning information.* Cheshire, CT: Graphics Press.

Tukey, J. W. (1977). *Exploratory data analysis.* Reading, MA: Addison-Wesley.

Vaught, R. S. (1977). What if subjects can't be randomly assigned? *Human Factors, 19,* 227–234.

Wainer, H. (1972). Draft of chapter for R. E. Lana and R. L. Rosnow's *Introduction to Contemporary Psychology.* New York: Holt, Rinehart & Winston.

Wainer, H. (1984). How to display data badly. *The American Statistician, 38,* 137–147.

Wainer, H. (1990). *Computerized adaptive testing: A primer.* Hillsdale, NJ: Erlbaum.

Walker, C. J., & Beckerle, C. A. (1987). The effect of anxiety on rumor transmission. *Journal of Social Behavior and Personality, 2,* 353–360.

Walker, C. J., & Blaine, B. (1991). The virulence of dread rumors: A field experiment.

Language and Communication, 11, 291–298.

Walker, H. M., & Lev, J. (1953). *Statistical inference.* New York: Holt.

Wallerstein, G., & Elgar, S. (1992). Shock waves in stellar atmosphere and breaking waves on an ocean beach. *Science, 12,* 1531–1536.

Wallis, W. A., & Roberts, H. V. (1956). *Statistics: A new approach.* New York: Free Press.

Weaver, C. (1972). *Human listening.* Indianapolis: Bobbs-Merrill.

Webb, E. J., Campbell, D. T., Schwartz, R. F., & Sechrest, L. (1966). *Unobtrusive measures: Nonreactive research in the social sciences.* Chicago: Rand McNally.

Webb, E. J., Campbell, D. T., Schwartz, R. F., Sechrest, L., & Grove, J. B. (1981). *Nonreactive measures in the social sciences* (2d ed.). Boston: Houghton Mifflin.

Webber, R. A. (1970). Perception of interactions between superiors and subordinates. *Human Relations, 23,* 235–248.

Weber, R. P. (1985). *Basic content analysis.* Beverly Hills, CA: Sage.

Wechler, J. (Ed.) (1978). *On aesthetics in science.* Cambridge: MIT Press.

Weick, K. E. (1968). Systematic observational methods. In G. Lindzey & E. Aronson (Eds.), *The handbook of social psychology* (2d ed., Vol. 2, pp. 357–451). Reading, MA: Addison-Wesley.

Weinberger, D. A. (1990). The construct validity of the repressive coping style. In J. L. Singer (Ed.), *Repression and dissociation: Implications for personality theory, psychopathology, and health* (pp. 337–386). Chicago: University of Chicago Press.

Weiner, B. (1991). Metaphors in motivation and attribution. *American Psychologist, 46,* 921–930.

Weiss, J. M. (1968). Effects of coping responses on stress. *Journal of Comparative and Physiological Psychology, 65,* 251–260.

Weschler, L. (1988, January 18). Onward and upward with the arts. *The New Yorker,* pp. 33–56.

Wickesberg, A. K. (1968). Communication networks in a business organization structure. *Journal of the Academy of Management, 11,* 253–262.

Wolman, B. B. (Ed.). (1977). *International encyclopedia of psychiatry, psychology, psychoanalysis, and neurology* (Vols. 1–12). New York: Van Nostrand Reinhold.

Woodrum, E. (1984). "Mainstreaming" content analysis in social science: Methodological advantages, obstacles, and solutions. *Social Science Research, 13,* 1–19.

Wyer, R. S., Jr., & Srull, T. K. (Eds.). (1989). *Advances in social cognition: Vol. 2. Social intelligence and cognitive assessment of personality.* Hillsdale, NJ: Erlbaum.

Yin, R. K. (1989). *Case study research: Design and methods.* Newbury Park, CA: Sage.

Zajonc, R. F. (1965). Social facilitation. *Science, 149,* 269–274.

Zechmeister, E. B., & Nyberg, S. E. (1982). *Human memory: An introduction to research and theory.* Monterey, CA: Brooks/Cole.

Zipf, G. K. (1935). *The psycho-biology of language.* Boston: Houghton Mifflin.

Zipf, G. K. (1949). *Human behavior and the principle of least effort.* Reading, MA: Addison-Wesley.

Name Index

Subject Index